PHONEY WARS

RAILWAYS
MAGAZINE
MARCH
1940
Vol. XIV. No. 12
6D.
FLAGS of FREEDOM

PHONEY WARS

NEW ZEALAND SOCIETY IN THE SECOND WORLD WAR

STEVAN ELDRED-GRIGG
with HUGH ELDRED-GRIGG

OTAGO

Published by Otago University Press
Level 1, 398 Cumberland Street
Dunedin, New Zealand
university.press@otago.ac.nz
www.otago.ac.nz/press

First published 2017

ISBN 978-0-947522-23-0

Published with the assistance of Creative New Zealand.

Arts Council of New Zealand Toi Aotearoa

A catalogue record for this book is available from the National Library of New Zealand.

Editor: Gillian Tewsley
Index: Diane Lowther

Cover: Margaret Thompson Harvey, *Casualty List*. *Collection of Charles Rose*
Page 6: Labour parties in New Zealand, Australia and Britain wished to put the wellbeing of the working class before the 'rearmament' demanded by the political right. This poster was printed for the British Labour Party in the mid-1930s. *Online Archive of California*
Page 8: Māori leaders and government advertisements encouraged volunteering. *Museum of New Zealand Te Papa Tongarewa*

Printed in China by Asia Pacific Offset

CONTENTS

ACKNOWLEDGEMENTS 7

INTRODUCTION 9

CHAPTER 1 **THE EVE OF WAR** 16

CHAPTER 2 **THE FIRST PHONEY WAR:**
SEPTEMBER 1939 TO JUNE 1940 60

CHAPTER 3 **A WAR FAR AWAY:**
JUNE 1940 TO DECEMBER 1941 114

CHAPTER 4 **WAR AT OUR DOOR?**
DECEMBER 1941 TO DECEMBER 1942 168

CHAPTER 5 **THE SECOND PHONEY WAR:**
JANUARY 1943 TO SEPTEMBER 1945 234

CHAPTER 6 **VICTORY?** NAPALM AND NUCLEAR BOMBS 316

NOTES 367

BIBLIOGRAPHY 397

INDEX 407

SMOKE
FROM CHIMNEYS
NOT FROM GUNS!
VOTE
LABOUR
PUBLISHED BY THE LABOUR PARTY, TRANSPORT HOUSE, SMITH SQUARE, S.W.1.
PRINTED BY ELM PRESS, LONDON, W.C.1.

ACKNOWLEDGEMENTS

Our goal with *Phoney Wars* was first to summarise and synthesise the best work done by the many writers who have looked at the society of New Zealand and its colonial territories in the Second World War, and second to fill some of the gaps by doing primary research, mostly in newspapers and the imaginative literature of the day.

Two historians have been especially important. Nancy Taylor, whose monumental *The New Zealand People at War: The home front* has never been widely read outside the closed circle of academic historians, provided us with a rich quarry. Frederick Wood, author of *The New Zealand People at War: Political and external affairs*, provided us with another rich quarry.

We did the bulk of our newspaper research in Papers Past (www.paperspast.natlib.govt.nz). We need to note, however, that during the war years newspapers now on the website were heavily censored by the state.

We are indebted to skilled archivists, librarians and technical experts who helped us to find and use texts or images in the Macmillan Brown Library, National Library, Archives New Zealand, Christchurch Art Gallery, Dunedin Art Gallery, Museum of New Zealand Te Papa Tongarewa, Air Force Museum of New Zealand, Auckland War Memorial Museum and Australian War Memorial. We are also indebted to oral historians who have done wonderful work, patiently and sensitively interviewing people who went through the war: Megan Hutching, Alison Parr, Judith Fyfe, Bee Dawson and Jim Sullivan.

Gillian Tewsley earns our thanks for being a skilled and careful editor. Publisher Rachel Scott looked after our book by encouraging, advising and critiquing in a generous way from the moment she first saw the manuscript until the completion of the finished work. Also, thanks to all others in the team at Otago University Press.

Stevan is also grateful to his grandmother, Barbara Hall, who when he was a boy had a lot of sharp things to say about world wars.

'All the people who went away,' she used to say. 'And where are half of them now? Sunnyside or six foot under. And what was it for? Nothing.'

TARINGA WHAKARONGO!
E TE IWI
"Awhinatia
Mai Matou"
HE KARANGA
NA TE
HOKOWHITU-A-TU

INTRODUCTION

The first task of any historical book is to outline briefly what will be covered and why the writer thinks it worth writing about, together with why the reader will want to read about it. The task is easy in this case.

I can scarcely imagine a reader not aware of the basic outline of the global conflict between 1939 and 1945; no other historical event looms so large in the popular consciousness. This is as true for New Zealand as for any other country in the world – perhaps more so than many, although the dominion was very remote from the main theatres of the war. And it remains true nearly seventy years after the signing of the last peace treaty.[1]

Any reasonably aware New Zealander, even today, is expected to know who Hitler and Churchill were, what happened in Auschwitz and at Pearl Harbor and how Rommel was stopped in Egypt. A historian of the Second World War does not need to brief readers with long boilerplate text about, say, the D-Day landings or the bombing of Hiroshima, or the basic political philosophy or social organisation of the United States during the Roosevelt years, of the Soviet Union under Stalin, or of Nazi Germany.

Freed from the need to persuade people that this book is about a subject worth contemplating, I still have to prepare readers for the treatment of the war in this book. First, though, some contexts and limits.

In comparison to similarly world-changing historical events, the war was relatively brief. The French Revolutionary Wars took twenty-six years to play out, the Thirty Years War lasted even longer than the titular thirty years, while the Chinese Civil War began in 1911 and, with occasional breaks, was not over until 1949. The Second World War lasted only six years.

But while the war was relatively brief, in almost every other sense it was expansive. Although not a global war in an absolute sense, it is easier to note the parts of the world that were not substantially affected (just Latin America and sub-Saharan Africa) than those that were. The war's reach was as deep as it was wide. More than any prior conflict, it came close to 'total war'. Civilians by the million were sucked up into the war machine, compelled to work in munitions factories, bombed by fleets of aircraft heavy with high explosives or subjected to ethnic cleansing in the wake of advancing armies. When Orwell wrote in *Nineteen Eighty-Four* about a perpetual, all-consuming war, he was taking only a single step forward from the war he had lived through. The war was the most economically intensive in history, swallowing more capital, labour and materiel than any before or since.

Any historian attempting to write about all of this faces a formidable task trying to frame such a huge, chaotic event in a way that is relatable and revealing. Luckily, as we are primarily interested here in the effect of the war on New Zealand, this allows us to take a very small slice of this vast pie. But even then we still have so many angles to examine that it can be overwhelming.

It may be easiest to begin by saying what this book is not. *Phoney Wars* is not a political or economic history: readers will need to go elsewhere if they seek close analysis of wheeling and dealing between politicians or political lobby groups, or if they seek to know a good deal about 'manpowering', trade talks with war allies or the workings of the Economic Stabilisation Commission. *Phoney Wars* is also not a military history. The tactics and strategies of military leaders, the course of individual battles and campaigns, are not of interest to us. Not only has this all already been extensively covered to the degree that you can read a detailed blow-by-blow account of just about any battle you wish to, it reveals little about the war as a whole. The entire sum of all military operations is only one aspect of the war; to go into these operations on a granular level is unrewarding for the author who wishes to take a broad view.

What this book does do is try to 'thaw' the history of the war in three ways, all of which will surprise most readers and repel or anger some.

First, the book unpacks and questions the assumption that the Axis was 'bad' and the Allies 'good'. This is a challenge to popular and even informed knowledge of the war. A book claiming that, say, the European Renaissance was a dreadful thing and that humans would collectively have been better off without it might seem strange or surprising to a general audience but nobody would feel personally attacked. Not so, however, with the Second World War. The public would deal very severely with any scholar who thinks Hitler 'had a lot going for him', as it does even with those who point out that collaboration was common in countries occupied by Hitler's army – or in China, Indonesia and other countries occupied by Japan. The bar for acceptance of such analysis – or, for many, heresy – is set very high.

A lot of readers will feel that the Second World War was an event so atypical, a conflict so extreme in its consequences, against an enemy so extraordinarily evil, that to indulge in moral calculus and the weighing of costs and benefits is a form of moral imbecility akin to counting the financial cost to oneself of pulling a child out of a burning building. The historian's task of seeking hidden dynamics and weighing up competing claims, it will be argued, must be set aside in the face of urgent humanist imperatives – or, now that the war has passed, out of respect for those who responded to those imperatives. Claims of this sort essentially seek to put the Second World War outside historiography. The overarching story of the Second World War, in New Zealand and elsewhere, is one of pain. Pain was felt all over the world by hundreds of millions of people for years on end. To argue that much of the pain may have been unnecessary is to probe a very tender spot. To argue that the 'enemy' may also have suffered has a similar effect.

But to remove the Second World War from an ongoing moral calculus is explicitly to remove it from history, if history is to be considered as anything more intellectually complex than a series of events in time, restating what we have already decided. This, we feel, is an argument that few would make overtly.

Further, students of metahistory – the history of the study of history and the discourses surrounding its practice – know of other events which, while once the subject of moral agreement, have subsequently been subjected to searching analysis. Medieval European 'crusades' against Muslims and 'pagans' were once seen as divine victories against satanic forces that historians had no ability or right to question; or at least not the historians of Western Christendom. The hindsight of centuries allows us now to take a view that is more nuanced. The Second World War can also be analysed using the tools we apply to other morally weighty, but more distant events. With the benefit of time simplistic moral viewpoints so seldom maintain their full force that anybody who makes a claim for the moral singularity of the Second World War risks being seen not as a historian but as a chronicler or propagandist.

This is not to say that the two sides were morally equivalent or that it should be a matter of indifference that the Allies defeated the Axis. The world can definitely do without the Thousand Year Reich, and probably also the Greater East Asia Co-Prosperity Sphere and the New Roman Empire. But that does not mean the defeat of the Axis was some kind of miraculous redemptive event outside the realm of analysis.

Nor are we prompted by a deep pacifism along the lines of the principles upheld by Mohandas Gandhi or Te Whiti o Rongomai or the Society of Friends, holding that there is no worthwhile goal that can be achieved with violence.

But while the book does not question the immorality of the Axis powers or the need to defeat them, it does question the morality of the Allies and the character of their victory.

Second, the book argues that New Zealand need not have involved itself in the war on the scale it did. The Second World War was essentially an external event for the people of New Zealand. While many citizens saw themselves as belonging to the British Empire and Commonwealth and felt ownership of British foreign policy, New Zealanders did not contribute to the inception of the struggle in any significant way.

Although nobody really predicted the way the war would play out, the New Zealand government's response to the fact of its involvement in the conflict never graduated beyond a series of ad hoc measures that were often contradictory. This confusion concerning war goals arose in part out of the reluctance of the New Zealand state to set goals independent of the larger British imperial system or, by 1941, the United States imperial system; and when we tell the story of the war as it affects New Zealand, it is a story of groups of citizens in and out of official positions responding to events rather than initiating them.

Ultimately there was no compelling reason for New Zealand to involve itself in the war. As a small state occupying a position of zero strategic significance, its contribution to a war waged between great powers was negligible. In our investigation of New Zealand's involvement in Allied operations we were not able to find a single setback to Japanese or German war goals in which New Zealand played even a modest role. Although at the time New Zealand's place in the war was often depicted as crucial, this seems simply to have been wartime propaganda. While the United Kingdom was very eager for New Zealand to involve itself in the war, its eagerness seems to have been based less on hard-headed assessment of the New Zealand contribution than a wish to present to the world, for political and diplomatic purposes, a picture of a united British Empire and Commonwealth.

We hope our readers will accept that our rejection of New Zealand's participation in the war is not prompted by some juvenile contrarianism that draws satisfaction from puncturing common conceptions merely because they are widely shared. We know we will not be accused of sympathy or advocacy for the regimes of wartime Japan or Italy, much less Nazi Germany. We do not go so far as to advocate that New Zealand's leaders should have pursued a stance of formal neutrality. Such a stance might have been optimal, but in a world where New Zealand faced external and internal pressures to fight, the same practical spirit that would be sceptical about New Zealand's contributions would also be pragmatic about New Zealand's freedom of action. The price ticket for formal neutrality would have been very high.

At the same time there are gradients of involvement between formal neutrality and total mobilisation. This was not something that the government of the time or the social groups who supported it seemed always to appreciate. New Zealand put itself on a serious and sweeping war footing in imitation of European and Asian countries that were actually in the front line of combat. The spectacle of blackouts in a country thousands of kilometres from the nearest enemy airbase was emblematic of the creation of a war economy and war society without any reasonable justification.

Third, the book argues that both these debates – the values debate and the interest debate – played out among New Zealanders throughout the whole length of the war. By New Zealanders, we are talking not only about soldiers, sailors and airmen, and definitely not only about generals and air vice-marshals. New Zealanders who were not serving in the armed forces were more able to distance themselves from the war than their Japanese, Polish or Libyan equivalents, but they were still deeply involved and affected. Children, the elderly, housewives, clerks, factory workers, shop assistants, farmhands and school teachers were all sucked into the war even if they never came anywhere near any actual fighting.

The war, contrary to the propaganda of the time and to subsequent memory, did not unite New Zealanders: it divided them. This was plainly the case, although the state was unable to overcome or even recognise the divided nature of its society and the competing responses of the various groups on either side of those divisions. Any history of New Zealand society's response to the war must take this into account, and must try to do justice to perspectives on either side of deep cleavages based on gender, class, race and culture. So when we observe the war through a New Zealand perspective, it is a perspective set as broadly as possible. *Phoney Wars* integrates the Second World War into the general course of New Zealand's domestic history as one event among many, like the evolution of Polynesian colonial society into Māori tribal society, or the growth of team sports among Pākehā in the late nineteenth century, or the development of a professional class among the offspring of New Zealand Chinese shopkeepers in the mid-twentieth century.

The Second World War was a 'normal' event in history.

We have called our book *Phoney Wars* because New Zealand always held back from complete mobilisation of its citizens, society and economy, even when the government spoke about 'peak' mobilisation after declaring war on Japan. Women, for example, were never mobilised fully. Nor were Māori. Workers kept many of their peacetime freedoms; so did capitalists. Allied governments, well aware of the way the dominion held back, had only limited success when they put pressure on Wellington to tighten the screws. A second reason why *Phoney Wars* seems an apt title for our book is because, as I observe above, there was no compelling reason for New Zealand to go to war against Germany and Italy, or later against Japan.

*

This book is the work of two writers, from two different generations.

Stevan Eldred-Grigg, my father, grew up in the immediate aftermath of the Second World War. The leaders, teachers and parents of the 1950s and 1960s had lived through the war and taken part in it. In many ways it felt as if the war was still going on. Books, comics, movies and songs about fighting Hitler or 'the Japs' were hugely popular. As schoolboys, Stevan and his friends imagined they were brave Kiwi battlers at El Alamein or on Guadalcanal. As he grew up, however, the widespread reverence for 'the War' – there was only one that could be described with a simple definite article, and it was not the New Zealand Wars – started to seem not quite fit for purpose in the Age of Aquarius.

I was born in 1980 and when I grew up the Second World War was a distant memory. The warriors who had crowded nearly every walk of life in the 1950s and 1960s were now dead or in homes for the elderly. In the 1980s and 1990s, teachers, parents and leaders had not experienced the war, or had experienced it only as very young children. But the Second World War was still a massive presence, and more recent wars such as Vietnam or Korea – let alone Bangladesh or Biafra – were seen as secondary. Books, movies and songs (and, increasingly, computer games) about blowing up Nazis were still proliferating, although references to the Second World War were not always explicit. The *Star Wars* trilogy, a defining piece of 1980s pop culture, was very explicitly a goodies-vs-baddies retelling of the Allied view of the Second World War in a sci-fi fantasy format. One of the very first video games I became addicted to as a pre-teen was *1942*; my friends and I spent hours acting out the role of an American air-force pilot in the Pacific trying to wipe out Tokyo. (Ironically, the game was produced by a Japanese game developer for the Japanese market.) Of course we played more traditional make-believe war games too, pretending to be British marines or Soviet riflemen. Outside in the 'real' world, meanwhile, social and economic developments such as Japanese dynamism in the 1980s or Eastern European nationalism in the 1990s were frequently explained first and foremost as outgrowths of the Second World War.

Now we live in a world different again, but not much has changed in the popular understanding of the Second World War. The ranks of those who lived through its struggles are dwindling – yet books, movies, music and computer games are still thick with references to the Second World War. One American webcomic writer presciently observed that 'Omaha Beach is the New Hoth'.[2] Novel developments in world politics, such as the rise of Islamic fundamentalism, the resurgence of Russian expansionism or flexings of power by China, are often handled as simply a retread of the events of the Second World War. Those who seek to understand them are urged to study not the history of Muslim thought or Russian statecraft or Confucian notions of hierarchy, but the great power politics of the 1930s and the military campaigns of the 1940s.

Surely one day we will escape the sense that we are living in the aftermath of the Second World War, but we are not there yet – not even close. While our understanding of the war has shifted, the idea that understanding the war is central to the task of understanding the world we live in stands unchallenged.

*

A note on sources: wartime news reports together with postwar memoirs and oral testimony have been used extensively in this book. We need to be wary, however, about their accuracy. Wartime news reports were compromised by censorship. War memoirs and oral testimony are compromised by the way we consciously or unconsciously change or misattribute memories whenever those memories are retrieved during our 'remembering', and also because our memories become contaminated by subsequent experience and shifts in language and thinking, not least for events that are still 'living' in the popular consciousness.[3] Nor can the speeches of politicians, the files of government officials, the statistics of number-crunchers, the dossiers of military authorities, the statements of chambers of commerce, the archives of trade unions or any other prosey reams tell anywhere near the whole story.

A good way to offset some of the weaknesses of conventional sources is by using novels, short stories and poems written during or soon after the Second World War. A novel, a short story or a poem speaks to us in the language of its day and conveys some of the values of its day. Fiction and verse are also likely to say things more honestly, more concisely and at the same time more subtly and memorably than anything else written or reported during the period, let alone anything ostensibly retrieved many years later by people writing memoirs, or speaking to an oral historian. Historians are perhaps too prone to think that bumf – to use a word spoken widely in the Second World War – has more authority as a historical source than a stanza written by a skilled poet, or a paragraph penned by a gifted novelist. Jane Austen anticipated such a point of view:

> *'I seldom look into novels ...' – Such is the common cant. – 'Oh! it is only a novel!' ... or, in short, only some work in which the greatest powers of the mind are displayed, in which the most thorough knowledge of human nature, the happiest delineation of its varieties, the liveliest effusions of wit and humour, are conveyed to the world in the best-chosen language.*[4]

Historiography has a very close kinship to the writing of verse, novels and the short story. Historiography, after all, is not science but story. The way the historian strives to weigh words, shape sentences, organise paragraphs, put in or keep out information – while asking readers to exercise their own judgement in the search for truth or truths – has many things in common with fiction and poetry. Hermann Hesse wrote during the war, 'we must not forget that the writing of history – however drily it is done and however sincere the desire for objectivity – remains literature. History's third dimension is always fiction.'[5]

Hugh Eldred-Grigg
Tallinn, Estonia
March 2017

A 1939 poster for the Centennial Exhibition in Wellington to celebrate the hundredth anniversary of the founding of the state of New Zealand. *Artist: Leonard Mitchell. Alexander Turnbull Library Eph-A-EXHIBITION-1939-01.*

CHAPTER 1 | THE EVE OF WAR

OUR OWN PEACEFUL PROSPERITY

New Zealand at the beginning of spring in 1939 was a peaceful, prosperous state flying its flag over 1.7 million people who lived either in the home islands or in its island colonies of Niue, the Cook Islands, Samoa and Tokelau. One in every ten citizens or subjects of the dominion was Māori, Samoan, Tokelauan or Niuean. A few thousand others were Chinese and nearly everyone else was European, mostly born in New Zealand. The dominion, having suffered heavy losses in the First World War, had not fought overseas for two decades other than in the late 1920s when troops 'pacified' restless subjects in Samoa.

The government said that it stood for peace at home and peace everywhere in the world. 'This does not altogether mean peace represented by freedom from war,' citizens were told by the prime minister, Michael Joseph Savage. 'It also means tranquility of mind, which is associated with lack of anxiety in sickness and old age.'[1]

A good many citizens thought that their booming economy rode on the sheep's back, or swung from the udder of dairy cows. Certainly the farms and stations were extraordinarily efficient, more advanced technologically than in nearly any other land, and yielded richly. Yet fewer than two out of every ten people in the workforce were employed in the primary industries of farming, mining, forestry and fishing. Wealth was won by workers in factories and shops, in offices and households.[2] Service industry employed four out of every ten people.[3] Wealth was growing swiftly. Gross domestic product in the last year before the war was 6.5 per cent bigger than the previous year[4] and many households were thriving. Average incomes were among the very highest in the world.[5]

The prime minister spoke soberly yet optimistically about the outlook for the world. A war was being fought in China. New wars were likely. Nations were wracked by 'an insane and gigantic scramble for armaments'. New Zealand, however, was 'well-

Wellington, capital of an apparently peaceful and certainly prosperous New Zealand.
Railways Magazine, 1939.

favoured'. The citizenry could 'remark the contrast of our own peaceful prosperity' with the 'anxiety and sorrow' harrowing so many lives in the outside world.[6]

TUGS AND TANGLES

Savage was parliamentary leader for the Labour Party. Conservatives seated in the opposition benches were provoked by his speeches because they believed that life in the dominion was now too easy for the working class. Wage earners were becoming spoiled and lazy. Along with prosperity had come 'lack of moral fibre' and neglect of stern virtues. 'Pleasures of all kinds hold first sway.'[7] Too many people cared too much about clothes and furnishings, dancing and cinema, sports and holidays.

A split between conservatives and democratic socialists was only one of many divisions within New Zealand. Loyalty to class, race, nationality, gender, generation, region and religion all tugged at or tangled up the workings of society.

Race and nationality, for example, split people into opposed groups.

Māori saw the world differently to Europeans. The two races had a long history of complex interrelations: they had worked together, played together and slept together, but were also often at odds. Nine out of every ten Māori lived in villages, well away from the streets and suburbs that were home for most other people in New Zealand. Contagious and infectious diseases sickened or killed them far more than other people in the country. A measles epidemic not long before the outbreak of war killed twenty-four out of every 10,000 Māori, compared with one in every 10,000 Pākehā.[8]

Māori children playing in the Waikato River, 1938. *Photographer: Leo White. Alexander Turnbull Library WA-12538-F.*

Nevertheless, the ranks of tribespeople were growing. The Māori birth rate more than doubled in less than twenty years before the war. The average Māori child was slightly taller and tended to have better eyesight than the offspring of the average Pākehā family.[9] Māori had a strong leadership, too. Tribal social organisation 'held out most tenaciously,' observed doctor, politician and scholar Te Rangi Hiroa.[10]

A deep divide between the two races concerned the legitimacy of the state. Pākehā New Zealand believed that sovereignty was held by parliament, while Māori New Zealand believed sovereignty lay in the Treaty of Waitangi. The treaty was a living truth for the tribes; the state for sixty years had deemed it a 'legal nullity'. A gathering of over 200 tribal leaders at Tokaanu, only months before the outbreak of war, agreed that the treaty should be written into law at the next session of parliament, or that the treaty rights of Māori should be 'defined by the Court of Appeal'.[11] The Labour Party in 1925 had promised mana motuhake to the tribes – autonomy within the state – and also the establishment of a commission to look into claims arising out of the treaty, but had done nothing.

European New Zealanders were divided by nationality too. Most were of British ancestry but a key group were Irish and others were German, Scandinavian and Croatian. Although government leaders during the coming war would speak of the citizenry as 'kinfolk' of the people of Britain, eleven of seventy-six parliamentary candidates endorsed by Labour in the last national election before the war bore family names that were not British. Cullen, Sullivan, Duggan and O'Brien were Irish. Schramm and Nordmeyer were German. Hansen and Hultquist were Scandinavian. Neilson was a name both Irish and Scandinavian. Māori names were Paikea, Kohere, Ratana and

Tirikatene. A twelfth name, Beck, could be found in both Britain and Germany. One politician with a British family name was in fact Romany. Savage, who also bore a British name, was Irish Catholic.

Irish Catholic New Zealanders saw the world differently to Anglo-Scots New Zealanders. They certainly did not think of themselves as British. Croatians, too, were Catholic. Catholics as a whole were wage workers who mostly voted for the Labour Party. The worldwide Catholic church had its own foreign policy, which by no means fitted snugly alongside the foreign policy of the government of New Zealand. Catholic clergy in the dominion nearly all agreed with Labour about the Nazi Party. James Liston, the senior Catholic bishop, spoke sternly about Hitler: 'his ideals, principles and methods are opposed to all that the Catholic church holds dear'.[12] At the same time the church was clear about which state and which political system was its worst enemy: 'The first peril, the greatest and the most general,' Pope Pius XI told the faithful, 'is certainly Communism in all its forms.'[13]

Not only were citizens often at odds with one another, the whole body of citizens was at odds with colonial subjects living willingly or unwillingly under the New Zealand flag. Samoans, Niueans, Tokelauans and Cook Islanders saw the world differently to their overlords in the main archipelago. Cantonese coolies in the tropical island colonies saw things differently too. Cantonese in the dominion, meanwhile, were yet another society within a society: they cared hardly at all about the British Empire or the Third Reich but backed the Guomindang dictatorship of China in its wars with Japan and the Communist Party.[14]

Class rivalry, another constant cause of tension between citizens, was closely linked with a wide gap in wealth between those at the bottom of the social heap and those at the top. The wealth gap had narrowed steadily since the turn of the century, but in the last year of peace the richest one tenth of people still owned over 51 per cent of all wealth, while the poorest half of citizens owned only 15 per cent.[15] 'The wealth of this country,' noted economist William Doig, 'is concentrated in the hands of a comparatively small group.'[16]

Family inheritance was the main source of wealth for the wealthy. The richest dynasties were landowners, merchants, financiers and industrialists. Kenneth Myers, for example, lived chiefly on inherited income from shares and fees as a company director.[17] Margaret Pirie, his wife, came from a family with inherited investments in coffee plantations and her income was drawn from those investments. The couple lived in a big house with white columns where a nanny took care of their children, a butler was head of staff, a chauffeur drove them, a cook worked in their kitchen, two maids cleaned the house, a washerwoman saw to the laundry and four gardeners looked after the grounds.[18] Myers, his biographers observe, 'was not feeling rich'[19] because the Labour government was hiking taxes on the wealthy. The gap between rich and poor was satirised by the poet A.R.D. Fairburn:

The working class: skilled workers in a railways workshop. Standard, *16 November 1939.*

old wealthy women, buyers of etchings, fondlers
of dogs, holders of stocks
in sweatshops where the young virgins,
the daughters of the poor,
housed with machines endure the hands of clocks ...[20]

Class was linked with conflict between the two main political coalitions, the National Party and Labour Party, as voting was closely based on social class.[21]

The Labour Party had come to power for the first time in 1935 and was building a welfare state. Labour members of parliament were men and women who had worked for wages or else came from households of the lower middle class. Savage, for example, was a former labourer whose assets amounted to around £4000,[22] quite a good sum for someone from the unskilled working class. The Labour Party worked hard to narrow the gap between rich and poor and make life easier for those on wages. A cornerstone of the new rights of the working class was a system of 'social security' begun in the autumn of 1939 with the aim of giving state help to anyone and everyone who was poor or struggling. Savage told citizens in a series of radio broadcasts that fairly sharing wealth was part of democracy.[23]

Labour was not wholly united, however, under Savage. The prime minister was drugged and dying. A succession struggle was stirring.

One group within the government, believing itself to be the left, spoke about a need to be more socialist. John A. Lee, the most quickwitted and quicksilver of politicians, early in 1939 attacked the government for 'shilly-shallying and drift' away from socialism and for not attacking the 'capitalist financial machine'.[24] A centrist group was strong in the party. Walter Nash, finance minister and one of its leaders, was worthy but wordy. Peter Fraser, tersely austere and another centrist leader, was already more or less acting prime minister. Social democracy, the two believed, could not be built overnight in a world of capitalist and imperialist great powers. Conflict between the left and centrist groups within Labour was based partly on nationality. Fraser and Nash, both born in Britain, felt a strong bond with what for them was the 'Mother Country'. The group opposing them was led by politicians born in New Zealand.

A new and powerful wing of the organised working class had been formed in 1937 when trade unions and district labour councils came together in the Federation of

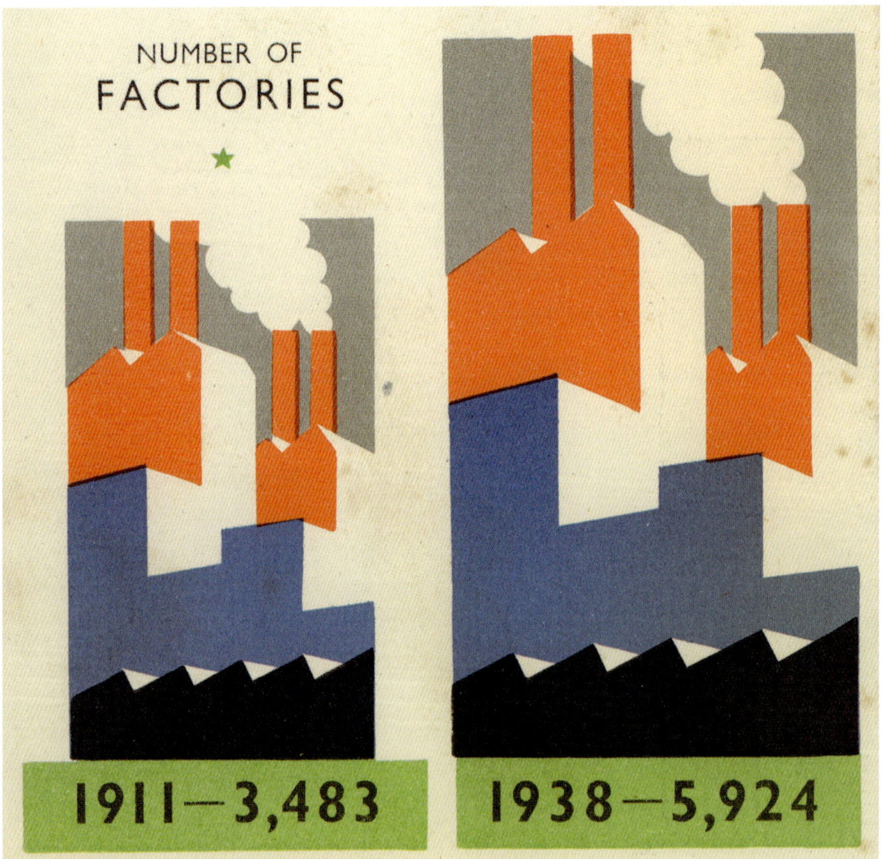

Manufacturing was a vital and growing part of the economy, although many people made the mistake of believing that the dominion depended economically on farming; by far the largest share of national wealth was earned by service industries and manufacturing.
Alexander Turnbull Library Eph-A-WAR-WII-1939-02.

American cars had been the most popular in the dominion until the late 1920s, but during the 1930s government tariffs and import licences favoured cars imported from Britain or assembled from British parts in New Zealand. *Press, 1 April 1939.*

Labour. A conference of the federation in 1938 voted to condemn Nazi Germany, fascist Italy and 'Japanese Military-Fascism' as a 'terrible threat to world peace' and called on the working class 'to more firmly unite its ranks, strengthen its organizations, sharpen its vigilance and generate greater activity in the struggle against Fascism and war'.[25] Foreign policy views in the Federation of Labour tended more to the left than the centrist group within the Labour Party.

The Communist Party, outside the government altogether, was small but lively. Mabel Howard, a trade union official, wrote a letter to Lee saying that the party was 'strong and well-organised' in Canterbury.[26] Wellington and Auckland were strongholds too. Communists worked towards a united front with the Labour Party. The Friends of the Soviet Union, a volunteer group, often worked alongside the party.

The Social Credit Association was another organisation jockeying for say inside and around the Labour Party. A mass movement among the lower middle class, the skilled working class and small farmers, its strongholds were in the North Island. This lobby group wanted to throw out capitalism and begin a new economic system that would be what its founding thinker called 'a Utopia of our own'.[27] One of thousands of households eager about the movement was the clever and talkative Scott family of Taradale. Lewis Scott, house painter, 'thought of all political events as evidence of international monetary plots' and believed there was a worldwide 'financial conspiracy, authorised and controlled by the Zionist faction of the Jewish people'.[28] Social Credit helped shape the opinions of many people within the Labour Party.

The deepest divide among class groups was not between organisations of the left but between the left and the right.

The National Party, the leading organisation of the political right, sat on the opposition benches in parliament. An alliance of farmers and landowners with city merchants, financiers, lawyers, doctors, shopkeepers and white-collar workers, it found common ground by seeking to safeguard the 'rights' of property. The party also spoke about bringing together everybody who believed in 'the political and economic unity of the Empire'. Adam Hamilton was parliamentary leader for the National Party. The son of a propertied family, educated at university and qualified as a clergyman after graduating from Knox College, he was a merchant and chairman of directors in Southland. National in the hands of such leaders was not a herd of hidebound conservatives but a modern mass party, willing to call for 'progressive and humanitarian legislation' to satisfy its following among the lower middle class.[29] The party wanted to provide a free health system for the poor, along with an old-age benefit for everybody.[30] At the same time, it was certainly a party of the right. A secret circular told its electoral candidates that the leaders of the Labour Party were 'traitors' to the British Empire.[31] Hamilton wanted 'equality of opportunity' rather than 'equality of everyone', which he said was the policy of the Labour Party.[32] He also told citizens that Savage wished to build a 'communist dictatorship' and was in thrall to the Soviet Union.

'Mother!' cried a party pamphlet. 'Do you want your child to drag out an existence as a wage-slave of a socialist state ... at the whim of a dictator?'[33]

The political right, like the left, suffered from strains and stresses.

Working farmers looked askance at large landowners, country voters at city voters, clerks at business owners. The unity of the right in the northern half of the North Island looked creaky for a while in 1937 when the Auckland Provincial Freedom League was set up among city company owners to fight the Labour Party. Working farmers were likely to see the league as a plot by 'townie capitalists'.[34] Queen Street and Hereford Street were by no means always good friends with Te Awamutu and Temuka.

Queen Street and Hereford Street needed to court farmers thanks to an electoral gerrymander, the 'country quota', giving country electorates 28 per cent more seats in parliament than was warranted by their share of electors. A strikingly undemocratic system, it boosted the power of farmers while sapping the power of the city. The quota was backed by an even less democratic polling system for county councils. Only people who owned property had the right to vote in a county; farm workers, forestry workers, fishers, miners and their spouses had no say. Raglan county, for example, was one of many where a majority of citizens, most of them belonging to coalmining or wage-earning households, had no right to vote for their own councillors.[35]

Newspapers spoke the language of class and occasionally class war. A press editorial in the last autumn of peace used the word 'armistice' to talk not about military matters but the struggle between workers and employers; it claimed that workers with their 'incessant demands for higher wages and reduced working hours' were an assault on the owner and the investor.[36] Almost all newspapers were loudspeakers for the right, being owned by moneyed conservatives who backed the National Party. Oliver Duff, editor, observed drily that 'the most influential newspapers' were 'firmly based on property and the flag'.[37] The daily press in every city, added a university essayist, weighed heavily in the lives of 'the masses who habitually devour the morning and evening paper and direct their lives accordingly'.[38] *Truth*, a widely read weekly, once had spoken for the radical left but now was on the reactionary right. The *Standard*, founded in 1935 as a socialist weekly, never won anything like the mass readership enjoyed by *Truth*. Socialist poet R.A.K. Mason, writing in the first issue of another new socialist newspaper, *People's Voice*, claimed that two voices could be heard in New Zealand:

> *One is the voice of our people. It is clear, bold and direct. It indulges in no high heroics, it is lacking in sentimentality, it turns and laughs at itself. Above all it is marked by vigorous independence ... The other is an old half-witted sheep. It is the voice of a front-page article in the 'Herald', of a leader in the 'Dominion' ... It is not the voice of the people at all. It speaks only for a few thousand money-addled reactionaries.*[39]

Conflicts between left and right that tugged so strongly during years of peace would not go away when the government decided to go to war.

EVERYONE DOING THE GOOSE-STEP?

The Labour Party was suspicious of the military. Arming, drilling, disciplining and above all conscripting citizens were seen by many of its followers as a way for the moneyed to weaken the working class. The party at its very first conference had condemned conscription as 'the negation of liberty'. Also from the start it had linked 'Militarism and Capitalism'.[40] Nor was the military looked upon too warmly by many other groups in society. The First World War had led people to ask whether 'patriotism' was a word that could mask an authoritarian way of looking at the world. 'Europe today,' wrote one correspondent to the *Standard*, 'proves that patriotism is the refuge for greater scoundrels and the cloak for more bestial brutality than ever before.'[41]

Teachers in state schools no longer preached the glory of war. A new generation of liberal and often leftish graduates of teaching colleges meant that the profession as a whole had mixed feelings about the military. Thomas Charters, retired army major and president of the Canterbury Navy League, noted that teachers responded in 'only a lukewarm' way when his group offered 'to educate school children and public opinion relative to the safety of the Empire'. The major went on to complain that schools no

Auckland War Memorial: war memorials in every city, suburb, township and sometimes even at country crossroads kept alive the grim memory of the First World War. Railways Magazine, *1939.*

longer offered prizes to students for the best essays on patriotic topics. William Cartwright, president of the North Canterbury branch of the Educational Institute, pointed out that schools had stopped giving such prizes because they strove instead 'to develop a true belief in democracy'.[42] The *School Journal*, which early in the century had been crammed with verse, stories and images about battles that had built the British Empire, now was telling children about 'the horror and waste' of fighting.[43]

Young people were more likely than older people to turn a cold shoulder to things warlike. William Pearson, student, felt 'a revulsion against the horror and futility of the First World War' and 'looked on nationalism as a dangerous passion'.[44] Lauris Scott, another student, on visiting the national war memorial in Wellington, reeled at the sight of 'revolting pictures' of 'colonels and captains in purple robes and smothered with medals, with pink faces and white moustaches'.[45] Young people as a whole, wrote one woman, felt 'great impatience' when 'their elders' talked about the First World War.[46]

Old soldiers could feel the same way. A wage worker and former soldier was portrayed by David Ballantyne in his novel *The Cunninghams* as saying to himself: 'no more fresh-faced New Zealand kids for Europe's battlefields'. The old soldier goes on to say it was 'cruel for the mothers when their children went to war'.[47] Wives and sisters of old soldiers could agree passionately. 'The annihilation of ten million men' in the First World War was lamented by a newspaper correspondent who called herself 'the mother of a young son'. She called the war 'mass murder' and lamented its 'hideous futility'.[48] Thousands felt much the same way when they stood in grieving crowds every Anzac Day.

A lot of young people and many of the middle-aged had shifted so sharply away from glorifying war that they were outright pacifists.

Pacifism drew its followers from among the ranks of working-class socialists, lower-middle-class Methodists and Baptists, doctors and lawyers and academics belonging to the League of Nations Union, and a wide variety of others throughout the country. A socialist writer commented on 'the most mixed, the most diverse, frequently the most contradictory' array of pacifist believers and beliefs.[49] Communists wrestled with the question, as did Christians. The Presbyterian church agreed to neither support nor oppose pacifist preaching.[50] One out of every three Methodist ministers joined the

Christian Pacifist Society.[51] The Peace Pledge Union, founded in Christchurch, drew many Christians and also many socialists. Of 890 organisations in the country backing a National Peace Council petition for a peace conference on the eve of the war, 258 were trade unions or Labour Party branches, 213 were school committees, 119 were friendly societies, 75 were churches, 73 were local bodies and 45 were branches of the Women's Christian Temperance Union.[52] A questionnaire among university students showed that nearly three out of every ten would not fight against an enemy invasion of the country, while nearly one in ten was unsure whether they would fight or not. Two out of every ten students thought peace could be won by the overthrow of capitalism.[53] The 'whole country' had 'gone defeatist', protested a letter to the *Dominion*.[54]

The swell of feeling against fighting was strongest fifteen or so years after the end of the First World War. However, during the late 1930s, more and more people thought it would be necessary to strengthen the military. The Labour government by the eve of the new war was spending millions on the army, air force and navy.

WHY?

The Labour Party had never been opposed in principle to strengthening the military; it said only that the state must field nothing but a voluntary citizen force whose soldiers, sailors and airmen must be paid a good wage. The government based its view of the world on a doctrine known as 'collective security', or in other words the theory that states should band together in order to work cooperatively against any state 'indicated as an aggressor by international authority'.[55] The League of Nations was the appropriate international authority. Almost everyone in the Labour Party earnestly hoped for good things from the League.

'Labour's passion for peace,' said Savage, 'makes it necessary for us to support the collective action of the League of Nations.'[56]

The government believed that the international body must be given good sharp teeth in the shape of weapons and troops. Citizens were warned that the dominion might go to war against an aggressive state if asked by the League of Nations. New Zealand in such an event would 'fight in sorrow for the good of the future,' said Nash.[57] The government was deeply unhappy about fascist states in Europe and the military dictatorship of Japan. Opposition to fascism and dictatorship was a core principle of the Labour Party.

Labour began strengthening the military. At first, the new government had been wary of spending for such purposes when its great goal was not to kill foreign foes but to better the lives of its own citizenry. A committee was set up in 1936 to look into war policy. Lee, the only one on the committee who had ever worn a uniform, said that no government leader knew 'the difference between a gas-mask and a tinopener'.[58] Frederick Jones was war minister, but in the words of one high official he was 'a non-

Michael Joseph Savage and eager citizens in the general election campaign, 1938.
Alexander Turnbull Library 1/2-051739-F.

entity' and the war portfolio was in truth run by Nash.[59] The war committee learnt that the previous conservative government had wanted an army and navy that would fit closely with the needs of the foreign and war policy of the British Empire. Lee spoke for many social democrats when he said that sending an army overseas for such purposes would be 'morally repugnant'.[60] A policy geared not towards imperial wars for imperial purposes but towards defending the dominion from attack was the goal of the new government.

Labour made up its mind to shell out, though thriftily, on what seemed to be the key things for the defence of the home islands: a modernised navy and a greatly strengthened air force. Year by year, allowances for the army, navy and air force were hiked, climbing slowly from less than 3.9 per cent to some 5.3 per cent of all state spending.[61] Savage spoke to parliament in the winter of 1938 to advise what was being done with such big sums of money:

> *The mechanisation of the Army on modern lines is proceeding, and the Territorial Force is being extended and improved. The most important advance has been the inauguration of an air defence scheme. The estimates for the Army, Navy, and Air Force account for £2,000,000, but in addition £1,000,000 is being provided for new landing fields and hangars and equipment.*[62]

The war budget trebled, in terms of sums spent, during the first three years of government by the Labour Party.

Although a governing party of social democrats was willing to spend more money on the military, the men of the social democracy were not very willing to sign up. Young and youngish men were asked from late 1937 to join the regular army, navy or air force, or else volunteer for a reserve territorial army. At first the hope was that the territorial army would number about 50,000 men, but volunteering was so lacklustre that the target was dropped to a mere 15,000, which in turn was not met.

Conservatives called for conscription. A group of businessmen and army officers late in 1936 had formed a body called the Defence League and branches now sprang up throughout the country. The league thought it 'imperative' that citizens should 'realise their responsibilities and immediately set in train preparations for their own safety, and that of their country'. The state, they declared, must 'develop an adequate system of defence on sea, land, and in the air', must 'mobilise and co-ordinate the country's resources' and must be ready to wage war on behalf of the British Empire.[63] Lee defined the leaders of the league as 'retired and liverish colonels who want to see everyone doing the goose-step'.[64] The League said it was not against the government nor tied up with class or party politics, but members were mostly conservative business people, landowners, farmers and Anglican clergy. William Perry, national president, was a wealthy lawyer who had been appointed to the upper house of parliament by the National government before it was defeated by the Labour Party.

'If New Zealand cannot produce another army like the one she sent overseas 1914–18 and do it quickly,' wrote a citizen, 'then we women may as well equip ourselves with revolvers and make a pact to save our children from the bayonet and ourselves from rape.'[65]

'Military service is good for youth,' wrote another, 'and helps to mould his character along the right lines.'[66]

The Defence League went in for widespread speechmaking and lobbying. The National Party beat the same drum, one of its election pamphlets in 1938 stressing the 'threat' posed by an unnamed foreign enemy:

> *Twenty years ago – the Dominion annually trained 30,000 territorials. To-day – only 3000 have attended camps this year … It is tragic that the socialist Labour Government should leave New Zealand women and children without proper protection!*[67]

Conscription was opposed by nearly the whole of the organised working class, which looked very coldly on the Defence League. The *Standard* linked the league with fascist ways of thinking. A lot of people on the left feared a right-wing coup. A Labour Party conference in the autumn of 1937 called for the state to step in and forcibly disband any 'armed forces not directly under the control of the Government'.[68] The Federation of Labour at its national conference the following year denounced the National Party and Defence League campaigns for compulsory military training, saying that drilling boys in barracks would be 'the prelude to a demand for conscription for overseas services in the event of an imperialist war'. The conference also condemned the way citizens had been 'subjected to what was virtually a military dictatorship' in the First World War.[69] The Labour government, while it was willing to boost spending on the military, right up to the eve of the new world war held out firmly against the notion of conscripting anybody.

'[T]he best reply to the conscriptionist,' said Savage, 'is to show that we are a free people, prepared to stand together in the case of an emergency.'[70]

THE GREAT POWERS

The world was more or less under the sway of eight great powers, three of which were democracies – at least in the opinion of their citizens – while the other five were uncompromising dictatorships. The 'democratic' great powers were France, Britain and the United States. The dictatorships were Japan, the Soviet Union, China, Italy and Germany.

Paris and Wellington had been allies during the Great War and were still thought by most citizens to be more or less on the same side. The *Press*, a leading conservative newspaper, told readers that 'no two countries' had 'closer community of interest than Great Britain and France'.[71] Social and economic links between France and New Zealand were slight, however, and not growing. The Front Populaire, a coalition of the centre and left, had governed France for two years and had spoken out about a need for more democracy in the worldwide empire held by Paris, but had broken up late in 1938 before anything much was done to make deeds out of words. The government now in charge of homeland and empire was a ministry of the centre right, led by Édouard Daladier.

French claims to democracy were badly compromised by the fact that women in the homeland had no right to vote and colonial subjects were governed by what was more or less imperial dictatorship. France denied voting rights and imposed a curfew and forced labour, for example, on the very doorstep of New Zealand in the colony of New Caledonia.[72] France had also killed many thousands of people between the two world wars by turning machine guns against unwilling colonial subjects in Morocco, Syria, Central Africa and French Indochina.

The Soviet Union was a vast state governed by the Communist Party and led by the 'Man of Steel', former seminarian and clerk Iosif Stalin. The economy was vast too. Gross domestic product accounted for nearly 10 per cent of the wealth of the whole world, second in size only to the United States.[73] Moscow claimed that its government was more truly a democracy than the governments of other states. It also claimed that the nationalities under its rule in Central Asia and Northeast Asia were not colonial subjects.

'Long live the mighty air force of the socialist nation!': Soviet Union Defence Ministry poster, 1939. *Artist: Viktor Dobrovolsky. www.pandia.ru*

New Zealand opinion was deeply divided over the rights and wrongs of the Soviet Union. Wage workers often saw the socialist republic as a ray of hope. Moneyed citizens were more likely to see it as a death ray.

A third great power was Guomindang China. The Guomindang, a political party modelled on old Confucian traditions of strict yet paternalistic governance and new fascist systems of governance, controlled many provinces of China. Jiang Jieshi, party leader – known in the dominion as Chiang Kaishek – claimed to speak on behalf of the whole of China. A basic principle of both fascism and his government, he declared, was that citizens must live to serve the state rather than the state serving the citizenry. The state was 'the most lofty entity'.[74] The deaths of nearly four million people in a flood along the lower Yangtze in 1931 and a famine that killed some five million people in several western provinces in 1936 showed that the state he headed was so far from being a lofty entity that it could not even save its subjects from drowning or starving. 'More Dead in China' was the weary headline above one of the very few reports on the 1936 famine in New Zealand newspapers.[75] Corruption was rife, criminal gangs and business groups were at loggerheads, warlords chased their own claims to power, bandits scoured the countryside, and peasants seldom gave the government anything other than passive obedience, or else worked hard to get around its laws.

Fascist Italy, a fourth great power, was a one-party state led by Benito Mussolini that held conquered colonial territory in Africa. New Zealand citizens had varying opinions about this dictator and his dictatorship. One out of every hundred or so people in the dominion was of Italian or partly Italian ancestry, but only a minority of them belonged to the Fascist Party.[76] The Labour Party believed that Italy, as one of the victors in the First World War, had no grounds for claiming new territory. Catholic New Zealand, however, was told by many of its clergy that heaven smiled upon fascist Italy. Conservative New Zealand thought Mussolini had done a good job in imposing order and law. The *New Zealand Herald*, a strong voice of the right, in 1933 praised the dictator for his work towards making a 'unified and orderly commonwealth' out of feckless Italy.[77]

Nazi Germany, led by Adolf Hitler, had its eye on new colonies in Eastern Europe, and only occasionally made noises about being handed back colonies in Africa, Asia and the Pacific – Samoa and Nauru among them – seized by the Allies during the First World War. Germany was rich – its economy the third largest in the world after the United States and Soviet Union – but its navy was weak and a very long way away.

Tens of thousands of people in the dominion and in Samoa were of German ancestry; few signed up as Nazis. However, New Zealand conservatives often looked approvingly upon the Third Reich. Nazism, for them, was less worrying than socialism and the Soviet Union. Donald Brown, a doctor, praised the way Germany had been lifted 'to a wonderful standard' by the Nazi Party.[78] Anthony Chorlton, a lawyer, wrote that Germany had become 'a very much cleaner country morally than it was a few years ago'.[79] John Laird, a clergyman, agreed that fascism had given Germans 'unity, peace, security, and hope'.[80] Ngaio Marsh, artist and writer, was aware that the Canterbury landowners with whom she hobnobbed were by no means opposed to the Nazi Party. A landed lady in her novel *Died in the Wool* could have backed the party, she wrote; while a young landowner in the same novel did indeed fall 'in love with' Nazism.[81]

Hitler and Mussolini shown as a pair of burglars stealing 'loot' from Europe and Africa, 1939. *Artist: Don Angus. Alexander Turnbull Library A-312-2-001.*

The Labour Party, meanwhile, looked very much askance at the Nazi Party. The fascists had crushed German trade unions, rounded up and killed German social democrats, and herded German young men into the military. Nazism was 'the antithesis of Socialism,' wrote a social democratic citizen in Wellington; it was 'monopoly-capitalism imposing its will on the masses whom it has deliberately transformed into its slaves'.[82] The Federation of Labour denounced the way the Nazi state behaved towards the working class of Germany.[83] The Matata branch of the Labour Party, when it called Nazism 'the dangerous enemy of democracy and world peace', typified the views of many working people in New Zealand.[84]

'This man believes something with passionate intensity. He believes his race is meant to dominate the earth'. This image, published with an accompanying caption by a church group, shows the point of view from which many people in New Zealand saw Nazi Germany. Only one in three German citizens voted for the Nazi Party, however, at least until free elections were stopped by the dictatorship. A 'passionate' and seamlessly united Germany was nothing more than propaganda. Evening Post, *3 October 1942.*

The government believed nonetheless that Germany had been wrongly victimised by the peace settlement at the end of the First World War. Nash declared that while Wellington was 'not in agreement with many aspects' of Nazi policy, Berlin 'had suffered some injustices' at the hands of the Allies.[85] Labour thought the German policy of adding territory to the Third Reich not wrong, so long as the territory was peopled by Germans and expansion was done peacefully. Also, the Labour government wanted to boost exports to the Third Reich. Germany had been one of the most important trading partners of the dominion before the First World War. Nash and his advisors flew to Berlin in 1937 to meet leading officials, industrialists and Hjalmar Schacht, economic minister and head of the

Reichsbank. Montagu Norman, head of the Bank of England, wrote to Schacht offering a pen portrait of Nash: 'He is,' said the great British banker, 'at once charming and dangerous – an extreme Socialist and a complete Christian.'[86]

In 1938 New Zealand and Germany signed a most-favoured-nation trade agreement, which was then ratified by parliament in Wellington. Labour politicians speaking in support of the deal talked about a need to build trade with such a rich market and also about binding the two nations peacefully. David Wilson, former tailor and national secretary of the party, said in the upper house that it was up to the Germans, and not 'the people of New Zealand', to decide what political system should govern their country.[87] The left of the party backed the agreement less strongly than the right. Lee wrote that it would be better for the government to 'import German technicians to eat our butter and manufacture goods here' than import German manufactured goods, but went on to say that 'the principle of the bill is good.'[88] National politicians broke out in what a newspaper called 'a storm of protest'[89] about how a trade agreement might weaken links with Britain, though in the end nearly all backed the agreement.

'I can offer no great objection,' said Hamilton, 'but I think most of us would stand for Britain first, Britain second, and Britain practically all the time, and anything likely to disturb our very valuable relations with Great Britain needs to be very carefully watched.'[90]

The government at the same time took a novel step by allowing a few refugees from the Nazi state to come and settle in New Zealand. Tens of thousands were keen to come. Labour was not keen on those tens of thousands coming. Opening the door to a throng of refugees, it was thought, would so seriously strain the finances of the government as to slow the building of the welfare state. Wellington agreed to let in only 1000 or so, almost all of whom were Jewish.

Jews were disliked by many New Zealanders. A jeering nickname used for Jews by working people was 'Ikey Mo'. A sneering nickname used by the middle class was 'Solomon and Company'. Conservatives said that socialism was in the grip of Jews. Socialists said that capitalism was in the grip of Jews. Arthur Field, who wrote for Social Credit, denounced 'the Jewishness of international finance' along with 'the Jewishness of Socialism'.[91] Jews, he added, were 'a definitely non-assimilable race'.[92] Lyla Matthews, a woman of the middle class who married a businessman of German-Jewish background, Bernhard Falck, wrote about him to her son as 'that slimy Hebrew'. The son, leftish poet Denis Glover, had an affair with a Jewish woman, Dorée Elkind, though he later called her 'a fat little Jewess!'[93] Merchants worried that the dominion was being invaded by an 'influx of alien businessmen' who were German Jews.[94] A nationwide chain of stores advertised in the *New Zealand Financial Times* telling readers that none of its company officials were Jews. Professional groups closed ranks to keep out Jews. The president of the Auckland Medical Association said 'that protective measures would have to be taken to safeguard against an influx of Jewish doctors to New Zealand'. The New Zealand Dental Association went further, asking for a complete ban on 'non-Aryans' seeking to come to the dominion from Germany.[95]

These five great powers could not do a lot to influence New Zealand. The same was not true of the other three: Japan, Britain and the United States.

JAPAN

New Zealand was not yet at war but many citizens worried about a murderous struggle under way in China. The Sino-Japanese War broke out when Guomindang and Japanese troops in the northern summer of 1937 opened fire on one another near Beijing. The war was not authorised by Tokyo. Japanese troops started shooting as a consequence of *gekokujo*, 'the head obeying the tail' or, in other words, a coup carried out by officers in the field taking matters into their own hands rather than acting upon orders from superiors. Afterwards, further *gekokujo* drew Tokyo into bewildering new entanglements.

Nanjing fell to an invading Japanese army. Chinese civilians in their tens of thousands were slaughtered while the world looked on and did nothing. Hundreds of thousands more died during the following months, too, killed or starved by Japanese troops. Thousands were also killed by their own troops in this ruthless war. Elwyn Jansen, from Otago, flinched at the sight of trigger-happy Guomindang soldiers; he noted 'how cheaply' they held the lives of their fellow Chinese.[96] The Guomindang withdrew inland, establishing its headquarters in Chongqing.

Japan was a dictatorship dominated by military and civilian reactionaries whose grip was so firm that they could afford to quarrel with one another about policy without risking losing their hold on the government. New Zealand had only weak links with Japan. The Labour government and the organised working class as a whole disliked the dictatorship in Tokyo. Conservatives on the other hand often saw Japan as a force for good in China, as we shall see.

The Japanese economy, like the New Zealand economy, was booming in the late 1930s and its industrial output was twice that of the whole of the rest of Asia outside the Soviet Union. Japan was one of the biggest exporters and importers in the world. Overseas trade was such a crucial part of its economy that its leaders were anxious about interwar hiking of trade barriers by most states.[97] Trading nations, by building tariff walls around themselves and their markets, were shutting the door on Japan. Japanese governing circles grew willing to think about war as a way to capture markets. Tokyo was able to point out, too, that Britain, France and the Netherlands for many years had deployed troops and gunboats to awe weak states in Asia and the Pacific. The British Empire during the nineteenth century had forced Beijing to cede treaty ports, the colony of Hong Kong and concessions over Guangdong and the Yangtze valley. The United States, by contrast, sought to exploit China neither by formal colonisation nor by staking out spheres of influence, but by an informal imperialism known as the 'Open Door'. Chinese nationalists of all political opinions wanted everybody out: the British, the Americans and the Japanese.

Japan found itself able to win impressive short-term victories in China but struggled to convert good outcomes on the battlefield into strategic advantage, as would happen later when Tokyo went to war with Britain and the United States.

British policy was to avoid provoking Japan.[98] New Zealand conservatives backed the policy. The *Otago Daily Times* told readers that territorial expansion by such a 'virile' nation as Japan was 'inevitable'.[99] Japan, added another newspaper, was 'the outpost of Western civilization and ideals' in Northeast Asia.[100] A conference of British Commonwealth prime ministers in 1937 talked about trying to put together a pact with Japan and Western powers to guarantee the status quo in Asia. Savage was not keen because of a Labour Party belief that the League of Nations should be guarantor of the independence of China. He agreed to a pact on condition that the Guomindang government become one of its members – and won his point.[101] This was perhaps the high point of Wellington's influence on the political shape of Asia.

New Zealand and Japan had been linked by a trade treaty signed in 1928, the first trade treaty ever made by New Zealand with any government outside the British Empire. Alan Richards, an Auckland traveller and journalist, foresaw the growth of a good market for butter and 'an almost limitless demand' for wool in Japan.[102] Japanese shipping companies launched direct sailings between their home ports and the ports of New Zealand. Japanese merchant firms opened branches in New Zealand. Japan became a key source of cottons, silks, earthenware, glassware, footwear and hosiery,[103] and it also supplied oak to the furniture industry.

Yet the Labour government did nothing to try to help trade along.[104] Shipments of goods between Japan and New Zealand boomed for two or so years then fell away. The government, when setting up a new system to control flows of money from 1938 onwards, made it easy for importers to swap New Zealand pounds for British pounds but hard to get hold of Japanese yen – and United States dollars, German marks and French francs. The Japanese consulate in Wellington spoke about the new policy as something that might prove 'a great mistake' for the dominion economy. The 'huge industrial activities' of his homeland needed such things as wool and casein, which could be supplied by New Zealand. The regional manager of Mitsui and Company added that not only was Japan a big buyer of wool imports from the dominion, it also exported big shipments of materials used by the secondary industries of New Zealand.[105] Wool exports to Japan dropped quickly, nonetheless, together with imports from Japan.

A lot of people on the political right still had hopes of making money out of Japan. Also, a lot of people still believed in the civilising mission of Japan. Warren Garland, exporter, early in 1939 after a trip to Shanghai, spoke warmly of the way the rising sun was lighting up life for those lucky enough to find themselves shone upon by its rays. 'The Japanese stand for law and order,' he told journalists. 'If Japan eventually controls China, I believe it will be the making of China.'[106]

Conservatives now worried, however, that Japanese business would push British business out of the hinterlands of Shanghai and Guangzhou. The National Party cared little what flag flew over those hinterlands but a lot about who made money. The *Evening Post* pointed out that the subcontinent was 'the last great open market of the trading world – to put the issue on a crude, material basis'.[107] Japan, it was feared, would close that market to the British Empire. Almost all leading newspapers now turned away from Tokyo in order to back the Guomindang. The *New Zealand Herald* declared as early as 1937 that Tokyo wanted to impose 'Japanese hegemony' over 'a large part of eastern Asia and … the north-western Pacific'.[108] Conservative views were coming close to those of the Labour Party.

Nagoya Pan-Pacific Peace Exposition poster, 1937. An international exposition in the city of Nagoya aimed to promote international peace while showcasing Japanese prosperity. Not long afterwards, unauthorised attacks by frontline troops drew Tokyo into a bloody war with Guomindang China.

The Labour government dealt with the Sino-Japanese War by holding talks with the Guomindang government – its consul in Wellington acting as go-between – and with the Conservative government in London. Additionally, the Labour government asked the League of Nations in Geneva to impose trade sanctions on Tokyo.[109] William Jordan, dominion representative to the League, bitterly attacked Britain in several speeches in London and Geneva. New Zealand was so strong in its statements that Maxim Litvinov, foreign minister of the Soviet Union, got the dominion onto a League of Nations committee to investigate the crisis between China and Japan.[110] Britain, by contrast, opposed stern measures against Japan.[111] New Zealand conservatives were edgy about the policy of the Labour Party. Melbourne, Paris and The Hague all disagreed with the position taken by Wellington.[112]

Worker unions went further than the government, calling for a trade embargo to put pressure on Tokyo. Watersiders refused to load Japanese ships. The Auckland chamber of commerce spoke up sharply, saying that wharf workers were behaving in an 'improper' way. The Labour government stepped in to stop the ban, not wanting to harm trade with Japan, and a deal was struck by which the unions kept up a ban on scrap iron, but went back to loading all other goods.[113] The *Standard* spoke against widening the trade embargo unless it was backed by states around the world.

'Any boycott,' it told readers, 'will not improve our commercial or diplomatic relations with Japan, and though this may appear to be a materialistic viewpoint, it should be remembered that we live under a capitalistic system in a generally capitalistic world.'[114]

The Federation of Labour the following autumn adopted a manifesto calling on the government to 'organise collective action to bring to an end Japanese aggression' in China.[115] At the same time, writers of the political left were penning prose and poetry about the Sino-Japanese War. Rewi Alley, organiser of an industrial cooperative for the Guomindang, published poetry. James Bertram, working as a newspaper correspondent and radio broadcaster, published *Crisis in China* in 1937, followed two years later by *North China Front*. Robin Hyde brought out *Dragon Rampant*.

The Labour government kept working away at the League of Nations. Wellington called for sanctions against Tokyo throughout 1938 and again early in 1939 but was supported only by Moscow. London opposed sanctions, as did Melbourne and Ottawa.[116]

Tianjin was the setting for another crisis in the middle of 1939 when Japan imposed a blockade on the treaty port. Cecil Davis, trade representative for New Zealand, was stripped naked by Japanese soldiers who wished to search the businessman from Canterbury. 'Stripping in itself means nothing to the Japanese,' Davis later observed.[117] Wellington, working with London, sent a formal protest to Tokyo. The Labour government seems not to have thought the matter so very grave. The National Party, on the other hand, was deeply stirred by what seemed an unwarranted insult to the dignity of both the dominion and the British Empire.

After the Tianjin crisis the Labour government brought its Japan policy wholly in line with the policy of the Conservative government in London. The first step was the Craigie–Arita Agreement, signed in the middle of the winter by Britain and Japan, which more or less acknowledged that Japan was now the paramount power in northern and central China. 'Britain has had to concede important points,' noted the *New Zealand Herald*.[118] Britain signed because its foreign policy was based on giving priority to Europe over Asia and the Pacific. Fraser told parliament: '[T]he earth is charged with electricity at the present time, and after all we are Members of the British community of nations.'[119] Wellington, in other words, was agreeing to give priority to Europe. The Labour government was not very keen to follow the British policy but did so because the League of Nations by then was clearly of no weight in the world.[120]

The left of the governing party was unhappy. Arnold Nordmeyer denounced the Craigie–Arita Agreement as 'the Eastern Munich'.[121] British policy, he added, meant that China was 'being sacrificed'.[122] John Robertson thundered that British policy was based on the desire of capitalists to safeguard their investments.[123] The British Commonwealth had 'sold out to a burglar', said William Anderton.[124] Britain was backing 'the aggressor' in order 'to maintain her power and prestige', added Robert McKeen.[125]

The Communist Party spoke up just as strongly, going so far as to say that Japan was a threat to democracy in the dominion as well as in China. 'New Zealand's first line of defence,' declared the *People's Voice*, 'is ... on the Yangtse.'[126]

Japan by the eve of world war was seen by nearly everyone in the dominion, whether on the left or right, as the wrongdoer in China. The Labour government looked on Japanese territorial expansion more sternly than it looked on expansion by Germany. Germany had been victimised after the First World War, while Japan had been one of the victors. Germany spoke about bringing together all Germans under one flag, following the principle that 'self-determination' was believed to be right and just by a wide array of people. Japan, on the other hand, was trying to impose its power over the Chinese and China. Tokyo was portrayed as aggressive and imperialist. The Guomindang, oddly, was portrayed as fighting for freedom and democracy.

Also, still more oddly, the rising sun was now being portrayed as a threat to New Zealand.

The dominion chiefs of military staff, when they surveyed the outlook for war in 1935, noted that only two powers were strong enough to attack New Zealand: Japan and the United States. The officer corps concluded that the 'only possible foe' was Japan.[127] The United States strongly backed the Guomindang and opened a trade war in the middle of 1939 by stopping exports of oil, copper and iron to Japan. The New Zealand government hoped that one day the Roosevelt administration would link itself in a common policy with the British Commonwealth and stop Japanese expansion in East Asia. One outcome of the new trade war, however, was that Tokyo felt more and more trapped and more and more urgently in need of some way to break out of what it saw as economic encirclement.

What would be the next step taken by Japan? Nobody knew; certainly not the government in Tokyo.

Japanese foreign policy was handled partly by cabinet, partly by the foreign ministry, partly by the army and partly by the navy.[128] Frank Hedges, a dominion journalist in Tokyo, wrote about the way Japanese army commanders often 'acted quite independently of and contrary to' the policy of the Japanese government.[129] Sato Naotake, who became foreign minister early in 1937, was applauded by parliament when he said that Japan should reverse its forward policy in China. He called for 'settling the China question peacefully and avoiding war with the Soviet Union'.[130] Tokyo signed an Anti-Comintern Pact with Berlin in 1936, hoping to 'contain' the Soviet Union. Japanese diplomats and politicians hoped, too, that the pact would be widened to bring in Britain and the Netherlands. The army was so much at odds with official foreign policy that a review of Japanese military planning at the same time took the novel step of providing for a possible war with the British Commonwealth. New Zealand, meanwhile, was now planning for a war with Japan.

The first steps were taken after autumn 1939 when the Labour government held a war conference in Wellington.

BRITAIN

Tokyo was not asked to send delegates to the war conference, but invitations were sent to London. Japan was a new player in the imperial game. Britain was an old player and the only great power whose doings stirred warm, sometimes passionate feelings in the hearts and heads of many people in New Zealand.

Trade and financial links between dominion and imperial motherland were strong. New Zealand importers bought nearly 49 per cent of their overseas purchases from Britain,[131] while exporters made 70 per cent of their earnings from selling to the British.[132] English and Scottish banking, furthermore, was at the heart of the banking and insurance system in New Zealand. Importers and exporters could have sought other sources of goods and capital, or other markets, but trade was constrained by a tangled skein of protective tariffs knitted around national and imperial economies during the interwar years.

It was also constrained by feelings – about nation, empire and loyalty.

Britain was not merely a centre of power and money but a sort of dream factory. The middle class and the rich called the homeland of their forebears 'Home'. The sons of landowners, merchants and manufacturers studied at Oxford and Cambridge. The daughters went to finishing schools in Chichester or Cheltenham. Well-to-do householders from the dominion consorted with well-to-do households in the Home Counties and the West End.

Helen Thomson, teacher at the University of Otago and descended from English and Scots colonists, found herself thinking 'constantly' when she was touring Britain on the eve of the war about the 'long dead figures of our race and spirits of our ancestors'.[133] New Zealanders, declared a conservative country editor, owed the motherland their 'love of freedom', their 'high traditions' and their 'pride of race'.[134] Almost every newspaper in the dominion bombarded readers with stories about Sandringham, not the Solomons; Twickenham, not Tonga. The *Press*, one of the worst offenders, observed that Fiji, the Cook Islands or Samoa 'meant less to the average New Zealander' than Europe.[135]

Trade followed the feelings of merchants, shipowners and exporters who loved the motherland and wanted to deal with nobody other than agents and friends and cousins and inlaws inside auction houses and counting houses and country houses at the end of well-worn grooves leading to Britain. The heavy focus on the British market for imports and above all exports was in many ways an outcome of the conservatism and lack of enterprise of New Zealand capitalists, who found life too comfortable to bother looking for and trying to open new markets.

Nor did the state do anything. The Labour government stuck so closely to trade with the 'old country'[136] that new import regulations guaranteed the British share of goods shipped into the dominion would not shrink and, indeed, could grow.[137] The National Party was still more strongly committed than the Labour Party to trade within the British Empire. Adam Hamilton in the autumn of 1939 took pains to claim that the dominion had 'no greater friend than Britain'. The Labour government, he went on, must not do 'any tinkering with our economic balance with the Motherland'.[138] The leader of the opposition was saying, in other words, that while profit was one concern of capitalists, another concern was national and imperial sentiment.

Only a few academics, capitalists or politicians called for new or strengthened trade links with states outside the British Empire. One was a young economist on the political left, John Condliffe, who spoke eloquently that same autumn about economic opportunities in the Pacific. The Pacific and the Americas, in his opinion, were 'the growing parts of the world' and the best prospect for trading wealth tomorrow.[139]

Yet trade – and above all export trade – stayed strongly tied to Britain.

New Zealand politicians and business people seldom thought of the strength of the British link as worrying or in any way risky. Conservatives and many social democrats viewed the British Empire as not only more generous, more just and more benevolent than other empires, but so rich and so strong it would go on thriving for hundreds of years. Also, it was evolving towards something new and still better: the Commonwealth.

The idea of a British commonwealth was tossed about by many people during the middle years of the 1920s. It was based on a political and constitutional understanding that Britain and the dominions – New Zealand, Australia, South Africa, Canada, Newfoundland and Ireland – were now equals in a collegial partnership. Cuthbert Alport, a prominent Conservative, in 1937 published *Kingdoms in Partnership*, in which he celebrated the new relationship between motherland and dominions as a sort of federation of kingdoms.[140]

New Zealand conservatives were slow to take to the concept of a Commonwealth. The *Auckland Star* editorialised that New Zealanders were 'content to belong to an Empire rather than a Commonwealth, and to be to some extent subordinate to Britain'.[141] Sons of conservative families were officers or officials for the British Empire, above all in Southeast Asia and South Asia. Adrian Hayter, for example, son of a landowning family in Canterbury and Marlborough, was an army officer in India. He wrote later about himself and his fellows: 'most of us young Army officers thought of ourselves as little tin gods … The fact that some Indians were highly developed in their own culture, and having passed through Oxford or Cambridge were far more advanced in ours than we ourselves, made no difference that to us all Indians were wogs.'[142]

Conservative citizens right up to the eve of the war still spoke not about Commonwealth but Empire. The word gave them pleasure and comfort. The National Party in its 1938 address-in-reply to parliament criticised the government for weakening 'the solidarity of the Empire'.[143] Nell Hartley, daughter of a Waikato farming family, won the junior oratory contest at her high school with a speech, 'Our Empire'.[144] The *New Zealand Herald* early in 1939 attacked the government for following a policy of economic nationalism and trying to make the dominion a state with 'a closed economy', which was a 'defection' from imperial unity.[145]

Citizens on the left, by contrast, were keen to talk about Commonwealth, not Empire. They disliked the imperial loyalty of the moneyed and middle class. John Beaglehole, an academic, wrote about the 'psychological retardation' of those who kept talking about Britain as 'Home'.[146] He and others on the left did not see the British Empire as the wonderful bulwark of law, order and civilisation admired by conservatives. They knew that Britain, like France, denied democracy to the vast majority of people under its imperial flag while squeezing wealth out of colonial holdings. British colonial governments taxed their subjects for the privilege of being subjects.[147] Poll taxes, hut taxes, village taxes and taxes on buying or selling covered the cost of controlling the typical colony while also levering its peasantry into growing cash crops for the imperial homeland.[148] Cash cropping, in turn, made peasants a more profitable market for manufactured goods imported from the imperial homeland. British colonial governments often imposed forced labour on their subjects, too.

British imperial subjects who were unhappy with colonial rule could be handled violently, even viciously, by imperial police and military. Nigerian women, for example, who protested against a capitation tax for ten years up to the eve of the war, were shot down by the colonial state.[149] At least they could be thankful that high explosives were not dropped on them by imperial warplanes. Villagers in Sudan were not so lucky. Nor were villagers in British Somaliland. Nor were Arabs who revolted against imperial rule in Palestine. Nor were villagers in the Northwest Frontier Province of India. Indian subjects were taxed to pay for soldiers to be sent to mop up villages after such bombings. The Indian Army, an immense force, was used by imperial authorities for such imperial purposes as putting down 'native rebels' not only in South Asia but in the colonies of the Middle East and Northeast Africa. 'The function of the army,' declared the internal affairs department of the government of India, was 'to suppress rebellion'.[150] A rebellion against imperial rule in Malabar was put down by killing some 10,000 subjects.[151] Village taxpayers, in other words, were paying to keep themselves suppressed while also giving imperial authorities free troops to keep hold elsewhere in the British Empire.

Pacific colonies meanwhile were sometimes run more or less as labour camps. Villagers found head taxes so harsh that they often took up weapons to fight for the

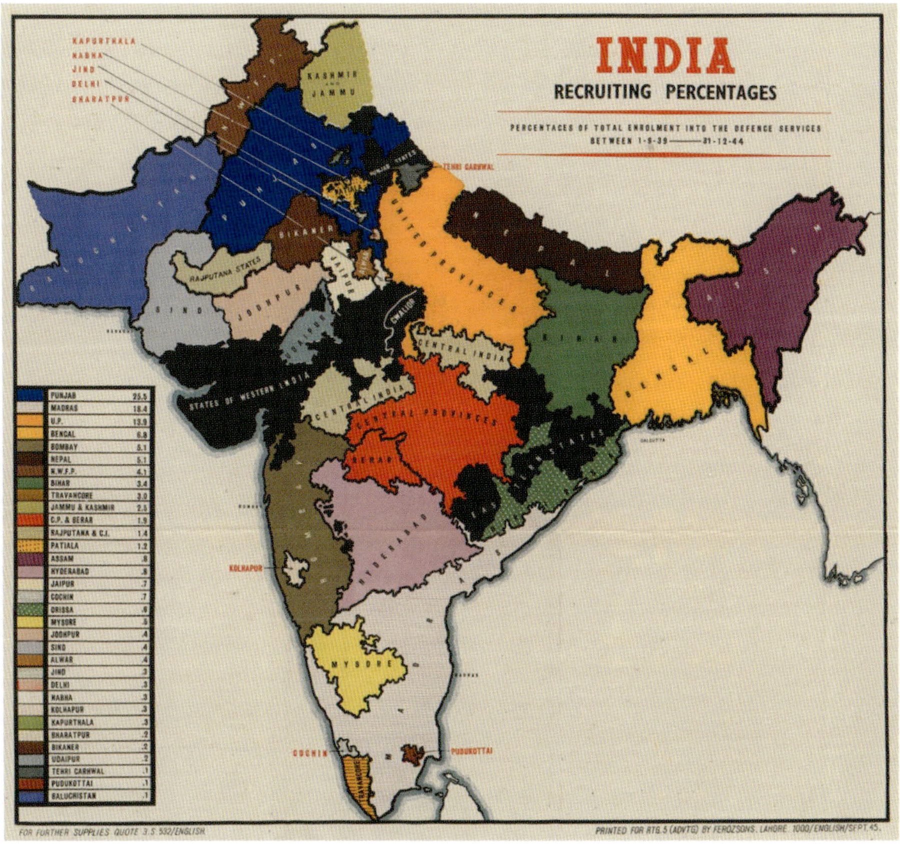

The Indian Army, one of the largest in the world, was imposed on the people of India by the British state and was used to control imperial holdings in South Asia, the Middle East and Northeast Africa. Almost all recruits came from only a handful of provinces. The great mass of people in British India were fearful of the army. *National Archives (Britain).*

right not to pay.[152] Imperial authority in the Solomon Islands was strongly disliked by nearly every tribe. British imperial flags flew less oppressively, however, over Tonga and the Gilbert and Ellice Islands.

The British Labour Party was opposed to imperialism in principle. The Conservative Party, which was governing the imperial homeland under the leadership of Neville Chamberlain, backed imperialism in principle; it was willing to widen rights and freedoms in India, but at the same time spoke about how colonies in Africa, Asia and the Pacific would also be given more rights and freedoms one day, though not tomorrow or the day after tomorrow. The New Zealand Labour Party spoke about empire as both wrong in itself and entangling New Zealand in aggression against colonial peoples and small states. One citizen pointed out that the word 'defence' was used as 'a cloak for aggression' by dominion conservatives who wanted to send an army overseas to support the imperial policies of Britain.[153] Wage workers, along with many teachers and some liberal doctors, lawyers, clergy, scientists and civil servants, often talked about the damage done by an aggressive British Empire. John Hodgson, an Anglican clergyman, knew from his own observations that imperial subjects were exploited in order to provide cheap goods for the households of New Zealand: 'I've been to Africa and seen the conditions of the native workers growing peanuts for the oil-extraction and cocoa growers.'[154]

Howard Wadman spoke up as a member of the Society of Friends: 'Have the British Herrenvolk repented the imperial swagger of 50 years ago? Have we? We may have dropped the swagger, but we've held on to the swag.'[155]

New Zealand had its colonies, too: sixty or so islands along with 'tiny islets without number' were governed by Wellington, making the capital of the dominion what a journalist called the capital of 'a minor Empire'.[156] New Zealand policy before 1935 had been to treat colonial subjects as people in 'tutelage' who were not yet ready 'to govern themselves'[157] even though, before colonisation, they had governed themselves for thousands of years. Whips were among the tools used to further that tutelage.

The Labour government after 1935 did very little to improve rights, health, schooling and earnings in Tokelau, Niue and the Cook Islands. Wellington set up a system of state control of fruit trading to earn cash for villagers, but also to make the islanders into taxpayers and to get cheap fruit to New Zealand. Whipping was banned.[158] Tokelauans, Niueans and Cook Islanders were nevertheless no better schooled and in no better health than they had been before the Labour Party came to power. One in every two Cook Islanders was infected with filarial roundworm,[159] which often caused serious injury and swollen limbs – even though the infection was easily treatable with cheap drugs. A curfew was in force throughout the islands. Tribesmen were forced to work on the roads at a very poor rate of one shilling a day. A large number of families had become landless because the colonial state had followed a policy of ending communal landownership by 'individualising' land title, copying the Maori Land Court in New Zealand. Nor was democracy in the offing: the colonies had no elected officials of any sort; power came from above, handed down by bureaucrats in New Zealand.

'We found them free,' wrote R.A.K. Mason, 'and we reduced them to servitude.'[160]

A Rarotonga Labour Party had sprung up in 1935: colonial subjects had thought that the new government on the mainland would want to build democracy in the Cook Islands. The party was disowned by the New Zealand Labour Party. Wellington did not welcome any talk in the villages about the right of islanders to elect their own parliament. A newspaper calling for freedom and democracy was founded by a young former headmaster, the 'ambitious, hugely energetic crowd-pleaser' and democratic socialist Albert Henry.[161] The tug towards independence was strongest in the Cook Islands, not so strong in Niue and weak in Tokelau.

Samoa was a special case, a colony masquerading as a mandate under the League of Nations.

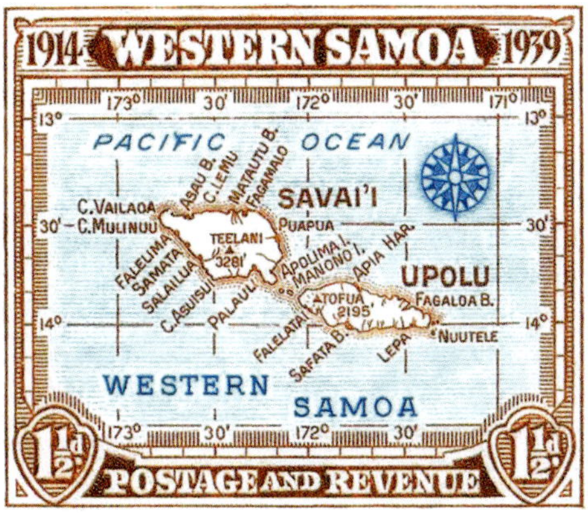

Postage stamp issued by the dominion government for Samoa commemorating the silver anniversary of the military occupation of the islands by New Zealand. Almost everybody in Samoa wanted their own independent state.

The mandate was a plantation society, organised in a racial hierarchy. Whites were on top, followed by `afakasi, Samoans and Cantonese. A journalist portrayed the complex and divided society as 'peaceful and contented',[162] but the truth was that the mandate was seething and most Samoans did not want Palagi government; they backed the independence movement, the Mau. The New Zealand Labour Party, before winning office, had promised to give new rights to Samoans. The Mau wrote to Savage in 1935 that his party's electoral victory was 'joyful tidings'.[163] Afterwards came some loosening of controls, but very slowly. Only a little was done even about handing over day-to-day clerical work to Samoans, let alone giving independence to the country.

The new government did stop the trafficking of Cantonese indentured workers between Apia and Hong Kong. The Labour Party was 'firmly opposed to the principles of cheap labour working long hours', declared the minister responsible, former shearer Frank Langstone.[164] However, the new policy was not one of runaway emancipation: a deal was struck with white plantation owners to soften the blow. Cocoa and rubber – or so the planters claimed – could not yield a profit without coolies to tend the crops. Labour allowed owners a few years of grace to find other ways of making the palm trees pay.[165] Wages were hiked, though, and working hours cut: Labour did not want anything like 'bond slavery'. Also, the government spelled out that it saw no need for householders in the mandate to employ Cantonese as private servants.[166]

Samoa policy was based, in other words, on a democratic socialist belief that no workers should be exploited; and on a rather muddled set of racist and paternalistic thoughts and feelings about 'protecting' the native people of the mandate.

Nauru was a special case too.

The island, rich with deep deposits of phosphate, was a mandate seized from Germany. Control of the mandate was shared between Australia, Britain and New Zealand. The Nauru policy of the Labour government was oppressive in a very straightforward way: Cantonese coolies bound by indenture sweated on the island. The phosphate they dug up was immensely important to landowners and farmers in New Zealand. Cleave Richwhite, manager of the Challenge Phosphate Company, declared that the dominion was 'fortunate indeed to have possession of such a veritable gold mine'.[167] Labour not only did nothing to soften the harsh treatment of workers and tribespeople on the island, it agreed to step up output and ship in more indentured workers from China.[168]

Social democracy was not for export, apparently – or not so long as the government of the dominion sought cheap phosphate.

Imperialism was debated by many voluntary organisations throughout the country, among them the Left Book Club. The Wellington club drew more than 1000 people to a series of meetings dealing with democracy and imperialism in the British Empire.[169] The Warkworth Left Book Club drew a big crowd in the winter of 1939 to talk over the topic of 'Empire or Democracy'. The little newspaper of the district wrote supportively of the proposal that Britain should give all its colonial subjects the right to vote in a true democracy:

> *the solution to the colonial problem is to view it from the point of view of the majority of inhabitants of those same colonies, instead of, at present, using them as pawns in the discredited game of 'power politics', or even worse, as sources of immense swollen profits sweated out of the hides of our black and brown skinned brethren in South African copper mines and tea and sugar plantations of Ceylon and the West Indies.*[170]

Charles Brasch, poet and editor, linked imperialists with fascists and capitalists:

> *The dead in Spain, the tortured in Germany,*
> *The oppressed in India and the lost in England*
> *Are victims of the one war.*[171]

Catholic Irish citizens in New Zealand were not always wholly behind the British Empire. James Liston gave voice to a widespread point of view when he said that the poor had been driven from Ireland because the British, 'their foreign masters', wanted to turn the land into 'a cattle ranch for the snobs of Empire'.[172] Centennial celebrations of the founding of the Catholic Church of New Zealand took place in 1938 – a big event – and Liston, as bishop of Auckland, took care to get a message sent by the prime minister of Ireland, Eamon de Valera, declaring that 'the Motherland' was 'deeply proud of the splendid story of one hundred years progress' of the faith in New Zealand.[173] Ireland was the motherland, in other words, not Britain.

Māori were divided in their opinions about the British Empire. Tribes who had fought as allies of the colonial state during the New Zealand Wars were often imperialist. Sir Apirana Ngata, a leader of Ngāti Porou, claimed in one speech that Māori were 'very glad that they had come under the British flag'. The tribes thought themselves 'as good Britishers as the next man'.[174] Eyes would have rolled in tribes whose forebears had fought against the colonial state during the New Zealand Wars. Spencer Westmacott, sheepfarmer and former army officer, told a 1938 conference of the Returned Soldiers Association that people like himself who lived in Māori districts were aware that tribes spoke about supporting Japan in the event of a war between the British and Japanese empires. 'Ask anyone who knows the Maoris,' he said. 'Contacts have been made in Japan.'[175]

Rātana was by far the most widely followed faith among Māori, and many of its flock felt warmly towards Japan. A bond between the church and the rising sun was first forged in 1924 when Tahupotiki Ratana, prophet and founder of the faith, sought to address the League of Nations at Geneva on questions of Māori sovereignty. He believed that the Japanese and Māori shared a common ancestry.[176] Sponsorship for his address was offered by the Japanese embassy. Sir James Allen, former dominion war minister and now high commissioner, told Japan to withdraw its backing. Japan did so. The prophet and his party travelled to Japan where they met ministers of the imperial government and were given an audience with the Taisho emperor in Tokyo. Ratana declared that he felt no loyalty to the governments of Britain or New Zealand.

'I will stand,' he said, 'upon the land of Japan and their government.'[177]

Also, of course, the colonial subjects of New Zealand in Niue and the Cook Islands, Samoa and Tokelau, together with Nauru, were not likely to look warmly on the British Empire. Nor were many Cantonese living and working in New Zealand, Samoa and Nauru.

The Labour government, meanwhile, found itself at odds with imperial foreign policy. Savage, Fraser, Nash and Jordan were the party leaders trying to navigate a course; they were helped by official advisors, notably Carl Berendsen and Alister McIntosh. The Labour government wanted to base its dealings with other states on internationalist rather than imperial needs. Also, unlike earlier governments, its leaders and many of its voters believed that wars were provoked by class and money. The *Standard* told readers that armaments manufacturers thrived 'on fear', that economic rivalry was the main cause of war and could be eased by a world economic conference, and that the League of Nations should be given military teeth.[178]

A war of words was now waged between Wellington and London.

The first serious crossing of swords came after Italy, in 1935, launched an attack on Ethiopia. Britain and France proposed a deal which would allow Italy some new territory. Wellington told London that it would not support such a deal because it would reward aggression and would be against the covenant of the League of Nations.[179] The League of Nations meanwhile had asked its member states to impose economic sanctions on the aggressor, but few did so. London had no strong wish to stop Rome from expanding its colonial holdings, so long as it was not done at the expense of the British Empire. Savage 'brusquely ordered' Sir James Parr, New Zealand high commissioner in London, a conservative appointed by the previous government, to follow the policy of his government and speak in favour of keeping up economic pressure on Italy.[180] Parr obeyed: New Zealand, he told Britain, wished 'to maintain, or even intensify' sanctions against Italy.[181]

A new high commissioner was soon appointed in the imperial capital: William Jordan. A working man, formerly a coach painter, he had no love for the governing groups of the British Empire.

Jordan first came to blows with the Conservative government on behalf of the Labour government when Edward Windsor, figurehead king of New Zealand, abdicated from his various thrones. Windsor wished to marry a divorcee, Wallis Simpson. Abdication was forced upon him late in 1936 by a Conservative government unwilling to allow Simpson to become the wife of the head of state. Wellington sent a message voicing 'dismay and deepest regret' at the policy[182] – the Labour government was not worried about its king being wedded to a divorced woman.

A third row between the two governments broke out in London at a 1937 conference of delegates from the Commonwealth. Official papers published afterwards were 'masterpieces of platitudinous reticence', in the words of a historian; but words spoken behind the closed doors of the conference were often passionate.[183] One hotly debated question was what the various governments would do in the event of a war with Germany. Ireland made it clear it would stay out. South Africa said that it would stay out too, unless a war involved something more threatening to its vital interests than borders in Europe. Australia said it was not eager to go to war simply to stop Germany from expanding in Europe. Canada said it could not make any promises.

New Zealand laid down its own position very clearly. Savage attacked the British government for the way it had handled Germany. He wanted the governments of the Commonwealth to work together to avoid war and help Berlin settle its true grievances. Savage spelled out the opinion of his government that the Versailles peace treaty at the end of the First World War had been punitive towards Germany. He proposed a world conference to review the treaty and 'give Germany a new start'. The prime minister added that New Zealand, as an outcome of such a conference, might be willing to hand back Samoa.[184] Savage also denounced 'secret diplomacy' and urged the Commonwealth to work with the League of Nations.[185] He spoke strongly about the way the Conservative government undermined the League of Nations. Britain, he said, had 'taken the lead in weakening the League'. He called for a world conference of nations to safeguard peace by reforming the international capitalist economy.

'New Zealand cannot maintain her assurance of aid in time of war,' Savage ended sternly, 'if Britain on her part refuses to pursue a policy based strictly on the principles of the League and of collective security.'[186]

A fourth quarrel between Wellington and London broke out in the winter of 1937 with the onset of the Sino-Japanese War. The disagreement sparked by this struggle has been considered above.

The Spanish Civil War led to more sharp words between Wellington and London. A republican government in Madrid was dragged into a civil war by rebellion among

'With weapons and culture the enemy is defeated': Spanish Civil War postcard. *Sandor Voros Spanish Civil War Collection, Adelphi University Archives and Special Collections.*

clerics, conservatives and fascists. The British government felt some sympathy for the rebels, believing that a conservative dictatorship in Madrid would be a good guarantor of British investments. The New Zealand government on the other hand wanted the British Commonwealth to intervene on the side of the republic. Jordan, late in 1937, lashed London for the 'farce of non-intervention'.[187] New Zealand failed, however, to talk any other dominion into backing its policy. The Labour government in the end did nothing more than give money to help feed Spanish children orphaned or impoverished by the struggle.

Yet another row emerged when the British government in the middle of 1938 gave diplomatic recognition to Italy as imperial overlord of Ethiopia.

The Labour government spoke up straightaway. 'This is a return to the law of the jungle,' declared Jordan in Geneva.[188] Savage, in words only a little less sharp, told London that Wellington disapproved and did not recognise the Italian claim to such overlordship.[189] New Zealand was the only state on the council of the League of Nations to join the Soviet Union in voting to uphold the independence of Ethiopia and denounce its conquest by Italy.[190] Conservatives in the dominion were so dismayed with Labour that the National Party brought a no-confidence motion before parliament, arguing that the foreign policy of the government was weakening the unity of the British Empire. The *New Zealand Herald* said that the policy was 'stupid folly' and that the government was 'biting the hand that feeds and protects New Zealand'.[191] The political right also made angry remarks about how New Zealand officials at the League of Nations seemed keener to 'keep company' with Soviet delegates than with the delegates from Britain.[192]

British dealings with Czechoslovakia during the middle of 1938 also brought a tart retort from New Zealand.

Germany was pushing to annex a strip of Czech territory. Edward Wood, aristocrat, former viceroy of India and now foreign secretary for the Conservative government, gathered the high commissioners of the dominions together and told them that Britain might do nothing if Germany chose to go to war with Czechoslovakia. Jordan spoke out against a policy of doing nothing. He was supported strongly by Savage. The quarrel over Czechoslovakia worsened when Chamberlain struck a deal with Hitler and signed the Munich Pact.

The British prime minister was following a policy of appeasement – by which he meant keeping the peace by holding talks and, when it seemed wise, giving ground. Chamberlain knew that his country was neither militarily nor economically strong enough to go to war, with any guarantee of winning, against a state as powerful as Germany. He also knew that a war could bring about national bankruptcy. The 'burden of armaments,' he told his cabinet, 'might break our backs.'[193] The Munich Pact was welcomed by the governments of Canada, Australia and South Africa – and by the New Zealand National Party. Hamilton called Chamberlain the 'saviour of peace'.[194] The Labour government was less happy. Although a message was sent to Chamberlain backing his 'efforts' for peace 'most earnestly', cabinet in Wellington was uneasy about violating the rights of a member of the League of Nations, Czechoslovakia.[195] Labour chose not to parrot 'the chorus of praise' heard on all sides about the Munich Pact.[196] Fraser, speaking for the government, picked his way carefully through a minefield of explosive words when he told citizens that 'everyone' was thankful to Chamberlain 'for saving the world' from bloodshed.[197]

The bitterest battles between Wellington and London, however, were over money. New Zealand on the eve of war found itself having to 'manage a boom, not a bust'.[198] A currency crisis early in 1939 led Wellington to make up its mind that the national economy should be safeguarded by imposing tight controls over imports and flows of money. The new controls would stimulate secondary industry, too, which would make more jobs for workers while helping the country to better fend for itself in the event of world war. The currency crisis was caused mostly by capitalists pulling their money out of the dominion, either in panic or in a calculated way, because of the government policy of founding a welfare state.[199] The National Party attacked currency controls as socialist madness, saying that the government should stop 'extravagant' social policy rather than try to engineer the economy. British Conservatives backed their peers in the New Zealand National Party. The Conservative minister for dominion affairs told

Cartoonist Minhinnick's response to the Munich Pact. New Zealand Herald, *1 October 1938.*

the Labour government that unless it cut back its 'expensive social services' and public works it would be punished by London.[200]

Nash set sail for the imperial capital in the winter of 1939 to try to sort out a new loan for his government to keep up and further its social policy. Chamberlain as parliamentary leader of the Conservative Party, together with Montagu Norman as head of the Bank of England, dealt with the finance minister austerely. New Zealand was bullied almost like a beaten enemy rather than welcomed like an ally. A deal was struck, but it was highly unfavourable for New Zealand. Savage thought that the 'intolerable' terms imposed on the dominion were 'unnecessary and humiliating'.[201]

Conservative newspapers in New Zealand upheld British Conservative opinion: 'The Dominion,' declared the *Evening Post*, 'must recognise that it cannot again saddle Britain with the burdens of its own extravagances and must order its affairs accordingly.'[202]

The raw feelings in the relationship between Wellington and London became clear when the Conservative cabinet talked secretly about demoting New Zealand from a dominion to a colony. Newfoundland had been dealt with that way. London made up its mind not to try such a step. Newfoundland was small, bankrupt, and its government had begged for help; New Zealand was rich, too big to be manhandled and its government was too stroppy. The willingness of Conservative leaders even to consider overthrowing the rights of the citizens of the dominion showed the depth of the divide between governing groups in London and the Labour government in Wellington.

THE UNITED STATES

One imperial power played the game in the Pacific according to rules not quite like those followed by Britain, Japan and France. American claims to democracy – loud to the point of braying – were in some ways hollow. Voting rights were denied to millions of blacks and millions of poor whites; even more of the latter than the former were allowed no say on polling day.[203] The federal government nevertheless spoke out against the imperialism of other states and was willing to allow autonomy and democracy to its three biggest colonies: Hawai`i, Puerto Rico and the Philippines. The United States was so competitive economically that it could elbow its way into markets without any need to carve them into colonies or protectorates. The heft of its economy was immense; every year it earned over 19 per cent of the gross domestic product of the whole world, slightly more than twice that of Germany, nearly thrice that of Britain, and well over four times that of Japan or France.[204]

Also, the republic was gaining 'soft' imperial power, mostly by selling films and pop music to the world.

American soft power stirred deep dislike among conservatives in many states. Anxiety was widespread among the middle class and those on the right in Britain, France and Germany. Swing, for example, a new style of popular music, was slated by many as 'nigger music'. Academicians in Paris were scathing, as were dons in Oxford and government officials in Berlin. Swing was either a 'bacillus' or a symptom of the

'British' New Zealand, embodied in such things as the myths of 'English' Canterbury and 'Scottish' Otago, did not always fit well with American cinema, swing music and other forms of mass culture sold in the dominion by Hollywood and Broadway. Railways Magazine, *1939.*

'inner crisis' sapping the strength of 'the entire white race'. At the same time, even in Germany an outright ban on swing was out of the question because too many citizens wanted to tune in to the beat.[205] One of the biggest prewar hits in the Third Reich was a swinging version by a Berlin big band, the James Kok Tanzorchester, of the American number 'At the Codfish Ball'.[206] Swing music heard throughout the war would help pave the way for young Germans to welcome occupation by the United States after the collapse of the Third Reich.

Many New Zealand conservatives felt much the same way. Oliver Duff noted that the middle class of the dominion worried about the corruption of core values and customs by American 'film stars and jazz bands'.[207] An Auckland citizen feared 'the pernicious and demoralising effect' of 'nasty American' comics and books, together with other 'vile stuff' shipped from the United States and broadcast on commercial radio stations in New Zealand.[208] A newspaper columnist wrote about a need to teach children to 'respect the British tradition' and 'stamp out anything in the way of Americanisation in speech'.[209] A governor of Wellington College spoke feelingly about 'the American accent and the use of slang over the radio'.[210] Americanisms, an elocutionist sighed, were now 'so ingrained' that many young people were not aware they were speaking in ways lacking 'taste and refinement'.[211]

The Labour Party was torn by contradictory feelings about Hollywood and Wall Street. American capitalism seemed on the one hand an enemy of social democracy, but on the other hand American socialist newspapers were widely read or quoted by unionists and democratic socialists in New Zealand. Social democrats thought the Democrat administration led by Franklin D. Roosevelt closely akin to the government of the Labour Party.[212]

The working class of the dominion, meanwhile, was irradiated by shining images on the silver screen and serenaded by spinning shellac on turntables. Of the 439 feature films approved for display in cinemas during the year up to the last autumn before the war, only 50 were British while 381 came from the United States.[213] The gloss of such images made many wage workers feel that life in the United States was somehow smarter, more alive, more modern, more exciting than life in New Zealand. A lot of young people who worked for wages or small salaries looked so warmly towards the land of swing music and moviemaking that they were ready to collaborate with it, and be emotionally colonised by it, should its troops ever make a landing in New Zealand.

Swing and the silver screen were not the only way, meanwhile, that the power of the dollar was stamping its image on other states. Washington also sought sterner types of power.

One way was to take control of strategic islands in the Pacific. Warplanes and commercial planes could now fly further than ever before, and imperial powers were scrambling for atolls to be used as fuelling stops. Japan, the British Empire and the United States quarrelled in 1935 when the stars and stripes were planted on Baker,

New Zealanders inside a cinema; untitled painting, late 1930s. *Artist: Russell Clark. Christchurch Art Gallery.*

Howland and Jarvis islands. Tokyo was unhappy, as was Wellington. The British Empire had already claimed the three islands and would 'assuredly have something to say', declared the *New Zealand Herald*.[214] The United States, after annexing the three atolls, eyed up Canton and Enderbury islands, which the British Empire had also claimed. American settlers carried out a 'surprise occupation' in 1938 and ran up the flag.[215] New Zealand took 'the lead' in such questions about ownership of islands, noted a British official; the government in Wellington did its best to negotiate with Washington on behalf of the whole British Commonwealth.[216]

Nor was the quarrel over tiny strategic atolls the only thing that divided the British Empire from the United States. The two powers had not got along well during most of the interwar years and had often been at outright odds in their foreign policy.[217] The United States had a blueprint for a war with the British Empire, called War Plan Red. A leading source of ill-feeling between the two powers by the late 1930s was their opposed foreign policies in East Asia. Washington saw Tokyo as its main rival for future dominance in China, while London on the whole was willing to work with Tokyo, and looked upon Japanese troops as policemen helping to protect British investments in the subcontinent. Chamberlain was one of many conservative people in the British Empire who so deeply disliked the United States that he talked about signing a non-aggression pact with Japan – he viewed the rising sun as less threatening than the stars and stripes to British wealth and power in East Asia.[218]

THE WAR CONFERENCE

The New Zealand government called the Pacific Defence Conference of April 1939 to talk over what might happen if war broke out in the Pacific. British, Australian and New Zealand government and military officials gathered in Wellington. The conference agreed that if Japan and the British Commonwealth were to go to war it was likely that Japan would try to land troops on some of the tropical islands and that the Japanese navy would attack merchant shipping in seaways to and from New Zealand. The conference agreed, too, that the Japanese navy might carry out small bombing and shelling raids on seaports in New Zealand, and maybe try to land about 200 men in 'hit-and-run' attacks on some of those seaports.[219] Why it would be worthwhile for Japan to stretch its strength so far, when other targets much closer to its home islands were much more tempting, seems to have been discussed only cursorily.

The conference also worried about what would happen if Britain was at war in Europe. A British navy tied down by struggles in the Atlantic would not be able to steam into the Pacific to fight the Japanese navy. The conference wondered if in such an event the Japanese military might even launch an outright invasion of New Zealand. Agreement was reached around the table that the dominion 'would be well advised' to think about building up its strength to be ready for an invading army.[220]

Officials and politicians at the conference talked about not only Japan but the United States. A war between the Japanese Empire and the British Commonwealth might give Washington leeway to seize more islands in the Pacific. American airlines, backed by their government, also might exploit a war to become dominant in the transpacific airways.

The conference did not come to any conclusion about how to cope with the ambitions of the United States, but did decide on a policy for Japan.

Tropical island colonies were seen to be the key. New Zealand, it was agreed, should straightaway strengthen its military presence in the tropics. A deal was done, too, between Canberra and Wellington. Although the governments in the two capitals were of opposing political stripe – a conservative Australian federal government led by Robert Menzies had few things in common with New Zealand Labour – they found it easy to settle on a common strategy for war in the Pacific. Australia would strengthen a line from Papua and New Guinea to the New Hebrides. New Zealand would take charge of building up army and air strength from the New Hebrides to Tonga.[221]

The island colonies, in other words, would become – or so it was hoped – fortresses against Japan.

Fiji was to be the core of the New Zealand zone, and troops were sent there swiftly. The colonial government, following orders from Wellington, quickly expropriated land for two military airfields at Vucimaca and Cawa on Viti Levu. Indian tenant farmers were evicted to free up the land, which plunged many into poverty.[222] Chinese market gardeners lost their land too. Fijians were 'uprooted from their villages'.[223] New Zealand, by militarising the colony, caused hardship to many people in Fiji.

Samoa was organised for war too. A territorial army was set up among the whites and `afakasi of the colony. The New Zealand army imposed what was called a 'fifty-fifty blood' ruling, which meant that men who were more than 50 per cent 'native' could not join the territorial army. Samoans were not thought trustworthy. Alfred Turnbull, head of the colonial administration, knew very well that most people in the islands did not want to be ruled by New Zealand. Arming and training them as soldiers, he believed, could lead to open rebellion. 'Our present policy,' he wrote, 'is to keep the Samoans quite apart from war participation in any way.'[224]

Wellington and Canberra, when coming to an agreement about getting ready for war, also agreed to step up the militarisation of their own homelands. The agreement was not welcomed by the left of the Labour Party, nor by many people outside its membership who hated the idea of a big army. The army officer corps was seen as a potential threat to social democracy. Also, the government during its first years in power believed that a nippy navy and swift air force were the best weapons for a state surrounded by sea and sky. Now, however, cabinet changed its mind. Savage told the citizenry he had come to believe in 'the necessity' of fielding 'not only a modern Air Force and Navy, but also an Army reasonable in numbers and efficient, with a proper scale of modern weapons'.[225]

The chiefs of military staff hoped that strengthening the army would allow troops to be sent away for a war in Europe rather than staying at home to garrison New Zealand. The officer corps was very conservative, and prone to glorifying the British Empire. Army officers wanted to fight overseas, to wage war for imperial purposes instead of staying at home cooling their heels quietly. At first, cabinet wondered how far to go. Savage spoke about 'a citizen army' in which men would wear civvies, not uniforms, and would be 'citizens and soldiers at the same time, not goose-stepping up and down the country'. At last, however, the government announced that its plan was to add 6000 more men to the army.

Savage spoke to the nation on radio. The men of the dominion, he said, would be armed and trained to defend their homes, not to fight on foreign battlefields. 'It is with a view to repelling attacks against our own shores that I ask them to prepare themselves,' he went on. 'I am not asking them to go to war, but to be prepared if war comes to them.'[226]

The young men of the country had not been keen to sign up for army training before the war conference, and proved no keener now that the government spoke more urgently. John A. Lee, who in early winter was given the task of recruiting, told his diary that the prime minister along with the war minister, Frederick Jones, had 'killed recruiting with half heartedness'.[227] Jones, he added a week later, had 'the recruiting appeal of Jack Rabbit'.[228]

Conservatives spoke the same way. 'Either from apathy or from a disinclination to make sacrifices not shouldered by all,' protested the *New Zealand Herald*, 'young men are hanging back.'[229]

The National Party held meetings. The Defence League held meetings. Worthy landowners, lawyers, company directors and factory owners called for compulsory military training. Josiah Hanan, lawyer and mayor of Invercargill, was one of many city and county councillors who wanted the young men of the country to be forced into the army. Anybody who opposed compulsory military training, he declared, was 'either a fool or a traitor'.[230] James Hargest, a well-to-do farmer and National member of parliament, said that what was needed was '40,000 or 50,000 men trained in the use of machine-guns and rifles' and that it was 'the duty of the young men to defend the country'.[231] A group of leading business houses together with the Returned Soldiers Association and the Territorial Association of Canterbury posted an advertisement, knotted with archaic grammar, across a whole page of the daily newspapers of Christchurch:

> *We must with all speed look to our Defences – Moral and Material: lay aside our social and political differences: where age and health permit, volunteer for Duty with the Army, Navy or Air Force, their Reserves, or some other National Auxiliary Service: but in every case by Personal Effort or Example or active Encouragement of others play a part that the world may know that a prepared British Commonwealth stands Intransigent and Implacable in the path of any aggressor who assails the Citadel of Freedom and Security.*[232]

The Labour Party was not willing to talk about compulsory military training, however, since its anti-conscription tradition was so strong.[233]

Voluntary recruiting went on slowly, meanwhile, until by the last week before the outbreak of war nearly 17,000 men were in the territorial army and another 10,000 or so in the National Military Reserve.[234] The navy was tiny yet well equipped and up-to-date; its two main vessels were the cruisers *Leander* and *Achilles*. Navy and army together built up a stockpile of weaponry at the seaports. Auckland was provided with materiel for 'four fast liners and forty-two defensively equipped merchant ships'.[235] Air-force training was strengthened, too: the De Havilland Company was to build 100 planes a year at a new factory in Wellington; the flying school in Christchurch took more students and a new flying school was set up at Woodbourne in Marlborough.

War planning as a whole was in the hands of the Organisation for National Security. At its top was the prime minister along with a leading bureaucrat and a leading army officer, backed by the cabinet, and it soon coordinated 'not only the activities of the fighting forces but the whole civil administration' by way of fifty separate committees.[236] The Emergency Precautions Committee, for example, was tasked to get the country ready for air raids, poison-gas attacks and shelling of coastal cities by warships. Savage gave an urgent order late in April 'that all preparations for a state

The mood on the eve of war. *Artist: Minhinnick.* New Zealand Herald, *26 August 1939.*

of war must be completed by July 31': this was when the government printed its *War Book*, a thick text bound in red that spelled out what was to be done to switch from a state of peace to a state of war. Government departments drew up their own protocols too.[237] State planners, believing that if war broke out the country might be cut off from the rest of the world, agreed that one way to cope was by strengthening economic autarky, or self-sufficiency. Already the government had a strong tool to handle war and other industry: the system of import controls set up in 1938 to limit money flows out of the country.[238]

A good deal of money was being spent on the military, yet planning for war was by no means the main priority.

The government still saw its chief task as building a welfare state, not a warlike state. Military spending before the Second World War was markedly less than before the First World War, even though cabinet seems to have agreed behind closed doors that in the event of a new war the dominion might send an army to fight far away from New Zealand.[239] The officer corps behind its own closed doors had got busy drawing up plans to do so.[240] The plans, had they been known to the government, could have been viewed as evidence that army bosses were not to be trusted because they thought themselves above democracy. Charles Brasch wrote a poem voicing the mood of many:

No one knows what his neighbour is called,
But fears him; defences go up; weapons are made
To keep the unknown constantly at bay.[241]

WHEN WILL IT START?

The last winter of peace was bleak with fears of war. The *Standard* wrote early in winter that citizens had stopped wondering whether there would be war but asked only where the struggle would break out and who would be the enemy. Germany? Japan? *Tomorrow*, late in winter, wrote that while many people were saying that war would be sidestepped, many others were saying that it was on its way.

'Will there be war?'
'When will it start?'
'Will we be in it?'[242]

Poland partitioned by the Third Reich and the Soviet Union.
Artist J.C. Hill. Auckland Star, *14 October 1939.*

CHAPTER 2 THE FIRST PHONEY WAR
SEPTEMBER 1939 TO JUNE 1940

THE OUTBREAK OF THE WAR

Germany attacked Poland on 1 September 1939. Wehrmacht tanks and Luftwaffe warplanes plunged towards Warsaw. Moscow, having failed to come to an agreement with Paris and London – an agreement urged by Wellington – stood aside after signing a non-aggression pact with Berlin. Britain and France declared war on 3 September 1939, having undertaken to back Poland. The declaration of war, beamed overseas by the British Broadcasting Corporation, was picked up by the New Zealand Broadcasting Service. Transmission towers quickly sent the news into kitchens and living rooms throughout the country.

'I am certain that the right will prevail,' said Chamberlain.[1]

New Zealand civilians in Europe found themselves caught up overnight. Geoffrey Cox, a newspaper correspondent, was in Paris. 'On the first night of it we waited in a blacked-out Paris for the mass bomber raids to begin,' he wrote. The bombers, however, did not come.[2] Mary Blair, a doctor, was in London. She was listening to the announcement of the declaration of war when the radio went silent and she heard an air-raid siren 'going all out'. At first she failed to grasp why the siren was sounding:

> *When one realised what it meant I called the household and we all went down to the air raid shelter. People did not seem to be grasping what was up and they were walking about in Belgrave Road. I went to the top of the basement steps and shouted to them to come into the shelter.*[3]

The siren proved to be a false alarm and, as in Paris, no bombers came winging their way towards the city.

Hector Bolitho, novelist, was another who took to shelter when the sirens first sounded in London. He was staying with a friend, the ambassador for Romania, after volunteering to do war work in the air ministry. Sleepy and annoyed, he sat in the basement. 'It all seemed such a bloody bore,' he wrote in his diary, 'waiting, with that humiliating gas mask: a snout of rubber in a brown cardboard box.'[4]

New Zealand civilians in Germany had to choose between heading for the border and staying.[5] Francis Garry, a headmaster from Northcote, together with his wife Elizabeth Scheele was about to enter Germany. The couple turned back.[6] Hundreds of other people from the dominion were fleeing continental Europe. John Marshall, a young lawyer and future prime minister, was in Brussels. He and his friend Ian Stevenson, another New Zealander, left straightaway for Ostend. They found hundreds of empty cars left behind by fleeing Britons on the wharves of Ostend before crossing on a ferry. 'We landed at Dover at dusk and drove up to London in the first blackout of the war,' wrote Marshall. 'It took us five hours, driving slowly and uncertainly through the gloom.'[7]

Others wanted to flee but found they were not able to get tickets. Edith Lyttleton, an elderly novelist, was in Norway. She tried to book passage by ship or plane, but every time she bought a ticket the sailing or flight was cancelled. 'There are spies everywhere,' she wrote. Norwegians, like many others, feared that they would be bombed. After three months Lyttleton was able to get to England.[8]

New Zealanders were also on ships at sea, or in seaports, when war broke out. James Jack, an accountant from Wellington, only found out about the war when his ship anchored at Goa. He watched two German ships steam into the neutral port, seeking safety. Jack had been in Germany earlier in the year and found its people 'very friendly'.[9] Stella Alexander, Auckland socialite, was sailing home from Europe with her husband Eliot Davis, wealthy company director, on the liner *Dominion Monarch*. The ship imposed a blackout before leaving Durban to cross the Indian Ocean.[10] A 'rush' of New Zealand civilians booked cabins on ships heading home from North America despite the lack of risk to their safety in the United States and Canada. The liner *Monterey*, for example, carried a record load of 723 passengers when it steamed out from San Francisco.[11]

The political leaders of the dominion, meanwhile, geared up government.

Military changes began days before the declaration of war, with men and machines being shifted about the country and sent to the Pacific islands. Soldiers set sail on the warship *Leander*, for example, to garrison Fanning Island.[12] The Samoan territorial army was mobilised, some of the Germans in the colony were interned, and the colonial government got busy with regulations to control prices and supply of food, petrol and oil. A state of emergency was proclaimed throughout the dominion and its colonies on 1 September. The announcement was made to the lower house of parliament, whose members listened 'in complete silence, the galleries being crowded'.[13] The weather, fittingly, was stormy. 'War regulations announced,' wrote Lee in his diary, 'as lightning flashes on the windows and to the sound of thunder.'[14]

Censorship was slapped onto the press, shipping was brought under state orders and citizens were forbidden to buy goods for hoarding. The Organisation for National Security worked around the clock. A cable came in the small hours of the morning of

2 September, saying that the British government was mobilising for war, and within forty minutes a bleary-eyed cabinet was seated around a table in the parliament buildings holding a conference with the service chiefs and the officers of the Organisation for National Security. Soldiers were ordered to awaken up and down the country, and coastal defences were got ready.

Cabinet sat almost without a break through the whole of 3 September, cabling to and from London, talking to the officer corps, and calling for reports from leading public servants. A cable turned up not long before midnight officially telling the government of the declaration of war. The cable had been sent by the British Conservative government two hours before, but had been slowed by the wires of the world becoming suddenly clogged with millions of messages.

The Labour government decided to declare war too.

George Galway, hereditary aristocrat, history graduate, former army officer and now governor-general, waited for orders in his office in Government House. Cabinet joined him soon after midnight. A string of over thirty orders-in-council were signed to put the country on a war footing. At nearly two in the morning of 4 September, a cable was sent to London. The telegram told the Conservative government there that the Labour government 'entirely' concurred with its decision that the declaration of war had been 'forced upon the British Commonwealth if the cause of justice, freedom, and democracy is to endure in this world'. The New Zealand government offered the British government 'the fullest assurance of all possible support'.[15] Wellington would later present its declaration of war officially by way of a neutral embassy in Berlin.

The news, when it was broadcast through the dominion, provoked strong feelings. Evelyn Scott, shorthand typist in Hamilton, 'just went cold inside'.[16] Gwenda Christophers, daughter of a bank manager in Lawrence, listened fearfully to the announcement. 'Dad had tears on his cheeks,' she said. 'He had lost his four older brothers in the First World War.'[17] A party of working people in Hastings had been enjoying themselves dancing and chatting before they heard the news. Harry Spencer, driver for a bakery, described what the announcement did to their mood: 'Everybody was knocked flat. It all went quiet, and half an hour later there was no party and everybody went home. It was the last thing in the world I thought would happen.'[18]

'I had never felt so shocked, so unreal,' wrote novelist Janet Frame. 'I had honestly believed that the days of war were over.'[19]

'I felt helpless and flattened,' said a nurse, Jean Bell.[20]

'I was plunged into the black fog-bank which for years past had been looming ahead of us, that terrible fog-bank of war in which all the landmarks of life would be obliterated,' wrote Brasch. 'Inside, however, it turned out to be not black, but grey.'[21]

The first New Zealanders to be killed were passengers on the liner *Athenia*, torpedoed on the opening night of the war while steaming along the coast of Ireland. Clare Carter of Napier had a 'miraculous escape'. She was in her cabin when the

The *Athenia*, a transatlantic passenger liner torpedoed in the evening of 3 September 1939 by the German submarine U-30 under the command of Fritz Lemp: 117 people died, among them several well-to-do New Zealanders. The sinking of the ship was the first naval action in the Second World War. *www.delcampe.net*

torpedo struck: she ran up on deck, where she had to lower herself down a rope to get into a lifeboat. Halfway down the rope she felt her hands burning so badly, and the pain 'so intense' from the friction, that she let go. She was lucky enough to fall into the sea near the lifeboat, and was dragged to safety. A 'wiry' grandmother from Dunedin was alone in the library when the vessel was hit. All lights went out. She stepped over dead and wounded people to get to a lifeboat.[22] Marjorie Whitton and Charles Tomlinson, husband and wife from Auckland, were two more who got away safely. He, a director of Motor Specialities Limited, was in the dining room and she was resting in their cabin when they heard and felt the blow.[23] The Hilton Porters, a showbiz couple from Auckland, also got off safely. Anne Fletcher, of Dunedin, was less lucky. 'I was fortunate to get the last berth on the *Athenia*,' she had written to her sister before the ship sailed.[24] She drowned, along with Sarah Harper of Christchurch.

Air-force men were next to be caught up in the fighting. Lawrence Edwards was the first – a young man from Taranaki, he was pilot of a British warplane shot down two days after the declaration of war. Others on the plane were killed but Edwards survived and was imprisoned in Germany.

The maiming, killing and seizure of New Zealanders was under way. The Labour government had thrown in its lot with warring states. Why?

WHY GO TO WAR?

The British declaration of war was not legally binding on New Zealand. All the dominions – New Zealand, Australia, South Africa, Canada and Ireland – were free, as historian Frederick Wood noted afterwards, to 'either take their stand beside the United Kingdom or proclaim neutrality'.[25] Australia, governed by a ministry on the political right, went to war straightaway. Canada declared war in a week. South Africa made up its mind after some wavering because, while many of the whites controlling the state wanted to back Britain, many others wished to proclaim neutrality – and some sought to fight alongside Germany.

Ireland, on the other hand, chose neutrality.

Eamon de Valera observed that 'whatever sympathies' the people of the dominion might have for one side in the war, they should nevertheless think first of their own country and 'consider what its interests should be and what its interests are'.[26] A war, his government had decided, was not in the best interests of Ireland. Britain, he later added in a more homely way, was like a house on fire asking Ireland 'to set our own house on fire in company with the other house' or, in other words, 'throw ourselves into the flames' and needlessly make an enemy of Germany.[27]

New Zealand's declaration of war was made by the Labour government without any debate in parliament. The National Party backed the government. Adam Hamilton spoke about a 'fateful hour' and promised 'unqualified support to the Motherland in her decision to stand with France and Poland'.[28] The lower house met two days after the declaration of war and quickly passed a resolution approving what cabinet had done; and the chamber then echoed to the sound of members singing 'God Save the King'.[29] The upper house dealt with the declaration of war the same way. David Wilson, Labour leader of the house, said that 'deeds and not words must decide the destiny of New Zealand'. He was supported by landowner and leading National Party member William Perry: 'We must win this war at whatever cost and at whatever sacrifice.'[30]

The speech that seized the imagination of most citizens, however, was made not in parliament but from a sickbed. Savage, shaky and dying, told his people over the radio, '[W]e range ourselves without fear beside Britain. Where she goes, we go. Where she stands, we stand.'

The speech was written not by Savage but by another government minister, solicitor-general and former lawyer Henry Cornish. At first the prime minister had been unwilling to give the war such strong support. He had bowed in the end to the strong wills of Fraser and Nash.[31] The fulsomely 'loyal' tone of the speech startled many on the left, while comforting the right.

New Zealand could have followed the example of Ireland and proclaimed neutrality. A neutral policy would have had strong advantages. The country would have been saved from much of the waste, misery and loss of war. Also, the policy could easily have been changed when the tides of war went one way or another, making neutrality a more or less prudent course to steer. Neutrality for the first years of war, followed by a declaration of war when the time seemed right, was the policy of the United States, Brazil and most of the other republics of the Americas.

Why not New Zealand?

Sir Harold Batterbee, newly appointed British high commissioner in Wellington, declared in a secret message to London that any New Zealand government that 'so much as hesitated' to declare war would not keep power 'for a day'.[32]

Two New Zealand historians have said recently that neutrality was 'completely unthinkable'.[33] But we need evidence to support such a strong statement. We have no such evidence: what most people thought, we do not know. A high commissioner, for example, mixed mostly with conservative and imperialist people. Newspapers, on the whole, were a guide only to the opinions of the political right. Most people did not keep a diary, nor did they keep letters or notebooks. Only a very few citizens later handed such documents over to any sort of archive or library. Opinion polls were not carried out during the war. Oral testimony would be gathered by oral historians long after the war, but people unwittingly change their memories as years go by.[34]

The government knew that many citizens were talking about neutrality and that most of them were Labour Party voters. 'Let us keep out of the struggle,' they were saying. 'If Britain wins without us, well and good; if she loses, it will make no difference to us.'[35] 'Why can't New Zealand keep out of the war?'[36]

A lot of households of the working class would very likely have supported, or at least not strongly opposed, neutrality. So, too, would many Catholics, most Māori and nearly everyone in the islands. Citizens on the political right would have been angry. The British government would have been upset too. The Labour government, by choosing neutrality, would have had to work hard to cope with protests and lobbying by conservatives within New Zealand. The National Party might perhaps have sponsored a political coup, backed openly by the governor-general and secretly by London. Motor cavalcades might have rumbled through city streets bearing troops – young middle-class men willing to do the job of putting down the working class as their fathers or grandfathers had done so thoroughly in the days of 'Massey's Cossacks'.

Quite apart from such considerations, however, the leaders of the Labour Party seem not to have considered neutrality as an option. Labour for four years had crossed swords with British governments over foreign policy. Why was it now willing to go to war?

Answers to that question were legion, but seldom cogent.

One answer can be found by looking at what the government said about 'war aims'. Fraser went to London soon after the declaration of war: he had been set the task of obtaining a straightforward set of war aims for the British Commonwealth. New Zealand citizens, the deputy prime minister told other Commonwealth leaders, would soon 'no longer be satisfied with broad generalities, no matter how eloquent, but will ask for a definite statement'. A lot of people in the dominion, he added, feared that the Allies and Germany might change their minds about fighting and team up instead against the Soviet Union.[37] Fraser said that his own government did not want another 'dictated peace' of the kind that had been so damaging at the end of the First World War. The Allies should make the most of any chance for 'sincere and constructive peace discussions' and must not push for a punitive peace treaty. The economic struggles that underlay war must be dealt with too. A peace treaty would have to boost the wealth of the working classes of all the warring states, for 'no peace is worthwhile which does not result in raising the living standards of the people'. The Labour government wanted to convince neutral states that the Allies were fighting for justice; to convince German citizens of the same thing; and, not least, to convince the people of New Zealand 'that the war was worth winning'.[38]

No statement of war aims was forthcoming. The Labour government, one historian observes, 'failed to induce' its partners to agree to spell out what they sought to gain by going to war.[39] Chamberlain, speaking to the other governments behind closed doors, said a statement of war aims would not be wise because it would stand in the way when it was time for peace talks with Germany. He told the world in a propaganda broadcast that the war aim of his ministry was 'to defend freedom and to establish peace', which of course meant nothing.[40]

At home in the dominion, politicians and editors also spoke about war aims loosely. 'Let me say, as forcefully as I can,' observed a magistrate, John Luxford, 'if we start public discussions on war aims before we have won the war we will be doing one of the things the enemy wants us to do.'[41]

Citizens had many opinions, often conflicting. 'Everyone has his own beliefs as to what we're fighting about,' wrote John McDonald, education officer in the army. 'We all see our post-war worlds differently.'[42]

The grounds given by the government for going to war can be grouped into two types: hardheaded and softhearted. Hardheaded reasons, in turn, were of two types: safeguarding the economy, and safeguarding the country against armed attack by an enemy. Softhearted reasons again were of two types: ethical beliefs about freedom and democracy, together with emotions about duty and loyalty.

*

Safeguarding the economy seemed to necessitate going to war against Germany. Exports were a weighty sector of the economy. One in every four pounds of gross domestic product was earned by shipping away gold, wool and food, and the main market by far was the imperial motherland.[43] 'Great Britain can live without us,' Frank Langstone told a meeting of trade unionists; 'we cannot live without her.'[44] New Zealand had to go to war – or so went the argument – in order to allow exporters to make money. Exporters had to make money because unless food and fibre could be sold overseas, the dominion would plunge into poverty.

The logic, in other words, was that the dominion needed to keep in the good books of Britain or, more bluntly, curry favour with Britain in order to safeguard the economy. The logic, however, was flawed.

First, what happened to the export markets of the dominion would depend partly on whether Britain would beat or be beaten by Germany; partly on how completely it might beat or be beaten by Germany; and partly on how costly it might prove for Britain to wage war until it was beaten or not beaten by Germany. Clearly, none of that could be guessed in the spring of 1939. A wise, low-risk, low-cost policy would have been to keep a watching brief while doing nothing. A second point is that defeat for Britain would have meant victory for Germany, which would have opened up another market for the dominion – Germany. Germany had been a big market in the past, before the First World War. Germany could have become a big market after the Second World War. John A. Lee pointed out that while the economic costs of a British defeat might be heavy, they need not be ruinous. 'Cut Britain's sea communications and Britain starves,' he noted. 'To interfere with ours is to dislocate our economy but not to afflict us with hunger.'[45]

Certainly it was not at all clear that waging war was the best way to protect the export market.

New Zealand exporters found themselves, as soon as war broke out, in a wonderful position anyway. London asked for, and got, a contract to buy the whole wool clip. Meat and dairy exports followed quickly. London cabled anxiously, only two days after declaring war, about buying all the meat the farms and freezing works of the dominion could ship out. The following day a cable asked for all the butter and cheese too. New Zealand exporters suddenly had a guaranteed market – at least for a year or so; and, in the case of wool, for every year of war and one year following. All that was needed was to say yes and then negotiate the best price. But the prices fixed were well below what was being paid on the open market, which meant the dominion gave away some of its wealth as a subsidy to Britain.

Britain might not have asked for the meat, butter and cheese had New Zealand not declared war. London might have wished to embark on economic warfare against a neutral dominion as a way of pressuring it to sign up to the alliance against Germany. Dairy products earned nearly 40 per cent of export earnings and went almost wholly to Britain; exporters would find it hard to sell their cheese and butter – though not their casein – elsewhere. Meat earned another 30 per cent or so of export earnings; a new

Exports were important to the economy: nearly two out of ten people in the workforce were employed in farming and mining, and much of their output was exported. The main market, worth some 70 per cent of all export earnings, was Britain. This poster, dated 1939, shows the contents of a typical cargo ship. *Alexander Turnbull Library Eph-E-SHIP-1939-01.*

market for meat would also have been hard to find. Wool, on the other hand, which yielded about 20 per cent of earnings, would have found a ready market. Gold, which accounted for about 12 per cent of earnings, was not a worry.

Exports were not quite as critical to the economy as most politicians believed, however, since the true wealth of households was based partly on goods and services not traded in the market. Home food growing, canning and bottling, poultry raising, sewing, knitting, cooking, baking, childcare and a good deal of other wealth production was done outside the cash economy. New Zealand also earned useful 'invisible' exports through banking, insurance and shipping. The shipping industry alone yielded good earnings with its fleet of more than 500 vessels, weighing over 195,000 tonnes. Well-to-do households owned shareholdings in big fleets like Shaw Savill, P&O, the New Zealand Shipping Company and the Union Steam Ship Company. 'Shipping is a means of obtaining invisible exports, it earns revenue from other lands,' observed shipowner Sydney Holm. 'As an island country we pay insufficient attention to this important industry.'[46]

Also, even if the British government had been so angered as to close the door on exports from New Zealand, the farmers of the dominion were strikingly modern and efficient, and with state help could have adapted to export challenges. Adaptation would have been costly in the short run, but it would also have been a very helpful way of switching the export economy from too much dependence on one market and on a limited range of goods. Changes would have begun somewhat earlier than they eventually did, later in the century.

A third and last flaw in the economic argument for declaring war was that the economic earnings from trying to safeguard the export market would need to be offset against the costs. The financial costs of waging war would be vast. Costs would come about not only because money would need to be spent to pay for armed forces and fighting but also because of forgone investment opportunities, lost production of goods and services, smashed or sunk assets, along with damage done to the health and strength of the citizenry. What, for example, would be the opportunity costs? Money spent on the military might be better invested in developing and diversifying the economy. A government trying to carry out a cost–benefit analysis of going to war would need to factor in the possibility that safeguarding the export market might not compensate citizens enough for losing immense sums of money. Maybe it would make better sense to take a sharp drop in national income as the cost of keeping citizens healthy, alive, and out of the fighting?

Nor was it obvious that declaring war was needed to safeguard the country against armed attack.

The government believed that if Britain lost the war the dominion would be prey to Germany. Fraser told a national conference of the Labour Party that the country was fighting because if the motherland was beaten the people of the dominion would 'lose everything'. New Zealand citizens would end up 'nothing more nor less than the slaves of a foreign ruling class'.[47] He was not asked for proof and nor did he offer any. Rex Mason, another leading member of the cabinet, told a nationwide radio audience that British defeat would turn the people of the dominion into 'spoils for the victors', helpless 'hewers of wood and drawers of water for a contemptuous and merciless conqueror'.[48] Nash portrayed a still bleaker outlook: the dominion would become 'one of the prizes, and a magnificent one', seized by a victorious Germany. The people of the dominion would be driven from their homes and 'shipped out of the country'.[49]

Citizens trying to make sense of the scrappy news they picked up from newspapers and radio broadcasts often spoke the same way. 'We've got to fight Hitler sometime or other or he'll never stop,' said a young businessman in the Bay of Plenty.[50] Whakatane, he seemed to think, could end up in the hands of the Third Reich.

New Zealand needed a strong protector, seemingly. The only strong state likely to wield weapons on its behalf was Britain. The government and many citizens alike thought that the dominion depended above all on what some historians have called 'the shield' of the Royal Navy.[51] Yet the watery half-world that lapped the shores of the dominion no longer lay within the British naval sphere of power: Japan and the United States were the big naval powers in the Pacific. A canny policy, perhaps, might have been for the government not to worry about the war in Europe but to give priority to working out ways to avoid annoying those two mighty neighbours. Tokyo and Washington would not have wanted Berlin to set itself up as a naval power in the Pacific. Berlin was not likely to spread itself so thinly anyway. Hitler was anxious to get his grip not on islands in the antipodes but on the European subcontinent from the Baltic to the Black Sea.

This map was published by the government after the outbreak of war with Japan. Critics of the government asked why, if the Southwest Pacific was the 'battle zone' in early 1942, the army had been shipped away to the other side of the world late in 1939. Auckland Star, *28 February 1942.*

Citizens not in the know about the true strength of the enemy were often swayed by wholly unfounded fears about the risk to New Zealand. Many of them dreaded fleets of bombers crowding the sky. Mervyn Browne, apprentice printer, walked out of a Whanganui cinema when a flashcard on the screen announced that Germany had invaded Poland. 'I looked up to the sky,' he said later, 'quite expecting there to be bombers coming over.'[52]

Working people were not the only ones who overestimated German power projection. 'Lowering grey skies dropping hopeless shafts of water, not the happy, laughing water gurgling on its way, but the dreary smoky wetness of a frightened city,' wrote a university student in Wellington. 'How soon will this city stand quiet, its grasping commercial sinews paralysed under a deadly fear, the drone of death high in the skies?'[53]

Very few citizens knew – partly because the government had not told them – that the only way enemy warplanes could fly over the dominion with a 'drone of death' was by taking off from aircraft carriers, and that Germany had no aircraft carriers. Not many were aware, either, that Germany was not in any way, for the foreseeable future, a military threat to New Zealand. The finding of the Wellington war conference earlier in 1939 – that the only likely enemy on the horizon was Japan – had not been widely publicised.

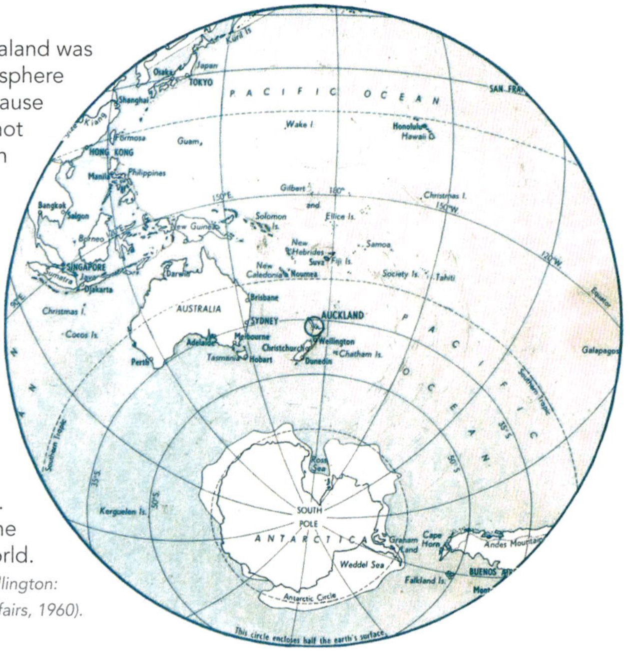

Where is the enemy? New Zealand was lucky to be surrounded by a hemisphere that was mostly water, but because few people owned globes it was not widely understood how very benign a strategic environment was enjoyed by New Zealand. This map, which makes it obvious, was not published until fifteen years after the end of the Second World War. Only one great power deployed a large army in this watery hemisphere: Japan. Although many citizens in the dominion were anxious about Japanese military power, Tokyo had only the slightest interest in faraway New Zealand. Germany, of course, was on the opposite side of the world.

A Descriptive Atlas of New Zealand *(Wellington: Department of Internal Affairs, 1960).*

A state, by siding with one group of states when a war breaks out, makes an enemy. Was it wise to declare war on Germany, and thus make it an enemy? The Labour government invoked the doctrine of collective security. New Zealand must go to war in order to save itself and other small states from war – or so went the somewhat contradictory narrative – because aggressive, militaristic and imperialist states could be stopped only by other states standing together as a group. The Labour government had hoped that the League of Nations would act as such a group, but now had fallen back on a narrower collective security. Nazi militarism, aggression and imperialism were to be stopped, ironically, by two of the biggest winners from imperialism, aggression and militarism in world history: the French Empire and the British Empire. Was it good policy? Collective security had not stopped war from coming. Was it wise to hope that war could be stopped in years to come by continuing to follow the same doctrine?

New Zealand could do little to help a collective of Britain and France. The Allies would lose or win the war no matter what was done or not done by New Zealand. The dominion was too small and weak to sway world destiny. New Zealand soldiers were soon 'under no delusions', as one officer wrote from Egypt, that the dominion army was anything other than 'a mere drop in the bucket'.[54] 'The forces in motion in the war are gigantic, defying full comprehension,' editorialised the *Auckland Star*.[55]

The government exposed the shipping of the dominion to risk by declaring war on Germany. The declaration meant that the seaborne property of the country was now on

Citizens of many states on the outbreak of war were terrified at the thought of bombing: people believed that as soon as war was declared massive fleets of bombers would take off and lay waste to the cities of the world. Governments handed out pamphlets and posters showing civilians how to cope with such bombing. This poster was published by the government of Japan. *https://za.pinterest.com/alicechiong18/*

a hit list in a way it would not have been had the government stood aside and followed a policy of neutrality. An editorial in the *Standard* pointed this out: 'New Zealand's Commonwealth membership renders her in this respect more likely to be attacked than if she stood alone.'[56]

A country of no strategic worth, lacking any very valuable booty, protected by an immense ocean, protected also by a small but disciplined army, navy and air force backed by a territorial army, was not a tempting target for any aggressive big power far away on the other side of the world. The left of the Labour government had been saying for some years that geography alone was enough to safeguard the country. 'Our isolation is our best defence,' argued Lee. Invasion, he went on to say, was a 'laughable prospect'.[57] Germany certainly had no plans and no ability to invade New Zealand.

The hardheaded reasons for going to war seem to have been woolly. What about the softhearted reasons?

*

A first group of softhearted reasons clustered around the concepts of freedom and democracy. Freedom and democracy were under threat – or so it was claimed – and war was the only way to safeguard those good things. David Wilson, speaking on behalf of the government to the upper house of parliament, said the war would 'preserve democracy and freedom' and that it was 'a fight between democracy and dictatorship'.[58]

The voiceover of *Country Lads*, a government propaganda film made by the National Film Unit, told citizens that the purpose of the war was to safeguard 'the right to be free'.[59] The National Party weighed in with the same sorts of words. Newspapers parroted the sentiment too. The *Auckland Star* declared that never in history had there been 'such a grim and ruthless challenge to the great institutions of Democracy'.[60] The newspaper spoke of 'the old German idea of world control', not giving its readers any hint that the only state that could be said to have conquered a worldwide empire was Britain, and perhaps France.[61]

A glaring weakness in the theory of the war being for freedom and democracy was Poland. 'Poland is a jackal,' wrote Lee in his diary.[62] The dictatorship in Warsaw certainly was not what anybody would call a bulwark of freedom and democracy. Isidor Reifer, a socialist Pole who had come to live and work in New Zealand, defined the dictatorship as 'a regime no better than Hitler's'.[63] The Labour Party was well aware that fighting on behalf of such a state with its 'illiberal landlord rulers' and its oppressed Jewish and other minorities was 'a curious cause' to be undertaken by a social democracy.[64]

A further glaring weakness in the theory was that the target was only one dictatorship. One-party police states were thick on the ground in Europe. Why was war not declared on Portugal, or Latvia, or Hungary? One-party police states were also thick on the ground elsewhere in the world. Brazil was a dictatorship. Mexico was a dictatorship. Thailand was a dictatorship. The Guomindang in China was a harsh dictatorship answerable by the end of 1939 for the deaths of far more civilians than the Nazi Party in Germany to that point.

Why not declare war on the Guomindang, or Brazil, or Thailand? Why single out Germany?

The colonial empires held by Britain and France were themselves far from bulwarks of freedom and democracy. The majority of people living under imperial flags had no right to vote, no voice in how they were governed and, when push came to shove, were kept in line by armed police or troops. The *Bay of Plenty Beacon*, like many other conservative voices, claimed that the British Empire had 'set the example of freedom to all its subjects black or white, brown or yellow',[65] but colonial empires were dictatorships, often very tough dictatorships.

The Labour government, while it was not keen on imperialism and colonialism in principle, often forgave the colonialism and imperialism of the British Empire. Opinion was based not so much on knowledge as wishful thinking. Frank Corner, member of the prime minister's staff, observed that Fraser thought the record of Britain – and the Netherlands – was fairly good.[66] The deputy prime minister did take the trouble to say in London, soon after the declaration of war, that one outcome of the struggle must be democracy in India. Also, he and many of his government colleagues believed that their own politics of democratic socialism upheld the very best traditions of

The government continued to boost the centennial of the New Zealand state, despite the dominion going to war, and stressed the coming of 'progress', prosperity, democracy and modernity. Although provincial and national sponsors of the centennial made free use of Māori motifs they ignored the belief of the tāngata whenua that the state had not upheld or even acknowledged the Treaty of Waitangi. *Artist: George Bridgman. Alexander Turnbull Library Eph-E-TOURISM-1940-01.*

civilised democracy. A civilisation was now under threat, they thought, and it was the civilisation from which social democracy had sprung.

'Under a social democratic system of government,' spelled out Ronald Meek, a communist university student, 'in moments of crisis it is more essential to save civilisation – i.e., capitalist civilisation – than to save social-democracy.'[67]

Labour Party leaders went further when speaking to their own voters; they claimed that the war was being fought not only for freedom and democracy but for a socialist society. The national executive of the party issued a manifesto on the outbreak of war, saying that Labour believed in 'the maximum freedom for the common people of all countries.' Anyone who gave any help to 'the aggressive Powers' was guilty of 'an act of treachery to the principles of democracy and Socialism.'[68] The manifesto took pains to avoid naming the aggressive powers – a wise step, since many of those on the left of the party would be willing to propose that one candidate for the honour was the British Empire. Outside the party, the empire was sold to newspaper readers as a haven for free folk, not as a citadel of capitalism or imperialism or what poet A.R.D. Fairburn satirically called 'the oil trust and the steel trust and the armaments trust and the chemicals trust and all that we deem holy and fightable and flaggable.'[69] The left, in other words, was trying to square a very awkward circle.

Imperial loyalty: almost one in five people living in the dominion was born in Britain. A lot of citizens were eager to help the 'motherland', even if giving help was costly and of no obvious advantage to New Zealand. A portrait of Britannia – one of the symbols of Britain – displayed on a field of imperial red, graced the cover of a programme for a 1940 concert in Oamaru. *http://oamaruoperahouse.co.nz*

A second group of soft-hearted reasons for going to war came from a sense of duty and loyalty. Many citizens of English or Scottish or Ulster ancestry wished to see themselves as fighting alongside kith and kin in the old country. The political right was a stronghold of such feelings.

'No doubt the Empire could win without New Zealand,' observed Thomas Hislop, lawyer and mayor of Wellington, 'but what New Zealander would want to shelter behind others?'[70] Adam Hamilton talked about 'our own blood brothers' on the other side of the world 'ready to daunt the horrors of mechanised warfare and frightfulness'.[71] John Martin, rich merchant, declared that the 'attachment and sympathy in this country with the Motherland' was so strong that 'any sacrifice that we are called upon to make in men, production, or money, will be cheerfully given'.[72] Cheviot Dillon Bell, son of an old family of southern gentry, was applauded when he told a National Party conference that the task of government now was to fight for 'my England right or wrong'.[73] A conservative citizen of Mount Eden wrote verse on the subject:

Sons of Empire take their stand,
By the land that gave them birth
Pakeha and Maori from
This England of the southern sea,
In their eager thousands come
Dear Motherland, to fight for thee.[74]

Labour Party leaders seldom wrote or spoke so fulsomely but they, too, often wanted to be loyal to Britain. Fraser talked in a nationwide radio broadcast about 'our kinsmen' on the other side of the world, 'the men, women, and children of our race and blood'.[75] Nash, about to leave London after having a harsh time dealing with financiers who disapproved of social democracy, was still able to write in a private letter: 'whatever New Zealand can do in its small way to help the Old Country will be done – even though the cost may be heavy'.[76] Nash was himself British by birth and upbringing, as were Fraser and many others at the top of the Labour Party. The mass of citizens – more than four in every five – were born in New Zealand.[77] John Mulgan, writer and army officer, wrote that a lot of people he knew 'didn't give a damn for England'.[78] Working people seldom spoke about 'Home'. Citizens of Irish, German, Scandinavian and Croatian ancestry were not likely to see themselves as kith, let alone kin, to the British. Nor, of course, were many Chinese, Samoans or Māori.

*

As we have seen, all the reasons for going to war – softhearted or hardheaded – were muddled and contradictory.

The question for the citizens of the dominion was whether it made sense for New Zealand to go to war against Germany. Te Puea Herangi, a chief of very high mana, wrote privately to Savage: it was 'not a time for much talk or heroics', she said, but 'a time for cool reasoning'.[79] The government was not reasoning coolly. The economy would not be safeguarded by declaring war; the costs of trying to safeguard it might not be worth the winnings. New Zealand would not be saved from attack by declaring war; it was not in any danger of attack. Freedom and democracy were flimsy reasons for going to war, given that freedom and democracy were not allowed to most of the people living under the flags of the Allies. Nor could anyone claim that anything like cool reasoning lay behind feelings of duty and loyalty to 'Home'.

Princess Te Kirihaehae Te Puea Herangi, 1937. *Photographer: Schmidt Studios. Alexander Turnbull Library 1/2-045546-F.*

Why waste lives and money going to war when none of the reasons given for weighing in were convincing – and when the dominion could not in any meaningful way help or hinder victory?

A VOLUNTEER ARMY

New Zealand, having made up its mind to declare war, next needed to decide what sort of war it was going to wage. A declaration of war did not mean that the whole state needed to be put on a war footing, nor that the government must mobilise and deploy an army.

The Labour government and its powerful ally the Federation of Labour both announced their goal was to give 'unqualified support' to Britain and France.[80] Yet 'unqualified' support could only be given by committing the whole wealth and work of the country. Was the government going to conscript? How could it conscript without stirring up the working class? Who would it conscript? Men only? Women too? Pākehā only, or also Māori? Was an army to be sent away? And if an army was to be sent, where was it to go? What was it to do? How long was it to stay in the field? Why? What were the specific steps and stages to be followed by the government of New Zealand in order to win whatever were its goals? Once the goals were scored, would the dominion withdraw? So long as the goals were not known, how could anybody draw up a timetable for getting to those goals?

One thing was clear: many options were open to the country.

A declaration of war did not mean the government need necessarily wage a fighting war. Wood noted that 'dominion status carried freedom not only to decide whether or not formally to go to war, but also to determine whether participation would be whole-hearted or merely nominal'.[81] The British government had talked early in 1939 about the question of whether, as it put it, dominions might occupy 'a half-way house between neutrality and participation' if a war was being fought by the British Empire.[82] Chamberlain was so well aware of dominion freedom of choice that he pointed out to the British parliament that it was 'a matter for each member of the Commonwealth to decide the extent to which it will participate in any war in which any other member of the Commonwealth may be engaged'.[83] Nash had said two months before the outbreak of war that it was 'unlikely' New Zealand would send an army overseas if war broke out, and that the dominion 'accepted responsibility' only 'for defending New Zealand ... and for defending Empire interests in the South Pacific'.[84] The declaration of war did not oblige the dominion to waste one single life of its citizenry, nor to squander any money.

A first option, in other words, was to do nothing warlike. The Labour government could work hard to try to cope with any awkward social or economic consequences of the outbreak of the war while otherwise carrying on with building up the welfare state. The election of 1938 had given a strong mandate for a welfare state. A lot of working-class voters now feared that war might shove that project aside and lead to the economic and other stresses and strains that poor and middling households had borne in the First World War.

The Labour government decided not to do nothing; instead it would actively go to war.

Once that decision was made, a second option was to wage an economic, not a military war against Germany. New Zealand could keep its people in their civilian walks of life and concentrate on boosting exports to help the Allies. This option was appealing to plenty in the Labour Party. Fraser, for example, soberly pointed out to others in the government that 'it might be of more value to the common cause to maintain farm production than to provide fighting men'. A citizen in Auckland agreed that the best policy was not to send troops overseas but to concentrate on 'producing the necessary material for England to overthrow Germany'.[85] *Tomorrow* ran an editorial supporting the declaration of war but opposed to fielding an army; 'we can most usefully contribute by the despatch of food supplies and the achieving of maximum self-sufficiency'.[86] A few people on the right shared the same view. Robert Nimmo, company director, told a gathering of Wellington business leaders that this war would not need as many troops as the First World War. 'It is an encouraging reflection for us,' he added, 'and if it proves sound we shall be all the better able to devote much of our civilian energies to increasing our export trade.'[87]

A third option was to call for volunteers and build up the military, but keep those strengthened armed forces in the home islands. The government could easily have told its allies that lack of certainty about Japan was a good reason not to send away an army. The government could also have pointed out that voters were far more anxious about war with Japan than war with Germany. The Labour left certainly saw things that way. So too did the left outside the Labour Party. The Catholic church was keen on keeping any volunteer army in New Zealand: the *New Zealand Tablet* told readers that sending troops overseas would be 'a traitorous disservice to our own country'.[88] Voices were also raised from the old Liberal side of the National Party. The *Auckland Star*, for example, argued that the dominion could 'chiefly play its part by bringing production of its primary industries to their maximum and arranging for its own defences'.[89] Many private citizens were not keen either for the government to deploy an army. 'I think New Zealand has every need for her own men without sending them overseas,' said a businesswoman in Whakatane. 'We don't know what might happen in the Pacific, and our shores should not be left unprotected.'[90]

The government thought it likely that Japan would join the struggle as soon as war broke out with Germany, and was 'rather taken aback' when Tokyo proclaimed its neutrality.[91] Batterbee wrote to London that 'the average New Zealander' had become 'convinced that New Zealand is the one country coveted by hostile Japanese'.[92] The Labour government during the early weeks of the war kept thinking it was too risky to send an army away to the other side of the world. Japan's continued neutrality, however, led to British pressure for dominion troops to be sent to Europe. Chamberlain said it was of the 'utmost importance' to send troops.[93] The Labour government could still have dealt with the pressure by quietly keeping most of the army in camp while sending away a symbolic regiment or two.

New Zealand government and military leaders flew to the imperial capital to explain that whether an army was sent overseas or not would be 'governed primarily by the attitude of Japan'.[94] London answered by saying that a southwards drive by Japan was 'highly unlikely'. Tokyo had 'her hands far too full in China', declared the British foreign minister, Edward Wood, and also was 'too apprehensive' of the Soviet Union and the United States.[95] Edward Chatfield, another British minister, added that even if Japanese troops did drive southwards they would be stopped at Singapore. A siege against that island colony would have to drag on 'at least four or five months' and would be a 'forlorn' task. Tokyo would not undertake 'such a mad enterprise'.[96] Leslie Hore-Belisha, the British war minister, said that as long as 'the attitude of Japan remained satisfactory' it was best for a dominion army to be sent to the Middle East.

Fraser, speaking as leader of the dominion delegation, pointed out that his country was not in Europe:

> *the New Zealand Government must obviously pay special attention to the defence of New Zealand ... Japan may not always be involved in China; Japan may not always be suspicious of Russia; the United States may not prove a sufficient deterrent to Japanese action southwards and, indeed, if the Commonwealth and its Allies were to receive a serious knock in the course of hostilities, the whole international situation might become entirely liquid again. These considerations are not absent from the mind of the New Zealand Government.*[97]

Wary words – yet the dominion delegation after a few days of talks said that as long as there was no sign of Japan joining Germany the dominion would be willing to send an army of 15,000 men to the Middle East. By bowing to British pressure, the New Zealand government was agreeing to follow an imperial war script. A 'complete reversal of military policy' had been 'quickly and easily achieved', observed Wood. The dominion would aim not to 'defend her own shores' but send an army overseas in order to kill or be killed in ways that had proved so costly in men and money during the First World War.[98]

Young and youngish men flocked to the colours, at least for a few days. One week after the first call had come for volunteers, nearly 12,000 had signed up.

Why did they volunteer to go to war?

Oliver Duff wrote that why men signed up was 'impossible to know, and foolish to pretend to know'. Volunteering was seldom done lightheartedly. Duff noted that there was 'certainly a deeper scepticism *in general*' than there had been on the outbreak of the First World War. War was no longer seen as 'an adventure into which youth can

The government spent heavily on advertisements using vivid images and stirring words to try to get men of military age to sign up. This advertisement sought volunteers for the air force. *Air Force Museum of New Zealand.*

rush with excitement'. The mood instead was more often 'sadness, touched indeed with bitterness'.[99] Haddon Donald, son of a family of manufacturers, wrote about his 'dread and a loathing' of war and how he felt 'no sense of adventure' when he signed up.[100]

A widespread belief afterwards, nevertheless, was that young men hoped for adventure, excitement and European travel by going into the army. This was true of some, certainly. 'I went because of the adventure,' said John Watson, who had been working as a steward in a gentlemen's club in Christchurch.[101] A lot of young men were so keen to get away from humdrum lives that they were 'relieved to get into camp', in the words of Jim, son of a dairy farmer in a story by Greville Texidor. 'It's a change from mowing the lawn and all that.'[102] Noel Gardiner, a farm appraiser from Te Kuiti, wrote that the war was 'an unexpected opportunity to escape', above all for 'younger chaps with dull, hole-in-the-corner jobs'.[103] Lindsay Buick-Constable wrote verse about his motive for volunteering:

I little thought
to find me
clothed in khaki;
polished, buttoned, beerful,
and yet,
I'm glad! I'm proud! I'm cheerful!
For I have found a new adventure;
found new reason
for my being
on the loose.[104]

This hope was a product of long years of social engineering. James Bertram wrote that before the fighting broke out he had thought of himself as having 'a certain immunity from war fever', but on the declaration of war found he had not. He wondered why. After noting that 'certain patterns of behaviour seem to be common in a war crisis', he added that to what degree they were 'conditioned by early training' was hard to say. The state deployed 'a formidable apparatus of public machinery' to 'persuade the individual' into the military.[105] 'A thousand primitive endocrines pour as the sweep of urgency and the drag of the social body in clumsy cohesion assault the young man in wartime,' wrote Richard Scott, son of a conservative churchgoing family in Palmerston North.[106]

Other young men agonised over whether or not to sign up. A university student wrote:

> *Must we fight? Tell us one good reason why, a reason you could equally well give to a German, Austrian, Russian, or Spanish youth ... Why is it shirking to refuse your body for the foulest dung-heap civilisation can keep steaming in its glory? To feed the flames of hate and corruption so that our children may reap the harvest of blood and steel a hundredfold.*[107]

A belief that the war was being fought for the forces of good swayed other young men. Richard Scott, on the political left despite his conservative family, made up his mind that fascism could only be beaten by fighting. He thought that 'as an internationalist' he had to be willing to 'maim and slaughter' for the sake of 'serving the world'.[108] Newspapers and film news worked hard to drive men into the army. Young men of the middle class came under heavy pressure from neighbours and family. 'I joined up because I was terrified of being thought unwilling to go,' said Douglas Debreceny, son of a business family in Opotiki. 'If I hadn't tried to do my duty, I'd probably have been ostracised by my family,' said a bank cadet, Jack Diggle. That same word was used by a young teacher, Ernest Warren: 'I think I would've been ostracised if I hadn't gone.'[109] Alistair Spence, a corporal in the army, wrote two years into the war about why he and others had volunteered:

> *Some hypocrites would say they are here to defend democracy. Some wished to get away from home for private reasons. But the majority of us fell into line partly from a hypnotic effect, partly because a change was offered, and partly because they were scared to stay at home and face public opinion inspired by the 'Glory' theme.*[110]

Civil servants found their lives made awkward unless they joined the army, and sports clubs, school old-boy networks and business employers often put pressure on men. Fathers did too, and clergy. 'When war broke out, my father was continually urging me to "Be a man",' said a soldier in a story by A.P. Gaskell. 'He would tell me the names of the boys who had joined up.' The young man found the pressure from his father so hard to bear that he sought advice from a clergyman. 'He told me to obey the dictates of my own conscience, but he said that if he were twenty years younger he would be right in there doing a man's job and striking a blow against the forces of Satan.'[111]

Young women told young men to sign up to show they were 'manly'. A few handed out white feathers; the angry mother of one soldier called them 'impudent, ignorant girls'.[112] Martin Medway, a young doctor in a wartime novel by Isabel Peacocke, one day opens his post and finds a white feather glued onto a sheet of paper along with the typed words: 'You are free, fit, and twenty-one – what about it?'[113] A young man in Taranaki was so shamed by white feathers that he signed up and left 'his mother, sick father and two young brothers' to run the family farm. Sidney Holland, businessman, former soldier and rising National member of parliament, was given a white feather and showed it to the lower house.[114] James Stark, who had been a brave soldier in the First World War, was sent a white feather too. 'I wouldn't have minded only one,' he said, 'but this is the second to come anonymously during the past few days, and I am sick of it.'[115]

Conservatives might urge young men to volunteer, but many working-class mothers and fathers urged their sons to stay away. James Cusack, shepherd and stonemason, signed up anyway. 'You're a bloody fool,' his father, who had been a soldier in the First World War, told him.[116] 'You'd be fools to be joining up,' said another former soldier to his stepsons in Wellington.[117] Friends often used that same word – called their mates 'fools' if they walked away from 'good jobs and prospects of marriage' to sign up for the military.[118] Volunteers got drunk before they could bring themselves to go into the army. One young man in a story by Gaskell stayed sober until he got to the recruiting office; 'although his mind was made up, he could not bring himself to go in, and walked on round the block, while knowing all the time that he would go in, and that he was only snatching a few more minutes'.[119] A volunteer soldier in the novel *Brave Company*, by Guthrie Wilson, asks himself about it on a battlefield:

> *Why are you here? Hmmm. I don't exactly know. For adventure? Suicide is not an adventure. For democracy? Obscenities upon democracy and all other abstractions. To destroy Hitler? Sorry, I have never met the man. Just caught up in a mass hysteria, a conforming type – is that it?*[120]

Young men jumped, and young men were shoved.

But most sat tight, waiting.

Volunteering had slowed down markedly by the end of the year. Only nine men stepped forward in the whole of Canterbury in the first week of December. The *Press* wrote about the poor turnout in the province and more broadly about 'New Zealand's complacency'.[121]

The government launched a charm offensive. Voluble politicians toured the country. Vivid posters were pasted on hoardings. Advertisements strewed the newspapers.

> *The 'Spirit of Anzac' CALLS YOU. There is a big job to be done in the world today. New Zealand has promised to do its part, and your Country now calls on every man to perform his duty. The need for men is urgent – which way does YOUR duty lie?*[122]

The campaign yielded recruits for a few weeks: the tally of those in the army doubled to 25,000 by the end of January. But the effect was temporary. The government tried again by setting up a National Recruiting Council. The country was divided into twelve recruiting districts, each governed by a volunteer committee made up of people from the working class and the middle class in the hope that members of each body would be able to 'speak to' men of their own class. Fraser and Hamilton toured the country calling for more men early in March, but by the end of the following month only 35,000 in total had signed up for the army. Volunteering was brisker for the air force and navy; the air force, in particular, seemed glamorous and attractive to young middle-class men.

Not many men of fighting age, however, were willing to go into the military. 'Recruiting has flopped,' wrote Lee in his diary.[123]

Citizens talked and wrote about why there was such a widespread unwillingness. A former soldier thought it 'very galling to see the very poor response to the call for recruits', and hinted that class politics was behind it. 'Party politics, political propaganda, and the petty utterances that go with it' must end, he declared, for the war to be fought 'with all the energy and vigour at our command'.[124] Others pointed at class politics. One citizen blamed the selfishness of the labour movement and its concern with 'minor trivialities, as to hours and wages' for the 'tiny' number of volunteers.[125] 'At no time in the last war was it necessary for the Prime Minister to go from one end of the Dominion to the other on a recruiting tour,' a conservative member of the Wellington recruiting committee pointed out unhappily.[126] The 'vigorous youth of the country are not doing all they could do,' complained Thomas Hislop.[127]

'If they want me they can come and get me,' some men said. 'I've a job worth six quid a week, I would be a mug,' said others.[128]

Young men knew, too, what war meant for soldiers. Sickness, wounds, lost limbs were some of the costs known and spoken about widely during the interwar years. George Clark and his siblings in a Waikato farming family listened to their parents talking about how two men of the family had been killed in the First World War:

> *We knew the horrors of war. We knew what our grandparents suffered, and our parents … We knew all about war and the misery. Loyalty to your country – I know it's good. If you have to go, you do; but if you didn't have to go, I wouldn't.*[129]

Conservatives blamed such men for putting their own needs ahead of the country. A wage worker or working farmer, however, was wise to weigh carefully the costs of giving up his freedom, taking a cut in earnings and risking his life by going into the army. Soldiers had struggled to get back onto their feet after the First World War. Going to war could set a wage worker or working farmer back years. He would not be able to build up savings. He would perhaps come home from the war so badly wounded that he could no longer work or farm. He might also come back neurotic or psychotic. The Labour government promised that the state would look after soldiers better than after the First World War. Savage said that anyone who volunteered would not come home after the war to find himself stuck with 'an unseemly struggle for the right to live'.[130] Wage workers and working farmers looked upon such promises sceptically.

The National Party, other conservative groups and the conservative press talked more volubly about a need to begin conscripting.

Conscription was one of the demands the political right had made during the last year or so before the war, and many more voices were now added to the chorus calling for the state to force men to join the army. The Otago Provincial Council of the Farmers Union, for example, told the government it must conscript. Alexander Cameron, a well-to-do landowner, spoke about his concern that 'the labouring classes were conspicuous by their absence' in volunteering.[131] The Defence League went further; it asked the government to impose compulsory war service on the whole citizenry.

Conscription was opposed, as always, by many of the voters who backed the Labour Party. The left of the party, the left outside the party, together with the unions of the left, saw conscription as a threat to the rights and freedom of the working class. William Barnard, lawyer, speaker of the lower house of parliament and on the left of the party, thought it odd that conservatives who got 'into a frenzy' when the Labour government tried to control capitalists should 'hysterically cry' to the same government about a need to control 'the flesh and blood of the young'.[132] The Catholic church spoke up against conscription, and many people not on the left pointed out that conscription would mean enslavement by the state. 'If we want to live up to our standards of liberty, freedom of thought and speech,' wrote one citizen, 'don't let us talk of conscription, otherwise we have all been deluded about the Empire's democratic principles.'[133]

The Labour Party and the Federation of Labour made a statement after they held a conference early in 1940 to discuss peace aims and war policy. The statement was straightforward, simple and widely welcomed by the working class: 'There is no conscription in New Zealand, and there will be no conscription while Labour is in power.'[134]

The volunteer army meanwhile was being shipped overseas. The media wrote it up fulsomely. Soldiers marching through city streets before boarding troopships were called 'brilliant and impressive'. Crowds thronged the streets. 'Whistles of officers shrilled and orders were rapped.'[135] The truth was that citizens, while looking on, often felt dismay. The prime minister himself found he could not bear to look at the first troopship steaming out of Wellington; Savage, who for so many years had led a political party with high hopes of peace, turned his back on the grim sight. Dorothy Norgrove, the daughter of a big working-class family, saw her father steam off by train from Auckland:

> *The crowd waved, unidentifiable khaki-clad figures could be seen waving back through windows ... and then there was nothing; only silence. What can the wives, parents, brothers and sisters, and children of men who have just left to be swallowed up in a war say to each other? We all filed through the barrier, and into the station. There were a few, insistently jovial voices, mainly those of older men. The complaining murmurs and cries of tired, uncomprehending small children lent an air of normality to the procession, but we were a bleak band.*[136]

Men who were crowded onto trains bound for the troopships nearly always drank heavily. Frank Sargeson saw one shipment while he stood on the platform of a railway station in the King Country:

> *Shortly it came at speed, a crammed trainload of young soldiers pretty much boozed up if one was to judge from their bawling and singing and the flung bottles that smashed on the platform and against the station building as the carriages flicked by. It was a fine midday and in a few moments the valley was quiet, river, hills and sky serene with sunlight as though saying, Here we are, the timeless conditions for all varieties of life on this part of the planet. By what error of judgement on somebody's part had there been this sudden intrusion of these soldiers? Trained to preserve and create? – but no, by the use of terrible weapons to devastate and destroy.*[137]

Not only civilians felt this way. Many of the volunteers had second thoughts about what they were doing. 'I sometimes wonder what all this cheering means,' wrote a young farmer, Keith Elliott.[138]

The next question for soldiers to ask themselves was: where were they going?

OCCUPYING EGYPT

The First World War had opened with immense armies plunging towards one another, shooting, machine-gunning, shelling, maiming and slaughtering. During the 1930s people had dreaded the same sort of charnel house in the event of another world struggle. They had supposed that a new war would be even worse than its forerunner; vast fleets of bombers would darken the skies above every city, dropping death onto the rooftops.

Not a lot, however, seemed to be happening.

German troops waited behind the Siegfried Line. They quipped that it was not a *Blitzkrieg*, a 'lightning war', but a *Sitzkrieg*, a 'sitting war'. English speakers called it the 'bore war' or the 'phoney war'. Judy Aitken, a New Zealand nurse with the medical corps of the British army, wrote to her family from France, 'one wonders if there really is a war going on somewhere,' and added that while she was on duty, she was 'having a proper holiday'.[139]

Poles, on the other hand, were not enjoying a holiday. Germany imposed forced labour and forced resettlement on its new colonial subjects, often brutally – not unlike Britain, France, the Netherlands, Belgium, Portugal and Japan in their own imperial holdings. Years of grimness were now under way for most people in Poland.

The Nazi government, having taken a firm step towards its overriding foreign policy goal of winning new eastern territory, was now willing to think about a peace treaty with the Allies.[140]

The New Zealand government was also willing to think about a peace treaty. A cabinet meeting sent instructions from Wellington to Fraser in London to work towards 'an armistice and a conference'. Fraser did so in the middle of November. 'It is obvious that sooner or later a conference must be held,' he secretly told other leaders, 'and it would certainly be better held before both sides have suffered enormous casualties.'[141] New Zealand, however, failed to convince the Allies. Britain had settled down to what Chamberlain called a 'waiting policy'. The navy was seeking and destroying vessels of the small German navy and imposing a tight blockade on Germany. The air force was bombing and skirmishing. Chamberlain was very unwilling to send troops into battle; he believed that shortages and other troubles would lead to a coup in Germany. Afterwards would come negotiations with a new government, led perhaps by Hermann Göring.[142] British opinion polls showed that the great mass of citizens supported this policy.[143]

Naval and air warfare, therefore, were the ways in which the fighting first entangled New Zealand.

On the outbreak of the war several hundred men from the dominion were in the British air and naval forces, and now they were busy. The New Zealand navy also got busy. Guns had been mounted on twenty cargo and passenger vessels at Devonport naval base by the end of the first four months of war. Each weapon was manned by a gun crew. 'The work of arming merchant ships and manning their guns is continuing steadily,' war minister Jones told citizens.[144] *Doric Star* and *Tairoa*, two ships laden with wool, meat, butter and cheese while plying from the dominion to Europe, had already been sunk.

The New Zealand navy first opened fire on the enemy in the South Atlantic. The *Achilles* not long before the Christmas of 1939 fought the heavy cruiser *Graf Spee* off the coast of Uruguay. Afterwards naval crew from the dominion met, drank and chatted with German sailors and gunners in the bars of Montevideo, lending the whole event a touch of chivalry. The *Achilles* then steamed back to Auckland. A crowd of nearly 100,000 people greeted the crew on a hot summer's day by hurling a 'snowstorm of paper' along Queen Street.[145] Sirens shrieked. Flags fluttered. Planes circled overhead. 'Auckland welcomed home the ship,' reported the *Evening Post*, 'and metaphorically garlanded her with the laurels of victory.'[146]

War widened to Scandinavia. Finland was attacked by the Soviet Union. The Allies talked about sending troops to violate the neutrality of Norway. Germany got in first, landing troops on 9 April and also occupying Denmark as a stepping stone to Norway.

New Zealanders were caught up in the fighting. One or two people from the dominion went to Finland. John Bonar Dunlop, an artist from Dunedin, was trained by the Finnish army for three months 'in the severest winter conditions' after he volunteered to help the small republic fight the Soviet Union.[147] Geoffrey Cox, working as a newspaper foreign correspondent, went to cover the war in Finland. He wrote news stories about wintry struggles 'where extreme cold turned the dead on the battlefields into scenes which resembled vast waxworks displays'.[148] Conservative newspaper editors told readers that the attack on Finland showed the Soviet Union to be worse than Nazi Germany. The *New Zealand Herald* said the 'brutal onslaught' on Finland was 'even more cowardly' than the German invasion of Poland. The *Otago Daily Times* noted that while the Nazi government had 'persecuted and degraded thousands' of people, the Soviet government had purged or starved 'hundreds of thousands'.[149] Finland was praised as a small and modern democracy like New Zealand.

Conservative newspapers dealt with the German invasion of Denmark and Norway in another way. Germany, they observed, claimed that they moved 'to forestall an Allied invasion'. The *Evening Post* labelled the claim a 'propaganda excuse' trumped up by Germany.[150] Citizens were not told that the Allies had themselves been about to invade Norway.

The Labour government had to make a decision about Finland. New Zealand had found ways to work civilly with the Soviets, drawing flak from Britain and Australia. The Labour Party lacked 'the axiomatic hostility' of conservatives towards the Soviet Union, although there was still some scepticism towards Moscow. Wellington throughout the war would work for a good relationship with the Soviets. The Labour government knew that the Soviet Union could be a counterweight to Japan. Labour leaders knew, too, that if war broke out between the Allies and the Soviet Union quite a few voters who backed the left of their party might well feel so troubled as to swing away from supporting Britain and France. The government therefore spoke out against Soviet aggression while at the same time asking London not to go to war with Moscow over Finland.[151]

The Labour government behaved the same way when Britain and France talked secretly in March 1940 about bombing Soviet oilfields in the Caucasus as a way to stop oil from being pumped to Germany. Wellington told London and Paris that such an attack would not only be an act of aggression but would likely 'rouse uncomfortably strong opposition' among the citizens of New Zealand. The opposition the government anticipated in such a case would come mostly from the Labour left.[152]

New Zealand troops, meanwhile, were landing in the Middle East. A first shipment of several thousand walked down the gangway and onto the sand in the middle of February.

The Middle East was almost wholly in the hands of imperial powers, above all the British Empire. Britain stationed an army of hundreds of thousands of men in Egypt to keep a good grip on the leaders of that supposedly self-governing state and also on

The *Achilles* attacking the *Graf Spee*. *Artist: Edward Annison. Archives New Zealand.*

the Suez Canal. The imperial hold was so strong that winning true independence was 'the predominant issue' in the politics of Egypt.[153] Gamal Nasser, who would one day become president of a postwar republic, wrote on the eve of the war about the 'weak and humiliated' people of Egypt.[154] The banks of the Nile were a 'curious' setting for dominion soldiers to wage what was supposedly a war for freedom and democracy.[155] New Zealand was helping an imperial overlord keep its power in Egypt. The *Union Record*, journal of the national Carpenters and Joiners Union, earlier had pointed out that a dominion army might be deployed not to fight fascism but 'for policing India or for any other imperialist activity'.[156] This was proving true – only in Egypt, not India.

Dominion troops tramping across an unwilling vassal state were not so very unlike German troops marching into Denmark.

Nor was occupation redeemed by a warm and friendly relationship between the subject peoples and the occupying troops. New Zealand soldiers behaved poorly in Egypt. One soldier said that 'most Kiwis, at times, acted in a high-handed arrogant manner'.[157] They bullied, stole, cheated and played 'funny' tricks, just as in the First World War. 'We are already tired of seeing niggers, who are a very degraded lot,' wrote one young man after two months in camp.[158] 'Egypt is awful,' said a young officer; he added that the 'wops' were 'mangy and full of dirt'.[159] Soldiers slapped Egyptians in the face, jostled them in the streets, punched them and pushed them off buses.[160]

Cosmopolitan scene on a street in wartime Cairo. *Artist: Neville Colvin. E.G. Webber,* Johnny Enzed in the Middle East *(Rotorua: Rotorua and Bay of Plenty Publishing Company, 1945).*

'If you run over a wog, make sure you kill him,' Reihana Rautahi was told at an army lecture for truck drivers. 'Back over him again if you think he's not dead.'[161]

Frank Varian was inside an army truck that broke its steering gear and ploughed into a market in Cairo. 'Killed four wogs and injured eleven,' he said afterwards. 'Bloody shame it wasn't more.'[162]

Joyce Macdonald, a nurse with the troops, wrote about the Egyptians as 'just one seething mass of screeching humanity'.[163] She added other comments when travelling with a fellow New Zealander on a riverboat on the Nile:

> *We were the only white people on board and never in your wildest imaginings could you picture anything so crudely raw and so grotesque. And the smells! – a deck caked with the dirt of countless ages, a hot, unrelenting sun pouring down, flies, flies and more flies clustering in the mixed cargo of unwashed humanity and animals!*[164]

Others saw the occupied people through the lens of not only race but class. Denis Caves, a young soldier, wrote that the people were 'very mixed'; the 'better class' were 'in some ways very fine' he told his fiancée. He used harsh words, however, for the mass of people: 'The lowest classes are detestable, filthy in body and mind and ignorant in everything but low earning and petty thieving.'[165] Winston Sargent wrote about the way dominion soldiers drove off street vendors by lifting 'our heavy army boots' and giving 'a smart kick to their buttocks'.[166] He saw one soldier push a streetwalker into the gutter. 'She moans,' he wrote. 'No one bothers to look whether she is all right.'[167]

A song on the lips of dominion troops cursed 'the dirty old harlots' of Cairo:

There was Susan and Tarzan and Lulu,
They did it this way and that,
They copied the gestures of animals,
Even the dog and the cat.[168]

Only a few of the more pensive men and women among the occupation army asked themselves what they were doing in Egypt. Sargent wondered 'what precisely' the people of Egypt thought about 'the great influx' of foreign troops. Certainly, he noted, there was evidence that the occupying army was being looked upon 'with some suspicion'.[169] Egyptians perked up whenever ground was won by Germany.

'You're finished,' the crowds called out. 'Goodbye the Kiwis.'

'We weren't very popular,' ruefully observed one soldier, Henry McRae.[170]

Egyptians dealt in varying ways with the burden of having to bow to an army of occupation. New Zealand soldiers were so well paid that a newspaper in Cairo dubbed them the 'millionaire soldiers'.[171] Money was made by those with goods and services to sell to troops. Winnings were good for industrialists whose factories ran red-hot on military contracts. Winnings could be good, too, for street vendors and sex workers, who found they could turn more than a few pennies by selling to the overbearing foreigners. At the same time, though, the occupation brought money worries to most households. The British Commonwealth use of the country as a military base brought ruinous rises in the cost of living for the poor and middle class. 'All prices have soared,' wrote an officer from Wellington.[172] Wages and farm earnings could not keep up with galloping inflation of the currency caused by army spending.[173]

Egyptians wondered whether throwing in their lot with Germany might help them drive out the British – and the New Zealanders. 'Ali Mahir, the prime minister, hoped that Germany would be victorious.'[174] The political leaders who wanted a British defeat were not very hopeful, however, and for the first nine months of the war they supposed that Germany would be beaten swiftly by the Allies.[175]

PAYING FOR WAR

Arming, training and deploying a modern military was already using up millions of pounds sterling. The First World War had cost vast sums to the dominion government of the day. State spending now needed to expand immediately and immensely in order to pay for the Second World War.

How was the government to get the money?

The First World War had been paid for in four ways. Volunteer groups had given money. War bonds were sold to the middle class and the wealthy. The money supply was boosted by spinning the printing presses and running off new banknotes. And the government made cuts to state spending on schools, hospitals, roads and railways. All four ways had brought trouble. Volunteer groups had not worked efficiently. War bonds had weighed the state down with a heavy burden of interest payments. Printing money had led to currency inflation and the subequent impoverishment of many households. Cuts to state spending had run down the material capital of the state and the social capital of the country.

Controversy broke out almost straightaway about how to pay for the Second World War.

Class was at the core of the controversy. The *Standard*, speaking for the government, claimed that 'shameless greed and sordid chicanery marked the handling of the finances for the last war'.[176] Nash, also speaking for the government, declared within a fortnight of the outbreak of the new war, 'no advantage or profit shall accrue to anyone on account of war conditions'.[177] Savage spoke more stirringly: 'The plain truth,' he told citizens, was that in the First World War 'while some men risked and sacrificed their lives for their country others took advantage of war conditions to enrich themselves at the country's expense'. The prime minister went on to say that it was 'quite clear' that capitalists were also willing 'to take advantage of the present war to serve their own political and economic ends'.[178] A new war would not, like the old war, be a struggle in which 'while men were dying, other men were getting rich'.[179] The National Party saw things the opposite way: it worried that a cunning government would exploit the war to build a socialist state.

Voluntary groups sprang up, as during the earlier war, to gather gifts of money, goods and services from the citizenry. Class tensions meant that well-to-do groups were fewer and weaker than in the First World War. Conservatives of the middle class and the elite who had been eager to sit on committees and give money during the earlier struggle were now in political opposition and not keen to help a 'socialist' government.

A few society hostesses got busy, nevertheless. A dressy ball was held in a Wellington cabaret, for example, to crown a carnival queen wearing a 'gown of gold threaded with glittering thread, and a flowing gold train edged with ermine'. Lucia Monckton-Arundell, wife of the governor-general, presided over the gathering.[180] People were 'not … very enthusiastic' about giving donations in most cities, towns and districts, though.[181] Warkworth citizens typically stayed at home or went to the cinema rather than fundraising; only seventeen people turned up to a first town meeting, and after that meeting was postponed in the hope of getting a better turnout, their ranks were swelled by a mere five extra people. 'Where is the old patriotic spirit of 1914–18,' wondered the chairman of the town board, 'when this district raised more money per capita than any other district in New Zealand?'[182]

The government, anxious about the inefficiency of fundraising, gazetted emergency regulations to control the work of voluntary groups. A National Patriotic Fund Board was set up. William Parry, a former miner now a government minister, was appointed controller of the fund. Provincial councils were delegated the task of fundraising regionally.

The government also asked citizens for interest-free loans, which it promised to repay after the war. Loans were handled by the finance ministry, led by Nash. A few landowners and business people gave large sums: the biggest was a loan of £10,000 from a Greymouth merchant firm, Wild and Robertson, and the next biggest was £2000 from Alfred Louisson, heir of a rich Christchurch brewing family. Working people signed away smaller sums. One man, who called himself simply 'Old Bill' and did not give his surname or address, sent a letter from One Tree Hill: 'Please find enclosed the sum of £5 as a small help towards the war fund from an old age pensioner who will endeavour to give at least one shilling in the pound while the war lasts.'[183]

A total of £1.3 million was handed over to the ministry in interest-free loans or war donations within six months of the declaration of war on Germany.[184] Money scraped together so scrappily could do very little, however, to cover the massive costs of the Second World War.

Companies and voluntary groups joined the government in urging citizens to give money to the military. This newspaper advertisement was paid for by the Timaru brewery of New Zealand Breweries. *Press, 28 December 1940.*

Controversy dogged the question of borrowing too. The Labour left, together with the left outside the party and those who believed in social credit, wanted the state to finance the war by taking over the banking industry. The Labour leadership was not willing to take such a step and instead chose to borrow in a more orthodox way. The War Expenses Act of 1939 gave the government authority to ask for £10 million, which was only a very modest beginning, given that hundreds of millions would need to be found for the war within a few years. Nash told citizens that borrowing from banks or the citizenry would be 'sparingly used to avoid a huge deadweight war debt'.[185] The government was stepping gingerly because it was well aware that wartime borrowing had become a heavy burden to the state in the First World War.

The government was not in favour of spinning the banknote printing presses because of the hardship this had caused for the working class during the previous war. Nash told the nation that increasing the money supply would only be done 'with care to see it is not simply inflationary'.[186] The policy of the government was to keep inflation as low as was workable in an economy where the military would be competing greedily with consumers for goods and services.

Nor was the government keen to use the method of slashing state spending that the government had followed in the First World War. The Labour Party believed in

The government bombarded citizens with advertisements urging them to lend money to the state to help pay for war. The loans came to be known as 'Victory' loans. *Artists: Abram Games and probably Albert O'Dea. Alexander Turnbull Library Eph-F-ODEA-1940/60-13.*

strengthening the state. 'We do not intend to let our social legislation lapse on account of the war,' declared Nash. 'Widows, children, and elderly people will be helped in times of war as well as peace.'[187]

A war of words broke out straightaway over this policy. Conservatives wanted the government to cut back on social spending. David Hogg, a leading businessman, called for sacrifice, discipline and thrift. The government during the First World War had 'faced the position in this way' and such a sound method of coping with crisis must not be undermined by any 'desire for luxury, comfort and self-indulgence'.[188] The *Otago Daily Times* said the government was 'persisting in implementing its Socialistic policies at a time when the need is for concentration of all resources on a single aim, New Zealand's war effort'.[189] The government, under cover of war spending, was 'continuing with Socialism until it had everything in its mesh', protested a businessman in Wellington.[190]

The Labour government chose a new way to fund the fighting: making the rich pay. Tax was to be the tool. Taxing the rich had been out of the question during the First World War because government during those years had been backed by those with money. Taxing the rich was orthodox policy for social democrats, however. 'For such a destructive purpose as war the obvious method of finance is taxation,' said Nash, 'and there is no doubt that we should pay as we go for the war to the limit that is practicable.'[191]

Taxing the rich to the limit would prove to be the key government policy for financing the Second World War. The contrast with the First World War, when the government had been so unwilling to tax the wealthy, could not have been more striking. A steep hike in the tax payable by those on high incomes, together with a steep hike in death duties payable by those who owned big estates, was imposed soon after war broke out. John A. Lee approved the government budget that brought in the new taxes as 'harsher to great wealth than any Labour budget yet'.[192] No government in the whole history of New Zealand, in fact, had ever struck such a heavy blow against the wealthy.

Conservatives publicly claimed that such wholesale taxation of the rich would have what the *Evening Post* called 'serious results in disorganising and lessening the capital available for industry'.[193] Conservatives, when speaking to one another in private, used words less carefully. The 'occupations of decent, industrious citizens, who had never asked the Government for a penny' were now being 'taken away', merchant Gordon Giesen told a group of businessmen.[194]

Taxing the rich was a crucial way for the government to pay for war. Wealthy people, while they were nearly always imperial loyalists on the political right, were not happy. This cartoon in the Labour Party newspaper shows a 'toff' in a gentlemen's club saying to another: 'The very idea! Other people are only giving their lives, but they ask US to lend money without INTEREST!' Standard, *3 October 1940.*

THE HOME FRONT

Class conflict over state spending and taxation was by no means the only division within the country after the outbreak of the Second World War. 'The present is no time for dissension, for altercation, for recrimination, and the undue ventilation of grievances,' the chief justice of the country, Sir Michael Myers, told a grand jury. 'The time calls for unanimity,' he went on, 'for the closing of the ranks of all sections of the community to meet a common danger.'[195] Yet the ranks did not close, and there was no unanimity.

The National Party and Labour Party used the faraway battlefields as tools for political purposes in New Zealand. The Labour government wanted to keep pressing forward with building a welfare state. The National opposition wanted to stop the building of a welfare state.

War controls over the economy caused angry wrangling within only a few weeks of the outbreak of the Second World War. At first, both big political parties backed a swift imposition of controls. The National Party agreed to the Emergency Regulations Act, giving the government sweeping powers to control the economy and society by way of undemocratic orders-in-council. The only concession National gained was that the government would use these powers in a politically neutral way. 'All of us dread the idea of a Government taking omnibus powers to do exactly what it likes,' observed a former conservative prime minister, Gordon Coates, 'but the people of this country must realise that their very existence may depend on the unification of effort.'[196]

An industrial council was set up under the new law. The council consisted of nine industrialists and nine trade unionists, led by the labour minister, Patrick Webb, who said its goal was to boost industrial production during the war 'as far as possible'.[197] A

Class conflict did not end with the declaration of war. Although both big political parties spoke of unity they did their best to fire 'torpedoes' at one another in and out of parliament. This cartoon portrays the parliamentary leaders of the National Party as officers of a U-boat. Hamilton has the ship of state in his sights. Coates tears up an agreement for political truce between Labour and National. Holland gives a salute. Standard, *12 October 1939.*

state building authority was set up under the new law too, with the aim of controlling the construction industry. A primary production council, whose task was to control farming, was a third emergency body set up under the new law. Landowners and farmers sat on this council, together with the president of the New Zealand Workers Union; at the head was agriculture minister W. Lee Martin. A price tribunal was founded three months after the declaration of war to systematically tackle price hikes caused partly by profiteering – a nightmare of the working class in the First World War.

Controls over the economy soon sparked testy quarrels inside and outside parliament. The new controls seemed likely to cost people on the political right. The moneyed, within a few weeks of the declaration of war, were saying that the government was using the struggle overseas as a pretext to push nationalisation of finance, trade, industry and even farming. A conference of chambers of commerce accused the government of imposing 'dictatorial control' on 'the whole trading system of New Zealand'.[198] The Labour government was 'taking advantage of the war situation to institute a system of bureaucratic control of the farming industry', claimed speakers at a meeting of the Waikato Farmers Union.[199] The *Evening Post* protested about 'the State octopus reaching out more and more'.[200] The National Party fought government economic controls 'tooth and nail' in the two houses of parliament, and the press backed the party in the fight.[201] The longest stonewall in the whole session of parliament that year came during a debate over banking. Hamilton attacked the government for trying to impose 'autocratic dictatorship of the State'. He was backed by Forbes and Coates, both former prime ministers.

'You can't get good government or wise government if it is government of the mob,' said Forbes.

'New Zealand is fast moving to National Socialism,' added Coates.[202]

Hamilton summed up the rhetoric of the right two months after the outbreak of war by saying that the government not only was keeping up its 'policy of State Socialism' but had done so 'deliberately … under the very first cloak of war'. Socialists were abusing democracy by bringing in 'revolutionary and objectionable' new laws.[203] Arnold Ely, president of the Auckland chamber of commerce, declared early in 1940 that the war had given the government an excuse for 'undue interference' in trade. He pointed out that price-fixing by the Labour government was 'a great deal' stricter than in Britain or Australia.[204] Holm made a similar claim as president of the chamber of commerce in Wellington: the state on the outbreak of war, he said, had taken steps to 'regiment practically all private commercial activities under various emergency regulations and enactments'. Those steps, he went on, 'cannot but give one the impression that we have gone considerably further along the road of complete State control of economic life than prosecution of the war demanded'.[205] He was more careful in his choice of words than many.

Landowners and farmers stirred restlessly over the way wartime economic controls withheld from them some of the wealth they believed was theirs by right. Although they spoke stoutly about the blessings of the British Empire, they complained about the way the government was letting the imperial motherland buy their wool, meat, butter and cheese too cheaply. Also, they complained about having to carry what Henry Blyde, vice-president of the Farmers Union, called 'the higher costs resulting from Socialism'.[206] Hamilton, who spent several weeks in the spring talking to landowners and farmers, claimed to have found among them 'intense dissatisfaction of the militant type'. At a time when many young men were going into the army, the government was keeping an army of other young men busy with its programmes of public works and pandering to 'spoon-fed' wage workers handling farm exports. Landowners and farmers found it hard to compete for unionised workers with a state willing to pay them good wages.[207]

Anger grew among people on the right about what seemed to be a lack of strong leadership in the National Party. The party came under fire from emerging conservative groups.

City business leaders formed a New Liberal Party in the autumn of 1940; they set up branches in all the main towns, aiming to carry on the policies of the Liberal Party that had merged itself, some years before, in the National Party. The New Liberals spoke about their belief in 'true Liberalism and in being fair not only to the capitalist, but also to the man in the street', and promised to 'represent all classes in the community to the detriment of no class'. A nationalistic tone was noticeable too: the party was calling for a government of 'New Zealanders for New Zealand'.[208] The new party seemed likely to draw support from the left of the National Party.

A striking, often strident new group on the right was the People's Movement. City business people late in the spring held secret meetings to work out a programme for the movement. Crowds were attracted by expensive advertisements to public meetings throughout the country. The first was in Wellington, where citizens heard that the government's 'socialistic trend of legislation' would lead 'ultimately and inevitably to dictatorship'.[209] Other meetings stressed the need to fight against the socialist state. Ernest Toop, company director and a leader of the movement, called for 'government freed from the domination of party and sectional interests' – by which he meant the working class and the Labour Party. A landed lady in Hawke's Bay said there could be 'no real progress' in society unless both the war with the foreign foe and the class war were settled on the basis of 'uprightness, fearlessness, unselfishness, and chivalry'.[210] Conservative newspapers backed the movement for the way it spoke for 'all classes' and upheld 'Christian and British' principles of democracy.[211]

War, meanwhile, had already shattered the Labour Party.

Although conservatives worried about a government steering full steam ahead towards socialist dictatorship, the true course of the ship of state was rather towards the right. A lot of people on the left felt that the governing group, by backing Britain so wholeheartedly, had sold out on the principles of social democracy. John Beaglehole complained, as a left academic, that the government two months into the war was not willing to 'do anything socialist'.[212] He noted that even old-fashioned liberals such as journalist Alan Mulgan were so exasperated by such timidity that they were 'going very red' and 'hailing the revolution & talking about state-action & the sins of Chamberlainism'.[213] Eric McCormick, a leftish young man of the middle class, was not alone in feeling 'not profoundly stirred by the cause of Poland' and in having 'no faith' in the British Conservative government. He also questioned Savage's statement 'that where Britain went, there New Zealand must follow'.[214] William Barnard, five months after the declaration of war, said that 'many thousands of New Zealanders' were not happy with 'the oft repeated declarations about liberty and freedom and democracy' given by the government as 'sufficient reasons for the present sacrifice'. He noted, too, that one word not spoken by the government was 'equality'.[215] R.A.K. Mason, further to the left, wrote a bold poem the day after the declaration of war:

We shall fight for freedom
– but we'll make sure it is freedom we're
fighting for.[216]

John A. Lee, gadfly of the Labour Party.
Photographer: Leo White. Alexander Turnbull Library WA-67319-G.

The Labour left was more and more unhappy about the way the leadership was refusing to finance the war by taking over the banks. And the left kept up its protest about the way the government had chosen to link the dominion closely with British war planning instead of giving priority to the needs of New Zealand. Controversy over war policy and other conflicts within the ranks ran so high that, six months after the declaration of war, Lee was expelled from the party; his expulsion was backed by 546 votes but opposed by 344. A group of other left members of parliament walked out in dismay and, with Lee, formed the Democratic Labour Party.

The followers of Social Credit, meanwhile, inside and outside the governing party, worried that the enemy was not fascism or dictatorship but the bankers of the world, backed above all by Jews. 'The enemy was all the more sinister for being hidden,' wrote Lauris Scott. Social Credit households like her family believed that the war 'brought further evidence of the power of the financial network, since it supported armament manufacture everywhere and was indifferent to national borders'.[217] The Douglas Social Credit Movement at a meeting three weeks after the outbreak of the war voted to support the government but urged it not to go to the banks but to use 'debt-free money' to finance the fighting.[218]

The Communist Party moved swiftly away from the government. The party's policy after the surrender of Poland was that there was no pressing need for a war against Germany. The *People's Voice* said that 'peace now would enable the peoples of the belligerent countries to get rid of those responsible for the war'.[219] A statement from the party two months after the outbreak of war went further: it defined the war as imperialist and said that the working class should try to hinder the war policy of the Labour Party. The West Coast Trades Council voted that 'the war in Europe is another imperialist struggle for markets and raw material between capitalist Britain and France on one side and capitalist Germany on the other, and which may involve the whole world with the accompanying slaughter of millions of workmen'.[220] A group of workers in Nuhaka agreed that 'all workers in all countries' were 'just chopping blocks for the capitalists'.[221] Gordon Watson, essayist, journalist and leading member of the Communist Party, agreed that the war was 'in essence a struggle for mastery between two great capitalist empires', Britain and Germany.[222] Douglas Martin, another writer on the left, was sent to prison for saying in a pamphlet that war had broken out not because there was any threat to the autonomy of the British Empire but because British capitalists wanted to attack the capitalists of Germany.[223] Communist delegates at the Federation of Labour conference early in 1940 called for the dominion to leave the war and proclaim neutrality, and for independence to be given to all colonies, especially India.[224]

Communist critiques of the war reached many people who were not members of the party. Crowds of up to 2000, for example, came along to meetings in Quay Street, Auckland, to listen to party speakers who opposed the war. The party published a string of pamphlets condemning the war as imperialist. The party also printed thousands of yellow stickers that its members or sympathisers in trade unions slapped onto boxes of goods for export to Britain. 'Down with conscription and Imperialistic war', the stickers said.[225] Communist Party membership grew quickly.[226]

The Labour Party, anxious about losing the moral high ground, attacked the Communist Party. The *Standard* scorned 'the Mental Slaves of Moscow' for saying 'a war between democratic Britain and Fascist Germany is an imperialist war'. Communists were not only wrong about that, they were 'Nazis in disguise'.[227] Robert Semple, public works minister, bitterly lashed communists: Stalin was 'the Red murderer' and communists in the dominion were traitors to democracy. 'I have opposed war all my life, but I have never subscribed to the belief that one must bare his chest submissively to the bayonet of an invader who will take his life and the liberty of the children who will come after him,' he stormed.[228] Frederick Schramm, lawyer, was another Labour member of parliament who spoke out against the 'subversive, untrue, malicious and disloyal' words of the Communist Party.[229] The Labour Party issued what came to be known as the 'black circular', banning party members from publishing anything opposed to government policy or helping the Communist Party.

The government for the first few months of war did not use the power of the state to silence protest, but tolerance ended early in 1940 when police barred communists from public speaking. Quay Street speakers were rounded up. Stern steps of this sort worried more than members of the Communist Party. One citizen, while a group of arrests was being carried out, jumped onto a windowsill and addressed onlookers. 'I have never spoken in public before, and I won't be much good,' he cried. 'But I am frightened, I am frightened for democracy.'[230]

War emergency powers were used now to stop communists from publishing anything critical of war policy. The first subversion trials of the war took place in the autumn of 1940 when the editor and publisher of the *People's Voice* were dragged into court, together with two committee members of the Auckland branch of the Communist Party. All were found guilty.[231] Other trials would follow.

Pacifists were rounded up too and herded into court.

Protest by pacifists began on the very day of the declaration of war against Germany. Ormond Burton, a former soldier and now a Methodist minister, stood in front of parliament and spoke to a crowd. Other protests followed swiftly. Meetings in the streets were backed by letters to newspapers and the publishing of pamphlets. 'War has never yet produced anything of permanent value to mankind,' wrote one pacifist.[232] Pacifists, together with people from groups on the political left, early in 1940 formed the Peace and Anti-Conscription Council. The council first met in Wellington, where its secretary, Ian Milner, wrote that it 'pledged to fight attempts to introduce conscription, to preserve civil liberties and living standards of the people, and to work for peace through the withdrawal of New Zealand from a war of which the real aims get more obscured month by month.'[233] Branches were formed throughout the country and crowds kept gathering; a throng of perhaps 6000 'men and women of all ages,' for example, flocked one night to a street meeting in Wellington.[234]

The state stopped pacifist protest. A strong signal was given the day war broke out, when Burton and two others were brought before a magistrate. A steady stream of arrests and trials kept up for the next few months. The laws used to stop the protests gave the police power to act against anyone who 'obstructed' them, or who seemed likely to cause disorder in a public place. The government, in other words, was waging a war for freedom and democracy by stamping hard on freedom and democracy. Citizens were often upset when constables bundled speakers away. 'I have just seen an example of what we are fighting against in Germany – Hitlerism,' said a man who climbed onto a soapbox in an Auckland park left empty by arrests; 'as a believer in free speech I protest.'[235]

The government invoked laws against disorder and obstruction because it did not wish to seem to be stifling free speech by hauling pacifists into court on charges of subversion.[236] Mabel Howard condemned fellow party members for forgetting what she believed were their socialist principles. The labour movement had been 'built out of suppression' by those in authority, she said at a city council meeting in Christchurch.[237]

The government took a key step towards tighter control over free speech at the end of the first summer of the war when it issued new Public Safety Emergency Regulations. Subversion was defined more sweepingly. The police were given stronger powers to stop public meetings. Fraser claimed that the regulations struck the appropriate balance while still punishing disloyalty. 'That is not freedom,' he claimed, 'but gross abuse of freedom.'[238]

One outcome was that the pacifist movement was forced more or less underground.

Nationality was another cause of conflict among people on the home front, although Germans living in the dominion were not harassed nearly as much as they had been in the First World War. Anybody who followed the news carefully knew that two out of every three German electors had voted against the Nazi Party in the last free poll held before the founding of the Third Reich. George Clark, for example, noted that his Waikato farming family 'felt sorry for the Germans getting led into another world war'.[239] The editor of a newspaper children's page told his readers that when the first war had broken out he had been a schoolboy and hated all Germans. Now he saw things differently. 'We must not "hate" the German people, who are men and women, boys and girls, just like ourselves,' he wrote. 'But we must hate and fight for the extermination of a system.'[240]

The government spoke the same way. The Nazi Party was the enemy – not the people of Germany. German music was played freely on the state-owned radio stations. The national conference of the Labour Party and the Federation of Labour early in 1940 proclaimed that 'the working people of Germany are in no important respect different from ourselves'. The New Zealand working class hoped 'to welcome them back some day to co-operation with the International Labour movement'.[241] The Federation of Labour proclaimed passionately:

> *The German people, who have given so much to human knowledge in every branch of science, literature, art, and philosophy, dare not express an opinion of their own. They dare not attempt to form their own scientific, cultural, and social organisations. The German trade unionists and Socialists who have given so many outstanding figures to the International Labour Movement cannot form a trade union of their own. We wish it to be clearly understood that we do not blame the German people for the present catastrophe, and that we are not animated by any feeling of bitterness towards them ... We extend the hand of friendship to the German people, and we pledge ourselves to help them to throw off the tyranny that is enslaving them.*[242]

The government nevertheless made up its mind to keep a close eye on any German citizens, or former German citizens, living in New Zealand.

All men and women of any foreign nationality were ordered, as soon as war broke out, to register their names and addresses under new Alien Control Emergency Regulations. All who had once been nationals of an enemy state, even if they were now citizens, were also ordered to register. The regulations gave police the power to ask enemy aliens or former enemy aliens, at any time and in any place, to show that they were carrying a registration certificate. A police constable also had the right to take any of those on the register into custody.[243] All registered people had no right to move, or even to leave home for more than a day, without notifying the police. All were forbidden from working on the wharves, or on ships.

Arrests and internments began in the last weeks of 1939, when nine Germans were locked up. Gregor Reithmaier was one, a young radio operator. Qualbert Fischer, nearly sixty and married with children, was another; he was 'an expert in the mining of mercury'.[244] Twenty or so others were added to the list of prisoners during the first half of the next year.

But the policy of internment was used only sparingly.[245] The Labour Party was concerned about repeating the mistakes of the First World War. The policy now was to intern only those who had spoken out strongly in favour of the Nazi Party, or who seemed in some other way to have links with the enemy. Two internees, for example, were the president and secretary of the Samoan Nazi Party.[246]

Kurt Stunzner, a young German Samoan, tending his pet seagull chicks while interned on Somes Island in Wellington Harbour. *www.germansinsamoa.net*

The political right wanted more arrests and internments. Conservatives often saw the war as a struggle not so much against fascism as against Germans and Germany. 'Every German must be viewed as a potential enemy,' said the Otago Returned Soldiers Association.[247] Newspapers, as the voice of the right, made sweeping comments about the supposedly aggressive, violent and lying 'Hun' or 'Teuton'. The *Evening Post* told readers that the two world wars showed 'no difference' in the aggressive ways of Germany.[248] The *New Zealand Herald* declared that Germany violated 'every basic conception of Western civilisation – righteousness, intelligence, and honour'.[249]

German New Zealanders nevertheless were playing leading roles as noteworthy politicians (such as Nordmeyer and Schramm) and as key army officers (such as Kippenberger, Voelcker, Dittmer and Freyberg).

German Jews who had fled from the Third Reich and sought safety in the dominion also had to register as enemy nationals. Citizens often denounced the newcomers as a threat to the country. 'Many of them are acting with brazen disloyalty to the Empire's cause,' protested one letter writer, 'and showing open sympathy with their former oppressors.'

Injury was added to insult because German Jews, as foreign nationals, were not allowed to volunteer for the military. Aliens could keep living their lives more or less as though there was no war, able 'to abuse British freedom with impunity and – worse still – to usurp the jobs of our own boys'.[250] Jews, many people muttered, were doing what they always did, looking after their own needs and making money.

Race divided citizen from citizen too.

Māori looked upon the war in varying ways. Ngāti Porou and Te Arawa were keen to fight the Axis powers. Te Arawa declared that 'the spirit' of their tribe 'flames at the deeds of wanton aggression' by Germany.[251] Sir Apirana Ngata spoke about waging war as 'the price of citizenship'. He wanted the government to set up a Māori battalion. Eruera Tirikatene and Paraire Paikea, two Rātana members of parliament, lent their backing. The government agreed. Ngāti Porou, an old ally of the state, within weeks sent more than 140 of its sons into the new Maori Battalion, followed by more than ninety from Te Arawa.

Other tribes held back. Waikato gave fewer than forty of its sons, and only fifteen signed up from Ngāpuhi, four from Ngāi Tahu and a mere three each from Whanganui and Ngāti Toa.[252] Ngata confessed that volunteering was 'not as good as one would wish' when he wrote a private letter about the matter to a colleague, Te Rangi Hiroa.[253] The key divide was between the 'loyal' and 'rebel' sides in the New Zealand Wars. Waikato was not at all keen to go to war. Te Puea Herangi told Savage that the people of the tribe were willing 'to render what help they can for the defences of our country', but to a friend she spelled out her true thoughts: 'Waikato are not going to the war.' She told young men who sought her advice about whether to volunteer: 'I'm not going to tell you to go; I'm not going to tell you to stay.'[254] Other leaders of the tribe opposed involvement in any way.[255]

The battle to get the Treaty of Waitangi written into law seemed more urgent to many, no matter what their tribe, than faraway battles against Germany. Tainui, Te Arawa, Takitimu, Kurahaupō, Aotea, Mātaatua, Tokomaru and Horouta at the end of 1939 petitioned the privy council to look into seven government violations of the treaty.[256] The privy council told the tribes that governments were not bound under law by the Treaty of Waitangi.[257] A group of Te Tai Tokerau tribes wanted the new military force being mobilised within the dominion army to be named the 'Treaty of Waitangi Maori Battalion' in order to 'draw the attention of both Maori and Pakeha to their respective obligations' under the treaty.[258]

Many tribal leaders were saying the war for freedom and democracy had not yet been won in New Zealand.

Chinese New Zealanders meanwhile were not keen to go to war against Germany. The true battle, for most of them, was the Sino-Japanese War. The Chinese consulate teamed up with the Chinese Association to wage a propaganda war, telling people they must show 'strong determination' and strive for 'national unity'. *Q-Sing Times*, published fortnightly by the Auckland branch of the Chinese Association, sought to foster 'the spirit of Nationalism among the Chinese overseas', in the words of its editor, Chau Yan Sham.[259] Song Meiling, forceful wife of Jiang Jieshi, sent letters of thanks for what she called the 'patriotic enthusiasm' of Chinese New Zealand.[260] The community continued to back the cause of the Guomindang after the declaration of war on Germany, and was vexed by the unwillingness of Wellington to take steps against Tokyo. Chinese workers in the colonies of Samoa and Nauru very likely felt the same way.

On the whole, the subject peoples of the island colonies were not keen to go to war against Germany, either. Some young men in the Cook Islands, Niue and Tokelau came forward as volunteers, but most felt that the war had nothing to do with the Pacific. The only meaningful step was taken by the Rarotonga Returned Soldiers Association,

Māori imagery was widely used by artists, companies and the state as emblems of New Zealand. Pan American Airways opened the first international passenger service between Auckland and San Francisco in 1937. *Los Angeles Public Library.*

whose ageing veterans volunteered 'for any duty, preferably active service'; but none could afford a ticket to Auckland.[261] Cook Island tribes as a whole were not willing to let their young men go into the army and the government did nothing to recruit actively.

Nor were colonial subjects in the two mandates of Nauru and Samoa itching to go to war for the British Empire.

Samoan feelings provoked a little skirmish in the propaganda war between the Allies and Germany. A radio broadcast from Berlin reported that the people of Samoa were disgruntled with colonial rule – which was true – and that the colonial state had to

A street scene in Apia, capital of Samoa, 1945. *Photographer: Whites Aviation. Alexander Turnbull Library WA-01106-G.*

use force to stop them from rebelling – which was also true. A radio broadcast from Britain attacked the German broadcast and told the world there had been 'no efforts at suppression' of the Samoans 'because none are necessary'. The British broadcast went on to claim that 'numerous' Samoans had offered to volunteer for the army.[262] The truth was that colonial officials worried that young men volunteering in the villages were driven by a wish to get arms and training in order to fight for freedom from New Zealand. Alfred Turnbull, head of the colonial government, wrote that words spoken by chiefs about letting young men go into uniform 'must not be misunderstood as to mean any loyalty towards [New Zealand] or indeed any wish to assist us in case of peril'.[263] The 'stubbornness of Europeans' or else the will of God had brought about the war, a spokesman for the Fono of Faipule (the congress of chiefs) observed rather dispassionately.[264]

Class, nationality and race kept tugging at, and tangling, the loyalty of citizens and subjects just as they had before the fighting. The home front did not close ranks seamlessly against a foreign enemy.

A RUSH TO THE PETROL PUMPS

Shortages, hoarding, profiteering and a widespread mood of crisis had swept the country on the outbreak of the First World War, but the new war met with a much more measured and muted response. Although the government had given itself sweeping powers under the emergency regulations, those powers were used gingerly. Citizens went on living and working more or less as they had before the declaration of war on Germany. Fears faded when people understood that life had not changed much from day to day. Radio and movie news about the war led New Zealanders to look upon the struggle with 'the attitude of spectators', wrote the *Auckland Star* late in the autumn of 1940;[265] and a citizen added that 'too many of our people' saw the faraway struggle 'as an interesting side-show concerning Europe alone'.[266]

Hoarding had been widespread for the first weeks after the declaration of war. Well-to-do women rushed to the shops to stock up on groceries, especially tea, sugar and flour. The wealthy and the middle class, who could afford to buy in bulk, swept some shops bare, leaving little for others. Nancy Taylor, a young historian, saw the panic and wrote that 'the private and petty greed contrasted with public professions of loyalty and co-operation'.[267] Newspapers spoke out against 'selfish hoarders'.[268] Christchurch grocers found that when their sales staff tried to stop customers from buying in bulk, they could be 'bullied into accepting orders'. The grocers decided to block hoarding by agreeing among themselves to sell only in small amounts and to serve only their regular customers; this, they hoped, would stop hoarders buying in bulk by going from shop to shop.[269]

Shortages were seldom serious, however, and two months after the declaration of war most people's buying habits had settled down.

Petrol was the exception to this, since as soon as the government declared war it imposed petrol rationing. Economic planners feared that Japan would join Germany and disrupt the dominion's oil supply from the Dutch East Indies. Citizens who wanted to buy petrol were ordered to go to a post office and apply for ration coupons. An 'extraordinary rush' followed up and down the country.[270] Thousands of coupons were issued every hour, and once drivers had their coupons they sat in long queues outside service stations where the pumps were ceaselessly busy. Hoarding was widespread. Petrol sales in the first week of war, before the ration system was in full swing, swelled to 'more than a million gallons above the weekly average'.[271] Japan was not planning to join the war, however, and sent clear signals to the government. 'The whole nation,' said the new Japanese consul-general, Toyokichi Fukuma, 'wants to cement the cordial and close association which exists between this country and Japan.'[272]

Petrol rationing ended at the start of summer thanks to Japanese neutrality. A lack of tankers during the following weeks, though, led the government to once more impose rationing, which in turn led to a jump in petrol thieving. Owen Swan, John

Petrol ration coupon. The government was anxious about petrol imports throughout the war because 56 per cent of the dominion's supply in the last years of peace came from the Dutch East Indies, a target of Japanese buyers and later the Japanese military.

Caulfield and James Keefe, for example, were three young men who worked as a gang to steal petrol from parked cars in the Bay of Plenty.[273] The Wellington Automobile Association warned motorists that petrol thieves were 'busy in and about the city'.[274] Petrol sales became a barometer of the anxiety of citizens about war news. Batterbee, writing as British high commissioner, told the government in London that whenever bad news came to the dominion it was 'signalled by a rush not to the colours but to the petrol pumps'.[275]

Civilian volunteering was as lacklustre as military volunteering. Quite a few citizens did step forward and offer their skills during the first fortnight of war. Ambulance services, for example, got busy. Over 1000 men and women signed up for training in first aid and home nursing with the Wellington Centre of the St John Ambulance Association.[276] Citizens everywhere volunteered to take on a wide array of tasks. After the first few weeks, though, the mood switched and most people went on with their lives in a workaday way. The *Evening Post* complained by the middle of the autumn of 1940 that for 'the great majority' of people life was going on 'with little change'. The paper thought it 'wrong that both men and women of the civilian population, whether eligible for active service or not, should sacrifice so little, if they sacrifice anything at all'. Only 'a small minority' were volunteering for war work.[277]

Mobilising the citizenry was provided for by emergency regulations, but the government let these powers lie unused.

Women, for example, found that they were not asked to do anything new. Young women were heard talking about how they would like to volunteer for auxiliary work in the army, air force or navy. Other than recruiting nurses for the military, however, the government did nothing to seek out the services of women, who sometimes took matters into their own hands. A group of nearly 200 Auckland women met weekly for voluntary drill and war training, calling themselves the Women's National Service Corps.[278] The state politely ignored their offer of service.

Working-class women found plenty of factory jobs, with good pay, in war industry. Military clothing manufacturers, for example, were soon employing thousands of workers paid to 'bend daily over machines throughout New Zealand'. Clothing factories grew swiftly alongside woollen mills and footwear factories, all busy with army contracts. 'Enormous quantities' of army uniforms and army boots were churned out weekly.[279] War boosted other types of manufacturing too. In Christchurch alone,

Factory workers: working-class women found themselves sought after by employers as never before, thanks to a boom in military supply industries. Women factory hands were praised as patriotic for their work. Evening Post, *18 December 1943.*

several big new factories opened their doors to make goods for the military. The rubber industry took off after the Skellerup family opened two rubber factories. The plastics industry began with the opening of a factory that was soon working three shifts every day and turning out nearly seven million plastic items every year.[280] Andersons, the main engineering company in the city, stamped out grenade casings and 'a large range of forgings for machine gun carriers'.[281] All these new factories offered plenty of work for young women of the working class.

Civilians who had been travelling overseas at the outbreak of the war sometimes volunteered for the military or other groups in Britain. Young men signed up for the British air force or army. Young women went into support work. Margaret Selby, for example, daughter of landowners in Canterbury, was on holiday when the war began, and joined the Women's Land Army. The farmhands, she wrote home, 'all seemed very amused when I first arrived', but soon she was in charge of a lot of stock.[282] Joan Skelton, daughter of a well-to-do farming family in the King Country, was also on holiday and also joined the Women's Land Army. 'I spent a lot of time spreading muck,' she noted later.[283] George Ward from Wellington, on a golfing tour when the war broke out, drove an ambulance in Kensington. Elsie Smith from the Wairarapa, travelling with her family, volunteered for the British air force and was set to what she called the 'dangerous work' of handling balloons aimed at stopping dive bombers.[284] Mary de

Beer, daughter of a wealthy merchant family in Otago, got a job as telephone operator at a fire-brigade station in London. 'Never having had to work, she had done nothing of this sort in her life before, excepting voluntary Red Cross work among people of her own kind,' wrote her cousin, Charles Brasch. 'Now, at nearly fifty, she was thrown together with men and women of every kind.' Dora de Beer, her sister, was not able to find war work and instead devoted herself to being housekeeper for her family, managing the house and servants, and knitting for men in the army.[285] Others from the dominion turned their hand to medical work. Norma Davidson, Elizabeth Manchester and Ellen Wilkinson, nurses, signed up. Davidson and Manchester were sent to Palestine, and Wilkinson went to France.[286] Doris and William Gordon, doctors from Taranaki, did voluntary health work. They were helped by their sons. 'The little boys,' wrote their mother, early in 1940, 'walked over a large tract of Wiltshire distributing leaflets on how to safeguard drinking water if bombs blew up the sewers.'[287]

New Zealand civilians living or travelling in Germany on the declaration of war were usually allowed to leave the country. Only a few of those who stayed on were viewed as a threat to the country and were interned. Almost all of those who were not put behind wire soon found themselves struggling financially: the state of war between the Allies and the Third Reich meant they could no longer be sent money from bank accounts and trust funds; nor were they, as enemy nationals, able to seek jobs.[288]

Others were stranded elsewhere in Europe. John McLaughlin of Christchurch got out of Germany just before the outbreak of the war and travelled through Hungary before finding himself stuck in Romania. 'Most days I stay indoors until late,' he wrote to his wife back home in Fendalton, 'and if I do go out it is to buy food.'[289]

A few New Zealanders had been living in Poland. Paul Falla, son of the chairman of the Union Steam Ship Company and an old boy of Christ's College, was an embassy official in Warsaw. He, like McLaughlin, ended up in Romania. The Mackenzie family, also living in Warsaw, lived through heavy shelling and air raids which 'made life unbearable', before they had to split up. Hugo Mackenzie, director of a language school, was ordered to stay in Poland. Maria Mackenzie and their son Herbert were allowed to leave by way of Germany. 'They treated me very nicely,' she said, 'but there was not enough food.'[290]

The island colonies, meanwhile, were finding that the outbreak of war mostly meant a heavy blow to their economy.

Military spending, which helped keep the wheels of industry and commerce spinning in New Zealand, did not go as far as the tropical islands. New Zealand troops were not sent to Tokelau, nor to the Cook Islands, Niue and Nauru. Samoa was given a small boost in military spending. War mostly meant a sudden collapse of the market for copra and a sharp drop in exports of tropical fruit thanks to an equally sharp drop in the tonnage of shipping. Wellington wanted ships for the more pressing job of getting goods from the dominion to Britain. The Cook Islands fruit industry 'overnight' was felled by a body blow.[291] The Samoan copra industry cut its yield, along with its earnings, by more than half, which meant that many villagers had to go back to living off the land.[292] The people of the mandate 'faced a lean time', noted the colonial government.[293] Nauru alone was doing well; its phosphate was a very high war priority.

Civilians jogged along, for now, in mainland New Zealand. Petrol had to be husbanded and tropical fruit was hard to find in the shops, but in general people were struck by how the mood of the country seemed very unlike the mood during the early days of the First World War. Fraser asked a secret session of parliament early in the summer whether only 'a bomb on the breakfast table' would awaken some New Zealanders to an awareness that the country was at war with Germany.[294] One citizen wrote to the *Evening Post* about the lack of a warlike mood:

> *How times have changed in this little country since that eventful year 1914 when the British Empire was at war with Germany! ... What do we find today? Apathy, indifference, subversive propaganda, and the prattle of pacifist organisations linked strangely with Communists. A desperate issue at stake and the voluntary system of enlistment a pitiable farce.*[295]

Frederick Wood was aware during the first war year of what he called 'a general feeling of futility'. He heard prominent people confess 'frankly', yet secretly, that they could not see how the war could be wound up.[296] Nancy Taylor wrote much the same way: a 'dull resentment was widespread', she observed, 'expressing itself almost unconsciously in forgetting the war as much as possible'.[297] James Bertram, coming home from China early in 1940, found himself confronted by a 'curiously intact' Auckland. The city seemed 'a great friendly garden suburb, where office-workers still came out in the lunch hour to gossip, bareheaded, in the sun' and where 'yachts still left at week-ends for islands in the Hauraki Gulf'. Parties at the beach 'remained as popular as they had ever been'.[298] The *Auckland Star* wrote about the city's peace and prosperity:

> *Apart from the presence in the city of a greater number of men in khaki than usual, it is hard for the people of this country to realise there is a war. Life is going on here almost the same as this time last year. Scarcely anything is changed. The war is so far away as to be almost unreal.*[299]

Agnes Loudon, principal of Auckland Girls Grammar School, urged students 'to be ready and willing' for a call to war that never came, noted one of the students, Dorothy Norgrove:

> *None of us took much notice; we were always being urged to greater virtue and industry ... And anyway, nothing much seemed to be happening here. All that fuss was on the other side of the world ... Meanwhile, nothing was as important as the onset of the cricket season, summer, and the long holidays.*[300]

The Savage funeral procession on one of the quays of Wellington.
Photographer: probably William Raine. Alexander Turnbull Library ATL 1/1-021743-G.

Denis Glover wrote a poem early in 1940 about the widespread lethargy:

> *Hope stands on broken stilts.*
> *Faith, time's poor refugee*
> *is ringed with hostile wire ...*
> *while practice bombs are bursting*
> *we just don't give a damn.*[301]

Savage, meanwhile, was slowly dying. He had never ceased to worry about the consequences of going to war, and at a cabinet meeting he said he worried that the New Zealand army might become facist and overthrow the government. On a cool autumn day, 27 March, the beloved prime minister died. Crowds watching his cortège pass through the streets of Wellington and Auckland were bigger than those that sent off the troops. A 'jammed mass of humanity'[302] looked at the coffin in Wellington. A 'vast concourse' of some 200,000 citizens then gathered in Auckland.[303] Fraser stood over the coffin of the founder of the welfare state and read out the words of a member of parliament and son of a prophet, Haami Ratana:

> *The world is disturbed, the country is throbbing violently, the earth is rent in twain, New Zealand has lost a leader, a Christian gentleman, a father of the Maori people. His memory will be revered by many and mourned by all.*[304]

Fraser was now prime minister of wartime New Zealand.

The fall of France: German soldiers relax in the summer sun on a French beach on the Atlantic coast. *Daily Mail.*

CHAPTER 3 | A WAR FAR AWAY
JUNE 1940 TO DECEMBER 1941

WAR HYSTERIA

The Phoney War ended only a month after the invasion of Norway. German troops tramped into the Netherlands, Belgium and France. France, with bewildering swiftness, on 22 June signed an armistice with Germany. The north and west of the French republic went under German occupation, while the south became a Catholic fascist dictatorship led by Philippe Pétain and governed from Vichy.[1] All the overseas colonies of France were to be governed by Vichy. Italy joined the struggle, declaring war on Britain and France.

New Zealand was swept by waves of hysteria, whipped up by newspapers and the movie news.

The first wave of feeling came when Germany invaded Belgium and the Netherlands. The Allies faced 'the certainty of a fierce and cruel fight', declared the *New Zealand Herald*. The government must no longer allow anybody opposing the war to 'spread disaffection and disloyalty'.[2] The *Evening Post* said the people of the dominion could no longer blind themselves 'to the fact that their own peril is not less than the peril of the people of the Mother Country'.[3] A chorus of chambers of commerce, National Party politicians and many other conservatives chimed in and called for the dominion to go onto a total war footing.

Parliament was not in session and was not due to meet again for a month, but the political right within three days of the invasion of Belgium and the Netherlands was asking for the house to be summoned immediately. Conservatives wanted a new government, something like the war coalition formed by the two strongest political parties in the First World War.[4] The British Empire was now in such danger, or so it was claimed, that party politics must be suspended in the common cause of fighting the foreign enemy.

The Labour government saw things less feverishly. 'I must point out the very grave danger of even well-intentioned people developing, or inducing in others, undue panic,' said Fraser.[5]

The next wave of hysteria hit after another week or so, following the collapse of the Netherlands and the first lunge by German troops into northern France. New Zealand 'need not be surprised to wake up some morning to learn of a hostile warship off the coast demanding our surrender', wrote one anxious citizen. 'What resistance could we offer to even a small landing party?'[6] The government, wrote another, might now 'wake up and start issuing gas masks, build air-raid shelters, practise black-outs and train every fit man to defend his country now, not wait until we are invaded'.[7] Almost every newspaper was now calling for a war cabinet to take control of the country.

'There is no doubt that public opinion is formed and growing firmer,' claimed the *Evening Post*, 'that New Zealand should set up a National War Cabinet.'[8]

The *Star-Sun*, which like the *Evening Post* was by no means among the most conservative newspapers, told its readers that if a plebiscite were to be taken it would show 'a 90 per cent vote in favour' of a 'truly national Government'.[9] Newspapers published column after column quoting those who wanted conscription and a national war cabinet, and very little or nothing from those who opposed them.[10] Conservative crowds gathered to call for a coalition government and mobilisation of the whole economy. William Mulholland, president of the Farmers Union, said that the dominion was 'standing four-square across the path of the very demons of hell'.[11] Allied surrender in the battles now being fought in Europe would mean there would be 'nothing to stand' between New Zealand and the military might of Germany.[12]

The National Party threw its weight behind such conservative protest, opening with a statement by Adam Hamilton. Citizens, he said, were worried by the 'shilly-shallying' and 'apparent ineptitude' of the government. The Labour Party, he went on, needed to know that the National Party would no longer 'stand aside and give it carte blanche'.[13] Parliament must be called quickly and the country must be governed by a war coalition, not by the Labour Party. There followed days of what Frederick Wood called 'bitter and confused controversy' between highly wrought gatherings. And a noisy new group, the National Service Movement, suddenly sprang into life.[14]

The National Service Movement began when a few hundred people, mostly on the political right, met in Auckland to call for the government to hand over its powers to a war council under the leadership of 'a strong and driving personality'. The meeting also called for everyone in the country to be conscripted into the military or for war work. The 'barbarian' was 'at the very gate', declared the lawyer chosen as chairman, Bryan Kingston. Labour and National must now shake hands with each other 'so that we may shake our fists together at the invader'.[15] Thousands of people in the city rallied, later that week, to hear similar speeches and cheer the head of the Presbyterian church in the province, Percy Hughes:

> *The country has been waiting for a lead. The great masses of the people in this country have been waiting for a lead. And so far we have not been asked to sacrifice a single thing. What is New Zealand doing?*[16]

The movement spread swiftly. Crowds gathered in every city in the North Island. Dunedin was active too: a throng of 5000 citizens swarmed into the centre of the city. Christchurch, on the other hand, behaved far more coolly – only a few hundred citizens went along to a meeting, perhaps because the city had such a strong pacifist tradition, and a strong tradition of working-class suspicion of warmongering.

The outcry everywhere in the country was led mostly by business people, landowners and speakers from the political right. The Labour Party did its best to dismiss the movement as a ploy by the National Party. Fraser spoke sternly about 'ill-informed hysteria' and an 'anti-Labour *blitzkrieg*'. Conservatives, he went on to say, were making a 'sinister attack' on the good things that had been brought to the mass of the citizenry by the welfare state.[17] A few politicians on the right of the Labour Party were nevertheless willing to go along to the big public meetings.

The Labour government went on, despite the war, with the expensive task of building a welfare state and 'social security'. Walter Nash in this cartoon admires a work of art called 'social surrealism' while Death seeks to draw the finance minister's attention away from the welfare state towards a painting that shows the bombing of London. *Artist: J.C. Hill.* Auckland Star, *31 May 1941.*

The government decided to try to gain the upper hand, driven by the need to quieten the fever on the right and also by its own belief that the war had taken a sharp enough turn for the worse to warrant sterner steps.

Fraser held talks with opposition leaders and late in May swore to the citizenry in a nationwide broadcast that the government was about to begin an 'all-in policy'. All manpower and all wealth in the country would be surveyed in order to organise capital and labour into war work. The government would also set up a war council. The council would handle everything to do with the war; and its members would be the cabinet and a few National Party politicians, together with leaders of unions, landowners and industrialists.[18] An Emergency Regulations Amendment Act gave the government wider powers than ever before over people and their property. The government asked for a mandate from an emergency congress of the Labour Party and the Federation of Labour. Nine out of every ten party members, and more than eight out of ten federation members, voted in support of the new policy. The government told them that the strengthened war effort was to be paid for by capitalists, not the working class.

National turned down the proposed war council: it demanded nothing less than a full wartime coalition. Chambers of commerce and organisations of landowners and other moneyed groups backed the coalition proposal too. The Rotorua chamber of commerce said that 'nothing short of a National Coalition Government would satisfy the country'. A crowd in Gisborne called for 'a united all-party War Cabinet'. The Nelson Farmers Union urged 'strongly' for a war coalition government, as did the New Zealand Manufacturers Federation. A petition was sent to the government from the business people of Invercargill:

> *We ask for an heroic Prime Minister and a Government that will devote itself to the formation of a National Government which will be fully representative of every class in this Dominion and devote itself to victory.*[19]

Many citizens on the political left were not happy about burying class warfare for the sake of foreign war; nor did they like talk of a heroic leader, which seemed not so very far from the *Führerprinzip* of the Nazi Party. At the same time, they were anxious about what was happening on the battlefields in northern France. Anxiety deepened when Germany was joined by Italy. Wellington declared war on Rome less than five hours after Italian troops first crossed the border into France. Fraser denounced what he called the 'cynical and cold-blooded' invasion by Italy.[20]

Two or three thousand young men were volunteering for the military every week now – far more than before the outbreak of the battles in France. Voluntary enlistment, as always, did not necessarily mean that men really wanted to go into the army or navy. A lot are likely to have signed up because there was renewed social pressure on them to go into uniform and they were not brave enough to stay out; or else because they believed the government was about to impose conscription and those who volunteered before the authorities came knocking on the door were more likely to get good billets. They were known as 'jumpers' because they went into uniform 'one jump ahead' of conscription. Eric McCormick was a jumper. He signed up when it was clear that conscription was on the way. 'Wishing to avoid the uncertainties and anxieties of the new system,' he wrote, 'I decided to enlist.'[21] The new infantryman made friends with three fellow soldiers and found that 'all three, like myself, were reluctant recruits who had volunteered under pressure'.[22] He wrote in his diary about 'this amateur army, with no real heart in the war'. Only a few of those who had queued with him outside recruitment offices seemed, in his opinion, to want to talk about patriotism or loyalty.[23]

A third wave of hysteria hit after the fall of France. The swift surrender of so powerful a state was something nobody had thought likely.

Fear grew stronger when a passenger ship sank in the Hauraki Gulf. The *Niagara*, 'a proud liner', one of the biggest and fastest vessels on the route to North America, struck two mines on a still, moonlit night after gliding away from Auckland. The blast from the mines was so heavy that the vessel 'shook from stem to stern'. Hatch covers were blown into the sky. Passengers were tossed out of their bunks. Quickly, the *Niagara* slid under the waters of the gulf. All on board managed to get off safely.[24] The sinking of a ship whose name was a household word throughout the country, followed quickly by the collapse of France, was a bitter blow.

War seemed at last to have come to New Zealand.

Conservative newspapers, unlike in the first weeks of the battles for France, wound back their complaints about the government for a week or two and felt obliged to show a stiff upper lip. 'We British have been in tighter corners before and fought a way out,' proclaimed the *New Zealand Herald*.[25] Citizens, however, often spoke or wrote in a less guarded way. The British Empire was at risk of being 'enslaved under the menace of dictatorship', thought Gainor Jackson, an accountant, company director and former army officer.[26] 'We may have the enemy at our doors at any time,' agreed a doctor, Thomas MacGibbon.[27]

'Work, family, fatherland': propaganda poster for the Vichy Republic. The three colours of the French national flag traditionally had been thought to stand for liberty, fraternity and equality.
Archives départmentales de la Drôme.

Citizens in private talked still more bleakly. Thousands, thinking the war was now nearly lost, spoke about surrendering. The people of the Bay of Plenty already had been prey to 'a certain despondency, a certain apprehension bordering on fear',[28] and now some spoke up as 'prophets of calamity'.[29] The voices of 'people who want to call the war off' were heard everywhere in Canterbury.[30] Timaru people were displaying 'a defeatist and despondent attitude,' observed the mayor of the town, William Tweedy.[31] *Truth* noted many people 'moping round the wireless, cackling about the war' or 'running round moaning and scare-mongering'.[32] *Tomorrow* told its readers that 'a wave of hysteria' was 'sweeping the country'.[33] A worker in Auckland wrote that the country seemed 'to have gone mad'.[34] So many 'dismal jimmies' were speaking glumly that 'one would think the end of the world was in sight', added a citizen in Ellesmere.[35]

The government wondered whether it might be wise to seek a peace treaty.

Winston Churchill, the new prime minister of Britain, cabled Wellington secretly for an opinion about whether to go on with the war or to open peace talks with Germany. The cable of support sent in reply was 'very feeble', wrote the British high commissioner, Batterbee. And even that feeble text was stronger than the first draft,

British loyalism lay behind much of the hysteria that swept New Zealand after the fall of France. Britannia here looks heavenward while in the foreground stand the young uniformed men of the dominion, together with three others: a worker, a uniformed woman and a Māori warrior. *Artist: Oriwa Haddon. A.R. Grimwood,* Flights and Fancies *(Wellington: Hutcheson, Bowman & Johnson, 1943).*

for the government was willing to open peace talks. Labour leaders knew that many working-class people were not keen on the war and that quite a few opposed it outright. The government was aware, too, that surrender by France might mean Japan would join the war in order to make the most of Allied disarray. A war in the Pacific would be far more risky to New Zealand than a peace treaty with Germany. Fraser told a secret session of parliament that he thought there was now one chance in three of Japan joining the war, and one chance in five of Japan raiding New Zealand.[36] Batterbee told London that he had found the cabinet so 'very defeatist' that only after he used what he called his 'influence' over Fraser was the cable to Churchill tweaked so as to become more 'useful' to the government of Britain.[37]

The Labour government, by giving in to this pressure, was agreeing to trim its policy according to the needs of the British government at the expense of the people of New Zealand.

The government did its best, next, to quieten the well-funded protests of the political right by setting up a new war cabinet. Hamilton and Coates took seats alongside Fraser, Nash and the war minister, Jones. Hamilton and Coates were elder statesmen from the 'old guard' of the National Party. Conservative newspapers damned the war cabinet with faint praise, arguing that it was only a proxy for what was needed: a true coalition that could yield the best 'from every individual, section and class'.[38] The war cabinet was to control only the war, or so went the theory. The other cabinet would keep the reins over all other departments of state. The left of the Labour Party were not happy. Nor were a group of young and thrusting newcomers in the National Party.

Citizens as a whole knew little about struggles for position within and between the political parties, let alone between the government of Britain and the government of New Zealand. A lot of people threw themselves instead into volunteer fundraising. The crisis on the battlefields led to what Nancy Taylor called a 'violent spurt' of gifts and loans of money to war funds.[39] The War Purposes Fund swelled by about 30 per cent over two months as many people, mostly from the middle class, organised gambling, games and sports to get together sums of money.[40]

AIR AND SEA WAR

Air fleets, fighting for control of the sky over England, loomed large in the imagination of people in New Zealand. The fight came to be called the Battle of Britain. Fraser, in a nationwide broadcast, declared that the struggle in the sky was 'the battle for New Zealand and the rest of the British Commonwealth – indeed, the Battle for Mankind'. Citizens were not always told the truth about the air war. 'Wave after wave' of enemy warplanes, the prime minister said, had been 'broken and hurled back with terrific loss'.[41] Newspaper readers and radio listeners heard that 185 German planes went down in one raid, for example, when fifty-six was probably the true tally.[42]

The Battle of Britain ended when the German air force changed its tactics and turned to bombing.

The British air force also got busy bombing.

Air raids during the closing months of 1940 and the opening months of 1941 brought terror from the sky for the first time to millions of ordinary people in both Britain and Germany. Among those were thousands of civilians from New Zealand. Hector Bolitho wrote in his diary about the 'thud of the bombs, the fear of death, the dreary discomfort of meals of endless sausages'.[43] Mary de Beer saw incendiary bombs raining and making the streets 'as bright as day'.[44] Rosemary Rees, novelist and producer, organised play readings among people who used her air-raid shelter regularly.[45] Charles Brasch was appalled by the 'rising and falling shriek or moan of the sirens', a sound 'piercing and chilling, like the howling of wolves'.[46] One afternoon he was having afternoon tea with the de Beers:

> *The sirens sounded, and soon through the clear hot day came the soft thud of bombs and the quicker guns, both far off, but intense, long-continued. Across Regent's Park we could see black puffs in the sky and a large number of planes flying very high; then, to the east, a great column of thick smoke … With darkness came a great red glow in the sky to south-east, like nothing I had ever seen except a New Zealand bush fire in the distance.*[47]

Dominion airmen, meanwhile, were up in the sky dropping bombs on Germany. The New Zealand Bomber Squadron, together with others, at the end of the northern autumn started what was called 'strategic bombing'. Duisburg and Dortmund were hit on 15 May, and other cities came next. New Zealand airmen were among those who on the night of 23 September carried out the first big air raid on Berlin. New Zealand airmen also strafed and machine-gunned Germans. James Swift, for example – a bomber pilot who had formerly been a motor mechanic – machine-gunned two trains near Rotenburg.[48] Two hundred airmen from the dominion were 'scattered among every squadron' of the British bombing fleet by the end of the first year of war.[49] One out of every four had already lost their lives. We do not know how many German civilians their bombs had killed.

The policy of strategic bombing was swapped at the end of 1940 for a more frankly murderous policy called 'area bombing'. Air fleets no longer sought strategic targets but instead bombed city centres or suburbs. The New Zealand squadron started by dropping explosives onto streets of civilian housing in Mannheim.[50] Three thousand and more airmen from the dominion had joined the British air force by the end of the second year of the war and soon there were no fewer than seven New Zealand squadrons: two were bomber squadrons, three were fighter squadrons and the other two were coastwatchers.

New Zealand newspapers, together with the radio and movie news, homed in on bombs laying waste to the streets of cities in Britain. Only occasionally were citizens invited to think about bombs laying waste to the streets of cities in Germany. New Zealand households heard over and over again how pluckily the people of Britain were behaving under the bombings. Nash spoke about 'amazing courage'.[51] Nobody told the households of the dominion that German civilians were also coping pluckily. Air raids after several months were killing far more civilians in Germany than in Britain, yet the news media in the dominion stayed eerily silent about their suffering. Ian Reid, bomber pilot and former Auckland journalist, wrote a typical news story about dumping a load of bombs on Berlin:

> *We swung in across the suburbs with our desynchronised engines beating out of harmony in a dissonance of irritating sound. Stray searchlights poked up on our left. To starboard were serried rows of official looking buildings, packed like neat teeth. If the bomb aimers found their mark, there would be smashed and blackened stumps over there in the morning. In front was the motionless, moonlit heart of the city, traversed by a few stray searchlights.*[52]

Reid of course wrote nothing about the women and children he was killing on the ground.

Airmen flying bombers on both sides were more or less equally brave, or reckless, or cowardly. Civilians living under the bombs on both sides found air raids equally wanton and pitiless.

As planes roared and spat across the skies over Britain and Germany another, far more silent, struggle was also under way. Allied fleets blockaded Germany and Italy. Germany and Italy sent out submarine fleets and surface raiders to blockade Britain. Karl Dönitz, commander-in-chief of the German submarine fleet at the beginning of the war, wrote that the 'one and only possibility' of beating Britain at sea was by 'attacking her sea communications'.[53] German submarines did so well for several months after the fall of France that they sank nearly 300 vessels. The losses could not easily be made good. Britain wondered whether it should cut back or even stop shipping wool, meat, butter and cheese from New Zealand. The naval war was seldom given much space in the newspapers of the dominion, however – even though the cargo and passenger ships sunk in the struggle were so important to the economy. New Zealand officials who handled propaganda knew that 'there was no advantage' to government war policy in letting citizens know about the successes of enemy submarines, observed Nancy Taylor.[54]

New Zealand women and men were on board many of the ships that went down in the Atlantic. Eveline Harcourt, for example, member of a Wellington business family, was a first-class passenger on the *Port Hobart* when that vessel was sunk off Puerto Rico. Also on the vessel was Phillipa Acland, from the Canterbury landed gentry. Gordon Simpson from Warkworth was a junior officer on the *Waiotira* when that gleaming new liner was torpedoed while he was standing at his post. 'It was pitch dark and on the eve of my birthday,' he wrote. The night was cold, with a heavy sea, but only one or two lives were lost. The *Waiotira* went down, watched by the boatloads of survivors. 'It would have made anyone cry to have seen such a beautiful ship sinking,' wrote Simpson.[55]

The *Rotorua*, one of the liners of the New Zealand Shipping Company, was still steaming at a speed of fourteen knots when, having been torpedoed, it 'ploughed … under the waves of an icy sea'. The vessel took twenty-two people down with it as it sank in 'a flurry of fume and frothing waves'.[56]

New Zealand civilians had many other torments on the Atlantic. The *Rangitiki*, by sheer luck, had 'a miraculous escape' from shelling. A raiding warship came upon the

Survivors from the sinking of the *Rangitane* arriving safely in Queensland, 1941. *https://northqueenslandhistory.blogspot.com*

magnificent modern liner when it was steaming in convoy. Ruth Shannon, a civilian on board, was 'just getting up from afternoon rest' when she heard 'a terrific crash'.[57] Other New Zealanders were on board ships that were mined, shelled or torpedoed on the Indian Ocean. The *Pinguin*, for example, a surface raider, sank three vessels that were plying the trade routes to New Zealand; and two crew were killed on the *Port Wellington*.

The Pacific Ocean was now the scene of naval war too.

The German raider *Orion* early in the winter of 1940 laid over 200 mines in the sea approaches to Auckland. The *Niagara* struck two of those mines.[58] The *Orion* later came upon the *Turakina*, a cargo liner, steaming out of a rain squall on its way to Wellington. The two vessels shelled one another: more than half the crewmen on board the merchant ship died. 'The vessel burns like a blazing torch,' wrote Kurt Weyher, captain of the *Orion*, describing the *Turakina* before his crew had picked up the survivors.[59]

The *Komet*, another raider, joined the *Orion* later in the year and the two ships patrolled the waters off New Zealand. The small cargo vessel *Holmwood* was a victim of the *Komet*. The raiders then scored a striking success when they came upon the sleek *Rangitane*, sister ship of the *Rangitiki*, one night off East Cape. The liner was carrying hundreds of people and a heavy load of contraband cargo. Weyher, who thought the big vessel looming up in the darkness was a warship, ordered his men to begin shelling. Women and men on board the liner were killed or wounded as the shells 'made a shambles'. A nurse who survived told her story of the sinking:

> *I was trapped like a rat, with flames all around. Then another explosion occurred below. Heavy fumes filled the cabin and my clothes began to sizzle and eventually were burnt off. I tried to find a place to escape through the ship's side. Two other women and a man on either side of my cabin were killed. I had resigned myself to my fate when suddenly I heard another woman's feeble cry for help. Then a man appeared through the flames in a section of the cabin which was not on fire. He spoke in calm tones and told me to walk to him. How he got me away I do not know.*

The shelling stopped when it became clear that the victim was a merchant vessel carrying women passengers. Survivors were taken off to safety, among them 'women whose faces were disfigured by shell splinters' and 'children with legs shattered by shrapnel'. The *Rangitane* was then shelled and torpedoed. Weyher noted that 'planks and debris shot to the surface, in a widening lake of oil'.[60] The liner sank swiftly.

'The Germans were very kind,' said one of the survivors. 'The doctors were excellent and treated us most respectfully.'[61]

The *Orion* and *Komet* sailed northwards to Emirau, in the Bismarck Archipelago. All civilians were landed safely and the *Orion* headed away to the Caroline Islands. The *Komet* went on to raid Nauru – the only territory under the New Zealand flag to be attacked during the whole of the Second World War. Shells were shot into the phosphate shipping plant on the island, along with the oil storage tanks. Oil, blazing fiercely, poured across the water and land.[62] Five ships were lost, too, when they were shelled by the *Komet*; three of them were fitted out solely for cargoes of phosphate. The *Triaster*, for example, sank bow first. 'As her bridge sank to the level of the sea,' noted Weyher, 'her compressed air siren suddenly uttered a grim lament, which only ceased when the sea surged over the ship's funnel.'[63] New Zealand seamen drowned in the sinking of the phosphate ships.

New Zealand landowners, farmers and industrialists found these attacks on the shipping plant and the cargo ships a heavy blow. The loss of the vessels, in particular, was 'a very severe blow to the industry', said the dominion phosphate commissioner, Sir Albert Ellis.[64] One outcome of the Nauru raid was that the New Zealand government was forced to impose a system of phosphate rationing.[65]

The *Adjutant*, a third German raider, later laid mines in shipping lanes outside Lyttelton and Wellington. The work was done so secretly that only after many years did anyone in New Zealand find out about it. The voyage was recorded in the log of the *Adjutant*:

> *It is a dark night. Godley Head light comes into sight at 2130; later, also the Christchurch aircraft homing beacons. They are all burning peacefully. A searchlight at Godley Head directed towards Baleine Point bars the main approach to the harbour*

> *... At daybreak, the* Adjutant *is about sixty miles off the coast. The high snow-covered mountains can be seen clearly; and as the sun rises, it might well be the Lake of Constance.*[66]

All naval raids were over by the early spring of 1941 and for a few months no vessel on or under the water sought to strike shipping off the coast of New Zealand.

CONSCRIPTION

Young men, as the months of war went by, were still not volunteering keenly enough to keep up the strength of the army. One option would have been to stop calling for troops and instead turn the wealth and manpower of the country into stepping up the output of wool and food for the Allies. Cabinet chose, instead, to keep fielding an army. The fall of France provoked most of its members into thinking that the stakes were now so high that the army must be kept strong.

The only way an army could be kept in the field was by conscripting.

The Labour Party and the Federation of Labour had to swallow hard before even speaking about conscription, not least because they had promised only a few months earlier that there would be no such thing so long as government was in the hands of the Labour Party. The question had been probed tentatively during the Phoney War. One or two government ministers had hinted that conscription might prove to be a necessary curtailment of the freedom of citizens in order to protect the wider freedom of democracy. At the same time, they took pains to say that conscription of manpower would be linked with conscription of the wealth of the wealthy. A few politicians and trade union spokespeople even went so far as to say that conscription could help to hurry forward a socialist state. Frank Langstone, for example, tried that tack when cornered on the question by workers at a big meeting in Auckland:

> *If there is going to be conscription, there is going to be conscription of wealth. It will mean that you and I will be on a soldier's ration and a soldier's pay, and if it is going to be that it will be the greatest step forward to collective Socialism because, when it is over, the psychology will have been established. If there are not enough volunteers for the next echelon and we have to take strong measures, it will be 100 per cent ... Everyone will be in it. There will be one common rule and regimentation and the greatest opponents to it will be capitalists and Communists.*[67]

Conscription became government policy in July 1940, with the backing of most unions and most of the Labour Party. The government's willingness to pay for the war by taxing the rich heavily – 'conscription of wealth' – allowed the organised labour movement to swallow the policy. The fall of France also led the movement to believe that democracy really was at risk. Fraser, even before the armistice with France, had told citizens that the government was willing to take very stern steps. 'Every person in

Advertisement for war bonds: a warplane flies above a surrendering German submarine, 1940–41. *Artist: William Krogman. Alexander Turnbull Library Eph-D-WAR-WII-1940/41-1.*

the Dominion, every atom of the country's services,' he declared, 'must be subordinated to the requirements of the Dominion and the British Commonwealth.'[68]

All men of military age could now be forced into the military. Men were not to be conscripted straightaway but called up in groups according to a system of balloting. Any balloted man who believed he should keep his civilian job for the good of the country, or who thought signing up would cause hardship to his family, could take his case to an appeal board. Conscientious objectors could also go to an appeal board if they had what government regulations called 'a genuine belief that it is wrong to engage in warfare in any circumstances', or if they held that it was wrong to fight but not to do other work for the army. The first group would stay out of uniform and be ordered to work for the war economy, while the second group would go into uniform and carry out non-combatant tasks.[69] The *New Zealand Law Journal*, before the boards began hearing appeals, published guidelines for finding out the true beliefs of objectors.

Six appeal boards were set up, each chaired by a magistrate. The Labour Party, well aware that the working class had chafed at the way bullying army officers sat in judgement over appeals during the First World War, would not allow anyone in the military to belong to the new boards. The magistrate chairing a board was to take advice from two other senior lawyers, together with a businessman who had knowledge of economic production and industry, and a trade union official who supposedly understood the needs of the working class.

The first ballot was held early in spring. Already some 65,000 men were registered as volunteers in the army and now another 16,000 had their names pulled out of the ballot box.

Conscripts felt fear, relief, anger, fatalism or dismay. Etna Bergen wrote after the war that she would 'never forget the ghostly look' with which her husband greeted the news

Air-force training; trainee crews enter a decompression chamber. *Artist: Nancy Adkin Ritchie. Air Force Museum of New Zealand.*

that he had been called up.[70] David Ballantyne, in *The Cunninghams*, gives a subtle portrait of the feelings of a young working-class conscript; Ballantyne based the story on his own experience. The young man worries intensely while waiting for the call-up card to come in the post. The card, when it does come, brings with it mixed feelings:

> *Might be okay. Might be better than I think. Chance to play cricket and football. Chance to get a sheila ... And there was no doubting that a man in uniform, even a thin goon like him, had a certain glamour for outsiders. At least he'd have the satisfaction of knowing that his mother and the rest of the family, plus all the old busybodies, would be proud of him, for what that might be worth. He didn't believe in fighting and killing and though he would wear the uniform he would not be proud of it and would take the first chance of getting out of it.*[71]

The muddle of vanity, hope and fatalism, together with a wish to please or at least placate those who put social pressure on young men to go off to war, was no doubt typical of many.

Thousands of those unlucky men did their best to keep their freedom by trying to fail the medical test. A man could make his feet swell by going for a long walk before reporting to the doctors, or could swallow drugs, or try other lurks to make his blood pressure look bad or cause other disabilities that would lead him to be classed as unfit for service. Tips about how to fail the test were spread by word of mouth, especially among the working class. Men who followed the tips – or so one writer claimed – 'met with a fair amount of success' at staying out of the army.[72] Others made their appeal to a board before taking the medical test.

The appeal boards first met early in 1941. They found that most of those appealing claimed that they could help the war best by staying out of uniform and sticking to their peacetime jobs. 'Why couldn't you help your Dad milking and get exempted?' Joy, daughter of a dairy farmer, asks Jim, son of a dairy farmer, in a short story by Greville Texidor. 'You don't want to go and get killed do you?'[73] Conscientious objectors were not thin on the ground, however; indeed, they were 'more common in New Zealand than in most other countries'.[74]

A religious objector found it hard to convince a board of his earnestness unless he belonged to one of the small Protestant sects with a long history of opposition to war, such as the Quakers. Catholics, Anglicans, Presbyterians and Methodists were told by boards that their churches backed the war and therefore nobody belonging to those flocks could claim the right not to be conscripted. Jews were given the same message. A rabbi told Wilfrid Franks, a painter, that he would no longer be a Jew if he stood out against going into the military. Franks answered the rabbi by saying that 'if Judaism stood for the killing of men' then he was not a Jew. The board ordered him into the army.[75]

Political objectors were on the left, nearly always. Cyril Chilvers, a young laundryhand, said he was a socialist, felt no loyalty to the state and did not care whether or not there was a British victory. The trade union member of the Auckland appeal board asked whether the young man would be willing to do what Soviet soldiers swore to do: fight for the life and property of the people. He answered that he would not, because New Zealand did not have a satisfactory system, unlike the Soviet Union.

'You have got me bewildered, brother,' said the trade unionist.

Chilvers was not granted the status of conscientious objector and had to go into the army.[76]

Charles Fury, a labourer, told the Wellington board that as a communist he was willing to fight for 'the interests of the working classes' but only if 'it would clear the way for a class war'. He opposed the war against Germany because it would make life worse for the working class. The board would not accept his appeal and he was ordered into the army.[77] Ronald Armstrong, a commercial artist, told the same board he was an international socialist. He was ordered into the army. Victor Hawkins, a ship rigger, said that he opposed wars where 'workers would kill workers and the war lords would gorge themselves on the blood of the workers'. He was ordered into the army.[78]

Feelings often ran high at appeal board hearings. Ronald Chilvers, a young fellmonger and brother of Cyril, could not control his feelings at a hearing of the board in Auckland. 'I will not go to war,' he cried out. 'No matter what happens I will never go to war. Even if you send for me I will not go. You cannot send me.' He knelt on the floor, weeping loudly.[79]

Appeal boards did not follow anything like a consistent policy. A man who appealed against conscription was so much at the mercy of the fixed opinions or whims of the nearest board that the outcomes of appeals varied greatly from province to province. John A. Lee protested in the winter of 1941 about the harsh behaviour of the board in Auckland. He thought it 'an outrage' that men coming before some boards got 'hectored for the attitude they took up', while those coming before other boards found themselves 'exempted for the same attitude'. Baptist, Presbyterian and Methodist clergy spoke out on the matter later that year. The Baptist Assembly, for example, was unhappy that some boards dealt in a 'humiliating and unfair' way with men who objected on religious grounds.[80] The harshest boards were those in Whangarei, Auckland, Napier and Wellington. The most generous boards were Hamilton, Dunedin and Christchurch.[81] A total of over 5100 men were conscientious objectors by the end of the war, of whom nearly 3100 came before the boards. Six out of every ten who pleaded their case to the boards were exempted from the military.[82]

A man whose objection was not upheld by an appeal board must either turn up at the barracks or else steel himself to fight the state and become what was known as a 'defaulter'. One out of every four chose to default. The state then wheeled in its coercive power, beginning with fines or imprisonment ordered by magistrates, and ending with locking up the most stubborn behind the barbed wire of 'detention' camps.

Defaulters, like conscientious objectors as a whole, found themselves at the mercy of magistrates whose views varied from province to province and city to city. 'The position is, roughly, that if you are sentenced in Southland you may be sent direct to the detention camp ... In Otago you receive one month,' noted an observer of the southern provinces, 'but if you belong to Canterbury or the West Coast you are sentenced to two or three months.'[83] The bleakness of detention camps was portrayed later by one defaulter, Ian Hamilton:

> *There was a barbed wire fence, ten feet high with a verandah all round the camp, then a patrol track and then another ten-foot fence. There were searchlights and sentry boxes on the hills and the whole camp was floodlit every night ... There was a hell of an atmosphere in the place. It was the first time I'd really had anything to do with men who had tried resistance and been broken, and it gave me the jitters. To come straight in from the outer to this was really something. I think the floodlights and searchlights at night put the whole thing, for me, over the edge and into the realm of nightmare.*[84]

The ranks of those in uniform, boosted now by conscription, kept growing. A year after the German invasion of France more than 40,000 of the men in those ranks were stationed far away from New Zealand.[85] Thousands already had been wounded, taken prisoner or killed in a hopeless struggle in the Balkans. Thousands more were soon to be wounded, taken prisoner or killed in more bloody struggles in the Middle East.

THE BALKANS AND THE MIDDLE EAST

The Nazi government, after the surprisingly swift victory over France in June 1940, needed to work out whether it was wise to keep waging war in the west or better to turn eastwards and attack the Soviet Union. New Zealand newspapers told readers that the great goal of Nazism was the conquest of the British Empire. Yet few military or foreign policy planners talked that way in Germany. Berlin had been willing to offer fairly easy peace terms to London after the seizure of Paris.[86]

The British Commonwealth, by turning down talks towards a peace treaty, made things awkward for Germany.

A plan was sketched out to invade Britain. Hitler gave the plan a rubber stamp but looked on invasion as a task he would rather avoid; he wanted to free his strength for going after the great goal, the Soviet Union. Alfred Jodl, German chief of the general staff, observed only weeks after the armistice with France that the Führer had resolved to destroy the communist state 'once and for all' by carrying out a surprise attack the following May. Hitler talked about attacking the Soviet Union as early as August 1940, which would have left Germany far too weak elsewhere to do anything more than hold its ground against the British Commonwealth.[87]

Japan came into the reckoning too. In September Berlin, Rome and Tokyo signed the Tripartite Pact. The three signatory states, together with several smaller partners, were soon nicknamed the Axis.[88] The new pact would bring Japan into a war against the Soviet Union – or so Germany hoped.

The Balkans got in the way.

German military planners were nervous about the southeastern corner of the continent becoming a threat to the flank. Greece was a worry, as was Yugoslavia. Germany, Romania, Bulgaria and Hungary invaded Greece and Yugoslavia in April 1941. Italy, which had been blundering about in Greece since late in the previous year, also joined the attack on Yugoslavia. The British Commonwealth poured planes and troops into Greece to try to hold back the Axis. Among them were nearly 17,000 soldiers from New Zealand, a huge body of men for such a small country.

These men found themselves trying to dig foxholes on the unlikely terrain of stony Greek valleys.

Why was the 2nd Division sent to kill or be killed in Greece? In large part it was because of a misunderstanding. Freyberg, the commander of the dominion army, believed the best use of New Zealand soldiers would be helping the British Empire keep hold of Egypt and in 'chasing the Italians out of Libya'.[89] He knew it would be a mistake to send men into Greece. The government, however, wrongly assumed that Freyberg favoured sending the men to Greece. Many New Zealanders were killed and wounded.

The word 'democracy' was cast about liberally when the government told citizens why dominion soldiers were fighting in Greece. New Zealand was 'rallying to the call of freedom' by fighting for Greece, Fraser told a crowd in Rotorua. The soldiers of the dominion were doing 'great, heroic, and hazardous work, never surpassed in the history of the world'.[90] New Zealand troops were the latest in a litany of heroes who had fought since classical times to safeguard Athenian freedom from totalitarian states such as Persia, Turkey and now Germany.

Greece, however, was not a democracy. A police state and dictatorship modelled closely on fascist Italy, its governing group had done its best to keep out of the war because while its sympathies were mostly with the Axis powers the country had to live with the knowledge that it belonged to what was seen as a British 'sphere' in the eastern Mediterranean.

New Zealand troops on the ground scrambled about on the stones. They shot and shelled and were shot and shelled. They were strafed by warplanes on whose wings were painted the black cross of Germany.

'The Black Cross certainly rules the skies,' wrote a gunner, 'and it seems that there will be more white crosses on the ground before we are finished.'[91]

One young man wrote more fully about what he and his fellow soldiers went through in the hopeless struggle:

> *We have been shelled and machine-gunned, and lain in partially completed trenches while hordes of dive-bombers screamed down on us dropping bombs and firing their machine-guns and cannon. We have marched miles on foot, covered many more in transport, often having to duck and dive as hideous Dornier bombers circled overhead*

The Alert at Dawn: a scene from the campaign in Greece. *Artist: Peter McIntyre. Archives New Zealand.*

> *dropping bombs and then coming down to allow the rear gunner to strafe us … It all came so suddenly after our long spell of doing nothing.*[92]

The campaign was a shambles, from which the troops were hastily withdrawn to Crete.

Crete was another shambles. German paratroopers blossomed in the sky. Nothing like it had ever happened in the history of warfare, wrote a soldier from Christchurch; the attack was 'like a Wellsian dream'.[93] The last days of May were spent trying to get Allied soldiers off onto ships. A 'great fear' seized a soldier from Masterton; his knees 'literally knocked together'. Other soldiers went 'as white as the whitest sheets'. Shocked and wounded soldiers were unloaded from the ships in Egypt. Civilians back home in the dominion were learning for the first time since the Great War what it meant to send an army overseas to the other side of the world. Peggy Dunstan wrote a poem about a young man killed in Crete:

> *My fingers*
> *trace the scars*
> *across your chest,*
> *but you have gone from me,*
> *you see, so far away …*[94]

Casualty List: the campaigns in Greece and North Africa brought home to civilians the grim truth that New Zealand soldiers were now dying wholesale for the first time since the Great War. *Artist: Margaret Thompson Harvey. Collection of Charles Rose.*

Almost four out of every ten men sent by the dominion to fight in Greece and Crete were killed or wounded, or driven into prison camps. Almost 1000 died in the battles, while over 4000 were rounded up behind barbed wire as prisoners of war.

War would chew its way through thousands more men, after they had regrouped, in gritty battles in North Africa.

German troops in the autumn of 1941 pushed the Allies back from eastern Libya into Egypt. Troops from both sides then slugged it out along the borderlands for the rest of the year. The battlefield was stark. A poem by Donald McDonald, a young Waikato farmer and now an army private, portrayed the desert as a land whose 'bones' lay below 'the old sun' and where men who had been 'children in sweet green lands' were now dying.[95] Joyce Macdonald wrote about the throngs of maimed men being shipped to her hospital; 'the big convoys rolled in almost daily and one never knew who or what one might find on a stretcher beneath the grey blankets'.[96] Almost 900 New Zealanders were killed, and nearly 2000 wounded, before the government withdrew its troops for a time to Syria.

Syria was one of many states in the region under colonial occupation by the troops of the British Commonwealth. France had been in control before the war but battles in mid-1941 wrested the territory from Vichy. Britain tightened its hold elsewhere in the Middle East. Iraq was invaded early in the year. Afterwards came an unprovoked attack on Iran. British Commonwealth troops landed in the south, without any formal declaration of war, while Soviet troops moved down from the north, as had been worked out in a secret agreement between London and Moscow. The invasion was not unlike the attack on Poland by Germany that had triggered the war and had been so indignantly condemned by the Allies.

A government party from New Zealand was fleetingly caught up in the fighting. 'MR. FRASER FIRED ON,' reported newspapers. A plane carrying the prime minister, together with government officials, was shot at by the anti-aircraft guns of Iraqi nationalist troops after taking off from near Basra. The shelling did not cause any damage.[97] The Labour government must in theory have supported independence for

The New Zealand army of occupation in North Africa: soldiers doing a haka in Egypt.
Alexander Turnbull Library DA-01067.

Iraq, but historians do not know whether the prime minister said anything about the matter to the British government on his landing in London.

New Zealand citizens were told very little about the fighting in Iran and Iraq. The *New Zealand Herald* claimed that Britain had 'clear treaty rights' in Iraq. British troops and bombers were 'restoring order' in a way good for 'loyal Irakis'. Nothing was said about the Iraq Petroleum Company, with its head office in London.[98] The same newspaper claimed that 'the Iranian people' would 'benefit' from being invaded by the British Commonwealth. Nothing was said about the Anglo-Iranian Oil Company, with its head office in London.[99]

MOBILISING THE NATION

Conscription of young men into the military was not the only goal of the government when it spoke about mobilising New Zealand. Labour leaders, as we have seen, sold conscription to the working class by saying that conscription would be imposed not only on men but money. The government went still further, claiming that it would use its authority to make everybody work for the war equally and share the costs democratically.

Conscription of wealth to pay for the ballooning costs of war was done in two main ways. First, the government stepped up the policy of borrowing from the citizenry, above all the wealthy. Second, the government stepped up the policy of taxing the wealthy.

The first policy got a big boost when the government in the winter of 1940 gave itself the power to borrow up to £40 million for war purposes, of which £10 million would come from a compulsory loan imposed on those with money. Nash told parliament it was 'not right' that not all citizens who were 'capable of affording assistance' were doing so. Compulsory loans were levied on 'all who have means' – not on the working class.[100] Sir Alfred Ransom, a sheep farmer and National Party member of parliament, asked whether the government would take not only the wealth but the credit of the wealthy. 'We will take everything,' answered Nash.[101] Malcolm McCaul, a company director, was typical of many rich people who denounced the compulsory loans as 'evidence of the pernicious system of class legislation' carried out by the government.[102]

The savings of the working class were gathered into the war kitty by means of a voluntary system of bond buying. Any citizen with a little spare cash could buy a bond for a sum as small as one pound sterling. Those of modest means could also open war savings accounts with the Post Office or with trustee savings banks. War savings accounts would help the government fight the enemy with the help of even 'the humblest worker' in the country, Nash told citizens.[103]

A stiffer policy of taxing the wealthy began when an excess profits tax was imposed in the spring of 1940 to soak up money made from war profiteering. The National Party could hardly oppose the tax in principle, at least not openly. Nobody wanted to say they supported profiteering. All they could do was try to talk the government into toning down the new tax. Conservatives claimed that they did not oppose 'the State's claim to tax war profits', but went on to say that the new tax would be 'injurious to morale' among the landed and business community.[104] William Goosman, landowner, company director and National Party member of parliament, worried that it would be 'a tax on industry, good luck or a good season'. He went on to say that the government would be wiser 'to risk somebody getting a little extra profit' than to drive down economic output by disheartening those who made a living from farming.[105] The New Zealand Manufacturers Federation spoke more boldly: the new tax was a 'blow to the maintenance of production in industry' as well as the development of industry.[106]

The government hiked other taxes too.

Gift and death duties went up: only the moneyed had to pay heavily. Income taxes went up: only the moneyed had to pay heavily. The rich, reeling, claimed that they were the victims of a class war being fought beneath the mask of war against a foreign enemy. Joseph Hodgens, a former carpenter and now a Labour member of

A victory wreath links flagpoles bearing the national banners of Britain and New Zealand. *Railways Magazine, 1940.*

parliament, told the opposition that since the state was going into the homes of the people to 'take the young men', then a 'due and proper contribution' must also be levied on 'the moneybags'.[107] Charlton Morpeth, chairman of directors of the New Zealand Investment, Mortgage and Deposit Company, spoke to shareholders about the 'staggering load of taxation' now weighing on the company.[108] A Christchurch businessman wrote with feeling about his own woes:

> *I am compelled to pay business tax, super-tax, school tax, gas tax, excise tax, sales tax, tariff tax, railway tax, petrol tax, and amusement tax, though I have no amusement. My business is so governed that I do not know who owns it. I am inspected, suspected, disrespected, rejected, examined, and reexamined, informed, required, summoned, fined, compelled and commanded, until I provide an inexhaustible supply of money.*[109]

Capitalists now and then volunteered to give up their profits freely. Sidney Holland announced that the engineering factory belonging to his family would do war work at cost. One or two other employers followed his lead, among them a motor engineering works in Invercargill and a marine engineering works in Port Chalmers. Nancy Taylor noted drily that such offers to waive profits 'did not multiply'.[110] Holland very likely made his own offer for political purposes, because his eye was now firmly on the parliamentary leadership of the National Party.

'Air force' costume design for the Wellington Victory Queen Carnival, 1941. Queen carnivals were organised by civilian volunteers in towns and cities throughout the early years of the war to raise money for the military. *Artist: Marion Rodie. Museum of New Zealand Te Papa Tongarewa.*

Voluntary fundraising went through a quick spurt at the time of the invasion of France. The Sick, Wounded and Distress Fund, a new body formed by the Red Cross and the Order of St John, collected nearly £750,000 within a few months, after which the nationwide fundraising organisation set up early in the war by the government sought £1 million for what was named the All-Purpose Appeal. Noisy fundraising fairs, carnivals, sports and other gatherings raised money. After the first sense of panic in the middle of the year abated, however, the sums of money raised dropped off. The National Patriotic Fund Board in the financial year 1940–41 spent almost £550,000 on gifts to soldiers and others, nearly twice the sum spent the year before,[111] but on the whole the wallets and purses of people throughout the country were not opened very wide by voluntary fundraising. Citizens were giving 'relatively little' for 'patriotic purposes' by the autumn of 1941, protested the Wellington promoters of a Victory Queen Carnival.[112]

Voluntary fundraising varied widely from suburb to suburb, town to town, district to district. Canterbury citizens, for example, gave war loans very unevenly. Waiau was willing to stump up money, which meant that by the winter of 1941 something like six out of every ten people in the district had subscribed to a war loan, as had around four out of every ten people in Akaroa. Only one in twenty people, though, subscribed in Leeston. The citizens of the dominion as a whole were also far less forthcoming with war loans than those in Britain, and even in Australia. The average Briton gave fifteen times more money to voluntary war loans, and the average Australian five times more than the average person in New Zealand.[113]

The economy was rich and still growing, which meant that lack of earnings was not the reason why people withheld voluntary gifts of money. New Zealanders had markedly higher average incomes than Britons, and were also more well-to-do than Australians. The gross domestic product of the dominion went up 5.5 per cent in 1940 and although growth slowed to 3.7 per cent in the following year, war was clearly not a setback for business and industry.[114]

The building industry, for example, enjoyed a widespread boom – above all in house building. 'Still buoyant after more than twenty months of war,' a newspaper noted, house building was 'little affected' by restrictions imposed by the government. 'There is a keen demand for a good type of house,' said an architect in Auckland. The typical new house was a bungalow with an emphasis on 'simplicity in design', but the well-to-do favoured 'the Georgian period'.[115] Citizens were spending heavily at the cinema, too; and they were gambling. Millions of pounds went into betting on horse racing. The sums fluttered at the Easter races in 1941 were the highest in racing history.[116]

Massive export shipments were still being sold on overseas markets. For the first year or so of the war, London stuck to the contracts to buy in bulk that had been negotiated with Wellington. Bulk contracts fitted British needs nicely because they kept prices pegged below the open market. Also they guaranteed supply. A third bonus was that the dominion was inside the sterling bloc, allowing London to save foreign exchange that was badly needed for buying goods from the United States.[117]

At the same time London had other trade worries, thanks to submarine warfare in the Atlantic. Torpedoes hit ships at such a rate that the British supply ministry by late 1940 was seeking supplies of dairy produce and frozen meat from sellers closer to home, above all Argentina and the United States. Britain agreed to keep taking about two out of every three tonnes of New Zealand's meat output, but the balance would have to go elsewhere or stay in cold storage.

'Only stern necessity made us demand such sacrifices,' wrote the British minister of supply, Frederick Marquis.[118] 'We want to keep the goodwill of the Dominions, whose business we are damaging a great deal.'

The sinking of still more ships in the following months led to talk in London of cutting back even more sharply on imports of meat from Australia and New Zealand.[119] Anxiety was widespread among dominion landowners and farmers, who feared that they would lose their biggest market. The Meat Committee of the Auckland Farmers Union spoke about the matter as 'what may be termed New Zealand's first great wartime emergency'.[120] Government planners were quite as anxious; they hastily tried to find other markets in Japan and the United States.

Export shipments were still massive, however, and still earning plenty of money.

Imports, too, were massive – initially. Shortages of imported goods had not been very noticeable in the first months of the war, but shop shelves started to look naked after the fall of France. Petrol was now rationed more strictly.[121] Phosphate rationing, provoked by the naval raid on Nauru, was organised by the government with the backing of the Farmers Union. William Mulholland, president of the union, observed that 'the amount available to farmers for topdressing and for each variety of crop was less than the amount known to give the best results', but that rationing was 'in the best interests of the farmers of the country'.[122] Paper was also running out. Imports had come mostly from Sweden and Norway, and from Canada. Civilians were now using a 'brownish paper, made locally with salvaged waste paper as a main ingredient'.[123]

Corrugated iron was in 'acutely short' supply by the time France signed its armistice, which caused problems for the building industry and for farming.[124]

Luxury goods could not always be imported as easily as before the war either – as women found when they sought to buy stockings. Silk imports from Japan and China fell away thanks to a lack of shipping, which meant that dominion hosiery mills could no longer get enough of the raw material to make fine stockings. A 'stockings scare' broke out when it became clear that most women would soon have to wear coarser and rougher rayon, cotton or wool stockings. Women fought bitterly for silk stockings. One spoke about having to 'struggle' to get only one pair.[125] 'I think it is disgusting the way the women of Auckland are behaving about the stocking problem,' added a shop saleswoman, and she went on to condemn 'the greedy, grabbing ones' who would 'get two and three pairs and brag about it to all their friends'.[126] Shop staff followed a policy of informal rationing. A female officer worker described battling to get stockings, late in 1941:

> *Yesterday morning one of the city stores had stockings available, and within two or three minutes the stockings counter was surrounded by a seething mass of pushing and scrambling women – and men! Having joined the fray, within a few seconds I found myself in the centre of the scrum, unable to move one way or another. In desperation I tried to leave, but found it was almost a physical impossibility. Finally, I left after a hard struggle and no stockings.*[127]

Civilians were beginning to suffer from serious shortages of luxury and some other goods by the time this department store advertisement was published late in 1941. George Court, the store, bought up a bulk run of serge cloth first imported for air-force uniforms but found to have a minor flaw: 'With an eye to opportunity we had it re-dyed in the best Indigo Navy and so are able to offer these Boys' Knickers of a far superior quality.' *New Zealand Herald, 13 September 1941.*

Spirits were another luxury in short supply. Whisky still came into the country – though less of it – from Britain. Gin could no longer come from the occupied Netherlands, however, nor cognac from occupied France, schnapps from Germany or vermouth from Italy. Hotels by the autumn of 1941 were selling whisky or gin by the glass. 'Sorry, sir, can't do it!' a hotel barman told a customer who asked to buy a small bottle of whisky in Wellington.[128]

Shortages worsened as the stocks that had been held in warehouses before the war ran out, and the loss of shipping made it harder to get new stock. Textiles, aluminium, steel, ironware, tyres, film, tea, cocoa and many other goods were now in short supply. Civilians were competing with the military for the shrinking pool of goods, too, just as they had done in the First World War. The country had plenty of wool, for example, but 'many jerseys remained unknitted' because stocks were being bought up in bulk by the army. Woollen mills spun their wheels to make military blankets and khaki cloth for the military, not for the warmth or comfort of households.[129] Khaki cloth nevertheless was in short supply, which meant the army had to buy shipments from Japan.

Yet the government still did not impose rationing. All goods, other than petrol and phosphate, continued to be bought and sold more or less freely. Mobilisation of the economy for war was far less sweeping than in Britain or Germany. Sums spent on the army, navy and air force kept growing, climbing to nearly 12 per cent of national income in the 1940–41 financial year,[130] but British economic mobilisation was so wholesale that military spending by 1941 accounted for 55 per cent of its gross national product.[131]

British politicians and officials spoke behind closed doors about what they believed was a very lacklustre commitment to war spending by the government in New Zealand. Wellington, they knew, wanted to keep up the supply of goods and services to its citizens and go ahead with building the welfare state, but London was not happy with such a policy. Batterbee, writing as high commissioner, secretly complained that 'nothing like the same attempt' was made by Wellington as by London 'to economise or to do without'. The government was not willing to give up 'any part of the labour programme' or lower the standard of living 'in any way'.[132] New Zealand, he believed, should impose austerity.

New Zealand did not impose austerity.

The thriving economy, along with Labour's policy of keeping up living standards and keeping on building the welfare state, meant that households were not too worried about losing income or wealth as a result of going to war against Germany.

The prices of goods and services were going up, however, and this stirred memories among working people of the frightening currency inflation that had hit them hard during the First World War. The government moved towards tighter control over wages, costs and prices. Emergency regulations in autumn 1940 gave the industrial court power to lift 'award' rates – the minimum wage allowed under

Civilians continued to buy private cars throughout the first two years of the war. The image in this advertisement, like many others for consumer goods, does its best to link consumer buying with the war by portraying luxury items against a military background.
Standard, 28 November 1940.

Shortages of some consumer goods were noticeable, but the country continued to be prosperous. This Wellington advertisement stresses the importance of 'Paris Style'; it was published in the month France surrendered to Germany. *Alexander Turnbull Library Eph-B-COSTUME-1940-03-front.*

law – to compensate workers for price hikes. Already nationwide retail prices were over 3 per cent higher than they had been on the eve of the war. The industrial court boosted wage rates by 5 per cent, which helped households. Yet still prices kept climbing. The government in the spring of 1940 called an Economic Stabilisation Conference. Sir Arthur Donnelly, lawyer and bank director, presided while seven capitalists and seven representatives of the working class sat down together to try to sort out ways to stop the upward spiralling of prices, costs and wages. The conference advised the government to fix nationwide rates of wages, salaries, rents and many goods and services. Two goals were to be pursued in fixing such rates:

The first is to stabilise prices, wages and costs so that the cost of the war is not thrown unfairly on one group to the benefit of another. The second is to increase all kinds of production and the efficiency of every type of service which will help, however indirectly, the national drive.

The government acted on the advice of the committee and fixed prices for many 'essential items', among them seventeen types of foodstuff, sixteen types of clothing and footwear, electricity, gas, coal and coke. At the same time, the government set up an Economic Stabilisation Committee – made up of five employers and five employees, led by two government ministers.[133] The committee drew up a plan that would soon solve most of the problems of wartime inflation but meanwhile a very controversial step was taken by the industrial court. Prices for goods and services were still going up. Workers went to the court to ask for another hike in award wages. The court turned them down, to the widespread dismay of many.

WAR WORK AND THE HOME GUARD

Conscription of young men into the army was backed up by a sketchy mobilisation of some other citizens into war work.

War work could be undertaken in two ways. Civilians could go into paramilitary or civil defence forces, set up by the government to support the true military. Civilians could also stick to their tasks for longer hours in weekday wage or salary work, or give their labour free for tasks done outside the paid workforce – thus boosting economic output.

'It is the clear duty of every New Zealand citizen in this time of crisis to come forward,' the prime minister declared in a leaflet handed out to all households. 'Every able-bodied man and woman has a part to play.'[134]

The paramilitary and civil defence forces drew tens of thousands of volunteers and were organised nationwide.

The Home Guard – the paramilitary – was a volunteer force founded in the winter of 1940 when the fall of France sparked fears about German invasion of New Zealand. The government, while it knew that such fears were foolish, bowed to pressure from old soldiers, landowners, farmers, merchants and imperial loyalists who wanted a nation in arms. All men aged sixteen or over who were willing to enrol for military training could go into the Home Guard. They would not be paid. Training would be done during evenings and weekends. Robert Young, national commander, told the citizenry that there would be 'no frills and ceremonial parades'.[135] The Home Guard, he added later, was 'the people's army'.[136] The truth was that the people who backed it were mostly from the middle class and from the countryside.

City people, above all the city working class, were far from keen about the Home Guard. There was a widespread fear among wage workers that the state would wheel in the paramilitary to break strikes. Semple, the government minister in charge, blamed such fears on seditious lies spread by the Communist Party:

> *What are we going to do? Are we going to give the invaders a cup of afternoon tea and sing 'For they are jolly good fellows?' or are we going to stand up like real he-men and fight for our country, our homes, our kiddies, and our liberty?*[137]

The ranks of the paramilitary were filled mostly by clerks, businessmen, doctors, lawyers, farmers and landowners. Patea, a small town in a farming district, fielded 320 men within the first few months, while only 1300 signed up in the biggest city in the country, Auckland. Sir Ernest Davis, the mayor, denounced the men of the city as 'defeatists – and escapists'. One young man answered by saying that many workers like himself did 'not fancy giving the State the benefit of our leisure time'.[138] Wage workers in southern cities were no more eager than those in northern cities to go into the paramilitary. The turnout of Dunedin men was 'disappointing in the extreme', declared the *Otago Daily Times*.[139]

The ranks of the Home Guard grew during the early months of the following year – they tallied around 100,000 by the middle of autumn – but the strongholds were still among the rural middle class. Christchurch, for example, fielded no more guardsmen than Whangarei, which had less than one tenth of the population of the southern city.[140] On the other hand, 'All the farmers and shepherds in the district joined,' wrote Jane Dare, who worked on a sheep station in Hawke's Bay. The landowner employing her was

The Home Guard: 'First Muster'. *Artist: L.C. Mitchell,* The Book of the Guard *(Wellington: Coulls Somerville Wilkie, 1943).*

'very keen' on the guards. The weekly training day on a beach was a 'social gathering' where the wives of guardsmen would 'bathe, gossip, and admire their husbands' pounding the dunes on horseback.[141]

A lot of men who signed up for the paramilitary quickly lost their keenness when they found that it meant tiresome training at the end of a working day or a working week. A lot of men stopped going. The *New Zealand Herald* described the Home Guard as 'the Cinderella of the country's defence forces, carrying out their training almost blindfold, finding it impossible to discover exactly what their part in an emergency would be, sparsely equipped, uniformed with promises'.[142]

The government in mid-1941 tightened control and imposed formal military authority over the Home Guard. Young spoke strong words: 'Before this show is over, the Home Guard will be the home defence of New Zealand.'[143]

Yet the switch to military control was not followed up with much in the way of weaponry, nor money. Home Guard turnout was still so poor by the middle of spring that there was, in the opinion of the *New Zealand Herald*, 'a widespread feeling of discouragement and despondency'.[144] The *Auckland Star* wrote early the following year about the way 'the patriotic enthusiasm which infused its ranks' during its early days had been 'allowed to ooze away'.[145] A Home Guard company in the city printed pamphlets calling for recruits; it delivered 1000 copies to households and found that the whole thing yielded only the 'magnificent total of three' new volunteers.

'What the hell is the use of the Home Guard, anyway?' citizens asked. 'Who is going to invade this country?'

'It can't happen here.'[146]

The Home Guard had not become the people's army.

Civil defence was in the hands of the Emergency Precautions Scheme. The scheme, set up before the war, was tasked with safeguarding civilians during air raids, poison-gas attacks and earthquakes. Volunteers were drilled in how to give first aid, fight fires, evacuate neighbourhoods, mend electricity, gas and water supplies and look after sewers. Wardens were appointed from among the men and women in each district who seemed most trustworthy. Cities and the countryside were parcelled out as over 300 districts. The scheme in each district was in the hands of a voluntary committee headed by a 'controller', but most committees were slow to draw up plans to cope with an emergency.

The Emergency Precautions Scheme drew many eager volunteers who quickly became 'paper tigers'. Volunteers got no pay. Committees got very little money from the government and mostly had to make do with equipment donated by citizens in the neighbourhood. 'The scheme exists only on paper,' the *Press* protested, and added that it was a 'story of delay, confusion and vacillation'.[147] A good turnout during the first weeks of some new recruitment drive would be followed by a steady falling off until, in the end, nearly everyone who supposedly belonged to the scheme was staying away.

Air-raid drills and blackouts were the main way most citizens were aware of the work of the Emergency Precautions Scheme.

'Air-raid warning!' a teacher might call, walking into a classroom. Students, having been drilled by volunteers from the Emergency Precautions Scheme, 'promptly disappeared from human ken and crouched unseen beneath their respective desks'.[148] Workers in factories, shops and offices carried out drills too. City and town councils were asked to survey the basements of their strongest buildings, to see which would make the best air-raid shelters; they did so slowly and haphazardly. Citizens were told that it might be wise to dig air-raid trenches or shelters in their suburban gardens, but hardly anyone dug. Citizens were also told that each household should build up a stock of sandbags so they could stifle fires caused by incendiary bombs. City, town and county councils were ordered to provide sand for the bags. Only the keenest householders took the trouble to go along to their local body to get the sand.[149]

Blackouts were imposed on coastal towns, cities and districts after the shelling of Nauru. The government thought German naval raiders might turn up off the coast and let loose 'a sudden salvo'.[150] At first the goal was brownout, not blackout. Street lighting was dimmed, as were lightbulbs and neon tubes in buildings visible from the sea. Cars, trams and other vehicles were also ordered to dim their lighting. A full blackout became policy later in the year, when the government started to believe there might soon be war with Japan. Citizens who disobeyed lighting controls could be fined stiffly or imprisoned, though the courts on the whole let offenders off with a warning.

Campaigns to get citizens to volunteer for the Home Guard and the Emergency Precautions Scheme went hand in hand with other campaigns to try to talk them into – or coerce them to – work harder and for longer hours at their daily tasks. The government asked wage workers to do so for 'victory'. Advertisements announced that war would be won not only on the battlefield but inside the factory. Patrick Webb, one of the leading ministers in the government, spoke stirring words:

> *Any miner who handles a shovelful less coal, any farmer who grows fewer turnips, any businessman who does not see that his business is conducted with the utmost efficiency, is helping the Hitler crowd to come out on top.*[151]

The government took steps to impose controls over the workforce, though haltingly. The Industrial Emergency Council set up on the outbreak of war had the power to lengthen working hours and tinker with working conditions and rates of pay. The council held talks with employers and workers, industry by industry. After the fall of France the government gave the labour ministry the right to step in and make any changes in working hours and working conditions in any industry. The ministry over the next year imposed such changes on workplaces ranging from ammunition works to woollen mills and from cement works to shearing sheds. The changes meant, overall, that workers were kept to task for longer hours and for less pay.[152]

A National Service Department was set up, also under emergency regulations, in the winter of 1940 to tighten control of manpower for industry. The government gave itself the power to declare industries 'essential' to the war economy and to 'direct' – in other words order – people to work in those industries. The theory, spelled out to workers and employers, was that this would be a fair and just conscription of workers, like the conscription of men into the military. However, many workers were by no means happy, and so the government did nothing. No industries were declared to be essential and nothing was done to direct people into work.[153]

Military contracts provided a powerful profit motive for manufacturers to make the most of their machinery and plant. Engineering works, for example, turned so assiduously to making munitions that the dominion by the end of 1940 was churning out many millions of cartridges, shells, mortar bombs and parts for machine guns. New Zealand became an exporter of weaponry. Shell fuses and hand grenades were shipped to Britain. The mining industry was geared to war thanks to very active oversight by the state. A Coal Mines Council, set up in the middle of 1940, went 'from coalfield to coalfield', working hard for quick understandings between workers and management whenever any industrial dispute broke out.[154] The tonnage of coal hacked out from the mines of the country went up year by year, slowly but steadily.[155]

Farmers were mobilised too. Primary production councils, founded earlier in the war, got deep down to the grassroots by means of new district committees. The committees, knowing their neighbourhoods well, were able to get farmers working together and pooling labour and machinery. Farmers toiled long hours to keep up or even boost the yields from their herds, flocks and crops. 'With their tractors often working far into moonlight nights, or with headlights searching along the furrow in the darkness,' wrote company director and racehorse owner John Carlyle Irving, such farmers 'kept faith' with 'their brothers at the front'.[156] Production councils and committees pasted up posters and spread the word about working the land for the sake of winning the war. They urged farmers to 'plough as you never did before. Plough your own land, plough your neighbour's land, plough for victory, plough for your kinsmen in the battle-line.'[157]

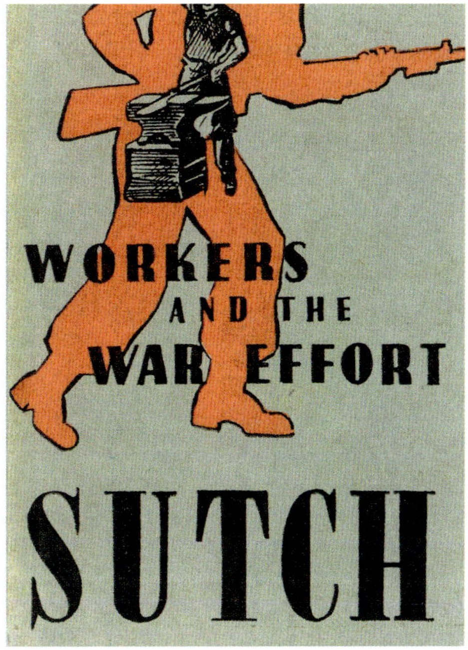

The government and volunteer groups published posters, pamphlets and books in the hope of talking workers into toiling harder, for longer hours, so as to back up the military. *W.B. Sutch,* Workers and the War Effort *(Wellington: New Zealand Co-operative Publishing Society, 1941).*

Farms and stations coped strikingly well with the loss of many thousands of workers to the military. A country newspaper observed by the middle of 1941 that there was 'a startling revolution going on'; farm owners were keeping up or boosting output by 'the greater use of female workers, the pooling of men and machinery, and the more complete mechanisation of farming'.[158] The wool yield of the country dropped slightly in the first months of the war but got back the lost ground the following year.[159] Butterfat weights churned out by dairy farms went up year by year.[160]

Yet a lot of citizens were still sceptical about the need to work harder and longer for the sake of fighting the faraway Axis. Overtime hours worked in factories nearly doubled during the first two years of the war, but most of those who did the overtime made sure they got overtime pay. Nor were wage workers willing to turn themselves into the obediently toiling troops of economic warfare. With young workmen being siphoned off to war, by 1941 labour was in very short supply and those who had stayed behind – men or women – were able to take days off at a whim without needing to worry that the boss might give them the sack.[161] 'Now that the worker is calling the tune and having a fair time for recreation, the employers are kicking and crying disloyalty,' wrote a clothing machinist whose son had enlisted and who herself had gone back to work. 'I say no, only getting a little of their own back.'[162]

Absenteeism was widespread. The 'normal attendance' in one factory, for example, was only 90 per cent of the staff on its payroll. On the first day back at work after the summer holiday at the beginning of 1941, four in every ten workers failed to clock in at factories in Christchurch and Wellington. One factory clocked in 48 per cent of its staff on the first day of the week, was lucky enough to get 90 per cent the next day, but then only 82 per cent the following day. 'The weather was too fine and the hands had sufficient money to take another holiday,' was the caustic observation of the manager. One employer had an even poorer turnout:

> *We have a staff of nearly 150 hands. On Monday last, when we reopened after Christmas, 65 turned up ... up to last night, with a full working week gone in the new year, there were still 40 missing. We are hoping that they will come back on Monday, but we have no guarantee that they will.*[163]

AUXILIARIES

Women had not been asked by the government to join the fighting ranks on the outbreak of the war. Nor would they be asked to do so throughout the rest of the war. Shooting and being shot, bombing, strafing, killing and being killed were not seen as womanly. Nursing was womanly, and doctoring too, which meant that the army from the beginning had recruited women into its medical corps. Otherwise, women were enlisted only slowly, and only into 'auxiliary' tasks, freeing up men to do the killing.

The air force took the first step, early in 1941: it called for women to volunteer as typists, clerks, telephone operators, cooks, kitchenhands and waitresses – jobs already done by women in the wider economy. A new door opened, however, when the air force asked women to take on the task of driving. Young middle-class women usually knew how to drive, which meant they could now do the work as members of what quickly came to be called the Women's Auxiliary Air Force. A newer opening still was in training women for technical tasks. Young women answered the call for volunteers so eagerly that within a few days the air force had far more than were needed, even though the pay was well below what women could earn in a factory.[164]

The army and navy waited more than a year before following the air force and opening up technical support jobs with the formation of the Women's Royal New Zealand Naval Service and the Women's Auxiliary Army Corps.

Women were sought more urgently for work outside the military.

The government made its first move to organise women war workers when it got busy sweeping with a new broom after the fall of France. A national conference of women in the winter of 1940 brought together the scattered and motley groups of volunteers who wanted to do something. The women who attended were mostly from the middle class and their leading light was an active, quick-witted doctor, Agnes Bennett. Semple oversaw this in his capacity as minister of 'national service'. Fraser kept a close eye on the conference too. Bennett and other delegates wanted to form an organisation with many of the trappings of the army, not least military titles and the saluting of women officers by women of lower rank. Fraser vetoed the proposal;

The air force was the first military service to recruit women into any units other than the medical corps. Advertisements sought to make the military attractive to young middle-class women. *Air Force Museum of New Zealand.*

he disliked such notions of hierarchy. All three groups agreed in the end to link up together in what became the Women's War Service Auxiliary.

The auxiliary was led by well-off women who seldom, during years of peace, would have dealt with anybody from the Labour Party. Member groups elected twelve to a national council. The government appointed four other councillors in a bid to give some voice to the working class. Janet Fraser, wife of the prime minister, became national president. Dorothy Atmore, clever and wealthy, former company director and now wife of an independent member of parliament, was national organiser of the auxiliary. The goal, she spelled out, was 'to make available through one centralised body the services of all women willing to assist should an emergency arise'. The government's role was 'only as a helper' and power was to stay in 'the hands of the women'. Women who worked for the auxiliary would only do so for pay, at award rates, so they could not be used by employers to undercut the wages of the working class.[165]

The Women's War Service Auxiliary swiftly formed provincial branches, and those branches got busy.

Women who worked for the auxiliary were nicknamed 'Tuis'. Ada Cocker, active before the war as a delegate to the Pacific Conference in Kyoto and now a member of the auxiliary national council, made it clear that it was intended to militarise women only as far as was 'necessary'. Auxiliary women were 'not allowed to wear military badges or have military titles', although they did wear a uniform and were drilled to carry out parades.[166] Tens of thousands of mostly young women who were willing to do war work were listed on the organisation's register of volunteers by the end of 1941, when the government ordered that all help given by women's organisations to departments of state and the army, navy and air force must be organised through the auxiliary. Thousands undertook canteen work, feeding, serving and cleaning up after soldiers, sailors and airmen in the kitchens and dining halls of military camps. Thousands took on clerical and typing work for the Emergency Precautions Scheme and the Home Guard. A few thousand women worked as drivers and mechanics in the civilian transport industry. The auxiliary also ran recycling drives for steel, aluminium, paper and other goods in short supply.

The war cabinet urged women to go into the civilian workforce too, to work for a wage or salary.

The manpower of the country, the minister of labour, Webb, pointed out early in 1941, had been 'reduced enormously'.[167] Only with the help of women, it was now obvious, could the economy keep growing. The daughters of the working class bent their backs to many tasks, but the daughters of the working class had always worked for pay. Webb asked other women to join the ranks. 'I am sure that many of our women, probably of the middle classes who are so keen and anxious to do valuable work,' he declared optimistically, 'would join with the rest of the workers by volunteering.'[168]

Shop and office work drew more young women from suburban bungalows, but few daughters of the middle class were willing to go into a factory. The choice was theirs to make, or not make, freely. Most suburban women chose to stay at home in those bungalows, or to go to the cinema, or to the races, or on picnics.

Only when Japan joined the war at the end of 1941 would such women feel political and social pressure intensify.

ALIENS

National prejudice grew nasty after the fall of France. Germans were spoken about in vicious ways. The government stuck to its position that the enemy was not the citizen of any enemy state but fascist dictatorship, but some still talked about the 'innate criminality' of the people of Germany. The Nazi Party, claimed the *Evening Post*, was 'the natural and continuous product of a breed which from the dawn of history has been predatory and bellicose'.[169] The 'German character itself' was 'almost sub-human'.[170] Anger, fear and hatred, buoyed by the waves of hysteria that swept through the country during the middle months of 1940, led many to demand that more enemy aliens be locked up behind the barbed wire of internment camps.

'I think the time has come when every German national should be interned at once,' declared an outspoken conservative, Allan Moody, lawyer and chairman of the Auckland Hospital Board.[171]

At the peak of the hysteria even Adam Hamilton, speaking as leader of the National Party, called for such a wholesale imprisonment policy.[172] Ronald Algie, a conservative university teacher, went still further when he spoke as president of the Freedom League. 'If the whole of the German race were wiped out now,' he declared, 'it would be no loss to the world.'[173] Citizens jeered at German women and men and threw stones at German windows. Edward Rothschild, for example, found all the windows broken when he turned up one morning to open his fruit and confectionery shop in Papakura. Rothschild had the windows mended, but soon they were broken once more, and nearby at Hunua three haystacks were set alight on a farm belonging to another German, Ernst Lion. A farm labourer aged seventeen, John Redman, was found guilty of both crimes.[174]

Lion and Rothschild were both refugee German Jews. Many of the harshest words spoken about Germans were about German Jews. Conservative professional and business people feared competition from such refugees, many of whom were highly qualified professionals or experienced business people who, as enemy aliens, could not go into the military.

Were these German Jews really opposed to the Nazi government, or had they instead been sent to the dominion to spy for Berlin, or to try to undermine the loyalty of the people of New Zealand?[175] Angry speakers on the political right called for laws or regulations to keep them out of the professions and business. Auckland was one city, they claimed, in which 'young and enterprising New Zealanders' had 'built up thriving businesses' that now had 'fallen into the hands of aliens, often at sacrifice prices'.[176] Sir Carrick Robertson, a leading surgeon and president of the Auckland Medical Association, elaborated on the point:

> *We do not suggest that all or any of these aliens are spies, but what we do know is that their roots for generations have been nurtured on German soil, and it is difficult to believe that just because of their mass expulsion during a political upheaval they are not at the bottom of their hearts loyal to Germany ... When the war is over our kith and kin will return to find their places taken by men of the very race they went forth to fight. Surely this is a monstrous thing.*[177]

The Labour government was not willing to do anything so high-handed as to round up every enemy alien, but it did decide to appoint an 'aliens authority' in every police district of the country. The job of the authority was to look into the backgrounds of each alien and report on them to Wellington. The government used its power sparingly – only 221 enemy aliens were interned during the whole course of the war.[178] An alien who was to be interned could seek to have the order overturned by an Aliens Appeal Tribunal.

'While we are vigilant,' said Rex Mason, the attorney-general, 'we shall endeavour not to be unjust.'[179]

At the same time the government narrowed the freedom of movement of enemy aliens by taking away their right to own cameras, cars and maps. Aliens were harassed by government officials, who often were obtuse in their judgements. Odo Strewe, a writer and thinker on the political left in Auckland, was interned as somebody who was 'potentially' an enemy of the state.

'Of course he's not a Nazi,' wrote an angry Frank Sargeson. 'Like myself he's simply a liberal intellectual, though a considerably more amusing one than I am.'[180]

Paul Schramm, a gifted musician who performed, broadcast, taught and composed in Wellington, was ordered to stop broadcasting. Officials feared that he might, while playing the piano, be sending 'coded messages' to Germany. He ended up driving a taxi.[181] As the war went on, enemy aliens were forbidden to buy property, mostly to placate people on the right who kept protesting about German Jews making themselves rich while 'our boys' were fighting for freedom and democracy.

Italians were looked at askance too. A few thousand people were of Italian birth, or else the offspring of Italians, mostly making a quiet living as wage workers, market gardeners, shopkeepers or in the fishing fleet. A lot of them felt loyal to Italy. A lot of them also felt loyal to New Zealand. Fascist leaders were interned after New Zealand declared war on Italy. Italian coalminers were interned too, or sacked, since coalmining was a key war industry. Italian shopkeepers, boycotted by former customers, went broke. Vincenzo Basile was one victim of strong 'public feeling': he had to give up his Wellington hairdressing salon and turn to labouring work.[182] Italians, however, generally evoked less fear and rage than Germans, and above all German Jews.

MĀORI AND PASIFIKA

Citizens were still divided by race too.

Māori fought as volunteers in Greece and afterwards in North Africa, most of them with the Maori Battalion. Newspapers, radio and movie news claimed that the tribes were wholeheartedly behind the war and ran gushing stories about their warrior spirit and bravery:

> *While some were singing their famous battalion song, a detachment in the sector was ordered to charge with fixed bayonets. They began to chant an ancient tribal haka – and led by a famous 'All Black' they charged. Into blazing Tommy gun fire they rushed*

> *never for a moment hesitating in their determination to destroy the power which seeks to destroy that personal liberty which is so dear to the Maori. At the bayonet point the forward Hun elements met their death, while our useful mortars cleaned out the others who were still in the wire. The slaughter was terrific.*[183]

Yet the Maori Battalion was not a striking testament of Māori support for war against the Axis. Waikato, Tūhoe, Taranaki and various other tribes questioned the war as they had from the beginning, and an overwhelming majority of iwi members wanted to stay out of the army. The government set up a parliamentary committee of the four elected Māori members of parliament, together with a legislative councillor, Rangi Mawhete, to encourage volunteering. Paraire Paikea, the chairman, stumped from marae to marae, speaking eloquently:

> *Greetings to you – oh you, the tribes of this island, dwelling each in your home marae, in Te Aotearoa in Te Waipounamu and hence unto Te Whare-kauri ... Oh kinsmen, work and toil while the sun shines. Clasp each your taiaha, clasp your ancestral mere pounamu, to safeguard indeed your land, your homes, your parents, your wives and children.*[184]

Waikato and allied tribes whose leaders came to an understanding with the government ended up sending 1000 of their young men away. A group of tribal stalwarts stuck nonetheless to their belief that the war was nothing but a hobbyhorse of Te Arawa and Ngāti Porou, iwi that had sided with the state since the New Zealand Wars. Te Kanawa, for example, did not mince words:

> *Why should the Maori people guard this island? ... What difference does it make if the Germans come here? The British have taken our land. They have killed our wives and children. The Treaty of Waitangi is only a delusion to make the Maori people believe that the British people will keep their word of honour.*[185]

The subject peoples of the island colonies, meanwhile, were no keener to help their governors now than when war was first declared.

The Cook Islands gave some sums of money. Atiu, for example, managed to scrape together £100 for the war chest within the first year of the fighting, a big sum for a poor island.[186] Villages sent knitted 'comforts'

Māori were not subject to conscription; the government was aware that forcing tāngata whenua into the military might provoke social disorder, even armed resistance, especially among the tribes that had fought against the state in the New Zealand Wars. Māori leaders and government advertisements encouraged volunteering. *Museum of New Zealand Te Papa Tongarewa.*

for men in the dominion army too. Fundraising and knitting were mostly organised, however, by white colonial officials who used their mana and power to talk villagers into helping. Hugh Ayson, the commissioner who oversaw the colony on behalf of Wellington, was a high-handed former judge who 'demanded respect', imposed a 'strict dress code' on his staff and 'and made his status clear by his demeanour, starched white shirt and white pith helmet'.[187] The white women who ran the Ladies Patriotic Guild of Rarotonga were a colonising group busy getting 'the native school children and Girl Guides' to knit under the overseeing colonial eye.[188]

The Rarotonga Island Council, an assembly of chiefs, did ask the colonial government to allow young men from the Cook Islands to volunteer after the fall of France. Once again, however, the chiefs were turned down. Several thousand people then signed a petition that was sent to Wellington:

> *We have received ... polite evasions for our offers of service – polite evasions that now say quite plainly we do not want you ... Two thousand of our sons await your answer to the petition which we ask to be direct, prompt and unequivocal; give us the opportunity of serving on terms of equality with the pakeha and our blood relations, the Maoris of New Zealand.*

The parliamentary Native Affairs Committee talked over the petition but made no recommendation; it told parliament there were 'difficulties' in letting men from the colony go into the army and that those difficulties could not be spelled out. National Party pressure in the house led one committee member to say that there had been 'heavy mortality' and even heavier physical and mental damage done to men from Rarotonga who had fought in the First World War. Another committee member said that in the earlier war 'the wastage rate in the case of Cook Islanders was terrific and we do not want a repetition'.[189] The government knew, too, that sick, wounded, restless and unhappy former soldiers had been both a burden and a threat during the interwar years to colonial authority in the Cook Islands. Colonial officials who saw old soldiers as 'troublemakers' were not keen to see sons and nephews sent away then brought back home to riot, as had happened after the First World War. Only twenty or so young men from the colony ever found their way into the New Zealand army; they did so by travelling to Auckland and volunteering.

Niueans were not touched much by the war, and nor were the people of Tokelau. One or two villages went to the trouble of fundraising. Fakaofo, for example – a Tokelauan community of fewer than 600 people – gave £111 to the 'war effort' and the Red Cross Society.[190] An official from New Zealand, on his annual visit of inspection to the colony, was given a further £30 that the inhabitants had subscribed to the bomber fund of Samoa.[191]

Samoans showed no more willingness to help New Zealand than they had in the first months of war. Chinese traders and white officials undertook a fundraising drive to pay for a fighter plane. Newspapers claimed that the money, scraped together in the autumn

Colonial administration buildings in Avarua, the capital of the Cook Islands. Although the administration buildings were simple, the colony had a steep hierarchy of authority. At the apex of power was the exacting Hugh Ayson. *Photographer: Whites Aviation. Alexander Turnbull Library WA-00998-G.*

of 1941, proved the 'loyalty and devotion to the cause' felt by the people of Samoa. The bulk of the cash, however, came from whites and Chinese rather than villagers. The banana exporting industry gave about a quarter of the money, and another quarter was the gift of white civil servants.[192]

Alfred Turnbull, head of the colonial government, kept to his policy of not allowing Samoans to sign up for the territorial army. 'The Samoans are not to be trusted,' he wrote to Wellington not long before the outbreak of the war. 'They are just as likely to betray us to an enemy as to help us.'[193]

War was having a grave economic impact on the islands. Samoa was 'in dire economic straits', wrote a newspaper correspondent, because the wartime shortage of shipping stopped it from exporting a good deal of its copra, cocoa, banana and rubber crops. Shipping shortages also meant that prices of imports were hiked higher and higher by traders, or by colonial governments in the case of wartime 'controlled' imports.[194] In the Cook Islands the cost of clothing went up by 40 per cent, and the cost of food by 50 per cent.[195] Climbing costs and sinking earnings caused hardship in every village. Thomas Herries-Davis, a young doctor from the islands, wrote about the growing poverty:

> *Some of the people could no longer afford to repair their European-type houses … families were reverting to living in the old-fashioned thatched houses; but the pandanus trees which in the old days had supplied all the building materials had, through parasite destruction, disappeared, and the Islanders were now stripping the leaves from the live coconut trees – of course injuring the valuable coconut crop.*[196]

The colonies were no more united than the dominion, and were even less systematically mobilising.

OPERATION BARBAROSSA AND SHIFTING ALLEGIANCES

Questions such as forming a war cabinet, going ahead with the welfare state, levying a paramilitary, tax, compulsory war loans, conscription, women's work and women in the military were all triggers for class conflict, as we have seen; and other disagreements about money and power set members of one class against others of the same class.

One question that sparked outspoken conflict along the class divide was the relationship between the Soviet Union and Germany.

Conservative hostility towards the Soviet Union had strengthened during the early months of the war thanks to the non-aggression pact signed between Berlin and Moscow. The political right believed the pact proved the Communist Party to be an enemy of the British Empire. The Labour Party, while it was no friend of the Communist Party, believed that the Soviet Union had good reason to forestall a struggle with the Third Reich. Also, the Labour government believed that the Soviet Union was not an enemy of New Zealand, nor of the British Commonwealth, and that it would be wise for London to come to an understanding with Moscow. Communists went further: they continued to argue after the fall of France that the war was still nothing but a fight for high ground between two capitalist imperialist systems, the British Empire and Nazi Germany: 'the rights of the people are being swept aside,' said the *People's Voice* that winter, 'in order that British Imperialism might strengthen itself in its struggle to maintain power and domination.'[197]

The balance between those who feared and those who felt some esteem for the Soviet Union started to sway in the winter of 1941 when the Nazi government launched the most enormous military operation in the history of Germany. Tanks, clanking across the western borders of the Soviet Union on 22 June, drove a murderous trident deep into the Ukraine and towards Leningrad and Moscow. The Commonwealth and the Soviet Union, swiftly signing a formal agreement, undertook to give each other as much help as they could, and also undertook not to sign a separate peace treaty. Nash, acting prime minister when the deal was struck, spoke about it favourably, and New Zealand took part in the talks leading to the agreement.[198] Henry Ramsbottom-Isherwood, a New Zealand air-force officer, was ordered to command a fighter wing of warplanes on the territory of the new ally. The Commonwealth, however, could not do a lot to help the Soviet Union. The Soviet Union, in the end, did not need a lot of help from the Commonwealth.

The Nazi government, by making this mighty throw of the dice, was gambling wildly.

Operation Barbarossa: the invasion of the Soviet Union by Nazi Germany.
Standard, *23 October 1941.*

The outlook for the whole war had been revolutionised overnight – revolutionised in a way that would mean, after a few more years of fighting, the crack-up and collapse of the Third Reich. Germany lacked the power to beat the Soviet Union. The Soviet Union, with its vast capacity to produce weapons augmented by shipments of war goods from other Allied states, possessed the power to beat Germany. New Zealand was even more on the sidelines, now, than it had been before the invasion of the Soviet Union. All the battles into which the dominion had so far thrown its army, and all the battles into which it would throw the army, were now sideshows. The British Commonwealth itself was now a sideshow.

Only a few people in the dominion understood that the impact of the new battlefield was so revolutionary. A good many people looked down on Soviet troops and weaponry. Richard Scott, a conservative builder in Palmerston North, said that the Soviet army would 'not last six weeks' and that the tanks rolled out on May Day parades in Moscow were 'a sham' made mostly 'of cardboard'.[199] Labour leaders as well as conservatives still saw the British Commonwealth as the key player in the Second World War. The *Auckland Star* told readers that the struggle between the Soviet Union and Germany, 'vast though it is', served as 'but a means to an end, and that end the destruction of the British Empire'.[200] Sir Cyril Newall, the governor-general, spoke about the question to a crowd in Canterbury:

> *Our Russian allies ... cannot win the war for us. No one can do that. We must win it for ourselves, and we would not have it otherwise. They can help us, and we can and must help them, but we must win our own war for ourselves.*[201]

Communists in New Zealand saw the new twist in the war in quite another way. A German attack on the Soviet Union made the war a straightforward struggle between a fascist state and a socialist state. The British Commonwealth was no longer in the wrong. R.A.K. Mason published a pamphlet called *Help Russia or Help Hitler*; Britain, he told readers, would be saved from 'a ghastly destruction' by the Soviet Union.[202] The Communist Party hoped it would be allowed to work in a close and friendly way with the Labour Party. After all, the official goal of both parties of the left was to destroy the fascist states.

The left, however, was still too deeply divided for the two parties to come together in a partnership that could be close, let alone friendly.

The Labour Party had drifted towards the right after John A. Lee was driven out. Fraser, notes one biographer, 'hated the Communist Party'.[203] Nor was the highhanded, often bullying, prime minister looked upon with warmth by communists; John Beaglehole claimed that Fraser was 'less & less highly thought of by the workers & the intelligentsia'.[204] Communists were dismayed when new war emergency regulations gave the government power to have 'subversive' workers sacked, and also to control unions more tightly. Coalminers – many of them communist – voted their opposition to the regulations, as did the Dunedin Federated Furniture and Related Trades Industrial Union of Workers, and the Carpenters Union, which called the regulations 'a most flagrant attack on the free basis of our New Zealand democracy'. Fraser in turn denounced the protests as 'obviously another step to oppose, frustrate, and sabotage the war effort' of the country.[205]

Communists and the government fought a bitter battle over the question of conscription. Communists were imprisoned for selling or handing out anti-conscription leaflets and pamphlets. The government censor ordered newspapers not to write anything about the leaflets and pamphlets, for fear that it would give wider publicity to communist points of view about the war; but still those worrying papers fluttered about and were passed from hand to hand, almost everywhere in New Zealand. Fraser himself confessed that they were 'flooding' the country. Two communists were put behind bars for slipping copies of *Soldiers and Workers* into Dunedin letterboxes, as were two others in Invercargill. Thomas Stanley went to prison for writing and publishing in Auckland a leaflet called *The Real Criminals*. Harold Darbyshire, roadman and father of four, was locked up for selling the pamphlet *The War and the Working Class* in Eketahuna. Alexander Galbraith and Douglas Martin, communists who campaigned in Wellington against conscription and the war, heard a judge who sentenced them to prison say that they were 'enemies within the gates'. The People's Voice office, headquarters of communist printing in the country, was seized by the police and forced to shut up shop.[206]

The military alliance between the Soviet Union and the British Commonwealth led thousands of people to take a new look at the Communist Party. Communists spoke about building a union of the peoples of the Pacific. They spoke, too, about the need for democracy instead of authoritarian hierarchy in the military. Communist Party membership trebled over the next eighteen months and tens of thousands of citizens sang, cheered and listened to speeches at nationwide rallies in support of international socialism and the Soviet Union.[207]

The Labour Party no longer openly attacked the Communist Party. At the same time, though, the government and its supporting unions stopped short of forming a common front with communists to work together towards victory. The Labour Party and Federation of Labour stated jointly in the spring of 1941 that they had 'carefully considered' but turned down the proposal for a common front. Communists had shown themselves to be too 'irresponsible and unstable' during the early months of the war; they were not answerable to 'democratic methods' and were not working 'with reference to the needs and purposes of the people of New Zealand'.[208] The meaning was that communists were the catspaws of Moscow.

The political right, meanwhile, was no longer in disarray.

A leadership coup in the spring of 1940 had overthrown the 'old guard' of the National Party headed by Adam Hamilton and brought to power a new leader, Sidney Holland. Hamilton was too scholarly to score many points inside or outside parliament against a strong and often stroppy Labour Party. Holland, on the other hand, was burly, a former army officer, could be rough when not hearty, hardly ever opened a book, and was above all a shrewd politician who knew how to work parliament. Gordon Coates wrote in a private letter about the 'lust to achieve office' that drove Holland.[209] A thriving manufacturer, the new National leader bought a sheep farm in order to sell himself to the landed as well as to the city capitalist. Calling himself 'a Britisher through and through', though he was born in Canterbury, he swore to keep the link with Britain and 'the British way of life'.[210] Also he claimed, in his first parliamentary speech as leader, that winning the war was the 'first and main' concern of the National Party.[211]

The new leader of the opposition quickly swept big right-wing groups into the National Party. The People's Movement, when he took over the helm, had been protesting against an 'apathetic acceptance' by the parliamentary opposition of a socialist state that violated 'British traditions'.[212] Holland, over the following weeks, got together with the leaders of such groups and managed to bring most of them into the same camp.[213] The camp, he told the nation, was committed to 'the maximum war effort, the restoration of personal liberty, the right of the people to live their own lives in their own way, and the fight against further socialistic encroachment'. Holland was a leader 'with not only the desire but the will to eradicate, by a constructive policy, the sectional strife and class bitterness' that dogged the country, said Ernest Toop, the leader of the People's Movement.[214]

Holland attacked the government when a new session of parliament opened in autumn 1941. The attacks homed in on working hours and wages.

Factory owners, landowners and most other employers wanted workers to give up what had become one of the core principles of the working class – a forty-hour working week. The National Party, flying the flag for employers, demanded that workers be kept to their tasks for longer hours, yet not be paid overtime. A battle over hours and wages had been fought from the beginning of the war; it hotted up after the fall of France when employers pushed the government to force longer hours onto workers,

Sidney Holland: city businessman, landowner, former army officer and new parliamentary leader of the National Party, portrayed as the member of a gentlemen's club. *Standard*, *11 January 1945.*

and unions said they would not sacrifice the forty-hour week 'on the altar of hysteria'.[215] Hamilton had condemned one union whose workers were given a boost in wages while German tanks were driving deep inside France, for demanding 'pillage'; the workers, he said, were guilty of 'a flagrant breach of the spirit of our nation today'. The working class must pull its weight to help win the war against the Axis.[216]

Unions asked in return why workers should be scapegoats: what about 'bankers, farmers, importers, investors, employers?'[217] Capitalists were exploiting the war to attack the wages, hours and conditions of the working class. The wife of a waterside worker wrote about her disgust with moneyed 'patriots' who talked about longer working hours as 'every man's duty'. She pointed out that some nights her husband already came home worn out with heavy work; was he now being told he 'should work himself till he is ready to drop'?[218] A wide array of working people shared her feelings.

Conservatives nevertheless made the most of their newspaper monopoly to keep up complaints against the working class. The *Auckland Star* late in 1940 told its readers that those who spoke about a capitalist 'attack' on the forty-hour week needed to know that 'the attack on New Zealand's forty-hour week was launched by Adolf Hitler'.[219] Workers were the 'only people allowed to profiteer' from the war, said Norman Spencer, chairman of the Auckland Chamber of Commerce, early in 1941, about the burden borne by capitalists under the welfare state.[220] 'The high standard of living will have to come down,' said Coates a month later, after stirring words about a need for 'sacrifice and hardship undertaken in a spirit of goodwill and comradeship'.[221] The Wellington Chamber of Commerce called for the government to impose a six-day working week in industry. Workers who opposed such a plan were 'traitors and enemies' of New Zealand.[222] The 'worst aspect of the forty-hour week', declared Mulholland, president of the Farmers Union, was 'the psychological effect' it had on citizens as a whole who believed they need not work any harder for victory because workers were sticking to only forty hours in industry.[223] The Wellington Employers Association near the end of 1941 said that everybody must 'understand and loyally accept' that they could not 'live in the same manner as in time of peace'. Workers must knuckle down for the sake of the British Empire.[224]

Capital was not always in conflict with the government, nor with the working class.

The welfare state led to new partnerships between government and capitalists. A cornerstone of the system was licensing imports in order to control international movements of money. A company that was awarded an import licence could find itself thriving. War led to new partnerships between capitalists and the state. The Fletcher family was widely known to have a very good understanding with the government over building state houses – one of the most emotionally charged policies of the Labour Party. Other wealthy families and companies came to similar understandings. Wright, Stephenson and Company, for example, a nationwide firm of merchants, did a good deal with the supply ministry. Ordinarily, seeds for winter fodder crops were imported from Europe. The government handed over to the company 'the organisation and supervision of the production of locally-grown seed'. Wright, Stephenson 'immediately proceeded with the enterprise, centralising their control from the seed department of their branch at Invercargill'. The deal worked so well that the country became self-sufficient in seed.[225] The Labour left chafed at the way so many companies were being turned into cronies of the government, while the political right asked the state for still more help in the form of skills and money.

Advertisement for the People's Movement, founded by business people, professional people and landowners late in 1939 as a lobbying organisation on the political right. Conservatives claimed that class and party politics should be set aside during the war so the dominion could concentrate its forces on beating the Axis. The People's Movement was brought into the National Party thanks to skilful political manoeuvring by Holland. *Auckland Star*, *2 August 1941.*

Capitalists as a whole, however, were still unhappy about the welfare state. The political right was still asking whether the government was taking advantage of the war to press ahead with socialism on the sly. 'It is evident,' said a circular published by Auckland merchants, 'that the Labour Party is using the plea of war necessity as a means to securing the full establishment of its long-desired Socialistic dictatorship.'[226]

Money was by no means the only cause of conflict between left and right, or between capitalists and the working class. Symbols could be important too. Flying the flag in state schools, for example, provoked conflict after the fall of France. Conservatives

Conservatives protested throughout the war against the forty-hour working week, arguing that the working class should be willing to make sacrifices and work longer hours to help bring about 'victory'. Standard, *12 June 1941.*

believed that schools should mark a mood of patriotic solemnity by gathering staff and students together to salute the flag. Mulholland criticised government politicians for being 'lukewarm' about patriotism. He saved his sharpest words for the 'anaemic patriotism' of the education minister, Mason, who was not keen on flag flying.[227] The Canterbury Education Board, which was dominated by business people, released a statement saying that it wished to 'keep prominently before the children what Britain and Britons stand for throughout the length and breadth of the Empire'. The board therefore ordered every school in the province to begin every school day with the students gathering to sing 'There'll Always Be an England'.[228] Clyde Carr, clergyman and Labour member of parliament, was scathing:

> *I know some people are dependent on ritual observances and that people with fairly primitive minds want to salute the flag and go through some mumbo jumbo. Teachers are people who have read widely and studied deeply and have got away from kindergarten methods of thinking and acting, and it is pretty hard to expect them to bow down before a totem pole ... I think that probably the loyalty of the conscientious objectors may mean a higher patriotism and a truer loyalty than some of those who outwardly salute the flag and bow before the god of war.*[229]

The National Party under its new leadership, meanwhile, pressed for a coalition government. The caucus of the party voted unanimously in the autumn of 1941 in favour of the two major political parties forming 'a truly national' government that would wage war in unity.[230] The *New Zealand Herald*, speaking as always for the party, claimed that it was 'the earnest hope of the great majority of the citizens' of the country that the Labour Party would awaken to popular 'contempt for party selfishness and its weariness of those who flout the demand for a National Government'.[231] The newspaper offered no proof for the unlikely claim that such views were held by most of the citizenry.

The Labour Party, wholly unwilling to think about a coalition throughout 1940, was not quite so clearly opposed to the proposal by the middle of 1941, even though uniting with the political right would slow down or bring to a sudden stop the development of the welfare state. A coalition might prove to be a necessary evil, at least for a year or two.

The Labour left, on the other hand, still spoke firmly against a war coalition. The Auckland Drivers Union voted unanimously against coalition, while the Auckland Amalgamated Society of Carpenters and Joiners not only 'strongly' opposed coalition but went on to urge the government to 'socialise all land, wealth, business and anything which might come to New Zealand for the duration of the war and in the future to be used for the benefit of the people'.[232] Nordmeyer told parliament that there was 'a great gulf' between the principles of the two major parties and that 'to disregard it would be the height of folly'.[233] The Upper Hutt branch of the Labour Party viewed the proposal for a coalition 'with disapproval'.[234] The Westland representation committee of the party said that a coalition would be an 'unholy alliance' which would bring about the 'greatest disaster' for the Labour Party.[235]

Social democrats, however, would soon be talking a good deal more eagerly about coalition government.

A LOVELY TIME SWIMMING

Although the government worried about war coming closer to home, few citizens seemed to share that worry. The waves of panic that swept the country during the autumn and early winter of 1940 ebbed swiftly and a humdrum mood once more gained ground. Germany was conquering new territory but the war was far away. Anton Vogt wrote a war poem published late that winter in a student university magazine, *Spike*:

We are so distant here
it is impossible to feel
that war is real
... and we are absent from our funerals
because our deaths no longer are
our own affair.[236]

Summer at the end of 1940 had been a season when most people went on with their lives more or less as though there was no fighting on the other side of the world. The war seemed 'a mammoth drama being acted out in some distant amphitheatre', noted a young librarian and university student, Sonja Vile.[237] Elsie Morton, a journalist, wrote about the contrast between 'care-free holiday-making' in the dominion and 'ruthless and cruel war' so far away.[238] Christmas shoppers thronged stores, picking and choosing between 'an amazingly wide range of goods in spite of difficulties imposed by war conditions and import control'. Shops often reported record sales. One suburban store, for example, 'doubled its takings of the previous year – and last year had been a record!'[239] Joanna Stevenson, a child of eight, wrote about the summer plans of her family:

> *On Christmas day, if it is fine, we have dinner out in the garden. It is lovely, because we have four apple trees, and we put the table and chairs under them, it looks so pretty. Our aunts and uncles and grandmother come and have a Christmas dinner with us. Every New Year we go down to the beach for a New Year's dinner ... We stay about two weeks at the beach and have a lovely time swimming and fishing.*[240]

The people of the dominion celebrated New Year 1941 in much the same way they had celebrated before the war. The *Auckland Star* noted that a new list of war dead had been released by the army, 'while hundreds of thousands of people' got ready for holiday. The list of those killed was 'negligibly small' compared with those in the First World War.[241] Trotting clubs and racing clubs ran their summer meets, bowls rolled and cricket balls were whacked on smooth turf. Family picnics strewed the sand in the Bay of Islands, the Bay of Plenty, Tasman Bay and Pegasus Bay. Yachts speckled the blue waters of the Hauraki Gulf, Port Nicholson, the Marlborough Sounds and Banks Peninsula.

A peacetime mood continued during the following months, no matter what twists and turns the fighting took in China, Europe, North Africa or the Middle East. Citizens were so casual about the war, reported the government censor, that many gave no 'active support and co-operation' to the government policy of not speaking about shipping movements but instead were 'indiscreet to a remarkable degree'.[242] Racecourses, as always, were a venue for wealthy women to show off the latest fashions in clothing and headgear. The latest in style – off-the-face hat, long jacket and pencil skirt – was worn by well-to-do women to the Auckland Racing Club's autumn meeting at Ellerslie:

> *Favoured colours were nature's tonings, rich browns, greens and beiges. All shades of blue and wine were also popular. The 'straight and narrow' silhouette made an appearance in a number of the silk and woollen frocks. It was no skimpy, economical style, however. Relieved by bows and drapes and cleverly concealed fullness, the frocks struck a graceful and thoroughly feminine note. They were worn in most cases with fitting coats or loose swaggers of lightweight material.*[243]

One woman lamented the way people were waging the war 'in their armchairs, in their gardens and on the tennis field and bowling green'.[244] An Anglican vicar told his congregation that the widespread lack of seriousness about the war made him

A wartime winter day in Wellington. *Artist: Harry Tombs. Art in New Zealand, Spring 1941.*

unhappy. 'This week hundreds of New Zealand boys have been reported missing on the battlefields of Greece,' he told a scanty turnout. 'How many in New Zealand care?'[245]

A lack of earnestness about the war was linked with a lack of any strong sense of why the country was fighting. The Labour government had tried, with no luck, to get other Allied governments to set out war aims clearly. It had not really worked out its own war aims and peace goals, however, let alone spelled out those aims and goals to citizens in a straightforward and systematic way.

Was one goal, for example, to bring the Axis and Allied governments to the table for talks ending with a peace treaty?

Or was the goal to destroy the Third Reich?

Or something else?

The lack of war aims grew so pressing that many people talked about the need for a wholly new order in the world. The Nazi Party had spoken for some years about building a *Neuordnung Europas*, a new order in Europe. Tokyo since 1938 had called for a *Tōa Shin Chitsujo*, a new order in East Asia. A third voice came from the Vatican:

a 'new order of the world' must be built upon 'the unshakable foundation of natural law and divine revelation', Pope Pius XII declared late in 1939, and his call was echoed in the dominion by not only Catholics but some Anglicans.[246] Allied statements about a new order dated from late in 1940 when a speech was broadcast by the British propaganda minister, Duff Cooper:

> *It is we of the British Commonwealth, not the apostles of Nazi and Fascist dictatorship, who are able to offer the world a real new order. The new order embodied in the Commonwealth has room for the aspiration of every country and race sheltering under it. It is not based on domination and the crack of the whip, but on freedom for men and nations.*[247]

New Zealand politicians, newspaper editors, broadcasters and clergy were willing to parrot such phrases in a loose sort of way. The right spoke about a new world order. The left spoke about a new world order. The president of the Auckland Farmers Union declared that the war would lead to sweeping changes in society. He told fellow farmers that while they could not guess what shape those changes might take, 'an entirely new order should come about'.[248] James Roberts, president of the Labour Party, got a 'most enthusiastic welcome' when he told the Nelson branch of the party that 'if a New World Order was to become a fact' it must be based on 'Socialistic doctrine'.[249] Hedda Dyson, editor of *Woman's Weekly*, called for 'a new spiritual order based on a conception of fellowship of people and nations'.[250] Joan Sutherland, speaking at a conference about social 'reconstruction' after the war, thought it of crucial importance to every woman: 'Women will be the trustees and bankers of the new order … Men are caught up in a net of materialistic machinery and the competitive spirit, and so are destroying themselves.'[251]

A new order must be based on a new economic system, in the opinion of Social Credit. John Hogan, talking to 2000 supporters of the movement in the winter of 1941, said that only with the help of the 'irresistible mobilised will of the people' would the world develop 'a new order consistent with real democracy'.[252] Others hoped for a new order based on a new system of schooling. The government wanted schools that would fit young people for peace and social democracy. 'Education alone,' the governor-general, Sir Cyril Newall, told students, 'will make possible a new order based on more real social justice.'[253] Others again spoke of a new order founded on religious sincerity. 'The new order must come from inwards outwards,' clergyman Eric Rich told his congregation in Masterton.[254] 'Christ has the New Order for the world,' declared tannery worker Richard Howe.[255]

'On every side to-day we hear of new orders,' an anonymous citizen wrote to a newspaper.[256]

Churchill and Roosevelt made a high-minded statement about supposed aims and goals when they met on shipboard in the winter of 1941 and cobbled together a joint statement known as the Atlantic Charter.

The charter outlined eight peace points for the world. The first point was that neither of the two signatory states sought to get hold of any new territory or sought any other 'aggrandisement'. The next two points were that the signatory states respected 'the right of all peoples to choose' how to govern their own country. Other points dealt with free trade and economic partnership between states so as to boost 'an improved standard of labour, economic advancement and social security', freedom of the seas, disarmament and the ending of 'the use of force' by the states of the world.[257] The charter as a statement of principle was widely applauded by many people in many countries, among them leaders of the New Zealand government.

'This historic meeting,' Nash enthused, 'has resulted in a declaration more potent for good than any other in the records of human history.'[258]

Yet while many – perhaps even most – citizens thought the charter noble, it was only words. None of the eight points was a very compelling motive for New Zealand to fight or keep fighting. Also, many people were cynical about those noble words. Who could really believe that Britain and the United States would not try to get hold of new territory? Who among the citizens of the dominion were so naïve about imperialist states as to think that woolly slogans about rights of self-government would mean the hauling down of the union jack from flagpoles in Africa and Asia and the Pacific, or the stars and stripes from flagpoles in such colonies as Guam or Hawai`i, or Samoa, or Puerto Rico? Churchill certainly did not intend anyone to take that as his meaning. He told his cabinet the charter did not apply to the British Empire.[259]

New Zealand citizens did not know what Churchill said to his cabinet, but cynicism about the war was widespread in the dominion throughout the whole of 1941, at least until the last few weeks.

Civilians muttered in private, complaining about propaganda, and doing their bit to 'drag the lead'. A railway ganger said that only 'a fool' would 'fight for the British Empire'.[260] Thousands of others spoke or thought the same way but, unlike the unlucky ganger, were too cautious or too shrewd to say such things to anyone who would dob them in to the police and get them dragged into court for speaking out 'seditiously'. The black market – above all in stealing and selling petrol – was now an ordinary thing for hundreds of thousands of people throughout the country, blurring the line between belief in noble words and a need to get on with workaday things.

Conservatives claimed that the mood was one of complacency. 'New Zealanders,' wrote a columnist at the end of spring, 'seem to require a terrible amount of urging to take the present war seriously.'[261]

The mood of cynicism or distant detachment ended suddenly, early in December 1941, when the government of New Zealand declared war on Japan.

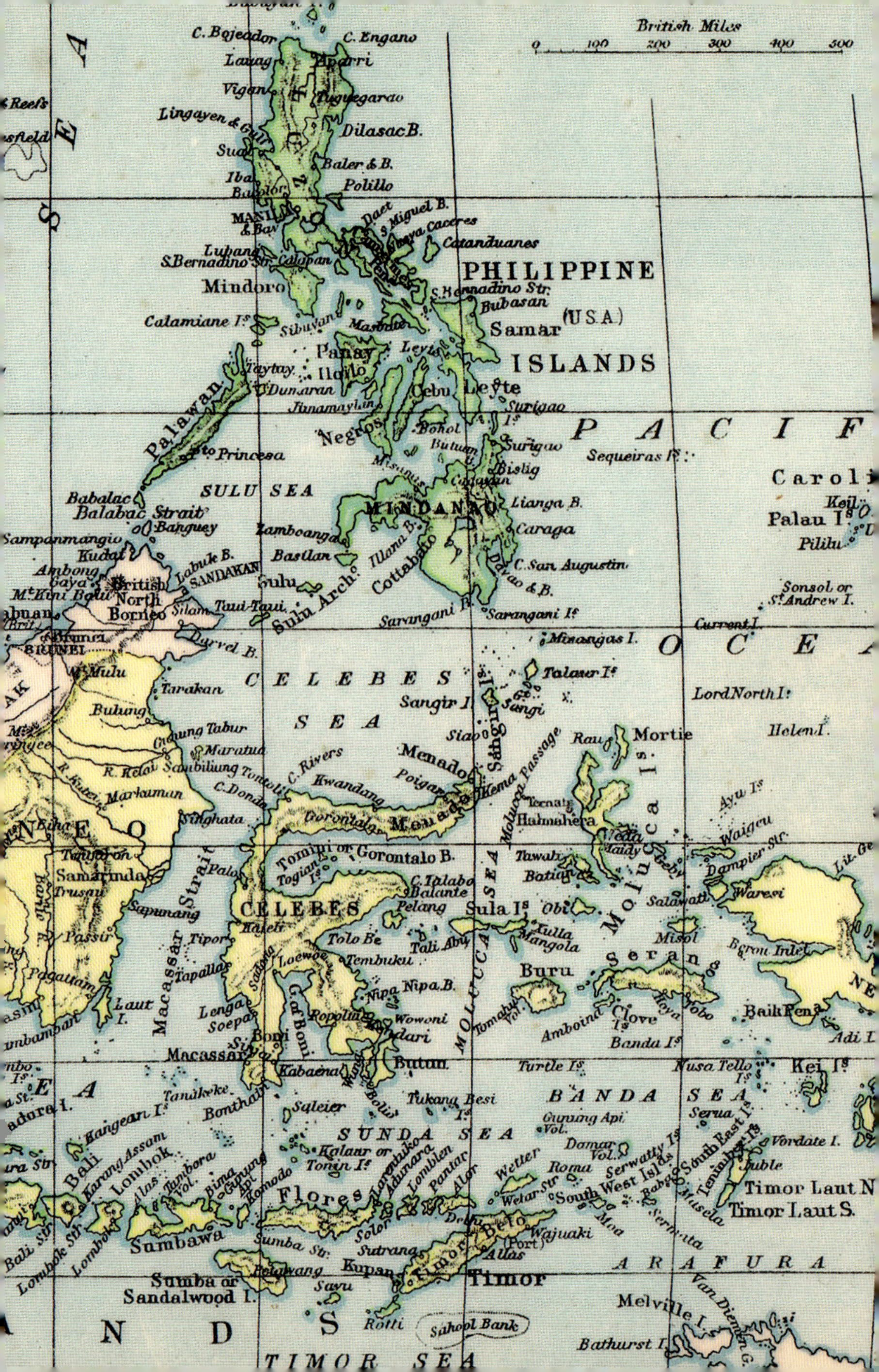

British Miles
0 100 200 300 400 500
PHILIPPINE
(U.S.A.)
ISLANDS
C. Bojeador
C. Engano
Laoag
Aparri
Vigan
Tuguegarao
Lingayen & Gulf
Dilasac B.
Baler & B.
Polillo
MANILA & Bay
Daet
S. Miguel B.
Nueva Caceres
Catanduanes
Lubang
S. Bernadino Str.
Calapan
Mindoro
Bubasan
Samar
Calamiane Is
Sibuyan
Masbate
Panay
Iloilo
Leyte
Taytay
Dunaran
Jinamaylan
Cebu
Surigao
Negros
Bohol
Butuan
Bislig
Palawan
Pto Princesa
SULU SEA
PACIF
Sequeiras Is
Caroli
Palau Is
Pililu
Babalac
Balabac Strait
Banguey
Kudat
Ambong
Gaya
Mt Kini Balu
British North Borneo
Labuk B.
SANDAKAN
Zamboanga
MINDANAO
Liang B.
Caraga
Bastlan
Illana B.
Cottabato
C. San Augustin
Davao & B.
Sulu
Sulu Arch.
Silam
Taui-Taui
Sarangani B.
Sarangani Is
Sonsol or St Andrew I.
Current I.
Brunei
BRUNEI
Darvel B.
Miangas I.
OCEA
Mulu
Tarakan
CELEBES SEA
Talaur Is
Sangir I.
Sangi
LordNorth I.
Bulung
Siao
Rau
Mortie
Helen I.
Gunung Tabur
Maratua
Menado
Kema Passage
R. Kelai
Sambiliung
C. Rivers
Tontoli
Kwandang
Poigar
C. Donda
Markaman
Singhata
Gorontalo
Menado
Ternate
Halmahera
Ayu Is
Waigeu
Samarinda
Tomini or Gorontalo B.
Togian Is
Tawali
Batian
Weda
Dampier Str.
Waresi
Makassar Strait
Palos
C. Talabo
Balante
Pelang
Sula Is
Obi
Salawati
CELEBES
Sapunang
Passir
Kaleli
Tolo Be
Tali Abu
Kulla
Mangola
Misol
Moluccа Is.
Berou Inlet
Tipor
Tembuku
Seran
Tapallas
Pagattam
Laut I.
Lenga
Soepa
Nipa B.
Buru
Macassar
Ropolin
Woworni
Kendari
Tomahu Vol.
Amboina
Clove
Banda Is
Bali-Fena
Adi I.
MOLUCCA SEA
Boni
G. of Boni
Sinjai
Kabaena
Butun
Turtle Is
Nusa Tello Is
Kei Is
Macassar
Tanakeke
Bonthain
Saleier
Tukang Besi Is
BANDA SEA
Serua
Gunung Api Vol.
Damar Vol.
Vordate I.
Bali
Karang Assam
Lombok
Kalaur or Tonin Is
SUNDA SEA
Bima
Komodo
Flores
Adunara
Lomblen
Pantar
Alor
Wetter
Wetar Str.
Roma
Serwatty Is
South West Isds
South East Is
Timor Laut N.
Timor Laut S.
Sumbawa
Sumba Str.
Solor
Sutrana
Dilli
Belo
Kupan
Wajuaki
Moa
ARAFURA
Sumba or Sandalwood I.
Savu
Rotti
Timor
Atlas
Sahool Bank
Melville Is
Bathurst I.
Van Diemen G.
ANDS
TIMOR SEA

CHAPTER 4 | WAR AT OUR DOOR?
DECEMBER 1941 TO DECEMBER 1942

PACIFIC BRINKMANSHIP

Japanese naval, air and land forces on 7 December 1941 struck suddenly at four colonies: Borneo, Malaya, the Philippines and Hawai`i. Malaya was attacked first, when Japanese troops landed at Kota Bharu. Hawai`i was attacked a little later when Japanese warplanes struck at Pearl Harbor.[1] The goal was to get oil, tin and rubber from British Malaya and the Dutch East Indies. The strategy was to crack the naval power of the one state that could step in and stop it – the United States – while the imperial army surged into Southeast Asia.

New Zealand political leaders moved swiftly. The war cabinet went into session 'almost continually' and armed guards stood outside the Japanese consulate in Wellington.[2] An emergency session of parliament followed within a few days. Newall opened with a speech on behalf of the government, accusing Japan of 'treacherous attacks'. The speech was very likely the shortest from the throne in the history of New Zealand.[3] Fraser then told the citizenry that they must go on to 'a war footing'. All would have to work together against the new foe.

'Now war is right at our doors,' he said. 'Everyone must work as never before, and men and women must answer to the call for war work and service.'[4]

Holland had spoken three days earlier, on behalf of the National Party, about 'this grave moment of national peril, when the lives of all New Zealanders are endangered'.[5] A chorus of other anxious voices throughout the dominion called for the country to go onto a full war footing.

'The machine must be got into top gear,' declared the *Auckland Star*, 'and every last ounce of effort must be put into every conceivable precautionary step which will help to keep our coasts inviolate.'[6]

'The war in a single night advances menacingly towards us,' said the *Evening Post*.[7]

Britain and the United States declared war on the Japanese Empire the day after the attacks on Hawai`i and Southeast Asia. The Netherlands declared war too. Wellington

A Dutch propaganda poster showing Japan as a threat to the colonial possessions of European powers in Southeast Asia. *Koninklijke Bibliotheek, Netherlands.*

proclaimed on 9 December that a state of war now existed between the government of New Zealand and the government of 'the Emperor of Japan', and word was sent to Tokyo.

Why had New Zealand chosen to go to war with Japan?

The choice, driven more by emotion than logic, followed a year-long complex and chilling game of brinkmanship in East Asia and the Pacific. Only two navies were of any importance in the hemisphere: those of Japan and the United States. Only two armies were of any importance in the island empires of the hemisphere: those of Japan and the United States. Britain and the Netherlands, while they owned colonies, fielded little in the way of naval or military hardware. France, Australia and New Zealand, while they owned colonies, fielded still less in the way of naval or military hardware. Britain had promised Australia and New Zealand that it would send a powerful navy should such help be needed.

The fall of France had led to struggles for power in its island colonies. The Vichy government claimed ownership of all French imperial territory, but ownership was also claimed by 'Free France', a government-in-exile under Charles de Gaulle. A struggle for colonial mastery broke out between these two – nicknamed *la guerre franco-française*. One by one the colonies were taken away from Vichy, often with the conspiritorial assistance of the British Commonwealth.[8]

New Zealand itself became involved in engineering a coup in the hundreds of tropical islands now known as French Polynesia, where the tiny white community was torn between loyalty to Vichy and to Free France. The majority Polynesian colonial subjects were not asked for their opinion. New Zealand had undertaken to Britain to help spread the influence of Free France in the French Pacific territories. Wellington sent a message to Jean de Géry, governor of the colony, ordering him to welcome a mission from New Zealand. The French administration tried to block the dominion by closing its consulate. The Union Steam Ship Company struck back on behalf of the New Zealand government by saying that none of its ships would now stop in Pape`ete.

Free French factions threw out the Vichy leadership; they claimed a plebiscite among the whites – which they had faked – had given them the authority to do so. New Zealand civil and naval officials steamed from Wellington to Pape`ete on the warship *Achilles* and landed in the colonial capital where they were met by leaders of the coup. The officials stayed for a month. The propaganda story was that the coup was a triumph for democracy.[9] French Polynesia became what one historian calls a 'stabilised' state 'on the side of the Allies'.[10] Fraser told citizens that the new regime in the colony had 'the support of the great bulk of the population, both French and Polynesian', and was 'freely and of its own desire co-operating' with the British Commonwealth.[11]

The sugar industry, the mainstay of the Fijian economy, was dominated by one of the richest businesses in all the island colonies of the Pacific: the Colonial Sugar Refinery Company. New Zealand soldiers sent to garrison the colony sang that their task was to safeguard the profits of company shareholders: 'There's fighting on in Egypt, but it's safer here by far; to hell with king and country, we'll defend the CSR'.

'WHITE MAN ALL GO HOME'

New Zealand did its best to play the brinkmanship game elsewhere, too, by strengthening its outposts in the Pacific. The war conference held in Wellington early in 1939 had agreed that the dominion should take on the task of building up army and air power in a line from the New Hebrides to Tonga.[12] The pivot of that line was Fiji.

Fiji was not a democracy. The biggest industry by far was sugar, and the biggest company by far was Colonial Sugar, owned by shareholders in New Zealand, Australia and Britain. Fijian tribes, which the colonial state saw as 'protected' people, had strong rights. Indian plantation workers, on the other hand, were not seen as protected people and had fewer rights. Wages and conditions for plantation workers, while they were set by the colonial state, were enforced by plantation owners who had the power of whipping. A 'reign of terror' was often the labour management method favoured by owners and their overseers, and the typical plantation was 'a self-contained autocracy'.[13] The government of the colony was autocratic too. A legislative council had some powers, but white settlers – a tiny minority in the colony – elected nearly one in three members of the council and the governor appointed most of the others; some were tribal chiefs of high rank.

New Zealand late in 1940 became the paramount power in the colony when Wellington cabled London to ask for – and was granted – the right to organise and oversee the whole military occupation of Fiji.[14]

Young men from many tribes volunteered for the Fiji Infantry Regiment, under the overseeing eye of officers from New Zealand. Fijians were quite keen to back the British Empire. Ratu Lala Sukuna, high chief with the most mana in the colony, believed, like many Māori chiefs, that going to war against the Axis would help the tribes gain ground in the government of their own country. Indian young men, however, seldom volunteered for the army. Indian businessmen set up a platoon and offered its services to the colony, but when those volunteers said they would only be willing to fight overseas if they were given the same pay and conditions as white soldiers, an angry colonial government disbanded the platoon.

Indians in Fiji on the whole saw the Fijians as pawns of imperialism, while Fijians on the whole grew 'increasingly resentful', in the words of an official report, of opposition to the war by Indians.[15] 'We found the Indian people generally on the island wary' and 'very anti-British', wrote a New Zealand army intelligence officer whose task was to spy on Indians.[16] He and other intelligence staff reported 'lots' of incidents of sabotage.[17] An airman in the New Zealand air force wrote about an encounter with a trader, one of the many thousands of unhappy Indians who wanted the men from the dominion to leave the colony.

Indian vendors at a market in Fiji. *Photographer: Leo White. Alexander Turnbull Library WA-03302-G.*

'All go home,' said the trader. 'Yes. White man all go home.'

'If we go, the Japanese might come,' said a companion of the airman. 'You mightn't like that.'

'Japan man no come here,' was the answer. 'White man go home now.'[18]

Indians were sometimes hanged for sedition by the colonial state.[19] Fijians were given praise and medals. The war, in other words, caused new conflict between the two racial groups in the colony. Indians were also subjected to taunting and bullying by men in the occupation army. Arthur Astwood, Maurice Hawker and James Bryant, for example, carried out a drunken attack and robbery against an Indian in Suva.[20]

New Zealand troops, together with the young men from the tribes who signed up, were too few for the colony to be occupied effectively. Troops were posted mostly at key strategic points: the harbours at Suva and Lautoka, and the airfields at Naurosi and Nadi. Armoured vehicles patrolled the roads in between, while commando units were set up at strong points.[21]

Tonga, another island state more or less a protectorate of New Zealand, was also pressed into mobilising. The kingdom, under the 'advice' of the dominion, had declared war on Germany in 1939 and set up the Tongan Defence Force. Officers for the new army were sent from New Zealand. Wellington further strengthened the military in the kingdom during the winter of 1941 by sending seventy officers and soldiers of the New Zealand army to train the troops fielded by Tonga, with a team of engineers to build a military airfield at Fua`amotu.[22]

Samoa was already able to field a little army. Turnbull, the colonial administrator, wondered now whether it would be wise to try to boost the ranks by allowing entry to

Queen Salote and New Zealand army officers reviewing barefoot troops of the Tonga Defence Force in Nuku`alofa, 1943. The Tongan army was both officered and organised by the New Zealand army. *Alexander Turnbull Library ATL: PA1-f-107-27-7.*

fit young men who were part white but mostly Samoan. The New Zealand army had laid down a 'fifty-fifty blood' ruling.[23] Berendsen, writing from Wellington, replied that it would be a good idea to loosen the ruling, because of 'the political consideration'.[24] He knew the Labour government would want a few Samoan faces in the ranks to make it seem as though the Samoan army was the army of the Samoans, not of the whites.

New Zealand also posted coastwatchers throughout the vast oceanic zone over which it had taken military oversight.

Coastwatchers had first been stationed on tropical islands soon after the outbreak of war, and during 1941 others were sent further north to set up new posts. Posts were built on seventeen atolls of the faraway British colony of the Gilbert and Ellice Islands. Wellington, by then, had become the radio headquarters of 'an immense network radiating north, south, and east across the Pacific'.[25] The task of coastwatchers was to observe and report on naval and air-force movements by Japan.

BRINKMANSHIP WITH JAPAN

The United States, meanwhile, pressed ahead with its brinkmanship against Japan. Roosevelt wanted his nation to become the paramount power in East Asia and the

Pacific.[26] He condemned the dictatorship of Japan. He strongly backed the dictatorship of the Guomindang in China and even secretly broke the neutrality laws of his government by financing and shipping arms to the Guomindang. He followed a policy of economic sanctions against Japan even though his administration knew that such a policy drove governing groups in Tokyo to look at do-or-die ways to break out of the stranglehold. United States military and economic planners were aware that they could afford to go to war against Japan and that, if they did so, they would win. Roosevelt was not only willing but in many ways eager to fight a war with Japan.[27]

The Japanese government since 1937 had been twisting and turning to find some way out of its nightmarish entanglement in China. Wellington kept to its policy of speaking about the Guomindang as the voice of democracy in China, despite a wealth of evidence to the contrary. 'China has withstood every crisis and shock,' wrote a book reviewer; 'each licking of her wounds leaves her more certain than ever that Japan will never be able to strike the knockout blow.'[28]

The Labour government found its head and its heart pulling in opposite ways. The heart was with the people of China against the Japanese air force and army. The head was aware of the need to back London, Canberra and Ottawa in a policy of trying to get along with Tokyo. The government propaganda office, on the outbreak of war with Germany, sent a secret circular to newspapers asking them not to publish any 'matter or comment which might in any way seem to reflect on Japan.'[29] The governments of Britain and New Zealand rubbed each other up the wrong way over the question for a few months in mid-1940, but those disagreements proved fleeting.[30]

The trigger for the war of words between Wellington and London was the fall of France.

The British government, wanting to reexamine its options now that it had lost such a key ally, asked the New Zealand and Australian governments what they thought about a plan to hold talks with Japan and the United States. Japan at the time was struggling with serious economic problems thanks to the burden of its fighting war in China and the trade war with the United States. The goal of talks between the three sides would be to get a guarantee of the 'territorial integrity' of the colonial holdings of Britain, France, the Netherlands and the United States, along with the 'independence and integrity' of China. The payback, for Tokyo, would be that the United States and the British Commonwealth would 'give Japan all financial and economic assistance and facilities in their power'. The British government also asked the New Zealand government what it thought of a proposal, should such talks not come about, to make concessions to Japan on matters 'not considered of capital importance' to the British Commonwealth.[31] Australia answered that it was willing to give ground to Tokyo.

New Zealand's answer was a provocative one.

The Labour government told the British and Australian governments that, while it agreed about the 'extreme undesirability of any act or omission on our part which might have the effect of unnecessarily precipitating trouble with Japan', it was 'most sceptical' about trying to talk Tokyo into cutting a deal with London and Washington. The Labour government spoke about what was 'morally right' as well as 'politically expedient'.[32] Wellington was once more trying to balance soft with hard motives in its foreign policy.

Wellington did not have enough weight in London to turn the imperial capital away from a temporising policy. The British government tried to keep in good with Tokyo by stopping military shipments to the Guomindang from British India. The Labour government was very unhappy. Wellington cabled London at the end of July to say, 'we neither understand nor sympathise with the policy'; the concession to Japan was 'at the expense of China' and 'a violation of international undertakings to which we are a party'. Also, the concession might cause 'misunderstanding and resentment in the United States of America'. The New Zealand government only made these points in secret diplomatic documents, however; it said nothing openly to its citizens.[33]

The Labour government at the same time was working hard to get closer to the United States. Fraser was so nervous about Japan that he and his government became prey to a longing for a powerful protector, prompted by a startling secret cable to Wellington from London saying that if Tokyo went to war the British would most likely not be able to send a large war fleet into the Pacific. The best thing to do, concluded the cable, would be to 'rely on the United States'. The Labour government found the cable 'almost apocalyptic', in the words of Frederick Wood. Fraser sent a stiff cable to Churchill. New Zealand, he pointed out, had done all its military planning on the understanding that Britain would make good its promise to send a war fleet into the Pacific if hostilities broke out with Japan.[34]

The Labour government decided to open direct diplomatic dealings with the government of the United States.

Japan, meanwhile, was wallowing in deep waters, not only stuck in China but also on the back foot in its relations with a very assertive United States, and not sure what to do about the Soviet Union or the British Commonwealth.

Tokyo had been shocked and downhearted when the Nazi–Soviet non-aggression pact was signed late in 1939, provoking fears of encirclement and breaking a promise by Berlin not to sign any separate treaty with Moscow.[35] A trade war with the United States opened that year too, when Washington ended a longstanding trade agreement with Tokyo. Tokyo turned elsewhere for help, signing a treaty of military alliance with Berlin and Rome in September 1940, hoping that the treaty also would be signed by Chongqing. Tension grew between Washington and Tokyo. Empires eyeballed one another in East Asia and the Pacific.

'JAPAN IS EVER READY TO NEGOTIATE'

Historians have sometimes portrayed the coming of war between Wellington and Tokyo as a tsunami sweeping down from the north, beyond New Zealand's control. The language they use is often doom-laden. Nancy Taylor, not prone to overstatement, called one chapter of her history of the home front 'The menace of Japan'.[36] Britain could no longer give naval 'protection' to the dominion – the argument goes – so the Labour government had to 'look to America'. The assumption, in other words, was that Japan was a threat to the dominion and that Wellington could do nothing other than seek a powerful ally.[37] The government itself used the metaphor of ocean waves: Fraser told factory workers in Christchurch that 'the tide of war' was 'rolling up' to the shores of New Zealand.[38]

The truth, however, was far more complex.

Tokyo was hard pressed by the manoeuvres of other states; it did not need more enemies. The imperial government would likely have been happy to talk with a delegation from Wellington, certainly from Canberra; and it may well have been willing to come to an agreement to draw some sort of line across the seas dividing a Japanese sphere of influence from a sphere held by Australia and New Zealand. It was known that the United States policy of blockading Japan was leading to a feeling of entrapment in Toyko. Nash, for example, spoke later about Western states sowing the seeds of war by not letting 'their goods flow' to Japan.[39] The influential *New Zealand Herald* asked astutely: 'Why did the Allies adopt a policy towards Japan that made war inevitable?' The 'primary responsibility for provoking war with Japan' could be laid at the door of Roosevelt, the editorial said, before dealing out some of the blame to Churchill.[40]

Matsuoka Yosuke was Japanese foreign minister when Fraser made the 'tide of war' speech. He never spoke about a need to gain control of Australia or New Zealand. China and the United States, in his opinion, were the two countries that held the key to prosperity and safety for Japan. He wanted a peace treaty with the Guomindang. He wanted friendship with the United States. The overall goal was to set up a free-trade zone in the western Pacific, led by Japan and China, alongside another in the eastern Pacific, led by the United States. The two zones 'would engage in friendly competition and cooperation'.[41] Matsuoka saw the main threat as the Soviet Union.[42]

Wellington would have been wise to send a mission or two to Tokyo, given the growing feeling that Japan was a 'menace'. Politicians and officials on such a mission could have taken a good look at the country, made contacts, spoken to the Japanese government and tried to come to some sort of understanding.

No mission was sent. The New Zealand government continued to get most of its news about Japan by way of London.

The unwillingness to talk to Tokyo can be blamed mostly on closed minds, a lack of independent thinking among political leaders in Wellington. Fraser, Nash and their colleagues nearly all wanted to stick closely to states that supposedly shared the same vital interests and whose people were 'kith and kin' – at least for those of British ancestry in New Zealand. Yet what was good for Britain, or its governing groups, was not always good for New Zealand. Once or twice some members of parliament wondered about handling things differently. A 'very distinguished' visitor from Japan called a gathering of members of parliament on one occasion to talk frankly about the risk of war breaking out. He proposed that the dominion convene an international conference to talk it over, and that invitations be sent to the Soviet Union, Guomindang China, Canada, the United States, Mexico, Peru, Chile and Australia. Some supported the idea – among them Clyde Carr, who spoke about it to Fraser.

'Well,' answered the prime minister, 'Japan might not like it.'

'Why not include Japan?' said Carr.[43]

The government was having none of it. Coates wrote in his diary that the war cabinet was, in his words, 'for action' if the Japanese government showed 'hostility'.[44] Only now and then did the New Zealand government speak to the Japanese government, and then only by way of the consulate in Wellington.

A typical encounter with the consulate occurred when Fraser called Nakafuji Norito, Japanese consul-general, to a meeting.

Tokyo at the time was trying to get some sort of trade deal with the Dutch East Indies. New Zealand imported oil from that vast colony, which meant among other things that it would be canny for the dominion to be on good terms with whatever state controlled its oilfields. New Zealand also imported most of its rubber from British Malaya. A government that aimed to look after the needs of New Zealand ought perhaps to deal very diplomatically with any strong state that might also see itself as having an economic stake in Southeast Asia. Fraser did speak some soothing words: he claimed that New Zealanders felt 'none but the most friendly feelings towards Japan' and that his government was 'most anxious' that there be 'no trouble' in the Pacific. The prime minister was stubborn and provocative, nevertheless. He told Nakafuji that the continued control of Southeast Asia by the Netherlands and the British Empire was 'vital' to New Zealand. He spoke about the 'need' for the British Empire to control Singapore. And he added a threat: if war broke out between Britain and Japan, New Zealand would go to war too.

Nakafuji replied that his own government found itself without any friends in the world. Tokyo had not yet joined the Axis. Presumably, he did not say that it was only through the use of war and threats of war that Britain and the Netherlands had taken control of Southeast Asia in the first place, and that they continued to use force to keep control against the wishes of most of the colonised people.[45]

The meeting ended, the two sides having achieved nothing.

The New Zealand government was wasting an opportunity. Fraser and other leaders of his government believed that there was a danger of war with Japan, and that if a

Japan and the United States vying to pick the 'forbidden apple' of the Dutch East Indies. *Artist: J.C. Hill.* Auckland Star, *20 April 1940.*

war broke out it might lead to raids, maybe even an attack, on New Zealand. They thought that the best way to try to stop such a war was by standing alongside London and Washington. Was that the best policy? London was a long way from Tokyo and the Japanese navy was never likely to be sighted anywhere near the English Channel. Churchill and his government saw Japan very much as a secondary problem for British policy. Washington, too, was not only a long way from Wellington and Tokyo but bent on expanding its power in East Asia even at the cost of war with Japan. Would it not have made sense to try to safeguard New Zealand by letting Japan know that the dominion would follow a neutral policy in any war in the Pacific?

A war in the Pacific, like the war with Germany, would be won or lost no matter what was done or not done by New Zealand. Wellington had the luxury of choosing to go in or to stay out.

Fraser did take care to make occasional public utterances of a diplomatic sort, which he knew would be sent on to Tokyo by Japanese consular staff in Wellington. On one occasion he announced, 'our Japanese friends know that we are friendly and will remain friendly'.[46] War, after all, was still only one of the options being weighed behind locked doors of governing groups in Washington and Tokyo. The two countries were both equally 'intent upon avoiding' war early in 1941. The balance shifted only when Germany attacked the Soviet Union. Washington straightaway hardened its stance in talks with Tokyo. Tokyo hardened its stance too, after agonising over whether to simply throw in its hand and let the United States become the dominant power in the western Pacific and East Asia.[47]

New Zealand diplomacy was not helped, meanwhile, by the speeches of some members of parliament. 'New Zealand,' announced conservative lawyer William Perry in the upper house of parliament, 'is living in the shadow of a menace that is growing, not daily, but hourly greater.'[48]

Tokyo heard about the tactless speech. Nakafuji made an answering statement in Wellington: he told the prime minister that economic expansion southward was 'indispensable' to the 'very national existence' of Japan. Tokyo, he offered, was 'ever ready to negotiate' with any state 'on the principle of mutual prosperity.'[49] The Labour government did not take up the offer to open a dialogue with Tokyo.

It did, however, decide to open direct dealings with the United States.

Wellington, along with Canberra, had been sending diplomatic feelers to Washington since late 1940. This made good sense, given the truth about naval power in the Pacific. What did not make good sense was that nobody in Wellington governing circles seems even to have considered that a mission to Tokyo might be helpful in light of the country's need to navigate a safe course for the small vessel of its own interests between the mighty battleships of the two great ocean powers.

Conflict was worsened, in many ways, by the aggressive brinkmanship of Washington. Cordell Hull, secretary of state for the Roosevelt government, in April 1941 presented Japan with a statement of four 'principles' which Washington claimed were the only acceptable basis for policy. The 'territorial integrity and sovereignty of each and all nations' was one of the principles, supposedly. The principle of 'non-interference in the internal affairs of other countries' was another; and a third was 'the principle of equality.'[50] The United States had a long history of not respecting the territorial integrity and sovereignty of its neighbours in the Pacific and Latin America, and a long history of interference in the internal affairs of states in both regions. It did not honour the principle of equality even when dealing with its own African American or Native American citizens, let alone its colonial subjects in Hawai`i, Samoa, Guam or Puerto Rico.

Fraser was working hard, by then, to let the United States know that the republic could do almost nothing wrong in the eyes of the government of New Zealand. 'There is no country,' he told Washington in a secret diplomatic message in February 1941, 'to the friendship of which we attach more importance than the United States.'[51]

A longing for protection quickly became a kowtowing towards the United States. The Labour government threw a state dinner for senior officers of a visiting American naval squadron at the beginning of autumn. Fraser spoke fulsomely about friendship between the two nations. Coates spoke as fulsomely.

'You have great friends here,' he told the officers. 'It is going to be a stern struggle, and we want your help.'[52]

Coates went on a mission to Washington soon afterwards to talk about weapons supply, along with Frank Langstone, who was to handle trade talks and begin setting up a diplomatic post. Fraser, when he was in London during the northern summer, spoke to the United States ambassador of his hopes and fears about Japan and the British Commonwealth; when he visited Washington afterwards he said that his government would agree to 'any' military understanding that the United States might offer New Zealand.[53] The state department in Washington responded by drawing up a proposal that was signed off by Roosevelt. India was to be given its own parliament and full freedom and democracy. New Delhi would then go into a military alliance with Wellington, Canberra and Chonqing, backed by Washington. The scheme came to nothing, however, because London vetoed it. Churchill was dead set against granting democracy to India.[54]

Coates and Langstone on their mission to court the Roosevelt administration in Washington. No such mission was sent to court the Konoe ministry in Tokyo.
Artist J.C. Hill. Auckland Star, *10 May 1941.*

New Zealand was now courting the United States eagerly because Tokyo had joined the Axis. Konoe Fumimaro, prime minister, wished to strengthen the position of Japan without going to war, and believed he could do so by linking up with Italy and Germany.[55] The Soviet Union and the United States would no longer view Japan as a state to be bullied easily, he thought, and instead would need to take account of its powerful friends. Tokyo was of the opinion, on the whole, that there was a need to stand up to the United States. 'A humble attitude will only prompt the United States to become domineering,' said Konoe.[56] Wellington made the mistake, however, of thinking that the alliance meant Japan was getting ready to go to war against the British Commonwealth.

British chiefs of staff looked into the matter and sent an appraisal of the military situation to New Zealand. The chiefs told Wellington that 'no serious threat' to New Zealand was likely unless Japan got hold of British Malaya and the Dutch East Indies. The British Commonwealth, they added, would be wise to 'induce the Dutch to resist any territorial demands' by Japan on its colonial holdings. Japan, for the foreseeable future, they believed, would 'try to avoid war with the British Empire and the United States'. A war, were it to break out, would not be a grave threat to the dominions in the Southwest Pacific. Japanese troopship convoys would need to be shielded by warships, which would be a heavy burden for the Japanese navy. 'The scale of attack on Australia or New Zealand would be likely, therefore, to be limited to cruiser raids,' concluded the

A Japanese propaganda poster: 'Manifesto for Greater East Asian Cooperation'. Tokyo saw Southeast Asia as crucial for the Japanese economy and, in the long run, for safeguarding Japanese status as a great power having to cope with the wealth and power of the Soviet Union and the United States. Japanese citizens were also encouraged to believe that they could help the peoples of Asia to be freed from control by the imperial powers of Europe.
http://2bangkok.com/wwiipropaganda.shtml

report, 'possibly combined with a light scale of seaborne air attack against ports.'[57]

Churchill backed up the military appraisal in a secret letter to Fraser. Japan, he wrote, was not likely to go to war unless Germany successfully invaded Britain. Japan was unlikely to attack Singapore, even in the event of such a war; and Singapore, if it was attacked, could cope with a long siege. Churchill then went on to talk about whether or not Japan might try to attack New Zealand:

> *We think this very unlikely, first because Japan is absorbed in China, secondly, would be gathering rich prizes in the Dutch East Indies, and thirdly, would fear very much to send an important part of her fleet far to the southward, leaving the American fleet between it and home.*[58]

The Dutch East Indies certainly had become the goal of much of Japanese economic and foreign policy. Ozaki Yukio, a leading politician, voiced the opinion of many when he told parliament in Tokyo early in 1941 that there was a pressing need for the British Empire, the French Empire, the Netherlands and the United States to end their monopolistic 'special privileges' in Southeast Asia. The oil, rubber, tin and other resources of colonies should be made available to all nations 'on a fair basis'.[59] A bureau had been set up inside the foreign ministry to try to make meaningful plans for developing trade and foreign policy in Southeast Asia. The bureau also handled trade and foreign policy for Oceania, Australia and New Zealand.[60] Military and naval planners now agreed with economic and foreign policy officials that the wisest way for Japan to widen its prospects was by peacefully moving southwards, above all into the Dutch East Indies. Matsuoka therefore opened negotiations with the colonial government in the capital, Batavia, asking for repeal of restrictions on Japanese economic activity in the colony, development of resources together, and stepped-up export of resources needed by Japan.[61]

The new policy of the Japanese government, in other words, was to try to gather Southeast Asia into an economic bloc led by Tokyo. The policy of the United States administration, as before, was to keep its investments in China and its colonial holdings in the Philippines. A deal of some sort was still a possibility. Tokyo, in March 1941, while it was talking earnestly with Batavia, also opened negotiations with Washington.

Not long after those talks opened, London asked dominion governments whether the British Commonwealth ought to tighten economic screws on Tokyo. Wellington answered that 'the circumstances are now exceedingly delicate' and 'any unnecessary irritation at the present juncture would be unwise'. The Commonwealth should apply economic pressure on Tokyo only if Japanese troops moved into Southeast Asia, and only 'in co-operation with or with the knowledge and sympathy' of the United States.[62] Wellington by now was unwilling to do anything that might not be backed by Washington.

The United States tightened the economic screws itself, in July. All assets owned by Japanese citizens or companies in all territories controlled by Washington were frozen, and at the same time Washington imposed a total trade embargo. The Netherlands quickly froze Japanese assets in its territory too, and imposed its own embargo. The British Commonwealth followed the same policy. New Zealand copied the others; the war cabinet sought to give what it called 'full co-operation to the United States'.[63] Wellington ended the trade treaty signed with Tokyo in 1928. Trade had withered away to nearly nothing anyway.

Tokyo reeled. A total trade war, thrust down its throat while it was holding diplomatic talks with Washington and Batavia, seemed like bullying and double-dealing. The trade embargo was a very heavy blow against the Japanese economy, as dominion newspapers noted:

> *Japan is almost wholly dependent on American and Dutch oil, on rubber from Malaya and the Dutch East Indies, on wool from the British Empire, on fertilisers from India and on minerals and metals from many sources, most of them controlled by Britain or the United States.*[64]

Tokyo was also troubled by the war between the Soviet Union and Germany. Moscow had only just signed a non-aggression pact with Tokyo. Germany went to war against the Soviet Union without asking for, let alone getting, agreement from Japan. One group of powerful people in Tokyo now argued that Japan should walk out of the Axis. Another group argued that the sow's ear could be turned into a silk purse if Japan broke the non-aggression pact and joined Germany in the attack on Moscow. Matsuoka, for example, spoke up for an invasion of Siberia, which nearly everyone in governing circles had long since seen as a good way to expand the Japanese Empire. Only, would such a war be winnable? Soviet armies two years before had beaten Japanese forces in Manchuria.[65]

Konoe and his government at an imperial conference on 2 July decided to make a bid for economic and, if need be, military power in French Indochina, British Malaya,

British Burma and the Dutch East Indies. Tokyo would still do its best, meanwhile, to work out some way to peacefully settle its disagreements with Washington.

The first step was to be in French Indochina.

JAPAN'S 'INDO-CHINA ADVENTURE'

French Indochina was in the hands of Vichy. Tokyo asked for the right to field troops in Tonkin and Vichy agreed. Japanese troops had been stationed elsewhere in the colony for some months already. Tokyo wished not only to get a springboard in Southeast Asia but to gain better access to the Guomindang provinces of China. Tonkin, together with Annam, Cochinchina, Laos and Cambodia made up what the French bureaucracy classed as a *colonie d'exploitation* – what one historian calls a 'cash cow' for France. The colony was so profitable for its imperial owner that on the eve of the war it had been sending a net yield of around $200 million yearly to Paris.[66] Wealth taken from its peasantry was spent on weapons, warplanes and warships in order to keep a grip on the colony while also boosting French imperialism elsewhere in the world.[67] The colony was a police state, too.[68] Nationalist revolts broke out late in 1940; they were put down by French troops, machine guns and warplanes going to work methodically.

'We were cruel,' said one French military man. 'We had to show our strength to those who remained loyal.'[69]

New Zealand behaved, in spite of this dark record of colonialism, as though French Indochina was somehow a bulwark of freedom and democracy. Nash said in a radio broadcast that the new move was 'Japanese aggression' and 'a matter of grave moment to all countries in the Pacific'.[70] Newspapers backed him, then went on to wonder what the next step might be in Southeast Asia.

'Pacific peace is menaced by Japan's new Indo-China adventure,' declared the *Evening Post*, 'and the outcome, either at short range or at long range, is unpredictable.'[71]

One outcome was the trade embargo, together with the freezing of Japanese assets, imposed by the United States, the Netherlands, Britain, Australia and New Zealand.

Thailand became the next hotspot.

France and Britain had browbeaten the Thai kingdom for many years, having annexed whole provinces and added them to their holdings in French Indochina, British Burma and British Malaya. Thailand was now making the most of disarray in its corner of the world by trying to get back territory seized over thirty years ago by France. A war between the kingdom and the Vichy colonial government broke out in the spring of 1940; it ended the following autumn when Tokyo acted as middleman between Hanoi and Bangkok. Tokyo had been wondering whether it might make sense to form an alliance with Bangkok but chose not to do so because it would upset London and Washington.

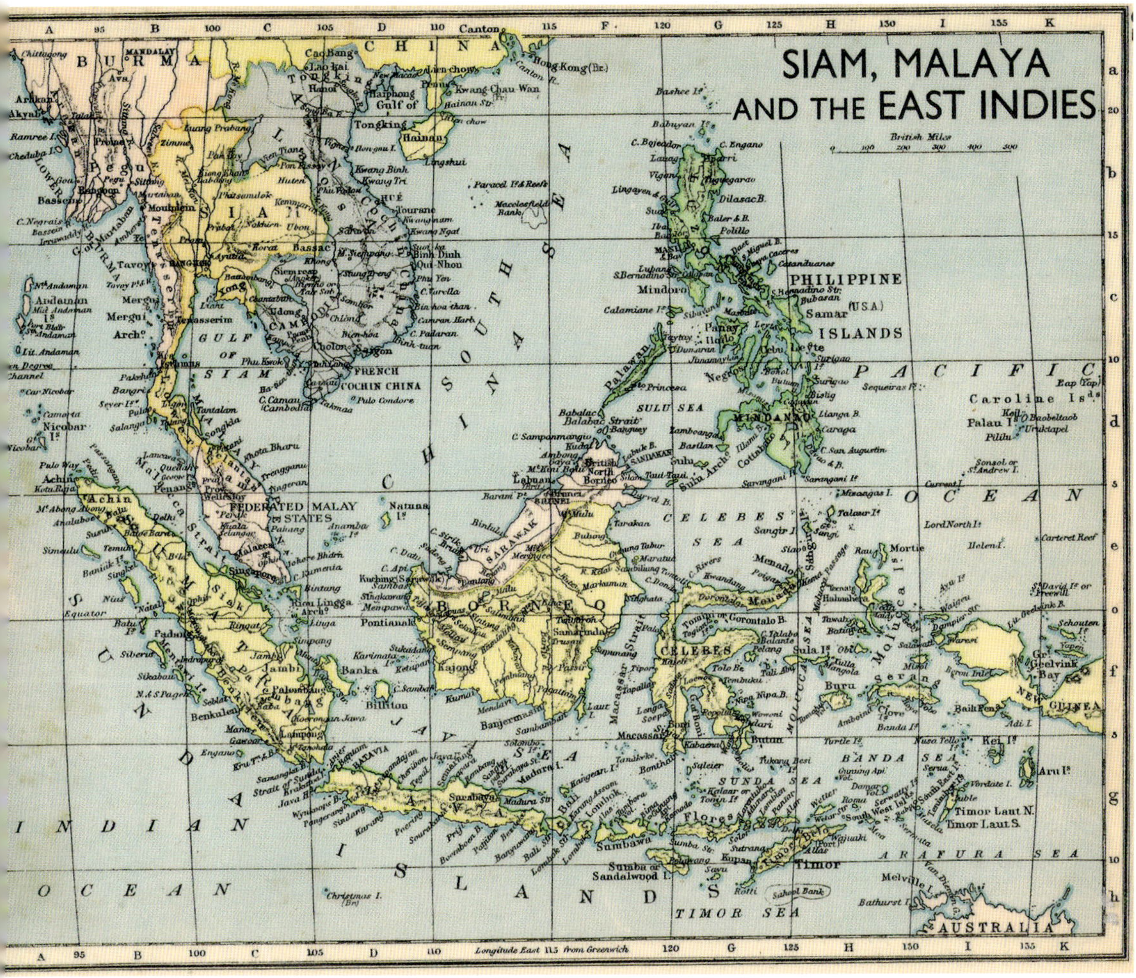

Southeast Asia in 1939. The region was almost wholly controlled by Western imperial states; Thailand had the only independent government. The Modern Pictorial World Atlas *(Auckland: New Zealand Newspapers Ltd, 1939).*

Bangkok now played its own card by sending secret messages to London and Washington. The messages sought what the Thai government called 'a public statement by London and Washington that they will not allow the sovereignty and neutrality' of the kingdom to be 'impaired' by pressure from Tokyo.[72] The United States and Britain decided to make such a statement. Canada agreed with Britain, as did Australia.

New Zealand, on the other hand, drew back.

National Party politicians and newspapers nearly all agreed that the dominion ought to give a guarantee to Bangkok. The *Auckland Star* claimed there could be no doubt of 'the peril' to the British Commonwealth if Japan gained power over Thailand.[73] The *New Zealand Herald* observed that many people now saw Thailand as 'the touchstone of war or peace in the Far East, just as Poland became the touchstone in the West'.[74] The Labour government, however, said that it doubted both 'the practicability' and 'the wisdom' of giving a guarantee to Thailand.[75] Churchill wrote to Fraser that the outlook was now good because ranks were closing against Japan; Tokyo was 'plunged in deep anxiety and hesitation'. The Soviet Union was 'coming into line' alongside the British Commonwealth and the United States in a common front against the Japanese Empire.

'I cannot believe that the Japanese will face the combination now developing around them,' concluded Churchill. 'We may therefore regard the situation not only as more favourable but as less tense.'[76]

Tokyo and Washington were still keeping up their negotiations, still seeking some sort of treaty, but as talks dragged on they yielded nothing. The two sides were now drawing up highly secret plans to attack one another should they not find a way to strike a deal. Tokyo decided in the first week of September that if nothing came of the talks after a month then it would need to go to war – and soon – against the United States, the Netherlands and the British Commonwealth. Army and navy planners got to work quickly.[77] Britain, the Netherlands and the United States, meanwhile, held a war meeting in the third week of September in Singapore to plan an attack on the Japanese Empire. The meeting was convened with the knowledge and approval of the government of New Zealand. The three powers agreed, in the words of the document they signed, to open a campaign of 'propaganda, terrorism, and sabotage'.[78] They also agreed to build up their firepower in the region as quickly as they could, ready to begin shooting.

The United States was working around the clock to amass military might in China and Southeast Asia. A fleet of bombers assembled in the Philippines and in the provinces of China held by the Guomindang.[79] George Marshall, a United States general, soon announced that the fleet was 'the greatest concentration of bombing strength in the world'. Japanese cities, he added, were 'very vulnerable', as were their naval bases.[80]

The British Commonwealth was also working around the clock to build up military strength in Malaya.

RUBBER, TIN, OIL

Malaya was a patchwork of colonies and protectorates centred on the big port city of Singapore. The *New Zealand Herald* declared that the frontier of the dominion was 'now in Malaya'.[81] The states of Malaya were no more a democracy than French Indochina or Guomindang China. Britain had taken the states bit by bit during the nineteenth century, mostly through 'gunboat diplomacy'. A last territory had been seized in 1909 from an unwilling Thailand. Malayan Chinese, who mostly wanted independence, backed either the Guomindang or the Communist Party. Malays seldom felt warmly about their imperial overlords.

'It has to be realised,' observed Lewis Moss, a mining engineer from Otago who worked for five years in Malaya, 'that the native races of the East would in many cases rather be controlled by Japan … than by Britain.'[82]

Malaya yielded about 60 per cent of the rubber and 30 per cent of the tin output of the whole world, and the biggest buyer was the United States.[83] Washington as well as London, therefore, had a strong stake in not letting that tin and rubber go to Tokyo. The white people who controlled the colony were often 'whisky-swilling rubber planters' seeking nothing more than 'the exploitation of the cheap native labour in order to reap fabulous fortunes from the rubber markets of the world', claimed the *Bay of Plenty Beacon*.[84] Workers were cheap – whether on rubber plantations, in tin mines or as servants in private households. 'In the intense heat of the day the hostess would just clap her hands and the boy would come and pass anything to her,' wrote novelist Nelle Scanlan about her stay with a white family during a visit to Malaya.[85] 'Rotten to the core' was how Max Boyd, a New Zealand air-force mechanic in a squadron sent to strengthen imperial forces in the colony, saw the colonial hierarchy.[86] William Mitchell, one of a group of dominion air-force riggers, was struck by what he called the 'luxurious lifestyle of the Europeans, and the poverty and dirt and degradation of the native population' in Malaya.[87]

Military strengthening of the colony was based on the notion of a fortress in Singapore. Ernest Bysshe sent reports to dominion newspapers about the build-up. 'Singapore,' he wrote breathlessly, 'key to military strategy in the Far East, sentinel for India and the Pacific.'

The city, he told readers, was the centre of eight shipping routes. Troops were encamped in its suburbs. Offshore were anchored 'great grey warships'. Churchill had said that the city would be held 'no matter what'.[88] The pilots of three fighter squadrons stationed in the region were nearly all members of the New Zealand air force, while other airmen from the dominion were in bomber and flying-boat squadrons, signalling, engineering and armoury.[89] New Zealand soldiers were also dotted through the officer ranks of the imperial army in Malaya and Burma. Others were officers in the 'Indian' army, deployed by Britain to attack Italian Somaliland, Eritrea and Ethiopia at the expense of the taxpayers of India. Now those taxpayers were to carry the cost of fighting a war against Japan, should war break out, although it would be hard to say why such a war would be of any help to many of the subject peoples of India.

Military strengthening was also under way in the neighbouring colony, the Dutch East Indies.

The Dutch East Indies was 'the last bulwark of democracy in the Far East' – or so said the *Auckland Star*.[90] The vast colony upheld 'freedom, democracy and international good faith', claimed the *Star-Sun*.[91] Wellington told London and Canberra as early as the spring of 1940 that it wanted the British Commonwealth to undertake to declare war if Japan attacked the colony.[92] The guarantee came at last in the first days of summer in 1941, when London announced that it had taken on 'the duty of safeguarding and

Japan's dilemma: to steer a path between coalitions of other great powers. Tokyo during 1940 and 1941 weighed up possible alliances, or at least understandings, with Germany, Italy, Vichy France, Thailand, the United States, the Netherlands and the British Commonwealth. *Artist J.C. Hill.* Auckland Star, *5 October 1940.*

restoring the possessions and rights' of the Netherlands. Nothing was said about restoring the rights of the subject peoples in the colony.[93] London asked for backing from Wellington. Wellington agreed, so long as the guarantee was also backed by Washington.[94]

All those capitals knew that getting an agreement with the colony for free trade in oil and other exports or, failing that, taking control of its islands, was vital to Tokyo.

The Dutch East Indies was a harsh and highly stratified colonial state whose cause was not very obviously the cause of democracy. The New Zealand government had a blind spot about colonies held by the Allies and the United States. Fraser, for example, warned Tokyo that it would not be good for any nation to try 'to impose, under any guise or any pretext, any particular conception of government or social conditions on other people'. Tokyo could have pointed out that such impositions were already to be found in British Malaya, British Burma, French Indochina and the Dutch East Indies, along with the New Zealand holdings of Nauru, Niue, the Cook Islands and Samoa.

'This is the Oil War,' wrote a shrewd journalist. 'No New Zealander can afford not to look at the world's oil map.'[95]

The Dutch East Indies and British Commonwealth trade and business were linked through Royal Dutch Shell, an oil company crucial to both Britain and New Zealand. The oil industry was worked by indentured coolie labourers, mostly Javanese. Coolies signed contracts as bond workers for three years; often they were rounded up by police and made to sign such contracts. Coolies spoke about the work as selling their soul, or *jual jiwa*.[96] Coolie ordinances imposed by the colonial state aimed to get work done at the lowest possible wage. Whipping, beating and kicking were used to keep workers in order on plantations, in mines and on the oilfields.[97]

Colonial subjects seldom took kindly to being worked or taxed by the faraway imperial overlord. Only small groups of people in the Dutch East Indies believed they did well from being imperial subjects; the mass felt indifference or hostility. A series of uprisings in western Java and Sumatra in 1926 ended only when the Dutch air force and army bombed or burnt villages, shot resisters and crammed the prisons with 13,000 people, more than 1000 of whom found themselves behind the wires of a concentration camp in New Guinea. Afterwards, other protesters challenged the state. The colonial government took the stern step in 1935 of outlawing the rights of the subject peoples to free association and assembly.

The Dutch East Indies officer corps held three rounds of talks in Singapore and Batavia with delegates from London, Wellington and Canberra. Washington sent delegates along too. The talks led the colonial government to believe it had more or less a blank cheque of military backing, at least from the British Commonwealth, to begin a policy of brinkmanship instead of diplomacy in dealings with Tokyo.[98] Batavia consequently called off trade talks with Japan and joined the trade embargo by the United States, Britain, Australia and New Zealand.

The colony was doing its best to back Tokyo into a very awkward corner likely to end in war.

Indonesian nationalists were unhappy: they were keen to get a treaty signed between Batavia and Tokyo. Japanese trade and investment, nationalists believed, would make life better for colonial subjects because goods would be cheaper and the economy would develop more quickly.[99] Indonesians as a whole were still less happy when the colonial government imposed military conscription in the middle of 1941, provoking nationalists to set up their own representative body, the Majelis Rakyat Indonesia, the Indonesian People's Council. A lot of its members looked to Japan for help.[100]

New Zealand never made its offer to back the colony conditional on democracy being granted to the subject peoples of the colony. Guests at a state lunch held in Wellington to welcome two powerful Netherlands politicians – the foreign minister and colonial minister – heard Nash speak fulsomely about a heritage of freedom shared by New Zealand and the Netherlands. The Dutch, he added, knew they could 'count on' New Zealand.[101]

ATTACK

The strengthening of colonial holdings in Southeast Asia was aimed at not only defence but attack. Marshall told the press in his secret briefing that the United States was 'preparing an offensive war against Japan',[102] even though Washington was still going through the motions of holding talks with Tokyo. A shake-up of power, meanwhile, was under way in Tokyo. Konoe hoped for a peaceful settlement with Washington, while Tojo Hideki, army minister, wanted to give up talks and start fighting. A widespread sense of encirclement and entrapment went with a feeling that the country was about to go bankrupt. Tojo summed up his viewpoint:

> *Two years from now we will have no petroleum for military use. Ships will stop moving. When I think about the strengthening of American defences in Southeast Asia, the expansion of the American fleet, the unfinished China Incident, and so on, I see no end to difficulties … I fear that we would become a third-class nation after two or three years if we just sat tight.*[103]

The only hope – a poor hope – was a quick war before the odds became even more overwhelming.

'We all wonder if there isn't some way to proceed peacefully,' said Tsukuda Keiji, army vice-chief of staff. 'On the other hand, it is not possible to sustain the status quo.'[104]

Konoe resigned. Tojo formed a cabinet. Foreign policy, the new cabinet decided, must somehow be shaped to stop the tightening grip of the embargo. Tojo told the Roosevelt administration that Japan would pull out of French Indochina and nearly the whole of China, and sign an agreement for free trade in Asia, on condition that the United States agreed to impose free trade throughout the whole world. He may have hoped that this proposal would work; or he may have hoped that Roosevelt would turn it down in a way that would outflank those in Tokyo who sought to appease Washington.

'I hope to reach an accommodation with the United States,' he said to one of his officials, 'whatever it takes.'[105]

Washington would not budge, however, and the question of whether or not to go to war was debated for one last time by governing groups in Tokyo. Hara Yoshimichi, president of the privy council, declared that Tokyo had made 'one concession after another' when dealing with Washington but had received no answer that was not 'utterly conceited, obstinate, and disrespectful'. The existence of the nation was so fundamentally threatened now that it must go to war, he said; 'there is nothing else we can do'.[106] The imperial council on 1 December resolved that war would begin within a few days.

Tokyo's perception of its own demands as reasonable and the demands of Washington as unreasonable was hardly the whole truth, it goes without saying. Japanese imperialists, like the British imperialists they followed in so many ways, were not given to wondering why others were upset by their expansionist policy. The fact remains, however, that Japanese leaders, not least those like Tojo who took a hawkish stance, justified their policy through the language of concessions and coexistence even when that policy caused something that was very much the opposite.

Japanese policy certainly led to outright war. At the same time, Japanese policy did not take place in a vacuum.

New Zealand meanwhile was kowtowing more and more deeply to the United States. Fraser and his inner group fretted nightly, now, about the likelihood of war with Japan. The United States was the sole possible counterweight and also, they believed, the only safeguard for New Zealand. A British foreign affairs official wrote secretly and sarcastically about the way Wellington was showing an 'increasing tendency to worship' Washington.[107] An 'almost pathetically enthusiastic reception', in the private words of the United States consul-general, welcomed two high-ranking officers from the American air force when they came to Wellington for talks early in November.[108]

Yet while the leaders of the Labour government were fretting, and flattering, many other leaders of public opinion were far more breezy. The Asian correspondent for the *Press*, for example, wrote an article outlining the military weakness of the Japanese Empire. He noted that although Japanese troops had driven deeply into China they had often 'found it impossible, or inexpedient, to hold their gains'. He noted also that Japan had been beaten in its border war with the Soviet Union. Tokyo would be behaving with 'sheer madness' if it sought to conquer new territory while it was still bogged down in China.[109]

The two sides – the Japanese and the Western powers – drew up secret plans for attack in Southeast Asia.

Tokyo hoped to gain enough ground to win what a general staff study called 'self-sufficiency and economic invincibility'.[110] Afterwards, the country would seek a peace treaty. The odds for the struggle, noted Tsukuda, were 'not bright'.[111] The nation would be ruined unless it went to war, thought Nagano Osami, chief of naval staff.

'Even if there is war,' he added, 'the country may be ruined.'[112]

Quick attacks were the chosen tactics. Japan would try to neutralise, or take, all territory held by other powers on the way to the Dutch East Indies. Thailand would become an ally. The Dutch East Indies would be safeguarded by occupying the two flanks, Burma and the Solomon Islands. The weight of weaponry brought to bear could not be imposing: some troops and planes would have to be kept back in case of attack by the Soviet Union, and others would need to stay in China to cope with communist guerrillas and the Guomindang. Only eleven of the fifty-one divisions of the army were to be deployed to fight for Southeast Asia. The Japanese navy was better off than the army – its fleet was the biggest in the Pacific – but its shipyards lacked anything like the building capacity of the United States.

The British Commonwealth, backed by the United States, decided to open the war by violating the neutrality of an independent state.

The plan was to land troops on the Kra isthmus and then take over the whole of southern Thailand. Britain sought backing from Australia and New Zealand. A message to Wellington pointed out that 'great tactical advantage lies with the side which gets there first'.[113] The war cabinet in Wellington answered that it would be 'desirable' to talk to the government of Thailand, and that the United States would need to be 'in general agreement'. Cabinet ended by saying, however, that it felt it was not 'in a position to pass any considered judgment of real value on some of the considerations outlined'.[114] Washington was less wishy-washy. Roosevelt privately promised Churchill that if war with Japan came about thanks to a British Commonwealth invasion of Thailand, then Washington would go to war against Tokyo.

Tokyo, as it happened, struck the first big blow.

'Surprise attack successful!' was the message sent to the imperial capital on 7 December by an attack fleet off Hawai`i.[115] Onozuka Kiheiji, retired president of Tokyo Imperial University, was dining with a colleague when he heard about the sinkings in Pearl Harbor.

'This means,' he whispered to a colleague, 'that Japan is sunk too.'[116]

JAPANESE COMING, REGARDS TO ALL

Japanese troops crowded into trains and troopships, were shunted out of the Japanese Empire and landed on the islands and peninsulas of Southeast Asia. Ooka Shohei, whose novel *Fires on the Plain* would later be one of the literary masterpieces of the Second World War, was on a troopship heading to the Philippines. He looked out at the warm water and saw a world of alienating colour and geometry.

> *The dark blue, monochrome sea stretched out in all directions to form a perfect circle girded by the horizon; the waters seemed to be forced up all round the circumference, so that we, who were in the centre, occupied a sort of hollow ... With the regular sound of waves lapping the sides of the ship, and the monotonous hum of diesel engines, the whole orderly scene suddenly struck me as very* strange.[117]

A few hundred New Zealanders, mostly civilians, were in lands under occupation by the Japanese army. Francis Herlihy, a priest working in Korea, met a policeman the morning after the attacks on Malaya and Pearl Harbor.

'There is war!' said the policeman. 'It is Japan with America and Britain!'

'Who began it?'

'I cannot say; I do not know.'[118]

Other civilians from the dominion were in mainland Japan. Gilbert Lennox-King, who ran an insurance office in Tokyo, was sent to an internment camp. The policeman who came to take him away was polite and before they set off the two of them drank a bottle of whisky. Samuel Lang, a missionary, was not interned and was allowed to spend the whole of the war in Tokyo, 'living a relatively normal life amongst friends and neighbours'.[119] Arthur Caro, former journalist, had been running a business in Tokyo for years when war broke out.

An air attack on shipping near Singapore: Japanese military broadsheet. *Pritzker Military Museum Library.*

> *I was allowed to attend office as usual, with instructions not to go to any place out of my usual routine ... After about a week the gendarme came and took me into the detention camp for what they said was 'for my protection only' ... When I arrived at my office, with my guard, after six months' internment, the skeleton staff, still there to wind up the business, gave me quite a welcome and helped with my packing.*[120]

Malaya and Borneo were the first British colonies to come under attack, followed soon by Burma and Hong Kong. New Zealanders who lived or worked in the colonies found themselves in the midst of the battle, some fighting but others doing their best to dodge the bombs. James Bertram awoke on the first morning of battle in Hong Kong. Lao Ma, a servant, brought his breakfast. 'Good morning, *Po xien-sheng*!' she said cheerfully. 'You hear the guns?' Suddenly, all the air-raid sirens of the city were wailing. Bertram rushed to a window and saw silver wings swooping low.[121]

He would end up in an internment camp.

Richard Wild, manager of South British Insurance in the colony, was another of the many civilians who were interned after the successful Japanese attack. His wife fled the colony, but only got as far as the Philippines; she was interned in Manila.[122] A few citizens of the dominion were not interned but were allowed to move about freely. Margaret Jennings gained permission from the Japanese occupation authorities to keep living in an orphanage she was running. Kathleen Thomson, a 'tall, serene' nurse, was chosen to be matron of a civilian hospital under the Japanese.[123]

New Zealand airmen came to blows with Japanese pilots in Burma. Victor Bargh, the son of a farming family in the Wairarapa, weaved and ducked over the stupas of Rangoon along with 'Willie' Williams, a builder's apprentice born in Hawke's Bay.

'Hell!' yelled Bargh upon sighting the first attacking air fleet. 'Showers of 'em, look Willie!'[124]

Others from the dominion who lived or were stationed in the colony worked for the imperial army. Elizabeth McCowen, for example, did cipher work at army headquarters in Rangoon.[125]

The Burmese seldom proved 'loyal' to their imperial overlords. Clifford Emery, an air-force pilot who was a doctor in Taranaki before the war, was shot down by a Japanese airman; he and his navigator survived the crash and crawled to a nearby village. The villagers felt so little warmth for these two representatives of imperialism that they robbed the intruders and handed them over to Burmese police, who in turn handed them on to the Japanese.[126]

Japanese troops, warships, fighters and bombers kept moving southwards through Malaya.

Malay villagers, thinking them liberators, gave goods and services to the incoming troops.[127] John Mulgan, army officer and writer, was pleased to see that most Malays, like most Burmese, did not 'really care a damn' about the British Empire.[128] New Zealand airmen and ground crews fought hopelessly against a weaker but far better organised enemy. William Mitchell was in Singapore when seventeen Japanese warplanes bombed the city. 'We were asleep, and the next thing there was an almighty explosion and we were more or less blown out of bed,' he said. 'We stumbled out of the barracks and fell into the concrete gutter outside.'[129]

The airfield at Kallang was bombed heavily, noted Geoffrey Fisken, flight sergeant in a New Zealand squadron. 'We tried to save our planes by sprinting to them, quickly jumping in and taking off, if there was time,' he added. 'We were sometimes even taking off as the bombs were dropping.'[130]

Max Boyd wrote in his diary about an air raid on Singapore: 'Hell on earth today.'[131]

Bert Wipiti, a refrigeration serviceman from Taranaki, was the first airman from any air force to shoot down a Japanese warplane over Singapore.[132] The two squadrons of warplanes manned by crews from the dominion ended up doing nearly all the fighting in the skies over Singapore.[133] The task was hopeless. The climax, an act of powerful symbolism, came on 15 February when the Allied army surrendered in Singapore. Never before had such a large British force given itself up to an enemy. The 'fortress' city that was supposed to stop or at least slow any foe who hoped to head towards New Zealand had proved hollow.

White people did their best to flee, leaving servants behind to fend for themselves

The anxiety of many people in the dominion about southwards Japanese military expansion peaked when the huge British Commonwealth army in Singapore surrendered to a smaller but more able Japanese army. This cartoon tries to be defiant. *Artist: Minhinnick.* New Zealand Herald, *17 February 1942.*

in the collapsed colony. Marie Ney, a New Zealand actress, was one of the throng. 'I left miserably at an hour's notice,' she told journalists, 'because my husband thought I should go.'[134]

Ian Newlands, a New Zealand air-force pilot stranded in Singapore, was lucky to get onto a ship crowded with other white people bailing out for Batavia. Japanese dive bombers attacked the ship. 'On deck there were corpses lying everywhere,' he recalled; 'just pulp.'[135]

The Dutch East Indies, though it was bristling with conscript soldiers and shielded by air squadrons, could not staunch the haemorrhaging of Allied strength in Southeast Asia. Japan attacked on 19 February. 'The Japanese will not get Java,' declared the commander-in-chief of the Dutch East Indies.[136] The colonial government did its best to rally subject peoples behind the flag of the Netherlands by speaking in a new way about the Indonesians sharing a 'common fate' with the Dutch. Indonesians, however, seldom helped the colonial military and often went out of their way to welcome the Japanese.[137]

The Dutch East Indies officially surrendered to Japan on 9 March. This meant that an overflowing wealth of tin, oil and rubber at last was in the hands of Tokyo.

Japanese submarines opened forays into territory that was under the flag of New Zealand. A submarine, on the lookout for troop transports, came into Cook Strait. The captain sighted one of the interisland steamships but did not attack the vessel because he was under orders not to do so. The submarine launched a plane to take a look at Wellington. A second submarine came into Cook Strait a few weeks later and also sent up a plane on another survey flight over Wellington, after which the vessel ploughed north to the Hauraki Gulf and flew the reconnaissance plane over Auckland. A third submarine slipped into the Bay of Plenty towards the end of autumn and also sent up a plane to reconnoitre Auckland.

New Zealand troops were taken, but not at home.

The dominion had set up coastwatching posts on a chain of atolls in the Gilbert and Ellice Islands. Japanese warships landed men on the atolls very soon after the attack on Hawai`i and Malaya. One by one the coastwatching posts were shut down and the operators rounded up.

'Japanese coming; regards to all,' was the last message sent by an operator on Maiana.

'Three enemy warships,' was the word from Beru. 'Good luck.'[138]

New Zealand men and women living and working in the Solomon Islands were able to run away, mostly. Estelle Field, a nurse from Invercargill, was working in a hospital on the island of Malaita, and John Thomson, also from Invercargill, was the hospital doctor. When a small party of Japanese landed, they both took to the bush 'in a hurry'. Field spent four months hiding in the hills before she got away and was brought back to New Zealand.[139]

Fiji and Samoa – or at least their offshore waters – were the setting for one or two bouts of fighting involving citizens from New Zealand. The *Monowai*, an armed merchant cruiser of the dominion navy, came across a Japanese submarine off Suva. The submarine shot a torpedo, which missed, then sped away. A launch with ten civilians aboard, several of them from the dominion, was strafed on another occasion by a 'savage onslaught of machine-gun fire' near Samoa. All the men dived into the sea; the launch caught fire and its hull was holed, but nobody was killed and in the end the crew patched up the craft and got home safely.[140]

AWAKE, NEW ZEALAND!

A wave of fear swept through New Zealand when word came of the opening Japanese strikes on Kota Bharu and Pearl Harbor. Batterbee, the British high commissioner, wrote almost gleefully that this was the end of the 'phoney war' New Zealand had enjoyed until now.[141] Other waves of fear followed as bulwark after bulwark fell in Southeast Asia. The enemy was 'practically at our gates', declared Andrew Hamilton, businessman and chairman of the Wellington stock exchange.[142] An 'unprecedented crisis' confronted the country, added the Returned Services Association.[143] The *Evening Post* told citizens it was time to stop living in the 'fool's paradise' where many had hidden themselves happily.

'This war is a total war,' it editorialised, 'and all of us without exception are in it, voluntarily or involuntarily, and until such time as dangers – the fruit of past neglect – are swept away.'[144]

Only the few citizens who owned a globe understood how very far away the troops of the enemy really were from New Zealand. School children, university students, office workers and householders mostly saw the world in flat maps drawn up along the lines of the very odd projection devised almost four centuries earlier by Mercator. Pearl Harbor and Wellington Harbour, on those maps, seemed more or less the same distance from Tokyo. The truth, as many air travellers learnt after the war, was that Tokyo was nearly as close to London as to Wellington.

An advertisement placed in newspapers by two shipping companies and an import merchant house begged citizens to rally behind the dominion and its military. 'Would you rather pull your weight in the country's war effort or pull a rickshaw? We are free – because throughout the British Empire our men and women have not hesitated to make sacrifices in the cause of freedom ... We will remain free – we will emerge victorious if we do our utmost – in every phase of our war effort. Lend your utmost through National Savings'. Evening Post, *5 February 1942.*

A lot of people believed, too, that the dominion was defenceless against the new enemy.

'Will they come this way?' they asked each other. 'What will you do? Where will you go? Say they come here? … The Japs, the Japs.'[145]

The strongest wave of fear swept the country after the surrender of Singapore. 'Not only air raids but actual invasion is imminent,' wrote a citizen; and another gloomed that what had happened to Singapore would happen next to 'Java, Darwin, Fiji, Auckland'.[146] The news was 'a terrible shock', Joan Macindoe, a young member of the Women's Auxiliary Air Force, said later. Singapore was supposed to be guarding New Zealand.[147]

'It is not now,' declared the *Dominion*, 'a question of *whether* we will be attacked, but *when*.'[148]

Citizens did their best to sweep bare the shelves of shops, and motorists to empty petrol pumps, to hoard against the landing of the enemy. On the morning on which the dominion declared war against Japan, anxious queues of people sat sweating inside their cars, wanting to buy. Lloyd Geering, a young clergyman, saw 'mile-long queues of motorists formed at every service station' in Otago.[149] The oil fuel controller early in the afternoon cancelled the validity of the last two rounds of petrol coupons handed out to the citizenry. He also forbade people from using anything other than standard petrol tanks. Wily citizens found ways around the law and went in for 'much boasting' about their 'smart instances of beating the ban', wrote Guy Scholefield. All civilians, a few days later, were forbidden to buy any petrol for private use.[150] The 'drastic' new regulation, wrote an editor, 'seriously curbed' the lives of many people. Streets looked empty. Shops lost trade. The new controls had 'a paralysing effect upon every walk of life, every sphere of business and every section of industry'.[151] Oil and petrol supply was loosened a bit soon afterwards, when the state found that it was indeed having a crippling effect on manufacturing and farming. Jokes and doggerel were prompted by the oil scarcity.

Mother loves her baby,
Loves the little lamb –
Takes him for an airing
In his squeaky pram.[152]

Civilians bought and filled sandbags to stack around walls and windows. Young lads, grown men and some keen women dug up their gardens to make air-raid shelters, or holes to hide things they prized. Marian Harvey, daughter of a working-class

An air-raid shelter in the grounds of a state primary school in Auckland. *Alexander Turnbull Library ATL PAColl-0783-2-0075.*

family, saw neighbours 'burying their treasures'. Nancy Bullen, a young secondary teacher, watched an internment within her own family. 'The cutlery was wrapped in the trousseau table linen from England. Most of the linen was hem-stitched or hand-stitched or that open work embroidery.'[153]

Women spoke about fighting invaders with whatever weapon was to hand. One pointed out that while some women were 'first class shots' they had no arms other than 'the wood axe' in their back yards. 'Give the women weapons, they can fight.'[154] Another told a crowd that 'a broken beer bottle would make an excellent weapon'.[155] The *Auckland Star* thought women, instead of allowing themselves to be 'trussed up in bundles and bayoneted' when the country was invaded, should grab whatever weapons they could in order 'to fight and to die fighting'. Weapons might be 'a jam-tin filled with dynamite, dad's old shotgun, the garden fork, a good sharp knife'. Husbands and fathers must take pains to 'leave no wife or screaming child or piteous invalid' at the mercy of the invading army.[156] Charlotte Hudson, a little girl at kindergarten in Christchurch, was kitted out by the teaching staff with 'a small bag containing a cork to bite on, cotton wool … and camphor'. The kit was 'designed to minimise the effects of a bomb blast'.[157] Valerie Forbes, a schoolgirl in the same city, together with her sisters in a working-class household, knew very little about either pharmacology or war strategy, but they worked themselves up into fits of tears about what would happen after an enemy landing.

'We thought they were going to come,' she said, 'and – the Japanese were going to *knife* us.'[158]

A few women evacuated with their children, leaving homes near the coast to stay with friends or family in the back country. Evadne Ashton-Warner, for example, afraid that Wellington would be bombed or invaded, left for Pipiriki.[159] Suicide was spoken about widely. Bunty Pemberton-Pigott, working for the army at a secret listening post in Marlborough, was ordered to destroy her code book and then kill herself after the enemy landed.[160] June Fleming, a clerk, daughter of a grocer, learnt that her mother had got hold of some suicide pills; the plan was for the whole family to take the pills in the event of an invasion by the enemy. 'I'm not going to allow any Japanese near you,' said her mother.[161]

'What shall I do if the Japs land?' a civilian woman asked her neighbourhood air-raid warden. 'Shall I kill my children?'[162]

Citizens crowded together inside town halls throughout the northern provinces of the country to listen to eager speakers uttering a new slogan: 'Awake, New Zealand!' The slogan was voiced first in Hamilton. Thomas Melrose, major in command of the Hamilton Home Guard, wrote articles in the *Waikato Times*, which were bundled together and published as a pamphlet, *Sound the Tocsin: Japanese menace*. The articles, and the crowded meetings that followed the publication of the articles, were not linked to any political party. Awake New Zealand grew into a mass movement, sweeping up followers by the thousand. One of the goals was to 'demonstrate that we are worthy custodians of this fair British Country'.[163] Melrose called for mobilising the whole nation, and this call was echoed by many others in what came to be a mass movement of citizens stirring from Northland to Taranaki.

> *Here in New Zealand are a million men and women. Arm every one of them; train every one; make them a million marching feet ... Let every pacifist and subversive impulse be rooted out and replaced by an impulse for victory.*[164]

A war dictatorship must be set up. The working class must stop speaking about class. The working class must begin speaking about duty and loyalty. The nation must rise above class, and also above party. Andrew Hamilton, chairman of the Wellington stock exchange, deplored the way leaders of the working class kept fostering 'that class hatred which, for the general good of the country, should be definitely uprooted'.[165] Melrose in *Sound the Tocsin* said there must no longer be 'class warring with class in a vain attempt to protect property and privileges'. All groups of people must work together as fellow citizens fighting the foreign foe.[166] A conservative dictatorship – or so some said – would be best in the hands of former soldiers from the First World War. Clive Hulme became poster boy. A farm labourer who could easily be portrayed as an honest working man, an army sergeant now home from battle, he had also won a Victoria Cross. Hulme sent out a message to the citizenry:

> *Where are the leaders – the men who in this day of the country's emergency should be in key positions, fighting grimly determined in an all-out effort to save New Zealand and those who belong to her? Men from the dust of Egypt and the mud of Flanders – have they not earned the right to guide us through our baptism of fire? ... Now is the time to act – strike at the enemy within our own gates, withstand opposition boldly, tolerate no strikers, no defaulters, no half-hearted weekend war effort: organise yourselves and lead this country.*[167]

The borough councillors of Pukekohe developed a scheme to put everything on a proper war footing. The Pukekohe Programme, as it came to be known, said that the nation was imperilled by 'the frequently recurring trials of strength between labour and capital'. New Zealand must be governed by 'a small Supreme War Council'. The war council would deal with any 'strikes, go-slow, offences against labour or attempts to profiteer' as sabotage.

'It's revolutionary,' said a startled borough councillor in Whakatāne. 'If that's democracy – it's a mockery.'[168]

The National Party made the most of the mood of crisis to attack the government for having sent away most of the country's air force and army. The policy of doing what Britain wanted by fighting Germany and Italy was wrongheaded, declared the party. An editorial in the *New Zealand Herald* lashed out at the diplomacy and war policy of not only Wellington but also Washington and London. Churchill, said the editorial, had only now confessed that Britain, while fighting Germany and Italy, 'never had sufficient

Japanese propaganda targeted the subject peoples of British India, most of whom were indifferent or hostile to the imperial Raj. *www.digitalposter.com*

arms to provide effectively' for war in Asia or the Pacific. Why, the editorial demanded, had Churchill not told people the truth?

> *Why, on the contrary, were they officially and repeatedly assured that all was well and, in the case of India, Australia and New Zealand, allowed to continue the despatch of fighting-men to the Middle East and to Britain? An even graver question arises. Why did the Allies adopt a policy toward Japan that made war inevitable, thus exposing one half of the human race to the savage attack of a well-armed adversary?*[169]

Curiously enough, the party of imperial loyalism was blaming the governing party for being too loyal to empire and not thinking enough about the needs of New Zealand.

The political left was busy making the same point. A forum for protest opened when the Federation of Labour held its national conference in April. Unionist leaders stood up to tear strips off the Labour government for sending to the other side of the world an army and air force that were needed to safeguard New Zealand. The federation voted that the government should 'adopt a more critical attitude towards' the war policy of the British government. The conference also voted that the New Zealand government should ask the British government to grant full self-government to India.[170]

India was not a priority, however, for the political leadership of the Labour Party. Fraser cabled Churchill to say that his government might 'have to face serious repercussions in the morale' of the country.[171] The prime minister was not convinced by cables coming back from London saying that it was not a Japanese objective to invade New Zealand; nor by his own chiefs of staff who told him that there were strong strategic and economic reasons why invasion was unlikely.[172] Fraser defied logic. A wise policy, he believed, would be to 'prepare against the worst' or, in other words, 'a possible attack on a substantial scale'.[173]

Nash was another senior politician who spoke about the possibility of an invasion of New Zealand.[174] Coates, too, wrote in private about a coming day when the 'yellow devil' would land in the country.[175] The government proclaimed a new policy: total war.

TOTAL WAR?

Calling up more men was the first step. Territorial and military reserve troops, tallying upwards of 5000 men, were mobilised as soon as word came about the attack on Malaya and Hawai`i. The troops were set to work guarding coasts and ports. A week later, mobilisation of another 21,000 territorials began, brought forward hastily. Volunteers were asked to step up for the military reserve, and draft papers were sent out to thousands of households. Fathers, no matter how many children they might have, were now to be conscripted willy-nilly.

At the same time, the government imposed a sweeping new system of control over people's working lives, a system that came to be known as Manpower.

A Manpower Office was set up early in the new year, with strong powers over industry deemed 'essential'. All men and women in certain age groups could now be ordered to work in essential industry. Any worker in any essential industry who wanted to quit, or any employer wanting to be rid of a worker, must get authorisation from a district Manpower official. Mines, timber mills, munitions, construction for the military, the electricity system, dairy factories and freezing works were the first industries deemed essential. The list grew quickly.[176] At first only men in their late forties, and women of twenty and twenty-one, were forced to register, but the net was soon cast so widely as to snare every youth or man below sixty, and every woman up to thirty. All were liable to what was, more or less, forced labour for the state.

Citizens were not only driven into essential industry, they could now be blocked from going into jobs in any other industry. An order-in-council late in the autumn gave Manpower officials the power to veto anybody from getting any job in 'non-essential' industry. Shops were non-essential, for example, as were factories making consumer goods. The power of the state to stop people getting the work they wanted, where they wanted, was further strengthened in the spring. Nancy Taylor heard the word 'Manpower' spoken over and over throughout the country.

'Manpower is holding on to him.'

'He's been Manpowered into cement.'

'Her firm came under Manpower last week.'[177]

Also, citizens were drafted wholesale into civil defence and the Home Guard.

The Emergency Precautions Scheme was boosted hastily. Bombs, or so the government feared, might soon start dropping on the cities of New Zealand. A conference of mayors met quickly and agreed to give priority to air-raid sirens, air-raid shelters and blackouts. A group of engineers, architects and other experts met alongside

All civilians who had volunteered to serve in the Home Guard or the Emergency Precautions Scheme were ordered, after the declaration of war on Japan, to stay in those organisations until further notice. Volunteer work had become conscript work. Civilians who had not previously volunteered to work in such groups were still free to use their spare time as they wished – by, for example, playing sports. The dividing of civilians into two classes led to acrimony. *Artist: Minhinnick.* New Zealand Herald, *14 November 1941.*

the conference and talked about how to protect civilians 'from blast and splinters from bombs'.[178] Military workers, together with volunteer bands of citizens, began digging. All men in the country between the ages of sixteen and sixty-six were ordered late in January to do work for civil defence or other war tasks. Women were not under orders, but were asked to volunteer their labour alongside the men and boys. An announcement by Ailsa Hislop, mayoress of Wellington, was typical: 'I ask any women who are able to handle tools to join me and other leaders at the working posts.'[179]

Anyone who signed up for such work would not have the right to step down if they found it too hard or wearying. All those on the rolls were now bound by law to keep toiling until the civil defence hierarchy, or some other official hierarchy, gave them leave to lay down their tools. The bigger and deeper trenches – luckily for those who were ordinarily typists, clerks or shop assistants and now found themselves handling shovels and spades – were dug with the help of bulldozers and other machinery. Air-raid shelters were soon everywhere, slotted into parks and gardens, walled in with mounds of spoil, along streets all the way from the smallest seaside township to the capital city.

'Parliament grounds now look like Gallipoli,' wrote Scholefield, 'or a relief map of New Guinea.'[180]

Blackout was tightened, and policed more strictly. Citizens who at night showed a light from a shop, office, house or shed could find themselves in court. A first offender might be warned or fined; those who kept being careless were locked behind bars. Wardens were often 'understanding' but often 'officious', and 'there was mounting worry if one's name were taken, for future slips could mean trouble'.[181]

Blackouts caused injury, too. Citizens stumbled, fell, broke bones, and sometimes were killed in road accidents caused by dimmed car lights. Women were molested in the darkness. Petty crime thrived too: handbags were snatched, and thieves found it easy to pilfer goods.[182]

The Home Guard was strengthened when the war cabinet met early in autumn and agreed on a policy of making 'utmost use of the man-power and woman-power' of the country. Guardsmen were to be paid by the state when mobilised for duty, and now for the first time could be used by the army as labourers on military works. A roll of 111,000 guardsmen was soon on the books, but while many of those men went about their tasks earnestly, many others did not. Only 63,000 even bothered to turn up for three out of every four parades.[183] The government responded by ordering all men not fit for military service to become guardsmen – which yielded another 30,000 troops – and fined those who did not report for duty.[184]

'Every New Zealander,' declared the government, 'must and will help to save New Zealand.'[185]

Rationing was stepped up too. The government was never keen to ration anything; it feared that the working class would become restless if the state started emptying the kitchen cupboard. Workers looked to the Labour Party as a guarantor of plenty, not scarcity. Japan upset such political sums by upsetting the supply of goods from the tropics and from Asia.

Rubber recycling promoted in an advertisement posted by the Ministry of Supply. *Press, 21 November 1942.*

After a week of war with Japan the government slammed rationing onto many rubber goods. 'In future no motor tyres or tubes may be removed, sold or otherwise disposed of,' declared the supply minister, Sullivan, 'except with the consent of or by direction of the secretary of supply.'

Citizens, guessing how things would go, swarmed into shops to stock up on sugar, tea and silk stockings. In autumn the government handed out ration books to everybody. Sugar 'came onto the ration', as people said, along with stockings. Footwear was next, together with textiles and clothing. Tea followed at the beginning of winter, when it had become obvious that shipments of leaf being landed on the wharves were no longer hefty enough to allow everyone to keep topping up their pots freely. India supplied most of the tea drunk by the working class, while the well-to-do liked tea from China. The two subcontinents were now on the wrong side of seas roamed by submarines taking orders from Tokyo.

Panic buying broke out every few weeks as householders whispered up and down the country about new rationing or new shortages. Wellington citizens rushed footwear, for example, crowding some shops so badly that the owners closed the boot and shoe departments.[186] The *Evening Post* wrote of a soap and cosmetics panic that broke out in the city during the winter:

> *The rationing germ seems to be as catching as its more virulent relative, the 'flu germ. Once bitten by it, the victim develops symptoms of a feverish rush, grabs all the spare cash, and dashes off to the city to buy as much as possible of the goods or commodity which rumour says will be next on the rationing list … One assistant said that he personally had sold to a lady, who appeared to be well over 70, enough lipstick and face powder to supply the wants of at least a dozen girls for a year.*[187]

Rationing was not the only tool for curbing consumption of goods. A Scrap Rubber Control Notice, for example, was gazetted to control recycling of old tyres and other rubber scrap. The order was made because of what Sullivan called the 'simply desperate' state of rubber supply.[188] The government imposed 'austerity' clothing. A set of regulations specified what clothes could be manufactured and sold to the citizenry. Children under eleven years of age were allowed to wear anything, as were pregnant women, and homemade clothes were not bound by the new sumptuary law, but factory sewing rooms were no longer allowed to stitch on capes, hoods, boleros, cuffs, pleats, full sleeves, too many buttons or too many pockets. Young women were to wear short skirts, to save on textiles, though skirts for older women could drop down to the calf. Men were no longer to wear the baggy trousers that had been all the rage between the wars.

Austerity clothing and rationing helped spread thinning resources more fairly, but in many ways the government was sabotaging the economy. Digging air-raid shelters was a waste of scarce labour; so was 'directing' workers into 'essential' industry, driving citizens away from their workaday tasks into the Emergency Precautions Scheme and drilling men in the Home Guard. Blackouts hindered production and trade. Rationing and manpowering caused economic inefficiency.

The costs of 'total war' were heavy.

The costs were unnecessary, too, because the enemy was not on its way.

JAPPY CHRISTMAS!

Although no less a leader than Fraser in his New Year's Eve speech at the end of 1941 told citizens that the dominion for the first time in its history was 'directly threatened by enemy attack',[189] the truth was that Tokyo gave no serious thought to attacking New Zealand. Japan was halfway around the world from New Zealand. The Japanese army, navy and, above all, economy lacked the depth and strength to win any long war, as governing groups in Tokyo, Washington and London well knew. Although ten aircraft carriers were among the pride of the imperial fleet when war broke out with the Western powers, all they carried were lightweight fighters and dive bombers that could attack ships and railways, or harry people on the streets of the odd city. Japan had no way to do heavy bombing in New Zealand. Nor was there any motive to do dive bombing, or to try to land troops.

A plan for raids or invasion may have been drawn up but later wiped out. We cannot know for sure, since the bulk of war records held by the Japanese government were destroyed before the country was occupied by the Allies. Yet it seems unlikely. Certainly nobody drew up an official plan to govern a conquered New Zealand. Japanese awareness of the dominion was not strong. The first book ever written in Japanese about the country, published in mid-1941, praised its social democracy. 'New Zealand is leading the world,' wrote the author, Kawase Isamu, a graduate of Lincoln and Massey; 'we must feel pleased for the happiness of our society in that the social facilities of our country have been gradually coming into line with those of New Zealand.'[190]

The Kokusaku Kenkyu Kai, an institute backed by money from banks, industrialists and the army and navy, came nearest to thinking about how to govern the dominion when some of its staff outlined a way in which conquered or friendly states might be administered within a system of colonies and protectorates known as Daitoa Kyoeiken, often translated as the Greater East Asia Co-Prosperity Sphere. A regional organisation would be wisest, the institute suggested – each region with its own government. One of those regions might be a New Zealand government-general which would administer all island groups from the middle of the Tasman across to French Polynesia. Citizens would be allowed 'self-government for internal affairs'. Tokyo would control military and foreign policy. The goal would be to strengthen Japan while forwarding 'the well-being of those peoples within the regions'. New Zealand, in other words, would get a taste of its own medicine and be handled not unlike its subjects in the Cook Islands, Nauru and Samoa – though more generously, since the citizens of the dominion were to have the right to elect their own parliament.[191]

The plan was merely paperwork, however, and was filed away.

Japanese attacks went so well for a few months that other planning groups, more or less backed by the state, drew up further documents looking at likely ways to govern the Co-Prosperity Sphere. The Total War Research Institute early in 1942 completed a plan for what it hoped would be 'an autonomous zone of peaceful living and common prosperity'. New Zealand, at some point, would join an outer rim of the sphere and become a multiracial nation of Māori, Pākehā and a new community of settler families from Japan.[192] The health and welfare ministry also proposed Japanese family settlement in New Zealand.[193]

Although such schemes were sweeping in scope, the authors were penpushers working well outside the inner sanctums of Japanese planning. Total War Research Institute bureaucrats and academics had no mandate to propose, let alone implement steps to be taken by either government or military. It was an organisation toiling tirelessly to draw up plan after impossible plan, but its blueprint for occupying New Zealand must be sized up alongside its blueprint for a war with Germany.

The printing of money known as Southern Development Bank Notes led to the belief for many years that Japan planned to conquer New Zealand. The Southern

'The enemy is routed on the roads of Burma': Japanese military broadsheet. *Pritzker Military Museum Library.*

Development Bank was set up under the imperial government and its notes were indeed used in Southeast Asia and the Solomon Islands.[194] The bank currency was meant for colonies under Japanese control, however, not for self-governing dominions like New Zealand. Japan never printed any money for an occupied New Zealand.

New Zealand chiefs of military staff early in 1942 told the government there were sound strategic and economic reasons why invasion was unlikely. Strategically, the first priority of Japan must be to 'destroy or neutralise Allied Naval power' in Southeast Asia. Economically, the priority was to get hold of 'oil, rubber, tin, nickel, coal, iron and rice'. New Zealand had good coal, but getting that coal onto ships and steaming those ships all the way across the ocean would be very costly and very risky. New Zealand had no oil, rubber, tin, nickel, iron or rice. A raid, concluded the chiefs, was the only real possibility.[195] Japan had so little power to do any serious harm to the dominion that Tojo spoke cajoling rather than threatening words during a parliamentary speech in Tokyo.

'New Zealand should avoid a useless war,' he declared, 'or relying on Britain and America, on whom no reliance can be placed.'[196]

Australian historians have searched tirelessly through war and occupation plans floated by various Japanese thinktanks, looking for evidence of an invasion scenario. The quest has yielded a blank. A group of 'visionary' naval officers did write a proposal for invading Australia 'in order to forestall it being used as a base for an Allied counter-offensive'. The officers who drew up the proposal, however, were only of middling rank and the navy general staff gave no backing.[197] The plan was 'too risky and fanciful', in the words of one authority. As for the army general staff, when they learned of the proposal they threw it out as 'gibberish'.[198] The army believed at least ten divisions and two million tonnes of shipping would be needed to invade Australia; they could spare only four divisions at the most, and did not have the shipping.[199]

The navy department did also look, rather academically, into the history, economy and society of New Zealand. Kawase Isamu in the middle of 1942 was asked to write five papers on the topic, and did so. Early the following year the army department asked him to give a talk about New Zealand.[200] A few officials in the navy department, too, murmured about whether Māori might join Japanese in a war against the government of New Zealand. Maybe Japanese radio could transmit broadcasts in te reo? One historian argues that this flutter of activity in Tokyo does imply some possibility of an invasion of New Zealand.[201]

The tide of war was already running strongly against Japan, however, even when the navy department commissioned the five papers, and an already acute shortage of troops, warplanes and warships was not likely to be helped by undertaking some quixotic mission against New Zealand. Navy blueprints, like the blueprints of the Total War Institute, must be seen as what nowadays would be called 'blue-sky thinking' – an exercise in looking at the unlikely. British plans for an invasion of Ireland were an equivalent bit of mostly meaningless paperwork.[202]

Nor, interestingly, did everybody in the dominion give in to fear about an attack by Japan.

New Zealand, while it was swept by waves of anxiety and even panic, at the same time kept up a good deal of optimism, cynicism or fatalism about the war in Southeast Asia. The mood, thought Frederick Wood, was marked by 'much less suggestion of hysteria' than at the time of the fall of France.[203] Citizens for ten days or so after the attacks on Malaya and Hawai`i wondered whether their workaday lives had suddenly become meaningless, but they then started shopping busily for Christmas. Gay Gray thought it 'strange that there are so many, even now, who want to play'.[204] A Wellington shop manager said shortly before Christmas Day that not even Japanese invasion would stop the city from celebrating yuletide as always. Trade in most towns was very brisk.[205] A Leeston editor wrote that people could be heard speaking as though 'nothing untoward' would happen to the dominion; it would 'be allowed to go on its own sweet way, prosperous, pleasure-loving'.[206] A Whakatāne editor was struck by the way many people clearly felt the dominion to be 'sorted out for special protection by the fates'. Citizens spoke equably.

'No, there's no chance of the Japs coming here.'[207]

The equable mood was often blended with a sense of black comedy.

'In the Home Guard, Jack?' one civilian asked another civilian.

'No, I suppose a man should be, but the fact is, I have no time for the crowd who are running it up there.'

'You'd prefer the Japs, eh?'

'Well, not exactly; but fair dinkum, do you think there is any need for a Home Guard here?'[208]

'Jappy Christmas!' people joked to one another during the festive season after the declaration of war on Japan.

A lack of hysteria was based to some extent on a feeling that not much could be done, one way or another, should the country come under attack. An enemy landing might best be met by surrendering. Harold Monaghan, an Anglican clergyman, worried about 'the spirit of defeatism which seems to be abroad'.[209] A lack of hysteria was also based on the skill of many people at guessing Japanese goals fairly shrewdly. A

The summer holidays in New Zealand at the end of 1942, the first anniversary of the declaration of war on Japan, were more straitened times than earlier war summers but were still extravagant compared with wartime Japan, Britain or Germany. Racing continued to attract spendthrift crowds. A lack of consumer goods in the shops meant that many people had spare cash; a lot of them chose to 'take a punt on the nags' rather than doing their patriotic, provident but dull duty by buying war bonds. *Auckland Star*, 20 December 1941.

staff writer on the *Evening Post*, for example, wrote with insight about war strategy:

> *Japan is conducting warlike activities over an area of land and sea more than twice as great as that in which Germany and Italy are engaged ... The more this framework, designed by Japanese architects, is examined, the flimsier it appears as a structure to withstand a heavy storm. Its weakness is ... in the enormous amount of power and material which it will ultimately require to sustain it. Japan ... must maintain the armies in all these distant places with convoyed supplies, over sea routes which are in some cases thousands of miles long; and she must at the same time keep an anxious watch on the vast expanse of the Pacific Ocean for fear of a possible heavy naval attack, which may not come that way, but also may.*[210]

The same journalist pointed out that Japan almost certainly sought territory much more strategically important than New Zealand.[211] Walter Maltby wrote that it would be 'an insane undertaking' for a country as far away as Japan to try to invade the dominion, 'a position of no strategic importance whatever'. He asked fellow citizens to do some sums about how many tens of thousands of soldiers would need to be landed, together with stores and weaponry, and how many troopships and escort warships would be needed to bring those troops.[212]

Also, people as a whole were well aware of the immense strength of the Allies.

The Declaration of the United Nations, signed after hasty paperwork at the very beginning of 1942, set up a military alliance between New Zealand, Australia, Canada, South Africa, Britain, Guomindang China, the Soviet Union, nine small American republics and two big American republics, Brazil and the United States. The signatory states declared they were fighting 'to defend life, liberty, independence and religious freedom, and to preserve human rights and justice in their own lands as well as in other lands'.[213] None, however, was willing to give liberty or independence to such colonial holdings as Nigeria or Niue, Rhodesia or Rarotonga, Sierra Leone or Samoa, Tanganyika or Tokelau or Tūhoe. The United Nations together held most of the wealth of the world. The United States owned a massive 42 per cent of all economic 'war potential' on the planet, the Soviet Union added another 14 per cent and Britain a further 10 per cent; the Axis, holding only 20 per cent, was outweighed massively.[214]

'Although Japan's surprise attack has given her an initial strategic advantage,' noted the *Press*, 'Japan cannot stand a long war.'[215]

'Three of the world's greatest nations are by our side,' observed Terence McCombs, Labour member of parliament for Lyttelton. 'Russia, the United States of America, and China are today our full allies.'[216]

OPPOSITE: The United Nations, the new alliance of powers fighting the Axis, upheld the Allied claim to be fighting for freedom and democracy. The colourful flags on this propaganda poster were flown by states that denied freedom and democracy to many – or, in some cases, all – people under their flags. Among them were Britain, France, the Netherlands, the Soviet Union, Guomindang China – and New Zealand.

UNITED
THE UNITED NATIONS FIGHT FOR FREEDOM

China, for military purposes of the Allied governments, meant the Guomindang. Gush about the Guomindang was pumped out more effusively than ever, now that it was an ally. Fraser spoke of the 'epic resistance' of 'China' to 'wanton aggression by Japan'. The Guomindang, he went on, had 'borne the brunt of the fight for freedom in the Pacific'.[217] Henry St Barbe Holland, Anglican bishop of Wellington, told his flock that 'China' had upheld 'the cause of freedom' for five years and was now 'playing a vital part' in safeguarding New Zealand. Jiang Jieshi, gangster warlord, was praised as one of 'the world's finest Christians'. The dictatorship under his thumb was 'a great ally, battling as we are for things that we know are dear to the heart of God'.[218]

One citizen who had lived and worked in China wrote scathingly of the 'laughable' propaganda heard about the Guomindang.[219]

Japan, meanwhile, struggled to secure its new holdings in Southeast Asia.

The Dutch East Indies was seen to be the key. A few planners flushed by short-term tactical success lost sight of Japanese strategic limits and talked eagerly about pushing towards India and Hawai`i. The agreed strategy, however, was to safeguard imperial flanks. The army was to take Tulagi and New Guinea. The navy was to engage the American navy near Midway. Afterwards, if all went well, the army might move into New Caledonia or Fiji. The whole Japanese sphere was then to be safeguarded with a 'ribbon defence'; one knot of the ribbon would be tied to the Aleutians, another to Fiji, while the rest of the ribbon would run westwards all the way to a third knot in Burma or northeast India.

New Zealand was not to be attacked.

COALITION AND QUAKE

The National Party seized on the outbreak of war with Japan to push once more for a coalition government. Holland, almost as soon as he heard the news of the attacks on Malaya and Hawai`i, spoke fulsomely:

> *At this grave moment of national peril, when the lives of all New Zealanders are endangered, I respectfully urge the immediate summoning of Parliament to consider the best course for ensuring the security of New Zealand and the Empire. Political differences should be dropped and a National Emergency Government formed, and all forces, economic, political, and industrial, should be organised on a full war footing.*[220]

The Labour Party, while saying nothing very welcoming to the National Party, gingerly weighed up behind closed doors the possibility of letting the right come into the government. A few feints and flirting words were tried during the early months of autumn before Fraser and his colleagues sat down to talk earnestly with Holland and his colleagues at the end of May. There followed a month of bargaining, backchat, catcalling, then more bargaining. The caucus of each party agreed at last, on 24 June, to set up what was to be known as the War Administration.

The War Administration was to consist of thirteen members of parliament: six from the opposition and seven from the Labour Party. The war cabinet was to go on, meanwhile, as the executive of the War Administration. Holland would get a seat in the cabinet. A law would be passed to postpone parliamentary elections one year at a time, and parliament would have the right to make up its mind at the end of each of those years that there should be no further postponement.[221]

'[T]he parties have declared,' said Holland, 'that in time of national emergency they are prepared to practise what they preach and that unity is strength.'[222]

Then a powerful earthquake rocked the lower North Island.

The lower house had not long risen on 24 June when parliament was shaken 'alarmingly'. Politicians ducked under tables or braced themselves in doorways. A bust of Seddon, on top of a stone pedestal, was beheaded after hitting the floor with a crash.[223] A tall brick chimney stack at a gasworks in the capital was felled too, and thousands of 'shattered chimney-pots' lay strewn on housetops throughout the city.[224]

Gwen Pollard, a young woman in the air force, jumped out of a window in her barracks. A second shock followed later in the evening. 'The whole place rocked,' she recalled. 'Everybody ran out to the front steps inside the main door, and all the rats ran out from the kitchen, great big rats. The girls were screaming.'[225]

Masterton was the town most knocked about by the tremors, with 'huge piles of brick and masonry sprawling across the footpaths and roadway, shattered shop windows, and trailing high-tension lines'. An Anglican church looked 'as if it had been bombed'. The front gable of a Presbyterian church was torn away. A water tower collapsed in a heap, as did 'huge sections of the engine building' at the town gasworks.[226] The whole of the Wairarapa was shaken badly:

King's Chambers building, Wellington, badly damaged by the big earthquake on 24 June 1942. *Alexander Turnbull Library ATL EP-Science-Earthquakes 1940s and 1950s-03.*

Houses swayed, chimneys crashed, residences became flooded with water from burst pipes, and the inside of buildings, business and private, were scenes of desolation with smashed crockery and other goods ... People rushed out into the streets as chimneys came tumbling down and wild scenes were witnessed. The crashing of chimneys and parts of buildings made the night hideous.[227]

The earthquake was one more untimely burden for an embattled country. The work of clearing streets, strengthening or demolishing damaged buildings and rebuilding could only be done by drawing on already thinly stretched manpower, machinery and money. Men were hurried into damaged towns and set to work. A state of emergency was declared for Masterton. The army was brought in to clear debris, help householders and guard shops.

On the war front, things were perking up, though. The *Mercantile Gazette* observed astutely as early as March that the turn of the tide for Japan, while 'almost imperceptible', had begun already:

In the three months she has been at war with the Allies she has certainly achieved a great deal, but it has cost her much in manpower and material. Japan cannot replace material for she has not the material and her industrial capacity is not equal to making good the daily losses. Moreover, the greater part of her able-bodied men must be in the firing line. Her lines of communication stretch from Burma to New Guinea, and those lines must be kept open. Japan needs a great deal more shipping than she possesses to keep these lines open, and those lines are vulnerable to attack ... Japan's war machine is getting rickety while the Allies' war machine is just beginning to take shape.[228]

The Battle of the Coral Sea was fought late in autumn, when the Japanese navy did its best to 'deepen' the defence of its new holdings in the Solomon Islands. Opening fire on the other side were the naval and air forces of Australia and the United States. New Zealand held its breath, waiting for news.

'The immediate future of New Zealand,' said Hon. D. Wilson, leader of the upper house of parliament, 'is wrapped up in the result of that battle.'[229]

New Zealand need not have worried about its safety, given that the Japanese fleet was not bound its way; but then and afterwards many people in the dominion had a wrongheaded but strong belief that the Japanese fleet fighting hard in the Coral Sea was indeed on its way to Wellington or Auckland. Although the gunners of the Japanese navy sank more enemy ships than their foes, their own imperial fleet was battered so badly that what warships did come floating out of the fight turned around and steamed away. New Zealand heard the news gleefully. A mistaken story of the battle as an event that saved the dominion from invasion was now embedded in popular history. 'The Battle of the Coral Sea saved New Zealand,' the victory supplement of the *Star-Sun* would proclaim after the surrender of Japan. 'It must be written into our history books.'[230]

The Battle of Midway, a few weeks afterwards, was the key that turned the lock on the Japanese Empire. Tokyo was well aware that it had not won what it wanted at Pearl Harbor. Yamamoto Isoroku, commander-in-chief of the Japanese navy, wanted to sink the aircraft carriers of the United States. Two monstrous fleets of warships opened fire on 4 June and pounded at one another for four days, ending not with the crippling of the United States fleet, but with gory carnage in the imperial Japanese navy.

Japan now had no hope of victory.

New Zealand was not quite aware of the implications of the Battle of Midway. Citizens still spoke about Japanese troops 'on their way'. A wide ocean, however, stretched nearly 3400 kilometres from Auckland to the nearest spot where the imperial army had dug in – Guadalcanal in the Solomon Islands. Soldiers under the rising sun would never get any nearer to New Zealand. Japan had nothing ahead but a grim, grinding, losing struggle.

'The real war,' prime minister Tojo told parliament, 'starts now.'[231]

THE ARSENAL OF DEMOCRACY

Troops sent by a foreign power now marched through the city streets of New Zealand. The troops were deployed not by an enemy, however, but by an overbearing ally.

The United States, gearing up its vast economy, was shipping out men and weapons to get ready to attack the Axis. The chiefs of staff in Washington decided how to tackle the Pacific. The strategy was to safeguard what they called 'the British antipodes and the islands and sea lanes between them and our West Coast and Panama'.[232] Headquarters for the South Pacific was to be Auckland. The first United States soldiers landed in the city in June 1942, followed by several thousand marines who disembarked at Wellington. The landing of so many strangers in foreign uniforms was top secret, but news spread quickly by word of mouth and huge crowds of civilians stood to watch and cheer as the newcomers paraded through Wellington and Auckland.

'It is doubtful,' wrote one United States war correspondent, 'if any alien troops ever received a warmer and more sincerely friendly welcome than the Second Marine Division got in New Zealand.'[233]

Japan, on the other hand, was finding the going so tough that it could hardly gain any new ground. Generals, admirals and politicians spoke behind closed doors about what might be the best 'exit strategy'. Clearly, unless Washington could be talked into signing a peace treaty, Japan would be smashed to smithereens in a few years. How could the country get out of the war without ending up in an even worse position than before the war? What territory won in the last few years of fighting was expendable, and what territory must be kept at all costs? Tokyo believed in its right to keep its grip on colonial holdings, but while empire as a whole was not negotiable, Japanese governing groups knew that some of the prizes must be given away.

The territory they thought the least expendable was in northern China. The territory they thought worth trying hard to keep was in Southeast Asia. The territory they thought least worth keeping was the scatter of tropical islands in the Pacific: only a few of those islands were worth money, and all were a long way away. The key war, for the governing groups, was the war in Asia. The 'Pacific War', as the Americans called it, was always a sideshow for Tokyo.[234]

New Zealand and the United States meanwhile, like all allies in any war, found themselves often working at cross-purposes.

The Labour government wanted any war in the Pacific to be waged under the banner not of the United States but of the United Nations. War planning should be done in a collegial way. Peace planning should too. The big powers must listen to the small powers and all the powers together should work out ways to set goals whose outcome would be good not only for the great powers but for the people of the world.

'We entered this war,' Fraser told millions of American radio listeners, 'with the object of securing for ourselves and others the right to live in peace and to return again to the task of building a better and a happier world for the ordinary man and woman.'[235]

Although many Democrats in the republic talked quite as earnestly as social democrats in the dominion about the needs of the ordinary woman and man, they also liked to talk about the power and authority of the United States. The policy of the Roosevelt administration was that Washington must be the boss when it came to war and diplomatic strategy in Asia and the Pacific, and it must do most of the fighting. New Zealand, Australia, the Netherlands, Britain and Free France must be elbowed out of the way to give the United States a good opportunity to impose its will on the postwar Pacific, Southeast Asia and East Asia.

A Pacific War Council was set up in Washington under the chairmanship of Roosevelt. New Zealand, Australian, Canadian, British and Dutch diplomats sat on the council, together with a politician from the Philippines and another from the Guomindang. The council, however, had no powers. All councillors were welcome to speak – when words could be got in edgeways between Roosevelt's sonorous phrases – but no decisions about peace or war were ever made at the meetings. The council was merely 'a press conference at the highest level', observed Geoffrey Cox, first secretary at the New Zealand legation in Washington.[236]

The United Nations in other talks agreed on a world strategy for the war. The Allies would work together first to beat Italy and Germany and afterwards would mop up Japan.

New Zealand was not happy. Fraser and Nash did their best to talk Roosevelt into attacking Japan as soon as possible, but with no luck.[237] New Zealand had to decide on its own strategy too. Germany was the priority target for the United Nations, but German troops were nowhere near as threatening as Japanese troops to Queen Street or Cathedral Square.

What ought the dominion to do?

A wise strategy, some people argued, was to keep pitting most of the military strength of New Zealand against Italy and Germany. Others wondered about dividing that strength more or less equally between the old enemy and the new enemy. Others again argued that it would be wise to ship the troops of the dominion away from the other side of the world and throw everything against Japan. Australia, dealing with the same dilemma, chose the third policy. New Zealand agonised over the question for a year or so. Citizens on both left and right felt strongly. One of the sharpest voices of the right was the *Auckland Star*:

> *It is on all sides admitted that if Japan had entered the war at the same time as Germany, Australia and New Zealand would not have sent expeditionary forces to the Middle East. It would then have been acknowledged that the proper and indeed the only course for both the Commonwealth and the Dominion was to employ their forces against Japan.*[238]

The government agreed, by the middle of the year, to keep most of the military strength of the country on the other side of the world while building up a new army to fight in the Pacific. Fraser told parliament that getting to grips with Japan by sending dominion troops into battle must be done in order for the dominion to 'carry weight' in the Pacific.[239]

The question of whether to pit troops against Japan, and if so how many, or whether to keep most of them on the other side of the world, was linked with a narrower question of how to garrison the dominion strongly enough to stop any raids or landings. Fraser sent a message to Roosevelt saying that it was 'essential for the successful prosecution of the war' to make the dominion a 'fortress' for freedom and democracy.[240] Churchill, keen to keep dominion troops in North Africa, backed the message by secretly asking Roosevelt to station a whole division of troops in New Zealand so long as Wellington agreed to let its own army division stay in Egypt.[241] All three sides agreed. The deal was done behind the backs of the citizenry.

American ships heavy with troops and weapons kept coming to New Zealand; during the course of the war around 100,000 marines, soldiers, sailors and airmen from the United States would land in the country. And at first, most citizens welcomed them as a guarantee of safety.

The island colonies and protectorates of the dominion were also garrisoned by the United States.

The strategy drawn up by chiefs of staff early in the year, of securing 'the islands and sea lanes' between New Zealand and the Americas, meant among other things sending troops to Fiji, Samoa, Tonga and the Cook Islands. The 'American military machine,' notes one historian, 'came into the Pacific in prodigious proportions, dwarfing anything that had ever come before.'[242] Thousands of men arrived, chewing gum, swilling Coke, swearing, unpeeling condoms and driving jeeps over the rutted little roads of tropical islands that until then had lived a quiet, poor, pious life of farming and fishing.

Fiji had already been garrisoned by troops from New Zealand. After the declaration of war on Japan, the dominion sent more. Khaki-clad men dug air-raid shelters, set up tank traps and a curfew and slapped a blackout on the colony. Suva 'looked grim in its war paint', wrote a journalist from the dominion, E.V. Sale.[243] Fijian chiefs ordered more of their tribespeople to sign up for the colonial army; within a year as many as 22,000 young men had left the villages and volunteered either as soldiers or to labour for the military. Indians, on the other hand, still looked askance at the war and the British Empire.[244]

The United States began troop landings early in winter when 15,000 infantry disembarked at Suva. Bomber squadrons arrived too. Fiji was so highly militarised that its facilities for military men on leave were 'heavily overtaxed' and the streets of the colonial capital by early evening were often no 'pretty sight'. Drunken men in uniform vomited in gutters, fought, and looked for sex or more drink. The two occupation armies spent freely. Military wage work, or sales of goods and services to the armies or to soldiers, put more money in the pockets of some Fijians than they had ever had before, and led to a mood of restlessness. A lot of colonial subjects were happy to tend to the occupation troops; others, though, felt exploited and angry.[245]

Washington and Wellington agreed secretly to take the dominion battalions away from Fiji. Ships brought them back home, where they were trained for jungle fighting.

Tonga also swarmed with a new occupation army. A force of over 9000 men was landed late in autumn, seemingly without anybody having warned the royal government or the 'protecting' powers of Britain and New Zealand. Queen Salote was welcoming, however, and for a few months the kingdom was as feverish as Fiji. The army spent money. The troops spent money. A lot of royal subjects tended happily to the occupation troops.[246] Tongans whispered to one another about having been given away by New Zealand to the United States.[247] The dominion did its best to uphold its mana in the kingdom by keeping artillery gunners stationed in Nuku`alofa.

Samoans wondered whether they might get caught up in the fighting. The leading chiefs did not want New Zealand or the United States to defend the mandate. 'Our people would suffer less if they remain quiet,' said one. The overall feeling was that the best course would be to welcome Japanese invaders peacefully, in much the same way as New Zealand invaders had been welcomed in the First World War.

Wellington, however, gave orders that the mandate must be got ready for fighting. Wellington and Washington agreed that American troops would be stationed on `Upolu and Savai`i. An advance party of marines landed quickly and from then on an average of 10,000 servicemen from the United States were usually on garrison duty.[248]

Samoa was turned upside down by the occupation army.[249] A 'fantastic outpouring of money' led to 'frenzied spending', wrote an observer from the dominion, Mills Rodger. 'Reckless spending' by troops led to 'sky-rocketing prices', added a journalist,

United States troops on parade in Apia. Charles Price, general and commanding officer, stands in the middle beside Alfred Turnbull, head of the New Zealand colonial administration in Samoa.

Mark Greene.[250] Gardens and plantations were abandoned for the sake of easy money.[251] Also there was 'a startling increase' in gambling, drinking, the sex industry and other types of 'moral delinquency.'[252] Colonial subjects were divided in their feelings about the occupation: some welcomed it as a new way of living; others looked on the 'unhealthy spasm of spending' as a betrayal of fa`a Samoa.[253]

Tokelau, Niue and the Cook Islands were less stressed than other tropical colonies by the landing of foreign troops.

New Zealand had no troops in any of the islands of Tokelau, and never sent any. Japan made no bid to take the colony. A group of young men from the atoll of Fakaofo volunteered to do war work in Samoa.[254] A few hundred American men were stationed a year later on the island of Atafu. Villagers and men in uniform swapped goods and services, and villagers bartered homemade handicrafts for foreign cloth and other goods.[255]

Rarotonga bustled after the declaration of war on Japan. Colonial officials organised a Home Guard. Weaponry was lacking, however – each platoon was given only 'one rifle and fifteen bullets.'[256] Niue got a Home Guard, too, but colonial officials were not sure whether to arm it with even one single machine gun.[257] New Zealand was not willing to do anything much, or to spend more than petty sums of money to arm or organise the people of Niue and the Cook Islands to fight any invading army. Nor did the United States send a garrison.

Aitutaki was the only exception: towards the end of the year nearly 1000 marines landed to set up a military base. The marines transformed life on the island almost overnight. They built an airfield, using 'massive technology'. Young men and some women on the island were paid wages to do labouring and other work for the military. 'Native' wages in the colony were officially very low, thanks to regulations imposed by New Zealand. The foreign troops, however, got good pay and had nothing on which to spend it other than food, 'bush-beer' and sex.[258]

A binge of dancing and laughing, drinking and gambling, prostitution, friendship and fighting also swept through cities and towns in the dominion garrisoned by troops from the United States. Hundreds of 'big grey' troopships over a year and more spewed out 'a rich armoury of tanks, jeeps, petroleum, machinery, ammunition and countless other war material' on the wharves of Wellington and Auckland.[259] A disembarking soldier saw the chaos of a quay where heavy rain fell on a 'fucked-up swamp of cornflakes, cigarettes, broken food cases, Hershey bars'.[260] American marines were the sons of poor farming families or the unskilled city working class, very unlike the wonderful gods seen on the silver screen in movies out of Hollywood. A marine seldom knew much about the world – perhaps only his own state or the 'scratch farm' his family toiled on.[261] Soldiers, by contrast, belonged to a wide range of social groups.

Marines and soldiers eyed one another suspiciously. Often they fought one another in the streets.

Almost all the young men of both groups saw their stay in the dominion as a fairly trifling break in the war, and were not likely – one historian suggests – to give much thought to the people of New Zealand.[262] The pay of marines and soldiers was good, at least by the standards of wartime troops. A monthly wage for a marine, for example, was £18 while he was stationed in New Zealand. Dominion soldiers were also paid well, but only upwards of £11 monthly. American troops usually had back pay in their pockets too, that they had not been able to spend before landing in New Zealand.[263] All troops tended to spend up big when they were on leave, whether they were Germans in Paris, Japanese in Shanghai, New Zealanders in Cairo or Americans in Wellington and Auckland.

New Zealand citizens were soon deeply divided over the troops from the United States, just as they had been divided on the eve of the war over the power and culture of the United States.

The official opinion always was that the troops were welcome guests in New Zealand. The United States was 'the great democracy'. The troops of the republic were 'Our Great Allies' fighting to save half the world in a 'life and death struggle with the savage millions of Japan'.[264] Citizens spoke about being indebted 'for our lives and all that we hold dear' to 'the timely aid of our great American friends'.[265] Maud Basham, a popular radio host known as Aunt Daisy, went as unofficial ambassador to the United States and gushed about the fellow feeling between the two peoples during an interview with a newspaper in New York.

'We want *all* the Americans to come and settle in New Zealand,' she said. 'We'd rather have Americans than anybody, because they're more like us – full of energy and go.'[266]

United States servicemen in Auckland.

A few marines and soldiers who came on ships flying the stars and stripes did grow very fond of New Zealand. John Zimmerman was struck, on disembarking, by the 'open-hearted friendliness' of Wellington.[267] And a few New Zealand citizens grew very fond of the troops from the United States.

'Oh heck,' wrote E.K. Green. 'We like 'em.'[268]

A lot was said about the newcomers being 'kith and kin' to the people of New Zealand. William Jordan, high commissioner for the dominion in London, claimed that 'both the United States and New Zealand were founded by settlers from Britain, prompted by the desire for greater liberty'.[269] The United States – or at least its officials when speaking publicly – saw things much the same way. Ernest King, head of the navy, declared that the United States must 'in honour' fight for New Zealand and Australia because their people were 'brothers' of the people of the United States. He put it less gracefully in a private letter, saying he and Roosevelt agreed that one of the reasons why the republic was willing to help the two dominions was to keep up the 'prestige of the white race' in the Pacific.[270]

Māori, of course, saw things another way. The racism so common among American troops struck them as shocking. Citizens whose forebears were Irish or German or Scandinavian also saw things another way, as did those whose forebears were Chinese. Germany, not England, was in fact the homeland of the largest group of migrants ever to settle in the United States. Roosevelt had a Dutch family name, and the surnames of two members of his cabinet were German: the head of treasury, Henry Morgenthau, and the secretary of the interior, Harold Ickes.

The feeling that Americans were somehow kinfolk of New Zealanders was linked with the strongly racist quality of the Pacific War. Citizens on both sides believed

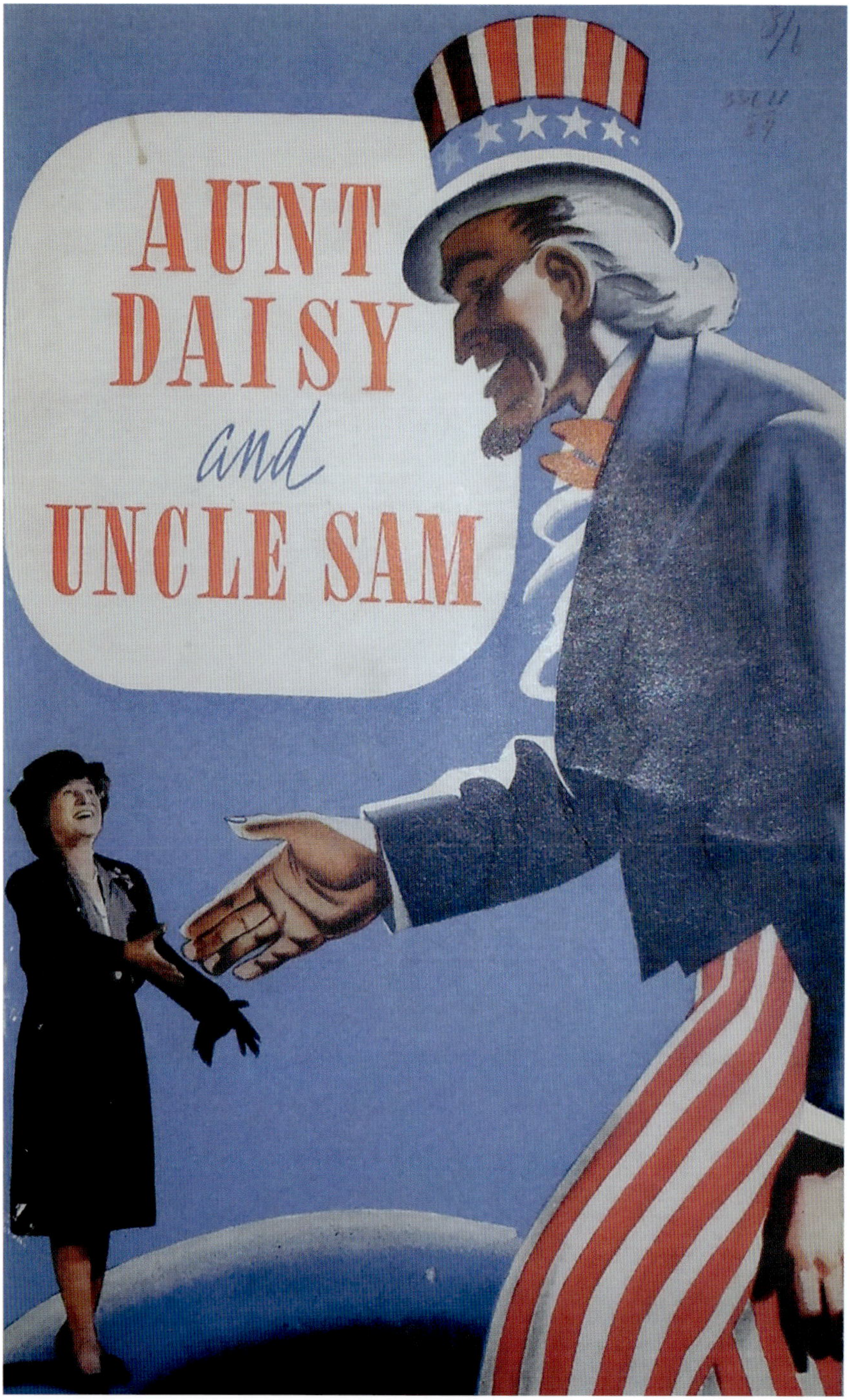

Maud 'Daisy' Basham: clever, talkative and pushy unofficial ambassador to the United States. *M.R. Basham,* Aunt Daisy and Uncle Sam: Aunt Daisy's wartime journey to the United States *(Wellington: Whitcombe & Tombs, 1945).*

in the racial character of the struggle. Japan had developed an elaborate taxonomy concerning the hierarchy of races in the world. At the top were the Japanese, the people most highly evolved racially, morally and spiritually. The mission of the Japanese, it was stressed, was to bring 'purity' to Southeast Asia. White people, by contrast, were coarse and dirty. 'I feel,' wrote Hino Ashihei about white prisoners of war, 'like I am watching filthy water running from the sewerage.'[271]

The Japanese feeling of superiority over whites ironically mirrored the feeling of white superiority over other races that was so widespread in the British Empire, including New Zealand. The war was a struggle of the white race against the 'yellow'. Japanese went about 'gibbering like idiots'.[272] The *Auckland Star* called them 'the bestial Japanese'.[273] Sir Ernest Davis, businessman and politician, spoke about 'the inhuman Japanese demons'.[274] Charles Chandler, clergyman, wrote that the Japanese were a 'sub-human' race and that civilisation would not be safe until they were 'either converted or exterminated'.[275] Hector Bolitho jotted in his diary about 'the little yellow ape who is now marauding in the Pacific'.[276] Gay Gray, newspaper columnist, wrote to her husband about the 'little brown-eyed monkey men'.[277] Paula Hanger, a minor poet, wrote verse about the Japanese as 'eerie and little-boned legions' of 'warriors, subtle in strategy, cold in their venom'. Isabel Peacocke, author of books for children, foamed over about their awfulness:

> *I do not regard the Jap as a man and a brother. God forbid! I think him the lowest and most bestial thing – with apologies to the beasts – that ever crawled out of the primeval slime, with most of the slime still adhering. I would thankfully see the earth purged of him.*[278]

The racism of civilians was mirrored by the racism of the military. Thomas White, a seaman in the New Zealand navy, thought the Japanese 'disgusting'. His captain called them 'the most vile race on the planet'.[279] Richard Mapp, an air-force flight sergeant, hated them as 'horrible little men'.[280]

Racist rage led to military atrocity. United Nations troops often slaughtered all or most surrendering enemy troops.[281] Ralph Williams, a tinsmith conscripted into the army, saw a fellow soldier in his platoon shoot a Japanese survivor at a post in the Solomon Islands. 'He had no weapon, nothing ... And someone just shot him.'[282] A New Zealand army officer said that his men slaughtered the Japanese 'in a wave of hate, such as one would kill rats'. The officer added that it was 'probably stretching one's imagination' to speak about any of the victims as 'a fellow man'.[283] The Fijian army, trained and led by officers from New Zealand, killed more than fifty Japanese for every one they took prisoner during six months of fighting on Bougainville.[284] The *Atlantic Monthly* at the end of the war published an article written by the military correspondent Edgar Jones:

A racist war: government and other propaganda portrayed the Japanese as apes or even monkeys, while also saying the enemy people were capable of nothing more than mimicking the Nazis. *Artist: J.C. Hill.* Auckland Star, *3 August 1940.*

> *We shot prisoners in cold blood, wiped out hospitals, strafed lifeboats, killed or mistreated enemy civilians, finished off the enemy wounded, tossed the dying into a hole with the dead … mutilated the bodies of enemy dead, cutting off their ears and kicking out their gold teeth for souvenirs, and buried them with their testicles in their mouths.*[285]

Only a few prisoners were taken in battle because Japanese troops were not willing to surrender – or so it was said – and would keep on fighting fanatically. The same sort of behaviour was called 'brave' rather than 'fanatical' when found among troops of the United Nations. The doggedness of Japanese troops was exaggerated anyway. Gordon Watson, an essayist and journalist in the New Zealand army, noted that the enemy, while they were 'good troops', were not 'outstandingly stubborn' when fighting.[286]

Civilians in the dominion found, meanwhile, like the peoples of the islands, that they could have fun – and make money – dealing with American troops. Manufacturers, transport companies and many other businesses sold goods and services to the military. Carrying firms, for example, 'worked the clock round for over a year'.[287] Entertainment was 'a very profitable pastime' for those selling goods and services on beaches and streets and in bars, brothels and nightclubs. Cash was spent so freely by marines and soldiers that Auckland, in the opinion of one citizen, became 'a second Cairo'.[288] Young women and young men had sex with the foreign troops. The working class, already besotted with American films and pop music, saw the newcomers as ambassadors of a way of living that was somehow more 'suave', more 'swinging'. Hollywood and swing music, having already become powerful tools for cultural colonisation before the war, swept up many young people. Lauris Scott was wowed:

> *Molly and I went into town for an ice cream. In the milk bar in the next little compartment were some American sailors (there are crowds and crowds of them all over the place) and they were black! I was really excited, especially when they talked – I never expected to hear real American voices except in the pictures. They wanted to shout us ice creams, but of course we didn't want that, it was just their charming way of talking (we told them so). Can you imagine the sheer joy of sitting there watching and listening to a true American accent and manner and style, in real life?*[289]

Yet suspicion, anger and anxiety were widespread too. A Canadian airman in New Zealand heard people speaking about American troops with 'intolerance'. The United States itself, he added, was 'belittled'.[290] New Zealand women chafed at the sexual harassment they suffered from the foreign troops. 'Hiya babe, hiya honey, going my way?' was a common question, often followed by manhandling. Alister Street, a nurse, noted that marines or soldiers would 'take your arm and drag you away'. She grew 'very adept at kicking them in the shins'.[291] Gwen Pollard, in the air force, made the most of being 'a very fast runner'; American troops otherwise would 'grab you' and 'push you into a doorway'.[292] Betty Tossman, also in the air force, taught herself how to deal with sexually aggressive foreign troops. 'We were continually fighting off hands, many hands, all the time. We had no legal protection against that. It was accepted. It wasn't acceptable, but it was accepted. I didn't like it a bit.'[293]

Lauris Scott quickly got fed up too. She wrote that she had become 'quite good at telling them to go away'.[294] She portrayed the scene one night at a Wellington nightclub:

> *A dimly-lit den full of American sailors and marines and weird female creatures dressed in satin and net, all jitter-bugging wildly, a blue smoke haze over everything. There was a real fight too, which drew everyone in the hall except a few blasé ones like us. We just danced grimly on.*[295]

The middle class often looked down on American troops, tending to see them as a rowdy rabble; a young woman from a well-to-do Wellington family, in a novel by Dan Davin, speaks disparagingly about their 'complete insensibility'.[296] Also, while many people on the home front were having fun or making money thanks to the arrival of laden troopships, those who found themselves suddenly competing with foreign marines and soldiers for goods and services were not so happy.[297] Citizens were often offended, too, by the way United States troops could be heard speaking brutally among themselves about 'pigs' – women who were willing to have sex with them. James Michener, a young novelist among the many thousands of incoming troops, wrote about fellow soldiers going into clothing shops and saying: 'I want something frilly for a pig.'[298] He wrote a short story about a family of middle-class Christchurch sisters whose menfolk are away fighting. Anne, one sister, comes home flushed and trembling one night from the city.

'A great oaf! Couldn't even speak the language. Pestered me in the store and then grabbed me as I was leaving. Leered at me and said, "You and me would be terrific in the hay, baby."'[299]

Dominion soldiers away on the other side of the world were upset at 'Yanks' being let loose among the women of New Zealand. The songs that they sang grew thick with anti-American obscenity:

> *They're a pack of Yankee bastards*
> *For reasons plain to see.*

They think they run New Zealand,
But they couldn't run latrines,
Yet they're fucking all our women,
Those United States Marines.[300]

Leslie Cleveland, a young soldier, wrote about what it was like for him to come home on leave from the battlefield and walk the streets of Auckland:

The city had become a garrison town. Queen Street was crowded with marines thronging the restaurants and spilling out of pubs that were trading after hours. Some soldiers were negotiating deals with black market operators, and sly groggers were peddling bootleg liquor. Every dark doorway was occupied by couples embracing.[301]

Sexual and other types of rivalry were so galling as to provoke what one observer called 'many regrettable incidents'.[302] Obscene yelling, bitter fistfights and nasty bashings agitated the streets. A young woman wrote about the 'filthy abuse' she and others who paired up with foreign troops had to bear from 'our own New Zealand boys'.[303] Whetukamokamo Pewhairangi was drinking in a crowded Wellington pub one day when two white Americans 'called him names'. He grabbed a bottle and hit them on the head. The outcome was a 'proper melee' in the pub.[304] Wellington was the setting for many fights between citizens and American troops. Two young men, Leonard Hindrup and George Murland, started one fight, apparently out of 'jealousy between these men and overseas servicemen'.[305] John Crawford, a young seaman, shot and killed two marines in Wellington, as well as firing three gunshots into the body of a young woman, Hazel Salmon. She and the murderer had been lovers, but she had left him and had several 'friends' among the foreign troops.[306] Clarence Bishop, a young labourer, that winter stood on a street 'challenging Americans to fight' and calling on fellow citizens to 'come and fight the Yanks'. Allan Murrell, a young seaman and labourer, did the same nearby: he stood outside a hotel 'challenging Americans to fight' and making a flying tackle at some of them as they went into the pub. 'Several hundred people gathered round and the position became ugly,' wrote a journalist. 'Had it not been for the police there would have been a riot.'[307]

One brawl in the streets of Wellington drew a throng of so many that it came to be known as the Battle of Manners Street. The affray pitched United States marines and sailors against New Zealand merchant seamen and soldiers.[308] Women struck a few blows too. Sonja Vile saw two middle-class matrons 'beating Americans over the head with their umbrellas'.[309] One was her future mother-in-law.

Auckland was the setting for the same sort of fighting. Derek Laver, a seaman in the New Zealand navy, got caught up in 'a pretty big brawl in Queen Street' and found that United States troops wrought 'a fair bit of damage' by whipping off their broad leather belts and wrapping them around their knuckles.[310] A 'drunken street brawl' one night ended when a United States soldier was killed by a blow to the skull.[311]

Fleet's In, painted in 1943, explores the sexual charge between young American servicemen and young women at the seaports and near military bases in New Zealand.
Artist: A. Lois White. McWhannell Stringer Collection.

Shots were fired another night when soldiers fought 'over women' and two men were wounded.[312]Arnold Rapana, a young labourer, and a United States seaman were stabbed when still another big fight broke out.[313] Domingo Eslava, of the United States navy, one day ran with a knife through the streets of Auckland. He had got 'mixed up in an affray', been knocked out 'and then, while still groggy, was given a knife by a bystander to go after his assailant'. He stabbed a policeman.[314] Charles Merrick, a seaman, did his best to kill his wife, Elsie Merrick, in New Lynn. She had left home to live with a United States serviceman and his wife; the serviceman paid her money for sexual favours, seemingly. Merrick took a knife and stabbed her several times, leaving her 'bleeding profusely'.[315] Thomas Beagle, a young soldier in the dominion army, shot a United States serviceman at a military camp near Papakura. The victim had said, 'openly and blatantly', that he wanted to have sex with Beagle and, when Beagle turned him down, had offered him money.[316] Thomas Haworth, a factory foreman, 'went mad' and struck thirteen blows to his wife Patricia's skull at Ōtāhuhu. She had been having sexual relations with Bernard Osgood, a corporal in the United States army.

'I killed her with a hammer,' Haworth told a hotel publican. 'She was rotten to the core; she was no good.'[317]

John Patara, a soldier, and Waitai Haare, a labourer, were found guilty in Auckland of causing 'grievous bodily harm' to a United States sailor, Jeremiah Magill.[318] Joseph Davis, a corporal in the United States army, was walking on a street when he was stopped and attacked by two dominion soldiers. 'Here's one of the —— Yanks who are taking out our New Zealand girls,' said one of the soldiers.[319]

The bashings, knifings and shootings only stopped when the last troopship steamed off from the wharves carrying the last troops away.

'THE TIDE OF WAR HAS DEFINITELY TURNED'

New Zealand by the middle of 1942 had achieved what officialdom called 'peak mobilisation' of the manpower and womanpower of the country. Almost 155,000 men and women were in the military. One out of every three was overseas, while the others were in the dominion, mostly in barracks. Already a lot of people were feeling that the worst was over and the war was not a worry. The *Evening Post* voiced the thoughts of many by pointing out, late in winter, that the 'heavy losses' suffered by Japan meant any sort of raid, let alone an invasion, was now 'extremely unlikely, if not wholly impossible'.[320] Citizens who had evacuated themselves into the backblocks drove or caught a train home to the city. Evadne Ashton-Warner, having spent six months in Pipiriki, went back to Wellington; she said she was sick of living amidst 'the mud and the Maoris'.[321] Civil defence conscripts complained about wasting their time doing pointless drills and firewatching. Home Guard drills thinned out.

A political sign of the new mood came in September when the National Party walked out of the War Administration. The trigger was a strike by coalminers at Huntly. The Labour Party dealt with the strike by bowing to the strikers – or so the National Party claimed.

'When a state neglects to enforce its own laws,' said Holland, 'it sows the seeds of anarchy.'[322]

'[T]here can be no trust between the two parties now,' said Fraser.[323]

The War Administration had lasted only three months, and the strike was not so much cause as pretext for a walkout. A lot of conservatives had been unhappy about the coalition from the beginning. The National Party, wrote one, had 'sold its birthright to the Federation of Labour'.[324] The War Administration never had a 'honeymoon', noted the *Auckland Star*.[325] Dealings between government members and opposition members of the coalition behind closed doors had not gone smoothly either.[326] Holland was not keen to be one among a group of ministers; he wanted to be prime minister of a government led by his own party, and very likely had agreed to a coalition only because he thought that many voters would accuse him of being unpatriotic if he stayed out.[327]

A scene in the North Africa campaign: *The Breakthrough, Mingar Qa'im.* *Artist: Peter McIntyre. Archives New Zealand.*

Nobody would try again to patch together a war coalition between the National Party and the Labour Party.

The need for coalition seemed less pressing anyway, thanks to the steady dimming of the stars of Japan, Italy and Germany. British Commonwealth troops had beaten back a last German drive into Egypt, and were now pushing forward into Libya. Britain tightened its grip on Egypt, forcing from office the prime minister, 'Ali Mahir, one of the key figures who was keen to get help from Germany.[328] New Zealand radio and newspapers hyped up the advance against the enemy in Libya as a key breakthrough in the war against the Axis. Kippenberger on the ground saw it the same way; he spoke to his troops about the fighting as 'the very beginning of the turning of the tide' in the Second World War.[329]

A far weightier struggle was under way, however, on a vast, shifting frontier between Germany and the Soviet Union. The Third Reich fielded up to 195 divisions on its eastern front; by comparison, no more than nine divisions were ever deployed to fight for North Africa. Millions of men, observed a New Zealand war correspondent, were 'locked in a life-and-death struggle' between the Soviet Union and Germany.[330] The Battle of Stalingrad alone, a murderous morass, was of enormously greater gravity than the Second Battle of El Alamein.

The Japanese, too, were 'signally defeated' by the end of spring when they tried to break out of the cordon set up by the United Nations.[331]

The Solomon Islands was the setting for a first big counterattack against Japan carried out by the United States, with help from Australia, Britain and New Zealand. New Zealand sent not only troops but an air-force squadron, which flew with the air arm of the United States navy. A tiny force from Fiji tagged along too, as did a few men from Tonga. Fighting began early in August and lasted for a gruelling six months, during which 38,000 men were killed, more than eight out of every ten of whom were Japanese.

Osmar White, a war correspondent from the dominion, went along with the invading army to observe landings on Guadalcanal. Troopships were escorted by warships:

> *All the destroyers in the Pacific seemed to be pacing up and down the channel like chained watchdogs, restless and vigilant, while the clumsy big ships disgorged men and guns in dun-green streams from hatches to barges. Security patrols of fighters were up. A formation of dive bombers winged its way west.*[332]

Solomon Islanders were not asked whether they wanted their villages to be shelled, bombed and fought over by Japan and the United Nations. Sydney and Auckland, Melbourne and Christchurch told radio listeners and newspaper readers that 'natives' in tropical island colonies were 'loyal' to the British Empire. Lendrick McMaster, a clergyman, spoke about such loyalty when he gave a talk in Leeston.[333] The truth was that most villagers were glad to see the back of their colonial overlords. The flight of the whites freed tribespeople from forced labour, indenturing, hut tax and poll tax.[334] Villagers often got along well enough with the Japanese army. Walter Baddeley, an Anglican bishop on Tulagi, saw occupying Japanese troops behave in a 'most apologetic' way when taking food from the villages. Villagers 'retired to their gardens in the bush, and remained there till the end of the occupation'. Only when the occupying army built an airfield were villagers rounded up to do some work, but the tribes just moved further back into the jungle.

'The Japanese treated the natives fairly well,' said Baddeley. 'It was remarkable how life in the villages in the bush went on normally.'[335]

Villagers in Papua and New Guinea for the most part rubbed along fairly well with occupation troops too. Michael Somare, a clever boy who later became prime minister of an independent Papua New Guinea, found the troops and officials sent by Tokyo 'extremely friendly' to the tribespeople of his country. Apo Amala, a tribesman, agreed that the Japanese were 'kind and just' to people in the villages.[336]

All year, meanwhile, the dominion was waging war in the air and at sea against Germany.

A Japanese victim of New Zealand weaponry: *Dead Sniper, Mono.*
Artist: William Reed. Dunedin Art Gallery.

Two new squadrons of warplanes set up within the British air force were manned mostly by young men from New Zealand. Airmen from the dominion were to be found in droves through the whole of the British air force, whose priority by late 1942 was 'ever-increasing air bombardment'.[337] Bombers no longer went after military and economic targets but instead sought to cripple or kill the civilians of Germany. A total of 1200 men from the dominion ended up flying or working as ground crew in this campaign of bombing.[338] The New Zealand bomber squadron in four months alone launched over fifty air raids and dropped hundreds of tonnes of bombs onto street after street of housing.[339] An airman told the story of a raid on Danzig:

The Angel of Death drops bombs on Adolf Hitler and Hermann Göring. The policy of 'carpet' bombing German cities was never portrayed by dominion newspapers, radio and cinema news as a policy of burning, wounding, shattering and killing civilians, although twelve German civilians were killed by New Zealand and other United Nations bomber fleets for every one British civilian killed by German bombing. *Artist: Minhinnick.* New Zealand Herald, *12 May 1942.*

Oh, Danzig. Neat little houses that all slowly slewed in the one direction as the blast hit them. Neat little houses that suddenly glowed gently and beautifully as the incendiaries took hold in their roofs. Have you ever seen those rows of coloured lights they string across the streets in New Zealand at Christmas? A string of incendiaries looks exactly like that, except that they're all red. Then a high-explosive bomb scatters the glow into a pattern like a rose garden – you know, a formal arrangement – geometrical, almost. After a while the scattered little roses run together into one big glow.[340]

The British navy at the same time struck hard against what was left of the German navy and merchant marine, along with any neutral shipping trying to get through the blockade of Germany. Denis Glover, one of many young New Zealanders in the British navy, was aboard a destroyer escorting convoys: 'one moment you see a ship, even though ablaze, and the next moment there is a great pall of smoke, and nothing on the surface of the Arctic water but a few small heads bobbing like pumpkins,' he wrote on the way to Murmansk.[341]

Thousands of households throughout the dominion by the end of 1942 were in mourning for sons, brothers, lovers, fathers and husbands. Almost 4200 soldiers, sailors and airmen were never coming back home to New Zealand. Another 1300 were 'missing'.[342] Throngs of men had become prisoners of war, too. The life they lived behind wire was nearly always dreary, sometimes grim, sometimes terrifying. A year that had begun with a mood of crisis ended nonetheless with a widespread feeling that the worst was over and that the outcome would be certain victory. Already the government had stopped many civil defence doings, eased blackout restrictions and lightened the hours of training for the Home Guard. Politicians acknowledged in Christmas speeches that the most taxing tasks were now behind the country.

'There is more cause to-day than ever since the outbreak of this war for reasoned confidence,' said Fraser. 'The tide of war has definitely turned this year and is with gathering strength now running with us.'

'[T]oday,' added Holland, 'the initiative everywhere has been wrested from the Axis.'[343]

Citizens often spoke far more bluntly.

'The Japs are as dead as Julius Caesar,' said a market gardener, George Parvin, at a hospital board meeting in Auckland.[344]

German civilians in the aftermath of a bombing raid. New Zealand squadrons nearly always flew with others in the British bombing fleet, which means we will never know which Allied nation was responsible for wiping out this group of people. Bombs dropped by New Zealand planes must have killed tens of thousands of women, children and old men in Germany. *Bundesarchiv Deutschland, Bild 146-1983-122-05A.*

New Year Holiday: the beach at Corsair Bay, Canterbury, early in 1943. *Artist: Evelyn Page. Hocken Pictorial Collections.*

CHAPTER 5 THE SECOND PHONEY WAR
JANUARY 1943 TO SEPTEMBER 1945

THE BEACH LOOMS CLOSE

The worst of the war was barely beginning for the unlucky people of Japan, and had been going on several years for the unlucky people of China. The most gruelling days of worry and fear were over already, however, for most of the lucky people of New Zealand. Although the going was still tough for soldiers, airmen and sailors on the fighting front, citizens at home knew that the dominion was safe and that the war was going to be won by the United Nations.

The last years of the war, at least for the dominion, might be called the Second Phoney War.

The United Nations drove forward nearly everywhere during the whole of 1943, almost always beating back the Axis. North Africa, where the mass of troops from the dominion were still fighting, was the stony and sandy setting for retreat after retreat by the troops of Italy and Germany. African battles were dwarfed, as before, by the struggle between Germany and the Soviet Union. The Battle of Kursk, in which both sides suffered dreadful losses, ended with defeat for Germany. Afterwards, the Soviet Union ground its way towards Poland. A sideshow opened in Italy when troops flying the flags of several states of the United Nations invaded from North Africa.

The war at sea and the war in the air, meanwhile, were being won wholesale by the United Nations.

The war at sea, though, was not won without heavy losses in the Atlantic. German submarines did so well in their attacks on shipping for one or two months early in the year that it seemed they might wreck the sea link between Britain and the United States. Germany's run of good luck ended in 'Black May' when the United Nations sank one out of every four working submarines in the German navy, the *Kriegsmarine*. Germany had lost the Battle of the Atlantic.

Japan, needing to keep shipping lanes open between China, Southeast Asia and its home waters, was too weak to be able to do much in the way of raiding. Submarines

John Fullarton, an officer in the New Zealand army, offered young readers a 'patriotic' portrait of the campaign in North Africa in his novel, *Troop Target* (London: Hutchinson & Co., 1943).

The Angel of Death plays a bombing symphony; as usual in such newspaper images, bombs are visible but not the victims of bombs. *Artist: Minhinnick.* New Zealand Herald, *28 February 1944.*

were sent out into the Pacific, but never very many. Ten or so burrowed up and down the Tasman Sea. A total of eighteen merchant ships on their way to or from the dominion were sunk by the middle of 1943 but then the Japanese navy, badly overstretched, stopped raiding in the Tasman. Other submarines and raiders worked the sea lanes in the Indian Ocean. The *Hauraki*, a cargo and passenger liner carrying military stores to Egypt, was taken, but dominion shipping on the whole was safe on the seaways. 'The trade routes which connect us with the Motherland still continue to be busy highways of commerce,' wrote a journalist, 'and our outward cargoes are at or near the highest ceiling ever touched in our history.'[1]

The war in the air was fought bitterly. New Zealand crews did most of their killing in Germany. James Insull, a navigator, was one of many men from the dominion who helped to sow a scorching whirlwind in Hamburg:

> *It was a shapeless mass of fire so far below that it all appeared like a badly focused technicoloured film of lights that seemed to move, twinkle and shimmer in a thousand shapes in colours of yellow, red and orange on a background of black velvet. I could soon distinguish bomb bursts and gun flashes among the blotches of light. I stared and stared. My heart was pounding and I felt I was not getting enough air.*[2]

Japan began losing ground when the United States started a strategy of 'island hopping'. The trick was to bypass island strongholds and take only islands that were not strong – and even then only enough to allow the United States to hop towards the mainland of Japan. One of the first islands in the chain was Bougainville. William Mitchell, an apprentice panelbeater in the dominion army, saw what the strategy meant when he was sent to the island after it had been taken by the United States:

> *It was frightening. The smell of death. The Americans had bulldozed great big holes and pushed all the corpses in and put in quicklime in the front line, but up in the hills you couldn't do that and there were arms and legs and limbs sticking out everywhere. The smell. Dead bodies.*[3]

United Nations strategy overall was still to throw most weight against Germany. The American military leadership on the sly followed a 'Pacific First' strategy of sending men and weaponry west rather than east, against the wishes and without the knowledge of the government in Washington.[4] As yet, though, the people of Japan felt the wretchedness of war less than those of Germany.

The United States, the British Commonwealth and lesser allies opened a new western front on 'D-Day', in the winter of 1944, with mass landings in France. Troops thronged onto beachheads while a fleet of warships rode the waves and a fleet of warplanes droned through the sky. Sir Arthur Coningham, an airman from the dominion, commanded the Allied Expeditionary Air Force. Hundreds of other airmen from the dominion flew warplanes to support the landing. Four squadrons crewed by men from New Zealand strafed, torpedoed and dropped bombs.[5] Elsie Carter, one of several young women from the dominion working on radar for the British air force, looked up as the battle fleet winged its way towards France. She noted that 'you couldn't see the sky for planes'.[6] Dewi Browne, a seaman from Whanganui, was on a hospital ship steaming to France:

> *On the way over I had two thoughts uppermost: goodness me, there's not that many ships in the whole world; and the other thing was, all these planes going over by the hundreds, all going the same way. I thought, they're all ours, and I thought, I know who's winning the war now.*[7]

Three thousand men from the dominion were on board warships. Denis Glover later wrote about the day:

> *Now eyes for everything, eyes for nothing. The beach looms close. There are people running up and down it. There are fires and the bursting of shells. Yes, and wrecked landing craft everywhere, a flurry of propellers in the savage surf … We are on those bristling stakes. They stretch before us in rows. The mines on them look as big as planets.*[8]

Germany fell back, and kept falling back. The Wehrmacht made a game bid to turn the tables in the west in the last days of 1944 during the Battle of the Bulge, but it was hopeless. German generals, like Japanese admirals after Pearl Harbor, found that while good tactical planning and a willingness to seize the initiative could temporarily put the enemy on the back foot, any offensive, no matter how successful at first, was doomed to strategic failure. The Battle of the Bulge was frightening for United Nations troops on the ground, who reeled back against attacking tanks, but it was not frightening for politicians and the officer corps in London, Washington or Moscow. The United Nations simply had far too many men, far too many weapons, and far too much money.

Japan throughout 1944 lost island after island, bringing the enemy and its bombers closer and closer to the homeland. Saipan, in the Northern Marianas, fell in July.

'Hell is about to descend upon us,' said the Japanese naval chief of staff after he heard about the loss.[9]

Tojo, taking responsibility, resigned as prime minister and into his shoes stepped another army general, Koiso Kuniaki. The new prime minister knew that the outlook was dismaying. A lot of political, military and other leaders had been saying for a year and more that the war could not be won and that the government should seek peace with the United Nations. The task now was to work out some way of losing while holding on to what governing groups believed to be the key things in the imperial state. Koiso and his cronies wanted to keep Japanese sovereignty and fend off democracy. Also they hoped to cling to a few scraps of overseas territory.

One option was to surrender straightaway to the United States. Another option was to wait until the Soviet Union came into the war in Asia. A group lobbied late in 1944 for the first option: the worst threat to Japan, or at least its governing groups, they argued, came from the Soviet Union and the Communist Party.[10] Yet even many of those leaders were wary of the United States. Takagi Sokichi, for example, an admiral who wanted peace, thought Washington sought a new world order revolving around the United States.[11] Others argued that the best hope for the nation was to be a middle power keeping its autonomy within a continent controlled by two superpowers – the Soviet Union and the United States. Japan made up its mind to follow the second strategy.[12]

A Japanese government poster showing civilians how to cope with bombing, 1943.
Mitchell Wolfson, Jr. Collection, Wolfsonian-Florida International University.

Air raids began to hit the mainland. James Bertram was a prisoner of war and saw the first bombs dropped on Tokyo:

> *The Ginza as one knew it in pre-war Tokyo was a built-up boulevard with a number of big department stores at its eastern side, and a string of cafés and shops that came within a few hundred yards of our working place. It was far from being a priority military target ... When at last the 'All Clear' sounded, a clear mile of the Ginza was spouting flame, with great sheets of fire meeting in the centre of the road beneath an arching roof of smoke.*[13]

The goal of the bombing, on the whole, was not to hit military targets but to spread terror, injury and death among civilians. Bertram noted that fire bombs were dropped in 'containers that exploded and broke asunder in mid-air', after which 'the sky was filled with a golden dropping rain'.[14] Napalm, developed in secret by the United States and first used earlier in the year on the people of Berlin, was the source of the golden rain. The chemical not only burnt buildings but stuck to the skin of people, making them shrivel up in agony.

The war at sea during 1944 was more or less a straightforward blockade of the Axis. Sea lanes were strewn with the sunken hulls of Japanese, German and neutral shipping, along with the corpses of passengers and crews. The Japanese merchant marine at the start of the war with the United Nations had weighed nearly 5.9 million tonnes but was down to less than 4.1 million by the beginning of 1944 and then not much more than 2.3 million by the end of that year.[15] The *Toyama Maru*, for example, a cargo passenger liner converted to a troopship, dragged 5400 crewmen and young Japanese soldiers down to their death thanks to four torpedoes shot into the hull by the United States submarine *Sturgeon*. The death toll was well over twice that of the sinking of the *Titanic*. Japan could not cope with anywhere near such a heavy loss of shipping.

One submarine of the German navy did get as far as the waters of the Tasman Sea, where it sank a cargo ship before fleeing eastwards in the first week of 1945 to cruise without luck up and down the shipping lanes to Auckland. The vessel looked gingerly over Gisborne, with the help of a periscope. Crew were amazed by the sound of music and the sight of couples dancing under bright lights. Günther Reiffenstuhl, first officer, wrote about it in his diary:

> *The pier is brightly lit, behind it is a big factory. One can see cars driving along the streets with their headlights on. The street lighting itself is also very bright, we are directly blinded by it. All the houses have their lights on, it looks like Christmas to us ... The people here are all so wonderfully unsuspecting.*

The submarine, nosing its way south, saw and heard much the same sights and sounds when reconnoitring Napier. 'The town on a hill glitters in a thousand lights,' wrote Reiffenstuhl. 'The people,' another crew member added, had 'no idea of a war and its sorrow.'[16] New Zealand had been feeling safe for two years by then and victory was so close that the British navy was moving many of its biggest and best warships into the Pacific. The *Howe*, flagship of a new British Pacific Fleet, anchored in Auckland.

'Our strategy can be expressed simply,' said Sir Bruce Fraser, commander of the fleet. 'It is to find and sink the Japanese Fleet.'[17]

United States troops smashed their way into western Germany during the first months of 1945, while eastern Germany was squeezed tight by the Soviet Union. Already, the winning powers were jockeying behind closed doors for advantage in the peace settlements. The British Commonwealth did its best to sell itself as a third superpower alongside the Soviet Union and the United States. The war had so badly weakened and impoverished Britain, however, that it was now in some ways a client state of the United States. The United States also talked up 'China' or, in other words, another client – the Guomindang. Stalin looked askance at such talk, worrying that once Hitler had been got out of the way the next foe he had to handle might be the United States.

FEED OR FIGHT?

New Zealand during these years had to work out its own war strategy. Political parties, the officer corps of the military, landed and farming groups, trading groups, bankers, industrialists, the professional unions, the unions of the working class, churches and many other groups talked long and hard through 1943 about what they thought made best sense, and needless to say found themselves disagreeing – often bitterly.

Two questions were key. The first was whether to keep waging a fighting war or, instead, to quit the battlefields and get down to doing what the dominion did well: growing, making and shipping food and other goods to the United Nations. The second question, linked with the first, already had been canvassed widely. Was it wise to leave the struggle in Europe to others, bring the troops back to the Pacific and throw everything against the Japanese Empire?

The debate over the first of those two questions livened up after the surrender of the Axis troops in North Africa.

Politicians, mayors, chambers of commerce and others claiming to speak for the citizens of the dominion trumpeted the surrender in words not only pompous but far from clear-sighted about what had happened in the sands and stones between Tunisia and Egypt. Fraser spoke about a 'truly great victory', even adding that it was 'one of the most complete military victories in history'. David Davies, an Anglican clergyman, told a distinguished congregation in the capital that 'the forces of evil' would now 'soon be overthrown'.[18]

After the boasting, the next step was to decide what to do with the army. The troops, backed by their loved ones, were asking for a break, and many people were saying that it no longer made sense to keep waging a fighting war when the country was suffering from a shortage of labour that threatened to become crippling. The United States and Britain were both asking the dominion for more food, too.

Britain had toyed with dropping the dominion as a food supplier during the height of submarine warfare, but when the submarines were beaten back, officials and politicians in the imperial capital became keen to ship more from New Zealand. The dominion was attractive as a supply source because it was so very efficient at producing food, and it was inside the sterling bloc. Britain needed to buy as much as it could within that bloc. London, therefore, during the last years of the war worked hard to beg, bribe and browbeat the dominion into shipping out food. A severe shortage of meat and butter, and a marked shortage of cheese, from late 1943 taxed the military and civilian planners of all states.[19] Britain was in such straits that cheese and butter rations had been halved since the start of the war, and then halved once more, after which the cheese ration was halved yet again; while food officials wondered whether citizens would have to be stopped from eating any butter at all.[20] John Llewellin, food minister, spoke of the 'overwhelming' dependence of Britain on butter and cheese from

The Soviet Union by the last months of 1942 was clearly winning the titanic struggle with Germany. *Artist: J.C. Hill. Auckland Star, 28 November 1942.*

New Zealand, together with lesser but 'still, very marked' dependence on the dominion for meat. 'If New Zealand's production declines below the present level,' he wrote early in 1944, 'I do not see how we can possibly maintain our present standards of feeding in this country.'[21]

'Look here,' Sidney Holland told a gathering of farmers and landowners in Canterbury, 'it is a question of whether we can save Britain from sheer and utter starvation.'[22]

The United States also wanted the dominion to plough and sow to feed the troops, while at the same time it was keen to keep elbowing small allies out of the fighting. Roosevelt did want some dominion troops to be pitted against Japan, but only to keep up the look of battles being undertaken by the whole of the United Nations. Theodore Wilkinson, an American admiral, pointed out that the United States was 'dependent' on New Zealand for food supplies to the military. The dominion supplied over half the food rations of American troops in the Pacific during 1943, and afterwards that share grew steadily.[23]

'You have certain food commitments to Britain,' William Calhoun, another American admiral, told a press conference in the last autumn of the war, 'and you have to feed yourselves, but we can take everything else, even if your output is trebled.'[24]

The dominion could not keep boosting its output of food, let alone of other goods and services, while also fielding an army in Europe and another in the Pacific. One in five men and women had been yanked out of the civilian labour force and into the military by the beginning of 1943, and the young and fit workers most needed by farming and other industry were those yanked out. One in two men of military age was now in barracks or on the battlefields instead of providing civilian services or making or growing food and other goods.[25] The loss of workers was hitting so hard that many industries were 'beginning to reach the limit of their ability to produce with their reduced staffs'.[26] The government wracked its brain over how to push production while keeping a strong military.

Why not fight on what people were now calling 'the food front', not the battle front?

At the very beginning of the war, plenty of people had argued that it would be better in every way for the dominion to feed, rather than fight for the Allies. Men would not be killed and the country could make money. Or, to put it less bluntly, efficiency would be best served by states nearest the battlefields doing the fighting while those farthest away put capital and labour into production to back those doing the fighting.

New Zealand, too, even when straining itself to the utmost, could field no more than a trifling number of troops, warplanes or warships alongside what was now being deployed by the big powers of the United Nations. The military strength of the dominion seemed quite beside the point when observers watched opening blows in the titanic struggle between Japan and the United States. Osmar White, a war correspondent born in Feilding, was awed by the massive scale of the American war machine in the autumn of 1943 when he was posted to Nouméa. The wharves were 'jammed with merchant shipping, much of it new and big'. A whole industrial town of 'new iron-roofed storehouses' had been built, the streets were noisy with 'streams of jeeps and trucks that squirted exhaust fumes so virulent that the leaves of the shade trees were oily and wilting'. The sky overhead was crowded with warplanes.[27] White saw 'steam shovels liquidating mountains, planes crossing oceans on schedules that read like rural train services, and tonnages with strings of ciphers that made the imagination giddy'. He found himself 'not entirely free from the feeling of being present at the birth of a juggernaut destined, before its life was done, to crush half the Orient'.[28]

Why should the dominion waste manpower and money by trotting out a regiment or two, or a score or so air squadrons, alongside such a juggernaut?

Advocates of that point of view often spoke out during the last months of 1942, and one thing that made the government listen was that those advocates stood on

New Zealand air-force men in an operations room in the Solomon Islands.
Artist: Maurice Conly. Air Force Museum of New Zealand.

both the political left and right. Employers wanted more workers; workers wanted not to go into the army. Fraser put the question before parliament in early December: the government, he said, now had to work out how best to balance 'the man-power requirements of the forces for the country's security and those of industry'. Holland replied that 'man-power and its organisation for war purposes' was 'causing more concern' to citizens than any other question and that it was time for 'a complete overhaul' of how workers were being used by the country.[29]

The question was canvassed more and more urgently. A conference of lobby groups and town and county councils in Christchurch at the end of the year agreed that keeping so many people in the military was 'wasteful of manpower, inefficient, costly, tedious, and frustrating'.[30] Auckland hosted conferences of trade unions and employers which concluded that the dominion needed to 'move from organisation of maximum concentration for military defence' towards 'maximum utilisation of manpower for production' – a conclusion backed by the Auckland Farmers Union.[31] Landowners and farmers were keen to get more workers into the paddocks, the woolsheds, the dairy factories and the freezing works.

The government by then was already winding down the military. Only two more conscript ballots followed peak mobilisation: a cohort of over 22,000 men in their mid-thirties were called up in early spring, and nearly 22,000 in their late thirties a month or so later.

Landowners, farmers and factory owners spoke out against taking workers to do 'useless routines' in the military when they could be freed for farming and industry.[32] The *Southland Daily News* early in 1943 talked about the pointlessness of conscripting men in order to keep them in camp where they did nothing more useful than 'eating and marching'.[33] Holland told parliament two months later there was 'no justification for the number of men who are under arms in this country'. The president of the Manufacturers Federation, he went on to say, was unhappy about the way the state had conscripted 'literally thousands of men' who were doing nothing but 'wasting their time' in barracks.[34]

Not all citizens or lobby groups were keen on thinning out the military, though. A few people on the political left argued that such a policy would be good for capitalists but not for freedom and democracy. Gordon Watson, a communist editor, wrote eagerly about the matter:

> *The idea of winning the war by growing food alone is a thoroughly petit-bourgeois idea, not a radical one ... Raising food crops to be sold for a profit would be a far 'better' way of winning a war than fighting in Burma or Borneo – but unfortunately there is no such choice for the Allies as a whole; the only argument is as to whether New Zealand should assume a responsibility for both forms of the war effort.*[35]

Conservatives spoke up, too, saying that the state must not sap the strength of the military. The officer corps wanted more, not fewer men and women on battlefields; it

Factory workers outside the Tattersfield mattress and rug factory, Auckland. The working class was driven harder and harder as the war went on, though at the same time the Labour government knew it must not push too hard or it would lose voter support. *Auckland Star, 26 October 1945.*

told parliament in a secret session in the spring of 1942 that conscription must be kept up until the full strength of the army, navy and air force grew to 185,000 – far more than most others thought fitting.[36] Conservatives remarked that switching from guns to butter was cowardly. The *Auckland Star* told readers the dominion should share 'the heat and burden of the struggle' instead of just supplying 'the biscuits and the jam', in order to 'enjoy an honourable status in the Pacific'.[37] The *Star-Sun* declared that citizens must not let the world say they 'defended their shores to the last drop of American blood'.[38] The conservative point of view voiced by such newspapers, however, was outweighed by an awareness among most of their readers that there was money to be made by supplying goods and services to the United States.

A first big step towards getting men out of the military came when all conscripts aged eighteen or nineteen years were freed to go back to their lives as civilians. The next step, taken in winter 1943, was to 'cut to its bones' the territorial army.[39] Slowly the huge herd of men and women wearing military uniform shrank; by the end of the year ranks were down to 137,000, which meant than one out of every nine people who had been under arms at the peak of mobilisation was now back on 'civvy street'. The Emergency Precautions Scheme was wound down, too, as was the Home Guard.

'New Zealand is faced with a most serious crisis, particularly in regard to the production of foodstuffs,' Nash wrote to William Halsey, admiral commanding in the South Pacific. 'Accordingly every effort is being made to effect the temporary release of any further men from the Armed Services.'[40]

Soldiers were marched out from barracks, and students Manpowered from university, to work in the paddocks. Only a few students welcomed patriotic work, noted Lauris Scott. Although she was keen – she wanted the wage – others were 'grumbling'. Students found the work hard. Janet Frame was among a student group Manpowered to pick raspberries in Central Otago:

> *Day and night we tried to endure the heat of the sun burning the air outside and stored in the corrugated iron walls and roof of the large shed where we lived and slept. Every day, all day, we picked raspberries as we'd been taught, crouched, milking them gently from their stalks, dropping the soft furry blobs into the tin bucket hanging by a cord around our neck. Our hands were stained with raspberry blood, and scratched with raspberry thorns.*[41]

Scott found the work hard, too. 'I'm … hot and dirty and tired,' she wrote in her diary. '*We are workers of the world* Molly says; *I know* I say and we are convulsed with laughter.'[42]

The need for workers on the land proved to be less than state planners had supposed, thanks to wartime mechanisation on farms and estates,[43] so the state Manpowered more workers into manufacturing. It also lengthened working hours for many of those on wages. Regulations were gazetted that ended treble-time pay, tightened other overtime pay and gave employers more freedom to play about with holidays. Construction workers, freezing workers, watersiders and factory hands were among those who had to put in longer hours at their tasks without overtime pay.

Hours had been extended in 'essential' industries even before the declaration of war on Japan. Clothing workers on some factory floors had been locked into fifty-six hours, freezing-workers as many as seventy hours, and some engineering and munitions workers seventy-five hours weekly.[44] At the start of the war with Japan the National Service Department urged the government to lengthen the working week for everybody on wages, speed up Manpowering, conscript all women who could work and ship them to cities where they were needed for industry, use children and old people, rationalise every essential industry through 'standardisation, simplification, pooling, zoning and the reallocation of orders' and, lastly, poleaxe every 'non-essential' industry.[45]

The Labour government found the proposals too harsh – needless to say, given it had been voted into power by the working class. A committee of officials of state and politicians was set up: the Cabinet Committee on Readjustment of Industry. The committee released a report that called for much the same measures as the National Service Department had proposed: state control of workers and state organisation of industry. The National Party now pressed for a sterner Manpower policy. The Farmers Union weighed in, too: it wanted state control of all industry, closing or curbing of production deemed not 'essential', and more hours at the grindstone for the working class.[46] Parliament went into secret session to talk over the whole Manpower question, after which the war cabinet agreed to impose a working week of 48 hours in war industry, 'concentrate' that industry, simplify and standardise production and get rid of 'non-essential' industry.[47]

The Battle of Midway helped the government in the hard task of selling the new policy to the working class; such a powerful blow against Japan ended the mood of urgency and meant the state could take steps slowly.

A meeting of union leaders, employers and state officials in Wellington early in 1943 talked about whether or not to go ahead with the longer working week and, if so, how. The meeting set up a 'very cumbersome and impractical process' to lengthen working hours 'industry-by-industry', which seems to have been done in order to 'thwart progress'.[48] The government wanted to look like it was working towards a tough policy, but without making life too hard for the working class. The building industry was a test case for the new policy. James Fletcher, commissioner for building, asked for a forty-eight-hour working week throughout the whole industry. The government vetoed the proposal and imposed those hours only on workers building for the military, or building hospitals or state housing. Workers fought back by holding stopwork meetings. A deal brokered, in the end, between unions and the minister of labour fell short of what capitalists had sought.[49]

The National Party, which throughout the war had keenly urged the government to impose longer hours on the working class, was having second thoughts now that it saw how easily such a step could stir wage workers into becoming stroppy.

Overtime was another way to squeeze more output from those working for wages – though at a cost to bosses, who were obliged by law to pay overtime wages at a higher rate than for standard hours on the job. Overtime worked by civilians had already gone up markedly during the early war years; now, it kept on going up. Workers put in more than six million hours of overtime during the second year of the war; nearly nine million hours the next year, and then over fourteen million hours when war began with Japan.[50] Overtime meant more money in the pockets of the working class but, of course, by keeping people on the treadmill away from their homes, it was also an attack on the family.

Wage workers were harried in other ways, too. The policy of feeding allies while still keeping an army in the field meant that screws were tightened on anyone who wanted to wriggle out of being Manpowered.

Raids for errant workers became widespread during the last years of the war. Police and Manpower officers hunted people down at beaches, parks, golf courses; in tearooms, hotels and cinemas. A worker who had no valid reason for being away from work could be hauled before a magistrate. Manpower officers seldom used their powers until the autumn of 1943, when the government ordered them to behave more sternly.[51] Phoebe Sanderson, for example, was tapped on the shoulder one day inside a cinema in Auckland. She turned to see a man and a woman.

'What are you away from work for?' they asked.

'Why, what do you want to know for?' she answered. 'I don't know you people.'

The man and woman showed her an identity card and told her they were from Man-

Government and corporate propaganda continued to urge the working class to be 'cogs' in the war machine for the sake of 'victory'. *Artist: John Harvey. Allan Sleeman,* They Work to Win: Cogs in the story of New Zealand industry geared to war *(Christchurch: Caxton Press, 1942).*

power.[52] Sanderson had been ill and was still convalescent, but most workers rounded up by state officials were taking a day or two off work because they were bored, weary or unhappy. Uru Rutini was one: a hand at the Whakatane Paper Mills, he had been injured at work and given leave for a while but, when he was declared medically fit, had not gone back to his tasks. He was found guilty of absenteeism by a magistrate.[53] Manpower officials by the end of the war had dealt with over 48,000 complaints about workers not clocking in for work.[54] Absenteeism was far more widespread than indicated by those complaints, as the *Auckland Star* noted early in 1944:

> *Absenteeism in industry is rife from end to end of the country ... thousands of workers ... regard it as the right of free men and women to work or not, as it suits them. That the war effort, the business of providing essential foodstuffs, equipment and services for the United Nations must inevitably suffer in consequence apparently does not weigh with them.*[55]

Managers and owners of workshops and factories often did not bother to report absent workers to state officials because absenteeism was hard to prove and took a lot of troublesome paperwork, and because the labour shortage was so bad that employers were reluctant to upset their staff. Also many of them were aware of research by economist Leslie Hearnshaw, whose pamphlet *Hours of Work in Wartime*, published in the spring of 1942, showed that the efficiency of workers dropped so markedly when they were kept for longer hours at their tasks as to wipe out any gains in output.[56] Nor were workers likely to do their best when Manpowering made them feel aggrieved and angry. Isobel Andrews wrote a short story called 'Bondsmen and Free', portraying a young man bound to his job in an essential industry.

'I'm stuck here in the blasted cheese factory for the duration,' he grumbles. 'No better'n a slave that's what I am. No better'n a slave. Is this a democracy?'[57]

Conscientious objectors and military defaulters, meanwhile, were perhaps the only ordinary people who gained with the shift away from a shooting war to fighting on the food front. A lot of liberal people were now saying openly that maybe it was not such an awful crime not to want to go into the army. The labour of those who objected to war on grounds of conscience, or on grounds of their own health and safety, could be given over to productive tasks on farms or in factories and workshops. The Catholic *Tablet* declared early in 1944 that letting objectors and defaulters out of prison would be 'in the national interest'. Petitions to parliament signed by several thousand citizens

Consumers were tantalised by advertisements promising that the reward for putting up with the shortages and makeshifts of war would come when military production switched back to peace production after 'victory'. This advertisement purports to show the switch taking place at the headquarters of General Motors New Zealand. *Allan Sleeman,* Prelude to Peace *(Christchurch: Jack Maybury, 1946).*

the following winter argued that imprisoning objectors and defaulters was 'wasteful both economically and in human values'.[58]

The war cabinet agreed in secret to loosen the strings: it set up 'revision authorities' to allow defaulters to apply for release on parole. Two out of every five defaulters had been given their freedom by the end of the war.[59]

The battle on the food front, in other words, was welcome news for defaulters and conscientious objectors.

Capitalists meanwhile were still pressing the government to wind down the military. The Manufacturers Federation lobbied the government early in 1944 to 'revise its military commitments, with a view to maintaining and increasing its industrial contribution to the war'.[60] The *New Zealand Herald* declared the shortage of workers to be 'the most clamant of those faced in this young year, and the one which will brook least delay'.[61] Fraser cabled Nash that soon there was likely to be 'a strong case' for withdrawing the dominion army from Europe in order to fight only in the Pacific 'and to maintain, and if possible increase, food production'.[62] Nash asked Roosevelt whether he thought boosting the output of food would be the best strategy for New Zealand.[63] The Federation of Labour, delegates from other working-class groups and capitalists sent along by chambers of commerce, groups of importers, the Employers Association, the Manufacturers Association and the Farmers Union, met together and resolved that 'in view of the shortage of labour, all suitable manpower be made available to farmers'.[64] Holland backed the resolution.

Fraser quickly loosened one or two new strings to get yet more workers onto the land.

New Zealand and the United States had signed a lend–lease agreement in which the two states undertook to swap goods and services with one another until the end of the war. The United States shipped in weapons and war machinery; New Zealand provided support services as well as shipping out food. The dominion was soon being praised as 'the largest victory garden in the world', in the words of Kyle Palmer, political editor of the *Los Angeles Times*:

> *The Dominion Government's gigantic garden project has been ticked off primarily in terms of thousands of pounds of cabbages, cauliflower, beets, carrots, lettuce, turnips, tomatoes, peas and beans. But secondarily the attendant release of ships is regarded as an equivalent of an entire new fleet of cargo vessels … Millions of pounds of fresh beef, mutton, lamb, pork, butter and cheese are being sent to the fighting fronts. You will find New Zealand butter in the messes on Guadalcanal, in the New Hebrides, New Caledonia, on ships at sea and all along the line in this theatre of operations.*[65]

Fighting on the food front, meanwhile, did not mean that the dominion was now willing to ship meat, cheese and milk to any land in the world whose people needed feeding. Neutrals were not to be fed, for they were not fighting for 'freedom and democracy'. The Axis was not to be fed, even though the mass of its peoples were now going hungry. Nor were people to be fed who could not pay for food, even when their hunger was an outcome of the bungling of colonial governments within the British Empire.

The Bengal famine left many bitter memories in British India. This cartoon, drawn when the imperial state hastily gave up the subcontinent in 1947, contrasts the bulging baggage of the fleeing foreigners with its legacy of hungry people, corpses and skulls. *Artist: Chittaprosad Bhattacharya. https://ridingtheelephant.wordpress.com*

A famine in 1943 killed up to four million people in the province of Bengal. The provincial and viceregal governments claimed the deaths were caused by a serious shortage of rice because of war and weather. Historians, however, have found that there were good enough yields of grain but that Britain would not allow trucks, railways and ships to be freed up to get food to the starving. Bengalis working in essential war industries were fed, but farm workers who grew the grain were left starving. Official policy was that 'the maintenance of essential food supplies to the industrial areas of Calcutta must be ranked on a very high priority'.[66] Canada offered to send several shiploads of grain to Bengal but Churchill vetoed the proposal.

'Winston so dislikes India and all to do with it,' wrote a fellow politician, Leo Amery, 'that he can see nothing but waste of shipping.'[67]

Shipping was earmarked instead for carrying food and oil and weapons to Britain. Archibald Wavell, the new viceroy, wrote angrily that starving people in his viceroyalty were being treated 'with neglect, even sometimes with hostility and contempt'.[68] New Zealand newspapers, while busily printing pages and pages about the hardships of civilians in Britain, found space for no more than snippets of news about Bengal, and they quoted anodyne statements put out by British imperial authorities that the deaths were due to bad harvests. A few citizens were moved to speak out. The Canterbury Trades Council urged that food be sent to ease 'the tragic situation in Bengal'.[69] The government did nothing but send a shipment of 7000 cases of condensed milk.[70] New Zealand could spare no more, since most of the massive shipments of food that the wealthy dominion exported were earmarked to fill the bellies of United States troops and thus help them in their task of killing, or were being spread on bread by the civilians of Britain.

Hunger was not a worry for many people in the dominion, but nearly everyone now became more aware of scarcity. Rationing was tightened in order to free up food and other goods for Britain and the United States.

Washington and London agreed that the citizens of New Zealand were dressing and eating too well for a people supposedly committed to fighting. The average person in the dominion was swallowing meat, for example, at a rate of 108 kilos a year, compared to 62 kilos in the United States and less than 49 kilos in Britain. London, backed by Washington, put strong pressure on Wellington to curb the eating habits of its citizenry. The two foreign capitals took the first step in autumn 1943 when they asked the dominion to look into cutting back the consumption of dairy foods. Wellington sent letters to and fro, trying to buy time while working out how to tighten rationing without provoking the working class.[71] Bankes Amery, a food official in Britain, wrote about the 'skilful way' the New Zealand government in its messages 'evaded all reference to rationing' and hid behind 'a smoke screen', claiming that its goal was to ship 'the greatest possible quantities' to Britain.[72]

Butter rationing began later that autumn, which did something to mollify Britain

Butter rationing was very controversial and was especially resented by the working class. This advertisement belongs to the years of abundant butter before the war. *Artist: Leslie Rykers. Alexander Turnbull Library B-185-003.*

and the United States. The government sold it to citizens on the grounds that the butter saved was to help brave Britons. The Labour Party caucus was not happy: it told the political leadership that the dominion had already done plenty for the war, without withholding food from the working class. Working people grumbled about the government stealing their 'bit of butter'.[73] A farmer remarked that only a few years ago the British had not been willing to pay a fair price for butter; he wondered why people must 'go without to give them butter now'.[74] A few strong unions won an extra butter ration for their workers.

The middle class, on the other hand, seems widely to have accepted the argument that rationing must be imposed in order to help the motherland.

A lot of the well-to-do, of course, felt a strong love for 'Home'. William Hindle, company director, spoke on behalf of the chamber of commerce in Wellington:

Nobody likes rationing in principle, but under war conditions, with the people of Britain standing up so magnificently, it would be a splendid gesture if we voluntarily imposed a ration on ourselves … We already stand high in Britain's estimation. A voluntary rationing of butter would be viewed as a fine contribution and would enhance our reputation – a reputation already gained by the great deeds of our sailors, soldiers, and gallant airmen.[75]

The same argument would be heard over and over again as rationing was tightened during the following years.

'The people of England and other countries are really suffering, and we have all we require,' said a widow in Herne Bay; 'we should accept any cuts like this in good spirit.'

'Well, it's a question of helping Britain, isn't it?' agreed a householder in Remuera.[76]

Meat was the next food to come under rationing, though the government moved very slowly on this. Batterbee complained about that slowness, and there were also complaints from the United States: New Zealand was not pulling its weight, not imposing a suitable wartime austerity.[77]

The government, as always, was worried about protest among the working class.

Pork had been withdrawn from the market already; sales to civilians were outlawed in order to free up all output for the troops of the United States. New Zealand working people ate little pork. The story was different with sheep meat, though.

The British food ministry told the governments of New Zealand and Australia that unless they could ship out more meat, meat rations for civilians might need to be axed in Britain. Conservatives in the dominion spoke up in support of meat rationing. James Begg, for example, a leading landowner, said that rations were 'the only way' the dominion could help Britain feed meat to its people, and that it was the 'obvious duty' of New Zealand.[78] The war cabinet bit the bullet. Meat rationing, it decided at the end of 1943, would be imposed in a few months; the goal would be to cut back by one third what the people of the dominion were eating. Sullivan, as supply minister, did his best to sell the policy:

> *New Zealand has a right to be called an arsenal of democracy because of her special ability to produce food, the fundamental munition of war. She is not the only source from which Britain can obtain food, but without New Zealand butter and meat the people of Britain will come perilously near to disaster.*[79]

Meat rationing spurred civilians to make jokes or write satirical verse about hollow pies and mint sauce with no lamb:

> *Turn it round tenderly,*
> *Baste it with care,*
> *Soon it must vanish*
> *From our bill of fare.*[80]

Eggs went 'onto the ration' during the winter of 1943. Other foods were cut back in ways that were not outright rationing. Honey, for example, was controlled by government regulations that told beekeepers what they could do with the yield from their hives. Vegetables were controlled by means of a sort of 'vegetable census' held at the beginning of 1943, in which all market gardeners and commercial glasshouse growers had to report to the state what crops they were growing and what crops they were about to grow. The government then bound private growers to provide vegetables to the state by way of war contracts. The state also grew crops by setting up a system of state-owned market gardens, worked by people on wages. A 'Dig for

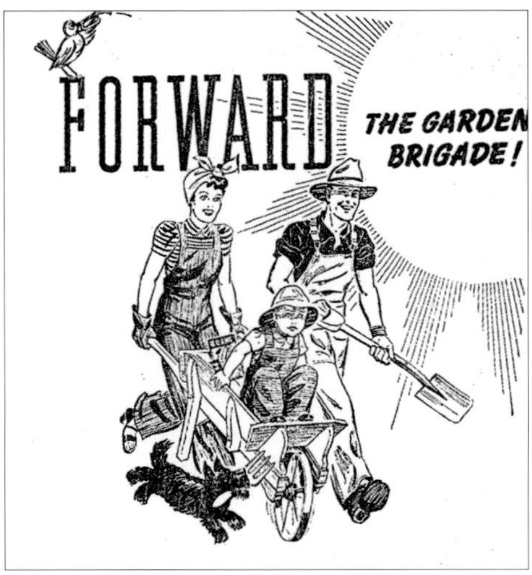

A Yates seed company advertisement boosting the government campaign asking civilians to 'Dig for Victory'.
New Zealand Herald, 22 September 1944.

A German ration card. The Third Reich at the start of the war imposed on its civilians strict rationing of meat, fats, sugar and coffee; as years went by more and more goods were brought 'on the ration'. A 'Normalverbraucher', average consumer, was at first allowed 700 grams of meat a week but by the last weeks of the war the allowance had dropped to only 250 grams – and often it could not be found in the shops anyway. The story was the same with other goods and in most other warring states. Rationing, with its tedious paperwork, was a dreary fact of everyday life for nearly everyone in nearly every country by the last years of the war.

Victory' campaign launched in the winter of 1943 sought to hector or jolly civilians into growing vegetables. Vere Hampson-Tindale, campaign chairman in Wellington, told people why they should get digging: 'the Dominion is faced with the need not only of supplying our normal civilian requirements,' he said, 'but also to meet our obligations to supply the chain of mess-rooms and kitchens which stretches from Oceania to the Mediterranean.'[81]

The state also controlled civilian consumption of goods by way of a wide array of regulations and other measures that stopped short of rationing.

Paper, for example, was regulated tightly. The state defined suitable sizes and weights for books and imposed a ban on making paper napkins and printing advertising leaflets. Getting wood for cabinetmaking was a growing worry, too. Almost all wood used to make furniture between the wars had been oak imported from Japan; the government early in 1943 forbade the use of any wood to make 'non-essential' items of furniture such as bookcases and cocktail cabinets. A schedule of allowable sizes and shapes was drawn up for other types of furniture, spelling out even the number of drawers and cupboard doors. Electricity was rationed by simply lowering the voltage or cutting supply for short spells. The state could do so since it more or less had a monopoly over electricity generation, and it could lean heavily on municipal and county power boards. The state also stopped people from installing new telephones, over which it had a monopoly. Manufacturers were forbidden to make civilian radio sets, electric stoves, electric radiators and many household gadgets.

Housing was now in seriously short supply. Margaret Dunningham, a children's storybook author, published *Three Brown Bears and the Manpower Man*. Bruno the bear is Manpowered from his home in the country. Juno his wife and Jonathan their cub go along too. They find, like 'lots of other people', that they cannot get a house or a flat in the city:

> *They answered all the advertisements*
> *They went to all the offices*
> *They telephoned*
> *They wrote letters*
> *And they walked*
> *And they walked*
> *And they walked*
> *But they couldn't find anywhere*
> *to live at all.*[82]

Although new houses had been built very briskly during the first year or two of the war, bungalows for civilians became a low priority after the declaration of war on Japan; the construction industry was ordered instead to build barracks, camps, airstrips and other military works up and down the country. City housing was hard to find and prices were going through the roof, above all in Christchurch, Wellington and Auckland. The cost of city bungalows was described as 'inflated', 'fantastic' or 'phenomenal' by the autumn of 1943, as houses changed hands at prices half as high again as on the eve of the war.

'We've just sold the old home for £4000,' said a couple in Auckland. 'And to think that it cost dad only £1800 three years ago!'[83]

Marjorie Paul, a land agent, claimed by the end of the war that 'a mad rush of buyers' clamoured after 'any and every kind of property', thanks to the military having drawn workers and materials away from the house-building industry.[84] The *Standard* noted that it was 'exceedingly difficult' for returned servicemen to buy a house. A black market had sprung up in which vendors would sell to buyers only if they paid a big sum of money 'on the side', on top of the market price, as a bribe.[85]

Rationing and other controls over consumer goods and services stayed tight until well after the end of the war and were a heavy burden on the working class and lower middle class. The wealthy, on the other hand, had ways and means to work around the worst of rationing. Landowners, for example, could cope with rationed petrol by driving carriages, as their forebears had done in the nineteenth century. Constance Barker of Four Peaks, an estate in Canterbury, bought a gig – and a carriage horse to pull it, which she named 'The Petrol Saver'.[86] She also made the most of her huge garden, growing and preserving fruit and vegetables with such method and thoroughness that her work gave rise, after the war, to a jam and wine factory.[87]

Helen Black, widow of a wealthy fur merchant and former mayor of Dunedin, was less enterprising when running her rationed household. The petrol shortage meant that tradespeople were no longer delivering goods, and Black lost 'a great deal of time'

The main house on Four Peaks, one of the estates of the Barker family of Canterbury.

doing her shopping. Servants were hard to find, too, thanks to Manpowering. 'Things became rather difficult in every way,' she wrote later, 'and so, to ease the situation, I sent my elder daughter to boarding school.' After a while, still unable to cope with trying to run a big house with rationing and no staff, she packed her two youngest children off to boarding school too. The private schools she chose charged fees far too high for any ordinary family of the working class. The widow was able to comfortably sit out the war shortages.[88]

Almost everyone, rich or poor, longed to buy more – and to buy it more freely. One woman stood in front of a shop window early in 1944 and looked at a display of tinned salmon and pineapple juice behind the glass. 'Display only,' said a notice posted in the display. 'Things to come – after the war.'

'Tantalising, isn't it?' said the woman.[89]

The mood on the home front undoubtedly was one of austerity. Almost every type of consumer goods, however – even for those not willing or able to buy 'under the counter' – were still enjoyed more lavishly in New Zealand than in nearly every other warring state. The butter ration that provoked such annoyance among working people was several times more generous than in Britain. The meat ration was, too. The money spent on Christmas shopping near the end of 1943 was 'phenomenal,' said the executive of a department store in the capital.

'People have money to spend,' added the *Evening Post*, 'and it appears that they haven't been frightened to spend it.'

The New Year's Day that followed was celebrated with picnics and sports. Shinya Michiharu, a Japanese prisoner of war behind wires at Featherston, saw a ceaseless stream of the 'latest models of beautiful passenger cars' passing his camp. The cars kept 'slipping past one after another pretty well without intermission' and were all going one way. At first he and his fellow captives thought the drivers must have taken to the roads because of 'some emergency'. Afterwards they learnt that the shiny vehicles belonged to members of the well-to-do horsey set on their way to the racecourse at Tauherenīkau.[90] The weather at the racecourse, noted a racing reporter, was 'brilliantly fine' and 'a very large crowd' enjoyed the event. Betting was very heavy. Races were run elsewhere, too. A 'large crowd' attended the races of the Marton Jockey Club. The Wyndham Racing Club drew 'a record crowd' from all over Southland. A new record for betting was set by punters at the Canterbury Park Trotting Club. And the Auckland Cup, the biggest race gathering in the country that day, also broke the record for heavy betting.[91]

'I felt a little disgusted with these horse races right at the height of a war,' wrote Shinya. 'Many of their soldiers were even now staking their lives fighting in the front lines, and didn't they feel it an utter contradiction that the nation behind the guns spent their time on horse races?'[92]

Spending and gambling carried on through the following year, breaking records not only on racecourses and in department stores but in cinemas, tearooms, dance halls

A Trentham racecourse crowd, c. 1943. *Photographer John Pascoe. Alexander Turnbull Library 1/4-000215-F.*

and nightclubs. The citizens of the dominion were thriving. Australians, even though they were themselves thriving in a way unknown by most of the people of Europe, lived more austerely than New Zealanders. Mark Greene was struck by the contrast between the two neighbouring states. Australia was 'hard up against it in many ways', he wrote from Melbourne towards the end of the war. Clothing, for example, was 'far less in variety' and 'inferior in quality' than in New Zealand.

'New Zealand is the favoured land of all the world,' he wrote; 'it enjoys a profusion of the essential things that none other to-day possesses, neither Australia nor yet America.'[93]

EUROPE OR THE PACIFIC?

The question of where the troops should fight grew into a heated controversy after the victory in North Africa. Should all dominion soldiers now be shifted to the Pacific? Or should they be thrown against Italy? Cabinet, when the question was talked over in the autumn of 1943, was split right down the middle. Afterwards the government asked for an opinion from the officer corps. The men in braid wanted the army to be used against Italy. The caucus of the Labour Party, when asked the same question, voted the same way as the officer corps, as did a secret session of parliament. Voting was close, however, among all groups. Alister McIntosh, head of foreign affairs, observed that among the political leadership as a whole there was only 'a very narrow balance in favour' of Italy.[94]

Fraser had been less than frank with his colleagues and with the citizenry, having made up his own mind that the troops must be fielded in Italy. He wrote for backing from Churchill:

> *A message from you, which I could read to Parliament in secret session, appealing for the retention of the Division 'on symbolic and historical as well as military grounds' would, I feel, have very great influence especially if you could associate President Roosevelt with yourself in the message.*

Churchill himself wanted to keep the dominion fighting in what he saw as his war rather than the struggle on the other side of the world. He wrote back fruitily:

> *There could not be any more glorious expression of the links which bind together the Commonwealth and Empire, and bind in a special manner the hearts of the people of the British and New Zealand isles, than the feats of arms which the New Zealanders ... have performed ... It is the symbolic and historic value of our continued comradeship in arms that moves me.*[95]

Roosevelt was then squared up too.[96] The National Party was angry at having been kept out of the loop. Fraser and Churchill had struck their deal 'without consultation with Parliament, and without its knowledge or concurrence,' complained Holland. The

A ragtag row of 'browned off' infantrymen in North Africa. The battles in the desert were over and soldiers found themselves – as soldiers so often found themselves during the war – hanging around, waiting to be given orders. *Artist: Neville Colvin. E.G. Webber,* Johnny Enzed in the Middle East *(Rotorua: Rotorua and Bay of Plenty Publishing Co., 1945).*

parliamentary opposition only learnt about the deal 'when cablegrams were read to us in secret session and the Prime Minister told us the War Cabinet's decision.' Holland went on to say that the decision would have been 'very different' had the opposition been properly briefed before the session and the question been debated fully.[97]

Cabinet governed, however – not parliament.

The troops were taken away from the field to rest and be refitted, after which they were thrown into the invasion of Italy.

Quite a few people within the government were restive about the choice that had been made, and throughout the first nine months of 1944 the leadership constantly weighed up whether or not to shift the army to the Pacific. Only in September 1944 did the war cabinet make up its mind.[98] The bulk of the army would stay in Italy. All troops would be withdrawn from the fighting in the Pacific.

The choice between the two fronts was made in a society where most people believed the centre of the world was Europe. Only a few people ever thought other than fleetingly about the islands of the Pacific. Europe, not the islands, crowded newspaper pages, radio airwaves and cinema screens. One reason was that most of the news received or published in the dominion was created by British Pathé, British newspapers and the British Broadcasting Corporation. British broadcasts alone were a 'paralysing infliction' in the opinion of the *Auckland Star*. 'Ten or eleven times a day, every day,' the newspaper complained, 'we may hear what London thinks about this and that affair,

Action, Falamai Village. New Zealand soldiers attacking a village in the Solomon Islands.
Artist: Russell Clark. Archives New Zealand.

including our own affairs'.[99] London spoke about the Pacific 'in a detached manner'. British editors and broadcasters did not mirror the 'direct and immediate interests' of New Zealand.[100] The *Press* noted that even when Japan joined the war the news came mostly from Europe.[101] The *Auckland Star* made the same point:

> *Although we live in a Pacific country we New Zealanders keep our eyes fairly firmly fixed on Europe. For almost a year, from about the time of Singapore's fall ... Port Moresby, Darwin, the Owen Stanley Ranges, Rabaul, Guadalcanal – the names of places which previously most New Zealanders would have had difficulty in locating on a map, suddenly became immensely important. But when the onrush of the Japanese forces was checked, and then reversed, our attention was again given mainly to events far beyond the Pacific.*[102]

One other cause of the focus on Europe was the policy of the United States. Robert Ghormley, commander of the South Pacific Area, had decided in the middle of 1942 that soldiers from the dominion would mostly be sidelined for garrison duty. New Zealand regiments were therefore parked quietly in New Caledonia and Tonga. Only late in 1943 were they allowed to fight alongside American troops, and even then only in lesser landings, well away from the key battlefields. Fraser was not happy: 'it would be neither wise nor proper,' he wrote late in 1942, 'to allow the offensive against the Japanese in the South Pacific to be conducted entirely by Americans.'[103]

Washington was clear from the first days that none of its allies would be allowed to land troops or warplanes on islands north of the equator; those islands were sequestered for occupation by the United States.[104] Roosevelt and his advisors set the timetable for how and where the dominion was to deploy its military.

Australia was a state that needed to be brought alongside, too. Canberra was upset when Wellington chose to keep the mass of its troops on the other side of the world rather than moving them to the Pacific. Canberra had chosen to do the opposite with its own troops. Fraser's fellow prime minister, John Curtin, sent him a 'terse note'.[105] Only when both governments found themselves elbowed aside at a conference in Cairo did they come together, and quickly.

An Australian Department of Aircraft Production poster hyping the construction of Bristol Beaufort warplanes by the department. New Zealand and Australia had common military and diplomatic interests in many ways. Australians, however, were prone to be far more fearful about possible invasion from their 'Near North'. *Artist: James Northfield. Australian War Memorial.*

The Cairo Conference in the spring of 1943 foreshadowed a newly assertive imperialism by the United States. Churchill sought an agreement with Roosevelt about what was to be done in Asia and the Pacific. Roosevelt sought an agreement, too, but wanted to bring along Jiang Jieshi, leader of the Guomindang. Churchill swallowed his anger at the conference being billed as a meeting of 'the Big Three' when it was clear that Jiang was a client of Roosevelt. Churchill could not swallow his anger when Roosevelt told him that he wanted the world, after the war, to be based on four superpowers: the United States, the Soviet Union, the British Commonwealth and 'China'. The president told the prime minister he saw the Guomindang as the 'worthy junior partner' of the United States.[106]

New Zealand and Australia were shocked, not only by the nakedness of United States imperialism but by the way they themselves had been left sitting on the sidelines. The two dominions had nobody speaking for them in Cairo. Cables were not sent asking the opinion of Wellington and Canberra. Herbert Evatt, Australian foreign minister, was outraged by the way the two dominions had been overlooked. He proposed that they hold their own conference where they could come to their own agreement about what was to be done in Asia and the Pacific. New Zealand was willing. McIntosh wrote that 'traditional' relations between Wellington and Canberra had 'very frequently' led them not to steer their ships of state the same way.[107] Now, though, it would be good to try to settle a common policy.

The two dominions held a conference in Canberra early in 1944 that ended with the signing of the Canberra Pact. Wellington bureaucrats nicknamed it the 'Anzaxis'.

The Canberra Pact was an agreement that New Zealand and Australia would work together on questions of foreign policy. The two states wanted a voice in any peace treaty and in the establishment of any new international body. The two proposed their own 'defence zone' from Papua and New Guinea to Samoa and the Cook Islands. Also they agreed to set up a commission to aid the economic, social and political development of the peoples of the 'South Seas'. Colonies were to be treated not as the property of imperial powers but as lands under 'trusteeship'. Fraser spoke about the pact in his typically wordy way:

> *I have every confidence that Australia and New Zealand will march forward together to better things for our own countries and for the whole world, and I hope that the ideals for which we stand will be accepted by all peoples. The occasion of the signing of this agreement is a historic one, in that it marks a common approach to great problems by two democratic British nations set apart from the Great Powers of the world ... without putting forward anything that cuts across the greater harmony and greater cooperation of the British Commonwealth of Nations and the world at large.*

Curtin spoke more snappily:

> *The agreement we have signed is of threefold importance. First of all, it is a landmark in international collaboration in the Pacific; secondly, it is a landmark in the development of Australian and New Zealand foreign policy; thirdly, it is a landmark in constitutional growth in the British Commonwealth of Nations.*[108]

Britain had mixed feelings about the pact. United States leaders greeted it coldly. Evatt had already told the United States that the two dominions were 'the trustees of democratic civilisation in the South Pacific' and for a while had talked about how the best thing would be for all British colonies and protectorates in the neighbourhood to be handed over to Australia and New Zealand. New Zealand could take Fiji and Tonga. Australia could take the Solomon Islands.[109] Now the two dominions were saying, quite sharply, that they would not allow the United States to create its own sphere of influence in the Southwest Pacific.

The British government, given its ostensibly warm intimacy with dominion governments, could not speak against the pact openly. Cabinet and the foreign office were supportive, on the whole, mostly because the pact was seen to be cocking a snook at the United States.[110] British representatives in Wellington nevertheless took 'little pains to conceal their annoyance' and were 'very sniffy', in the words of McIntosh.[111] Afterwards they stayed sniffy.

'I think they are becoming high-handed these days,' wrote Berendsen towards the end of the year.[112]

'I can never remember a period during which there have been so many tart telegrams exchanged between ourselves and the British,' agreed McIntosh.[113]

The United States administration, like the government of Britain, did not speak out against the pact openly, but the civil and military leadership understood that the two dominions had proclaimed a sort of Monroe Doctrine for the Southwest Pacific.[114] Cordell Hull, as American secretary of state, spoke and wrote sharp words.[115] The Anzaxis also galvanised opinion in the Pentagon that it would be a mistake to allow New Zealand troops to do any active fighting in the Pacific.[116]

New Zealand warplanes bombing Kavieng in the Solomon Islands. *Artist: Maurice Conly. Air Force Museum of New Zealand.*

Supplying the military, meanwhile, was still weighing heavily on the social and economic life of New Zealand.

Although the roll call of men and women in the military kept dwindling, the number stationed on or near battlefields was growing. At the peak of mobilisation in the middle of 1942 the tally of men and women stationed overseas was 53,000, but by the end of the following year this had been boosted to 76,000 servicemen and servicewomen. The roll call of those trapped inside prisoner-of-war camps grew, too.

New Zealand troops slogged northwards through Italy. A formidable dominion air fleet of twenty-six squadrons, among them ten bomber and twelve fighter squadrons, strafed and bombed the Solomon Islands.

'The reduction of Rabaul continues with unabated vigour,' gloated a journalist in the autumn of 1944. 'The town itself is a charred skeleton of rubble and ruins with few buildings left standing amid the shambles.'

'It was as pretty a piece of bombing as I have ever seen,' said the commander, Charles Nicholls, after one raid.[117]

Nothing was said in newspapers or on the radio or cinema news about how the bombing was maiming or killing villagers and townspeople in the Solomon Islands.

MUTINY

The highly regulated, controlled, rationed, hectored and chivvied people of the dominion did not unite any more seamlessly behind the 'war effort' during the last years of the war than they had at the beginning. Growing pressure on civilians led many to evade the law. Citizens in and out of uniform knitted together a complex and widespread web of cynicism, wagging, pilfering and black marketing.

The black market grew in step with tightened controls over the economy. Trade in fruit and vegetables was done so freely under the counter in Christchurch by the autumn of 1943 that more pears, for instance, were being sold on the black market than through 'regulation channels'.[118] Cream was widely traded outside the law, too. John Thomas, rationing controller for the city, noted not only that milk vendors were selling cream to 'special' customers but that householders were playing milk vendor against milk vendor – blackmailing milkmen who would not sell cream outside the law by threatening to go to others who were willing.

'Working warily at first,' wrote a journalist, 'the black marketers are reported to have become bolder in the last few weeks and illegal selling of cream is extensive in some districts.'[119]

Tea was not widely traded on the black market, in the opinion of the dominion rationing controller. Nor was butter, evidently. Sugar was 'a different story'.[120] Sugar black marketers were usually the owners of grocery shops. A raid carried out in Nelson netted three grocers who were tried for 'having supplied sugar without coupons or permits'. They had been dobbed in by rival grocers. Archibald Smith had sold 106 kilos on the black market, William Blue, more enterprisingly, had offloaded 415 kilos, while the biggest dealer, Arthur Best, had handled 453 kilos.[121]

Meat became a very hot black market commodity after rationing was imposed. One citizen wrote unhappily about a 'class of people' who 'laugh at meat rationing; they get all they want, and they think it is a joke to beat the ration'.[122] Farmers sold meat on the black market; Nelson Creed, for example, slaughtered and sold three sheep a week.[123] Butchers also sidestepped rationing. They did it to make money – or they did it as a kindness. Florence Macey, from a working-class family in Wellington, was sold 'ham and lovely stuff' by the family butcher to help with her wedding. A bakery shop made a wedding cake using 'currants and sultanas and things' – also outside the law – while a dress shop broke the law by making 'nice clothes' for the bride and bridesmaids.[124]

Alcohol was a big seller on the black market. Civilians were willing to pay good money for drink, and 'sly grog' vendors were keen to get some of that good money. The *Evening Post* probed the trade in Wellington during the autumn of 1943 and found it widespread:

> *Sly-groggery in its worst phases, especially in areas where servicemen are quartered, is keeping the police particularly busy. Convictions, when secured, are usually followed by heavy fines. But such punishments seem to be failures as deterrents, considering the*

magnitude of the traffic, for fines, heavy as they may be, can generally be met out of the princely profits of the trade.[125]

Agnes McIntyre, a munitions worker, was hauled into court in Wellington after a raid; she pleaded guilty. Charles Applebee, a wool classer, was also hauled in and also pleaded guilty. Yue Noy Sum, a laundryman, pleaded guilty. Sylvia Shaw was fined for selling, too; and Una Tasker was fined for being found 'on the premises'.[126] Auckland was the setting for the biggest black market in drink. The *Auckland Star* portrayed the industry as so 'rich in profit' that one vendor alone sold 1500 bottles of beer in one night. Touts and 'droppers' sought out buyers on behalf of sly grog shops.[127] Dorothy Stone, tailoress, was one of many who had 'considerable experience in the sly grog trade' before she was jailed for a month by a magistrate.[128]

Petrol and rubber were widely sold on the black market, and this led to a good deal of stealing. Cars were 'converted' then 'stripped of wheels and tyres', noted the Automobile Association.[129] A 'group of gangsters' got so good at counterfeiting petrol coupons by the winter of 1944 that they were 'debauching the coupon currency and endangering the very limited supply of petrol, so vital to the life of the nation', declared the oil fuel controller. The law was tightened so that no civilian could redeem any coupon unless it was signed on the back and marked with the number plate of the vehicle, and even then the petrol would only be supplied if pumped 'direct into the tank of the vehicle'.[130]

Civilians were not the only people buying and selling on the black market. Soldiers, sailors and aircrew did it, too. Kelso Beyer was a young soldier nabbed for stealing 640 rounds of rifle ammunition from the army camp at Trentham. He was unlucky. 'Others were implicated,' noted a newspaper, but the police had not been able to track them down.[131] Theft of military supplies by servicemen was so widespread in 1944 that it was denounced as 'sabotage' by a magistrate who found four aircraftmen guilty of stealing tyres, tubes, wheels and kits of tools.[132] Thousands of ordinary soldiers did what they could to pilfer things. Military stores fetched a good price on the black market. Officers were not

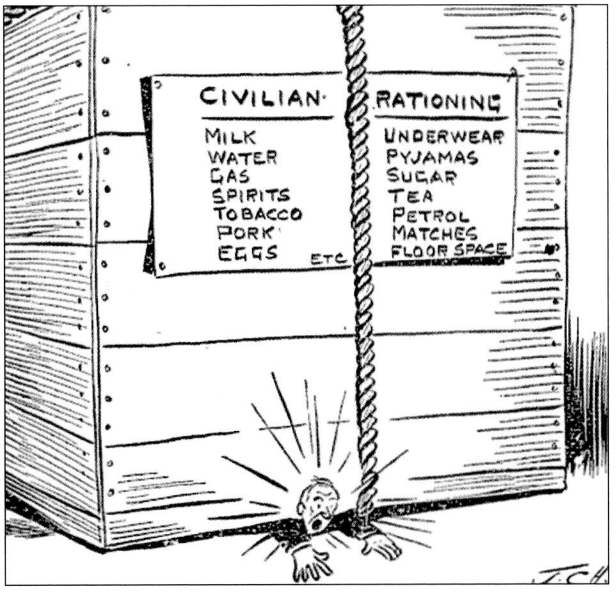

The burden of rationing. *Artist: J.C. Hill.* Auckland Star*, 26 May 1943.*

above pilfering, either. Cream was poured over puddings in the officers' mess on the air-force base at Whenuapai.

'A pig farmer used to bring us a gallon of illegal cream each day,' said one of the mess cooks, Trevar Donaldson.[133]

Pilfering was common throughout the country. Rationed goods were lifted, together with goods that were simply in short supply thanks to the broken shipping lines caused by war and the tight controls imposed by the government. Theft on the wharves of Wellington had grown by late 1942 to what one official called 'alarming proportions'. The comment was made after two young men, Noel York and Hawerati Heihei, were convicted for stealing meat from the army, and two others, Eric Menzies and Francis Randolph, were found guilty of theft from the Patriotic Fund Board.[134] Goods gathered by fundraising groups were often pillaged. Coffee, oysters, and tins of cream collected on behalf of troops overseas were stolen in New Plymouth, provoking the mayor of the town to note that 'patriotic parcel-packing centres' in the province were 'frequently broken into'.[135] Drinking glasses were nicked from hotels and restaurants; the Hawke's Bay Jockey Club president protested about 'the widespread belief that a person who bought a drink at the bar also bought the glass'. Cutlery went the same way, as did crockery.[136] The *New Zealand Herald* early in 1944 spelled out what was happening:

> *Auckland hotels and restaurants are losing hundreds of pounds' worth of property every week through petty pilfering by guests and customers. Although experiences differ, the general opinion is that thefts are increasing in spite of various preventive measures taken by managements. The pilfering is partly attributed to servicemen in search of souvenirs and to civilians seeking articles in short supply or unobtainable in the shops … 'We are losing 30 dozen glasses from the bar's lounges and bedrooms a month,' said a member of the staff of a leading city hotel yesterday.*

The hotel had lost around 300 towels in a year, too, while electric lightbulbs were stolen almost as soon as they were screwed into their sockets. Mats, china and cutlery were walking, together with other fittings. Eight table covers were taken one day, and two days later two matching cushion covers, very likely lifted by the same light-fingered guest. Shoes were stolen from outside the doors of hotel rooms, where guests left them overnight for polishing. Two hotel managers had their own shoes stolen that way.[137]

Cynicism about the war underlay a lot of pilfering and racketeering.

A cynical attitude was easily understandable during the Second Phoney War. The dominion was churning out food and other goods. The enemy was far away. Why should citizens have to go short? A businesswoman early in 1942 said that through her whole career of forty years serving behind counters she had 'never known such a discontented public' and so much 'selfishness'.[138] Doris McLean, a journalist who had joined the air force, was buffeted by a rowdy crowd fighting for rationed goods inside a menswear shop. 'Hundreds of men, women and children were fighting, screaming, grasping, snatching and yelling over the counters,' she wrote. 'The noise was incredible.'[139]

Authority figures protested over and over about such ways of behaving. Clearly, though, cynicism had got a strong grip. Alfred Averill, the Anglican archbishop of the dominion, spoke up about 'the outbreak of lust and self-interest which is disfiguring our fair land'.[140] The *Evening Post* complained about the 'disturbing signs recently of a tendency by many people to take their responsibilities to the nation less seriously'.[141] A 'slackening effort' was slated by the *Auckland Star*:[142]

> *There is a recklessness, a prodigality with money such as this country has never known. Allied with this is a growing spirit of greed and selfishness ... a quickening pace in the pursuit of pleasure. Thus the heroism of New Zealanders abroad, the sweat and outpoured blood of our boys in the Pacific combat zone, has a sharp and gravely disturbing contrast at home.*[143]

Pep talks did not stop the mood from spreading. Frederick Baskett, company director and president of the Auckland chamber of commerce, lamented the 'growing disregard of the law' and 'serious deterioration in the attitude of a large section of our people towards their country'. He feared that its root was 'sheer selfishness'.[144] Bertram Jacobs, company director and national president of the Returned Services Association, lambasted people for their widespread cynicism and breaking of laws. He called on people to 'banish all selfishness' and 'make the Spirit of Anzac a real live thing'. He asked citizens to 'challenge all abuses of the laws of our country – particularly those specially passed to help the war effort'. He also asked people not to 'grouse' and to accept wartime sacrifices cheerfully.[145]

Thousands of citizens who read his words in the newspaper doubtless rolled their eyes.

Soldiers who had come home from the battlefields were often shocked by the mood of society. Charles Barron was one: weary and knocked about from the fighting in North Africa, he found a 'strange atmosphere' in his homeland. Afterwards he said he had 'never been so disillusioned' as when he saw how civilians were behaving.[146] Leslie Cleveland was another one who was struck by the way so many people were 'racketeers, shirkers, under-the-counter merchants and black market dealers'. He thought that morale 'was eroding' in the homeland. On top of society was a blanket of 'emergency regulations, tight censorship and unceasing propaganda' while

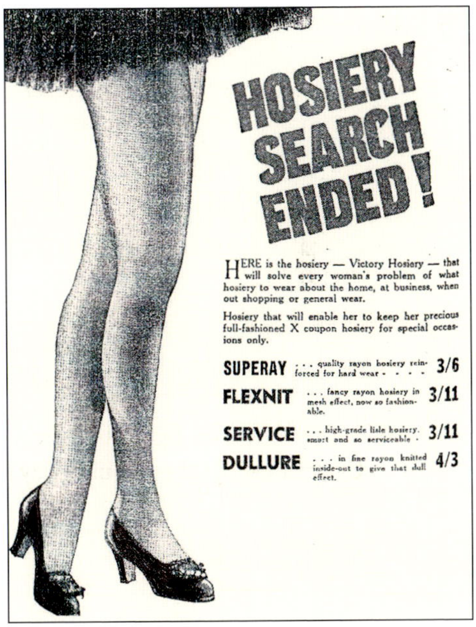

Stockings were never 'on the ration' during the war but, because silk was in short supply thanks to conflict with Japan, the hosiery mills of the dominion used various ersatz silks that were hot, scratchy and lost their shape after washing. New Zealand Herald, *1 December 1944.*

underneath was a layer of 'feverish excitement and self-indulgence'.[147] A soldier who had been away from home for a long while thought he saw 'a very ugly spirit abroad in our land – a spirit selfish, greedy, hostile'.[148] A fellow soldier said that civilians were 'more interested in making money and having a good time' than in beating the Axis. He heard people hinting that soldiers were 'fools for being in the Army'.[149] Hubert Witheford, writing as a poet rather than as a dismayed soldier or a businessman prone to pep talk, portrayed the late wartime suburbs of the country:

Launched from a merciless bow the sun-shafts strike
The iron roofs on a thousand bitter houses.
Whose surfaces, bright coloured and corrupt,
Contain their victims with a vice's power.[150]

The dismayed troops, meanwhile, were themselves restless and often close to a mood of mutiny.

After the end of the fighting in North Africa, the government let all soldiers who had been in the army from early in the war come home on furlough for three months. The men had been asking for a break. The officers were keen for them to have a break. Women who had waved goodbye to the men from the wharves were asking for them to be given a break, too. 'We willingly gave up our sons,' wrote a mother, but it was 'imperative' that those sons now be allowed to come back to New Zealand.[151] The last three years had been years of 'anxiety and loneliness', added a young woman engaged to a young man in the army. 'Surely after all the brave deeds our sweethearts have done,' she wrote, they would be allowed a furlough in New Zealand.[152]

Troopships brought some 6000 soldiers home in the winter of 1943.

A 'furlough man' at home with his family, portrayed sentimentally in a tobacco advertisement. The truth was that many men on furlough were suffering badly from stress and were dismayed by the widespread mood of cynicism in New Zealand. *Auckland Star*, 23 May 1942.

The men soon asked themselves whether they were willing to go back to the front at the end of their furlough. Family and friends often urged the 'furlough men' not to go, saying they had done enough and should now stay. Newspapers, gagged by war censorship, were not allowed to canvass the question openly, but the whole country was talking about it and feelings ran very strong.

The National Party took up the matter in the general election campaign in August. Holland told a nationwide radio audience that 'no man should be sent to the war twice before everybody has gone once'.[153] The war cabinet had already agreed that any furlough man who was married with children, as well as any man in his forties or older, and any who was Māori, could quit the army. All those who failed a medical check would also be allowed to quit. A long list of nearly 2700 ended up 'failing' those medicals, often because doctors were highly sympathetic towards men who confessed that they did not want to go back into the army. Other furlough men were given the right to quit if they could prove to an appeals board that they had 'special reasons' to do so.

Controversy then broke out about the 'special reasons'; many citizens said that every single furlough man who made up his mind to appeal to a board should be allowed to get out of the army.

'I am going to recommend that every man stay in New Zealand,' declared one member of an appeals board, Thomas McCready. 'When a man has done three years' service he has done enough.'[154]

Mutiny loomed in the first weeks of 1944 when furlough men were ordered back to camp. Hundreds showed what they thought of being sent back to the war by simply staying away. A crowd at Hamilton railway station urged men not to obey the order but to stay. Police were told to track down those who would not go, but did not always do what they were told. Laurie Walker, for example, was a furlough man who had got a job as barman at a hotel in Richmond. The police in the town took pains to 'search' for him only when they knew he would not be where they were searching.[155] Other furlough men reported back too late to camp. Others again, who did report back, said they would not leave the country. A troopship steamed away in the end with only 663 furlough men on board, leaving the government knitting its brow about what to do with the men who had chosen to mutiny.

Army regulations were very clear: any soldier who deserted could be executed by firing squad. Men had been shot for such a 'crime' during the First World War. The Labour Party, however, would not allow such ferocious punishment, since the men in uniform were supposedly 'citizen soldiers'. Men who disobeyed the order to go to camp and embark on the troopship were court-martialled, which was the law, but the courts simply sentenced each man to detention for ninety days. The next step was to say that detention would be suspended if the men left on the next troopship. A crowd of furlough men protested in the streets of Christchurch. The war cabinet held talks with spokesmen for those who did not want to go back to the front and some then agreed to sail on the next troopship. Almost all of those who had been found guilty of desertion were still so stubborn, and so strongly backed by friends and family and many others in society, that they stayed at home instead of embarking on the troopship.

The Court of Appeal made matters still more vexing for the government by looking into the case of furlough defaulters early in April. The court ended up by overruling the sentences for desertion handed out by the courts martial, but it added that the men were perhaps guilty of mutiny. The war cabinet slowly felt its way forward. Furlough men who would not go back to the front were laid off from the army but without pensions and other privileges.

The same saga had to be battled through all over again when a second shipment of 1900 furlough men landed in the country. Citizens still had strong opinions, and spoke out about them strongly. Furlough men kept being stroppy. The government kept giving ground. Frederick Wood noted how thoroughly and how well the soldiers, together with a wide array of people who backed them throughout the country, were able to defy the state:

> *The Government's inability to get more than a portion of the first furlough draft back to the Middle East is a striking instance of the limited effectiveness of the impressive array of wartime powers which it had been given in law ... No one could well deny that any country which accepted the principle that soldiers could retire on their own initiative after three years' service would be withdrawing itself from effective participation in the war.*[156]

Troops took the law into their own hands in other ways, too. A group of soldiers in camp in Marlborough sent an ultimatum demanding that they be moved to another camp. The 'threat of mutiny', which never made it onto radio or into the newspapers, was acted on quickly. The regiment was disbanded and its men pepperpotted through other regiments. Richard Scott, one of the troublemakers, wrote about how they were lambasted by a group of 'grotesquely fierce' sergeant majors.[157]

Other men chose to mutiny. Troops who boarded the troopship *Dunnottar Castle* at Wellington in the spring of 1944 found it so overcrowded and dirty that they stormed back onto the wharf and broke down the wharf gates. Afterwards, 'led by sailors with a piper playing', they marched on parliament.[158]

New Zealand troops on the other side of the world, meanwhile, often behaved restively. Morale had been fairly good in the army during the fighting in North Africa but was low for most of their time in Italy. There were twice as many men who ran away or would not follow orders on Italian battlefields as in Egypt.[159] A whole platoon of soldiers did not want to go into battle one day late in 1943; they were backed by their sergeant, who told his officer that the men had 'had it'. One soldier was crying in his trench, and although some of the others did join the attack, fourteen stayed out.

'Fuck that!' said one. 'I can't go up there. I can't stand it!'[160]

Ten were court-martialled.

A mutiny followed in the middle of 1944 when fifteen men in a platoon refused to follow orders and join an attack. A fellow soldier in the company, though not the mutinous platoon, wrote about the mood in his diary: 'This war is getting me down for my nerve is all to hell ... I know I am afraid of action now and really scared.'[161]

The army was riddled with rivalry between various groups, too. Men in the field felt anger towards those not in the field. Foot soldiers, the infantry, suffered most of the hardest fighting, and most of the death and wounding. 'What a life,' wrote one infantryman late in 1943; 'the toughest and most nerve-wracking life there is.'[162] Thousands of soldiers, on the other hand, never came anywhere near the fighting;

Into Cassino. New Zealand soldiers on a battlefield in Italy. *Artist: Peter McIntyre. Archives New Zealand.*

fewer than half the men sent overseas by the dominion army ever went into combat.[163] Soldiers in the field looked with envy or rage at drivers who were free to come and go, and at clerks and others back at base behind the lines in Italy; 'Johnny Base Bludger' was a nickname used widely. Guthrie Wilson portrayed an infantryman slagging the people back at base:

> *Bloody little small-town nobodies doing the big-shot act all over Italy, it makes you want to cry. Dolled up like territorials on parade day, fawned on and waited on – the runts! Makes you want to spew. Makes you want to kick their comfortable arses through their teeth … Jesus! the bloody little pimps!*[164]

Base bludgers were often just as wretched as the men in the infantry, however, and longing to get back to New Zealand. Soldiers in all ranks and walks of life sang a gloomy song in Italy:

> *Oh, Peter Fraser,*
> *won't you send us home?*
> *We've had your army*
> *now we've been to Rome.*
> *We've had the tears, the sweat, the blood,*
> *we've had the rain,*
> *and we've had the mud.*
> *So please just send us home.*[165]

WOMEN AND WAR

The phrase 'total war' was bandied about very freely by the government during the first year or so after the declaration of war on Japan. Women were now needed for the struggle. Total war, citizens were told, could only be brought about by wives, mothers and daughters serving the nation with their strength and their knowhow. People spoke breezily about the relationship between women and men being transformed by war, not only in the economy but the whole of society.

'There can be no question of the willingness, or rather eagerness, of the women of New Zealand to play their full part,' declared the *Evening Post* soon after battle began with Japan.[166]

Janet Fraser, wife of the prime minister, gave a radio speech that was broadcast throughout the country. 'There is a place,' she said, 'for every woman to do her share.'[167]

Women flocking into the dominion army, air force and navy was something wholly new to society. Women had not been allowed into the military during the First World War. Now, they were recruited actively. Quick-witted women could end up being trained as officers, which among other things meant learning how to handle weaponry. Hazel Davis, who worked before the war in a department store, went into the army and was taught to be an officer at Trentham. She learnt military law and 'did cross-country marching, cross-country night map-reading, shooting with Bren guns, .303, Vickers, pistol'.[168]

Women went into the military in other warring states, too. June Howden flew warplanes for the British air force, ferrying them from base to base. 'Seeing all the new planes was exciting,' she said.[169] Jane Winstone, another who ferried warplanes, was killed in 1944 when she crashed a Spitfire. Cynthia Wilson, daughter of a landowning family, joined a Scottish brigade and then signed up for the army of Poland.[170]

Women were keen, in some districts, to set up their own private army. A group formed what they called an 'Amazon Battalion' at Edgecumbe. The goal was to shape the group into 'an offensive and attacking force'.[171] Other women were eager to go into the Home Guard. A band in Southland wanted not only to join the guard but to 'do anything, including fighting'.[172] Military life for such women was both challenging and liberating. Edith Lewis, a nursing sister in the army, found her work so deeply satisfying, she was not sure how she would cope when the war ended and she had to give it up:

> *It was going to be a strange turn in my life to wake up in the morning with no responsibility beyond my own need, and I was not sure I was going to like it. I knew I would miss the bugle calls, and the comings and goings of the camp life with the men in khaki, who had been so much in my life, and who were so much my friends.*[173]

Nell Hartley, trained by the air force as an instrument repairer, was given the specialised task of removing instruments from the flying panel of warplanes:

Woolshed Interior. Three land girls at work in the foreground and two men shearing in the background on the Rydal Downs estate of the Ensor family in Canterbury. *Artist: Juliet Peters. Macmillan Brown Library.*

> *I was in my element. I knew the work was important and I felt equal to the task. With my equipment in the pockets of my overalls I squeezed, slid, wriggled and twisted my sinuous way into the small space behind the panel and worked lying on my back.*[174]

Rosemary Clark-Hall, from Christchurch, was also in the air force, where she was a driver of ground transport. She later recalled the song she and her workmates sang:

> *Oh, the transport girls are happy,*
> *The transport girls are free,*
> *The transport girls are happy,*
> *When they're out upon the spree.*[175]

Thousands of women did 'man's work' in farming, which the government began marketing as a fit field of work for women in the spring of 1941 when a land corps was set up under the Women's War Service Auxiliary. Women volunteering to join the corps, it was hoped, would take over farm jobs left vacant by men who had been conscripted into the military. Land corps workers would wear a uniform with a green tie.

The corps was very slow to get going: only 104 women were working under its direction even in early 1943, when the corps was reorganised as the Women's Land Service – quickly nicknamed the 'Land Army'. Women working in the service were known as 'land girls'. The roll grew steadily, peaking at nearly 2100 land girls, helped by advertisements in the press and on radio:

> *Food is the biggest gun in the whole war. Food to feed our own people, Great Britain, our Allies ... food to strengthen our drive to victory ... food to help the United Nations write the peace. An urgent call is made to all women over 17 years of age irrespective of present occupation to apply to help our farmers increase their output ... It's a healthy life and a vital war job.*[176]

Women of rank spoke out, too, urging young women to go into the paddocks, the milking sheds, the woolsheds, and to work for victory. The first of those women of rank were Mary Dreaver, church minister, journalist and a sister member of parliament, and Mary Grigg, daughter of a wealthy landowning family. The two – one standing for the left and the other the right – toured the dominion, speaking to women and asking for them to step forward as land girls.

'Every day the war goes on,' said Grigg, 'shows more clearly the terrific responsibility that rests on the shoulders of the primary producer.'[177]

Land girls worked mostly not on small farms but big estates. Okirae, for example, an estate in Hawke's Bay, at the peak of Manpowering was staffed by six men and four land girls.[178] Jane Dare, already working as a land girl, signed up for the new Land Army and was sent to another estate in Hawke's Bay. Her tasks were to milk cows, mow lawns, 'spray a large orchard, and do the vegetable gardens'.[179] Dora, a workmate on the estate, was an office worker who 'knew not the first thing about the country' but was 'very useful at odd jobs' in the sheds 'and when it rained would rush in and offer to cook or do housework'.[180] Dare then went to another estate in Hawke's Bay. She milked cows, separated milk, fed calves, made butter, looked after poultry, dug up vegetables, washed them for the cook, chopped wood, sawed small logs, cleaned out drains, washed the car of her mistress, blacked the shoes of her master and helped the gardener look after the grounds.[181]

Land girls, like young women in the military, often spoke with eagerness about how their tasks made them feel free and happy. Judy Parkes, an office worker on Queen Street, made up her mind to join the Land Army. She went to the Glenburn estate in Hawke's Bay. 'I had such fun learning how to use a stockwhip,' she said; 'the first time I cracked it – I couldn't stop grinning!'[182] Mavis Gilbertson, who worked in a newspaper office before becoming a land girl, wrote: 'I am very happy in my work and like it more each day.'[183] Mary Granville, who before the war was a clothing model and cosmetics assistant in a Christchurch department store, found her life changing markedly. Her husband joined the navy. She joined the Land Army. She loved it, and gave radio talks about the work. Granville told her husband that her life seemed to have opened up far more widely.

> *I myself am conscious of the fact of having 'grown up'. Sounds queer, doesn't it from a woman of my age. But I think I must have been retarded mentally & you going away made something snap. I find things, little irritations, pin pricks etc, that used to infuriate me, don't matter a tinker's cuss now. I don't give a damn now whether I've said or done 'the right thing'. It doesn't seem to matter. So much larger things are at stake.*[184]

Farm tasks had always been done by wives and daughters on many small farms, far more often than ever showed up in official statistics. A woman on a working farm was likely to take it for granted that she might need to put in many hours alongside brothers or father or husband in the sheds or paddocks. The shortage of men during the last years of the war simply meant that they did more such tasks, squeezing them into their already full working day. One farm woman with two sons, one at school and the other in the military, did what she could to help her husband on the land by milking and driving a tractor. 'I find it no hardship,' she wrote, 'besides doing my own housework.'[185]

The wife or daughter of a wealthy landed family was less likely to do such tasks, thanks to a sharp line being drawn around what could and could not be done by a lady. A well-bred woman did not drive tractors or milk cows. Helen Swinburn, one daughter of a landowning family, shocked her mother by leaving an expensive private school at seventeen to become a land girl. 'I think my mother thought I was going to grow up into a sort of hairy baboon with a fag hanging out of my mouth, swearing and tough! She could not even boil water when she was seventeen.'[186]

Yet even the women of landowning families sometimes did light work on estates and could nearly always sit well in a saddle, and look with some knowledge at fences, crops, grass, woodlands, cattle and sheep. A lot of those women during the last years of the war took on jobs left vacant by men who had gone into the military. Airini Woodhouse was one; she became the manager for her absent husband on Blue Cliffs in Canterbury. The estate had been worked before the war by eight or more men on wages but by early 1942 only one was left on the payroll. Woodhouse, a 'serious and exacting' mistress, tended to the stock and the paddocks with five land girls, together with her daughter, Carne Woodhouse. The housekeeper, who during peacetime was head of servants in the big house, pitched in when it was time to do dipping and shearing.[187]

Woodfield, another estate in the province run during the war by women, belonged to the Jones family. The grounds were overgrown around 'an enormous derelict-looking house', approached through 'the remains of once-handsome gates'. Only one woman servant was left working inside the house, and no men were left working in the paddocks. Bertha Jones, sister-in-law of the mistress, did all the tractor work on the cropping land. The mistress sweated on the land daily:

She was dressed in filthy corduroy trousers, a man's shirt, a woollen balaclava helmet rolled up like a beret, and huge hobnailed boots ... Her hands were absolutely ingrained with dirt and nicotine, her black hair was cut like a man's.[188]

The roll call of women from farming and landowning families who took on the job of working the land was long, though we have no way of knowing how long. Certainly they were hard at work throughout the country. Kathleen Hawkins portrayed one in verse, calling her Sally. A young wife who before the war had 'pretty hands' and 'read good books' and never felt the soil with her fingers other than when she was flower gardening, she now rolls up her sleeves when the farm hands go away to war and sets to work alongside her young husband:

Her hands are roughened now, her hair and dress
Lack some of the past care and daintiness,
Weeds flourish where rare garden plants lie dead –
Sally is serving in the milking shed.[189]

Manufacturing drew a wide array of women into factories and got them doing new things. Pay in a factory was far better than on the land. State propaganda was printed and screened to tell women it was their duty to go onto the assembly lines and begin a new way of living and working:

No longer dainty hands and pretty dress. Steel now, for the guns! No longer lily-fingered loveliness. Steel fingers now! Dirty fingers now! Working fingers now! Bombs now! Metal now! Now it is war, and now it is women working for war. No longer peace and prettiness for women![190]

Amy Kane, president of the Women's Institute, said early in 1942 that many women who had never been in factories were responding to the call for workers 'magnificently'.[191] A foundry spokesman said the following year that women were in some ways doing better than men at tasks until then thought of as men's work. 'We have women working drills and milling machines, and doing moulding jobs in connection with munitions,' added a spokesman from another foundry. Women were working hydraulic steam presses at a rubber factory, 'jobs never before given to women', and although the tasks were 'pretty strenuous' they were 'standing up well to the heavy work'.[192] Alister Street was a young woman who went into armaments manufacturing at a Wellington works where she and other women made tails for mortar bombs:

The assistant handled the red-hot bomb tails as they came out of the welder – we had a long pair of forceps like hospital theatre forceps – you'd lift up these red-hot mortar bomb tails, dip them in an oil and then stack them on pegs on trays.[193]

Manpowering meant that these tasks were sometimes done by women of the middle class. Young ladies who lived in City Rise, Fendalton, Khandallah and Remuera sweated on assembly lines alongside daughters of the working class from Caversham,

A woman factory worker assembling bombs in an advertisement for Lifebuoy soap. The implication is that the young woman was a daughter of the middle class and not used to factory work, although on the whole 'the Manpower' was careful not to 'direct' middle-class women into factories but instead sent them to less gritty types of industry. *Evening Post*, 18 *December 1943.*

Sydenham, Newtown and Arch Hill. Zita Pritchard worked in a clothing factory alongside one such 'delicate little thing' who had been Manpowered and 'used to cry nearly every day'.[194] Optimists welcomed the way women from both sides of the tracks were thrown together on the factory floor, thinking it a wholesome sign of the new social democracy.

The war also led many women, above all young women, to dress and speak and otherwise behave in ways not until now deemed womanly. Trousers, for example, were worn widely, though in order to lessen the trespass they were called 'slacks'. Women had worn trousers in the First World War, too, but only as a fundraising novelty. Now they wore them at home, at work, in the street – and, in the words of Nancy Taylor, they came to be 'highly respected' for their practicality.[195] Mary Dreaver lauded slacks as 'the modern working apparel of thousands of war workers'.[196] A journalist wrote with gentle satire about the way young women were now 'rushing about in slacks and sweaters, and smoking more than usual' while carrying out war work.[197]

Wartime changes would carry on when peace came back, or so many people believed. 'This generation, later, when the dust clears from the battlefields, will see that women have proved finally that they need no longer be dependent, and therefore inferior to men,' wrote Darry McCarthy, who wore the uniform of the Women's Auxiliary Air Force. 'The last war partly emancipated women, this one should finalise the liberation.'[198]

'This war has put women in their rightful place,' Mabel Howard told parliament.[199]

Yet the truth was that the warring dominion never came anywhere near total mobilisation of its economy, let alone its society. Women were never used fully. The way women were used did not mark a striking break with conventions of masculinity and femininity. Changes were only piecemeal, and always provoked disagreements. Although some people said women must take on new tasks, others said they must keep behaving in the old ways.[200] Nor did the war shove many women of the middle class into factories or other workplaces where they would have to do gritty tasks. A journalist wrote that they looked with 'dread' on the threat of being Manpowered into such jobs. 'Will I be sent to a mental hospital to work,' middle-class women asked, 'or to a freezing company?'

Officials who did the Manpowering took pains to keep those who came from the middle class out of hospital kitchens or workshops. A 'wise discrimination' was used to choose 'horses for courses' – or, in other words, the Manpowering system was tender towards 'young ladies' and sought to find them jobs that were ladylike and would not 'sink' them to the ranks of the working class. A young woman from the middle class was typically sent to work as a clerk, while a young woman from the working class was packed off to a kitchen or workshop.[201] Women of the unskilled working class did not necessarily mind that they were treated as fodder for assembly lines, because most of them had grown up taking it for granted that when they left school they would work in a factory. Almost all those on wages throughout the war came from the working class; few were the daughters of the Manpowered middle class.[202]

An advertisement for women's slacks. *Auckland Star, 2 September 1940.*

Tasks did not change a lot; most had long been seen as women's work, anyway. Men's work was still men's work. 'I think the authorities are a bit shy of calling on women for that sort of work,' noted Amy Kane.[203] Of nearly 23,000 'directions' of women into paid work by way of Manpowering, very few involved women taking over men's work.[204] Thousands of daughters of the working class did stop toiling as servants for the rich and the middle class,[205] but only to clean and cook, bake and sew, fetch and carry inside hospitals, hotels and barracks instead of inside the houses of those with money. The hours were a lot better; so was the pay. Women pocketing the pay, though, were still servants.[206] The daughters of the middle class who went into the military found themselves stuck, too, cooking, washing or sweeping. The lucky ones typed, kept the books, were clerks, drivers, or were given technical tasks.

The military never allowed women anywhere near the fighting. Killing was manly, not womanly. William Bell, colonel in the Southland Home Guard, said that while he appreciated the 'courage and determination to take part in the defence of the country' shown by women in the province who wanted to sign up, it was 'impossible'.[207] No women were allowed to join any guard regiment anywhere in the country. The Edgecumbe Amazon Battalion was disbanded after only a few months: men had not backed it, and it was damned with faint praise by the newspapers of the Bay of Plenty.

'We know definitely in our heart of hearts,' wrote one editor, 'that war is no place for a woman.'[208]

Women were more likely than men to be withheld from the military even when the army, air force or navy went out of their way to get women by Manpowering. The army on one occasion wanted 982 women to work as clerks and to run stores on bases and in camps, but all they got were 20 typists. Women doing essential jobs in the civilian workforce, one historian notes, somehow were more 'essential' than men doing such jobs.[209] The ranks of women in the military were always fairly thin, too. Only some 8000 women wore uniform at the peak of mobilisation, and the tally dropped to around 5000 by the end of the war.

The truth, in spite of propaganda about the war opening new doors, was that women were never allowed to be anything other than 'auxiliary' to men in the military.

A lot of young women greasing axles or scrubbing toilets or scouring saucepans felt angry, because they were daughters of the middle class and had volunteered for the military in order to avoid being Manpowered onto a farm or into a factory. A woman in the air force wrote a satirical story about the life

A member of the Women's Auxiliary Air Force seated ornamentally in barracks, as pictured by male eyes. *Artist: Maurice Conly. Air Force Museum of New Zealand.*

of 'Wendy the WAAF' who patriotically signed up for the military but was ordered to do nothing better than 'clump around in clogs and feed starving erks'. An erk, in air-force slang, was an airman of low rank.[210] The daughters of the middle class nevertheless begged, wept, jumped before they were pushed, or pulled strings in order to avoid going into a freezing works or any other sort of factory. Janet Cooke was one who took matters into her own hands when she was told she must go into a factory. 'That's the last place I'll be,' she told herself before buying a ticket and running away to another city.[211]

'I got a telegram from the Manpower people telling me to report at the freezing works,' said Gwenda Christophers, daughter of a bank manager. 'I rushed to the bank and told Dad to sign the air-force papers so that I wouldn't have to go to the freezing works.'[212]

'I was working in an office in Wellington and I heard rumours that the Manpower people were going to be getting active,' said Marjorie Lee. 'That decided me to do something of my own choice rather than go to the jam factory or the battery factory.'[213]

She signed up for the navy.

Rosalie Seddon wrote a comic poem about a young woman 'of the luscious languid type' who spends the first three years of the war doing nothing and then at last makes up her mind that she must do her bit. She weighs up in a leisurely way the pros and cons of going into the air force, the army or the navy:

And while she contemplated …
The Manpower Board just packed her off,
To Westfield Freezing Works.[214]

A member of the Women's Auxiliary Air Force doing 'military' work – washing dishes. Contact *magazine, 1942.*

The bulk of women in the military came from middle-class backgrounds, only a few from the skilled working class and almost none from the unskilled working class. A survey of the Women's Auxiliary Army Corps showed that 18 per cent, before they joined the army, had been living at home and not working for pay, which meant they were mostly young women of the middle class. Of the others in the corps, 4 per cent had been working in professions, 27 per cent in offices and 21 per cent in shops. Only some 28 per cent had come from jobs in hotels, catering or manufacturing.[215] A middle-class family was more likely than a working-class family to see the war as ennobling. A working-class young woman was less likely than a middle-class young woman to like the stiff discipline, rank and hierarchy of the military. 'I loved the discipline,' said Lorna Smith, daughter of a conservative member of parliament.[216] A working-class young woman knew that a factory job meant fairly good hours, fairly good pay, often a fairly easygoing workplace and no orders to dress in a certain way, behave in a certain way or live in barracks.

New Zealand women went through experiences not unlike those of their sisters in Japan and Germany.

Japanese women, while they were sought for war work by their government, were told they embodied what soldiers were fighting for – the 'warm fountainhead' of the country.[217] The state registered young women as possible war workers, but throughout the whole of the struggle the government could not bring itself to conscript any women into factory or other service, even though labour was needed urgently. Tokyo urged women to do voluntary war work instead, backed by a new body called the Greater Japan Women's Society. The society, led by women of the middle class, behaved very much like the New Zealand Women's War Service Auxiliary.[218]

German women, too, were allowed to stay at home carrying out household tasks rather than stand on assembly lines or shoulder weapons in defence of the Third Reich. The Nazi government knew that mass protest against war hardship by women during the First World War had been a serious source of social, political and military stress not only on the home front but on the fighting front. Soldier sons, soldier brothers and soldier husbands had been badly upset by reading angry letters sent from their mothers, sisters and wives. Berlin bureaucrats throughout the new struggle conscripted women into war work quite sparingly.[219]

The idea of femininity was very strong everywhere from Otago to Osnabrück, from Ottawa to Osaka. John Allum, company director and mayor of Auckland, said it was 'most undesirable' to take young mothers away from their 'primary task', which was tending to the family.[220] Mavis Hill praised woman as homemaker in awkward poetry:

She is the true foundation of the Empire,
Expecting neither gratitude nor praise
For unrewarded years of quiet devotion,
The moulding of its Youth to manhood days.[221]

The worry that women were becoming 'unsexed' provoked Gilbert Ward to publish a comic novel, *The League of the Brown Skirts*. Mrs Warrington Cumber-Glubber, a member of the landed gentry who wears brown tweeds and has 'a nose like a vulture',[222] has founded a group called the Daughters of Zealandia. Madge Heatherway, a young newspaper reporter, masquerades as her maid in order to get the dirt on the group. Madge thinks her boss 'a budding Hitler'.[223] The Daughters of Zealandia secretly call themselves the League of the Brown Skirts and their objective is to found 'a Totalitarian State in New Zealand ruled exclusively by women'.[224] After it carries out a coup, it will abolish votes for men and make them 'Chattels of the People'.[225]

A woman railway guard, smartly dressed and competently smiling, working for what was the world's largest capitalist business before and during the war: the Deutsche Reichsbahn. The warring states produced many images that showed women taking on new tasks. The truth, however, was that most women in Germany, Japan – and New Zealand – were not allowed to 'wear the trousers' but instead kept carrying out work traditionally seen as 'womanly'.

Ward was on the political right, as were Hill and Allum, so their views were perhaps not too surprising. The leaders of the left, however, also spoke of women as the cornerstone of home life and the family. Janet Fraser gave an 'inspiring' speech on the topic to the National Council of Women. 'In the strength of the family lives the strength of the nation,' she said.[226] Wellington members of the National Council of Women worried that, thanks to women being caught up in the war 'home life, with all its influence' seemed 'in danger of disappearing'.[227] Mary Dreaver, while lauding the wearing of slacks, ended with: 'who will question their still being quite ladylike?'[228] The mass of women did not find that the war caused any big changes, whether they were working for pay or without pay.

A lot of women did their best to go on as though there was no war. Women could always be found 'idle in hotel lounges', noted one citizen, and were 'not war conscious' but 'pleasure conscious'.[229] Barbara Lorigan wrote indignantly that forcing women into war work would bring the dominion 'down to the levels of Germany'.[230] The typical woman of her type was nicknamed 'Florence Fussipance'. A writer portrayed her satirically:

> *I'm simply LIVID. I ACTually am ... Stopping us girls from using lipstick, rouge, and facial cream. CAN you Beat it? I mean they couldn't be RUDER it's not even RESPECTable, and no stockings; making us go about raw ... I mean it's positively grim; it's too shaming.*[231]

New Zealand was not fighting a total war, and women were even less likely to be fighting such a war than their menfolk. Thousands of women put up with the war 'passively', noted Nancy Taylor. They dealt with domestic tasks. They looked after 'children, households'. They complained – vexed by the rationing of petrol, the shortages in the shops.

'This beastly war,' they said.[232]

WE MATE LIKE CATS

A mood of sexual excitement seemed widespread in wartime society. Truth might be the first casualty in war, wrote a clergyman and former soldier, Ormond Burton, but 'chastity is probably the second'.[233] Ernest Beaglehole, scholar, thought that sexual relationships 'come into sharper focus in wartime because of the hysteria, the excitement and the lack of emotional balance'.[234] Alice Greville, poet, wrote about 'the War-tempo speeding up sex to a climax'.[235] The sight of sweethearts kitted out in khaki before boarding troopships led many lovers not to wait till their wedding night.

New Zealand troops overseas sought sexual opportunity. The wages of a dominion soldier were high by the standards of the day, and the earnings of sex workers were low in Egypt, Italy, Fiji, Samoa and Tonga. 'There was a good deal of whoring,' said army medical officer Hec Levien.[236] Gordon Slatter, infantryman, noted that civilian poverty was so bad in Italy that the body of a young woman could be bought 'with tins of bully and cakes of soap'.[237] Men went to brothels in groups and watched each other take turns with prostitutes. Gordon Williams talked about such a session when he and two fellow artillerymen paid to go with a woman. One friend was too shy to do anything; the other was not shy.

'I'll ride her! But you blokes make sure no one puts cigarette butts on my arse.'

'Yes, she'll be right!' said Williams.[238]

A lot of men went out sexually exploring because they were freed from the ties of home and family. Denis Glover, although he had left a wife at home in Christchurch, had many sexual encounters while in the navy. 'A Sailor Finds Love' was a poem he wrote about one of those meetings:

It was an hour of need, Oh
I know now it was meant to be ...
Love struck like a torpedo ...[239]

A young soldier, airman or sailor living cheek-by-jowl with other young men might also try out what psychologists of the day called 'situational homosexuality'. Edgar Gornall, doctor, wrote about the topic in a sexual guidance book published in 1944; he explained to readers that some who would only look at women in civilian life would be willing, when in uniform, to have sex with another man.[240] Men who before the war were sexually attracted by other men found, too, that they could behave more freely than when living at home where they might be seen by neighbours or family. Eric McCormick wrote in occupied Egypt about 'charming boys'.[241] Owen Roberts, another young soldier, took many fellow soldiers as lovers and said afterwards that he had the 'time of his life' while in the army. 'The sex was incredible,' agreed an air-force navigator, Simon Sydney, who went with many men while in the military.[242]

Women at home in the dominion, having been left alone by lovers or husbands, turned to other men or sometimes other women for pleasure and comfort. Colleen

Stage shows during the war were often more sexualised than during the years of peace. Programme cover for a show staged at His Majesty's Theatre, Dunedin, 1944. *Alexander Turnbull Library Eph-A-VARIETY-1944-01-front.*

Most servicemen sent overseas had sex with prostitutes while they were there. This sketch shows a streetwalker in Cairo. *Artist: Neville Colvin. E.G. Webber,* Johnny Enzed in the Middle East *(Rotorua: Rotorua and Bay of Plenty Publishing Co., 1945).*

Dee 'found out about lesbians' when in the air force and learnt 'to accept that they had their way of life and I had mine'.[243] Peggy Bulfin, who handled confidential letter files for the air force, noted that the 'usual problem' among single women in her squadron was unwanted pregnancy.[244] Lorna Smith, also in the air force, came across a case where one young woman who complained about lack of promotion was told in reply that she needed to show more responsibility.

'You've had one baby – anyone can make one mistake – but you've had two.'[245]

A Manpowered young woman – or a young woman evading Manpowering – could be more or less sure of picking up a soldier, airman or sailor simply by strolling down

Army life was intimate and gave openings for sexual play between men well away from the eyes of family and community back home in New Zealand. *Washing Clothes, New Caledonia.* *Artist: William Reed. Dunedin Art Gallery.*

the street. New Zealand and United States troops, when they steamed into the seaports or railway stations of the dominion, sought sex – and many women and quite a few men were happy to offer it for fun or a fee. Passionate love affairs followed, as did fleeting one-night stands. Women broke their engagement to lovers away overseas, or sent letters to husbands, asking for a divorce. A chaplain with the army in North Africa spoke of 'the suffering of many of our men because of broken engagements among unmarrieds and unfaithfulness among marrieds'.[246] George, a sensitive young soldier, was portrayed going through such heartbreak in a story by Winston Sargent. George loves his fiancée Betty, but when he goes away to war he has sex with a young woman called Maia. He struggles with his feelings:

> *Maia is on my mind. My conscience pricks me when I think of Betty. No, I can't do without Betty. But Maia … I decide that I won't mention this incident to Betty – she wouldn't understand.*[247]

Betty meanwhile dances with young soldiers and airmen in Christchurch. One night one of them gives her a kiss. She writes about it to George:

> *I felt as if I was in your arms. He was naughty and did hold me so very tightly. It took me all my time to drag myself away from him. You understand how a woman misses that sort of thing. You know I prefer your kisses to anyone else's, but there comes a time when the urge to be loved is so strong that you can't do anything about it.*

The story ends when George comes home on furlough and finds Betty has dumped him.[248]

Mary Whitelaw, a social worker, observed that war often threw women and men 'into the frequent company of someone who awakens in them a deeper and more enduring passion than their own spouse has ever done.'[249] Charles Mergendahl, a lawyer stationed in the dominion as a lieutenant of the United States army, portrayed a young officer very like himself who has a sexual relationship with a young woman in Wellington. The husband of the young woman has gone away as an officer in the dominion army. The two young people feel lonely.

'I'm tired,' says the young woman. 'It seems I never stop being tired.'

'Everyone's tired,' says the young man. 'It's that kind of time.'[250]

They become lovers and she falls pregnant.

Lyndahl Chapple Gee, mother of future novelist Maurice Gee, wrote a short story about two young mothers with husbands away at the war dealing with their loneliness in opposite ways, 'Louise romantically, Millie remedially'. Louise stays faithful to her husband. Millie sleeps with men from the air force, army and navy. 'I guess you just can't be faithful and patriotic too!' she says to Louise.[251] The point of view of women like Millie was portrayed subtly in 'The Girl Who Stayed at Home,' a poem by M.K. Joseph:

> *My love put on his battledress*
> *And then he went away*
> *I kissed him at the station*
> *But that was yesterday*
> *That was yesterday my love*
> *And now the tears are dried*
> *And I sit upon the beach*
> *With a new love by my side.*[252]

Nor was it only young people who looked for sex while going out fundraising, or square-bashing in barracks, or working in essential industry. Frank Sargeson wrote a short story portraying an ageing gentleman who, by doing voluntary war work, wins 'the right of free entry' into a group of matrons and finds 'even the most respected citizeness' in the group willing to go to bed with him on the sly.

'What it all added up to,' adds Sargeson, 'was that the perks of the war years were wonderful beyond anything he had for years dreamed of.'[253]

Conservatives were dismayed by what they saw on city streets. Couples made the most of the blackout to have sex in shop doorways. The *Observer* noted that sex between young women and young servicemen was common 'in side streets', even in daylight.[254] Condoms strewed the pavements. A soldier back on furlough was 'amazed' that even 'the street women of Cairo' were 'not half so brazen as many seen in Queen Street'.[255] The *Evening Post* worried about 'looser relations between the sexes' in Wellington. Hislop, the mayor, said that a 'plague of indecency' had swept the city thanks to 'an extraordinary slackening of control and discipline'.[256] Auckland city councillors and clergy got together to find ways to make citizens follow 'stricter standards of personal conduct'.[257] The chief commissioner of the Boy Scouts Association spoke about the 'state of moral depravity, especially of a sexual nature' that was overwhelming the country.[258] Nor were such scenes to be found only in the city. Harold Heaslip, a vicar, denounced what he saw in Stratford:

> *There must be few people who do not know that this town of ours, like many other towns, has become a monkey house, because some of its citizens – and not a few – have respect for neither the laws of God nor the dictates of common decency. Sexual laxity has become so common that many people consider it no longer shame or sin ... This town, like many others, is reeking with impurity.*[259]

A country town in the spring evening is portrayed in a short story by Maurice Duggan. A young woman has come across a young man lying naked in the grass. Now the two stroll the streets:

> *In town they went to the milkbar, past the crowd of boys outside the billiard-room and past the crowd emptying from the theatre. Half-time and icecream and bottles of gaseous, brightlabel softdrinks, the people crushed into the tiny confectionery shop or gathered in lax groups about the filmboards.*[260]

The shift in sexual behaviour during both world wars was perhaps not so much a matter of people behaving more freely as more openly. The years of war caused no obvious change in the number of babies conceived before wedlock. One in every four babies before the war was either 'illegitimate' or born within seven months of wedlock;[261] late in the war the number was somewhat more than one in every four.[262] A group of Auckland women, anxious about war babies born out of wedlock, set up the Motherhood of Man Movement.

'The little children must be given a welcome,' said its booklet. 'They are citizens of the future.'[263]

Young men and women often sidestepped pregnancy, of course, by unrolling rubber. They may well have done so more readily than they had before the war because the military taught servicemen and servicewomen about contraception with a thoroughness that until then had seldom come their way. Roma Watson, an air-force nurse, noted that often it was 'the girls who knew the least' who 'got into trouble' with an unwanted pregnancy.[264] Also, young men and women may have bought more abortions than before the war. All towns had 'backstreet' abortionists.

Ottilia Binswanger wrote a short story about Phyllis, who loves a man in the army. 'The young soldier led her through the dark park under the oak trees where underneath the smooth grass grows … Phyllis awoke to a passion … and she gave herself with all her young vigour.' She finds herself pregnant after the soldier has gone away, and talks with a hospital matron about whether to abort the baby.

'You know,' says the matron, 'girls are very clever at abortions these days.'[265]

Cleverness was not always helpful. Sonja Vile, a trainee nurse, was on ward duty when a staff nurse 'dropped' onto her lap 'the corpse of a young woman of about my own age' who had got pregnant to a marine and gone 'to a back street abortionist who had botched the job and the result was septicaemia, which killed her'.[266] Officially the rate of unlawful abortions stayed much the same throughout the war – about thirteen for every hundred births – but that rate was almost certainly lower than the true tally.[267]

A feeling was certainly growing that sex was out in the open now. Conservatives thought it was losing its mystery. Rex Fairburn wrote a poem, 'Modern Love':

We often speak
of our technique
as though we handled spanners;
we mate like cats
in modern flats,
our morals match our manners.[268]

RELIGION, RACE

Clergy who agonised about the way the war was changing sex lives were not a group of people who had much authority in New Zealand. The dominion was only a thinly religious society. The 'indifference of a large majority' of people towards faith was noted on the eve of the war by an Anglican bishop, George Gerard.[269] Charles Chandler wrote on the first anniversary of the declaration of war that the god he worshipped had 'little or no claim upon the lives of over half the population' of New Zealand.[270] Although the census made it look as though nearly everyone belonged to a religious group, only a minority bothered going to church or temple or synagogue. Among those who did go, faith was seldom passionate. Joseph Brocklehurst, another clergyman, spoke about the matter in the last year of the war:

> *Many Church folk are at one with the enemies of religion in thinking that religion is a kind of hobby, like folk dancing or stamp collecting. It stands apart and alone and has no practical meaning.*[271]

Lay people agreed about the thin veneer of religious faith in the country. Oliver Duff, a journalist, said nobody who stepped inside a church would suppose 'zeal for

God's house is eating us up'. Congregations were small and most of those worshipping were 'not young'.[272] Another journalist penned a slightly more nuanced portrait:

> *Outside the churches is a relatively large majority of people who never enter a place of worship, comprising people in all walks of life and classes of society. They are not necessarily hostile to religion or anti-Christian, in fact very few of them are so; and they may even call in the minister, when they want him, as they would ring up the plumber when the bath leaks. But they seem to have quite nebulous ideas of God and Jesus Christ and the principles of the Christian faith or of any faith. They don't want to be bothered about these things; they are frankly materialistic, living for today.*[273]

Military and political leaders nevertheless invoked the god of Christianity as an ally. Christian principles were 'at stake' in the war, Adam Hamilton said, as leader of the parliamentary opposition on the first war Christmas.[274] 'Godspeed to you all,' said Walter Nash to the troops five years later, on the brink of a big attack in northern Italy:[275] Parliament every year during the war pledged its 'firm and unswerving devotion' to fighting for 'Christian civilisation'.[276] William Perry, opposition politician and president of the Returned Soldiers Association, was one of many leaders who spoke religiously about the war:

> *This monster who rules Germany has torn down the Cross of Christ from its altars and erected in its place the swastika, or the crooked cross of paganism ... You know that you are fighting to rid Europe and the world once and for all of the terror and menace of Nazi ruthlessness and Nazi paganism.*[277]

War strengthened the religious faith of some people; for others it dealt their faith a sharp blow.

Soldiers were among those who found that waging war led to a strengthened religious feeling. A private waiting to go into battle, or when in the thick of battle, might pray. 'I turn to God in my troubles more than ever I did when at home,' said an infantryman, Owen Gatman.[278] Prisoners of war sometimes 'experienced a return of religious fervour or perhaps turned to religion seriously for the first time in their lives', wrote one of their number, Walter Wynne Mason.[279] Civilians, also, could feel their faith quickening. Protestant churches grouped together in the autumn of 1941 to form the Campaign for Christian Order, whose goal was to crusade for a newly living faith that would reshape society. Christian Order was linked with a wave of thought called Moral Rearmament. Crusading hopefully, members of the movement published books with such titles as *For Faith and Freedom, The White Army of Peace, Arise and Build, A New World Order* and *Work and Wealth in Christian Order*.

Yet while faith stirred among a few thousand souls, there was no flocking to places of worship.

Church attendance seems to have grown somewhat after the fall of France but afterwards fell away.[280] 'Even now, in the midst of war,' wrote Chandler not long after the declaration of war on Japan, 'the common people do not hear us gladly.'[281] Nor was the Campaign for Christian Order welcomed any more gladly. The crusade flagged as the war dragged on year after year.[282] The Catholic church stayed out of the campaign.[283]

War led, too, to further eroding of religious feeling among many, perhaps most, citizens of New Zealand.

The theory of a good and wise god who governed benevolently in heaven seemed less than persuasive when there was so much maiming and massacring. Also, most people knew that among the citizens and subjects of both groups of warring states were millions of Christians – and, indeed, Muslims, Hindus and Buddhists. Dorothy Norgrove, a schoolgirl, listened to religious hymns being sung in honour of girls' brothers who had been killed fighting.

'It occurred to me that there must be *German* relations of soldiers and sailors singing the same or similar hymns,' she wrote. 'And couldn't God, if he existed, have prevented all this unreasonable mayhem from happening in the first place?'[284]

Christianity was meaningless to most soldiers, in the opinion of an infantryman, Gordon Slatter. 'Religion didn't matter at the war. A man was a man, a soldier was a soldier, and religion was letters stamped into the identity discs slung around the neck.'[285]

Soldiers who prayed when under fire often did so not from strong religious faith but because they were frightened and grasping at any straw, even prayers from childhood. 'We weren't religious until we were in danger ourselves and bleated out silently for God to help us and God save us,' wrote a gunner, James Henderson; 'you'd start whimpering for God and Christ.'[286]

Soldiers liked to cover all religious bases by calling on a goddess who had been worshipped in the Western world for thousands of years: Lady Luck. She had been brought back to lusty life on the battlefields of the First World War, and now had a new outing during the Second World War. 'Lady Luck,' said Ronald Stewart, a wireless operator in bombers, 'certainly played some part' in helping bomber crews to survive raids over Germany. Aircrew 'went to a considerable extent to try to be lucky'. A tiki or a St Christopher's medal might be tied to the dogtag worn around the neck. A teddy bear might be taken onto a warplane. Airmen on one base always took care to pat the bald head of a man in the ground crew when about to set off on a raid. One man 'always peed on the plane's tail wheel before he went up on an op'.[287] John McDonald, an air-force officer, wrote about the way religion and superstition tugged on the mind:

> *Superstition wins hands down. Or perhaps I should say that simple homely good luck charms have it all over the organized trappings of religion ... And, for myself, I'd hate to go off on a shaky do without my little tiki. That's not superstition, I'd just feel lonely without it. Of course I don't ascribe any magical powers to it, that'd be very silly and most unscientific, yet ... I take no chances and I wear it all the time.*[288]

New Zealand and British military power linked mythically with the war god Tū. The artist, whose iwi was Ngāti Ruanui, worked as a Methodist minister and radio broadcaster before the war; he then joined the air force. *Artist: Oriwa Haddon. A.R. Grimwood,* Flights and Fancies *(Wellington: Hutcheson, Bowman & Johnson, 1943).*

Men in the military gave a lot of wit and feeling to mocking Christianity. A short story by Gaskell portrayed the way life in the army seemed shockingly pagan to a pious young private. A sergeant talks 'with great lewdness'. Other men joke about 'unclean matters'. The 'filthy' talk is backed up by 'low and worldly edicts' of the army.[289] Richard Scott, a soldier stationed at camp in Marlborough, wrote a new version of a hymn sung by children in schools:

I am Jesus' little lamb
My fucking oath I am.[290]

Civilians, too, seemed more likely than before to make fun of Christianity. The church, wrote a newspaper editor, was 'being made the favourite theme of criticism and ridicule'.[291] Yet while religion was not strong, many people still saw themselves as belonging to a community of people whose forebears had shared the same faith. Presbyterians, for example, whether they went to church or not, were likely to mix with people whose backgrounds were also Presbyterian. A sense of community was very strong when people thought of themselves as either Protestant or Catholic. Community was based partly on faith and partly on notions of race or nationality. At its most intense, it was split between Irish Catholic and British Protestant.

The split between the two groups had led to heated words and fists flying between rowdy crowds during the First World War. Words were less heated during the Second World War. The Catholic church and the Labour Party had become confederates between the wars and the church on the whole was willing to back the government going to war against Germany. The Nazi Party, after all, was not only pagan but actively anti-Christian. The Soviet Union and the Communist Party were pagan and actively anti-Christian, too, making a godsend of the 1939 non-aggression pact between Berlin and Moscow. '[T]he issue is simpler and clearer for us from the alignment of Soviet Russia and Nazi Germany,' declared the principal of St Patrick's College, Wellington. 'The foes of religion are our country's foes today.'[292]

Catholic clergy and laity were thrown somewhat, two years later, when the tables turned and the Soviet Union became an ally of New Zealand. How could the sons of good Catholic households fight alongside the sons of such a state? War with Japan made things easier, once again, for Catholics to side with Protestants. Japan was wholly outside the world of Christendom, unlike Germany, Italy or 'Holy Russia.' Thomas O'Shea, archbishop of the dominion church, after the outbreak of war in the Pacific issued a pastoral letter to the clergy and laity in which for the first time he spoke of the war as a crusade:

> *Perhaps there has never been another Lent in our lives, more than this one, when we feel nearer to the Christ of the Garden of Gethsemane … We do well in these days of national emergency, when there is a menace over all our lives, to enter the Garden of Gethsemane in spirit and make our way to the Christ of the Agony.*[293]

Yet there was always a strong latent hostility between Catholics and Protestants. Quite a few of the latter were on the lookout for signs of disloyalty.

Catholics as a whole backed the proclamation of neutrality by Ireland. Irish New Zealanders could feel a sort of grim gladness that Britain was being bombed by Germany, seeing the blitz as payback for what Britain had done to Ireland. 'British people to-day,' wrote one, 'are enduring something of the terror inflicted on the Irish people.'[294] Protestant conservatives, by contrast, believed it treasonous for Ireland to follow a policy of neutrality. The *Evening Post* thought it 'deplorable' for any state belonging to the British Commonwealth not to go to war against Germany.[295] The *New Zealand Herald* said the republic was giving 'assistance to Germany.'[296] Protestant zealots linked Catholics with the Nazi Party. *Totalitarianism and Christianity*, a booklet published by Allan McDiarmid, told readers that the church had 'always been totalitarian, never democratic,' and that its sympathies in the war were 'with the totalitarian states.' Protestants on the other hand were 'the religious counterpart of democracy.'[297] *No Friend of Democracy*, a booklet by British freethinker Edith Moore that was shipped into the country, claimed among other things that 'Catholic and Fascist are synonymous terms'.[298] The booklet was seized and suppressed by the state.

War censorship meant that the most abrasive words spoken for or against Irish neutrality never found their way into print.

Jews, too, were often looked on as people of suspect loyalty.

The overwhelming majority of Jews in the dominion were people whose forebears had come from Germany. German Jewish families who had long ago settled in the country loved German music and literature, and sometimes chatted at home in German. Jewish refugees who had landed on the wharves only lately were even more clearly German: German was their mother tongue, and most of them did their best to live in the new land in the ways they had known in Germany. All – above all the newcomers – were at risk of being seen by neighbours as 'enemy aliens', which by the end of the war had become code for refugee Jew. One irony was that every Jewish rabbi in the dominion wholeheartedly backed the war against the Axis. Wellington rabbi Solomon Katz voiced a typical point of view:

> *A new barbarism, trained in the science of destruction, has broken through the barriers of civilisation and, moving forward with terrific force, is menacing the very existence of civilised humanity. This satanic force has now come within striking distance of our own shores. Our fair land and its people may any day become the target for the enemy's onslaught, an object of desolation and destruction. In these times of danger and imminent calamity, we must shed our smugness and self-complacency and lift our hearts to God.*[299]

News leaked to the government in 1942 about genocide being carried out by the Third Reich prompted a speech from Fraser, who was in Golden Bay. Millions of people were being killed, he had learnt, not for breaking any law but merely for being Jews. He told the country that the government wished 'to express its horror and that of all New Zealanders at the shocking and inhuman cruelties now being perpetrated against the Jewish people'.[300] Although the prime minister undoubtedly felt horror, conservatives who looked down on Jews, and working people who disliked Jewish employers and moneylenders, tended to have more mixed feelings.

'The majority of New Zealanders,' wrote one unhappy citizen, 'are infected, to some degree, by a germ which has a paralytic effect on the heart ... the anti-Semitic germ.'[301]

Jews whose families had been in the dominion for many years were seldom targeted, but refugees who had come on the eve of the war found themselves parrying verbal blows. Attacks were not common early in the war, but they became widespread during the last two years. One claim that many whisperers and slanderers made was that the refugees had been sent to the dominion to spy. Another was that they made money out of the war because, as they were not citizens, they could not join the military and therefore were free to use their low Jewish cunning to buy up shops and other businesses left vacant by the patriotism of 'our boys'. *Truth* spoke about 'extraordinary

Liberty Loan advertisement, 1943. The government did its best to get not only the moneyed but the working class to buy war bonds. Advertisements like this targeted factory hands. *C.M. Banks Ltd. Museum of New Zealand Te Papa Tongarewa.*

inroads' being made by refugee Jews into commerce and industry. 'The fur, the clothing and the manufacturing trades,' readers learnt, 'are already experiencing the results of this foreign invasion.'[302]

The mood darkened when some citizens called for the state to cut back on the civil freedoms of refugee Jews. The New Zealand Manufacturers Federation asked the government to 'implement restrictive measures' on 'certain aliens' selling, buying and running businesses. Or the government could force aliens, as a second-best option, 'to work 100 per cent on war and essential civilian production'.[303]

Nor was it just words. Jews were driven out of jobs.

Pianist Paul Schramm, whose broadcasts had been banned had ended up driving a taxi to earn himself a wage, but his right to hold a taxi licence was then taken away; licences were not for enemy aliens but for citizens of New Zealand.[304] Schramm was allowed to play again in 1944 and gave concerts that were broadcast on state radio. He also did a nationwide tour interpreting Beethoven and Chopin. Angry citizens nevertheless still denounced him as an enemy.[305]

The government tried to calm controversy about enemy aliens by speaking soothing words – and by using censorship. The National Party, however, kept bringing it up. Polson, on one occasion, told parliament that enemy aliens were causing a 'great deal of uneasiness'. Senior public servants, he said, had given him secret information about how they were able to buy businesses in New Zealand. The country was 'alive with rumours'. Mason, justice minister, answered soothingly.

'Let me assure the public,' he said, 'that we are not being overrun by aliens.'[306]

Attacks were kept up during the very last months of the war when many citizens worried about the need to find jobs for soldiers, sailors and airmen coming home to the country. Jobs clearly should not go to refugee Jews. The Wellington Hospital Board, for example, went out of its way to say that its wartime policy had been to veto the employment of any enemy aliens. Herman van Staveren, president of the Wellington

Hebrew congregation, protested that the policy of the board was 'a veiled attack against the Jewish peoples as a whole'. A member of the board answered that van Staveren's words were 'a piece of impertinence and impudent'.[307] Some citizens said that the state ought to round up refugee Jews, lock them in camps and then, when the fighting was over, lease a 'large transport' ship and send 'Jewish and alien refugees back to Europe'. The state could then acquire businesses bought during the war by Jews and sell them to 'our own lads'.[308] At the national conference of the Returned Services Association in the winter of 1945 nearly every delegate supported the following proposal:

> *That any person or persons who arrived in New Zealand from Germany, Austria, Hungary, or Italy since 1939 must return to their own countries within two years after hostilities with Germany cease, and that they be allowed to take out of New Zealand the same amount of money or property, or both, that they declared to the Customs Department on entering New Zealand; any further money or property that they possess to be sold and the proceeds handed to the New Zealand Government for distribution among the wives and dependants of those who fought while the enemy aliens enjoyed peace and plenty in New Zealand.*

'The sole purpose of most of them,' said one delegate about the refugee Jews, 'is the aggregation of property and control of industry.'

'These people,' added another, 'came here to save their own skins.'[309]

MĀORI

The Second World War brought deep and abiding changes to the lives of New Zealand Māori –and less striking change to the lives of Cook Island Māori. Nine in every ten New Zealand Māori before the war were living in villages, where they tilled the land to make scanty earnings or went out fishing. A lot of young men and some young women did wage work – mostly labouring on roads for county councils or in paddocks or shearing sheds or in the kitchens of private landowners on farms and stations – which yielded some cash for the whānau.[310] Villages and villagers in their daily doings were governed on the whole by chiefs and old tribal ways.

The war made many thousands of those villagers into a new working class in the growing cities of New Zealand.

Chiefs and religious leaders in many tribes urged their young men to go into war industry and the military. Chiefs and religious leaders in many other tribes urged their young men to stay out of the war. As always, the key divide was between 'loyal' and 'rebel' sides in the New Zealand Wars. Te Puea stuck to her early stand of neither approving nor disapproving of the declaration of war on Germany and Italy; she behaved the same way after the declaration of war on Japan.[311] Rātana congregations in some villages spoke approvingly about the troops of Japan.[312] Frederick Bennett, a Māori Anglican bishop, observed that Rātana flocks 'in several districts' were 'making unwise and disloyal statements.'[313] On the whole, however, most tribes ended up agreeing that only through fighting, and giving support to the fighting, could they win more say in New Zealand.

All tribes grouped together, too, in a remarkable new body, the Maori War Effort Organisation.

The organisation was set up by the tribes after a group of rangatira talked the government into giving its blessing. Paraire Paikea, chosen as national chairman, spoke about grouping Māori 'around their tribal system and Spirit' in order to 'compete on equal terms with their Pakeha brothers and sisters in the present and future economic, commercial, industrial and social life of New Zealand.'[314] Waikato and Taranaki were willing to lend their backing, once they agreed that the body could lead to the settlement of land grievances and an improvement in the political position of their tribes. Other tribes, which had held back from supporting the organisation out of a wish to show their respect for the grievances of Waikato and Taranaki, were happy to follow.[315]

The Maori War Effort Organisation spread throughout the whole of the country, growing up swiftly from the flaxroots. All meetings followed kaupapa Māori. Tasks were sweeping. One task was to recruit young tribesmen as soldiers for the Maori Battalion, together with others as warriors with the Home Guard. Another task was to grow crops to feed the military. A third task was to work alongside government departments to find men and women workers to take over jobs in freezing works, fertiliser works, sugar refining, dairy processing and other industries that had been left vacant thanks to so many men being rounded up by the military. A last task was to carry out fundraising. Tribes worked hard to get people to give money. A 'Gala Monster Polynesian Victory Concert', for example, drew crowds to the town hall in Auckland.[316] Altogether the tribes coaxed well over 10,000 men and women into working for essential industry. Also, right up to the last days of the war, they fielded the Maori Battalion. One out of every four Māori men of military age went into military uniform or worked in essential industry.[317]

The government gave no funding to the organisation because the point was to show tribal autonomy. Tribes had never before come together with anything like such striking unity. Whanganui chiefs sat alongside those from Te Tai Rāwhiti. Murihiku worked for the war just as Te Tai Tokerau did. Paikea, summing up what was being done, called it 'revolutionary' for the tribes to do so much and to be given so much authority and autonomy.[318]

'In the minds of the Maori people,' he said, 'the Maori War Organisation is the greatest thing that has happened in the history of the Maori people, since the signing of the Treaty of Waitangi.'[319]

War, craving young men and women to work in essential industry, also drew into the dominion a whole new group of labourers from the Cook Islands.

Rarotonga shipped out hundreds of young people to work in 'labour-starved factories, hospitals and construction sites'. Young women landed as servants. The government allowed recruitment of those young women when the rich started lobbying – triggered by a servant shortage in one of the households of the Williams family, who were wealthy landowners on the East Coast. Nio Are and Agnes Parakoti were the first to come under the scheme; they were sent to one of the Williams estates at Tokomaru Bay. Others soon followed. Sir Ernest Davis took two young women servants for his house in Auckland, and another three for his country house near Rotorua. Wages were low. A left-wing newspaper protested about 'strong girls, willing girls, who have never heard of trade unions' being paid badly to work 'far into the night' to serve at the bridge parties of white mistresses.[320] The government took heed of the protest and stopped supporting the trade in servants.

A task far more vital to the dominion economy began when several hundred men in Rarotonga signed indentures to hack out phosphate on the island of Makatea.

New Zealand needed a new source of phosphate to make up for what it could no longer get from its lost mandate of Nauru. Makatea belonged to French Oceania. The Compagnie Française des Phosphates de l'Océanie offered indentures to villagers willing to bind themselves to dig for a year on the island. Villagers who signed up came from households made so poor by war that they were willing to do such work in hopes of breaking out of their poverty. The Labour Party, which between the wars had often spoken out against the use of indentured labour in island colonies, was keen to set them to work. Wives and sisters and mothers went with the workers, as did many children, but none found the island to be anything like their gentle homeland. Makatea was a bleak and barren lump. The work was gruelling. Rarotongans in their sweating homesickness sang a song of longing:

Oh Rarotonga, land that nourished me,
How far I am from thee.[321]

Cook Island Māori who harnessed themselves to the dominion war economy were nevertheless few alongside the trainloads of New Zealand Māori making their way to the city. The warriors of the Maori Battalion, and those trains disgorging young people from the villages, led many other citizens to think about the wider question of what was owed to the tribes and colonial subjects in the tropical islands. The *New Zealand Herald* went so far as to ask readers whether they had 'been fed far too long' on a 'sentimental affirmation' that there was racial equality. The leader writer went on to say bluntly that the affirmation was 'of course, untrue'.[322] A citizen wrote to a newspaper about 'the unhappy story' of the way the colonial state had confiscated land from tribes during the New Zealand Wars. Pākehā, added the writer, seemed to have 'a lot to repay to the Maori people, both for what happened long ago, and for sacrifices in these days of war'.[323] George Cruickshank, bishop of Waiapu, gave an outspoken speech about how

the treatment of Māori by governments in New Zealand was in some ways not unlike what the Nazi government had done in Poland.[324]

Yet while the tribes as a whole were willing to work for the war, we must not overlook the fact that many villages continued to withhold their full support right to the end of the struggle.

Thousands of tribesmen went to war – but thousands also stayed away. The Maori Battalion fielded only 3600 troops during the whole of the war, and while a few thousand more waited for an empty spot on the roll, and several hundred others served in the air force or navy or elsewhere, tens of thousands of men of military age lived in the villages and could not be made to go to war by hook or by crook. Absenteeism was widespread among the young people who did leave the kāinga, too. A lot did not like being manpowered by the state. A lot did not want to go to a city. A lot did not like being told what to do and where to work by the busybody committees of the Maori War Effort Organisation. The state stepped in with a big stick only when the committees found they could not wangle or wheedle stubborn workers into doing what they were told.

A Rotorua magistrate, for example, dealt with several such workers one day. Wiha Curtis was found guilty of failing to obey an order from a Manpower officer to report for work. Ellen Te Kiri and Cora Low were also found guilty. 'These young girls are roaming the streets,' complained a state official, 'and don't want to work.' Rotahi Mohaia, who had already been imprisoned for absenteeism, pleaded guilty to leaving his forestry job. John Te Aonui, another errant forestry worker, was also found guilty. Bert Witariana, who had left his job but had gone back to it after a warning, was convicted and ordered to pay costs. Isaac Matenga was sent to jail. Sydney Moke, who had walked away from an essential job making mine props, said he would rather be sent to jail than go back to war work. The magistrate obliged by having him locked up. 'And when you come out you will get another instruction to return to work,' was the warning. 'If you don't obey it you will go back to prison for a longer term. If you don't want to work outside you'll work inside.'[325]

Māori found ways to continue sidestepping work in war industry. A farmer told the Whangarei Primary Production Council that although the land of the district badly lacked labour there were throngs of 'able-bodied Maori youths doing no regular work'.[326] A Bay of Islands farmer the following year protested to the Farmers Union about the supply of tribal farm workers being 'unsatisfactory'. Hands were 'needed urgently' yet a 'large body of natives' was not willing. A delegate from Whangarei added that young village men cared about nothing but 'beer and benzene'. Māori wage workers, even when they could be found, often 'would not work more than a certain

OPPOSITE: Four young women pose beside an air-force transport plane, Rarotonga.
Photographer: Whites Aviation. Alexander Turnbull Library WA-00961-G.

number of days in a week,' noted a farmer near Te Kuiti.[327] The Rotorua Manpower officer spoke about how employers in his district 'grumbled' at the idea of taking on Māori. Absenteeism was said to be too high, and the work not 'reliable'.[328]

The war threw the two main races of the country together in ways that provoked new tensions and conflict.

A colour bar quickly became obvious, noted Kahi Harawira, a clergyman and army major who worked to place young villagers in city jobs. He found that many of those young people were turned down by employers on no other grounds than that they were Māori. City landlords often turned a cold shoulder, too:

> *He himself had had the door slammed in his face at one boarding house, even though he had been in uniform at the time. A young woman, a university student with high qualifications, was turned away on making application for a room, on the grounds that she was a Maori. She said to the woman who had turned her away, 'Is that what my brother died for?' She had just received word of her brother's death while serving with the Maori Battalion.*[329]

Harawira was backed by some other clergy. Māori knew there was a colour bar, said John Laughton, head of the Presbyterian Maori Missions, and were 'made to feel that colour bar in a conscious way'.[330] Chiefs also spoke out. Eruera Mita told the Uenukukōpako tribal committee how two men who had been in the Maori Battalion were treated in a racist way by other workers at Karapiro:

> *Much has been written and said of the outstanding exploits of the Maori Battalion, but apparently there are still some Europeans who think that the Maori people are not worthy of the much vaunted 'freedom' their comrades died to preserve. It is most unfortunate that detestable racial discrimination which smacks of Hitlerism should, in these enlightened days, still spoil the relationship between Maori and Pakeha.*[331]

John Reece Cole described in a short story how two young Māori men squeezed their way onto a crowded city tram among Pākehā commuters. One of the young men, formerly a soldier in the Maori Battalion, loses his stick. He tries to fumble for it beneath a seat where two women are sitting. A sudden lurch of the tram shoves him against the knees of one of the women, who shrieks and pushes at him with her gloved hands.

'Revolting creatures!' she says.

'Chuck him off!' someone shouts.

The young Māori man straightens himself up, and he and his companion get off the tram and walk away. The stick is found inside the tram by an old woman – and it proves to be a white stick.[332]

Arthur Richards, member of parliament, was worried enough by the question of a colour bar to look closely at rented housing in his electorate of Roskill. He got a 'disturbing' glimpse of the 'overcrowded and squalid conditions' braved by many Māori.

Ten people had been crowded into one dark basement room with a bare earth floor. Ten people were living in a room about three metres by six metres in another basement:

> *Despite the wretched conditions under which the Maori people live in the localities visited, it was obvious in many instances that an attempt was made to make the best of circumstances. In the restricted quarters there was a pervading smell of boiled clothing, and there was white linen hanging on the line.*[333]

The changes going on were so deep that the balance between races and cultures would never be the same as before the war, when most white people seldom set eyes on tribespeople. Māori were becoming less likely to live in a world of villages and farming and fishing. One in four dwelt in towns or cities by the end of the war, and within a generation the streets of suburbs, not the creeks and paddocks of the countryside, would be the setting for the daily lives of most Māori. Children brought up in the suburbs did not belong to the old village world; nor were they bequeathed its old ways of thinking, feeling and behaving.

The tāngata whenua, together with growing groups of other Polynesians, would find those suburbs both bitter and hopeful.

CLASS WAR

Class still divided society too. A lot of the well-off worried about 'the reds' and saw 'a "bolshie" behind any pair of whiskers' observed a clergyman, Eric Rich, of Masterton. A lot of working people, on the other hand, were still anxious about 'the excesses of capitalism'.[334] Angry words were still spoken, and edgy battles waged, over who was to pay for the war, and how. Class war was also fought over the question of whether or not the government should be going ahead with building a welfare state.

The state, by the end of the struggle, had spent £780 million on the military.[335] War spending during the three years of peak mobilisation took away more than half the national income of New Zealand.[336] The money was found in the four ways it had been found from the beginning: voluntary fundraising yielded some money; borrowing from the citizenry yielded a lot more; and taxation yielded by far the most money. Also, the government did its best to cut costs in the running of the state, thus saving money to be spent on the military.

The National Patriotic Fund Board kept its grip on voluntary fundraising, paying out between £1.6 million and £1.9 million every year after the outbreak of war with Japan.[337] Volunteers worked hard to gather more money. The wealthy and the middle class now and then stumped up with handsome cheques and gave services or goods. Ellesmere county landowners, for example, gave a 'wonderful collection of antiques and heirlooms' to a fundraising event presided over by the society hostess Agnes, Lady Wigram. Antique books and manuscripts from the seventeenth century were given, together with a violin from the eighteenth century and a 'great display' of silver and jewellery.[338] Eye-catching gifts by the moneyed were offset by secretive gifts from those of more modest means. A widow sent in a few rings:

> *I can't help any other way. I get a pension of £7 19s a month, for which I thank God. I have to pay £1 per week rent and keep myself and son aged twelve years. So you see I can't help much by way of giving money. My fingers are swollen with arthritis, so I am not able to wear my rings. You are quite welcome to them if they can help in any way.*[339]

The rich were being taxed so heavily, however, that they often looked askance at a collection cup. Also, wealthy and middle-class conservatives continued to oppose the government politically. Auckland capitalists were slow to stir themselves in 1943 when the mayor sent invitations to 'about 35' leading businessmen to meet and talk about fundraising. Only 'about 15' turned up, talked 'a lot' and did a lot of 'passing the buck'. Some moneyed men found 'the physical exertion of lifting a pen and signing a cheque too great'.[340] Women of the middle class were not so likely to go onto the streets fundraising as during the First World War. A lot of them, even when they did so, seemed to spend much of their time chatting or yawning. A citizen, one day, saw 'at least three groups of collectors talking among themselves' rather than soliciting for money. All three groups were women, most likely from the middle class. The citizen then saw another group of women fundraisers but they seemed 'fed up'. He went on to say that there had been 'no really enthusiastic collection day in Queen Street for many a long day'.[341]

Working people, too, often looked askance at going out collecting or dropping coins into collection cups. Many believed that nobody should have to beg for money. A group of unions and other worker organisations in Dunedin opposed voluntary fundraising so strongly that they said people who went out collecting were 'mutts'. The state, they believed, should pay for the war by conscripting the wealth of the wealthy.[342]

Voluntary fundraising varied widely, as always, from suburb to suburb, district to district and province to province. Canterbury and Wellington were a lot less open-handed than Auckland and Otago.[343] The whole sum collected by voluntary fundraising was markedly smaller than in the First World War. A typical account came from a newspaper in the Bay of Plenty:

> *If we were permitted to publish some of the experiences of the voluntary collectors who are now combing the Borough in the interests of the All Services Patriotic Appeal, our readers would be astounded at the utter selfishness and apathy of some of our so-called citizens. In some instances the callers have been met with point blank refusals, others want to argue on political grounds, others raise moral and ethical points.*[344]

Borrowing was a much more efficient way for the state to get money. The government continued to sell war bonds to the citizenry. War bonds were loans, not gifts. The moneyed were willing to buy. The poor were willing to buy. Bonds, which were backed by the state, were a safe way of saving. Selling bonds meant, though, that the state was shouldering a big burden of debt. The burden was 'tremendous', said Thomas Bloodworth, a former carpenter now a Labour Party politician and member of the upper house of parliament. The 'vast increase in the amount borrowed,' he added, was 'almost terrifying.'[345] The state during the six years of war borrowed £260 million, or 33 per cent of everything spent in the struggle against the Axis. Only £3 million, or less than 0.4 per cent of total war spending, was overseas lending. All the rest was borrowed or found in other ways inside New Zealand.[346]

The willingness of citizens to buy bonds was often striking.

'Bomber bonds', when they were marketed soon after the declaration of war on Japan, drew crowds to government buildings up and down the country. A 'magnificent patriotic response' was noted in Wellington, where citizens stood in the rain patiently queueing.[347] Rosina, Lady Norwood alone bought bonds worth £500, and her businessman husband Sir Charles Norwood shelled out another £1000.[348] A Liberty Loan the following winter was heavily oversubscribed; the government had hoped to sell bonds worth £15 million but got well over £17 million by the time they stopped selling.[349] Sales, however, had gone slowly.

'There is plenty of money in the country,' noted the *Star-Sun*, 'and if the people had shown any real enthusiasm for victory or any readiness to make a sacrifice the fifteen millions called for would have been raised in the first week.'[350]

Bond buying, like volunteer fundraising, varied widely between suburbs, towns and provinces. Greymouth bought nearly six times as many bomber bonds as Westport, though the two districts had roughly the same population and were very similar socially and politically. Hamilton bought bomber bonds worth £220,000 while only £76,000 sold in bigger and richer Invercargill.[351] Sales flagged nearly everywhere within half a year of the outbreak of war against Japan. A new round of bonds went onto the market in 1943, leading to an almost piteous appeal on behalf of the government by Fintan Walsh.

'Would it be too much of a sacrifice for the workers of this country to subscribe,' he pleaded, 'to defend their liberty, their standards of living, their culture, and their happiness in this the loveliest of all lands?'[352]

'Canterbury is not making a very creditable showing,' wrote an editor the following year, during another round of bond selling; 'nor is the progress made throughout the country anywhere near commensurate to its ability to find the money.'[353]

The bonds did get sold, but in the end the state always had to use compulsion to cover the bulk of the costs of fighting.

Tax was the tool for that compulsory levy. Wealth was taxed, and incomes were taxed, and as war went on those taxes were hiked higher and higher until the biggest incomes were losing up to 90 per cent to the state, driving many of the rich to impotent fury. Kenneth Myers found himself facing an income tax bill one year that was 'almost

The rich and the middle class continued to chafe at the way the Labour government taxed their incomes and wealth remorselessly. *Artist: J.C. Hill.* Auckland Star, *18 July 1942.*

double' what he had formerly had to pay. He called it 'persecution, and … nothing else.'[354] Company tax, also, was hiked steadily. The Waikato Farmers Co-operative Auctioneering Company, for example, one year made net earnings of over £74,000 but had to pay £52,000 in tax, or in other words 70 per cent of those net earnings. 'The huge burden of taxation,' said the chairman of directors, 'is stifling all industry, preventing enterprise and killing initiative.'[355]

Duties were levied on the estates of the dead, too, at rates that cut deep into the wealth of the wealthy. Alice Merry, a property hoarder in Wellington, was worth around £105,000 on her death but nearly £56,000 was taken in death duty.[356] Sir Henry Horton, a rich newspaper owner, was worth nearly £200,000 when he died, but 'slightly more than half' went as death duties to the state.[357] The middle class was also hit, though less heftily. Charles Winder, a Thames motor dealer, died worth nearly £66,000 but his estate shrank to less than £50,000 after death duty had been paid.[358] James McDougall, a farmer in the Wairarapa, was worth £51,000 when he died in the last year of the war, but only £31,000 after death duty.[359]

Taxes levied on the well-to-do supplied £471 million, or 60 per cent, of the vast sums spent by the state on the military.[360]

Taxing the rich was a popular policy among households of the working class, needless to say. The way the state took the knife to social services to pay for the war was not so fetching, however. Schools went short of money. Hospitals went short of money. The Labour government took pains not to wield the knife too sharply, seeking to save what could be saved in the running of the state but without becoming skinflint, since paring things back very severely had led to protest by workers during the First World War.

The government, while it was scraping the bottom of all sorts of barrels to find money to pay for war, was also speeding up the development of a welfare state. The broad outlines of the welfare state, commonly known as 'social security', had been sketched during the last two years before the war, but while the fighting raged overseas the government kept widening the rights the new system gave the citizenry. A child allowance, for example, had been granted on the eve of war to the first baby born to every mother; the same boon was awarded from 1940 onwards to every second baby as well. The following year a big step was taken when the state began giving a new family benefit to all mothers of young children whose household earnings were less than 110 shillings weekly. The benefit was generous – ten shillings a week for every child – and a boon to the poorest people in the working class.[361] One in six families qualified for the benefit and were now able to spend more to feed and clothe their youngsters. Health spending was boosted, too. Citizens were given free outpatient care in public hospitals, a benefit allowing them to get free drugs, and a benefit allowing them free physiotherapy.

Conservatives protested doggedly about the steady spread of the welfare state. The more moderate right declared that social security, while it was a noble principle, was not something to be sought during years of war but was best saved for the years to follow victory. The *Evening Post*, for example, slated it as an 'unfair burden which thrifty individuals have to carry'.[362] The less moderate right declared social security to be parasitic, the enemy of thrift, destructive to the economy and to the values of personal responsibility.

Class war came to a head during 1943 with a general election held for the lower house of parliament.

The collapse of the War Administration meant there was a need for a new mandate for the government. War was going so well that an election was settled on for the spring. The Labour Party and National Party were the key players, but various small groups on both left and right also fought for seats in the house, among them the Democratic Labour Party, the Communist Party and the Social Credit Movement. Censorship was loosened to allow for open debate, and soon the parties were 'going at it hammer and tongs', in the words of the head of foreign affairs, Alister McIntosh.[363]

The Labour Party told electors it had won for the people a high 'standard of prosperity and social security' and waged war 'with vigour, efficiency and unsurpassed success'. Fraser said the party would 'make the post-war future of New Zealand better than even the best of the past'. The National Party, he went on, spoke about a need for more freedom but what it wanted was 'freedom for predatory vested interests, which simply means freedom to grab the highest possible profits from industry, trade and financial investments and the right to grind the faces of the poor'. True freedom was not freedom to make money but 'freedom from want, freedom from exploitation and freedom from the fear of slumps and depressions', and could only be guaranteed by the Labour Party.[364]

Two parties wanted more socialism: the Democratic Labour Party and the Communist Party.

The Democratic Labour Party drew good crowds in many electorates, and it told those crowds they must stop the rightward drift of the governing party. John A. Lee, as party leader, gave most of his energy to attacking not the National Party but the party that had driven him out, 'Fraser-Labour'. The Labour Party 'once possessed transforming zeal' but now was no more than 'a tired group of paid caretakers of the status quo'.[365] Lee also savaged his other rival on the left, the Communist Party. The 'Communist scum' he called them one day when backing up Clare Jowsey in her campaign for the seat of Ōtahuhu. His speech, to over 1000 railway workers, was greeted by angry shouts.[366]

The Communist Party hoped to win an electorate or two. Only upwards of 2000 people belonged to the party, but many thousands more read the *People's Voice*. Harold Silverstone and Connie Birchfield, party members who stood for election to city councils in the last year of the war, each won more than 9000 votes. Communist opinions were common among university students as well as the working class.

'All the enlightened people here are Communists,' wrote Lauris Scott.[367]

The National Party, while it was aware it need not think too hard about arguments put forward by communists, took pains to say it was willing to keep a good deal of the welfare state. Conservatives knew that social security had been welcomed by a wide swathe of voters, among them citizens of the lower middle class and the skilled working class. The National Party hoped to win those voters for their own camp. Party leaders therefore said that they also stood for 'security, including social security', while at the same time they spoke about a need 'to cut the strangling cords' of the welfare state.[368] The party goal, they claimed, was 'a country of free and prosperous people', and the way to score that goal was with the help of four policy planks. One plank was to guarantee everyone 'well-paid creative employment under good working conditions, with the Government sharing the responsibility'. A second plank was to end 'avoidable causes of want'. A third plank was to give back to the people 'their fundamental British right of freedom to live their own lives in their own way without bureaucratic dictation in a system of competitive private enterprise'. Lastly, 'justice for the family' would be won by the government helping citizens own their own homes and bring up healthy offspring. All social welfare benefits would be kept up. Wages would not be cut. The National

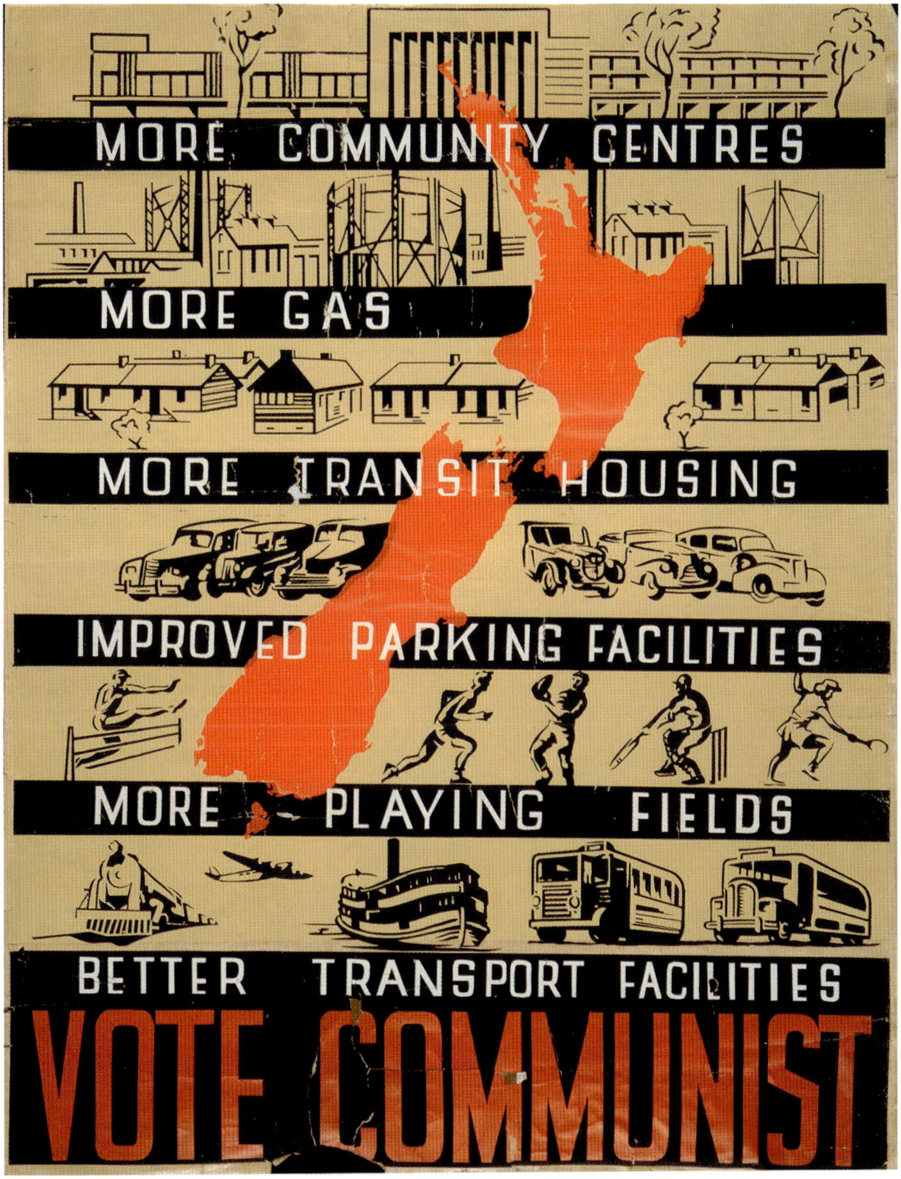

A Communist Party poster; electoral support for communism was stronger during the last years of the war than at any other point in New Zealand history. This poster was printed to support the 1944 city council election campaigns. *Alexander Turnbull Library Eph-D-ROTH-Communist-1944-02.*

Party nevertheless would not allow socialists to hide any more behind the mask of social democracy.

'Competitive free enterprise to be restored,' summed up the party manifesto; 'liberty of the subject to be reinstated; bureaucratic dictation to cease.'[369]

Social Credit followers were divided about whether or not to organise themselves into a political party. A national conference spoke worriedly about the war government with its 'growth of bureaucracy' and 'loss of democratic rights'.[370] The Labour Party was becoming a tool of international financiers who sought to sink the citizens of the dominion into a 'state of servitude through a fear complex of poverty amidst plenty'. The 'Capitalist Party' – the National Party – would seek to sink citizens into another sort of 'servile state'.[371] Social Credit hired a young organiser, John Hogan. He toured the country speaking to 'industrial workers, farmers and business men' and set up and edited a fortnightly newspaper, *Democracy*. The paper, banned under war censorship, was only allowed to roll its presses once more in election year.

'The present Government,' declared Hogan, 'consists mainly of old, tired men, whose radicalism and progressive ideals have become stale and timid.'[372]

Social Credit followers grouped themselves into what they called the Real Democracy Movement.

A wide array of lobby groups, unions, professional associations and many other organised bands of citizens also threw their weight into electioneering. The People's Movement, for instance, was one group on the right that sought a wholly new sort of government, in both war and peace, by throwing out a 'totalitarian' and 'vicious' system of party politics that 'kept Capital and Labour fighting over rewards like dogs over a bone'. The movement spoke of setting up a sort of corporate state.[373] Other groups were not opposed to the party system but wondered about which party. Worker unions were divided about whether members ought to put their tick alongside a candidate for the Communist Party or the Labour Party. Capitalist unions knew that some of their members, above all smallholders, were quite keen on Social Credit. The Farmers Union, for example, was far from hardline in its statement of policy. State ownership of 'certain public services, especially where, by their nature, they must be of a monopolistic character' was a good thing; it would be a mistake, however, for there to be too much state ownership.[374]

Newspapers in nearly every city openly backed the National Party. The *Evening Post* told readers that the policy of the party was 'attractive, progressive, and liberal'.[375] The *Standard* was the only newspaper of any size backing the Labour Party. Frederick Doidge, who had been a journalist for the right-wing press in Britain before going into politics on the side of the National Party, rubbished that paper as 'the lie factory of the Labour Party'.[376] The feelings of a deeply divided society led to a bitter campaign up and down the country.

'In some respect and in some electorates it was the bitterest that we have experienced,' said Fraser.[377]

Election day was 'electric with excitement', queues of people waiting for doors to open at polling booths. Queues were still standing outside some booths at midday.[378] A fair few citizens, however, stayed at home: only 83 per cent of those on the electoral rolls cast a vote, compared with 93 per cent in the last election before the war. The government lost several seats and tens of thousands of voters, the latter mostly to the Communist Party and the Democratic Labour Party. The National Party picked up a few new seats. All other parties did poorly. The government had won well enough to keep governing but voters had given a strong signal of restlessness. Fraser told the country that the Labour Party had been given 'a definite, decisive, and full mandate' to stay at the helm of the country.[379]

The Labour government, with the blessing of its renewed electoral mandate, takes the dominion for a stroll.
Standard, *3 December 1944.*

The National Party said that before long it would be governing.

'The Government can be in no uncertainty,' declared the strongly conservative daily, the *Press*. 'The electorate has not hesitated to show which way its confidence is turning.'[380]

The Labour Party saw its victory as a mandate to go on with building the welfare state. Nash spoke warmly about the principles behind the welfare state when he was elected president of the International Labour Organization. His speech was widely quoted throughout the Western world. The word 'freedom', he said, had been bandied about by the warring states. Freedom to speak or to vote a government into or out of power, he went on to say, was not enough to satisfy democratic socialists in New Zealand:

> *There can be no freedom where there is hunger. There can be no freedom where there is ill health … I don't want to get rid of poverty just to ensure that prosperity is maintained. I want to get rid of poverty because it is bad, it is wrong.*[381]

The Labour Party throughout the war had seen social security as the keystone of a just society. 'I feel we are all fighting for that,' said Fraser; 'it makes life worthwhile for every man, woman, and child in the country.'[382]

The government for the first years of the war had been able to preside over the very demanding twin tasks of fighting a war while building a welfare state, thanks to brisk growth in the economy. War, without question, was costly. The welfare state, without question, was costly. Yet the country was booming. Gross domestic product grew by 5 per cent even in the year of crisis after the war with Japan began. The next two years saw breakneck growth of 11.1 per cent and then 8.1 per cent.[383] Nash worked very hard to stop the economy from swinging about too wildly under the pressure of war by underpinning everything with what was known as 'stabilisation'. The First World War had frightened the working class and the lower middle class with runaway inflation of the currency. The keys to keeping them happy now were 'stable' wages and 'stable' costs.

Food prices were stabilised, for example, with the help of consumer subsidies for butter, bread and milk. Fruit and vegetables came under price control next, followed by the sale and lease of land. A complex array of other regulations sought equipoise for the economy: zoning production, standardising goods, simplifying goods, 'government importation and selling below cost, absorption by traders of some cost increases, transference of others from essential to non-essential goods'.[384] Nash was proud of how well he saved households with low or modest incomes from the price hikes and war profiteering of the First World War. He was proud, above all, of how well he controlled the supply of money.

'In New Zealand,' he declared in the spring of 1944, 'control is more complete than in any country except Russia.'[385]

The boom, however, suddenly went bust. The economy shrank during the last year of the war; gross domestic product went down by 2.0 per cent,[386] enough to trigger fears that with peace would come a slump. A slump had followed the First World War. Working people were nervous about the likelihood of another one – as were many farmers, shopkeepers, tradespeople and others in the middle class. The sudden shrinking of the economy, linked with awareness that huge hunks of national income were still being gobbled up by the military, led citizens to jostle with one another to try to get a bigger share, or at least to keep the share they had already, of whatever wealth was not being devoted to fighting the Axis.

Class conflict seems to have stepped up during the last two years before victory.

Strikes, lockouts and other rows between workers and employers took up many more working days during those years than earlier in the war: strikes climbed from a low yearly rate of 15,000 working days to a new high of nearly 53,000 working days. Workers earning the lowest wages grew 'increasingly restive', noted Nancy Taylor. Living costs seemed to be going up, no matter how much the government claimed that it had stabilised prices, while at the same time hours of overtime were going down, or seemed likely to go down when an end came to the overseas fighting.[387]

The most obvious social divide shown up by strikes was between the more militant unions and the more conservative people with property.

The National Party led a campaign against any group of workers who thought about striking. Holland, speaking to parliament after the coalminers' strike that gave him the pretext to walk out of the War Administration, said he had asked the government to arrest and imprison the leaders of the union and send all other miners back down the shafts or else to military camp. The union leaders were 'wreckers'. The government was dealing with them weakly, following 'a policy of appeasement, a policy which is an enemy to the Empire and the world'.[388] Holland carried on in the same vein. He slated the 'strikes and policies of go slow' that were 'sabotaging the war effort'. He announced that strong unions were subjecting the dominion to 'something very nearly akin to tyranny'. William Goosman, owner of a big transport company and member of parliament for the National Party, backed his leader by saying that militant unions were 'holding the Government up to ransom' and 'emulating highwaymen of the days gone by'.[389]

Chambers of commerce, employer unions, magistrates and other conservative voices echoed the National Party. A court in Kaiapoi was told early in 1944 that a group of slaughtermen from a freezing works were 'traitors to those men who are fighting, being maimed and dying in the cause of democracy'.[390] The *Bay of Plenty Beacon* denounced 'the maggot of class' that stopped citizens from falling in line to form 'a common front' against the overseas enemy.[391] The *New Zealand Herald* declared that the 'great question' was 'whether a democracy is prepared to use a firm hand against those who sabotage its war industry'.[392] A series of columns in that newspaper late in 1944 told readers that while unions had a part to play in a modern society, class conflict must not be allowed to overcome social unity. 'Acrimony and class hatred eventually paralyse industrial advancement.' Workers who spoke about the supposed power of a 'junta of capitalists' needed to understand that capitalists had less power now than unions of seamen, coalminers and watersiders.[393]

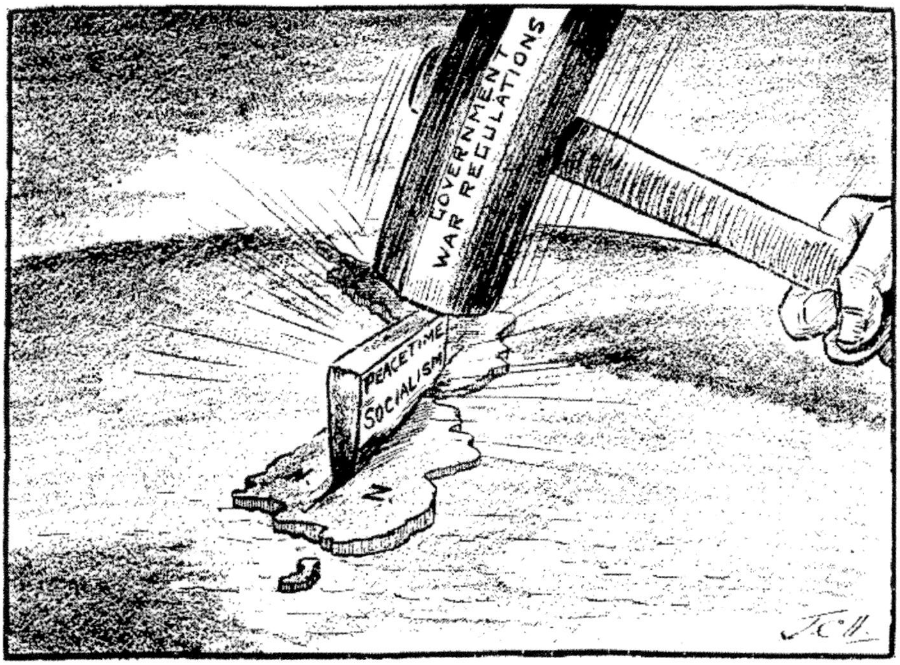

Conservatives continued to accuse the Labour government of using the war to advance socialism in New Zealand. *Artist: J.C. Hill. Auckland Star, 14 November 1944.*

A war of words between militant unions and moneyed conservatives was hardly surprising. A war of a less open sort, meanwhile, pitted unions of the left against unions of the right and also the socialist left against the less socialist right inside the Labour Party.

The government did its best to mask such struggles by keeping up a strong parliamentary front against the National Party. Sullivan answered a strident speech by Holland in words spoken quite as stridently. The leader of the opposition was carrying out the 'old attack' on working people that he and his party always carried out. The working class had 'nothing to be ashamed of' when compared with 'the employing and capitalistic class' whose spokespeople were the National Party.[394]

Yet a lot of unions and citizens in the left of the Labour Party were unhappy. The measures taken by the government to mobilise the economy for 'total war' were seen as attacks on the freedoms, rights and livelihood of the working class. Southland freezing workers spoke out only a few weeks after controls were tightened following the declaration of war on Japan. The 'burden of war should not be borne by labour and conscripted manpower alone,' they protested; 'we demand that the Government put into operation its policy of conscription of wealth immediately'.[395] The Auckland Harbour Board Employees Union protested at 'an unjust penalty on the workers' and pledged that they would 'resist in any lawful way any attempt to lower the workers' standard of living'.[396] The Federation of Labour, very potent in politics, a few months later called upon the government to impose strict 'limitation of profits' and 'heavier taxation of the higher incomes' to offset what was being asked of the working class.[397]

The government stuck to the right on such questions during the Second Phoney War.

Sullivan, in the spring of 1942, when it was already obvious that the tide had turned against the overseas enemy, told coalminers that going on strike had 'exactly the same effect as the torpedoing of a New Zealand supply ship by the Japanese'. Strikes in the coal industry hampered the power of the nation 'to fight the war, preserve the country against aggression and invasion, and to protect the people of New Zealand'. The striker was in league with the Japanese as 'the internal or external aggressor, each of whom equally threatens the security of the nation'.[398] Semple said strikers 'declared civil war on the civilian community'.[399] Fraser fretted so badly about strikes by coalminers, watersiders and other workers that he had even threatened to resign from the prime ministership:

> *I want to say that that sort of thing is defeatism of the worst kind – stabbing the country in the back. If, as Prime Minister, I cannot get better support from the industrial workers of the country, my duty to the country is to step down altogether. I am not going to occupy the position of Prime Minister and see the country betrayed … The limit of my endurance with that sort of thing has been reached, and I would appeal to the ordinary, decent thinking person in the country to support the Government.*[400]

The government continued to speak about disloyalty to the nation whenever unionists went out on strike in the last years of the war against the Axis. Webb, speaking as labour minister, early in 1944 went so far as to claim that anybody 'holding up production in this war' was not just an enemy to the state but 'an enemy to unionism'.[401] The government position was that most unionists were 'responsible' and that 'trouble' was caused by a minority. Semple, speaking as railways minister, early in 1945 praised the 'commonsense' of most railway workers who chose not to follow an 'impatient, impetuous, unthinking minority'. He wound up, as he did often, with sweeping words:

> *a halt must be called to industrial irresponsibility and harmful insurgency. The men fighting overseas and those who have returned from service have never complained about their conditions in front of the enemy. Is it too much to ask all workers in this relatively peaceful country to do the same and never less than their best to maintain untarnished New Zealand's great war effort?*[402]

Yet the split within the socialist camp did nothing to stop the building of the welfare state. The Labour Party was still officially a socialist party and waved a red rag in front of the conservative bull when a party conference declared that 'ultimate socialism' was still its goal.[403] The National Party now made the most of every opening to attack the Labour Party. Holland grew more abrasive and pushing. Keith Holyoake, a tobacco farmer and one of the rising stars of the right, talked of a need to fight the 'parasitic growth' that would lead to 'the dictatorship of Socialism'.[404] John Acland, a wealthy landowner and another rising star of the right, announced that what was needed was not to banish private property but to spread it 'amongst all the people in this country'. Soldiers coming home from the war did not want to live under a socialist state that would behave towards them 'like drill sergeants or a wet nurse'.[405] A nationwide newspaper advertisement warned citizens to oppose 'the Socialist dictatorship, towards which this country is rapidly approaching'; it was written and paid for by the Associated Chambers of Commerce.[406]

Conservatives still linked the supposed socialism of the government with the supposed national socialism of the Nazi Party. One conservative groaned early in 1944 that the dominion had suffered 'eight and a half years' of a 'National Socialism' based on 'class hatred' and 'endless strife in industry'.[407] St Barbe Holland told his Wellington synod that the 'fight for freedom' would 'enter a new and critical phase' after the defeat of the Axis. Freedom lovers would have to turn from the foreign foe and give their strength to battling the 'evil seed' of national socialism sown by the Labour Party.[408] Richard Gerard, a large landowner and a National Party member of parliament, a year later told the lower house that government policy was 'leading to National Socialism'.[409] The Dominion Council of Co-ordinated Business Associations was founded that winter to unite 'all classes of society' behind 'free enterprise versus National Socialism'.[410] The lobby group called on citizens to march through the streets. A crowd of perhaps

10,000 people answered the call by marching; but they backed the government, not the opposition, and mocked the claim that the government was fascist. Angus McLagan, former coalminer, spoke as president of the Federation of Labour:

> *Not only do we repudiate the slander – we hurl it back in the teeth of those who have uttered it and say that they and they alone are the friends of Fascism ... The people of New Zealand know only too well that Labour has always fought Fascism, and that wherever Fascism has come to power, Labour has been its first victim. The people are not likely to forget that many of those who are now raising the National Socialist bogy were themselves in the past the friends and admirers of the Nazis and Fascists.*[411]

Other political questions provoked wild words during the last two war years.

A typical class controversy greeted a move by the government to give hundreds of thousands of landless citizens the right to vote for county councils. Farmers and landowners fought a bill that went before parliament in the autumn of 1944 because they knew that it would end their monopoly over county government. William Horrobin, treasurer of the Farmers Union, called the bill 'revolutionary'. Holland added that it had unleashed an 'immense amount of feeling'.[412] The debate was long, and many members spoke passionately.

'The war against the landowners has begun,' said landowner and leading National member of parliament William Polson. 'It is evidently a crime to own a piece of land.'

'May the galloping horses be reined before they have ridden to the devil,' added a conservative lawyer, Rollo Ramsay.[413]

The Labour Party answered that the new law was simple democracy. 'Democracy, to my mind,' said Charles Chapman, linotype operator, unionist and Labour member of parliament, 'means every man and woman should have the right to vote.'[414]

Angry talk about class conflict marked many debates inside and outside parliament, but shrewd conservatives kept up the strategy of not altogether opposing the welfare state. The Annual Holidays Act, for example, passed in the autumn of 1944, which gave a yearly paid holiday of two weeks to all workers on wages and salaries, was a measure 'long awaited' by the National Party – or so claimed Holland.[415] Charles Camp, secretary of the New Zealand Employers Federation, voiced the private opinions of bosses when he spoke about 'the disappointment of many employers' in the new law and protested at the way it was railroaded through parliament by the Labour Party.[416]

War could not forge unity between the middle class and the working class. Nor could it link left with right, the Labour Party with the National Party. Wage workers wanted a welfare state, a social democracy, social security. The middle class and wealthy wanted a state in which they were free to earn more, own more, get better schooling, enjoy better health and live longer lives than the working class.

Fighting a foreign foe overcame class conflict, in other words, no more than it overcame any other serious source of disunity.

New Zealand air-force ground crew at work in the Solomon Islands. *Artist: Maurice Conly. Air Force Museum of New Zealand.*

CHAPTER 6 VICTORY?

NAPALM AND NUCLEAR BOMBS

Germany surrendered on 7 May 1945. The news was sent quickly by radio and cable to New Zealand. The government told citizens they must wait to celebrate until 9 and 10 May, which would be set aside for a public holiday. Workers clocked in on the morning of 8 May and children trudged to school. The mood was restless, however, with many people 'complaining bitterly' about the government not declaring a public holiday. Citizens ended up taking matters in their own hands. A 'peace fever' gripped so many within an hour or two that droves of them simply walked out of factories, offices and shops. Crowds sauntered through streets singing, swinging rattles, letting off firecrackers and tooting on trumpets.

'Why wait for to-morrow?' people said. 'To-day's the day!'[1]

Dunedin was the only city where anything like an official celebration was held on the first day, partly because the yearly graduation procession by students spilled over into wider festivities; the mayor sponsored merrymaking in the Octagon. All other towns and cities waited until the following morning when bells started pealing and sirens screaming. Christchurch was 'in carnival mood': a throng of several thousand joined a civic service of thanksgiving in the King Edward Barracks, while tens of thousands enjoyed 'high carnival in the gaily decorated and illuminated streets'.[2] Apia celebrated with 'the ringing of church bells, and sounding of sirens and steamer whistles', after which 'a large concourse of Samoans and Europeans' heard speeches and watched a parade by the little army of the mandate.[3]

Politicians and clergy everywhere spouted worthy words. Edward Gibbard, mayor of Dannevirke, was pious: 'I believe that our sailors, soldiers and airmen, along with those who helped them, were the instruments of Divine intervention to bring to naught the greatest armies ever arrayed against righteousness.'[4]

Only a minority of citizens went down on their knees to pray, though; the mass of people instead chose a knees-up. Joyce Stables, a young woman in the air force, joined others who headed to Blenheim from the airfield at Woodbourne. 'The town went absolutely berserk with people drinking everywhere and broken glasses all around. We just wandered about and laughed at it all.'[5]

The next day began quietly but grew loud as more and more people got drunk. Wellington saw scenes of 'increasing abandon, culminating in scenes of revelry unprecedented in the history of the city'.[6] Hitler was hanged in effigy from the top of a tall building. The swastika flag was laid down as a doormat in front of a shop.[7] Christchurch, too, got carried away:

> *Men and women, boys and girls, soldiers, sailors and airmen, elderly people and infants in arms, on shoulders and in prams, formally-dressed citizens and citizens in the most bizarre attire, sober citizens and citizens in 'an advanced state of celebration' marched through the streets in a great column of flag-waving, banner-carrying, singing and shouting people ... a hilarious crowd, brimming over with good-humour. The smallest incident was the pretext for wild cheering.*[8]

Yet the war was not over; the government wanted to keep fighting Japan.

Not many people in the dominion as a whole, however, seemed keen to keep fighting. Wage workers were sick of the war. Farmers were sick of the war. Capitalists were worried about the shortage of hands in factories and on the land. William Hale said as chairman of the Dairy Board that the 'man-power position in dairy factories and on farms' was 'desperate'.[9] Gilbert Grigg, a wealthy landowner, said the same about sheepfarmers when speaking as chairman of the Meat Producers Board. The National Party took up the call on behalf of conservatives. The Democratic Labour Party spoke out on behalf of wage workers. All said it would be wise to bring home the troops. War could now be waged not by fighting on battlefields but by getting busy on the food front.

The government stuck to its guns. Nash attacked the National Party:

> *The responsibility is very clear that our work as a nation at the present time is to take our part with Australia, with Great Britain, and with the other members of the British Commonwealth to see that the Japanese are defeated at the earliest possible moment ... Should we pull out and leave Australia to fight? But, further still, should we pull out and leave Britain to send her troops 10,000 miles to fight our battles?*[10]

Almost everyone agreed that the United States needed no help in beating Japan. A lot of people with inside knowledge were well aware, too, that the United States did not want anybody else to 'help' shape a 'new order' in the Pacific. The war cabinet knew better than anybody, which was the very reason why the government wanted to keep fielding troops. New Zealand, by going on with the bombing and shooting, might be allowed a say in any peace treaty in the Pacific. The logic was coldly calculating. Men were to be sent to kill or be killed for the purposes of postwar diplomacy – although government leaders spoke warm words rather than cold. Morality, not policy, was to be served by going on with the killing.

United States bombing of Japan 1944. The cartoonist jokes about the slaughter; the caption for the cartoon is 'Alterations and additions to Hon. Rising Sun'. *Artist: Minhinnick.* New Zealand Herald, *27 November 1944*

'Out of gratitude and for our own honour,' said Nash, 'we have no alternative but to continue to fight with our comrades.'[11]

The National Party shot flak.

'The Dominion has made a great effort, an effort far beyond the capacity of our man-power and woman-power,' declared Walter Broadfoot, a lawyer and National Party member of parliament. 'Surely we have already won our place at the peace table without shedding more blood.'[12]

The National Party dropped its call to give up the shooting war only when it became clear that London was as keen as Wellington to send troops to fight against Japan. The British government shared with the dominion government a wish for a say in any peace treaty with Tokyo. National Party politicians stopped speaking out and parliament voted unanimously to field what Fraser called 'a reasonable number of men' against Japan.[13] The military was to be cut down in size from 100,000 to 55,000 men and women, of whom 16,000 would join an army to be deployed by the British Commonwealth.

A fear shared by most people was that the war would drag on for two or more years. Japanese soldiers and citizens were fanatics – or so said the war propaganda – who would fight tooth and nail until they had spilled their last drop of blood.

'The Japanese,' pontificated the *Evening Post*, 'have been indoctrinated for centuries past with the idea that they are a chosen people, chosen to rule the world.'[14]

The editorial writer did not point out that the British had been indoctrinated in much the same way.

Japanese people were far from fanatical about fighting, however; many millions of them were praying for peace. War had brought fear, hunger, sickness, poverty – and now firestorms when the bomber fleet of the United States, having killed hundreds of thousands of civilians in Germany, loomed over their rooftops. Napalm was used freely. Lachie McDonald, a journalist from Auckland, saw fires 'raging, leaping from block to block' when he went as an observer on a raid over Tokyo.[15] A single raid laid waste to a quarter of Tokyo. Prisoner of war James Bertram witnessed the holocaust:

> *Occasionally a twist of the great fires sent a wave of heat that smote our faces across miles of water. Beneath our wall, where we watched, we were in shadow. But behind us the barrack roofs, the wooden watch-tower with its Japanese sentry, the feathery tops of trees, were all clearly bathed in the glow, as in the light of some strange dawn. And faces looking towards the city were like the faces of Aztec priests in ritual around a temple pyre.*[16]

Bombs dropped on the cities of Japan left the same wreckage of burnt and broken people as bombing had left in London and Lübeck, Berlin and Birmingham, Darwin and Düsseldorf. Bertram saw 'singed and blackened faces'. He saw 'fathers with the bodies of their children in their arms' and 'the wild eyes and drunken movements of those who have looked on unspeakable horrors'. A Japanese survivor spoke about the shambles among women and children at a primary school in Toyokawa:

> *An arm lay on the ground. There was a skull split in half. A headless torso. A girl's head hung from a tree by the road, the hair caught in the branches. A young worker with no legs, face burned black, crawled around on her hands.*[17]

Almost every civilian was war weary. A peace cabinet was formed under Suzuki Kantaro. The new prime minister believed the best way to stop the war was to ask for a settlement with Washington to be brokered by Moscow. A telegram was sent to Moscow on 13 July. Stalin sat down at the Potsdam Conference with the British and United States leaders, however, before he got word from Suzuki. The Potsdam Declaration, which came out of the conference, called on the Japanese government to surrender unconditionally.

New Zealand was not happy. Fraser wrote to the British government voicing 'regret' that Britain, the Soviet Union and the United States had agreed on unconditional surrender 'without previous consultation' with New Zealand, even though the dominion had 'actively participated' in fighting Japan and was 'vitally interested' in any peace settlement with Tokyo.[18] The regrets of a small dominion had no weight, needless to say.

A negotiated peace was now out of the question. Tokyo had no choice left other than to choose when to surrender.[19]

Tokyo after firebombing, 1945; more than twice as many civilians were killed in only one air raid on the Japanese capital than in all wartime air raids on the cities of Britain. Other bombing raids on the cities of Japan followed incessantly. *Saotome Katsumoto,* Haha to Ko de Miru Tokyo Daikushu *(Tokyo: Kusanone Publishing, 1988).*

New Zealand was still waging war against Japan. The air force kept up its bombing in Bougainville. The navy deployed three warships off the coast of the imperial mainland. The cruiser *Gambia* shot shells as one of several British Commonwealth vessels carrying out the last naval bombardment of Japan. The target was the steelworks at Kamaishi, in northern Honshu. United Nations prisoners of war were killed, along with many Japanese civilians. One of those killed by the shelling was William Brodie, a prisoner from Lyttelton, whose burns were so bad that he died after a day of suffering. One of those quailing under the shelling was William Hall, a prisoner who had been a ship's engineer in Port Chalmers:

> *They lay off about four miles and belted us with 16-inch shells. They were so close you could see the big shells in the air, and the damage and chaos were unbelievable. They dropped a shell within a few feet of me and that's why I'm deaf ... They shelled us for about three hours and killed a lot of people, a lot of Japanese.*[20]

The attack on the steel works was one event in a week crowded with events for the people of Japan. A bright new light had shone, three days earlier, over Hiroshima. A bright new light shone, the same day as the steelworks were shelled, over Nagasaki.

Rātana clergy, when they heard the news, were aware of prophetic words spoken over twenty years before by Tahupotiki Ratana, the founder of the faith, to the Taisho emperor in Tokyo.

'Your people will be turned to dust,' he had said, 'when you see two bright lights above you.'[21]

Prisoners of war freed from the camps, heading home on a troopship. *www.kiwiveterans.co.nz*

The Soviet Union, the day before the shelling of the steelworks, began a massive attack on the Japanese Empire. The attack was highly planned, very efficient, and moved swiftly. Tokyo decided to give up. The decision was sent to the United Nations on 10 August and five days later, after complex manoeuvres on both sides by diplomats, politicians and military leaders, the Showa emperor told the nation by radio that his government was going to surrender in accordance with the Potsdam Declaration. The radio speech meant, but did not say outright, that the government was surrendering unconditionally.

The news had already been sent by radio and cable to New Zealand.

The citizens of the dominion kicked up their heels upon the surrender of Japan in more or less the same way they had upon the surrender of Germany. A few towns jumped the gun. Timaru spilled its citizens into the streets on the afternoon of 13 August:

> *Sirens shrieked, bells pealed, and in a few minutes shops and offices emptied and the town gave itself up to gaiety. Brass, pipe, and tin-can bands headed processions of young and old, swinging rattles, singing, and scattering confetti.*[22]

Official news came late in the morning of 15 August, a working day. Factory workers ditched their tools and hoofed it into the streets. Shop and office workers ran away from their desks and counters. Farmers and farm workers heard the news later, when they stopped work to eat at midday. Crowds spent two days singing, dancing and drinking.

Dunedin broke into a 'spontaneous outburst of rejoicing'. Factory, train and ship sirens let out 'a deafening din' as soon as the news came over radio. Crowds were soon 'pouring into the streets'.[23] Christchurch seemed less 'boisterous' that first day,[24] but a procession the following day drew a crowd that was 'in every way greater' than any seen before in the city.[25] Auckland swarmed with 'a mass of excited, carefree people' from late morning onwards on 15 August, with crowds dancing to band music in the streets. Avarua was noisy with ringing bells, as was Apia. Samoan workers stopped working. The first day of celebration in the mandate ended with a dance in the Tivoli, and the following day several hundred Chinese marked the end of eight years of war by going to government house at Vailima on the breezy heights above Apia.[26]

Children, meanwhile, saw strange sights in the Hutt Valley. Barbara Adams was seated at her desk when the school principal stepped into the class, whispered something to the teacher, then hurried away. The children looked at the teacher:

> *She had a stunned, almost haunted look, and sat down in her chair with her head in her hands. Then the teacher from the next classroom flung open the door and raced into the room. She put her arms around our teacher, and they danced and laughed and cried, all at the same time. Our nine-year-old faces looked on in amazement.*

Children, freed from their desks, were told to run home for the rest of the day. Shirley, an ace at athletics, broke school rules by crossing the teachers' lawn before shinning to the top of the flagpole. 'She was hooting and shouting out to the children gathered below,' Barbara saw. 'We looked up in wonderment.'[27]

Confetti, bunting and streamers whirled about in nearby Wellington:

> *In Manners and Lower Cuba Streets there were scenes of wild jubilation. Flags immediately appeared, streamers and showers of confetti poured down from the buildings, and crowds, arm in arm, blew whistles and waved rattles and hakas were organised by students ... The swift transition in city shop windows from everyday to carnival displays was one of the most amazing features of yesterday's celebrations. In a few moments flags, flowers, bunting, and Victory motifs were placed as deftly and artistically as new stage settings.*[28]

Crowds got rowdy. Partying gave way, here and there, to edgy standoffs between crowds and the state, between working people and the middle class, and between Pākehā and Māori.[29]

Sex was also a keynote of the story. Young people paired up and unbuttoned in alleyways and shop doorways. A former soldier wrote unhappily about 'our young men and women, many of them in their teens, openly abandoning themselves to drunkenness' and losing 'all sense of control and self-restraint' in the streets of Wellington.[30] Wesley Parker, a Methodist minister, thought that the 'hooliganism' of drunken crowds in the streets of Auckland was 'the logical sequel and crowning disgrace to the mounting licence of the war years'.[31] James Blundell, a young marine engineer, said that 'the whole city went bloody mad ... nuts'. One of his cousins, who was in the navy, fell from a tram and 'nearly killed himself, pissed'. Blundell also saw wild lovemaking.

'Christ, they were rooting in the bloody house bar, they were rooting in … Oh, it was all on.'[32]

Three people were killed in accidents in the capital, and many others were injured in fights. John Colson, a soldier, died when he was hit by a railcar on a level crossing. Beatrice Higgins was knocked over by a car in Waterloo Quay. William MacLean, a waterside worker, was helping an injured woman when he collapsed and died. The most common injuries in the city came from blows to the head by bottles.

Aucklanders died in car accidents, too, and others suffered from 'lacerations after being struck by bottles and glasses hurled among the crowds'.[33] A lot of people seem to have been feverish rather than happy. Errol Brathwaite, an airman, later wrote about it with pensive hindsight:

> *Victory, for most of us, came like a thief in the night. It was hard for most of us to realise that it had come. Oh, we celebrated wildly, but wildly celebrating was something that we had done frequently through the past six years, at the drop of a hat. We threw off constraints, let ourselves out of the cage of duty and strain for brief periods, mainly to release the strains and tensions which were building up in us. Our victory celebrations, I think, were largely in the same spirit. Someone said, 'It's over! We've won!' And we had another party.*[34]

The party was followed by hangovers.

Atom bombs caused widespread dismay. Was it right to have dropped the two bombs? Washington claimed that without those two bright lights the 'fanatical' people of Japan would have fought to the bitter end, at the cost of countless hosts of Japanese along with one million soldiers from the United States. This sum, however, was plucked from thin air by politicians in Washington. Pentagon experts estimated far fewer losses to their military. Spying in the streets, together with surveillance from the sky, gave American governing groups a very good understanding not only of the low morale but of the economic and military weakness of Japan. Truman had been

A troopship about to land service people home in New Zealand, 1945. *Artist: Maurice Conly. Air Force Museum of New Zealand.*

aware for three weeks that the Japanese government had agreed on surrendering.

Leonard Isitt, head of the New Zealand air force, knew nothing of the agreement to surrender but saw widespread evidence of economic and military weakness when he visited Yokohama and Tokyo. 'Militarily, Japan is a completely defeated nation,' he summed it up. 'They were beaten without the atomic bombs.'[35]

Atom bombs had been developed with the backing of both the government in Wellington and the scientific community of New Zealand. Ernest Marsden, the physicist working as dominion head of scientific research for war projects, first heard about the bomb project nearly two years before Hiroshima and Nagasaki were flattened. He told Washington he could send the best physicists in the dominion to help. The Labour government supported the project keenly. Daniel Sullivan, scientific and industrial research minister, told parliament that government policy was 'to give all the scientific help we could' to work on the weapon.[36]

Conservatives were pleased the bombs were dropped. Japan warranted being bombed because it was a 'monster' nation, wrote one citizen of Auckland.[37] The 'rape, torture and other bestialities inflicted by the Japanese', agreed another, meant it was right to use 'any means in our power to force them into submission'.[38] Ruth Patrick wrote more guardedly: the bomb was 'terrible', she thought, but it seemed 'perfectly plain' that the weapon had ended the war early. The deaths of a 'comparatively small number' of Japanese allowed the saving of 'many precious' young men from New Zealand, Australia, Britain and the United States.[39] Clergy spoke up for the bomb, too. Presbyterian ministers welcomed the new weapon, on the whole, as did most Methodists.[40] Anglican priests, while they were more divided in their opinion, spoke about the bomb as a gift of 'Divine Providence'. Frederick Bennett believed that the god he worshipped had handed the secret of the bomb to the United Nations.[41]

The atom bomb worried more and more people as days went by. A Canterbury woman, for example, spoke of her 'horror and dread'.[42] Another citizen of the same province said that the people of the two doomed cities had been killed like 'lambs in the slaughtering pen at the freezing works'.[43] A third Cantabrian said the atom bomb was a 'monstrosity'.[44] One more pointed out that the United Nations could no longer claim that they were only willing to bomb 'military objectives'.[45] A letter of angry eloquence poured from the pen of M.G. Townend:

> *Are we so bereft of pity and imagination, so numbed by the horrors of six years' warfare, that we cannot call a halt to this nightmare of mass-murder and destruction? The Japanese are not insects to be wiped out by the million. They are people very like ourselves; they, too, love their children, their homes, and countryside. But we, if we acquiesce mutely in their insensate blind extermination, are less than human.*[46]

Citizens wrote so many letters to newspapers on the question that editors stopped publishing them. Voices were still heard in newspaper feature columns, however, and on the radio, in church and at the lecture hall. Scientists spoke up. Marsden, having helped develop the weapon, wrote that atom bombs must not be 'shackled by prostitution to nationalistic military ends'. Also, he added, it would be wrong for the weapon to be in the hands of 'one master nation', by which he meant the United States.[47] Catholic laity and clergy spoke out. *Tablet* noted many people voicing their 'horror at this latest hell-spawned weapon'.[48] Lillian Keys, a laywoman, felt 'overwhelmed' by news of the bomb. 'Our newspapers,' she wrote, 'display sickening hypocrisy in attempting to gloss over these horrors.'[49]

A wounded soldier welcomed by women and children in Wellington after landing from a hospital ship. *Alexander Turnbull Library, EP-Days of Commemoration-VE Day-01.*

Liston, the senior Catholic bishop in the country, spoke gravely. 'Our good and just cause has, let us confess it in sorrow, been dishonoured in the sight of God and men.'[50]

The surrender of Japan was carried out formally on 2 September in Sagami Bay, near Tokyo. The dominion warship *Gambia* lay at anchor with other vessels in a vast fleet flying the flags of the United Nations. A bulletin sent by the New Zealand navy dwelt on the beauty of the 'wide sweeping bay'. Crew on board the warship looked at the famous Fujiyama and talked about whether it was more or less beautiful than Taranaki. They discussed how the landscapes of Japan looked so much like the landscapes of New Zealand.[51] Isitt, dominion delegate, waited with the other United Nations delegates on the deck of the American battleship *Missouri* to witness the surrender of the enemy.

'There was an air of tense expectancy,' he said later; the Japanese party 'preserved a fixed calmness until General Umizo showed some emotion when it came to his turn to sign the document.'[52]

Ceremonies of surrender followed elsewhere in the Pacific. Sir Albert Ellis and two other dominion delegates flew from Auckland to join Australian and British delegates in accepting the surrender of Japanese troops on Nauru. The ceremony took place aboard the Australian warship *Diamantina*. Naval officers stood in uniforms of tropical white. Soeda Hisayuki, the Japanese commanding officer, wore a long samurai sword. Ellis wrote a portrait of the ceremony:

> *The Japanese were received with grave military etiquette and similarly responded. The conditions of surrender were then read … A Japanese rendering following, read by an interpreter. Captain Soeda gravely bowed his assent and the signing then took place. The ceremony struck me as being most impressive.*[53]

Meanwhile an airman at Rukuhia, Peter Crispe, was listening to everyone on the base say they were aching to get out of the military.

'I wonder how soon we can get discharged, now it's over? ... I want to get out now.'[54]

WHY?

The Second World War had starved, sickened, maimed and murdered more people than any other war in human history. New weapons had torn open, shredded, crushed or burnt soldiers and civilians. A mechanised system of mass murder, killing ordinary people for pseudoscientific 'racial' reasons, had minced millions. The halo of bright light that shone over Hiroshima, then Nagasaki, marked an awful new genie let out of a bottle. Would the world ever again know anything like peace or safety?

Citizens felt a 'sense of fearful responsibility', according to the *Evening Post*.

Death knocked most heavily on the doors of the Soviet Union, where at least 24 million, and perhaps many more, were killed by bullets, shells, bombs, disease and starvation. China lost nearly as many, Germany nearly 9 million, Poland nearly 6 million, and over 3 million died in Japan. India lost millions of people who starved to death or were felled by disease after being fatally weakened by going hungry. After the war, death went on knocking.

A soldier being welcomed home.
Artist: Pamela Kelliher. New Zealand Mirror, *1945.*

Why had the dominion been fighting?

The Labour government never made anything other than vague statements about why. Cabinet chose to declare war on several states, and the declarations of war were given the rubber stamp by the National Party. Yet no group of politicians or state officials ever sat down to draw up a list of goals to be won for the dominion by going into the struggle. New Zealand had no 'war aims', to use the jargon of diplomacy, other than the very woolly one of helping the motherland and other states fight Japan, Italy and Germany.

And why had the motherland been fighting? A lot of sonorous phrases were spoken, but in many ways the British government went to war in order to follow its old policy of stopping any one state from being overwhelmingly strong in Europe.

New Zealand citizens wanted something more moving than that very humdrum motive, and from the beginning of the war they had got together in groups to draw up their own plans for a postwar world.

A 'new order' was to be built after 'victory'. The president of the Counties Association in the winter of 1945 said that throughout the war the phrase 'new order' had been 'in the minds of and on the tongues of many people', and that it was understood to mean 'a new era in life, with peace, equity and satisfaction supreme everywhere'.[55] Labour politicians spoke about this or that new order, as did National politicians. Clergy spoke up, too. St Barbe Holland explained that a new order 'must arise to take the place of the order which this war is mercilessly destroying' and that the churches must work together towards 'creating a world free from the abuses and corrosive elements of the past' by building on a 'strong and constructive' Christianity.[56] The New Zealand Educational Institute, the national union of primary school teachers, spoke about a new order based on a new sort of schooling that would be free, democratic and questioning.[57] Social Credit wanted to build the new order by taking over the banks, a policy outlined in a booklet, *The People's Plan for a New Order*.[58] Auckland waterside workers called on their 'working class comrades' to come together 'to secure a new order of peace and prosperity'.[59] Women called for a new order, too. 'In this "New Order" let us build a new society, and not just patch up the old,' wrote Christina Guy; 'a new society which includes equal pay for equal work; equality of the sexes.'[60]

Rex Fairburn wrote an essay:

> *If this war has given us any cause for hope, it is the hope that in the years ahead of us, clear thinking and generosity of feeling, expressing themselves in resolute action, will supplant the defeatism, the muddling, the sloth of mind, the half-hearted vainglory and the selfishness that have plagued us throughout the last two decades. If we fail to set our house in order – if we content ourselves with foolish heresy-hunting, and the singing of hymns of self-praise – then all will have been in vain.*[61]

The Second New Zealand Expeditionary Force Association, a body of servicemen home from the fighting, told citizens that the task was 'to see that this new order which has been promised us, and for which we surely fought, is not strangled at its birth'.[62] Groups of former servicemen disagreed with one another about what that new order might be, however; and so too did groups on the left and groups on the right, and church groups, groups of women, teachers and tellers, merchants and machinists, supporters of Social Credit and comrades of the Communist Party.

Wellington, lacking its own war aims, for six years had wandered along the warpath without gaining any clarity. The doctrine of 'unconditional surrender', for example, caused coded messages to hum down the wires during the early days. The doctrine was

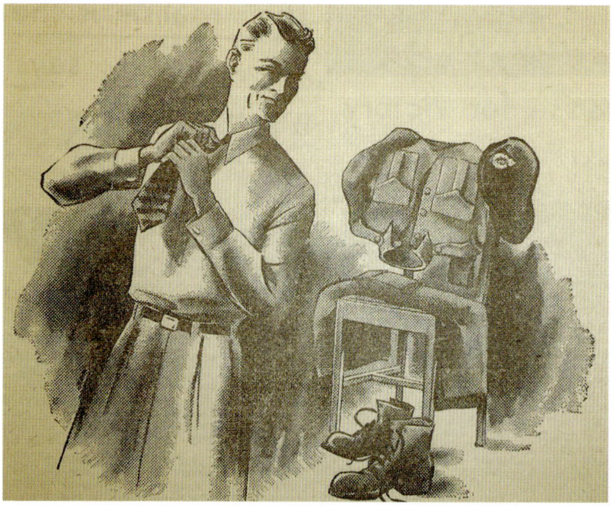

A 'demobbed' serviceman in a tobacco advertisement.
Standard, *18 October 1945.*

not welcome to Wellington. Germany, the government believed, must not be ground into the dust. A peace treaty must be negotiated on an 'equal and rational' basis, unlike at the end of the First World War.[63] Wellington was willing to go into peace talks with Berlin after the fall of France. Only during the last years of war did the government submit to the doctrine of unconditional surrender when it was announced as policy by Roosevelt. The Labour government knew it could do little to sway such a powerful ally; but a responsive government would have sat down with its advisors and opened talks with the citizenry to work out in an orderly and systematic way just why it was fighting.

The costs of fighting, as everyone had been well aware from the beginning, were bound to be heavy.

What were to be the winnings? And would those winnings outweigh the costs?

The winnings had always been spoken about as economic, military, political and emotional. War would show duty and loyalty to the 'motherland'. War would shield the dominion against armed attack. War would uphold freedom and democracy. War would safeguard the economy.

A SAFEGUARDED ECONOMY?

Safeguarding the economy was a goal agreed on by nearly everybody. The key to keeping up a modern and prosperous society, citizens thought, was shipping out and shipping in trade goods. Imports could be bought more or less from anywhere, but seven out of every ten pounds earned from exports came from shipments to Britain. The dominion, so the thinking went, must fight to keep that export market strong.

How well was the economy safeguarded by going to war?

The economy not only kept up its output during the years of fighting but grew strikingly. Gross domestic product swelled by 50.5 per cent; or, put another way, in spite of the waste and wreckage brought about by fielding an army, the dominion was half as wealthy again when the enemy surrendered as it had been at the beginning of the struggle.[64] Waging war and building a welfare state were challenges, but capitalists worked out ways to make money. John Martin, wealthy company director, told the shareholders of Wright, Stephenson in 1942 that since employers could no longer go 'untrammelled along the old beaten paths' they must now adjust themselves 'to the requirements of what might be called the new age'.[65] Capitalists grew more willing to fit war and the welfare state to their own purposes. Exporters found it fairly easy to make good earnings. Importers also found it fairly easy. Manufacturers did good business by getting war contracts, or by developing new industry inside a shelterbelt provided by the wartime shortage of shipping. The finance industry did good business, too. South British Insurance, for example, opened new branches in Africa, where prices boomed for raw war materials.[66] The company also made huge profits from marine insurance during the war, because premiums shot up thanks to war risk. Shareholder dividends averaged more than 18 per cent yearly.[67]

British observers were aware from the beginning that while war was costly it could yield the dominion good winnings.

'Undoubtedly the war will impoverish New Zealand to the extent that stocks are run down, repairs and capital works suspended, etc,' wrote a British treasury official; 'but we shall be impoverished to a much greater extent and there seems some reason to hope that New Zealand will be less impoverished than most countries.'[68]

London grew impatient, even angry, when it became obvious that the opposite of impoverishment was happening in New Zealand. The wish of the dominion 'to be enriched during the war at our expense' was lambasted by another official of the British treasury. Britain had lost all its savings and 'gone into the red'. New Zealand, on the other hand, was coining cash.[69] The dominion did so well out of the war that it gave away tens of millions of pounds to subsidise the war efforts of Britain and the United States. One subsidy came from selling wool and food to the imperial homeland at prices below what those goods were worth on the open market. Fraser pointed out somewhat tersely to London that the dominion, by not 'seeking world market prices for our produce', was

Civilians grew so restless during the last years of the war that many companies and the government started to show shining images of what would come after 'victory'. The caption of this 1943 advertisement for men's suits was: 'With Peace in 194X'.
Standard, 21 October 1943.

'following a policy of not embarrassing' the government of Britain.[70] A second subsidy came two years after the war when £10 million sterling was handed over as an outright gift to Britain; London had wanted twice as much and had also demanded £25 million sterling as a gift from Australia.[71] The United States also got a big subsidy from New Zealand because the dominion sold food and other exports to the republic at prewar prices while buying imports at wartime prices. John Condliffe, an economist, pointed out that if the dominion had bought from the United States on the same terms as those on which it sold to the republic, it would have come out of the war as 'a substantial creditor of the United States'.[72] Jack Baker, another economist, noted that the dominion government in 1942 felt 'considerable alarm' at the way it was shelling out so freely to subsidise its mighty ally in the Pacific.[73]

Waging war, in other words, did in some ways hold back the economic growth of New Zealand. The growth of gross domestic product during the first three years of the struggle, while it was handsome, may have been up to 3 per cent less than the peacetime potential.[74] The opposite was true of the last war years. Gross domestic product ballooned so amply that in 1943 it may have been 8 per cent higher than the potential; overall the years of good growth during the war more than offset the less good years.[75] State finances stayed well afloat, too.

'From a book-keeping economist's viewpoint,' wrote Taylor, 'the war achievement was admirable, a bargain.'[76]

Allied purchase of goods and services from the government and many of the capitalists of the dominion was good for the economy in another way. New Zealand strengthened its trading links by going to war alongside Britain. London was so keen to get wartime supplies of wool and food, and so keen to pay with sterling rather than with dollars, that it was willing to offer 'bulk contracts' to Wellington.[77] Bulk contracts were good for Britain because they allowed prices to be fixed, saved foreign exchange, and at the same time meant that the state could plan well ahead on the basis of known supply. Bulk contracts with the imperial homeland were good for New Zealand because they allowed exporters and the government to do long-term planning, too.[78] Shipping was guaranteed, moreover, which was a boon during the war years. Bulk contracts meant, lastly, that trading was 'stabilised', to use a word beloved by Nash.

Bulk contracts did not always work smoothly. Quarrels broke out between the two sides now and then over prices and shipping. New Zealand grumbled that the prices paid were too low. Britain threatened to stop sending ships and to get its supplies instead from the United States, Argentina and Uruguay. The quarrels were patched over, and trade kept humming.

New Zealand was not behaving very wisely, however, by tying itself to trade with Britain. The dominion was hitching its wagon to a train wreck.

The Chamberlain government in 1939 had been slow to go to war because it knew Britain no longer had the economic strength to beat a state as powerful as Germany.

New Zealand, by linking itself so closely with 'the motherland' during the war, entrenched for one more generation its risky economic dependence on exports to Britain. The strength of the trade link is suggested by this 1950 poster for a shipping company: the size of Britain and Ireland has been exaggerated to make them seem bigger than they really are in comparison with New Zealand. *Alexander Turnbull Library Eph-E-SHIP-1950-01.*

A long war was bound to break up trade routes and at the same time empty the state coffers.[79] Churchill replied that victory should be won 'at any cost'. Victory was won – if indeed it was victory – and the cost was overwhelming. Britain before the war had been the biggest creditor in the world: it had loaned about £4000 million. Britain by the end of the war was a debtor and owed about £3000 million, mostly to the United States. The British state was nearly bankrupt. Almost all its overseas investments had been sold. All its gold had been shipped to Fort Knox.

Warfare had turned a rich creditor nation into the biggest debtor nation in the world.

New Zealand should have been doing its best to diversify from rather than to back up its trade with Britain. Alternative markets were not easy to find, admittedly, but neither the government nor exporters did a lot to look for those markets, even though they saw that waging war was wrecking the British economy. The *Auckland Star* as early as 1943 pointed out that the imperial homeland would be poor when the war was over: 'She has put everything she has into the war, and there is nothing left in the till.'[80] Imperial loyalty led many people to say that the dominion should stick with Britain in spite of its new poverty. Other allies, though, were seeking their own advantage. Why not New Zealand?

Washington was seldom sentimental in its dealings with London. Churchill wrote a letter – never sent – protesting to Roosevelt about the way the United States behaved towards Britain as 'the sheriff collecting the last assets of a helpless debtor'.[81] Roosevelt spoke frankly to a colleague in his cabinet: 'We have been milking the British financial cow.'[82] Washington stopped lend–lease arrangements as soon as the war ended, and then handed over the bill. A few days later, the United States imposed almost crippling terms when it agreed to give London a loan to bail out the finances of the state.

'Comparable terms,' declared a member of parliament, 'have never hitherto been imposed on a country that has not been defeated in war.'[83]

The mood was bitter, noted a journalist from New Zealand:

> *Britain has no alternative but to accept the loan ... The black mood has been caused by this realisation, and the fact that in the hour of her weakness, wholly due to her unique and deliberate sacrifices, the country has been compelled to accept terms at which she cannot but feel resentment. The bitterness is due to the plain fact that the country must, as in 1940, settle down to a long period of real hard slogging work to rebuild her fortunes, while at the same time being shackled to America until at least the year 2000 by the terms of the loan.*[84]

Additionally, while the economy of the dominion had done very well out of war, a good deal of what was spent was wasted spending.

New Zealand lavished hundreds of millions of pounds on barren things that vanished into thin air as though exploded, which of course they often literally were. War expenditure used up 31 per cent of national income.[85] The military was a tool for smashing things, and for killing or maiming, not for building, tilling, tending and nurturing. Money was sunk into guns, shells, tanks, planes, bombs and torpedoes when it could have gone to schools, research institutes, clinics, hospitals and state houses. The government cut back not only social spending but spending on roads and railways. A decision was made in 1941, for example, to build no more goods wagons in railway workshops.[86] A very obvious way the state made savings was by not keeping up highways.

'The roads are just dreadful nowadays,' said a young woman in a postwar short story by John Reece Cole. 'We went for a run out to Newhaven this afternoon and had to crawl all the way. Soon as the needle moved over fifty we got shaken to pieces. It was simply brutal!'[87]

Potholed roads meant more than just a rough ride for anyone wanting to go on a pleasure jaunt. Roads and railways were sinews of the economy. Goods could not be transported as cheaply or efficiently thanks to money being withdrawn from tarmac and rolling stock.

The economic waste of going to war was most obvious when retreating troops wrecked or dumped their costly equipment. David Strang was among many soldiers toiling hard one morning after a battle in Greece to put 'a pickaxe through tins of grub, tinned milk, tinned bully beef' and then to swamp guns in the sea in order to keep them from being taken by the enemy. Keith Arkinstall, busy on the same spot on the same morning, was one of a group wrecking army trucks.

'Put the picks through all the tyres. A pick through your battery, a pick through your radiator core. Drained the oil, started the motor and let her go until she went bang, and that was the end of her.'[88]

The economic waste of going to war was also obvious during the early days of peace when the state dumped military goods wholesale. Errol Brathwaite was shocked to see rows and rows of warplanes parked at Rukuhia. Hundreds of planes, bought for good money and then 'faithfully flown' against the enemy, were now useless, 'the weeds already growing up to their wings, their paint flaking, their engines rusting, their sleek forms collapsing wearily into the long grass'. Afterwards the costly machines were 'sold cheaply, hacked to bits with axes and saws and crowbars, and melted down in crude furnaces, to be sold as aluminium and duralumin ingots'.[89] The military got back only a few pennies for every pound that had been spent, despite such recycling. The dominion threw away a lot of its earnings on war rather than prosperity.[90]

War also wrought havoc with the most valuable economic resource of all, the people of New Zealand.

Men and women of military age, the strongest and fittest people in the country, were withdrawn wholesale from the productive economy. Military life meant not only spending rather than making money, it also meant getting those workers to waste most of their time doing nothing more worthwhile than waiting. Millions of hours of manpower were wasted by men in the military. The long hours of military training were 'dull and unprofitable' to those undergoing the training, noted a general, James Burrow.[91] Training was unprofitable in a way he did not mean, too: it yielded no goods or services to the economy. After training, soldiers, sailors and airmen then spent most of their years in uniform doing nothing, often deeply bored, killing time rather than killing the enemy. Guthrie Wilson wrote that he 'marched for hours, stood for hours, sat for hours' during his years in the infantry.[92] 'Monotonous days,' added another soldier. 'I have never seen so much patience played as over here,' wrote another.[93] The waste of manpower was worst when servicemen became prisoners of war and were

The cost of war: soldiers and other service people spent a lot of the war wasting their intelligence and their labour hanging around waiting for orders and doing nothing. This painting was entitled *The Soldier Resting*.
Artist: P.M. Hutchison. Archives New Zealand.

locked up inside camps. Tony Vercoe, an intelligent and musical young man from Nelson, described loitering with his mates in an Italian camp in North Africa:

> *As the days and weeks moved on, as life became more nauseous, more irksome, as monotony, hunger, filth and disease took their toll, all these mates were reduced to silence. While never wholly giving up they became listless shadows … Men's lives reduced to periods of lying in the bivvies, holding on as long as possible before the next forced trip, staggering or crawling to the bog.*[94]

The economic consequences of going to war were not straightforward, in other words.

On one hand, the wealth of the dominion grew strikingly. The economic bond with Britain stayed strong. On the other hand, by fighting to safeguard its British market the country was keeping itself stuck in an old economic groove while squandering goods and services in a reckless way. Men, women and children – the key economic resource of the country – were wounded, sickened, stressed, worn down or killed. Roads, railways and bridges grew the worse for wear, leading to lessened production

The Labour government worked hard to keep in good with Churchill, but Churchill was working hard to keep in good with Roosevelt and Stalin while struggling to handle many other Allied states, too. This cartoon appeared on the cover of a German satirical magazine. *Simplicissimus, 1 January 1942.*

and lowered efficiency. A lack of labour and a lack of raw materials also led to lessened production and lowered efficiency. Farms and factories were starved of workers and raw materials, which instead went to the military. The schooling gained by youngsters was poorer than during years of peace, which meant that the workforce after the war would be less well equipped for a modern economy.

The policy of going to war in order to keep the dominion safe from enemy states was not very effectual, either: like the economic policy, it was based on the notion of backing Britain. Britain and its navy, many people believed, were a strong shield.

That belief was wrong. Britain was not a naval power in the Pacific. The navies of Japan and the United States, not the British navy, were the only fleets with any meaning in the hemisphere surrounding New Zealand. At the end of the war only one of those two fleets was left: the navy of the United States. Britain ceased being a world power early in the war and by the end of the war was only what a diplomat called 'junior partner in an orbit of power predominantly under American aegis'.[95] Wellington, ironically, worked hard to keep in good with London while London worked hard to keep in good with Washington and Moscow. Churchill confessed: 'every morning when I wake my first thought is how I can please President Roosevelt, and my second is how I can conciliate Marshal Stalin'.[96]

Flinging men and money to the other side of the world in order to help the imperial homeland was not a wise policy.

MAIMING, SICKENING, KILLING

Killing, sickening or maiming the workforce is an odd way to safeguard an economy, yet that was what happened when the dominion declared war on the Axis. A total of 12,000 soldiers, sailors and airmen died during the fighting. New Zealand killed a higher percentage of its troops than any other country of the British Commonwealth. Patriots took pride in that death rate, thinking it evidence of bravery, but the tally might instead be seen as proof that the policy of going to war had gone badly wrong.

Why kill so many when New Zealand was so far away from any enemy?

Bullets, bombs, shells and shrapnel brought death, as did falls, collisions, overturnings, sinkings and smotherings. Death was often very messy. James Murphy was an officer on board the warship *Leander* when it was hit by a torpedo in the Solomon Islands. 'Hot blood is a terrible smell,' he said.[97] Archibald Scott, a soldier, was a prisoner of war who saw 'human entrails on the rigging and the rails' of a ship torpedoed by a British submarine while on the way to Italy. Body parts were 'splattered and squashed against winches'.[98] Thomas May saw men burning to death when trapped in army tanks. A gunner scrambled out of one flaming tank 'with part of his face shot away, all of his jaw'; he then dropped dead. 'The drivers were burning.'[99] Guthrie Wilson portrayed a young infantryman from the dominion who had been caught by shelling in Italy. 'The top of his head has been lifted like a boiled egg,' he wrote. 'His legs terminate at the shins in squashy pulp and bloody strings.'[100]

The weapons of the United Nations killed whole battalions of men in 'friendly fire'. The lives of five prisoners of war, for example, ended when a bomb was dropped on an air-raid shelter in Oderburg, Germany:[101] the victims would have been safely at home had the dominion not chosen to declare war on the Axis. Military training, too, killed some servicemen who never even got around to fighting. Peggy Bulfin saw such deaths while working on an aircrew training station at Ohakea. 'The hardest part on a station was the fairly large number of people who were killed during training,' she observed. 'You'd be with somebody one night and the next day they'd be killed.'[102]

Viruses and bacteria helped the killing. Military camps and barracks were a crowded, flimsy, unhealthy type of housing, and slit trenches on the battlefield were even worse. Health was sapped by poor food, lack of water, and marching in all weathers – the cold, wet winters of Italy and wearying heat in the deserts of North Africa and the jungles of the Solomon Islands. New Zealand soldiers had little or no immunity to many diseases endemic in the Middle East and North Africa. Military wards were crowded with cases of 'infective hepatitis, dysentery, malaria, and sandfly fever'.[103] The same was true of troops sent to Fiji, Tonga, New Caledonia and the

'Aurora Orientalis'. The war began with two great powers in the Pacific: Japan and the United States. At the end of the war there was only one: the United States. *Artist: Minhinnick. New Zealand Herald, 4 September 1945.*

Solomon Islands. Tropical skin diseases were widespread, as were septic sores, malaria, dengue fever, diarrhoea and dysentery.[104] All troops sent overseas were prone to diseases flaring up that were not threatening when they lived in New Zealand.[105]

Also, of course, war led to wounding. Official figures stated that nearly 16,000 men and women were wounded while in the military. Winifred Vautier, a nurse, tended former servicemen in a hospital in Rotorua. 'The returned men at Rotorua had been sent home after losing arms, legs, bladders – all sorts of things,' she said. 'Men of my age who were crippled or maimed for life.'[106]

Military medical staff toiled to do the best they could, but death took hold in ways it would not in civilian society. Soldiers, sailors and airmen often lay sick or hurt for a long time before they were found. A sick or wounded man found in the field had to be handled hurriedly and in makeshift ways at frontline dressing stations, before being jolted to a base hospital.

'Many of them had very dirty wounds because they'd been lying out there until the stretcher-bearers found them,' said Mavis Thyne, an army nurse in Italy. 'I had to do about seventy penicillin injections every four hours but it wasn't very easy to find somewhere that wasn't bandaged up.'[107]

Men suffered agonising pain when injections had to be driven into open wounds; often they wept with fear when they knew it was time for another injection. Base hospitals were not as good as civilian hospitals in New Zealand. Nursing staff had to make and mend, noted Jack McKinney, a member of the army medical corps:

> *Many times a sister's thoughts, as she stoked a copper fire or tinkered with a temperamental primus that at a critical moment refused to do anything but gush a sooty smoke-screen, must have turned to the hospital she had left, where the gleaming faucets at a touch would pour forth gallons of boiling water and where the behaviour of the steam sterilisers never gave a moment's worry.*[108]

Men who were taken as prisoners of war had to deal with further hardships.

The Italian army, during the first two years of fighting, often treated surrendered soldiers in a bullying or slipshod way. A soldier spelled out the misery of prisoners of war on board a ship steaming to Taranto, for example: he wrote in his diary of the 'appalling spectacle' of men who looked like 'lousy animated bags of bones draped in torn and greasy rags'.[109] Men died in some Italian camps simply because they were starving.[110]

The German army treated prisoners of war more tolerably. Over 6000 men from New Zealand were behind wires in the camps of the Third Reich by the last year of the war, and many of them said they were better off than in Italy.[111] The stress and strain of being a prisoner was wearing, nevertheless.

'Barbed wire and steel bars predominate so much that it is little wonder our minds become crabbed and rusty,' wrote Denis Caves while inside a camp near Teschen; 'one begins to doubt himself, life, God and the use of living in a world of madness.'[112]

The Japanese army handled prisoners of war very poorly. Men were often close to starving. Men were driven to work, too, on farms or in factories or the construction industry. All the warring states on both sides got prisoners of war to do such work, and it was allowed by international law. Germany and Italy paid workers a good enough wage for their trouble, however, and guards seldom drove them ruthlessly. Japanese guards, on the other hand, often punched, kicked, stabbed and shot prisoners who were ordered to work. Neil Docherty, a captive from the dominion air force, saw such things while slogging on a railway:

> *I saw men murdered for no reason at all just taken into the jungle and shot. Men suffering with dysentery, malaria, and terrible tropical ulcers were carried to the railway on stretchers when it was humanly impossible for them to walk, and were forced to lie there holding the drills while other prisoners, a little fitter, hammered them. If a man suffered a rigor he was bashed for it, and, believe me, they were bashings. I saw men with their faces smashed in with rifle butts, others cut to the ground and terribly lacerated with thrashings from bamboo cane.*[113]

The cost of war: maiming, sickening and killing New Zealanders. This painting is entitled *Stretcher Bearers*. *Artist: Herbert Coe. Archives New Zealand.*

All those who came home from the war, whether or not they had been behind barbed wire, were likely to be sick in mind and body. A total of 53,000 were in such bad shape that doctors deemed them eligible for a War Disablement Pension.[114]

Psychological illness was widespread, for fear, stress, anger and hatred corroded the minds of airmen, soldiers and sailors. Adrian Hayter felt 'gnawing, intense fear' when fighting. Fear was so corrosive that 'at times it came near to physical sickness'.[115] Gordon Slatter wrote about 'misery and fear and spewing up the stew before an attack'.[116] Clifford Barkle saw 'big, strapping' men turn into 'blubbering kids … crying pitifully for their mothers'.[117] Tony Vercoe spoke about 'the terrible sound of a man howling … sobbing with shock and terror, the wailing rising and falling'.[118] James Henderson, an artilleryman, wrote that the causes of the 'great shuddering sobs welling uncontrollably from within us' were not physical pain but 'utter forlornness, utter despair, utter abandonment, the absolute plumbing of the depths of woe.'[119] Max Boyd, an air-force mechanic, confided in in his diary about how he and his friends grovelled in their foxholes like terrified rabbits. 'We were all fearful,' he added. 'I now know what stark fear is … You sweat terrifically, shiver all over uncontrollably.'[120]

Guthrie Wilson wrote about the psychological stress more fully:

> *Manifestations of shattered control vary in intensity from reluctance to move into danger at the one end, to a form of paralysis whereunder the subject becomes incapable of moving any muscle of his body. It may be reflected in tears or in adamantine dourness. Or it may end in sheer screaming insanity … The best of us breaks eventually. The pitcher goes so often to the well but of a sudden it can go no more. I have seen men, good men too, soldiers of long and honourable service, burst into unpremeditated weeping … Fatigue, exposure, nervous exhaustion do their work of wastage and the wastage can never be repaired.*[121]

Men were often so wan and wasted that those waiting to welcome them home from war were shocked by what they saw. Lauris Scott thought they 'looked so thin and haggard and even the young ones so old'.[122] Nancy Ellison, a young teacher, waited at Rotorua railway station to greet her husband Terry:

> *The train had stopped. People were surging forward, others struggling in the opposite direction. I stood still, letting the stream of passengers flow round me, watching and waiting for Terry. Then I saw him, his kit bag on his shoulder. 'That Army cap doesn't suit him,' was the first thought that flashed through my mind. He looked different somehow, tired, taut, not smiling at all. I caught his eyes. He had seen me and was struggling towards me, but it wasn't the same Terry I had said goodbye to on the same station four years before. He never came back.*[123]

The toll of such stress meant that by the middle of the war 40 per cent of men in the wards of one army field hospital were suffering from psychological illness; some were in what was called a 'panic state'.[124] A total of over 7300 men were so badly traumatised during the course of the war they were discharged from the military.[125] Duncan Stout, an army doctor, wrote that the most common symptoms of psychological damage among servicemen and former servicemen were irritability, weariness, difficulties with mental concentration and an unwillingness to meet people or 'go out to social engagements'. Almost all men who had been away for any length of time, he added, suffered from such symptoms.[126] Charles Bevan-Brown, a civilian doctor, published a booklet giving advice on how to deal with psychologically traumatised former servicemen in the family. He pointed out that the custom of encouraging men to forget any bad memory and get on with living was not helpful and would often deepen the trauma, leading to 'attacks of panic or anxiety'.[127] Victims of trauma needed professional treatment. The list of professionals qualified to give such treatment, however, was 'lamentably small'.[128] The burden of care fell mostly on family. Within forty years of the end of the war, 10,070 former servicemen had been given state pensions for psychiatric sickness.[129] John Reece Cole portrayed a 'flak-happy' pilot who flew his 'kite' on sixty bombing raids before coming home to New Zealand:

> *I begin to think I'm all right. Then suddenly something sets me off again. I got on a tram one night. You know how they swing and jolt? Well, it's just like a kite bumping through heavy flak. I couldn't even wait until the next stop, and nearly broke my neck jumping off. I retched in the gutter, until a cop came and moved me on. He thought I was drunk.*[130]

Nightmares troubled many. 'I didn't sleep very well and I used to yell and scream,' said John Watson, who had been in the army. 'And there was always a war on. There was always a war in dreams.'[131] Also it was common to have fits of crying. 'I'd just disappear and I'd have a little weep,' said Thomas May, another man out of the army. 'I just couldn't stand it, I couldn't stand people.'[132]

James K. Baxter published a poem soon after the war portraying a young soldier who had come home from the fighting:

> *The boy who volunteered at seventeen*
> *At twenty-three is heavy on the booze.*
> *Strafed in the desert and bombed out in Crete –*
> *With sore dark eyes and hardened by the heat*
> *Entitled now to call himself a man ...*[133]

Trauma suffered by former soldiers, airmen and sailors was passed on to those trying their best to help fraught sons, fathers, brothers, lovers or husbands. A man who had been in the military was far more likely than other men to be depressed, to become alcoholic, and to strike, beat, rape or in other ways attack other people. Aggression was provoked and rewarded in the military. Soldiers often found it hard to stop being aggressive when they once more became civilians. The victims of that aggression were now their own wives, lovers, daughters and sons.

Civilians were killed, too.

The fight on the home front wore people out. War working hours were long. War stress was sapping. Houses in winter were often cold, because the military and war industry had priority for supplies of coal and electricity. Old people and babies got sick or even died thanks to a lack of heating. Civilians died doing paramilitary things for which they had no training. William Parkes and John Pavlovich, for example, were electrocuted while serving in the Home Guard; they were trying to hang telephone wire near Wellsford.[134] The blackout killed civilians, too. A coroner in Wellington protested about such deaths, saying that motorists must drive more carefully.[135] Petrol rationing, on the other hand, saved the lives of several hundred people who otherwise would have been knocked down by cars; 246 were killed on the roads in the year before the war started, but only 140 in the last full year of the war.[136]

Civilians who needed medical care during the years of fighting could not count on the same help as they would have found had the dominion not chosen to fight the Axis. Hospitals were stripped of some of their equipment and many of their staff. Mary Lambie, director of the nursing division in the government health department, wrote about the 'difficult years' from late 1942 onwards when there were 'shortages of many requirements for hospital and medical practice, and all kinds of makeshifts'. Nurses and doctors came back from war sick or wounded, too, which meant they needed medical care themselves instead of giving it to civilians on the home front.[137]

Atrophy in the public health system did not trouble the wealthy, though. William Anderson, son of a Christchurch family of factory owners and a schoolboy at Christ's College, was diagnosed with spondylitis. 'It was not a good time for anyone to be in bad health as most of our younger doctors were overseas,' wrote his father, Hugh Anderson, 'and it was extremely difficult to know what to do.' Anderson money could pay for private injections of gold and the services of a private nurse, luckily,[138] but sick citizens of more modest means went downhill. Civilians who lacked good medical care were likely to be sick or injured for longer spells than before the war, which led to the loss of their labour and, in turn, a weaker economy.

Civilians, just like servicemen and servicewomen, suffered from psychological stress caused or worsened by war. A few were so stressed that they killed themselves, or died of shock. A young woman in Wellington 'slit her two wrists' after learning that her lover had died at the battlefront.[139] The young wife of a crewman killed in the blast of a torpedo that struck the *Leander* was 'so overcome' by grief that she turned on a gas oven and put her head inside, and her little daughter's too, until they were both dead.[140]

A lot of civilian women who were not driven to such extreme steps were nevertheless gripped by restlessness, fear and worry.

Mary Whitelaw wrote about the way such feelings went so deep in 'many girls and women' on the home front that they fed 'a secret spring of bitterness, born in rebellion against an unjust fate, poisoning the whole of life'.[141] Janet McKinnon wrote in verse about the way her life would be 'full of aching voids' if her husband were to be killed in the fighting. 'For if he goes, a part of me will go with him.'[142] Neva Morrison, a young woman from Gisborne, wrote more than fifty years after the end of the war about the day she learnt that her lover, an air-force pilot, had been shot down.

'I screamed and screamed and screamed, and a part of me is screaming still.'[143]

Mavis Hill, the mother of a soldier, wrote verse shaped in orderly stanzas as a reply to a letter from her son in North Africa. The orderly stanzas fell apart at the end, finishing with a postscript:

I think I'll walk … it's very cold inside,
I've just received their message … and it's late …
You – won't – be – coming – home – again … they say …
My breaking heart … is swaying … with the gate.[144]

A short story by A.P. Gaskell portrayed a group of young men and women getting together for Christmas Day. Eleanor, one of the group, has just heard that her fiancé has been killed in North Africa. All try to keep up her spirits by singing, dancing, joking and drinking.

'We're not going to let her sober up,' says one, May. 'That's the plan … Don't you think that's a good idea? We're not going to sober up either.'

At the end of the evening, however, things have got worse for Eleanor.

'She says she can't drink any more or she'll be sick, and if she's sick she'll sober up,' says May to the others. 'And if she doesn't drink she'll sober up. So what can she do?'[145]

Men on the home front also were gripped by restlessness, fear and worry. The war was 'an unrelieved horror', wrote Frank Sargeson. The tension that came from 'one moment trying to face it, and the next trying to shut it out completely' drove a lot of people 'half barmy'.[146]

New Zealand patriots carefully counted up the tally of men from the dominion who were killed while fighting, but few cared to do a reckoning of how many citizens of other states were killed by the dominion and its military. Not that awareness was lacking among the men who did the killing. Artillery gunners and bomber crews seldom witnessed the mayhem they brought to those on the other side, but air-force pilots and army infantry saw nasty sights. Colin Larsen, infantryman, wrote about the way jungle fighting in the Solomon Islands was 'a very personal affair between yourself and the enemy, who is so close at times that you can almost see the whites of his eyes'. After one glance the face of a man fighting on the other side would be imprinted on the mind 'indelibly'. After a second glance it would seem that the two men had known each other 'for years'. Jungle warfare, added Larsen, could be 'so much of a man to man affair, that it strikingly reveals the true nature of war – murder'.[147] David Scott, a fighter pilot, was stunned by what he saw when he shot down a young enemy pilot whose name, he later found out, was Detlef Walter:

> *I could clearly see the horrified look on his face … I slid in behind and gave his aircraft another burst of cannon fire. Both he and his aircraft hit the sea at the same moment and quickly disappeared under a huge fountain of spray. That second burst of my cannons was neither wise nor necessary. A spur of the moment action that even to this day still troubles me deeply … A German pilot whose terrified young face will haunt me for the rest of my days.*[148]

Lewis Howard, another pilot, was well aware of what he did to his fellow men when he flew with a fighter squadron in the Solomon Islands.

'The Jap pilot was thrown clear of the machine and was terribly shot up. What a sight! He was a young chap.'[149]

Airmen were aware, too, that women and children were cowering under the bombs. New Zealand bomber crews killed civilians in the Solomon Islands. Dominion pilots dropped 1876 tonnes of bombs, for example, on the one town of Rabaul.[150] Phillip

The cost of war: 'enemy' people killed by the dominion military. Japanese young men, victims of New Zealand airmen or soldiers, are seen here on a battlefield in Guadalcanal.
Artist: Allan Barns-Graham. Archives New Zealand.

Wilson and crews of other warplanes from the dominion 'indiscriminately' strafed and bombed thatched villages in which they knew that women and children could well have been sheltering.

'We were never certain,' he wrote, 'whether we were really attacking the enemy or merely innocent islanders.'[151]

Any assay of the winnings and losses in the war must take account of those killings. How many Germans, Italians, Japanese, Indians, Burmese, Solomon Islanders and others were killed by the dominion going to war? How many enemy soldiers, sailors and airmen were shot, smothered, torn open by the soldiers, sailors and airmen of New Zealand? How many enemy civilians came in for their share of the killing? Germany lost around 635,000 civilian lives when bombs came shrieking down from the sky,[152] and hecatombs of those lives were taken by air crews from New Zealand. Thousands of dominion airmen flew bombers over Germany and they must have slaughtered tens of thousands of women and girls, men and boys. We need to think about those women and children and old men stumbling through the streets or huddling inside air-raid shelters when we seek to weigh the winnings and losses brought about by the dominion going to war. The deaths of many of the civilians in Hiroshima and Nagasaki must be added to the weighing, given that the atom bomb project was actively supported by New Zealand.

New Zealand also aided and abetted death by starvation of civilians, some in enemy states and others in allied states.

The dominion government did almost nothing when millions of people were starving in Bengal. The war was the cause of the starvation, but a shipment of condensed milk was the only help given by the war cabinet even though New Zealand at the same time was sending massive shipments of food to the citizens of Britain and the troops of the United States. Civilians were starving in Southeast Asia too. Food yields fell appallingly because the armies of the imperial powers, when hurriedly withdrawing, blew up oil supplies, wrecked bridges, roads, railways and rolling stock, sank shipping and smashed up seaports. Japan was too badly overstretched to get the sabotaged transport systems working. United Nations bombers and submarines worsened the wreckage. Rice shipments from Vietnam, for example, sank to the bottom of the sea when cargo ships were torpedoed by American submarines, some working out of the ports of New Zealand. The rice was needed to help feed the people of the Philippines. Tonkin alone suffered from a famine that is thought to have killed some 2 million people, a toll caused partly by flooding and a cold snap but greatly worsened by United Nations attacks on shipping, bridges and railways.

After the war, the dominion did no better when millions of people starved in Japan and Germany.

The Japanese government, which had been struggling to feed its people during the years of fighting, now lost the struggle. The imperial food ministry ruled that each adult needed to eat around 2200 calories a day in order to be able to carry out light work or other activity. Rations within four months of the surrender were barely more than half, and in the following two years went as low as a quarter of that allowance.[153] New Zealand voiced no official protest against the policy of starving Japan. New Zealand shipped no food; nor did it do anything else to bypass the policy. Japanese soldiers died, too, when they were set to work by the victorious powers as forced labour in French Indochina, British Malaya and the Dutch East Indies. Altogether, some 300,000 of those captives were worked to death in the mines, fields and factories of Southeast Asia.[154] No protest came from New Zealand.

Germany also went hungry for two years after the war because the winners withheld food shipments. As many as 6 million civilians may have been killed by the policy.[155] New Zealand newspapers spoke about the deaths occasionally. 'Germany is faced with famine,' reported the *Evening Post*.[156] The *Auckland Star* added that 'the calorific value of the present German ration is little more than half of life's essential demands', and went on to say that it was neither wise nor humane 'that millions of the people of Germany should perish by starvation and disease if that can reasonably be prevented'.[157] One or two groups of citizens spoke out. The Methodist synod of Wellington asked the government to 'take immediate steps to assist in relieving the extremely grave food situation'.[158] The government, however, voiced no official protest about the policy of starving a defeated enemy and did nothing to ship food to bypass the policy.

FREEDOM AND DEMOCRACY: EMPIRES AND THE WORLD

The war supposedly had been fought to uphold freedom and democracy. The government said so at the beginning of the struggle. The government kept saying so. A speech from the throne early in 1942 made the point when telling parliament about the declaration of war on Japan.

'We who uphold freedom and democracy,' said the governor-general, 'know now beyond the possibility of doubt whom we must fight.'[159]

The National Party, doing its work as parliamentary opposition, did not question the speech by saying that neither the Guomindang nor the Soviet Union was a democracy. Nor, of course, were freedom and democracy easy to find in the colonies controlled by the British Empire. Almost everyone agreed that the parliamentary system in the dominion embodied freedom and democracy. The same system still governed at the end of the war, which means that the struggle in one way at least had upheld freedom and democracy. Canada, Australia and Britain kept parliamentary systems running throughout the war, too, as did South Africa. This last was nothing like a democracy, however, given that most of the people within its borders had no right to vote or to be represented in parliament. France, though it lost its democracy during the war, by the end had restored the republic.

So far, at least, the war had upheld freedom and democracy, although it is doubtful whether it was ever seriously in danger outside France, Belgium, the Netherlands and Scandinavia.

Dictatorships were turned into parliamentary states, moreover, which was a big step forward.

Japan quite quickly became a democracy. At first, some politicians and officials in New Zealand wanted to impose a very long period of occupation on the defeated state. Berendsen, a key official, wanted the country under military control for at least twenty years. Fraser saw things less sternly. He wanted to stamp out the military strength of Japan but at the same time sought 'radical changes' in Japanese politics, economy and society.[160] The dominion could help the beaten foe develop a social democracy in which people would enjoy 'a wider and more equitable distribution of income' and life would be better for 'the poorer classes'.[161] New Zealand also wanted the abolition of the Japanese monarchy.[162] The dominion soon found that any settlement with the defeated enemy was to be more or less dictated by the United States. Washington decided how to dispose of the Japanese navy, for example, without consulting either Wellington or Canberra. The two dominion capitals were angry.[163] Tokyo, under the oversight of Washington, was turned into the capital of a constitutional monarchy whose political system was not unlike New Zealand's.

Germany, or at least its western and southern provinces, became a republic in some ways more advanced and democratic than New Zealand. The constitution of the new Bundesrepublik was based on closely and clearly defined human rights, unlike the constitution of the dominion. The voting system was more democratic, too, and there was no monarchy. Italy was another success story for freedom and democracy. The dictatorship was thrown out, as was the monarchy.

Freedom and democracy gained very little ground elsewhere, and in some ways slipped backwards.

New Zealand played some part in the settlement of affairs in several states of Europe. Dominion politicians and officials were among delegates seated around a table at the Conference of Paris, in the northern summer of 1946, drawing up peace treaties with Italy, Finland, Romania, Bulgaria and Hungary. Rex Mason, a cabinet member, led the delegation from New Zealand. Jordan, another old political campaigner, was also in the delegation, along with historian and public servant Alister McIntosh, the young 'brilliant and highly individual scholar' Patrick Costello,[164] and Frank Corner. The conference dragged on for weeks.

'Here we sit,' said Jordan, 'listening to "Quack, quack, quack," day after day.'[165]

'I reflect ironically,' wrote Costello, 'this is the goal towards which, in our scuffles in Greece … our going and comings in the Western Desert, we were all the time striving.'[166]

New Zealand could do little at the meeting other than try tinkering. The dominion backed Czechoslovakia, for example, in a border disagreement with Hungary. Britain and the United States backed Hungary. The group from Wellington were able to get Budapest to make some concessions to Prague in spite of London and Washington.[167] Gains were trifling, though, and delegates at the Conference of Paris were well aware that the end of the war had not brought freedom and democracy to Eastern Europe. Poland was not a democracy when the dominion declared war; nor did war bring democracy to Poland. London and Washington, ever since the Teheran Conference in 1943, had agreed more or less that the land whose freedom had ostensibly been at stake when war began would be handed over to the Soviet Union as a colony or, at best, a protectorate. Wellington protested against handing it over, but had no say. Nor were Estonia, Latvia, Lithuania, Czechoslovakia, Hungary, Romania, Bulgaria, Yugoslavia and Albania added to the roll of countries that could claim in any meaningful way to embody freedom and democracy. None had been a parliamentary state before the war anyway, other than Czechoslovakia.

Europe, where the war had begun, was in other words the setting for some growth in freedom and democracy.

Asia, Africa and the Pacific were another story.

The New Zealand government argued that ownership of colonial empires must be turned into 'trusteeship'. Fraser was so strong a believer in trusteeship he was chosen as chair of the Trusteeship Committee at the United Nations conference in San Francisco. Nash, too, spoke about the need to bring in trusteeship. 'The End of Imperialism' was a topic on which he could be warranted to talk wordily.[168] The 'first consideration' of the trustee power had to be 'the wellbeing and development of native peoples'. Colonies must be held in trust under the supervision of the United Nations. Churchill was so angry when this principle was laid down by Wellington that his government, in an 'unusually sharp' retort, said it would not allow any oversight of its colonies by any international body.[169]

Trusteeship was embedded in the constitution of the new international body, the United Nations Organisation.

The Labour government put in long hours trying to turn wartime alliance into world parliament. Labour strongly supported the United Nations Organisation. The first step towards founding the new body was taken when delegates from China, the Soviet Union, Britain and the United States met at Dumbarton Oaks. Although no small state was allowed to send delegates, Berendsen, dominion ambassador in Washington, seized the chance to tell British delegates what New Zealand wanted. He told them that only a few changes needed to be made to the covenant of the old League of Nations.

'If we were to attempt to draw up a plan for a new organisation,' he said in a lucid and eloquent speech, 'we would begin by taking a copy of the Covenant and a pencil, and we would not pencil very much.'[170]

A conference of fifty states, held in the middle of 1945 in San Francisco, talked over, shaped and then signed the United Nations Charter. A preamble to the charter told the world that the purpose of the new body was to save people from war, to uphold human rights, to safeguard international law and to help forward 'social progress and better standards of life in larger freedom'.[171] Conservatives in the dominion were cynical. So, too, were many liberals, such as Charles Chandler:

> *The mere publication of such a charter will mean less than nothing unless other factors are taken into consideration … If we are prepared to accept it as something which of itself can give us assurance of future peace, then we are doomed to disillusionment, and that far sooner than we dare suspect.*[172]

The struggle over trusteeship and other questions brought the dominion into conflict with the Soviet Union, the United States – and Britain. The British Labour government was not too keen on a new world parliament; it wanted instead to bring back the old system in which diplomats sought a 'balance of power' between big states.[173] Sir Alexander Cadogan, under-secretary of state at the foreign office, sneered at the way the 'tiresome' Fraser went on about trusteeship.[174] The small states won the struggle to write the doctrine of trusteeship into the constitution of the new body. Trusteeship did not apply to every colony, however, only to those held before the war as mandates of the League of Nations. Berendsen wrote bleakly that the postwar world would be not only a world of great powers but a world in which those great powers would never come to any agreement.

'Therefore,' he added, 'what I see is the same old struggle for balance of power, spheres of influence, etc. etc.'[175]

The cost of war: brutalising the people of New Zealand. This painting, *Jungle Patrol*, shows a dominion soldier alongside a Solomon Islander. *Artist: William Reed. Museum of New Zealand Te Papa Tongarewa.*

The gifted diplomat was right, needless to say.

Africa stayed subject to Britain, Belgium, Spain, Portugal and France. The French celebrated liberation from Germany while Algerians marched through streets calling for liberation from France. Paris, sending in a squadron of bombers, killed thousands of Algerians.[176] Wellington did not put pressure on London to grant independence to colonial holdings on the continent. Nash, for example, was against British withdrawal from Egypt. Imperial occupation of the country was 'sound', he said, because there was 'no practicable alternative' as a way of keeping control over the Suez Canal.[177] The National Party agreed wholeheartedly. Also the big daily newspapers wanted to keep Egypt under imperial sway. Mahmud Nuqrashi, prime minister, told the British late in 1945 that they must evacuate all troops. Crowds of workers and students swarmed into the streets and began attacking buildings belonging to the British. New Zealand was tarred with the same brush, having backed Britain so strongly. The New Zealand Forces Club was stoned in Cairo.[178]

Asia and the Pacific were a complex story. France, Britain and the United States sent troops and officials to colonies they had lost and found that many people in those colonies now took up weapons to stop the imperial powers from coming back.

Washington had declared at various points during the war that it did not wish to acquire new territory. Wellington knew that such declarations were politics, not policy. The war cabinet early in 1944 agreed that the dominion would support the republic in any takeover of the Japanese island colony of Micronesia. Cabinet was not thinking about the rights and freedoms of the subject peoples of Micronesia but about how to keep the United States committed to the Pacific. Fraser wrote that giving the islands to the big ally 'should increase the direct interest of the United States in the maintenance of the Pacific settlement'.[179] Micronesia, in other words, was to be a bribe. The Labour government was playing the old game of using small nations as bargaining chips in order to try to protect the power or position of other states. Micronesia was indeed taken by the United States and then militarised in a way unknown during the years of Japan's overlordship.

France set up the Union Française in an attempt to create constitutional unity for its colonial holdings. A weakness in the scheme was that many colonial subjects wished not to be colonial subjects. Pouvanaa a Oopa, a Tahitian politician, led a protest movement seeking independence for French Oceania; he was put behind bars for five years.[180] New Caledonia was not allowed to begin working towards independence until fifty years after the end of the war for freedom and democracy. Nor did its neighbouring dominion do anything to try to help shape a more democratic outcome for the villagers of the French colony. Fraser at the end of 1945 sent seasonal greetings to 'the French people of New Caledonia' and 'the French people of French Oceania'; he was looking forward to 'still greater friendship and co-operation in our work in the Pacific'. He said nothing about the Kanak people, nor about Pouvanaa a Oopa, nor about independence for New Caledonia and French Oceania.[181]

Postwar imperialism: a postage stamp showing the Netherlands 'helping' Indonesia. *www.nmm.nl/zoeken-in-de-collectie*

The dominion welcomed the Netherlands back into Southeast Asia, too. Nash, as acting prime minister, sent a message to the government of the Netherlands after the surrender of Germany. 'We look forward with you,' he said, 'to the early liberation of the Indies.'[182]

Liberation, it turned out, meant backing British and Dutch invasion of a colony that, two days after Japan's surrender, proclaimed itself the republic of Indonesia. Afterwards came four gruelling years of fighting. Indonesian nationalists were shocked by the way the Netherlands and the British Commonwealth deployed Japanese troops against the Indonesians.[183] The three imperial states, Japan, Britain and the Netherlands, killed thousands of people in their bid to crush the republic. Sukarno, its president, appealed for help from the international community: 'We urge the justice of the Indonesian claim for independence under the Atlantic Charter.'[184]

Only a few groups of dominion citizens spoke up for Indonesia. Waterside workers protested against the British Commonwealth sending troops. Wellington wharfies stopped loading a ship bound for Batavia.[185] One or two other unions protested, too. Hutt Valley railway workers voted in support of the 'demands for freedom and independence' of the people of Indonesia. They also voted for the government and the Federation of Labour to back the young republic.[186] The federation and the government handled the question warily. On the one hand, they knew how awkward it would look were they to say openly that they wanted colonial empires restored in Southeast Asia. On the other hand, that was indeed their policy.

The Labour government showed its true opinion in a small but significant gesture early in 1945 when it invited 'a great number of Dutch families with children' to come from Indonesia for a holiday in New Zealand. The costs were paid by the government of the dominion and the government of the Dutch East Indies. The families were all white, mostly people who had spent the last few years in internment camps as prisoners of Japan. A holiday would be good for them, observed Willem van Panhuys, the Netherlands consul-general in Wellington, because they had been living 'in filthy living quarters without proper food and clothing, under conditions of oppression, anxiety, and tension'.[187] The New Zealand government said nothing about the way such conditions were workaday reality for millions of colonial subjects under the Dutch.

Britain, meanwhile, was doing its best to work out how to fit into a new world – one in which it lacked the strength to foot it with the Soviet Union and the United States. A new Labour government, led by Clement Attlee and elected to power shortly before the surrender of Germany, quickly organised full independence and democracy for British India. The foreign and colonial policy of the Attlee government turned out in other ways, however, to be not so very sweeping. London during the first two years after the war did not propose to allow democracy and independence anytime soon to its holdings in Southeast Asia, Africa and the Pacific.

Fiji, for example, was another colony in which principle was trumped by power politics. Wellington wanted to keep Britain strong and engaged in the Pacific. The war cabinet agreed early in 1944 to try to talk London into propping up its grip on Fiji and stationing 'substantial forces' in the Pacific.[188] Fijians would have to wait nineteen years before they were given the right to vote, and another four years before independence was granted to the colony. The British government never formally accepted the

Postwar imperialism: the government and the big newspapers spoke of the 'restoration' of 'order' when they wrote about British, French and Dutch police and military taking back control of colonial territory. People's Voice, *12 December 1945.*

principle of trusteeship during all those years, and nor did New Zealand strongly urge the case of Fiji.

The Labour government, in other words, backed imperialism in the Pacific, so long as the imperial powers were Britain, France, the Netherlands and the United States – and New Zealand. At the end of the war Fraser sent a message to the peoples of Samoa, Tokelau, Niue and the Cook Islands.

'We must give thanks to God that our lands and islands have been spared,' he said; 'we are able to turn immediately to the tasks of peace.'[189]

The dominion had long governed its island colonies in a slipshod way, as the prime minister learned when he visited Niue, Rarotonga, Samoa and Tokelau towards the end of 1944; he was the first Labour Party leader to pay such a visit for well over twenty years. Fraser was dismayed at how poorly his government was administering the islands.[190] The war boom was over and many people were struggling. Thomas Herries-Davis, a young doctor practising in Rarotonga, wrote that 'the villages were unkempt and the general appearance was one of dejection'.[191] Banana and coconut plantations had been left to run wild and were no longer making money. Young people were seeking to get out. Cook Islands leaders were calling for independence more urgently.

Niue, on the other hand, was not so keyed up; nor was Tokelau.

Samoa was well ahead of the others politically. Tribal leaders knew what had been promised by the Atlantic Charter. Tupua Tamasese Mea`ole, speaking on behalf of the three royal dynasties, told Fraser that the charter had guaranteed small nations the right to govern themselves, and went on to point out that the prime minister himself had upheld the principle in parliament. Wellington decided the colony must be made fit for independence by a period of trusteeship. Samoa was not happy. Tribal leaders sent a petition to the United Nations calling for independence without delay. The Labour government argued that the colony was not yet ready. Talks between the two sides ended in some autonomy but with several years under trusteeship.[192]

Trusteeship, while it was seen to be good for the people of Samoa, was not seen to be good for the Māori of New Zealand.

Māori were as eager as other colonial subjects to be given autonomy, if not full independence. The Treaty of Waitangi had guaranteed their autonomy. Tribe after tribe had sought for nearly a century to have the treaty upheld by the state. Sir Apirana Ngata had told the tribes that by paying 'the price of citizenship' – in other words fighting in the war – they would be rewarded with full rights of citizenship.[193] Hopes were high, lifted even higher by the way the tribes worked together in the Maori War Effort Organisation. After the war, or so it was said on many marae, the government would very likely reward them by honouring the Treaty of Waitangi.

The treaty was not honoured after the war, and most politicians continued to view it as a curiosity that meant nothing. The Maori Social and Economic Advancement Act of 1945 did set up tribal committees, and gave them some state funding. The task of the committees was to behave as middlemen – committee members were men, mostly – between villagers and departments of state.[194] A seat on a tribal committee, however, was slim pickings. The cost of such a modest gain had been very heavy. One in every six Māori men who joined the army was dead by the end of the war: their death rate was markedly higher than that of Pākehā.

Was the cost worth the winnings?

'I doubt,' wrote Henare Ngata, army officer and son of Sir Apirana, 'if Maori people can point to any specific benefit and advantage which can be attributed to the participation of their men in World War Two.'[195]

Thirty more years would pass before the treaty gained any status under law.

Māori leaders hoped that the Maori War Effort Organisation would carry on after the war as a way of embodying the promise of autonomy written into the Treaty of Waitangi. Fraser was not opposed to the notion and nor were some other Labour members of parliament, but the matter was handled mostly by officials in key state departments that opposed anything like autonomous institutions for Māori. Treasury advised the government to order the organisation to stop its work. The Native Department – few of whose officials were Māori – agreed with Treasury, as did Mason, the minister responsible.[196] Slowly, the props were pulled out from beneath the Maori War Effort Organisation.

Māori were not going to be granted autonomy.

Ceylon Wickliffe, a sergeant in the Maori Battalion, visiting a city school in Wellington, 1943. At the time, most Māori children still lived in the country and went to village schools; within twenty years, most Māori children lived in city streets and went to city schools.
Photographer: John Pascoe. Alexander Turnbull Library 1/4-000840-F.

MILITARISM, CENSORSHIP, PROPAGANDA

Freedom and democracy were compromised in more subtle ways by the things that war brought with it: censorship, propaganda, and citizens being herded into camps where they were subjected to drilling and the barked orders of the military.

Censorship was so stifling that not only was it very hard for people to know what went on during the war years but, to this day, it remains very hard for us to know. Newspapers, film news, radio broadcasts and private letters were censored closely. All civilian letters were liable to be opened and censored, together with all letters from soldiers not sent in a 'green envelope' – only allowed for private letters not dealing with anything military – and even then, letters in green envelopes were checked at random by censors.[197] The Labour government imposed censorship as soon as war broke out, and then added a second layer of censorship when the United States was dragged into the struggle. A task for cadets on the *Auckland Star* was to take proofs of the newspaper to American military officers 'to be read and approved, amended or excised'.[198] Monte Holcroft wrote about his toils as editor of the *Southland Times*:

> *I was receiving a steady stream of 'defence notices,' directives and warnings which had to be filed and checked when sensitive issues reached the news columns or required editorial comment. Restrictions and restraints seemed to come almost physically around the old brick building, giving it the semblance of a barracks or (on very bad days) a prison.*[199]

Holcroft also carried out voluntary censorship. The owner of his newspaper, Robert Gilmour, a financier, knew that editorials when in 'the right hands' could help 'the war effort, guiding opinion and stiffening morale at crucial points'.[200] Holcroft did his best to keep the mood warlike in Southland. Newspaper owners and editors, in other words, were unofficial censors who supported the state and military by playing up any news that might seem good while downplaying news that might cause people to be gloomy.

Citizens censored themselves, too.

Servicemen told only some of the truth, or none of the truth, when they wrote home to friends and family. *Brave Company*, a novel by Guthrie Wilson, opened with the words of a soldier on a battlefield in Italy: 'This morning I wrote to my wife … Much that one could write would make unhappy reading ... we all lie in letters home.'[201]

John Caves wrote to his fiancée from Italy:

> *My Own Darling, Sometimes I realise how unfair we are to ourselves when we write home only reassuring letters of the bright side of our life and leaving out ugly heart-rendering and sordid facts. Many thoughtless ones at home are to think our part easy … But of course civilian morale must be kept up – hence lies and more lies.*[202]

The mass of men and women in the military were not skilful writers, of course, and found it very hard to put into words what they were going through, let alone what they were feeling and thinking. The struggle to choose words was hard even for poets and novelists who wound up in the army, air force or navy. The contradictions, the complexities, the ambivalences of war were so unlike what civilians back in New Zealand were experiencing.

'I feel overcome with the difficulty of trying to write an intelligible letter to you,' said John Mulgan, army officer and novelist, to his wife.[203]

Citizens often knew when they opened a letter, leafed through a newspaper, sat down in a cinema or switched on a radio that they were reading or listening to lying words. The elderly and middle-aged had lived through the censorship of the First World War. Citizens sharpened their wit by mocking the censorship. A soldier in *Brave Company* speaks cynically.

> *We've got to win this war, you know. Don't you read your papers? Have a look at them sometime. They tell you all about it. They are most insistent that we should win this war. Highly important war, this one. Gold cup to the winner, I understand.*[204]

Radio broadcasters, filmmakers and newspaper editors, meanwhile, were not happy. The Newspaper Proprietors Association was chafing at the bit so badly by 1942 that it made a public statement about the misuse of censorship. Editors told the country they were aware of 'the evil consequences' of the state making them withhold the truth, when truth should be told to 'the people of a democratic country'.[205] A country editor complained a year later about radio broadcasts in which 'every piece of bad news has been sugar-coated until it assumes the appearance of a strategic gain to the Allies irrespective of whether our armies are advancing or retreating'.[206] The *Star-Sun*, straight after the war, told its readers that newspapers had struggled against 'the synthetic fogs' of 'rosy censorship'. A columnist confessed that he and others portrayed the dominion army as one in which nobody wept, grumbled – or died. 'Don't blame the war correspondents,' he went on, pointing out that nobody had been allowed to print anything but stories in a 'brass-bound, hug-me-tight style' that would stir people to want to keep fighting.[207]

Propaganda was a close ally of censorship in the war against freedom of speech in what supposedly was a democracy. *Return at Dawn*, the 'official story of the New Zealand bomber squadron' written by Hilary Saunders and published by the state during the war, was a good example of how the government did its best to brainwash the citizenry. New Zealand bombing crews were portrayed in the book dropping their payloads onto 'the abodes of the guilty'.[208] Saunders did not say that among the guilty inside those abodes were millions of children and millions of women and men who never voted fascist, never wanted a war and could not help being on the receiving end of bombs. Film propaganda was spun by the National Film Unit. Radio propaganda was beamed over the airwaves by the New Zealand Broadcasting Service and the British Broadcasting Corporation. The two state radio broadcasters worked hard to lull listeners into thinking their 'news' was trustworthy. Allen Curnow wrote a satire:

By sedative Communiques
May I be soothed
And gently by the B.B.C.
My Pillow smoothed.[209]

The war crimes trials that the winning powers held after the war were another way to keep up the propaganda. Trials in Nuremburg and Tokyo grabbed the headlines; and United Nations states convened hundreds of other courts throughout Asia and the Pacific.[210] All those in the dock were military, political or other leaders who had fought or worked for the Axis.[211] No trials looked into war crimes carried out by those who had fought or worked for the United Nations.

New Zealand sent a judge and a prosecutor to the trials in Tokyo. Erima Northcroft, the judge, secretly protested that the trials were being treated like 'Hollywood'. United States lawyers and judges seemed incompetent 'almost to childishness'.[212] Northcroft, a key figure at the trials, did not speak out openly, however.[213] Only three of the eleven judges at Tokyo were Asian. Radhabinod Pal, from India, was the only one of the eleven who protested about the trials there being used not for justice but as propaganda.

'I would hold,' he said, 'that every one of the accused must be found not guilty of every one of the charges in the indictment and should be acquitted on all those charges.'

Pal pointed out that while there was plenty of proof of war crimes committed by the Japanese state and its military there was also plenty of proof of war crimes carried out by the United Nations. Why were no trials being held to interrogate those war criminals?[214] Washington, he said, had provoked the war with Tokyo. The trials, he went on, were a 'sham employment of legal process for the satisfaction of a thirst for revenge' by Washington, London, Paris, The Hague, Ottawa, Wellington and Canberra.[215]

Herding citizens into camps was another way the wartime government weakened freedom and democracy.

Coaxing people to volunteer for the military was, arguably, an attack on freedom and democracy, since the state was able to exploit its massive power and wealth when doing the coaxing. Conscripting people into the military was an outright attack on freedom and democracy. And the military, in itself, was an organisation based not on freedom and democracy but authority and hierarchy. Admittedly, those who held military authority were not only people from the top of society; the army promoted so many men and women from the lower ranks into the officer corps that three out of every ten people given their 'pips' in the last year of war had been labourers before signing up.

'There is no doubt the army is a great leveller,' wrote Robert Wilson, a soldier from Northland; 'we have captains who were navvys and privates who were solicitors.'[216]

Meritocracy is not freedom, however; nor is it democracy. Military orders came from the top downwards, were to be obeyed without question and were enforced by strict discipline. Officers also had a good deal of arbitrary say.

A scene from the war crimes trial in Tokyo. *www.macarthurmemorial.org*

'I think the whole business of rank needs looking into with a coldly inquiring eye,' wrote John McDonald, himself an army officer. 'No man should be compelled to call another "sir". It's an affront to human dignity.'[217]

Democracy thrives, on the whole, when citizens behave with tolerance and respect towards one another and towards the people of other states. New Zealand, by going to war, weakened the hold of such things in society. Civilian laws and customs were based on avoiding violence, dealing with disagreements by talking, living and letting live, being good neighbours. Military laws and customs were based on being violent, dumbly obeying a superior, attacking an enemy, starving the neighbours, bombing the neighbours, burning the neighbours and killing the neighbours. Phillip Wilson agonised about how he ended up dropping bombs on towns and villages:

> *I couldn't understand why we had to do it … we'd been turned, by our air force training, into automatons that resembled, not men of warm flesh and blood any longer, so much as objects constructed out of wire and paper, which responded to signals from a faceless machine – signals such as 'Shoot. Bomb. Kill. Destroy' … We no longer had any sense of human fairness, or justice, or compassion. Our traditional code, of a fair go for everyone, had been obliterated … we were men who'd deliberately shut off our thinking minds, and had refused to consider any longer whether what we were doing was right or wrong.*[218]

Patrick Sheehan, who came back home after being in the army, agonised about the question in the same way:

> *You're confused. You don't know right from wrong any more … From now on, you're not allowed to kill, doesn't matter what people do to you, you can't kill, not allowed to kill. And yet you were killing for just no reason at all beforehand. And now you go back into civilian street and just pretend it never happened and be kind, don't destroy anything. Which you had. You'd destroyed a whole country and its people.*[219]

The warring state, by telling people to obey without questioning, by spending scarce money on weapons, by imposing censorship, by propagating propaganda, won few or no obvious gains for freedom and democracy.

A 'HOLYOAKIAN' WAR?

Nor was the dominion ever in any danger from any enemy. Germany and Italy lacked the power to attack New Zealand. Japan, the only opponent strong enough in the region to be able to mount a serious attack, knew such an attack would yield little worth gaining. Not that its leadership always thought about things coolly. Japanese generals and admirals sometimes did launch attacks that were against their own interests – Pearl Harbor was a striking example – yet as the war ground on they faced tougher and tougher strategic choices and lost the luxury of thinking about flamboyant displays of bellicosity.

New Zealand, by choosing to declare war, made an enemy of Japan, Italy and Germany.

A war in the 1960s would show how to placate an overbearing ally while being thrifty with the lives and the money of the citizenry. The Vietnam War was in some ways not unlike the war against Nazi Germany. A powerful ally wanted Wellington to wage war in both struggles. The powerful ally in both wars was seeking its own gain, fighting for its own purposes, rather than seeking any gain for New Zealand. The battlefields in both struggles were far away. The powerful ally in both wars denounced the foe as an ideological enemy. Fascism was the enemy ideology in the earlier struggle;

communism the enemy ideology in the new struggle. The Nazi state was indeed appalling. The socialist state of North Vietnam was appalling, too, killing a million or more civilians in purges of well-to-do peasants, intellectuals, anti-communists, non-communist nationalists and 'pro-imperialists'.[220] Admittedly there were clear differences between the two wars, but some of those differences might well have made the government eager to get involved in Vietnam. The Labour cabinet led by Savage in 1939 was not only somewhat pacifist but markedly anti-imperialist. The National cabinet led by Keith Holyoake in the 1960s was strongly anti-pacifist and by no means anti-imperialist.

Why did the Holyoake government not conscript young men in thousands and send them off to Vietnam?

Holyoake and his cabinet, like their Labour predecessors, believed that they must keep in good with a powerful overseas ally. Yet, unlike their predecessors, they were by no means convinced about the necessity of the war that ally was asking them to wage. Holyoake, while he was a conservative anti-communist, did not think that the Vietnam War could be justified on grounds of either hardheaded pragmatism or high-minded morality. The National government was left with the awkward task of trying to 'help' the powerful ally just enough to keep in good without paying too high a cost.

At first, when the United States was propping up the French colonial regime in Vietnam, New Zealand bought approval not by sending troops but simply by shipping out some of its stock of surplus materiel left over from the Second World War. After the flight of the French the American policy was to prop up its own puppet dictatorship in Saigon. Washington had to talk allies into believing they were threatened by the spread of socialist governments in Asia. The National government was willing to use such language when speaking to parliament and the citizenry.

'The crux of the matter for us is that Communist aggression in Vietnam is a threat to us,' John Marshall, deputy prime minister, told the house. 'Our security and way of life are at stake and we cannot stand aside.'[221]

National politicians privately took such apocalyptic warnings with many grains of salt. So, too, did the officer corps. The chiefs of staff in 1961 said that the 'vital issue' for New Zealand was 'not the need to restore stability' in Vietnam but 'to preserve our position with the United States as our major ally'.[222] Alister McIntosh, now a very seasoned diplomat, wrote secretly four years later that the policy of the government when supporting Malaysia in its struggle with Indonesia was to do little, and do it slowly. Allies, he noted, would always put the country 'under constant pressure' to do more; 'therefore we should feed our help out in dribs and drabs'.[223] The Holyoake government followed exactly that strategy in Vietnam. New Zealand never sent anything other than what McIntosh called 'some token force' to support the war being waged by the United States.[224] Frank Corner, by now ambassador to the United States, wrote in 1967:

> *Given the great distance of New Zealand from Asia, the improbability of any direct military threat – except as a result of involving ourselves through the alliance – and given the failure of the United States for many years to take any action directly helpful to New Zealand, the fact that New Zealand is making any contribution is the notable thing.*[225]

An astute official or politician in 1939 could have written in much the same way:

> *Given the great distance of New Zealand from Europe, the improbability of any direct military threat – except as a result of involving ourselves through the alliance – and given the failure of Britain for many years to take any action directly helpful to New Zealand, the fact that New Zealand is making any contribution is the notable thing.*

Warm words backed by coolly token troop shipments proved enough for the task at hand – a task not so much of swapping blows with North Vietnam as of pleasing the United States. American government and military establishments spoke gratefully, even fulsomely, about such lukewarm backing. A president in office visited New Zealand for the first time in history as a way of saying thank you for sending troops.

The cost to the country was fairly slight. Only smallish sums of money were spent on training, kitting out and paying the troops. The United States agreed to give a subsidy for many costs, too, among them supply and transport. New Zealand only ever stationed a few hundred soldiers in the field at any one point. Only a few dozen died in the fighting.

Any weighing of deaths against the goodwill of a powerful ally will always be fraught, of course; some would say wrong. Comparison and contrast between Holyoake and his ministers in the 1960s with their counterparts in the 1930s need not be an exercise merely in weighing up two different political deals to see which was a better 'bargain'. It can also be a more fundamental weighing up of two opposed approaches to decisionmaking.

Holyoake saw the demands of a powerful overseas ally in the context of a wide and tangled network of costs and benefits – economic, social and political – to be negotiated warily. The leader kept his eye on gaining maximal advantage at the cost of minimal disadvantage. He was able to do so even when handed a demand that his political mandate, together with his own personal philosophy, led him to view favourably. Holyoake saw his job, first and foremost, as one of soberly negotiating his cabinet, his party and the state of which he was prime minister through a complex set of competing demands.

A 'Holyoakian' approach to strategic thought was lacking in the leadership of the Labour Party.

Savage, Nash and Fraser were more or less uncritically compliant when the call to arms came from London. All three gave way to a surge of feeling. The leadership as a whole did not sit down and think things through coolly. A policy of outright neutrality was not likely to have been workable: a big group of voters felt so loyal to Britain that where the motherland stood, they stood. Although that loyalty was wrongheaded, arguably, nobody could change such feelings. Also, while trade with Britain was not quite the key to the economy that many people thought, it was nonetheless very valuable and would have been hard to offset with trade from elsewhere – above all, overnight. New Zealand could very likely have weathered British economic sanctions without collapse but no pragmatic politician would be keen to take on such a task. The hypothetical 1930s 'Holyoake' would have to work out what was the least that his government and the country could do to avoid upsetting Britain, and local Anglophiles, without paying too high a price in blood or gold.

A small volunteer army of a few thousand men could have been sent to fight Italy and Germany. All other men and women could have stayed at home and stuck to their ordinary tasks. London would have done its best to screw more out of the dominion, in the way Washington would during the Vietnam War, but Wellington could have kept saying that given its distance from the battlefields the best way for it to help would be to keep up production of wool and food. Also, during the first years of the war the dominion could have pointed out that it needed to husband its strength in readiness for any fight with Japan. London knew that Wellington and Canberra were anxious about Tokyo.

New Zealand, by not sending tens of thousands of men and not flying squadrons of bombers, would not have delivered victory to the Axis. All military effort by the dominion was more or less meaningless. New Zealand could have enjoyed the blessings of its safety without going onto a gruelling and wasteful war footing.

Was it worth blowing up old ladies in Hamburg? Or girls and boys in Berlin?

And why not send food to starving villagers in Bengal?

THE STAIN OF BLOOD

Victory was disillusioning. The dominion and the whole world seemed to have spent six years running very hard, very expensively and exhaustingly, to stay in more or less the same spot. 'Worry is dead – long live worry' commented the *Evening Post* when pointing out at the end of 1945 that many people who looked towards the future felt 'a misgiving and a shrinking'.[226] Stresses and strains had become obvious in the relationship between the Soviet Union and the United States. Although the dominion worked hard to keep on an even keel in its relationship with Moscow, the same was not true of Washington. The *New Zealand Herald* saw worldwide signs of 'discord, suspicion and distrust'.[227]

Citizens wondered how the dominion would fit into a new world now split between two superpowers. A new world that proved to be not the 'new world order' so many had sought so hopefully. A world that proved new only in the sense that the old balance of power between a few big states had tilted in a terrifying new way.

A world, too, with nuclear bombs.

Poets, novelists, essayists and historians throughout the years of fighting had asked whether the game of war would prove worth the playing. Denis Glover got 'much sardonic pleasure' from knowing that when the fighting was over it would be followed by fifty years of 'quarrelsome confusion all in the name of liberty'.[228] Dan Davin wrote about what seemed to be the bleak outlook for a world divided between Washington and Moscow. The Soviet Union stood for 'autocracy, secret police'. The United States stood for 'hysteria, hopeless confusion about the meaning of words, a materialism proclaiming its democratic spirituality'.[229] Rex Fairburn wrote that the world was being 'nicely partitioned' between the 'two barbarisms'.[230] Lauris Edmond wrote with more feeling when she described her younger and less cynical self, watching men on the streets who were home from the fighting:

> *I couldn't help wondering if any belief or any country has the right to demand what has been demanded of those men – and taken too. It isn't as though conditions after the war will be so much better – if they were, it might be worth it, but they won't be.*[231]

New Zealand for several years had bled itself heavily. Money and men and women were shovelled into the task of trying to safeguard the economy, keep the country safe from military attack, keep up the link with the imperial homeland and, nobly, support freedom and democracy. The dominion had done well economically; however, the economy had not been much at risk. The dominion had avoided being invaded by the enemy; however, it had never been at risk of invasion. The dominion had kept up the link with the imperial homeland; however, the imperial homeland was a sinking ship. Freedom and democracy had gained ground in a few states; however, most people in the world were still the subjects of empires or dictatorships.

Also, of course, the Axis would have lost the war anyway, whatever the dominion did or did not do.

Curnow wrote a poem during the war to mark the three-hundredth anniversary of landfall by Abel Tasman. The poet was aware of the way so many politicians and so many of the moneyed were twisting words while claiming to speak for history. The past was something they wished to pin on their chests 'like a decoration for merit that congratulates itself'. New Zealand has often pinned the two world wars on its chest as though they were gold medals. New Zealand has often spoken of itself as meritorious, worthy of congratulation, for having gone to war against the Axis.

The Second World War, the meritorious war, the war for a new world order, the war for freedom and democracy, needs to be weighed up carefully.

Was the dominion strikingly brave and bold?

Or was the dominion quixotic?

Why so much blood?

Curnow, having written about sailors crossing a strange sea, ended with cool yet warm words:

Only by a more faithful memory, laying
On him the half-light of a diffident glory,
The Sailor lives, and stands beside us, paying
Out into our time's wave
The stain of blood that writes an island story.[232]

Postwar optimism; a sketch for a window in the Otaki War Memorial Hall.
Artist: E. Mervyn Taylor. Museum of New Zealand Te Papa Tongarewa.

NOTES

ABBREVIATIONS

AJHR *Appendices to the Journals of the House of Representatives*
NZJH *New Zealand Journal of History*
NZPD *New Zealand Parliamentary Debates (Hansard)*
NZYB *New Zealand Official Yearbook*

INTRODUCTION

1. The last peace treaty was signed in 1951 between Japan and forty-eight member countries of the United Nations. Japan and the Soviet Union did not sign a peace treaty; nor has a treaty been signed yet between Japan and the Soviet successor state, the Russian Federation.
2. www.penny-arcade.com/comic/2005/05/24. Hoth is the name of a planet used by 'the Alliance' (the Allies) as a base for warfare against 'the Empire' (the Axis) in the *Star Wars* film *The Empire Strikes Back*. Omaha Beach was the Allied military name for a section of Normandy coast on D-Day. The irony is twofold, given that, as is already discussed, Hoth was simply a retelling of Omaha Beach in the first place.
3. E.L. Loftus, 'Planting misinformation in the human mind: A 30-year investigation of the malleability of memory', www.learnmem.org/cgi/doi/10.1101/lm.94705. A review of the literature in false memory can be found at http://onlinelibrary.wiley.com/doi/10.1002/0471264385.wei1109/full
4. Jane Austen, *Northanger Abbey*, www.gutenberg.org/files/121/121-h/121-h.htm#link2HCH0005
5. Hermann Hesse, *The Glass Bead Game*, (London: Vintage, 2000), 39.

1: THE EVE OF WAR

1. *New Zealand Herald*, 27 December 1938.
2. Factory production alone was worth £30.5 million yearly, compared with £45.8 million for farming. These figures do not include dairy production, which was primarily factory processing of farm products. J.B. Condliffe, *The Welfare State in New Zealand* (London: Allen & Unwin, 1959), 146.
3. www.teara.govt.nz/en/graph/24347/industrial-structure-of-workforce-1936-2006
4. Statistics New Zealand: www.stats.govt.nz/methods_and_services/access-data/tables/long-term-data-series/national-income.aspx, table-e1-2-1
5. Angus Maddison, 'Statistics on world population, GDP and per capita GDP, 1-2008AD': www.ggdc.net/MADDISON/oriindex.htm
6. *Auckland Star*, 31 December 1938.
7. *Evening Post*, 4 November 1939.
8. H.B. Turbott, 'Health and social welfare', in Ivan L.G. Sutherland (ed.), *The Maori People Today* (Wellington: New Zealand Institute of International Affairs and NZCER, 1940), 234–35.
9. Ibid., 230–31.
10. Peter Buck, 'Foreword', in Sutherland (ed.), *The Maori People Today*, 7.
11. *Evening Post*, 14 March 1939.
12. Nicholas Reid, *James Michael Liston: A life* (Wellington: Victoria University Press, 2006), 232.
13. Quoted by *Zealandia*, 3 July 1941. *Zealandia* supported this policy.
14. Stevan Eldred-Grigg & Zeng Dazheng, *White Ghosts, Yellow Peril: China and New Zealand 1790–1950* (Dunedin: Otago University Press, 2014), 288–94.

15. The figures are for 1938. M.N. Galt, 'Wealth and income in New Zealand: c. 1870 to c. 1939', PhD thesis, Victoria University of Wellington, 1985, 24.
16. W.T. Doig, *Rich and Poor in New Zealand* (Christchurch: Christchurch Co-operative Book Society, 1942), 13.
17. Paul Goldsmith & Michael Bassett, *The Myers* (Auckland: David Ling, 2007), 164.
18. Ibid., 167.
19. Ibid., 164.
20. A.R.D. Fairburn, 'Dominion', in Jane Stafford & Mark Williams (eds), *The Auckland University Press Anthology of New Zealand Literature* (Auckland: Auckland University Press, 2012), 346.
21. Miles Fairburn & Stephen Haslett, 'How far did class determine voting in New Zealand general elections, 1911–1951?' *New Zealand Journal of History*, vol. 39, no. 2, 2005, 230.
22. *Evening Post*, 23 May 1940.
23. Quoted in Barry Gustafson, *From the Cradle to the Grave: A biography of Michael Joseph Savage* (Auckland: Penguin, 1988), 258–59.
24. N.M. Taylor, *The Home Front*: *New Zealand People at War* series (Wellington: Department of Internal Affairs, 1986), 48.
25. *Workers' Weekly*, 22 April 1938, cited in Taylor, *The Home Front*, 24–25.
26. David Gee, *Our Mabel* (Wellington: Millwood, 1977), 56.
27. C.H. Douglas, *Major C.H. Douglas Speaks* (Sydney: Douglas Social Credit Association, 1933), 41.
28. Lauris Edmond, *Hot October* (Wellington: Bridget Williams Books, 1989), 60–61.
29. Barry Gustafson, *The First 50 Years: A history of the New Zealand National Party* (Auckland: Reed Methuen, 1986), 9–10.
30. Ibid., 30.
31. Ibid., 31.
32. Ibid., 19.
33. Ibid., 32.
34. Ibid., 20.
35. *Auckland Star*, 22 April 1944.
36. *Ellesmere Guardian*, 14 April 1939.
37. Oliver Duff, *New Zealand Now* (Wellington: Department of Internal Affairs, 1941), 37.
38. *The Spike; or Victoria College Review*, 1940, 12–13.
39. Rachel Barrowman, *Mason: The life of R.A.K. Mason* (Wellington: Victoria University Press, 2003), 256.
40. *Weekly Press*, 1 October 1916.
41. *Standard*, 9 September 1936.
42. The controversy occurred early in the war, but referred to the years between the wars. *Press*, 15 June 1940.
43. D.R. Jenkins, *Social Attitudes in the New Zealand School Journal* (Wellington: New Zealand Council for Educational Research, 1939), 24.
44. Bill Pearson, 'Beginnings and endings', *Sport* 5, Spring 1990: www.nzetc.org/tm/scholarly/tei-Ba05Spo-_div1-N10638.html
45. Edmond, *Hot October*, 85.
46. *Evening Post*, 27 January 1940.
47. David Ballantyne, *The Cunninghams* (Christchurch: 1976) (first published 1948), 179; set in the last years before the war.
48. *Rodney and Otamatea Times, Waitemata and Kaipara Gazette*, 2 August 1939.
49. Taylor, *The Home Front*, 174.
50. P.J. Lineham, 'The religious face of patriotism', in John Crawford (ed.), *Kia Kaha: New Zealand in the Second World War* (Auckland: Oxford University Press, 2000), 206.
51. Taylor, *The Home Front*, 177–78.
52. The remainder were other groups. John Crawford & James Watson, '"The most appeasing line": New Zealand and Nazi Germany, 1935–40', *Journal of Imperial and Commonwealth History*, vol. 38, no. 1, March 2010, 89.
53. The validity of the questionnaire is compromised by the fact that only 49 per cent bothered to fill it out. Taylor, *The Home Front*, 175.
54. Letter to the *Dominion*, 1938, quoted by *The Spike; or Victoria College Review*, 1938, 15–16.
55. Editorial, *New Zealand Herald*, 4 December 1934.
56. Quoted by Gustafson, *From the Cradle*, 204.
57. Keith Sinclair, *Walter Nash* (Auckland: Auckland University Press, 1976), 198.
58. John A. Lee, *The John A. Lee Diaries 1936–40* (Christchurch: Whitcoulls, 1981), 58.
59. Interview by John Henderson, March 1970, quoted by Brian Easton, 'Fraser and the development of the nation-building state', in Margaret Clark (ed.), *Peter Fraser: Master politician* (Palmerston North: Dunmore, 1998), 127.
60. Crawford & Watson, '"The most appeasing line"', 79, 83.
61. Taylor, *The Home Front*, 23.
62. *Evening Post*, 22 July 1938.
63. *Evening Post*, 15 October 1936.
64. Taylor, *The Home Front*, 29.
65. Letter to the *Dominion*, 1938, quoted by *The Spike; or Victoria College Review*, 1938, 15–16.
66. *Evening Post*, 18 September 1936.

67. Gustafson, *The First 50 Years*, 33.
68. Cyclostyled paper, 'New Zealand Labour Party, 1937 Annual Conference: Recommendations to the Government', 1, quoted in Taylor, *The Home Front*, 26–27.
69. *Workers' Weekly*, 22 April 1938, quoted in Taylor, *The Home Front*, 24–25.
70. *Press*, 31 May 1939.
71. *Press*, 3 June 1938.
72. Stewart Firth, 'Colonial administration and the invention of the native', in Donald Denoon, Stewart Firth, Jocelyn Linnekin, Malama Meleisea and Karen Nero (eds), *The Cambridge History of the Pacific Islanders* (Cambridge: Cambridge University Press, 1997), 274–75.
73. 'Statistics on world population, GDP and per capita GDP, 1–2008 AD': www.ggdc.net/MADDISON/oriindex.htm
74. Bai Shouyi, *An Outline History of China* (Beijing: Foreign Languages Press, 2002), 540.
75. *Auckland Star*, 8 April 1937.
76. Taylor, *The Home Front*, 118–19.
77. *New Zealand Herald*, 23 August 1933; Reid, *James Michael Liston*, 233, 372.
78. *Evening Post*, 14 December 1936.
79. *Evening Post*, 28 October 1935.
80. *Evening Post*, 6 October 1934.
81. Ngaio Marsh, *Died in the Wool* (London: Collins, 1944), 138–39, 252.
82. *Evening Post*, 13 June 1939.
83. J.N. Bade, 'Count Felix von Luckner's 1938 "propaganda" visit to New Zealand and its consequences', *NZJH*, vol. 35, no. 2, October 2001, 224–25.
84. Ibid., 226.
85. *Auckland Star*, 13 May 1937.
86. Sinclair, *Walter Nash*, 143.
87. *NZPD* 248, 7 October 1937, 668–69.
88. Lee, *Diaries*, 36.
89. *Ellesmere Guardian*, 12 October 1937.
90. *NZPD* 248, 623.
91. A.N. Field, *To-day's Greatest Problem* (Nelson: A.N. Field, 1938), 2.
92. Ibid., 32.
93. Gordon Ogilvie, *Denis Glover: His life* (Auckland: Godwit, 1999), 104, 210.
94. Ann Beaglehole, 'Refugees from Nazi Germany and Austria 1933–45', in J.N. Bade (ed.), *Out of the Shadow of War: The German connection with New Zealand in the twentieth century* (Melbourne: Oxford University Press, 1998), 30.
95. L.M. Goldman, *The History of the Jews in New Zealand* (Wellington: Reed, 1958), 224–26.
96. E.G. Jansen, *Jade Engraved* (Christchurch & Dunedin: Presbyterian Bookroom, 1947), 24.
97. John Dower, *Japan in War and Peace: Essays on history, culture and race* (London: New Press, 1995), 13.
98. Gerald Chaudron, *New Zealand in the League of Nations: The beginnings of an independent foreign policy, 1919–1939* (Jefferson (NC): McFarland & Co, 2012), 92–93.
99. Ibid., 90–91.
100. W.D. McIntyre, 'New Zealand, Japan, and the twenty-year last contest of empires, 1931–1951', in Roger Peren (ed.), *Japan and New Zealand: 150 years* (Palmerston North: Massey University, 1999), 93.
101. M.P. Lissington, *New Zealand and Japan 1900–1941* (Wellington: Department of Internal Affairs, 1972), 96–97.
102. *Evening Post*, 13 February 1934.
103. *NZYB* 1940, Wellington 1940, 281.
104. Lissington, *New Zealand and Japan*, 135.
105. *New Zealand Herald*, 14 December 1938.
106. *Evening Post*, 6 March 1939; *Auckland Star*, 9 March 1939.
107. *Evening Post*, 17 December 1937.
108. *New Zealand Herald*, 16 July 1937, quoted in Lissington, *New Zealand and Japan*, 119–20.
109. C.J. Elder & M.F. Green, 'New Zealand and China, 1792–1972', in Ann Trotter (ed.), *New Zealand and China: The papers of the twenty-first Foreign Policy School* (Dunedin: Foreign Policy School, University of Otago, 1986), 34.
110. Gustafson, *From the Cradle*, 211.
111. Ibid., 34–35.
112. *Auckland Star*, 9 October 1937.
113. Lissington, *New Zealand and Japan*, 115–19.
114. Taylor, *The Home Front*, 11–12.
115. Ibid., 24–25.
116. Lissington, *New Zealand and Japan*, 107–08.
117. *Auckland Star*, 8 January 1945.
118. *New Zealand Herald*, 26 July 1939.
119. Quoted in Lissington, *New Zealand and Japan*, 110.
120. Elder & Green, 'New Zealand and China', 34–35.
121. Lissington, *New Zealand and Japan*, 122–23.
122. *NZPD* 254, 738.
123. *NZPD* 255, 357.
124. Ibid., 787.
125. Ibid., 698–99.
126. *People's Voice*, 20 October 1939.
127. Quoted in Lissington, *New Zealand and Japan*, 115.
128. Ian Nish, *Japanese Foreign Policy in the Interwar Period* (Westport & London: Praeger, 2002), 76.
129. *The Star-Sun*, 7 August 1939.
130. Nish, *Japanese Foreign Policy*, 115–16.

131. A total of £55.4 m of imports came into the country in the last full year of peace, of which £26.9 m came from Britain; some of those millions came from Britain as an entrepôt, not as an ultimate source. *NZYB* 1940, Wellington, 1940, 281.
132. Many people believed that 80 per cent of all money made by selling goods overseas came from selling to the British, but a lot of goods sent to Britain were sent straight on to other ports in Europe. Wool, above all, was re-exported in this way. 'The last year for which particulars of re-exported goods are available is 1933, when the total value was £5,264,000', *Auckland Star*, 23 April 1937. Or, in other words, around 16 per cent of exports to 'Britain' in 1933 went to elsewhere in Europe. The total of New Zealand exports in the last year of peace, 1939, was £58 m, of which £46.7 m went to British ports; and if we assume the same percentage of re-exporting as in 1933, then only £39.2 m really went to Britain.
133. Helen Thomson, *Happy Voyage, Part 2* (Christchurch: Helen Thomson, c. 1987), 16.
134. *Bay of Plenty Beacon*, 25 August 1939.
135. *Press*, 26 December 1942, quoted in Taylor, *The Home Front*, 710.
136. M.A. McKinnon, *Independence and Foreign Policy: New Zealand in the world since 1935* (Auckland: Auckland University Press, 1993), 83.
137. Ibid., 83. The trade agreement signed with Berlin was not the first choice of the Labour government, earlier unsuccessful talks having been held about an agreement with London. Nash had tried his best to get an understanding that would safeguard the market for dominion wool and food exports to Britain and, as payback, safeguard the market for manufactured imports going the other way. The offer had been turned down by London. Only then did the government look to Germany. Crawford and Watson, '"The most appeasing line"', 80.
138. *Auckland Star*, 29 April 1939; discussed by McKinnon, *Independence and Foreign Policy*, 85.
139. Condliffe still saw trade with Britain as crucial, arguing that if imports were encouraged from the United States then such imports would in turn encourage the United States to import more from Britain, and allow Britain to buy more butter from New Zealand. *Evening Post*, 2 May 1939.
140. C.J.M. Alport, *Kingdoms in Partnership: A study of political change in the British Commonwealth* (London: Lovat Dickson, 1937).
141. *Auckland Star*, 30 May 1928.
142. A.G. Hayter, *The Second Step* (London: Hodder & Stoughton, 1962), 148.
143. *NZPD* 251, 405–14.
144. Nell Hartley, *Swagger on Our Doorstep* (Tauranga: Moana Press, 1987), 199.
145. *New Zealand Herald*, 9 January 1939.
146. *Evening Post*, 12 March 1941.
147. Michael Havinden & David Meredith, *Colonialism and Development: Britain and its tropical colonies, 1850–1960* (London: Psychology Press, 1993).
148. Cash cropping – or so colonial officials believed – was the most obvious way peasants would be able to raise cash to pay the taxes. Ben Naanen, '"You are demanding tax from the dead": The introduction of direct taxation and its aftermath in South-eastern Nigeria, 1928–39', *African Economic History* 34, 2006, 80.
149. Ibid.
150. Quoted by Gyanesh Kudaisya, '"In aid of civil power": The colonial army in Northern India, c. 1919–42', *Journal of Imperial and Commonwealth History*, vol. 32, no. 1, June 2004, 43–34.
151. Ibid., 50.
152. Donald Denoon, 'New economic orders: Land, labour and dependency', in Denoon et al., *The Cambridge History of the Pacific Islanders*, 229.
153. *Evening Post*, 24 September 1936.
154. *Waiapu Church Gazette*, 1 October 1942.
155. *Waiapu Church Gazette*, 1 February 1943.
156. *Star-Sun*, 23 September 1939.
157. S.D. Wilson, 'The record in the Cook Islands and Niue 1901–45', in Angus Ross (ed.), *New Zealand's Record in the Pacific Islands in the Twentieth Century* (London & New York: Longman Paul, 1969), 32.
158. Dick Scott, *Years of the Pooh-Bah: A Cook Islands history* (Rarotonga & Auckland: Hodder & Stoughton, 1991), 213.
159. Wilson, 'The record in the Cook Islands and Niue', 52–53.
160. R.A.K. Mason, *Frontier Forsaken: An outline history of the Cook Islands* (Auckland: Auckland Labourers Union, 1947), 6.
161. Scott, *Years of the Pooh-Bah*, 221.
162. *Star-Sun*, 19 August 1939.
163. Quoted in Mary Boyd, 'The record in Western Samoa to 1945', in Ross (ed.), *New Zealand's Record*, 175.
164. *Evening Post*, 3 January 1938.
165. D.R. Haynes, 'Chinese indentured labour in Western Samoa, 1900–1950', MA thesis, Victoria University of Wellington, 1965, 60–64.

166. *Evening Post*, 3 January 1938.
167. *Auckland Star*, 12 September 1934.
168. Bill Willmott, *The Chinese Communities in the Smaller Countries of the South Pacific* (Christchurch: Macmillan Brown Centre for Pacific Studies, 2007), 27–40.
169. Rachel Barrowman, *A Popular Vision* (Wellington: Victoria University Press, 1991), 76.
170. *Rodney and Otamatea Times, Waitemata and Kaipara Gazette*, 21 June 1939.
171. Charles Brasch, *Collected Poems* (Auckland: Oxford University Press, 1984), 12.
172. Reid, *James Michael Liston*, 23.
173. Ibid., 218.
174. *Evening Post*, 25 August 1938.
175. *Evening Post*, 29 July 1938.
176. Keith Newman, *Ratana the Prophet* (Auckland: Penguin, 2009), 203.
177. Ibid., 99.
178. Taylor, *The Home Front*, 24.
179. F.L.W. Wood, *Political and External Affairs*, *The New Zealand People at War* series (Wellington: Department of Internal Affairs, 1958), 43–44.
180. Gustafson, *From the Cradle*, 204–05.
181. *Evening Post*, 3 July 1936.
182. Gustafson, *From the Cradle*, 205–06.
183. Wood, *Political and External Affairs*, 54–55.
184. Ibid., 90–91.
185. *Standard*, 11 November 1937.
186. Gustafson, *From the Cradle*, 208.
187. Ibid., 210–11.
188. *Auckland Star*, 13 May 1938.
189. Gustafson, *From the Cradle*, 210.
190. Ibid., 208, 211.
191. *New Zealand Herald*, 14 May 1938.
192. Quoted in Gustafson, *From the Cradle*, 211–12.
193. Robert Self, *Neville Chamberlain: A biography* (Aldershot: Ashgate, 2006), 333.
194. *Evening Post*, 1 October 1938.
195. Wood, *Political and External Affairs*, 91.
196. Ibid.
197. *Evening Post*, 3 October 1938.
198. A full discussion of the 1938–39 financial crisis can be found in M.A. McKinnon, *The Broken Decade: Prosperity, depression and recovery in New Zealand, 1928–1939* (Dunedin: Otago University Press, 2016), 385–92.
199. Simon Boyce, '"In spite of Tooley Street, Montagu Norman, and the Reserve Bank's Governor": Recolonization or the eclipse of colonial financial ties with Britain in the 1930s?' *New Zealand Journal of History*, vol. 39, no. 1, April 2005, 88.
200. Gustafson, *From the Cradle*, 244.
201. Ibid., 246.
202. *Evening Post*, 28 July 1939.
203. Glenn Feldman, *The Disfranchisement Myth: Poor whites and suffrage restriction in Alabama* (Athens (GA): University of Georgia Press, 2004), 135–36.
204. World GDP was approximately 4500 billion (in the $US of 1990) of which the biggest imperial powers were: US 863 billion or 19.2% of world GDP, USSR 430 billion or 9.6% of world GDP, Germany 375 billion or 8.3% of world GDP, UK 301 billion or 6.7% of world GDP, Japan 204 billion or 4.5% of world GDP, France 201 billion or 4.5% of world GDP, Italy 154 billion or 3.4% of world GDP. Angus Maddison, 'Statistics on world population, GDP and per capita GDP, 1–2008AD': www.ggdc.net/MADDISON/oriindex.htm
205. M.H. Kater, 'Forbidden fruit? Jazz in the Third Reich', *American Historical Review*, vol. 94, no. 1, February 1989, 11–43.
206. www.youtube.com/watch?v=BHunO4EUfRc&list=RDBHunO4EUfRc#t=51
207. Duff, *New Zealand Now*, 117.
208. *Auckland Star*, 25 January 1936.
209. *Auckland Star*, 21 May 1937.
210. *Evening Post*, 31 May 1939.
211. *Evening Post*, 4 September 1941.
212. Michael Bassett & Michael King, *Tomorrow Comes the Song: A life of Peter Fraser* (Auckland: Penguin, 2000), 204.
213. *Auckland Star*, 19 August 1939.
214. *New Zealand Herald*, 28 June 1935.
215. *New Zealand Herald*, 6 April 1938.
216. http://archive.atlantic-archive.org/524/. For a discussion of the rivalry see M.R. Megaw, 'The scramble for the Pacific: Anglo-United States rivalry in the 1930s', *Historical Studies*, vol. 17, October 1977, 458–73.
217. David Reynolds, 'From World War to Cold War: The wartime alliance and post-war transitions, 1941–1947', *Historical Journal*, vol. 45, no. 1, March 2002, 212–13.
218. One historian has criticised this view of Anglo–American relations, arguing that while London and Washington might have come close to blows at times in the 1930s, by 1939 they had come to link their positions in East Asia and the Pacific. Greg Kennedy, *Anglo-American Strategic Relations and the Far East 1933–1939* (London & Portland: Frank Cass, 2002).
219. Taylor, *The Home Front*, 24.
220. Historical Publications Branch, *Documents Relating to New Zealand's Participation in the Second World War 1939–45*, vol. 3 (Wellington:

Department of Internal Affairs, 1963), 538–39.
221. *Evening Post*, 20 March 1943.
222. Quoted in J.A. Bennett, 'Wartime emergency and the displacement of Indians in Fiji: Cost and compensation', *Journal of Pacific History*, vol. 37, no. 2, 2002, 210.
223. Ibid., 212.
224. Turnbull to Berendsen, 21 March 1940, Western Samoa Administration, Archives New Zealand R17709272, 1939–1941.
225. Wood, *Political and External Affairs*, 72.
226. Ibid., 81–82.
227. Lee, *Diaries*, 159.
228. Ibid., 160–61.
229. *New Zealand Herald*, 12 June 1939.
230. *Star-Sun*, 21 August 1939.
231. *Evening Post*, 30 June 1939.
232. *Star-Sun*, 5 August 1939.
233. Wood, *Political and External Affairs*, 82–83.
234. Ibid.
235. Historical Publications Branch, *Documents Relating to New Zealand's Participation in the Second World War 1939–45, vol. 1* (Wellington: Department of Internal Affairs, 1949), 18.
236. *Evening Post*, 7 September 1939.
237. Ibid.
238. J.V.T. Baker, *War Economy*, *The New Zealand People at War* series (Wellington: Department of Internal Affairs, 1965), 61.
239. Wood, *Political and External Affairs*, 78.
240. Crawford & Watson, '"The most appeasing line"', 83.
241. Brasch, *Collected Poems*, 30.
242. *Tomorrow* 16, 30 August 1939, vol. v, 649, 677, quoted in Taylor, *The Home Front*, 20–21.

2: THE FIRST PHONEY WAR

1. www.bbc.co.uk/archive/ww2outbreak/7957.shtml?page=txt
2. Geoffrey Cox, *Eyewitness: A memoir of Europe in the 1930s* (Dunedin: Otago University Press, 1999), 274.
3. *Evening Post*, 4 November 1939.
4. Hector Bolitho, *War in the Strand* (London: Eyre & Spottiswoode, 1942), 12–13.
5. *Evening Post*, 7 September 1939.
6. *Auckland Star*, 4 November 1939.
7. John Marshall, *Memoirs, vol. 1, 1912 to 1960* (Auckland: Collins, 1983), 58–59.
8. Terry Sturm, *An Unsettled Spirit: The life and frontier fiction of Edith Lyttleton (G.B. Lancaster)* (Auckland: Auckland University Press, 2003), 254.
9. *Evening Post*, 27 September 1939.
10. E.R. Davis, *A Link with the Past* (Auckland: Oswald Sealy, 1948), 180.
11. *Evening Post*, 30 September 1939.
12. Historical Publications Branch, *Documents Relating to New Zealand's Participation in the Second World War 1939–45, vol. 1* (Wellington: Department of Internal Affairs, 1949), 18.
13. *Auckland Star*, 2 September 1939.
14. John A. Lee, *The John A. Lee Diaries, 1936–40* (Christchurch: Whitcoulls, 1981), 176.
15. Historical Publications Branch, *Documents, vol. 1*, 6–7.
16. Jim Sullivan (ed.), *Doing Our Bit* (Auckland: HarperCollins, 2002), 125.
17. Ibid., 37.
18. Megan Hutching (ed.), *Last Line of Defence: New Zealanders remember the war at home* (Auckland: HarperCollins, 2007), 60.
19. Janet Frame, *To the Is-land* (London & Auckland: The Women's Press/Hutchinson, 1983), 217–18.
20. J.C. Williams, *Slate Pencil to Word-Processor* (Christchurch: Waverley Press, 1995), 78.
21. Charles Brasch, *Indirections: A memoir 1909–1947* (Wellington: Oxford University Press, 1980), 350.
22. *Evening Post*, 4 October 1939.
23. *Evening Post*, 25 November 1939.
24. After buying her ticket she had had second thoughts and decided to stay longer in Britain, 'but they were so busy at the shipping office when I went to cancel my berth that I decided to keep to my original intention and leave by the Athenia'. *Evening Post*, 30 October 1939.
25. F.L.W. Wood, *Political and External Affairs*, *The New Zealand People at War* series (Wellington: Department of Internal Affairs, 1958), 7.
26. Clair Wills, *That Neutral Island: A cultural history of Ireland during the Second World War* (London: Faber & Faber, 2007), 41.
27. Ibid., 122.
28. *Evening Post*, 4 September 1939.
29. *Evening Post*, 6 September 1939.
30. *Evening Post*, 7 September 1939.
31. Margaret Hayward, interviewed by Stevan Eldred-Grigg, Wellington, 15 November 2010.
32. Gerald Hensley, *Beyond the Battlefield: New Zealand and its allies 1939–45* (Auckland: Penguin Viking, 2009), 52.
33. John Crawford & James Watson, '"The most appeasing line": New Zealand and Nazi Germany, 1935–40', *Journal of Imperial and Commonwealth History*, vol. 38, no. 1, March 2010, 79.
34. E.L. Loftus, 'Planting misinformation in the human mind: A 30-year investigation of the

malleability of memory': www.learnmem.org/cgi/doi/10.1101/lm.94705. A review of the literature in false memory can be found at http://onlinelibrary.wiley.com/doi/10.1002/0471264385.wei1109/full
35. *Rodney and Otamatea Times, Waitemata and Kaipara Gazette*, 28 February 1940.
36. *Auckland Star*, 16 March 1940.
37. Wood, *Political and External Affairs*, 104–05.
38. Ibid., 107–08.
39. Keith Sinclair, *Walter Nash* (Auckland: Auckland University Press, 1976), 193.
40. Robert Self, *Neville Chamberlain: A biography* (Aldershot: Ashgate, 2006), 401.
41. *Evening Post*, 15 March 1940.
42. J.D. McDonald, *The Pitcher and the Well* (Hamilton: Paul's Book Arcade, 1961), 64.
43. John Gould, *The Rake's Progress? The New Zealand economy since 1945* (Auckland: Hodder & Stoughton, 1982), 40.
44. *Evening Post*, 20 December 1939.
45. I.C. McGibbon, *Blue-water Rationale: The naval defence of New Zealand 1914–1942* (Wellington: Department of Internal Affairs, 1981), 263.
46. *Evening Post*, 20 March 1940.
47. Quoted in Michael Bassett & Michael King, *Tomorrow Comes the Song: A life of Peter Fraser*, (Auckland: Penguin, 2000), 212.
48. *Rodney and Otamatea Times, Waitemata and Kaipara Gazette*, 28 February 1940.
49. *Evening Post*, 27 April 1940.
50. *Bay of Plenty Beacon*, 22 September 1939.
51. I.C. McGibbon, *New Zealand and the Second World War: The people, the battles and the legacy* (Auckland: Penguin, 2003), 18–21.
52. Hutching, *Last Line of Defence*, 72.
53. *Spike; or Victoria College Review*, 1939, 15.
54. *Evening Post*, 27 March 1940.
55. *Auckland Star*, 11 May 1940.
56. Quoted in I.F. Milner, *New Zealand's Interests and Policies in the Far East* (New York: Institute of Pacific Relations, 1940), 95.
57. McGibbon, *Blue-water Rationale*, 263.
58. *Evening Post*, 7 September 1939.
59. www.nzonscreen.com/title/country-lads-1941
60. Editorial on the page for returned servicemen, *Auckland Star*, 9 September 1939.
61. *Auckland Star*, 4 September 1939.
62. Lee, *Diaries*, 176.
63. *Evening Post*, 10 February 1940.
64. N.M. Taylor, *The Home Front: The New Zealand People at War* series (Wellington: Department of Internal Affairs, 1986), 18.
65. *Bay of Plenty Beacon*, 31 May 1940.
66. Corner, in an interview with Michael King, cited in Bassett & King, *Tomorrow Comes the Song*, 408, n. 123.
67. Rachel Barrowman, *A Popular Vision* (Wellington: Victoria University Press, 1991), 199–200.
68. *Evening Post*, 2 September 1939.
69. Lauris Edmond (ed.), *The Letters of A.R.D. Fairburn* (Auckland: Oxford University Press, 1981), 123.
70. *Evening Post*, 1 May 1940.
71. *Evening Post*, 23 December 1939.
72. J.C. Irving, *A Century's Challenge: Wright, Stephenson & Co., Limited, 1861–1961* (Wellington: Wright Stephenson & Co., 1961), 181–83.
73. *Evening Post*, 24 April 1940.
74. *Auckland Star*, 26 October 1940.
75. *Evening Post*, 10 January 1940.
76. Sinclair, *Walter Nash*, 188.
77. www.stats.govt.nz/Census/2013-census/profile-and-summary-reports/century-censuses-population/born-oseas.aspx
78. Vincent O'Sullivan, *Long Journey to the Border: A life of John Mulgan* (Auckland: Penguin, 2003), 233.
79. Michael King, *Te Puea: A life* (Auckland: Reed, 2003), 230.
80. *Evening Post*, 8 September 1939.
81. Wood, *Political and External Affairs*, 57.
82. Andrew Stewart, *Empire Lost: Britain, the Dominions and the Second World War* (London: Continuum, 2008), 18.
83. Wood, *Political and External Affairs*, 57.
84. *Evening Post*, 5 July 1939; Hensley, *Beyond the Battlefield*, 50.
85. *Auckland Star*, 20 September 1939.
86. Quoted in James Bertram, *The Shadow of a War: A New Zealander in the Far East 1939–1946* (London: V. Gollancz, 1947), 58.
87. *Evening Post*, 20 March 1940.
88. *New Zealand Tablet*, 25 October 1940, quoted in Taylor, *The Home Front*, 83.
89. *Auckland Star*, 9 September 1939.
90. *Bay of Plenty Beacon*, 22 September 1939.
91. Hensley, *Beyond the Battlefield*, 54–55.
92. Quoted in Crawford & Watson, '"The most appeasing line"', 90.
93. Hensley, *Beyond the Battlefield*, 60.
94. Historical Publications Branch, *Documents, vol. 1*, 333–34.
95. Ibid., 531–34.
96. Ibid., 535–37.
97. Ibid., 538–39.
98. Wood, *Political and External Affairs*, 99.
99. Oliver Duff, *New Zealand Now* (Wellington: Department of Internal Affairs, 1941), 121.

100. Donald Haddon, *In Peace and War: A civilian soldier's story* (Masterton: Fraser Books, 2005), 6.
101. Alison Parr, *Silent Casualties: New Zealand's unspoken legacy of the Second World War* (Auckland: Penguin, 2010), 28.
102. Greville Texidor, 'An Annual Affair', in Dan Davin (ed.), *New Zealand Short Stories* (London: Oxford University Press, 1953), 310.
103. Noel Gardiner, *Freyberg's Circus: Reminiscences of a Kiwi in the North African campaign of World War II* (Auckland: Ray Richards, 1981), 38.
104. L.M.B. Constable, *Poet in Khaki* (Wellington: Handcraft, 1940), 12.
105. Bertram, *The Shadow of a War*, 39.
106. R.G. Scott, *Dick Scott: A radical writer's life* (Auckland: Reed, 2004), 55–57.
107. *Spike; or Victoria College Review*, 1939, 15.
108. Scott, *Dick Scott*, 55–57.
109. Martyn Thompson, *Our War: The grim digs: New Zealand soldiers in North Africa, 1940–1943* (Auckland: Penguin, 2005), 13, 17, 18.
110. John McLeod, *Myth and Reality: The New Zealand soldier in World War II* (Auckland: Reed Methuen, 1986), 21.
111. A.P. Gaskell, *All Part of the Game* (Auckland: Auckland University Press, 1978), 101.
112. *Evening Post*, 7 October 1939.
113. I.M. Peacocke, *April, May, June* (London: Ward, Lock & Co., 1943), 167.
114. Taylor, *The Home Front*, 80–81.
115. *Auckland Star*, 6 January 1940.
116. Parr, *Silent Casualties*, 25.
117. Ibid., 57.
118. *Auckland Star*, 16 September 1939.
119. Gaskell, *All Part of the Game*, 79.
120. Guthrie Wilson, *Brave Company* (London: Robert Hale, 1951), 204.
121. W.H. Scotter, *A History of Canterbury, vol. III: 1876–1950* (Christchurch: Canterbury Centennial Historical and Literary Committee, 1965), 448–49.
122. *New Zealand Herald*, 3 January 1940.
123. Lee, *Diaries*, 204.
124. *Evening Post*, 11 May 1940.
125. Ibid.
126. *Evening Post*, 8 May 1940.
127. *Evening Post*, 1 May 1940.
128. *New Zealand Herald*, 17 and 18 May 1940, quoted in Taylor, *The Home Front*, 73–74.
129. Hutching, *Last Line of Defence*, 193.
130. Taylor, *The Home Front*, 73–74.
131. *Evening Post*, 23 December 1939.
132. Ibid.
133. *Auckland Star*, 20 September 1939.
134. *New Zealand Herald*, 22 February 1940.
135. *Evening Post*, 3 January 1940.
136. Dorothy Butler, *There Was a Time* (Auckland: Penguin, 1999), 154.
137. Frank Sargeson, *More than Enough* (Wellington: Reed, 1975), 97.
138. Keith Elliott with Rona Adshead, *From Cowshed to Dogcollar* (Wellington: A.H. & A.W. Reed. 1967), 34.
139. Anna Rogers, *While You're Away: New Zealand nurses at war 1899–1946* (Auckland: Auckland University Press. 2003), 301.
140. Hitler addressed the Reichstag on 6 October 1939 in words aimed not just at foreign governments but his own citizens – most of whom were upset by the outbreak of war. He spoke about the wisdom of good relations with Britain and France and went on to propose a peace conference between the nations of Europe. Vyacheslav Molotov, chief of foreign affairs in Moscow, suggested that the Soviet Union might act as a mediator to bring about such a conference. The New Zealand government, when discussing the German peace proposal, knew, as Wood notes, that it was 'echoed by' the Soviet Union. Wood, *Political and External Affairs*, 105.
141. Wood, *Political and External Affairs*, 108–09.
142. Self, *Neville Chamberlain*, 394–97.
143. Ibid.
144. *Evening Post*, 16 December 1939.
145. *Auckland Star*, 24 February 1940.
146. *Evening Post*, 24 February 1940.
147. *Evening Post*, 24 April 1942.
148. Cox, *Eyewitness*, 275.
149. *New Zealand Herald*, 4 December 1939; *Otago Daily Times*, 30 December 1939; quoted in Taylor, *The Home Front*, 59.
150. *Evening Post*, 10 April 1940.
151. Wood, *Political and External Affairs*, 357–58.
152. Ibid., 359–60.
153. Selma Botman, 'The liberal age, 1923–1952', in M.W. Daly (ed.), *The Cambridge History of Egypt, vol. 2* (Cambridge: Cambridge University Press, 1998), 190.
154. David Hirst & Irene Beeson, *Sadat* (London: Faber & Faber, 1981), 56.
155. McGibbon, *New Zealand and the Second World War*, 61.
156. Taylor, *The Home Front*, 84–85.
157. McLeod, *Myth and Reality*, 131.
158. *Auckland Star*, 13 April 1940.
159. *Auckland Star*, 8 June 1940.
160. W.G. Stevens, *Problems of 2NZEF* (Wellington: Department of Internal Affairs, 1958), 217.
161. Thompson, *Our War: The grim digs*, 281.

162. Ibid.
163. Joyce Macdonald, *Away from Home* (Christchurch: Bookroom, 1945), 30.
164. Ibid., 22.
165. Paul Grey & Sally Grey, *Private J.D. Caves: The long journey home* (Auckland: Paul Grey & Sally Grey, 2004), 15.
166. Winston Sargent, *The Palms Bend Down* (Christchurch: Caxton, 1945), 27.
167. Ibid., 29.
168. http://faculty.buffalostate.edu/fishlm/folksongs/les01.htm
169. Sargent, *The Palms Bend Down*, 43.
170. Thompson, *Our War: The grim digs*, 93.
171. [Anon.], *A Digger's Diary: Ramblings in Egypt with the First Echelon* (Wellington: Organ Bros, 1940), 6.
172. *Evening Post*, 27 March 1940.
173. Joel Beinin, 'Egypt: Society and economy, 1923–1952', in M.W. Daly (ed.), *The Cambridge History of Egypt, vol. 2* (Cambridge: Cambridge University Press, 1998), 329.
174. Selma Botman, 'The liberal age, 1923–1952', in Daly, *The Cambridge History of Egypt, vol. 2*, 298–99.
175. Ibid.
176. *Standard*, 5 October 1939.
177. *Evening Post*, 16 September 1939.
178. *Evening Post*, 21 October 1939.
179. Quoted in Barry Gustafson, *From the Cradle to the Grave: A biography of Michael Joseph Savage* (Auckland: Penguin, 1988), 252.
180. *Evening Post*, 16 March 1940.
181. Taylor, *The Home Front*, 146.
182. *Rodney and Otamatea Times, Waitemata and Kaipara Gazette*, 15 November 1939.
183. *Evening Post*, 1 April 1940.
184. *Evening Post*, 20 March 1940.
185. *Evening Post*, 16 September 1939.
186. Ibid.
187. *Evening Post*, 20 April 1940.
188. *Auckland Star*, 18 November 1939.
189. *Evening Post*, 6 December 1939.
190. *Auckland Star*, 18 November 1939.
191. *AJHR*, 1940, B-6, 2.
192. *NZPD*, 3 July 1940, vol. 257, 336.
193. *Evening Post*, 27 September 1939.
194. *Auckland Star*, 18 November 1939.
195. *Evening Post*, 7 February 1940.
196. *NZPD*, vol. 256, 46, and *Evening Post*, 13 September 1939, quoted in Taylor, *The Home Front*, 34–35.
197. *Evening Post*, 20 September 1939.
198. *Evening Post*, 7 October 1939.
199. Ibid.
200. *Evening Post*, 18 October 1939.
201. Wood, *Political and External Affairs*, 121–22.
202. *Evening Post*, 7 October 1939.
203. *Auckland Star*, 14 November 1939.
204. *Evening Post*, 24 February 1940.
205. *Evening Post*, 20 March 1940.
206. *Evening Post*, 1 May 1940.
207. *Otago Daily Times*, 8 November 1939, quoted in Taylor, *The Home Front*, 41.
208. *Auckland Star*, 16 April 1940.
209. *Evening Post*, 29 November 1939.
210. *Evening Post*, 1 May 1940.
211. *Evening Post*, 29 November 1939.
212. Tim Beaglehole, *A Life of J.C. Beaglehole: New Zealand scholar* (Wellington: Victoria University Press, 2006), 236.
213. Ibid., 232.
214. E.H. McCormick (Dennis McEldowney, ed.), *An Absurd Ambition: Autobiographical writings* (Auckland: Auckland University Press, 1996), 150.
215. Wood, *Political and External Affairs*, 111–12.
216. Rachel Barrowman, *Mason: The life of R.A.K. Mason* (Wellington: Victoria University Press, 2003), 263–65.
217. Lauris Edmond, *Hot October* (Wellington: Bridget Williams Books, 1989), 61.
218. *Auckland Star*, 26 September 1939.
219. D.S. Carter, 'The attitude of the New Zealand Communist Party to foreign affairs, 1930–1941', MPhil thesis, University of Auckland, 1981, 60–61.
220. *People's Voice*, 15 December 1939.
221. *People's Voice*, 29 September 1939.
222. Elsie Locke, *Gordon Watson: His life and writings* (Auckland: Forward Press, 1949), 174.
223. D.M. Martin, *The War Behind the War* (Christchurch: Left Book Club, 1940), 12.
224. Taylor, *The Home Front*, 222.
225. *Evening Post*, 13 March 1940.
226. Taylor, *The Home Front*, 211–12.
227. *Standard*, 7 and 21 September 1939, quoted in Taylor, *The Home Front*, 53–54.
228. *Evening Post*, 7 February 1940.
229. *NZPD*, vol. 256, 47, 87, 96.
230. *New Zealand Herald*, 29 January, 1, 5 & 12 February 1940, quoted in Taylor, *The Home Front*, 209–10.
231. Taylor, *The Home Front*, 213.
232. *Evening Post*, 13 December 1939.
233. *Evening Post*, 7 February 1940.
234. *Evening Post*, 10 February 1940.
235. *New Zealand Herald*, 27 January 1940, quoted in Taylor, *The Home Front*, 189–90.
236. Taylor, *The Home Front*, 182.
237. Ibid., 186–87.
238. *New Zealand Herald*, 26 February 1940.

239. Hutching, *Last Line of Defence*, 200.
240. *Auckland Star*, 9 September 1939.
241. *New Zealand Herald*, 22 February 1940.
242. *Evening Post*, 8 September 1939.
243. *Evening Post*, 4 September 1939.
244. *Evening Post*, 23 December 1939.
245. Wood, *Political and External Affairs*, 157.
246. W.W. Mason, *Prisoners of War* (Wellington: Department of Internal Affairs, 1954), 17.
247. *Evening Post*, 25 October 1939.
248. *Evening Post*, 4 September 1939.
249. *New Zealand Herald*, 30 September 1939.
250. *Auckland Star*, 20 April 1940.
251. *Evening Post*, 16 September 1939.
252. *Evening Post*, 21 October 1939.
253. McLeod, *Myth and Reality*, 24.
254. King, *Te Puea*, 235–36.
255. Ibid., 230–31.
256. *New Zealand Herald*, 26 December 1939.
257. *Evening Post*, 7 May 1941.
258. *Evening Post*, 20 September 1939.
259. C.P. Sedgwick, 'The politics of survival: A social history of the Chinese in New Zealand', PhD thesis, University of Canterbury, 1982, 406–07.
260. Ibid., 422.
261. *Auckland Star*, 19 April 1940.
262. *Evening Post*, 2 December 1939.
263. Turnbull to Berendsen, 2 March 1939, Western Samoa Administration, Archives New Zealand R17709272, 1939–1941.
264. Wood, *Political and External Affairs*, 333–35.
265. *Auckland Star*, 11 May 1940.
266. *Evening Post*, 11 May 1940.
267. Taylor, *The Home Front*, 33–34.
268. *Bay of Plenty Beacon*, 8 September 1939.
269. *Evening Post*, 7 September 1939.
270. *Evening Post*, 16 September 1939.
271. Taylor, *The Home Front*, 742–44.
272. *Evening Post*, 27 April 1940.
273. *Bay of Plenty Beacon*, 1 November 1940.
274. *Evening Post*, 1 May 1940.
275. Quoted in Bassett & King, *Tomorrow Comes the Song*, 226.
276. *Evening Post*, 16 September 1939.
277. *Auckland Star*, 27 April 1940.
278. *Auckland Star*, 4 November 1939.
279. *Auckland Star*, 20 July 1940.
280. Scotter, *A History of Canterbury*, 439–40.
281. H.B. Anderson, *The Day's Run* (Christchurch: Caxton, 1977), 264–65.
282. *Evening Post*, 4 May 1940.
283. Sullivan, *Doing Our Bit*, 180–81.
284. Ibid., 63–65.
285. Brasch, *Indirections*, 351.
286. *Evening Post*, 17 April 1940.
287. Doris Gordon, *Backblocks Baby-Doctor* (London: Faber & Faber, 1956), 221.
288. Mason, *Prisoners of War*, 6.
289. *Auckland Star*, 1 April 1940.
290. *New Zealand Herald*, 9 February 1940.
291. Dick Scott, *Years of the Pooh-Bah: A Cook Islands history* (Rarotonga & Auckland: Hodder & Stoughton, 1991), 225.
292. Copra production fell from 12,536 tons in 1939 to 5644 tons in 1940. G.R. Lewthwaite, 'Land, life and agriculture to mid-century', in J.W. Fox & K.B. Cumberland, *Western Samoa: Land, life and agriculture in tropical Polynesia* (Christchurch: Whitcombe & Tombs, 1962), 174.
293. *Auckland Star*, 5 October 1940.
294. Bassett & King, *Tomorrow Comes the Song*, 202; *Standard*, 12 December 1940.
295. *Evening Post*, 8 February 1940.
296. Wood, *Political and External Affairs*, 127.
297. Taylor, *The Home Front*, 69.
298. Bertram, *The Shadow of a War*, 49.
299. *Auckland Star*, 23 December 1939.
300. Butler, *There Was a Time*, 146–47.
301. Sinclair, *Walter Nash*, 190.
302. *Evening Post*, 30 March 1940.
303. *Evening Post*, 1 April 1940.
304. Ibid.

3: A WAR FAR AWAY

1. The most thorough investigation of the peculiarly Catholic quality of fascism in Vichy France is John Hellman, *The Knight-Monks of Vichy France: Uriage, 1940–1945* (Montreal & Kingston: McGill-Queen's University Press, 1997).
2. *New Zealand Herald*, 11 May 1940.
3. *Evening Post*, 15 May 1940.
4. *Evening Post*, 20 May 1940.
5. *Evening Post*, 11 May 1940.
6. *Auckland Star*, 18 May 1940.
7. *Auckland Star*, 11 May 1940.
8. *Evening Post*, 25 May 1940.
9. *Star-Sun*, 5 June 1940.
10. *Evening Post*, 25 May 1940.
11. *Evening Post*, 29 May 1940.
12. *Auckland Star*, 18 May 1940.
13. *Evening Post*, 20 May 1940.
14. F.L.W. Wood, *Political and External Affairs, The New Zealand People at War* series (Wellington: Department of Internal Affairs, 1958), 132.
15. *New Zealand Herald*, 21 May 1940.
16. *New Zealand Herald*, 24 May 1940.
17. *Evening Post*, 22 May 1940.

18. *Evening Post*, 27 May 1940.
19. *New Zealand Herald*, 31 May 1940.
20. *Evening Post*, 11 June 1940.
21. E.H. McCormick (Dennis McEldowney, ed.), *An Absurd Ambition: Autobiographical writings* (Auckland: Auckland University Press, 1996), 150–52.
22. Ibid., 158.
23. Ibid., 165.
24. *Evening Post*, 20 June 1940.
25. *New Zealand Herald*, 24 June 1940.
26. *New Zealand Herald*, 26 June 1940.
27. *Press*, 15 June 1940.
28. *Bay of Plenty Beacon*, 31 May 1940.
29. *Bay of Plenty Beacon*, 26 June 1940.
30. *Star-Sun*, 8 June 1940.
31. *Evening Post*, 26 June 1940.
32. *Truth*, 10 July 1940.
33. Quoted in Michael King, *Frank Sargeson: A life* (Auckland: Auckland University Press, 1995), 191.
34. *Auckland Star*, 1 June 1940.
35. *Ellesmere Guardian*, 28 June 1940.
36. Gerald Hensley, *Beyond the Battlefield: New Zealand and its allies 1939–45* (Auckland: Penguin Viking, 2009), 92.
37. Batterbee, quoted in John Crawford & James Watson, '"The most appeasing line": New Zealand and Nazi Germany, 1935–40', *Journal of Imperial and Commonwealth History*, vol. 38, no. 1, March 2010, 94, n. 77.
38. *New Zealand Herald*, 17 July 1940.
39. N.M. Taylor, *The Home Front: The New Zealand People at War* series (Wellington: Department of Internal Affairs, 1986), 133.
40. The War Purposes Fund held £1,692,140 on 27 April 1940 and £2,197,921 by 24 June 1940. Taylor, *The Home Front*, 145–46.
41. *Evening Post*, 19 August 1940.
42. Taylor, *The Home Front*, 286.
43. Hector Bolitho, *War in the Strand* (London: Eyre & Spottiswoode, 1942), 40.
44. Brasch, *Indirections*, 368.
45. *Evening Post*, 23 April 1941.
46. Brasch, *Indirections*, 363.
47. Ibid., 364–65.
48. B.G. Clare, *Early Operations with Bomber Command* (Wellington: Department of Internal Affairs, 1950), 28.
49. Ibid., 31.
50. H.L. Thompson, *New Zealanders with the Royal Air Force, vol. 1* (Wellington: Department of Internal Affairs, 1953), 187.
51. *Evening Post*, 28 May 1941.
52. *Evening Post*, 24 May 1941.
53. S.D. Waters, 'German raiders in the Pacific', in *Episodes and Studies, vol. 1* (Wellington: Department of Internal Affairs, 1948), 3.
54. Taylor, *The Home Front*, 288.
55. *Rodney and Otamatea Times*, 5 March 1941.
56. *Evening Post*, 7 March 1941.
57. *Evening Post*, 28 December 1940.
58. Waters, 'German raiders in the Pacific', 5.
59. Ibid., 7–8.
60. Kurt Weyher & H.J. Ehrlich, *The Black Raider* (London: Elek Books, 1955), 128.
61. *Evening Post*, 14 January 1941.
62. *Evening Post*, 3 January 1941.
63. Weyher & Ehrlich, *The Black Raider*, 136.
64. A.F. Ellis, *Mid-Pacific Outposts* (Auckland: Brown & Stewart, 1946), 13.
65. Waters, 'German raiders in the Pacific', 24.
66. Ibid., 26.
67. *Evening Post*, 20 December 1939.
68. J.E. Martin, 'The National Service Department and New Zealand's manpower crisis of 1942', in John Crawford (ed.), *Kia Kaha: New Zealand in the Second World War* (Auckland: Oxford University Press, 2000), 221.
69. J.E. Cookson, 'Appeal boards and conscientious objectors', in Crawford (ed.), *Kia Kaha*, 176.
70. Mrs E. Bergen of Palmerston North, 20 September 1969, quoted in Taylor, *The Home Front*, 725.
71. Bryan Reid, *After the Fireworks: A life of David Ballantyne* (Auckland: Auckland University Press, 2004), 33–34.
72. *Auckland Star*, 30 November 1940.
73. Greville Texidor, 'An Annual Affair', in Dan Davin (ed.), *New Zealand Short Stories* (London: Oxford University Press, 1953), 310.
74. P.J. Lineham, 'The religious face of patriotism', in Crawford (ed.), *Kia Kaha*, 199.
75. *Evening Post*, 19 February 1941.
76. *New Zealand Herald*, 5 March 1941.
77. *Evening Post*, 19 February 1941.
78. *Evening Post*, 12 February 1941.
79. *Evening Post*, 5 March 1941.
80. Taylor, *The Home Front*, 252–54.
81. Ibid., 264.
82. Cookson, 'Appeal boards and conscientious objectors', 196, n. 2.
83. Taylor, *The Home Front*, 267–68.
84. Ian Hamilton, *Till Human Voices Wake Us* (Auckland: Oxford University Press, 1984), 22.
85. *Evening Post*, 23 April 1941.
86. The truth about the diplomatic and military goals in the Third Reich has proved notoriously tricky to disentangle, but Hitler gave a speech on 19 July 1940 offering a peace treaty with Britain. The terms were that Britain

would keep its empire and Commonwealth, while Germany would keep its territorial gains in Europe. Roderick Stackelberg & Sally A. Winkle, *The Nazi Germany Sourcebook: An anthology of texts* (Oxford: Taylor & Francis, 2003), 263.
87. Walter Warlimont (translated by R.H. Barry), *Inside Hitler's Headquarters, 1939–1945* (Novato, CA: Presidio Press, 1991), 111–12.
88. 'Axis' was a word first used in this context in 1936 when Germany and Italy signed a number of understandings that led propagandists to air extravagant claims about a new world spinning around an axis of power from Berlin to Rome.
89. Historical Publications Branch, *Documents Relating to New Zealand's Participation in the Second World War 1939–45, vol. 1* (Wellington: Department of Internal Affairs, 1949), 341–46.
90. *Evening Post*, 23 April 1941.
91. The name of the gunner is unknown. Winston Sargent, *The Palms Bend Down* (Christchurch: Caxton, 1945), 107.
92. *Evening Post*, 11 June 1941.
93. Sargent, *The Palms Bend Down*, 117; Anonymous soldier in Jim Henderson (ed.), *Soldier Country* (Wellington: Millwood, 1978), 149.
94. Peggy Dunstan, in Jim Henderson (ed.), *Soldier Country* (Wellington: Millwood, 1978), 77.
95. Donald McDonald, *Sidi Resezgh and other verses* (Wellington: Progressive Publishing, 1944), 11.
96. Joyce Macdonald, *Away from Home* (Christchurch: Bookroom, 1945), 45.
97. *Evening Post*, 19 May 1941.
98. *New Zealand Herald*, 2 June 1941.
99. *New Zealand Herald*, 18 September 1941.
100. J.V.T. Baker, *War Economy: The New Zealand People at War* series (Wellington: Department of Internal Affairs, 1965), 265.
101. *Evening Post*, 5 October 1940.
102. *Evening Post*, 2 October 1940.
103. *Evening Post*, 10 October 1940.
104. *Evening Post*, 12 October 1940.
105. *New Zealand Herald*, 9 October 1940.
106. *New Zealand Herald*, 12 October 1940.
107. *Evening Post*, 23 July 1941.
108. *Auckland Star*, 3 May 1941.
109. *Evening Post*, 9 October 1940.
110. Taylor, *The Home Front*, 134.
111. Ibid., 156.
112. *Evening Post*, 9 April 1941.
113. *Ellesmere Guardian*, 29 August 1941.
114. Statistics New Zealand: www.stats.govt.nz/methods_and_services/access-data/tables/long-term-data-series/national-income.aspx, table-e1-2-1
115. *Auckland Star*, 31 May 1941.
116. *Evening Post*, 23 April 1941.
117. M.A. McKinnon, 'The impact of war: Anglo-New Zealand economic diplomacy 1939–1954', PhD thesis, Victoria University of Wellington, 1981, 67–68.
118. Ibid., 96.
119. Ibid., 98.
120. *Auckland Star*, 12 April 1941.
121. Taylor, *The Home Front*, 743.
122. *Evening Post*, 5 July 1941.
123. Taylor, *The Home Front*, 755–56.
124. Ibid., 756.
125. *Auckland Star*, 27 September 1941.
126. *Auckland Star*, 9 August 1941.
127. *Auckland Star*, 15 November 1941.
128. *Evening Post*, 2 April 1941.
129. Taylor, *The Home Front*, 761–62.
130. Baker, *War Economy*, 76.
131. Mark Harrison, 'Resource mobilization for World War II: The USA, UK, USSR, and Germany, 1938–1945', *Economic History Review*, vol. 41, no. 2, 1988, 171–92.
132. McKinnon, 'The impact of war', 40, 43.
133. Baker, *War Economy*, 280–84.
134. *Bay of Plenty Beacon*, 21 March 1941.
135. *Evening Post*, 30 November 1940.
136. *Evening Post*, 17 February 1941.
137. *Evening Post*, 22 October 1940.
138. *Auckland Star*, 14 December 1940.
139. Taylor, *The Home Front*, 456.
140. Ibid., 460–61.
141. Jane Dare, *Rouseabout Jane: A land girl in New Zealand* (Christchurch: Whitcombe & Tombs, 1956), 48.
142. *New Zealand Herald*, 28 October 1941.
143. *Evening Post*, 7 May 1941.
144. *New Zealand Herald*, 28 October 1941.
145. *Auckland Star*, 27 March 1942.
146. *Auckland Star*, 15 November 1941.
147. Taylor, *The Home Front*, 491–92.
148. *Auckland Star*, 16 August 1941.
149. Taylor, *The Home Front*, 488.
150. Ibid., 497–98.
151. *Evening Post*, 4 December 1940.
152. Taylor, *The Home Front*, 138.
153. Martin, 'The National Service Department', 223.
154. Taylor, *The Home Front*, 399.
155. *NZYB* 1945, Wellington 1945, 270.
156. J.C. Irving, *A Century's Challenge: Wright, Stephenson & Co., Limited, 1861–1961* (Wellington: Wright Stephenson & Co., 1961), 186.

157. *Bay of Plenty Beacon*, 17 July 1940; see also Taylor, *The Home Front*, 142–44.
158. *Bay of Plenty Beacon*, 15 August 1941.
159. *NZYB* 1946, Wellington 1946, 302.
160. Ibid.
161. Taylor, *The Home Front*, 684–85.
162. *Evening Post*, 10 January 1941.
163. *Evening Post*, 11 January 1941.
164. *New Zealand Herald*, 6 February 1941.
165. *Evening Post*, 8 August 1940.
166. *Auckland Star*, 2 December 1941.
167. *Evening Post*, 12 February 1941.
168. *Evening Post*, 2 April 1941.
169. *Evening Post*, 24 May 1941.
170. *Evening Post*, 27 July 1940.
171. *New Zealand Herald*, 16 May 1940.
172. Wood, *Political and External Affairs*, 156.
173. *New Zealand Herald*, 26 June 1940.
174. *New Zealand Herald*, 24 July, 6 August, 13 August 1940; 24 January 1941.
175. Ann Beaglehole, 'Refugees from Nazi Germany and Austria 1933–45', in J.N. Bade (ed.), *Out of the Shadow of War: The German connection with New Zealand in the twentieth century* (Melbourne: Oxford University Press, 1998), 31.
176. *Auckland Star*, 23 August 1941.
177. *Evening Post*, 28 May 1940.
178. Wood, *Political and External Affairs*, 160.
179. *Evening Post*, 17 July 1940.
180. King, *Frank Sargeson*, 189.
181. Ross Somerville, 'Schramm, Bernardina Adriana and Schramm, Leo Paul', from the *Dictionary of New Zealand Biography*: www.TeAra.govt.nz/en/biographies/4s13/schramm-bernardina-adriana
182. Taylor, *The Home Front*, 119–23.
183. *Ellesmere Guardian*, 13 June 1941.
184. *Auckland Star*, 6 August 1941.
185. The full name of Te Kanawa is not known. Michael King, *Te Puea: A life* (Auckland: Reed, 2003), 231.
186. *Evening Post*, 13 July 1940.
187. Ron Crocombe, 'Ayson, Hugh Fraser', from the *Dictionary of New Zealand Biography*: www.TeAra.govt.nz/en/biographies/4a27/ayson-high-fraser
188. *Evening Post*, 11 September 1940.
189. Dick Scott, *Years of the Pooh-Bah: A Cook Islands history* (Rarotonga & Auckland: Hodder & Stoughton, 1991), 224–25.
190. *Evening Post*, 5 October 1940.
191. *New Zealand Herald*, 18 December 1940.
192. *Auckland Star*, 12 March 1941.
193. Turnbull to Berendsen, 2 March 1939, Western Samoa Administration, Archives New Zealand R17709272, 1939–1941.
194. *Auckland Star*, 9 June 1941.
195. Scott, *Years of the Pooh-Bah*, 225.
196. T.R.A. Davis & Lydia Davis, *Doctor to the Islands* (London: Michael Joseph, 1955), 26–27.
197. *People's Voice*, 21 June 1940.
198. Taylor, *The Home Front*, 580.
199. Scott, *Dick Scott*, 48.
200. *Auckland Star*, 20 September 1941.
201. *Evening Post*, 22 November 1941.
202. Quoted in John Caselberg, *Poet Triumphant: The life and writings of R.A.K. Mason (1905–1971)* (Wellington: Steele Roberts, 2004), 176.
203. Gustafson, *From the Cradle*, 270.
204. Tim Beaglehole, *A Life of J.C. Beaglehole: New Zealand scholar* (Wellington: Victoria University Press, 2006), 238.
205. *Evening Post*, 12 October 1940.
206. Taylor, *The Home Front*, 213–21.
207. Rachel Barrowman, *Mason: The life of R.A.K. Mason* (Wellington: Victoria University Press, 2003), 279.
208. Taylor, *The Home Front*, 587–89.
209. Quoted in Michael Bassett, *Coates of Kaipara* (Auckland: Auckland University Press, 1995), 267.
210. Barry Gustafson, *The First 50 Years: A history of the New Zealand National Party* (Auckland: Reed Methuen, 1986), 41.
211. *Evening Post*, 27 November 1940.
212. Ibid.
213. Gustafson, *The First 50 Years*, 42.
214. *Evening Post*, 19 February 1941.
215. Taylor, *The Home Front*, 136–37.
216. *Evening Post*, 12 June 1940.
217. *Evening Post*, 13 July 1940.
218. *Auckland Star*, 3 August 1940.
219. *Auckland Star*, 7 December 1940.
220. *Evening Post*, 24 January 1941.
221. *Auckland Star*, 22 February 1941.
222. Martin, 'The National Service Department', 224–25.
223. *Evening Post*, 4 June 1941.
224. *Evening Post*, 3 December 1941.
225. Irving, *A Century's Challenge*, 185–86.
226. *Evening Post*, 5 July 1941.
227. *Evening Post*, 16 July 1940.
228. Taylor, *The Home Front*, 124–29.
229. *Auckland Star*, 8 August 1941.
230. *New Zealand Herald*, 17 April 1941.
231. *New Zealand Herald*, 12 July 1941.
232. *New Zealand Herald*, 7 August 1941.
233. *Evening Post*, 31 July 1941.
234. *Evening Post*, 10 June 1941.
235. *Auckland Star*, 4 June 1941.
236. *Spike; or Victoria College Review*, 1940, 10.

237. Sonja Davies, *Bread and Roses* (Auckland: Australia & New Zealand Book Co., 1984), 30.
238. *Auckland Star*, 21 December 1940.
239. *Auckland Star*, 26 December 1940.
240. *Auckland Star*, 21 December 1940.
241. *Auckland Star*, 31 December 1940.
242. *New Zealand Herald*, 2 April 1941.
243. *Auckland Star*, 12 April 1941.
244. *Auckland Star*, 3 May 1941.
245. *Evening Post*, 2 June 1941.
246. Pius XII, quoted approvingly by *Waiapu Church Gazette*, 1 February 1940.
247. *New Zealand Herald*, 9 October 1940.
248. *Bay of Plenty Beacon*, 20 June 1941.
249. *Standard*, 19 October 1944.
250. *Auckland Star*, 6 May 1941.
251. *Auckland Star*, 27 November 1941.
252. *Auckland Star*, 13 August 1941.
253. *Evening Post*, 30 May 1941.
254. *Evening Post*, 7 May 1941.
255. *Auckland Star*, 19 June 1941.
256. *Auckland Star*, 26 June 1941.
257. *New Zealand Herald*, 15 August 1941.
258. Ibid.
259. Andrew Stewart, *Empire Lost: Britain, the Dominions and the Second World War* (London: Continuum, 2008), 85.
260. *Truth*, 23 July 1941.
261. M.H.C. [women's columnist], *Evening Post*, 29 November 1941.

4: WAR AT OUR DOOR?

1. The International Date Line misleads many people into thinking that Pearl Harbor was the first target; the true sequence, using Tokyo time, began at 0030 hours on 8 December with occupation of the International Settlement in Shanghai; 0215 hours landings in northeast Malaya; 0325 hours attack beginning at Pearl Harbor. W.D. McIntyre, 'New Zealand, Japan, and the twenty-year last contest of empires, 1931–1951', in Roger Peren (ed.), *Japan and New Zealand: 150 years* (Palmerston North: Massey University, 1999), 99.
2. *Evening Post*, 8 December 1941.
3. *Evening Post*, 11 December 1941.
4. *Evening Post*, 12 December 1941.
5. *New Zealand Herald*, 9 December 1941.
6. *Auckland Star*, 9 December 1941.
7. *Evening Post*, 8 December 1941.
8. Robert Aldrich, 'Imperial mise en valeur and mise en scène: Recent works on French colonialism', *Historical Journal*, vol. 45, no. 4, December 2002, 919.
9. Gerald Hensley, *Beyond the Battlefield: New Zealand and its allies 1939–45* (Auckland: Penguin Viking, 2009), 100–03.
10. Ibid., 99–103.
11. *Evening Post*, 2 October 1940.
12. *Evening Post*, 20 March 1943.
13. Donald Denoon, 'New economic orders: Land, labour and dependency', in Donald Denoon, Stewart Firth, Jocelyn Linnekin, Malama Meleisea and Karen Nero (eds), *The Cambridge History of the Pacific Islanders* (Cambridge: Cambridge University Press, 1997), 231.
14. Hensley, *Beyond the Battlefield*, 160.
15. Stewart Firth, 'The war in the Pacific', in Denoon et al., *The Cambridge History of the Pacific Islanders*, 302–03.
16. D.R. Eliot, 'Where the hawk flies', MS, Canterbury Public Library, New Zealand Collection, 140.
17. Ibid., 142.
18. Phillip Wilson, *Pacific Star* (Wellington: Alister Taylor, 1976), 66–67.
19. Ibid.
20. *Evening Post*, 22 January 1941.
21. C.R. Larsen, *Pacific Commandos: New Zealanders and Fijians in Action: A history of Southern Independent Commando and First Commando Fiji Guerillas* (Wellington: Department of Internal Affairs, 1946), 15–16.
22. I.C. Campbell, *Island Kingdom: Tonga ancient and modern* (Christchurch: Canterbury University Press, 1992), 176.
23. Turnbull to Berendsen, 14 February 1941, Western Samoa Administration, Archives New Zealand R17709272, 1939–1941.
24. Berendsen to Turnbull, 4 March 1941, Western Samoa Administration, Archives New Zealand R17709272, 1939–1941.
25. O.A. Gillespie, *The Pacific* (Wellington: Department of Internal Affairs, 1952), 230.
26. One historian observes that the Roosevelt administration wanted 'America in Britain's place'. R.S. Thompson, *A Time for War: Franklin D. Roosevelt and the path to Pearl Harbor* (New York: Prentice Hall, 1991), 405.
27. 'Here was no deterrence; here was deterrence that amounted to provocation. Was the provocation deliberate? Three times, twice to Lord Halifax and once to British premier Winston Churchill, Franklin Roosevelt intimated that he was trying to force "an incident" that would bring America more deeply into the fray. He may have hated war, but he presided over policies that came to be indistinguishable from incitements to war'. Ibid., 401.

28. *Evening Post*, 5 July 1941.
29. F.L.W. Wood, *Political and External Affairs: The New Zealand People at War* series (Wellington: Department of Internal Affairs, 1958), 191–92.
30. Ibid., 200.
31. Historical Publications Branch, *Documents Relating to New Zealand's Participation in the Second World War 1939–45, vol. 1* (Wellington: Department of Internal Affairs, 1949), 1–4.
32. Ibid., 8–9.
33. Ibid., 14–15.
34. Wood, *Political and External Affairs*, 194.
35. Ian Nish, *Japanese Foreign Policy in the Interwar Period* (Westport & London: Praeger, 2002), 134.
36. N.M. Taylor, *The Home Front: The New Zealand People at War* series (Wellington: Department of Internal Affairs, 1986), 314.
37. Ibid.
38. *Evening Post*, 24 October 1940.
39. Keith Sinclair, *Walter Nash* (Auckland: Auckland University Press, 1976), 233.
40. *New Zealand Herald*, 29 January 1942.
41. D.J. Lu, *Agony of Choice: Matsuoka Yōsuke and the rise and fall of the Japanese Empire, 1880–1946* (Washington: Rowman & Littlefield, 2002), 173.
42. Ibid., 170.
43. This incident is obscure; the only known source so far is a parliamentary speech by Carr on 26 July 1945. The identity of the 'distinguished visitor' is unknown. *NZPD*, vol. 2268, 1945, 692.
44. Bassett & King, *Tomorrow Comes the Song*, 203.
45. M.P. Lissington, *New Zealand and Japan 1900–1941* (Wellington: Department of Internal Affairs, 1972), 156–57.
46. *Evening Post*, 29 March 1941.
47. Akira Iriye, *The Origins of the Second World War in Asia and the Pacific* (London & New York: Longman, 1987), 140.
48. *Evening Post*, 23 August 1941.
49. *Evening Post*, 27 August 1941.
50. Lissington, *New Zealand and Japan*, 169.
51. Quoted in Bassett & King, *Tomorrow Comes the Song*, 204.
52. *Evening Post*, 19 March 1941.
53. *Evening Post*, 27 August 1941.
54. Hensley, *Beyond the Battlefield*, 157.
55. J.B. Crowley in J.W. Morley (ed.), *Japan's Foreign Policy* (New York: Columbia University Press, 1974), 82.
56. Quoted in ibid., 88.
57. Historical Publications Branch, *Documents, vol. 1*, 543–52.
58. Ibid., 17–20.
59. Nish, *Japanese Foreign Policy*, 147.
60. Lu, *Agony of Choice*, 183–84.
61. Ibid., 192.
62. Historical Publications Branch, *Documents, vol. 1*, 25.
63. Ibid., 50.
64. *New Zealand Herald*, 28 July 1941.
65. Nish, *Japanese Foreign Policy*, 151.
66. H.K. Smith, *The State of Europe* (Sydney & London: Angus & Robertson, 1950), 141, 228.
67. Martin Thomas, 'Economic conditions and the limits to mobilization in the French Empire, 1936–1939', *Historical Journal*, vol. 48, no. 2, June 2005, 493.
68. The term 'police state' is accepted even by the most sympathetic recent historians of French Indochina – Brocheux and Hémery – who argue that although the colonial experience was damaging in some ways, it was creative in some other ways. Pierre Brocheux & Daniel Hémery, *Indochine: La colonisation ambiguë, 1858–1954* (Paris: La Découverte, 2001), 112.
69. E.J. Hammer, *The Struggle for Indochina, 1940–1955* (Stanford: Stanford University Press, 1954), 24–26.
70. *New Zealand Herald*, 28 July 1941.
71. *Evening Post*, 24 July 1941.
72. http://archive.atlantic-archive.org/465/
73. *Auckland Star*, 9 August 1941.
74. *New Zealand Herald*, 11 August 1941.
75. Historical Publications Branch, *Documents, vol. 3*, 55–57.
76. Ibid., 62–63.
77. Nish, *Japanese Foreign Policy*, 162.
78. Quoted in R.S. Thompson, *Empires on the Pacific: World War II and the struggle for the mastery of Asia* (New York: Basic Books, 2001), 94.
79. Michael Schaller, 'American air strategy in China, 1939–1941: The origins of clandestine air warfare', *American Quarterly*, vol. 28, no. 1, Spring 1976, 3–19.
80. Quoted in Thompson, *Empires on the Pacific*, 96–97.
81. *New Zealand Herald*, 31 July 1941.
82. *Auckland Star*, 8 February 1941.
83. *Evening Post*, 26 June 1940.
84. *Bay of Plenty Beacon*, 7 September 1945.
85. Nelle Scanlan, *Road to Pencarrow* (London: Robert Hale; Christchurch: Whitcombe & Tombs, 1963), 109.
86. Brian Cull & Paul Sortehaug, *Hurricanes over Singapore* (London: Grub Street, 2004), 147.
87. Megan Hutching (ed.), *Against the Rising Sun: New Zealanders remember the Pacific War*

(Auckland: HarperCollins, 2006), 73.
88. *Auckland Star*, 14 December 1940.
89. H.R. Dean, *The Royal New Zealand Air Force in South-East Asia 1941–42* (Wellington: Department of Internal Affairs, 1950), 3.
90. *Auckland Star*, 20 December 1941.
91. *Star-Sun*, 30 December 1941.
92. Historical Publications Branch, *Documents, vol. 3*, 25–26.
93. Ibid., 93–94.
94. Ibid., 101.
95. *Auckland Star*, 14 September 1940.
96. John Breman, 'New thoughts on colonial labour in Indonesia', *Journal of Southeast Asian Studies*, vol. 33, no. 2, June 2002, 334.
97. Ibid., 336.
98. H.T. Bussemaker, 'Paradise in peril: The Netherlands, Great Britain and the defence of the Netherlands East Indies, 1940–41', *Journal of Southeast Asian Studies*, vol. 31, no. 1, March 2000, 119, 123.
99. Elly Touwen-Bouwsma, 'The Indonesian nationalists and the Japanese "liberation" of Indonesia: Visions and reactions', *Journal of Southeast Asian Studies*, vol. 27, no. 1, March 1996, 3–4.
100. Ibid., 4.
101. *Evening Post*, 21 May 1941.
102. Quoted in Thompson, *Empires on the Pacific*, 96–97.
103. Quoted in Nicholas Tarling, *A Sudden Rampage: The Japanese occupation of Southeast Asia 1941–1945* (Honolulu: University of Hawai`i Press, 2001), 76–77.
104. Quoted in W.D. McIntyre, 'New Zealand, Japan, and the twenty-year last contest of empires, 1931–1951', in Peren, *Japan and New Zealand*, 99.
105. J.L. McClain, *Japan: A modern history* (New York: W.W. Norton & Co., 2002), 480.
106. Ibid., 481.
107. Hensley, *Beyond the Battlefield*, 150.
108. Ibid., 161.
109. *Press*, 22 November 1941.
110. Iriye, *The Origins of the Second World*, 171.
111. Quoted in McIntyre, 'New Zealand, Japan', 99.
112. Quoted in Tarling, *A Sudden Rampage*, 76–77.
113. Historical Publications Branch, *Documents, vol. 3*, 81–82.
114. Ibid., 83–84.
115. 'Attack at Pearl Harbor, 1941: The Japanese view', EyeWitness to History, www.eyewitnesstohistory.com (2001).
116. Saburo Ienaga, *Japan's Last War: World War II and the Japanese, 1931–1945* (Canberra: Australian National University Press, 1979), 141.
117. Shohei Ooka, *Fires on the Plain* (London: Corgi, 1980), 18.
118. Francis Herlihy, *Now Welcome Summer* (Melbourne: Hawthorn Press, 1946,) 208.
119. Ken McNeil, 'Encounters, 1860s to 1940s', in Peren, *Japan and New Zealand*, 51.
120. *Auckland Star*, 22 October 1942.
121. James Bertram, *The Shadow of a War: A New Zealander in the Far East 1939–1946* (London: V. Gollancz, 1947), 105–06.
122. C.W. Vennell, *Risks and Rewards: A Policy of Enterprise* (Auckland: South British Insurance, 1972), 133.
123. Anna Rogers, *While You're Away: New Zealand nurses at war 1899–1946* (Auckland: Auckland University Press. 2003), 311.
124. Dean, *The Royal New Zealand Air Force*, 26.
125. *Bay of Plenty Beacon*, 4 June 1943.
126. *Evening Post*, 11 May 1945.
127. Thompson, *Empires on the Pacific*, 124.
128. Vincent O'Sullivan, *Long Journey to the Border: A life of John Mulgan* (Auckland: Penguin, 2003), 235.
129. Hutching, *Against the Rising Sun*, 75.
130. Lawrence Watt, *Mates and Mayhem: World War II: Frontline Kiwis remember* (Auckland: HarperCollins, 1996), 77.
131. Cull & Sortehaug, *Hurricanes over Singapore*, 33.
132. Dean, *The Royal New Zealand Air Force*, 8.
133. Ibid., 11.
134. *Evening Post*, 29 August 1942.
135. Hutching, *Against the Rising Sun*, 56.
136. *Evening Post*, 28 February 1942.
137. P. van Vliet, 'The Dutch East Indies', *Fourth International*, vol. 4, May 1943, 149–52.
138. Gillespie, *The Pacific*, 235.
139. *Evening Post*, 16 January 1943.
140. *Auckland Star*, 28 March 1942.
141. Hensley, *Beyond the Battlefield*, 165.
142. *Evening Post*, 11 December 1941.
143. Ibid.
144. Ibid.
145. A.P. Gaskell, *All Part of the Game* (Auckland: Auckland University Press, 1978), 41.
146. *Auckland Star*, 17, 18 February 1942.
147. Bee Dawson, *Spreading Their Wings: New Zealand WAAFs in wartime* (Auckland: Penguin, 2004), 40.
148. *Dominion*, 14 February 1942.
149. Lloyd Geering, *Wrestling with God: The story of my life* (Wellington: Bridget Williams Books, 2006), 64.
150. Taylor, *The Home Front*, 747.
151. *Bay of Plenty Beacon*, 17 December 1941.
152. *Evening* Post, 13 June 1942.

153. Alison Parr, *Home: Civilian New Zealanders remember the Second World War* (Auckland: Penguin, 2010), 98.
154. Taylor, *The Home Front*, 345–46.
155. *Evening Post*, 27 March 1942.
156. *Auckland Star*, 12 March 1942.
157. Charlotte Hudson, *Seawrack and Moonbeams* (Christchurch: Hazard, 2005), 16–17.
158. Macmillan Brown Library, accession number MB 857.
159. Sylvia Ashton-Warner, *I Passed This Way* (New York: Knopf, 1979), 299.
160. Jim Sullivan (ed.), *Doing Our Bit* (Auckland: HarperCollins, 2002), 145.
161. Parr, *Home*, 100.
162. Harry Bioletti, *The Yanks are Coming: The American invasion of New Zealand 1942–1944* (Auckland: Century Hutchinson, 1989), 3.
163. *Auckland Star*, 9 May 1942.
164. T.H. Melrose, *Sound the Tocsin: Japanese menace* (Hamilton: Waikato Times, 1942) (unpaginated).
165. *Evening Post*, 11 December 1941.
166. Melrose, *Sound the Tocsin*, n.p.
167. *Bay of Plenty Beacon*, 6 March 1942.
168. *Bay of Plenty Beacon*, 27 March 1942.
169. *New Zealand Herald*, 29 January 1942.
170. *Auckland Star*, 8 April 1942.
171. Wood, *Political and External Affairs*, 210–11.
172. COS, no. 115, Archives New Zealand, EA1, PM 81/4/3, pt 3.
173. Historical Publications Branch, *Documents, vol. 3*, 122–28.
174. Sinclair, *Walter Nash*, 214.
175. Quoted in Michael Bassett, *Coates of Kaipara* (Auckland: Auckland University Press, 1995), 264.
176. Taylor, *The Home Front*, 665.
177. Ibid., 666.
178. *Evening Post*, 12 December 1941.
179. *Evening Post*, 17 December 1941.
180. Taylor, *The Home Front*, 521.
181. Ibid., 545.
182. Ibid., 546.
183. Ibid., 473.
184. Ibid., 474.
185. *Evening Post*, 14 March 1942.
186. *Evening Post*, 22 August 1942.
187. *Evening Post*, 6 June 1942.
188. *Evening Post*, 18 July 1942.
189. *Dominion*, 31 December 1941.
190. Penelope Griffith, 'Dr Isamu Kawase and the first book on New Zealand in Japanese', *Turnbull Library Record*, vol. 9, no. 1 (May 1976), 13.
191. Archives New Zealand, Navy Department, EA1, 85/1/22 General, 'Japanese plans for the Invasion of New Zealand'.
192. McIntyre, 'New Zealand, Japan', 101.
193. Ibid.
194. www.armymuseum.co.nz/museum-news/recent-acquisitions/japanese-invasion-money/
195. COS, no. 115, Archives New Zealand, EA1, PM 81/4/3, pt 3.
196. *Evening Post*, 17 February 1942.
197. Peter Stanley, '"He's (not) coming south": The invasion that wasn't': www.awm.gov.au/events/conference/2002/stanley_paper.pdf, pp. 2–3. Stanley bases this on H.P. Frei, *Japan's Southward Advance and Australia: From the sixteenth century to World War II* (Melbourne: Melbourne University Press, 1991), 160–74; also Ike Nobutaka, *Japan's Decision for War: Records of the 1941 policy conferences* (Stanford: Stanford University Press, 1967).
198. These quotes from Frei, *Japan's Southward Advance*, 163, 166.
199. Carl Bridge, 'Australia, New Zealand and Allied Grand Strategy, 1941–43', in John Crawford (ed.), *Kia Kaha: New Zealand in the Second World War* (Auckland: Oxford University Press, 2000), 57–58.
200. Griffith, 'Dr Isamu Kawase', 15–16.
201. James Belich, *Paradise Reforged* (Auckland: Penguin, 2001), 282.
202. A discussion of British ideas about invading the Irish republic, together with the mobilising of the Local Defence Force of Ireland to cope with such an invasion, can be found in I.S. Wood, *Britain, Ireland and the Second World War* (Edinburgh: Edinburgh University Press, 2010), 49–55.
203. Wood, *Political and External Affairs*, 210–11.
204. *Evening Post*, 20 December 1941.
205. Taylor, *The Home Front*, 317–18.
206. *Ellesmere Guardian*, 6 March 1942.
207. *Bay of Plenty Beacon*, 15 December 1941.
208. *Auckland Star*, 27 December 1941.
209. *Ellesmere Guardian*, 13 March 1942.
210. *Evening Post*, 31 January 1942.
211. *Evening Post*, 14 March 1942.
212. *Auckland Star*, 21 December 1940.
213. http://avalon.law.yale.edu/20th_century/decade03.asp
214. Paul Kennedy, *The Rise and Fall of the Great Powers* (London: Random House, 1989), 430.
215. *Press*, 9 December 1941.
216. *Evening Post*, 13 December 1941.
217. *Evening Post*, 10 October 1942.
218. Ibid.
219. *New Zealand Herald*, 9 October 1944.
220. *Evening Post*, 8 December 1941.

221. Wood, *Political and External Affairs*, 230–34.
222. *Evening Post*, 25 June 1942.
223. Ibid.
224. *Evening Post*, 27 June 1942.
225. Megan Hutching (ed.), *Last Line of Defence: New Zealanders remember the war at home* (Auckland: HarperCollins, 2007), 180.
226. *Evening Post*, 26 June 1942.
227. *Evening Post*, 25 June 1942.
228. 4 March 1942, quoted in *Bay of Plenty Beacon*, 20 March 1942.
229. *Evening Post*, 9 May 1942.
230. *Star-Sun*, 9 May 1945.
231. McClain, *Japan*, 499.
232. Quoted in Stewart Firth, 'The war in the Pacific', 312.
233. R.W. Johnston, *Follow Me: The story of the Second Marine Division in World War II* (New York: Random House, 1948), 83.
234. The Imperial Japanese Army raised a total of 223 divisions during the war, of which only thirty-five were deployed in the Pacific. An overview of the centrality of China throughout the war can be found in Koshiro Yukiko, 'Eurasian Eclipse: Japan's end game in World War II', *American Historical Review*, vol. 109, no. 2, April 2004, 418.
235. *Evening Post*, 21 March 1942.
236. Sinclair, *Walter Nash*, 218.
237. Ibid., 220.
238. *Auckland Star*, 5 December 1942.
239. *NZPD*, 18 March 1943, vol. 262, 496.
240. Historical Publications Branch, *Documents, vol. 3*, 226–27.
241. Ibid., 249.
242. Firth, 'The war in the Pacific', 312–13.
243. E.V. Sale, *Shovel, Sword and Scalpel: A record of service of medical units of the Second New Zealand Expeditionary Force in the Pacific* (Wellington: Department of Internal Affairs, 1945), 41.
244. J.A. Bennett, 'Wartime emergency and the displacement of Indians in Fiji: Cost and compensation', *Journal of Pacific History*, vol. 37, no. 2 (2002), 215.
245. *Bay of Plenty Beacon*, 14 May 1943.
246. Campbell, *Island Kingdom*, 177.
247. Historical Publications Branch, *Documents, vol. 3*, 330–31.
248. Wood, *Political and External Affairs*, 335.
249. Mary Boyd, 'The record in Western Samoa to 1945', in Angus Ross (ed.), *New Zealand's Record in the Pacific Islands in the Twentieth Century* (London & New York: Longman Paul, 1969), 185.
250. *Auckland Star*, 11 September 1945.
251. *Auckland Star*, 3 July 1945.
252. *Auckland Star*, 7 November 1942.
253. G.R. Lewthwaite, 'Land, life and agriculture to mid-century', in J.W. Fox & K.B. Cumberland, *Western Samoa: Land, life and agriculture in tropical Polynesia* (Christchurch: Whitcombe & Tombs, 1962), 174.
254. *Matangi Tokelau: History and traditions of Tokelau* (Apia: Office for Tokelau Affairs, 1991), 126–28.
255. Ibid., 129–30.
256. Dick Scott, *Years of the Pooh-Bah: A Cook Islands history* (Rarotonga & Auckland: Hodder & Stoughton, 1991), 225.
257. Leslie Rex & Vivian Young, 'New Zealand period', in Institute of Pacific Studies (ed.), *Niue: A history of the island* (Niue: Institute of Pacific Studies, 1982), 129–30.
258. K.M. Johnston, *Village Agriculture in Aitutaki, Cook Islands* (Wellington: Dept of Geography, Victoria University of Wellington, 1967), 88.
259. *Auckland Star*, 21 August 1945.
260. Bioletti, *The Yanks are Coming*, 96.
261. Ibid., 37.
262. Deborah Montgomerie, 'GI Joe down under: American infantrymen in New Zealand during World War II', *NZJH* 34, no. 2, October 2000, 262–76.
263. Taylor, *The Home Front*, 643.
264. *Auckland Star*, 9 May 1945.
265. *Auckland Star*, 5 August 1944.
266. A.S. Fry, *The Aunt Daisy Story* (Wellington: Reed, 1957), 112–13.
267. J.L. Zimmerman, *Where the People Sing: Green land of the Maoris* (New York: Alfred A. Knopf, 1946), 38.
268. *Auckland Star*, 21 November 1942.
269. *Evening Post*, 18 July 1942.
270. Hensley, *Beyond the Battlefield*, 180.
271. Quoted in John Dower, *Japan in War and Peace: Essays on history, culture and race* (London: New Press, 1995), 275.
272. *Auckland Star*, 2 May 1944.
273. *Auckland Star*, 22 November 1944.
274. He did take pains to say that only the former, not the latter, was acceptable to a Christian. *Auckland Star*, 29 September 1945.
275. *Auckland Star*, 6 February 1943.
276. Hector Bolitho, *War in the Strand* (London: Eyre & Spottiswoode, 1942), 179.
277. Deborah Montgomerie, *Love in Time of War: Letter writing in the Second World War* (Auckland: Auckland University Press, 2005), 76.
278. *Auckland Star*, 25 August 1945.
279. Hutching, *Against the Rising Sun*, 253.

280. Ibid., 224.
281. McClain, *Japan*, 503.
282. Hutching, *Against the Rising Sun*, 204.
283. John McLeod, *Myth and Reality: The New Zealand soldier in World War II* (Auckland: Reed Methuen, 1986), 82.
284. R.A. Howlett, *The History of the Fiji Military Forces 1939–1945* (London: Crown Agents for the Colonies, 1948), 122.
285. www.theatlantic.com/past/docs/unbound/bookauth/battle/jones.htm
286. Locke, *Gordon Watson*, 232.
287. *Auckland Star*, 21 August 1945.
288. *Auckland Star*, 19 September 1944.
289. Lauris Edmond, *Hot October* (Wellington: Bridget Williams Books, 1989), 89.
290. *Auckland Star*, 20 September 1944.
291. Judith Fyfe (ed.), *War Stories Our Mothers Never Told Us* (Auckland: Penguin, 1995), 120.
292. Hutching, *Last Line of Defence*, 178.
293. Ibid., 115–16.
294. Edmond, *Hot October*, 121.
295. Ibid., 148.
296. Dan Davin, *The Sullen Bell* (London: Michael Joseph, 1956), 72.
297. J.V.T. Baker, *War Economy: The New Zealand People at War* series (Wellington: Department of Internal Affairs, 1965), 75.
298. James A. Michener, *Return to Paradise* (New York: Random House, c. 1951), 281.
299. Ibid., 280.
300. Les Cleveland, *The Songs We Sang* (Wellington: Editorial Servies, 1959), 22–23.
301. Les Cleveland, 'Where the heart is', *New Zealand Books*, Winter 2011, 23.
302. *Auckland Star*, 19 September 1944.
303. *Auckland Star*, 11 September 1944.
304. *Evening Post*, 26 December 1942.
305. *Evening Post*, 27 April 1943.
306. *Evening Post*, 11, 12 May 1943.
307. *Evening Post*, 22 June 1943.
308. Bioletti, *The Yanks are Coming*, 149–58.
309. Sonja Davies, *Bread and Roses* (Auckland: Australia & New Zealand Book Co., 1984), 55.
310. Hutching, *Last Line of Defence*, 234.
311. *Press*, 27 November 1942.
312. *New Zealand Observer*, 17 February 1943.
313. *Auckland Star*, 4 May 1943.
314. *Evening Post*, 1 February 1944.
315. *New Zealand Herald*, 8 February 1944.
316. *New Zealand Herald*, 11 May 1944.
317. *New Zealand Herald*, 16 May 1944.
318. *Auckland Star*, 4 August 1944.
319. *Evening Post*, 10 October 1944.
320. *Evening Post*, 29 August 1942.
321. Ashton-Warner, *I Passed This Way*, 299.
322. Wood, *Political and External Affairs*, 235–37.
323. Ibid.
324. *Auckland Star*, 27 June 1942.
325. *Auckland Star*, 11 July 1942.
326. Wood, *Political and External Affairs*, 230–34.
327. Barry Gustafson, *The First 50 Years: A history of the New Zealand National Party* (Auckland: Reed Methuen, 1986), 44.
328. Selma Botman, 'The liberal age, 1923–1952', in M.W. Daly (ed.), *The Cambridge History of Egypt, vol. 2* (Cambridge: Cambridge University Press, 1998), 298–99.
329. Angus Ross, interviewed and quoted in Glyn Harper, 'From darkness to light: Kippenberger and a tale of two battles', in Crawford (ed.), *Kia Kaha*, 133–34.
330. *Evening Post*, 2 July 1941.
331. *Evening Post*, 14 November 1942.
332. Osmar White, *Green Armor* (Sydney: Angus & Robertson, 1945), 201.
333. *Ellesmere Guardian*, 23 June 1944.
334. Firth, 'The war in the Pacific', 322.
335. *Evening Post*, 30 October 1943.
336. Firth, 'The war in the Pacific', 309–11.
337. H.L. Thompson, *New Zealanders with the Royal Air Force, vol. 1* (Wellington: Department of Internal Affairs, 1953), 246–47.
338. Ibid., 249.
339. Ibid., 268.
340. J.D. McDonald, *The Pitcher and the Well* (Hamilton: Paul's Book Arcade, 1961), 84–85.
341. Denis Glover, *Hot Water Sailor and Landlubber Ho!* (Auckland: Collins, 1981), 143–44.
342. *Evening Post*, 5 December 1942.
343. *Evening Post*, 26 December 1942.
344. *Auckland Star*, 24 November 1942.

5: THE SECOND PHONEY WAR

1. *Auckland Star*, 24 April 1942.
2. Max Lambert, *Night after Night: New Zealanders in Bomber Command* (Auckland: HarperCollins, 2007), 200, 256.
3. Megan Hutching (ed.), *Against the Rising Sun: New Zealanders remember the Pacific War* (Auckland: HarperCollins, 2006), 82.
4. M.A. Stoler, *Allies and Adversaries: The Joint Chiefs of Staff, the Grand Alliance, and US strategy in World War II* (Chapel Hill: University of North Carolina Press, 2000).
5. H.L. Thompson, *New Zealanders with the Royal Air Force, vol. 2* (Wellington: Department of Internal Affairs, 1956), 256–67.
6. Jim Sullivan (ed.), *Doing Our Bit* (Auckland: HarperCollins, 2002), 66.

7. Neill Atkinson (ed.), *Hell or High Water: New Zealand merchant seafarers remember the war* (Auckland: HarperCollins, 2005), 188.
8. Gordon Ogilvie, *Denis Glover: His life* (Auckland: Godwit, 1999), 195.
9. J.L. McClain, *Japan: A modern history* (New York: W.W. Norton & Co., 2002), 501.
10. Koshiro Yukiko, 'Eurasian eclipse: Japan's endgame in World War II', *American Historical Review*, vol. 109, no. 2, 2004, 428.
11. Ibid., 432.
12. Ibid., 434.
13. James Bertram, *The Shadow of a War: A New Zealander in the Far East 1939–1946* (London: V. Gollancz, 1947), 249.
14. Ibid., 256–57.
15. M. Parillo, *The Japanese Merchant Marine in World War II* (Annapolis: Naval Institute Press, 1993), 242.
16. Gerald Shone, *U-boat in New Zealand Waters* (Auckland: Pahiatua Publications, 2016), 128, 134, 147.
17. *Auckland Star*, 12 December 1944.
18. *Evening Post*, 17 May 1943.
19. M.A. McKinnon, 'The impact of war: Anglo-New Zealand economic diplomacy 1939–1954', PhD thesis, Victoria University of Wellington, 1981, 133.
20. Ibid., 63.
21. J.V.T. Baker, *War Economy: The New Zealand People at War* series (Wellington: Department of Internal Affairs, 1965), 490–93.
22. *New Zealand Herald*, 12 April 1944.
23. I.C. McGibbon (ed.), *Undiplomatic Dialogue: Letters between Carl Berendsen and Alister McIntosh 1943–52* (Auckland: Auckland University Press, 1993), 27.
24. *Auckland Star*, 21 April 1945.
25. Baker, *War Economy*, 481.
26. Ibid., 484–85.
27. Osmar White, *Green Armor* (Sydney: Angus & Robertson, 1945), 188.
28. Ibid., 194.
29. *Evening Post*, 5 December 1942.
30. N.M. Taylor, *The Home Front: The New Zealand People at War* series (Wellington: Department of Internal Affairs, 1986), 712–13.
31. *New Zealand Herald*, 23 December 1942.
32. Taylor, *The Home Front*, 699.
33. *Southland Daily News*, 26 January 1943.
34. *NZPD*, vol. 262, 66, 3 March 1943.
35. Locke, *Gordon Watson*, 180–81.
36. Baker, *War Economy*, 482–83.
37. *Auckland Star*, 23 December 1942.
38. *Star-Sun*, 23 December 1942, quoted in Taylor, *The Home Front*, 714.
39. Taylor, *The Home Front*, 701.
40. Baker, *War Economy*, 486–89.
41. Janet Frame, *An Angel at My Table* (Auckland: Hutchinson of New Zealand, 1984), 36.
42. Lauris Edmond, *Hot October* (Wellington: Bridget Williams Books, 1989), 145.
43. Baker, *War Economy*, 493–95.
44. J.E. Martin, 'The National Service Department and New Zealand's manpower crisis of 1942', in Crawford (ed.), *Kia Kaha: New Zealand in the Second World War* (Auckland: Oxford University Press, 2000), 231.
45. Ibid., 228.
46. Ibid., 230.
47. Ibid., 231.
48. Ibid., 232.
49. Ibid., 233.
50. Baker, *War Economy*, 482–83.
51. Taylor, *The Home Front*, 690.
52. Deborah Montgomerie, *The Women's War: New Zealand women 1939–45* (Auckland: Auckland University Press, 2001), 112.
53. *Bay of Plenty Beacon*, 8 September 1944.
54. Taylor, *The Home Front*, 687.
55. *Auckland Star*, 8 January 1944.
56. Taylor, *The Home Front*, 690, 693.
57. Isobel Andrews, *Something to Tell* (Wellington: Progressive Publishing Society, 1944), 24.
58. Taylor, *The Home Front*, 282.
59. Ibid., 284–85.
60. *Evening Post*, 3 January 1944.
61. *New Zealand Herald*, 3 January 1944.
62. F.L.W. Wood, *Political and External Affairs, The New Zealand People at War* series (Wellington: Department of Internal Affairs, 1958), 280–81.
63. Taylor, *The Home Front*, 1222.
64. *Auckland Star*, 4 April 1944.
65. *Auckland Star*, 24 July 1943.
66. Amartya Sen, *Poverty and Famines* (Oxford: Clarendon Press, 1981), 56.
67. Janam Mukherjee, 'Hungry Bengal: War, famine, riots, and the end of Empire 1939–1946', PhD thesis, University of Michigan, 2011, 225.
68. Sen, *Poverty and Famines*, 79.
69. *Evening Post*, 23 October 1943.
70. *Evening Post*, 8 November 1943.
71. McKinnon, 'The impact of war', 57–59.
72. Ibid., 60.
73. *Auckland Star*, 22 November 1943, quoted in Taylor, *The Home Front*, 827.
74. R.G. Scott, *Dick Scott: A radical writer's life* (Auckland, Reed, 2004), 84.
75. *Evening Post*, 28 August 1943.
76. *Auckland Star*, 2 June 1945.
77. McKinnon, 'The impact of war', 61–62.

78. *Auckland Star*, 17 December 1943.
79. *New Zealand Herald*, 27 December 1943.
80. *Evening Post*, 4 March 1944.
81. *New Zealand Herald*, 10 September 1943.
82. M.M. Dunningham, *Three Brown Bears and the Manpower Man* (Hamilton: Paul's Book Arcade, 1945), n.p.
83. *Auckland Star*, 13 March 1943.
84. Marjorie Paul, *Profit Motive v. Returned Servicemen and Social Security Pensioners* (Auckland: Auckland Service Print, 1945), 8.
85. *Standard*, 1 February 1945.
86. Bee Dawson, *Spreading Their Wings: New Zealand WAAFs in wartime* (Auckland: Penguin, 2004), 65.
87. The factory was so successful that it grew into the preserving company Barker's of Geraldine, which still operates more than seventy years after the end of the war.
88. Helen Black, *Sunshine and Shadow* (Dunedin: John McIndoe, 1947), 283.
89. *Evening Post*, 12 February 1944.
90. Shinya Michiharu, *The Path from Guadalcanal* (Auckland: Outrigger, 1979), 93.
91. *Evening Post*, 3 January 1944.
92. Shinya, *The Path from Guadalcanal*, 93.
93. *Auckland Star*, 21 April 1945.
94. McGibbon, *Undiplomatic Dialogue*, 23–24.
95. Historical Publications Branch, *Documents Relating to New Zealand's Participation in the Second World War 1939–45, vol. 2* (Wellington: Department of Internal Affairs, 1951), 190–91.
96. Taylor, *The Home Front*, 718–19.
97. *Evening Post*, 23 January 1943.
98. Wood, *Political and External Affairs*, 290–91.
99. *Auckland Star*, 28 February 1942.
100. *Auckland Star*, 31 October 1942.
101. *Press*, 14 April 1945.
102. *Auckland Star*, 13 January 1945.
103. Historical Publications Branch, *Documents, vol. 2*, 148, 196.
104. M.P. Lissington, *New Zealand and the United States 1840–1944* (Wellington: Department of Internal Affairs, 1972), 69.
105. Michael Ashby, 'Fraser's foreign policy', in Margaret Clark (ed.), *Peter Fraser: Master politician* (Palmerston North: Dunmore, 1998), 170–71.
106. Quoted in R.S. Thompson, *Empires on the Pacific: World War II and the struggle for the mastery of Asia* (New York: Basic Books, 2001), 255.
107. Quoted in Ashby, 'Fraser's foreign policy', 172–73.
108. *Evening Post*, 22 January 1944.
109. Wood, *Political and External Affairs*, 312.
110. Andrew Stewart, *Empire Lost: Britain, the dominions and the Second World War* (London: Continuum, 2008), 120–22.
111. McGibbon, *Undiplomatic Dialogue*, 65.
112. Ibid., 90.
113. Ibid., 94.
114. Stewart, *Empire Lost*, 123.
115. Ashby, 'Fraser's foreign policy', 173.
116. Wood, *Political and External Affairs*, 317–18.
117. *Auckland Star*, 15 April 1944.
118. *Auckland Star*, 22 May 1943.
119. *Auckland Star*, 26 February 1944.
120. *Auckland Star*, 10 February 1945.
121. *Auckland Star*, 16 June 1945.
122. *Auckland Star*, 15 April 1944.
123. *Auckland Star*, 21 October 1944.
124. Judith Fyfe (ed.), *War Stories Our Mothers Never Told Us* (Auckland: Penguin, 1995), 104.
125. *Evening Post*, 10 April 1943.
126. *Evening Post*, 7 November 1942.
127. *Auckland Star*, 15, 16 March 1943.
128. *Auckland Star*, 19 June 1943.
129. *Evening Post*, 20 October 1945.
130. *Evening Post*, 1 July 1944.
131. *Evening Post*, 15 October 1943.
132. *Evening Post*, 20 May 1944.
133. Dawson, *Spreading Their Wings*, 180.
134. *Evening Post*, 7 November 1942.
135. *Evening Post*, 31 March 1945.
136. Taylor, *The Home Front*, 764–66.
137. *New Zealand Herald*, 14 January 1944.
138. *Auckland Star*, 31 January 1942.
139. *Contact*, July 1942, 63–64. Doris McLean was a journalist on the *New Zealand Woman's Weekly* before joining the air force; under the pseudonym 'Wendy the WAAF' she wrote a regular column in the air force magazine *Contact*.
140. *Auckland Star*, 4 September 1943.
141. *Evening Post*, 18 December 1943.
142. *Auckland Star*, 31 December 1943.
143. *Auckland Star*, 3 January 1944.
144. *New Zealand Herald*, 25 February 1944.
145. *Evening Post*, 13 May 1944.
146. Macmillan Brown Library, accession number MB 857.
147. Les Cleveland, 'Where the heart is', *New Zealand Books*, Winter 2011, 23.
148. *Auckland Star*, 15 January 1944.
149. Ibid., 24 April 1944.
150. Hubert Witheford, *Shadow of the Flame: Poems 1942–7* (Auckland: Pelorus, 1950), 26.
151. *Auckland Star*, 28 November 1942.
152. *Auckland Star*, 26 November 1942.
153. Wood, *Political and External Affairs*, 267.
154. *Auckland Star*, 20 October 1943.

155. Peter Cox, *Good Luck to All the Lads: The wartime story of Brian Cox 1939–43* (Christchurch: J.J. Angerstein, 2008), 120.
156. Wood, *Political and External Affairs*, 270–71.
157. Scott, *Dick Scott*, 64.
158. J.H. Albany, in Jim Henderson (ed.), *Soldier Country* (Wellington: Millwood, 1978), 14.
159. John McLeod, *Myth and Reality: The New Zealand soldier in World War II* (Auckland: Reed Methuen, 1986), 77.
160. Ibid., 78.
161. Ibid., 81.
162. Ibid., 54.
163. Ibid., 26.
164. Guthrie Wilson, *Brave Company* (London: Robert Hale, 1951), 202–03.
165. Gordon Slatter, *A Gun in My Hand* (Christchurch: Pegasus, 1959), 74.
166. *Evening Post*, 15 December 1941.
167. Ibid.
168. Megan Hutching (ed.), *Last Line of Defence: New Zealanders remember the war at home* (Auckland: HarperCollins, 2007), 154.
169. Sullivan, *Doing Our Bit*, 109.
170. *Evening Post*, 29 May 1943.
171. *Bay of Plenty Beacon*, 1 April 1942.
172. *Evening Post*, 17 January 1942.
173. E.M. Lewis, *Joy in the Caring* (Christchurch: N.M. Peryer, 1963), 295.
174. Nell Hartley, *Swagger on Our Doorstep* (Tauranga: Moana Press, 1987), 210.
175. Dawson, *Spreading Their Wings*, 60.
176. *New Zealand Herald*, 5 October 1943.
177. *Evening Post*, 14 November 1942.
178. Dianne Bardsley, *The Land Girls: In a man's world, 1939–1946* (Dunedin: University of Otago Press, 2000), 53.
179. Jane Dare, *Rouseabout Jane: A land girl in New Zealand* (Christchurch: Whitcombe & Tombs, 1956), 116.
180. Ibid., 134.
181. Ibid., 146.
182. Bardsley, *The Land Girls*, 105.
183. Ibid., 132.
184. Ogilvie, *Denis Glover*, 66, 67, 74, 159, 168.
185. *Press*, 9 April 1941.
186. Bardsley, *The Land Girls*, 123.
187. Ibid., 57–62.
188. Dare, *Rouseabout Jane*, 88.
189. Kathleen Hawkins, *The Pup and other poems for parcels*, Tauranga: *Tauranga Times*, c. 1942, 'Sally in the Shed', n.p.
190. *Women at War*, National Film Unit, Wellington, 1941: www.archway.archives.govt.nz/ViewFullItem.do?code=24038371
191. *Evening Post*, 10 January 1942.
192. *Evening Post*, 16 January 1943.
193. Fyfe, *War Stories*, 125.
194. Montgomerie, *The Women's War*, 29–30, 119.
195. Taylor, *The Home Front*, 841.
196. *New Zealand Herald*, 7 August 1942.
197. *Auckland Star*, 27 July 1940.
198. Errol Brathwaite (ed.), *We'll Be Home for Christmas ...* (Christchurch: Caxton, 1994), 256.
199. Quoted in David Gee, *Our Mabel* (Wellington: Millwood, 1977), 67.
200. Montgomerie, *The Women's War*, 18.
201. *Auckland Star*, 31 October 1942.
202. Montgomerie, *The Women's War*, 65.
203. *Evening Post*, 10 January 1942.
204. Montgomerie, *The Women's War*, 87–88.
205. Taylor, *The Home Front*, 1092–93.
206. Montgomerie, *The Women's War*, 29–30.
207. *Evening Post*, 17 January 1942.
208. *Bay of Plenty Beacon*, 1 April 1942.
209. D.O.W. Hall, *Women at War* (Wellington: Department of Internal Affairs, 1948), 31–32.
210. Brathwaite, *We'll Be Home for Christmas*, 121.
211. Anna Rogers, *While You're Away: New Zealand nurses at war 1899–1946* (Auckland: Auckland University Press, 2003), 251.
212. Sullivan, *Doing Our Bit*, 37.
213. Ibid., 133–34.
214. R.L. Seddon, *Whims of a WAAF* (Auckland: Oswald Sealy, 1945), 3.
215. The percentages have been rounded out and hence come to a total less than 100 per cent. Taylor, *The Home Front*, 1113–14.
216. Sullivan, *Doing Our Bit*, 98.
217. McClain, *Japan*, 88.
218. Ibid., 492.
219. German historians have written extensively on the topic; one recent title is Christina Löffler, *Die Rolle und Bedeutung der Frau im Nationalsozialismus: Antifeminismus oder moderne Emanzipationsförderung?* (Saarbrücken: VDM Verlag, 2007). Two accessible publications in English are Claudia Koonz, *Mothers in the Fatherland: Women, the family, and Nazi politics* (New York: St Martin's Press, 1987); Jill Stephenson, *Women in Nazi Germany* (Harlow: Longman, 2001).
220. *Auckland Star*, 27 February 1943.
221. M.E. Hills, *War Poems* (Wellington: Gordon & Gotch, 1943), 5.
222. Gilbert Ward, *The League of the Brown Skirts* (Timaru: G.F. Ward & Co., 1944), 10.
223. Ibid., 26.
224. Ibid., 30.
225. Ibid., 75.
226. *Evening Post*, 28 May 1941.

227. *Dominion*, 9 December 1942.
228. *New Zealand Herald*, 7 August 1942.
229. *Auckland Star*, 15 May 1943.
230. *Auckland Star*, 7 March 1942.
231. *Evening Post*, 23 May 1942.
232. Taylor, *The Home Front*, 1053.
233. O.E. Burton, *The Silent Division* (Sydney: Angus & Robertson, 1935), 24.
234. Clubs Co-operating Committee, *Men–Women Relationships in War Time: A series of four articles* (Wellington: G. Deslandes, 1943), 8.
235. A.J. Greville, *War Days: New Zealand* (Auckland: self-published?, c. 1945), n.p.
236. Martyn Thompson, *Our War – The Grim Digs: New Zealand soldiers in North Africa, 1940–1943* (Auckland: Penguin, 2005), 44.
237. Slatter, *A Gun in My Hand*, 113.
238. Thompson, *Our War*, 265.
239. Ogilvie, *Denis Glover*, 174.
240. E.A. Gornall, *Sex Instruction for the Adolescent Boy and Young Man* (Auckland: Gornall Instructional Publications, 1944).
241. E.H. McCormick (Dennis McEldowney, ed.), *An Absurd Ambition: Autobiographical writings* (Auckland: Auckland University Press, 1996), 175–76.
242. Chris Brickell, *Mates and Lovers: A history of gay New Zealand* (Auckland: Random House/Godwit, 2008), 180.
243. Sullivan, *Doing Our Bit*, 229.
244. Ibid., 232.
245. Ibid., 98.
246. *Waiapu Church Gazette*, 1 July 1943.
247. Winston Sargent, *The Palms Bend Down* (Christchurch: Caxton, 1945), 90, 98–99.
248. Ibid., 213–14.
249. M.D. Whitelaw, *When the Boys Come Home: Marriage, reunion and readjustment after the war* (Blenheim: H. Duckworth, 1943), 9.
250. C.H. Mergendahl, *This Spring of Love* (New York: Doubleday, 1948), 49.
251. Lyndahl Chapple Gee, 'Double Unit', in Elizabeth Webby & Lydia Wevers, *Goodbye to Romance: Stories by New Zealand and Australian women writers 1930–1988* (Wellington: Allen & Unwin, 1988), 52–59.
252. Lauris Edmond (ed.), *New Zealand Love Poems: An Oxford anthology* (Auckland: Oxford University Press, 2001), 180.
253. Frank Sargeson, *The Stories of Frank Sargeson* (Auckland: Penguin, 1982), 294–95.
254. *New Zealand Observer*, 14 March 1943.
255. *Auckland Star*, 8 February 1944.
256. *Evening Post*, 3 April 1943.
257. *Evening Post*, 24 July 1943.
258. *Evening Post*, 9 October 1943.
259. *Waiapu Church Gazette*, 1 November 1943.
260. C.K. Stead (ed.), *Maurice Duggan: Collected stories* (Auckland: Auckland University Press, 1981), 52–56.
261. *NZYB* 1940, Wellington 1940, 94.
262. *NZYB* 1946, Wellington 1946, 44.
263. Motherhood of Man Movement, *Children First is the Motto of the Motherhood of Man Movement* (Auckland: Motherhood of Man Movement, c. 1943), n.p.
264. Dawson, *Spreading Their Wings*, 108.
265. O.M.W. Binswanger, *And How Do You Like this Country? Stories of New Zealand* (Christchurch: Brookes, 1945), 45–56.
266. Sonja Davies, *Bread and Roses* (Auckland: Australia & New Zealand Book Co., 1984), 43.
267. Margaret Sparrow, *Abortion Then and Now: New Zealand abortion stories from 1940 to 1980* (Wellington: Victoria University Press, 2010), 1–3.
268. Denys Trussell, *Fairburn* (Auckland: Auckland University Press, 1984), 214.
269. *Waiapu Church Gazette*, 1 January 1939.
270. *Auckland Star*, 14 September 1940.
271. *Waiapu Church Gazette*, 1 November 1944.
272. Oliver Duff, *New Zealand Now* (Wellington: Department of Internal Affairs, 1941), 35.
273. *Evening Post*, 28 March 1942.
274. *Evening Post*, 23 December 1939.
275. Historical Publications Branch, *Documents, vol. 2*, 402.
276. *Auckland Star*, 31 August 1940.
277. *Evening Post*, 3 January 1940.
278. Thompson, *Our War*, 222.
279. Mason, *Prisoners of War*, 121.
280. P.J. Lineham, 'The religious face of patriotism', in John Crawford (ed.), *Kia Kaha: New Zealand in the Second World War* (Auckland: Oxford University Press, 2000), 202.
281. *Auckland Star*, 31 January 1942.
282. Lineham, 'The religious face of patriotism', 208–09.
283. Ibid.
284. Dorothy Butler, *There Was a Time* (Auckland: Penguin, 1999), 170.
285. Slatter, *A Gun in My Hand*, 202.
286. Thompson, *Our War*, 233.
287. Lawrence Watt, *Mates and Mayhem: World War II: Frontline Kiwis remember* (Auckland: HarperCollins, 1996), 145.
288. McDonald, *The Pitcher and the Well*, 81.
289. A.P. Gaskell, *All Part of the Game* (Auckland: Auckland University Press, 1978), 100–06.
290. Scott, *Dick Scott*, 60.
291. *Bay of Plenty Beacon*, 4 February 1944.
292. *Evening Post*, 9 December 1939.

293. *Evening Post*, 7 March 1942.
294. *Auckland Star*, 11 September 1940.
295. *Auckland Star*, 8 November 1940.
296. *New Zealand Herald*, 12 July 1941.
297. A.B. McDiarmid, *Totalitarianism and Christianity* (Wellington: G. Deslandes, 1941), 18–19.
298. Edith Moore, *No Friend of Democracy* (Auckland: Lee's Weekly, c. 1945), 12.
299. *Evening Post*, 30 March 1942.
300. *Evening Post*, 18 December 1942.
301. *Auckland Star*, 12 April 1943.
302. Ann Beaglehole, 'Refugees from Nazi Germany and Austria 1933–45', in J.N. Bade (ed.), *Out of the Shadow of War: The German connection with New Zealand in the twentieth century* (Melbourne: Oxford University Press, 1998), 33.
303. *Evening Post*, 27 May 1944.
304. www.teara.govt.nz/en/biographies/4s13/schramm-bernardina-adriana
305. Edmond, *Hot October*, 215.
306. *Evening Post*, 30 September 1944.
307. *Evening Post*, 1 June 1945.
308. *Auckland Star*, 7 April 1945.
309. *Evening Post*, 22 June 1945.
310. McKinnon, *The Broken Decade*, 165.
311. Michael King, *Te Puea: A life* (Auckland: Reed, 2003), 230–31.
312. Ibid., 232.
313. *Auckland Star*, 25 February 1942.
314. Quoted in Claudia Orange, 'The price of citizenship? The Maori War Effort', in Crawford (ed.), *Kia Kaha*, 241.
315. Claudia Orange, 'An exercise in Maori autonomy: The rise and demise of the Maori War Effort Organization', *NZJH*, vol. 21, no. 1 (1987), 159.
316. *Auckland Star*, 15 September 1944.
317. *New Zealand Herald*, 23 March 1945.
318. Orange, 'An exercise in Maori autonomy', 161.
319. Ibid., 162.
320. Dick Scott, *Years of the Pooh-Bah: A Cook Islands history* (Rarotonga & Auckland: Hodder & Stoughton, 1991), 227.
321. Ibid., 229.
322. *New Zealand Herald*, 18 October 1944.
323. *Bay of Plenty Beacon*, 16 January 1942.
324. *Waiapu Church Gazette*, 1 October 1945.
325. *Bay of Plenty Beacon*, 14 March 1944.
326. *Auckland Star*, 8 August 1942.
327. *Bay of Plenty Beacon*, 29 October 1943.
328. *New Zealand Herald*, 23 March 1945.
329. *Auckland Star*, 16 October 1944.
330. *Auckland Star*, 4 November 1944.
331. *Auckland Star*, 20 June 1944.
332. J.R. Cole, *It Was So Late, and other stories* (Christchurch: Caxton, 1949), 24–28.
333. *Auckland Star*, 13 November 1943.
334. *Evening Post*, 7 May 1941.
335. This sum is in floating pounds sterling, not in pounds sterling indexed to one particular year. *Evening Post*, 8 September 1945.
336. Baker, *War Economy*, 258–59.
337. Taylor, *The Home Front*, 156.
338. *Ellesmere Guardian*, 31 May 1940.
339. *Evening Post*, 10 July 1943.
340. *Auckland Star*, 18 September 1943.
341. *New Zealand Herald*, 31 July 1944.
342. Taylor, *The Home Front*, 153–54.
343. W.H. Scotter, *A History of Canterbury, vol. III: 1876–1950* (Christchurch: Canterbury Centennial Historical and Literary Committee, 1965), 450.
344. *Bay of Plenty Beacon*, 13 March 1942.
345. *Evening Post*, 3 July 1943.
346. *Evening Post*, 8 September 1945.
347. *Evening Post*, 28 March 1942.
348. *Evening Post*, 4 April 1942.
349. *Evening Post*, 6 June 1942.
350. *Star-Sun*, 4 June 1942.
351. Greymouth bought bonds worth £56,826; Westport £9,998. *Evening Post*, 4 April 1942.
352. *Evening Post*, 12 June 1943.
353. *Ellesmere Guardian*, 22 September 1944.
354. Paul Goldsmith & Michael Bassett, *The Myers* (Auckland: David Ling, 2007), 174.
355. *Auckland Star*, 17 October 1942.
356. *Evening Post*, 27 October 1941, 25 February 1942.
357. *Evening Post*, 7 August 1943.
358. *Auckland Star*, 6 October 1943.
359. *Evening Post*, 14 December 1945.
360. *Evening Post*, 8 September 1945.
361. 110 shillings were £5½.
362. *Evening Post*, 1 July 1943.
363. McGibbon, *Undiplomatic Dialogue*, 34.
364. *Auckland Star*, 24 September 1943.
365. *New Zealand Herald*, 24 September 1943.
366. *Auckland Star*, 23 September 1943.
367. Edmond, *Hot October*, 119.
368. *Ellesmere Guardian*, 27 August 1943.
369. *Evening Post*, 28 August 1943.
370. *Hutt News*, 3 February 1943.
371. *Bay of Plenty Beacon*, 26 April 1944.
372. *Auckland Star*, 18 September 1943.
373. *Evening Post*, 24 July 1943.
374. *Evening Post*, 15 May 1943.
375. *Evening Post*, 28 August 1943.
376. *Evening Post*, 11 September 1943.
377. *Evening Post*, 29 September 1943.
378. *Auckland Star*, 25 September 1943.

379. *Standard*, quoted in *Evening Post*, 29 September 1943.
380. *Press*, 27 September 1943.
381. Keith Sinclair, *Walter Nash* (Auckland: Auckland University Press, 1976), 238–39.
382. *Evening Post*, 21 March 1942.
383. Real GNP, taking into account inflation, during the same three years grew by 4.8 per cent, 10.6 per cent and 10.6 per cent. Statistics New Zealand: www.stats.govt.nz/methods_and_services/access-data/tables/long-term-data-series/national-income.aspx, table-e1-2-1
384. Taylor, *The Home Front*, 1290–91.
385. Quoted in Keith Sinclair & W.F. Mandle, *Open Account: A history of the Bank of New South Wales in New Zealand, 1861–1961* (Wellington: Whitcombe & Tombs, 1961), 207.
386. Statistics New Zealand: www.stats.govt.nz/methods_and_services/access-data/tables/long-term-data-series/national-income.aspx, table-e1-2-1
387. Taylor, *The Home Front*, 428–29.
388. *New Zealand Herald*, 15 October 1942.
389. *Evening Post*, 3 March 1944.
390. *Press*, 19 January 1944.
391. *Bay of Plenty Beacon*, 13 March 1942.
392. *New Zealand Herald*, 22 September 1942.
393. *New Zealand Herald*, 30 December 1944.
394. *Evening Post*, 3 March 1944.
395. *Auckland Star*, 30 January 1942.
396. *Auckland Star*, 17 January 1942.
397. *Evening Post*, 9 April 1942.
398. *Evening Post*, 15 September 1942.
399. *Auckland Star*, 15 September 1942.
400. *Evening Post*, 21 March 1942.
401. *Auckland Star*, 24 February 1944.
402. *Auckland Star*, 30 January 1945.
403. Marshall, *Memoirs*, 95.
404. *Evening Post*, 14 July 1945.
405. Ibid.
406. *Evening Post*, 31 July 1945.
407. *Auckland Star*, 1 April 1944.
408. *Waiapu Church Gazette*, 1 August 1944.
409. *Evening Post*, 14 July 1945.
410. *Evening Post*, 30 June 1945.
411. *Evening Post*, 3 August 1945.
412. *Auckland Star*, 29 March 1944.
413. *New Zealand Herald*, 3 April 1944.
414. *Auckland Star*, 1 April 1944.
415. *New Zealand Herald*, 16 March 1944.
416. *Evening Post*, 13 April 1944.

6: VICTORY?

1. *Star-Sun*, 8 May 1945.
2. *Press*, 11 May 1945.
3. *Auckland Star*, 10 May 1945.
4. *Waiapu Church Gazette*, 1 June 1945.
5. Jim Sullivan (ed.), *Doing Our Bit* (Auckland: HarperCollins, 2002), 61.
6. *Press*, 10 May 1945.
7. *Evening Post*, 8 May 1945.
8. *Press*, 11 May 1945.
9. *Evening Post*, 2 May 1945.
10. *Evening Post*, 26 May 1945.
11. *Evening Post*, 11 May 1945.
12. *Evening Post*, 21 July 1945.
13. *Evening Post*, 4 August 1945.
14. *Evening Post*, 17 August 1945.
15. Lachie McDonald, *Bylines: Memoirs of a war correspondent* (East Roseville: Kangaroo Press, 1998), 59–60.
16. James Bertram, *The Shadow of a War: A New Zealander in the Far East 1939–1946* (London: V. Gollancz, 1947), 257.
17. Ienaga Saburo, *Japan's Last War: World War II and the Japanese, 1931–1945* (Canberra: Australian National University Press, 1979), 200.
18. Robin Kay (ed.), *Documents on New Zealand External Relations, vol. II: The surrender and occupation of Japan* (Wellington: Department of Internal Affairs, 1982), 27.
19. J.L. McClain, *Japan: A modern history* (New York: W.W. Norton & Co., 2002), 511–12.
20. Neill Atkinson (ed.), *Hell or High Water: New Zealand merchant seafarers remember the war* (Auckland: HarperCollins, 2005), 96.
21. Keith Newman, *Ratana the Prophet* (Auckland: Penguin, 2009), 103.
22. *Evening Post*, 14 August 1945.
23. *Evening Post*, 16 August 1945.
24. *Press*, 16 August 1945.
25. *Press*, 17 August 1945.
26. *Evening Post*, 18 August 1945.
27. *New Zealand Memories*, no. 109, 2014, 19.
28. *Evening Post*, 16 August 1945.
29. Jock Phillips, 'New Zealand celebrates victory', in John Crawford (ed.), *Kia Kaha: New Zealand in the Second World War* (Auckland: Oxford University Press, 2000), 315.
30. *Evening Post*, 20 August 1945.
31. *Auckland Star*, 21 August 1945.
32. Atkinson (ed.), *Hell or High Water*, 263.
33. *Evening Post*, 16 August 1945.
34. Errol Brathwaite (ed.), *We'll Be Home for Christmas …* (Christchurch: Caxton, 1994), 253.

35. McClain, *Japan*, 513.
36. *NZPD* 1945, vol. 272, 368, quoted in Owen Wilkes, 'New Zealand and the atom bomb', in Crawford (ed.), *Kia Kaha*, 270.
37. *Auckland Star*, 22 August 1945.
38. *Auckland Star*, 13 August 1945.
39. *Auckland Star*, 18 August 1945.
40. P.J. Lineham, 'The religious face of patriotism', in Crawford (ed.), *Kia Kaha*, 207.
41. *Evening Post*, 20 August 1945.
42. *Press*, 11 August 1945.
43. Ibid.
44. Ibid.
45. Ibid.
46. Ibid.
47. Quoted in Wilkes, 'New Zealand and the atom bomb', 269–70.
48. *New Zealand Tablet*, 15 August 1945.
49. *New Zealand Tablet*, 29 August 1945.
50. Nicholas Reid, *James Michael Liston: A life* (Wellington: Victoria University Press, 2006), 215.
51. *Ellesmere Guardian*, 28 September 1945.
52. *Evening Post*, 10 September 1945.
53. A.F. Ellis, *Mid-Pacific Outposts* (Auckland: Brown & Stewart, 1946), 54.
54. Megan Hutching (ed.), *Last Line of Defence: New Zealanders remember the war at home* (Auckland: HarperCollins, 2007), 218.
55. *Ellesmere Guardian*, 31 July 1945.
56. *Waiapu Church Gazette*, 1 September 1942.
57. New Zealand Educational Institute, *Wealth: Reconstruction in primary education* (Wellington: New Zealand Educational Institute, 1944).
58. C.E. Phillips, *The People's Plan for a New Order* (Auckland: Unity Press, 1942).
59. *Auckland Star*, 27 July 1945.
60. C.K. Guy, *Women on the Home Front* (Wellington: Progressive Publishing Society, 1943), 19.
61. A.R.D. Fairburn, *Hands off the Tom Tom* (Wellington: Progressive Publishing Company, 1944), 15.
62. *Auckland Star*, 13 December 1945.
63. F.L.W. Wood, *Political and External Affairs: The New Zealand People at War* series (Wellington: Department of Internal Affairs, 1958), 308.
64. New Zealand GDP during the 1938 financial year was $16,989 m when figures are converted to a base of $NZ in the year 2000, and had grown to $25,549 m by the 1946 financial year: www.stats.govt.nz/methods_and_services/access-data/tables/long-term-data-series/national-income.aspx - e1–2, column AK
65. J.C. Irving, *A Century's Challenge: Wright, Stephenson & Co., Limited, 1861–1961* (Wellington: Wright Stephenson & Co., 1961), 189.
66. C.W. Vennell, *Risks and Rewards: A policy of enterprise* (Auckland: South British Insurance, 1972), 159.
67. Ibid., 233–34.
68. M.A. McKinnon, 'The impact of war: Anglo-New Zealand economic diplomacy 1939–1954', PhD thesis, Victoria University of Wellington, 1981, 138.
69. Ibid., 157–58.
70. Jim McAloon, *Judgements of all Kinds: Economic policy-making in New Zealand 1945–1984* (Wellington: Victoria University Press, 2013), 70.
71. Ibid., 66–69.
72. J.B. Condliffe, *The Welfare State in New Zealand* (London: Allen & Unwin, 1959), 94.
73. J.V.T. Baker, *War Economy: The New Zealand People at War* series (Wellington: Department of Internal Affairs, 1965), 77.
74. Phil Briggs, 'Looking at the numbers: A view of New Zealand's economic history' (Wellington: New Zealand Institute of Economic Research, 2007), 52.
75. Ibid.
76. N.M. Taylor, *The Home Front: The New Zealand People at War* series (Wellington: Department of Internal Affairs, 1986), 1287.
77. McKinnon, 'The impact of war', 67–68.
78. Ibid., xviii.
79. John Charmley, *Churchill: The end of glory* (London: Hodder & Stoughton, 1993), 355–67.
80. *Auckland Star*, 4 December 1943.
81. Charmley, *Churchill*, 438.
82. Ibid., 443.
83. Robert Boothby, quoted in H.K. Smith, *The State of Europe* (Sydney & London: Angus & Robertson, 1950), 84–85.
84. *Auckland Star*, 15 December 1945.
85. Baker, *War Economy*, 258–59.
86. *Evening Post*, 25 June 1941.
87. John Reece Cole, 'It Was So Late', in Dan Davin (ed.), *New Zealand Short Stories* (Christchurch: Caxton, 1949), 356.
88. Martyn Thompson, *Our War – The Grim Digs: New Zealand soldiers in North Africa, 1940–1943* (Auckland: Penguin, 2005), 60.
89. Brathwaite (ed.), *We'll Be Home for Christmas*, 268.
90. Brian Easton, 'Fraser and the development of the nation-building state', in Margaret Clark (ed.), *Peter Fraser: Master politician* (Palmerston North: Dunmore, 1998), 121.
91. John McLeod, *Myth and Reality: The New Zealand soldier in World War II* (Auckland: Reed Methuen, 1986), 105.

92. Guthrie Wilson, *Sweet White Wine* (London: Hale, 1956), 64.
93. Quoted in Matthew Wright, *Pacific War: New Zealand and Japan 1941–45* (Auckland: Reed, 2003), 120.
94. Tony Vercoe, *Yesterday's Drums: Echoes from the wasteland of war* (Wellington: Steele Roberts, 1996), 99–100.
95. B.J.C. McKercher, *Transition of Power: Britain's loss of global pre-eminence to the United States, 1930–1945* (New York: Cambridge University Press, 1999), 343.
96. Charmley, *Churchill*, 558.
97. Megan Hutching (ed.), *Against the Rising Sun: New Zealanders remember the Pacific War* (Auckland: HarperCollins, 2006), 158.
98. Tony Williams (ed.), *Anzacs: Stories from New Zealanders at war* (Auckland: Hodder Moa Beckett, 2000), 186–87.
99. Alison Parr, *Home: Civilian New Zealanders remember the Second World War* (Auckland: Penguin, 2010), 65.
100. Guthrie Wilson, *Brave Company* (London: Robert Hale, 1951), 131.
101. W.W. Mason, *Prisoners of War* (Wellington: Department of Internal Affairs, 1954), 373.
102. Jim Sullivan (ed.), *Doing Our Bit: New Zealand women tell their stories of World War Two* (Auckland: HarperCollins, 2002), 231.
103. T.D.M. Stout, *War Surgery and Medicine* (Wellington: Department of Internal Affairs, 1954), 748.
104. Ibid., 751.
105. Ibid., 750.
106. Sullivan, *Doing Our Bit*, 200.
107. Ibid., 47.
108. J.B. McKinney, 'Wounded in battle', in *Episodes and Studies, vol. 1* (Wellington: Department of Internal Affairs, 1948), 30.
109. Mason, *Prisoners of War*, 202.
110. D.O.W. Hall, 'Prisoners of Italy', in *Episodes and Studies, vol. 1*, 25–26.
111. Mason, *Prisoners of War*, 388.
112. P. Grey & S. Grey, *Private J.D. Caves: The long journey home*, (Auckland: Paul & Sally Grey, 2004), 108.
113. *Auckland Star*, 21 September 1945.
114. Stout, *War Surgery and Medicine*, 761.
115. A.G. Hayter, *The Second Step* (London: Hodder & Stoughton, 1962), 173.
116. Gordon Slatter, *A Gun in My Hand* (Christchurch: Pegasus, 1959), 128.
117. Thompson, *Our War*, 219.
118. Vercoe, *Yesterday's Drums*, 52.
119. J.H. Henderson, *Gunner Inglorious* (Wellington: Whitcombe & Tombs, 1945), 75.
120. Brian Cull & Paul Sortehaug, *Hurricanes over Singapore* (London: Grub Street, 2004), 73.
121. Wilson, *Brave Company*, 91–92.
122. Lauris Edmond, *Hot October* (Wellington: Bridget Williams Books, 1989), 173.
123. Nancy Ellison, *Whirinaki Valley* (Hamilton: Paul's Book Arcade, 1956), 142.
124. McLeod, *Myth and Reality*, 74.
125. Ibid., 81.
126. Stout, *War Surgery and Medicine*, 651.
127. C.M. Bevan-Brown, *War Neurosis: Designed for the guidance of relatives and friends of ex-service men and women* (Christchurch: J.W. Baty, 1945), 4–5.
128. Ibid., 7.
129. Parr, *Home*, 14.
130. Cole, *It Was So Late*, 107.
131. Alison Parr, *Silent Casualties: New Zealand's unspoken legacy of the Second World War* (Auckland: Penguin, 2010), 120.
132. Ibid., 121.
133. J.E. Weir, *Collected Poems: James K. Baxter* (Wellington: Oxford University Press, 1979), 42–43.
134. *Rodney and Otamatea Times*, 9 December 1942.
135. *Evening Post*, 5 July 1941.
136. *NZYB* 1946, Wellington 1946, 225.
137. M.I. Lambie, *My Story: Memoirs of a New Zealand nurse* (Christchurch: N.M. Peryer, 1956), 121–22.
138. H.B. Anderson, *The Day's Run* (Christchurch: Caxton, 1977), 264–65.
139. Judith Fyfe (ed.), *War Stories Our Mothers Never Told Us* (Auckland: Penguin, 1995), 107.
140. Hutching, *Against the Rising Sun*, 161.
141. M.D. Whitelaw, *When the Boys Come Home: Marriage, reunion and readjustment after the war* (Blenheim: H. Duckworth, 1943), 8.
142. Quoted in Brathwaite, *We'll Be Home for Christmas*, 215.
143. N.C. McKenna, *Angel in God's Office: My wartime diaries* (Auckland: Tandem, 1996), 17.
144. M.E. Hills, *War Poems* (Wellington: Gordon & Gotch, 1943), 28–29.
145. A.P. Gaskell, *All Part of the Game* (Auckland: Auckland University Press, 1978), 41–50.
146. Michael King, *Frank Sargeson: A life* (Auckland: Auckland University Press, 1995), 208.
147. C.R. Larsen, *Pacific Commandos: New Zealanders and Fijians in Action: A history of Southern Independent Commando and First Commando Fiji Guerillas* (Wellington: Department of Internal Affairs, 1946), 121–22.
148. Quoted in Brathwaite, *We'll be Home for Christmas*, 244–46.

149. Ibid., 176.
150. J.M.S. Ross, *The Assault on Rabaul* (Wellington: Department of Internal Affairs, 1948), 31.
151. Phillip Wilson, *Pacific Star* (Wellington: Alister Taylor, 1976), 177–78.
152. Jörg Friedrich, *Der Brand: Deutschland im Bombenkrieg 1940–1945* (Munich: Propyläen Verlag, 2002).
153. John Dower, *Embracing Defeat: Japan in the aftermath of World War II* (London: W.W. Norton & Co., 1999), 96–97.
154. Ibid., 52.
155. Giles MacDonogh estimates 2.5 million deaths in his book *After the Reich: The brutal history of the Allied occupation* (New York: Basic Books, 2007). The higher figure of nearly 6 million is estimated by James Bacque, *Crimes and Mercies: The fate of German civilians under Allied occupation, 1944–1950* (New York: Little, Brown & Co., 1997).
156. *Evening Post*, 20 October 1945.
157. *Auckland Star*, 6 October 1945.
158. *Evening Post*, 17 November 1945.
159. *NZPD*, vol. 261, 1942, 2.
160. Kay, *Documents, vol. II,* 44.
161. Ibid., 220–21.
162. Gerald Hensley, *Beyond the Battlefield: New Zealand and its allies 1939–45* (Auckland: Penguin Viking, 2009), 375.
163. Ann Trotter, *New Zealand and Japan 1945–1952: The occupation and the peace treaty* (London: Athlone Press, 1990), 95.
164. James McNeish, *The Sixth Man: The extraordinary life of Paddy Costello* (Auckland: Penguin, 2007), 319.
165. Ibid., 187.
166. Ibid.
167. Ibid., 189–91.
168. Keith Sinclair, *Walter Nash* (Auckland: Auckland University Press, 1976), 223.
169. Wood, *Political and External Affairs*, 320–22.
170. Ibid., 324–25.
171. www.un.org/en/documents/charter/preamble.shtml
172. *Auckland Star*, 7 July 1945.
173. M.A. McKinnon, *Independence and Foreign Policy: New Zealand in the world since 1935* (Auckland: Auckland University Press, 1993), 58–59.
174. Ann Trotter, 'Personality in foreign policy: Sir Carl Berendsen in Washington', *NZJH*, vol. 20, no. 2, 174.
175. I.C. McGibbon (ed.), *Undiplomatic Dialogue: Letters between Carl Berendsen and Alister McIntosh 1943–52* (Auckland: Auckland University Press, 1993), 100.
176. www.massviolence.org/Setif-and-Guelma-May–1945?artpage=3–5
177. Sinclair, *Walter Nash*, 247.
178. *Auckland Star*, 3 November 1945.
179. Kay, *Documents, vol. II*, 228.
180. Robert Aldrich, 'Imperial mise en valeur and mise en scène: Recent works on French colonialism', *Historical Journal*, vol. 45, no. 4, December 2002, 920.
181. *Evening Post*, 29 December 1945.
182. *Press*, 9 May 1945.
183. Peter Duus, untitled review article, *International History Review*, vol. 27, no. 2, June 2005, 419.
184. *Evening Post*, 10 November 1945.
185. *Evening Post*, 17 October 1945.
186. *Evening Post*, 27 October 1945.
187. *Evening Post*, 30 November 1945.
188. McKinnon, *Independence and Foreign Policy*, 51.
189. Kay, *Documents, vol. II*, 47.
190. Michael Bassett & Michael King, *Tomorrow Comes the Song: A life of Peter Fraser* (Auckland: Penguin, 2000), 281–82.
191. T.R.A. Davis & Lydia Davis, *Doctor to the Islands* (London: Michael Joseph, 1955), 52.
192. McKinnon, *Independence and Foreign Policy*, 66.
193. Apirana Ngata, *The Price of Citizenship* (Wellington: Whitcombe & Tombs, 1943), 18.
194. Claudia Orange, 'The price of citizenship? The Maori War Effort', in Crawford (ed.), *Kia Kaha*, 245, 248.
195. www.nzhistory.net.nz/war/maori-and-the-second-world-war/impact
196. Orange, 'The price of citizenship?', 241.
197. Deborah Montgomerie, *Love in Time of War: Letter writing in the Second World War* (Auckland: Auckland University Press, 2005), 13.
198. Bryan Reid, *After the Fireworks: A life of David Ballantyne* (Auckland: Auckland University Press, 2004), 40.
199. M.H. Holcroft, *The Way of a Writer* (Whatamongo Bay: Cape Catley, 1984), 184.
200. Ibid., 183.
201. Wilson, *Brave Company*, 5.
202. Grey & Grey, *Private J.D. Caves*, 85.
203. Vincent O'Sullivan, *Long Journey to the Border: A life of John Mulgan* (Auckland: Penguin, 2003), 255.
204. Wilson, *Brave Company*, 284.
205. *Auckland Star*, 17 October 1942.
206. *Bay of Plenty Beacon*, 22 October 1943.
207. *Star-Sun*, 9 May 1945.

208. H.A.StG. Saunders, *Return at Dawn* (Wellington: Director of Publicity, 1942), n.p.
209. Allen Curnow, *Whim-Wham: Verses 1941–1942* (Christchurch: Caxton, 1942), 26.
210. Timothy Maga, '"Away from Tokyo": The Pacific Islands war crimes trials, 1945–1949', *Journal of Pacific History*, vol. 36, no. 1, 2001, 37.
211. Ibid., 50.
212. Trotter, *New Zealand and Japan*, 82.
213. Takatori Yuki, '"America's" war crimes trial? Commonwealth leadership at the International Military Tribunal for the Far East, 1946–48', *Journal of Imperial and Commonwealth History*, vol. 35, no. 4, 2007, 549–68.
214. C.M. Cameron, 'Race and identity: The culture of combat in the Pacific War', *The International History Review*, vol. 27, no. 3, September 2005, 564.
215. W.A. Schabas & Nadia Bernaz (eds.), *Routledge Handbook of International Criminal Law* (New York: Routledge, 2010), 123.
216. Montgomerie, *Love in Time of War*, 43.
217. J.D. McDonald, *The Pitcher and the Well* (Hamilton: Paul's Book Arcade, 1961), 20.
218. Wilson, *Pacific Star*, 177–78.
219. Parr, *Silent Casualties*, 124.
220. www.hawaii.edu/powerkills/SOD.CHAP6.HTM
221. David McCraw, 'Reluctant ally: New Zealand's entry into the Vietnam War', *NZJH*, vol. 15, no. 1, 1981, 59–60.
222. Roberto Rabel, *New Zealand and the Vietnam War: Politics and diplomacy* (Auckland: Auckland University Press, 2005), 45.
223. Ibid., 86.
224. Ibid., 98.
225. Ibid., 114.
226. *Evening Post*, 31 December 1945.
227. *New Zealand Herald*, 31 December 1945.
228. Gordon Ogilvie, *Denis Glover: His life* (Auckland: Godwit, 1999), 190.
229. Davin, *The Sullen Bell*, 210.
230. Denys Trussell, *Fairburn*, (Auckland: Auckland University Press/Oxford University Press, 1984), 198.
231. Edmond, *Hot October*, 173.
232. Allen Curnow (ed.), *The Penguin Book of New Zealand Verse* (Auckland: Penguin, 1966), 208.

BIBLIOGRAPHY

PRIMARY

Macmillan Brown Library, Christchurch; MB 857.

Archives New Zealand, Wellington; COS, no. 115, EA1, PM 81/4/3, part 3.

Archives New Zealand, Wellington; EA 1, 85/1/22 General 'Japanese plans for the invasion of New Zealand'.

Archives New Zealand, Wellington; Western Samoa Administration, R17709272, 1939–1941.

Archives New Zealand, Wellington; 'Women at war', National Film Unit: www.archway.archives.govt.nz/ViewFullItem.do?code=24038371

BOOKS, ARTICLES AND THESES

Aldrich, Robert, 'Imperial mise en valeur and mise en scène: Recent works on French colonialism', *Historical Journal*, vol. 45, no. 4, 2002, 917–36.

Alley, Rewi, *Yo Banfa!* (Auckland: Pelorus Press, 1976).

Alport, C.J.M., *Kingdoms in Partnership: A study of political change in the British Commonwealth* (London: Lovat Dickson, 1937).

Anderson, H.B., *The Day's Run* (Christchurch: Caxton, 1977).

Andrews, Isobel S., *Something to Tell* (Wellington: Progressive Publishing Society, 1944).

Ashton-Warner, Sylvia, *I Passed This Way* (New York: Knopf, 1979).

Atkinson, Neill (ed.), *Hell or High Water: New Zealand merchant seafarers remember the war* (Auckland: HarperCollins, 2005).

Bacque, James, *Crimes and Mercies: The fate of German civilians under Allied occupation, 1944–1950* (New York: Little, Brown & Co., 1997).

Bade, J.N., 'Count Felix von Luckner's 1938 "propaganda" visit to New Zealand and its consequences', *New Zealand Journal of History*, vol. 35, no. 2, October 2001, 221–37.

Bade, J.N. (ed.), *Out of the Shadow of War: The German connection with New Zealand in the twentieth century* (Melbourne: Oxford University Press, 1998).

Bai, Shouyi, *An Outline History of China* (Beijing: Foreign Languages Press, 2002).

Baker, J.V.T., *War Economy: The New Zealand People at War* series (Wellington: Department of Internal Affairs, 1965).

Ballantyne, David, *The Cunninghams* (Christchurch: Whitcoulls, 1976).

Bardsley, Dianne, *The Land Girls: In a man's world, 1939–1946* (Dunedin: University of Otago Press, 2000).

Barrowman, Rachel, *Mason: The Life of R.A.K. Mason* (Wellington: Victoria University Press, 2003).

——, *A Popular Vision* (Wellington: Victoria University Press, 1991).

Basham, M.R., *Aunt Daisy and Uncle Sam: Aunt Daisy's wartime journey to the United States* (Wellington: Whitcombe & Tombs, 1945).

Bassett, Michael & King, Michael, *Tomorrow Comes the Song: A life of Peter Fraser* (Auckland: Penguin, 2000).

Beaglehole, Tim, *A Life of J.C. Beaglehole: New Zealand scholar* (Wellington: Victoria University Press, 2006).

Belich, James, *Paradise Reforged* (Auckland: Penguin, 2001).

Bennett, J.A., 'Wartime emergency and the displacement of Indians in Fiji: Cost and compensation', *Journal of Pacific History*, vol. 37, no. 2, 2002, 205–19.

Bertram, James M., *The Shadow of a War: A New Zealander in the Far East, 1939–1946* (London: V. Gollancz, 1947).
Bevan-Brown, C.M., *War Neurosis: Designed for the guidance of relatives and friends of ex-service men and women* (Christchurch: J.W. Baty, 1945).
Binswanger, O.M.W., *And How Do You Like this Country? Stories of New Zealand* (Christchurch: Brookes, 1945).
Bioletti, Harry, *The Yanks Are Coming: The American invasion of New Zealand, 1942–1944* (Auckland: Century Hutchinson, 1989).
Black, H.McK., *Sunshine and Shadow* (Dunedin: John McIndoe, 1947).
Bolitho, Hector, *War in the Strand* (London: Eyre & Spottiswoode, 1942).
Boyce, Simon, '"In Spite of Tooley Street, Montagu Norman, and the Reserve Bank's Governor": Recolonization or the eclipse of colonial financial ties with Britain in the 1930s?' *New Zealand Journal of History*, vol. 39, no. 1, April 2005, 75–92.
Brasch, Charles, *Collected Poems* (Auckland: Oxford University Press, 1984).
——, *Indirections: A memoir 1909–1947* (Wellington: Oxford University Press, 1980).
Brathwaite, Errol (ed.), *We'll be Home for Christmas* ... (Christchurch: Caxton, 1994).
Breman, John, 'New thoughts on colonial labour in Indonesia', *Journal of Southeast Asian Studies*, vol. 33, no. 2, 2002, 559–60.
Brickell, Chris, *Mates and Lovers: A history of gay New Zealand* (Auckland: Random House/ Godwit, 2008).
Briggs, Phil, 'Looking at the numbers: A view of New Zealand's economic history' (Wellington: New Zealand Institute of Economic Research, 2007).
Brocheux, Pierre & Daniel Hémery, *Indochine: La colonisation ambiguë, 1858–1954* (Paris: La Découverte, 2001).
Buick-Constable, L.M., *Poet in Khaki* (Wellington: Handcraft, 1940).
Burton, O.E., *The Silent Division* (Sydney: Angus & Robertson, 1935).
Bussemaker, H.T., 'Paradise in peril: The Netherlands, Great Britain and the defence of the Netherlands East Indies, 1940–41', *Journal of Southeast Asian Studies*, vol. 31, no. 1, 2000, 115–36.
Butler, Dorothy, *There Was a Time* (Auckland: Penguin, 1999).
Cameron, C.M., 'Race and identity: The culture of combat in the Pacific War', *International History Review*, vol. 27, no. 3, 2005, 550–66.
Campbell, I.C., *Island Kingdom: Tonga ancient and modern* (Christchurch: Canterbury University Press, 1992).
Carter, D.S., 'The attitude of the New Zealand Communist Party to foreign affairs, 1930–1941', MPhil thesis, University of Auckland, 1981).
Caselberg, John, *Poet Triumphant: The life and writings of R.A.K. Mason (1905–1971)* (Wellington: Steele Roberts, 2004).
Charmley, John, *Churchill: The end of glory* (London: Hodder & Stoughton, 1993).
Chaudron, Gerald, *New Zealand in the League of Nations: The beginnings of an independent foreign policy, 1919–1939* (Jefferson (NC): McFarland & Co., 2012).
Clare, B.G., *Early Operations with Bomber Command* (Wellington: Department of Internal Affairs, 1950).
Clark, Margaret (ed.), *Peter Fraser: Master politician* (Palmerston North: Dunmore, 1998).
Cleveland, Les, *The Songs We Sang* (Wellington: Editorial Services, 1959).
——, 'Where the heart is', *New Zealand Books*, winter 2011, 23).
Clubs Co-operating Committee, *Men–Women Relationships in War Time: A series of four articles* (Wellington: G. Deslandes, 1943).
Cole, J.R., *It Was So Late, and other stories* (Christchurch: Caxton, 1949).
Condliffe, J.B., *The Welfare State in New Zealand* (London: Allen & Unwin, 1959).
Cox, Geoffrey, *Eyewitness: A Memoir of Europe in the 1930s* (Dunedin: University of Otago Press, 1999).
Cox, Peter, *Good Luck to All the Lads: The wartime story of Brian Cox 1939–43* (Christchurch: J.J. Angerstein & Associates, 2008).
Crawford, John, (ed.), *Kia Kaha: New Zealand in the Second World War* (Auckland: Oxford University Press, 2000).
Crawford, John & James Watson, '"The most appeasing line": New Zealand and Nazi Germany, 1935–40', *Journal of Imperial and Commonwealth History*, vol. 38, no. 1, 2010, 75–97.
Cull, Brian with Paul Sortehaug, *Hurricanes over Singapore* (London: Grub Street, 2004).
Curnow, Allen, *Whim-Wham: Verses 1941–1942* (Christchurch: Caxton, 1942).
Curnow, Allen (ed.), *The Penguin Book of New Zealand Verse* (Auckland: Penguin, 1966)
Daly, M.W., (ed.), *The Cambridge History of Egypt, vol. 2* (Cambridge: Cambridge University Press, 1998).
Dare, Jane, *Rouseabout Jane: A land girl in New Zealand* (Christchurch: Whitcombe & Tombs, 1956).

Davies, Sonja, *Bread and Roses* (Auckland: Australia & New Zealand Book Co., 1984).

Davin, Dan, *The Sullen Bell* (London: Michael Joseph, 1956).

Davin, Dan (ed.), *New Zealand Short Stories* (London: Oxford University Press, 1953).

Davis, E.R., *A Link with the Past* (Auckland: Oswald Sealy, 1948).

Davis, T.R.A. & Lydia Davis, *Doctor to the Islands* (London: Michael Joseph, 1955).

Dawson, Bee, *Spreading Their Wings: New Zealand WAAFs in wartime* (Auckland: Penguin, 2004).

Dean, H.R., *The Royal New Zealand Air Force in South-East Asia 1941–42* (Wellington: Department of Internal Affairs, 1952).

Denoon, Donald, Stewart Firth, Jocelyn Linnekin, Malama Meleisea & Karen Nero (eds), *The Cambridge History of the Pacific Islanders* (Cambridge: Cambridge University Press, 1997).

Doig, W.T., *Rich and Poor in New Zealand* (Christchurch: Christchurch Co-operative Book Society, 1942).

Douglas, C.H., *Major C.H. Douglas Speaks* (Sydney: Douglas Social Credit Association, 1933).

Dower, John, *Embracing Defeat: Japan in the aftermath of World War II* (London: W.W. Norton & Co., 1999).

——, *Japan in War and Peace: Essays on history, culture and race* (London: New Press, 1995).

Duff, Oliver, *New Zealand Now* (Wellington: Department of Internal Affairs, 1941).

Dunningham, M.M., *Three Brown Bears and the Manpower Man* (Hamilton: Paul's Book Arcade, 1945).

Duus, Peter, untitled review article, *International History Review*, vol. 27, no. 2, 2005, 419.

Edmond, Lauris, *Hot October* (Wellington: Bridget Williams Books, 1989).

—— (ed.), *The Letters of A.R.D. Fairburn* (Auckland: Oxford University Press, 1981).

—— (ed.), *New Zealand Love Poems: An Oxford anthology* (Auckland: Oxford University Press, 2000).

Eliot, D.R., 'Where the hawk flies', MS, Canterbury Public Library, New Zealand Collection.

Elliott, Keith with Rona Adshead, *From Cowshed to Dogcollar* (Wellington: A.H. & A.W. Reed, 1967).

Ellis, A.F., *Mid-Pacific Outposts* (Auckland: Brown & Stewart, 1946).

Ellison, N.H., *The Whirinaki Valley* (Hamilton: Paul's Book Arcade, 1956).

Episodes and Studies, vol. 1 (Wellington: Department of Internal Affairs, 1948).

Fairburn, A.R.D., *Hands off the Tom Tom* (Wellington: Progressive Publishing Company, 1944).

Fairburn, Miles & Stephen Haslett, 'How far did class determine voting in New Zealand general elections, 1911–1951?' *New Zealand Journal of History*, vol. 39, no. 2, 2005, 215–41.

Feldman, Glenn, *The Disfranchisement Myth: Poor whites and suffrage restriction in Alabama* (Athens (GA): University of Georgia Press, 2004).

Field, A.N., *Today's Greatest Problem* (Nelson: The Examiner, 1938).

Fox, J.W. & K.B. Cumberland, *Western Samoa: Land, life and agriculture in tropical Polynesia* (Christchurch: Whitcombe & Tombs, 1962).

Frame, Janet, *To the Is-land* (London & Auckland: Women's Press/Hutchinson, 1983).

Frei, H.P., *Japan's Southward Advance and Australia: From the sixteenth century to World War II* (Melbourne: Melbourne University Press, 1991).

Friedrich, Jörg, *Der Brand: Deutschland im Bombenkrieg 1940–1945* (Munich: Propyläen Verlag, 2002).

Fry, A.S., *The Aunt Daisy Story* (Wellington: Reed, 1957).

Fyfe, Judith (ed.), *War Stories Our Mothers Never Told Us* (Auckland: Penguin, 1995).

Galt, M.N., 'Wealth and income in New Zealand: c. 1870 to c. 1939', PhD thesis, Victoria University of Wellington, 1985.

Gardiner, Noel, *Freyberg's Circus: Reminiscences of a Kiwi in the North African campaign of World War II* (Auckland: Ray Richards, 1981).

Gaskell, A.P., *All Part of the Game* (Auckland: Auckland University Press, 1978).

Gee, David, *Our Mabel* (Wellington: Millwood, 1977).

Geering, Lloyd, *Wrestling with God: The story of my life* (Wellington: Bridget Williams Books, 2006).

Gillespie, O.A., *The Pacific* (Wellington: Department of Internal Affairs, 1952).

Glover, Denis, *D Day* (Christchurch: Caxton, 1944).

——, *Hot Water Sailor and Landlubber Ho!* (Auckland: Collins, 1981).

Goldman, L.M., *The History of the Jews in New Zealand* (Wellington: Reed, 1958).

Goldsmith, Paul & Michael Bassett, *The Myers* (Auckland: David Ling, 2007).

Gordon, Doris, *Backblocks Baby-Doctor* (London: Faber & Faber, 1956).

Gornall, Edgar A., *Sex Instruction for the Adolescent Boy and Young Man* (Auckland: Gornall Instructional Publications, 1944).

Gould, John, *The Rake's Progress? The New Zealand economy since 1945* (Auckland: Hodder & Stoughton, 1982).

Greville, A.J., *War Days: New Zealand* (Auckland: self-published[?], c. 1945).

Grey, Paul & Sally Grey, *Private J.D. Caves: The long journey home* (Auckland: Paul & Sally Grey, 2004).

Griffith, Penelope, 'Dr Isamu Kawase and the first book on New Zealand in Japanese', *Turnbull Library Record*, vol. 9, no. 1, 1976, 12–17.

Grimwood, A.R., *Flights and Fancies* (Wellington: Hutcheson, Bowman & Johnson, 1943).

Gustafson, Barry, *From the Cradle to the Grave: A biography of Michael Joseph Savage* (Auckland: Penguin, 1988).

——, *The First 50 Years: A history of the New Zealand National Party* (Auckland: Reed Methuen, 1986).

Guy, C.K., *Women on the Home Front* (Wellington: Progressive Publishing Society, 1943).

Hall, D.O.W., *Women at War* (Wellington: Department of Internal Affairs, 1948).

Hamilton, W.I., *Till Human Voices Wake Us* (Auckland: Oxford University Press, 1984).

Hammer, E.J., *The Struggle for Indochina, 1940–1955* (Stanford: Stanford University Press, 1954).

Harrison, Mark, 'Resource mobilization for World War II: The USA, UK, USSR, and Germany, 1938–1945', *Economic History Review*, vol. 41, no. 2, 1988, 171–92.

Hartley, Nell, *Swagger on Our Doorstep* (Tauranga: Moana Press, 1987).

Hastings, J.R., *A Digger's Diary: Ramblings in Egypt with the First Echelon* (Wellington: Organ Bros, 1940).

Havinden, Michael & David Meredith, *Colonialism and Development: Britain and its tropical colonies, 1850–1960* (London: Psychology Press, 1993).

Hawkins, Kathleen, *The Pup and other poems for parcels* (Tauranga: Tauranga Times, c. 1942).

Hayter, Adrian, *The Second Step* (London: Hodder & Stoughton, 1962).

Hellman, John, *The Knight-monks of Vichy France: Uriage, 1940–1945* (Montreal & Kingston: McGill-Queen's University Press, 1997).

Henderson, J.H., *Gunner Inglorious* (Wellington: Whitcombe & Tombs, 1945).

—— (ed.), *Soldier Country* (Wellington: Millwood, 1978).

Hensley, Gerald, *Beyond the Battlefield: New Zealand and its allies 1939–45* (Auckland: Penguin Viking, 2009).

Hills, M.E., *War Poems* (Wellington: Gordon & Gotch, 1943).

Hirst, David & Irene Beeson, *Sadat* (London: Faber & Faber, 1981).

Historical Publications Branch, *Documents Relating to New Zealand's Participation in the Second World War 1939–45, vol. 1* (Wellington: Department of Internal Affairs, 1949).

Historical Publications Branch, *Documents Relating to New Zealand's Participation in the Second World War 1939–45, vol. 2* (Wellington: Department of Internal Affairs, 1951).

Historical Publications Branch, *Documents Relating to New Zealand's Participation in the Second World War 1939–45, vol. 3* (Wellington: Department of Internal Affairs, 1963).

Holcroft, M.H., *The Way of a Writer* (Whatamango Bay: Cape Catley, 1984).

Howlett, R.A., *The History of the Fiji Military Forces 1939–1945* (London: Crown Agents for the Colonies, 1948).

Hudson, Charlotte, *Seawrack and Moonbeams* (Christchurch: Hazard, 2005).

Hutching, Megan (ed.), *Against the Rising Sun: New Zealanders remember the Pacific War* (Auckland: HarperCollins, 2006).

—— (ed.), *Last Line of Defence: New Zealanders remember the war at home* (Auckland: HarperCollins, 2007).

Ienaga, Saburo, *Japan's Last War: World War II and the Japanese, 1931–1945* (Canberra: Australian National University Press, 1979).

Ike, Nobutaka, *Japan's Decision for War: Records of the 1941 Policy Conferences* (Stanford: Stanford University Press, 1967).

Institute of Pacific Studies (ed.), *Niue: A history of the island* (Niue: Institute of Pacific Studies, 1982).

Irving, J.C., *A Century's Challenge: Wright, Stephenson & Co., Limited, 1861–1961* (Wellington: Wright Stephenson & Co., 1961).

Iriye, Akira, *The Origins of the Second World War in Asia and the Pacific* (London & New York: Longman, 1987).

Jansen, E.G., *Jade Engraved* (Christchurch & Dunedin: Presbyterian Bookroom, 1947).

Jenkins, D.R., *Social Attitudes in the New Zealand School Journal* (Wellington: New Zealand Council for Educational Research, 1939).

Johnston, K.M., *Village Agriculture in Aitutaki, Cook Islands* (Wellington: Dept of Geography, Victoria University of Wellington, 1967).

Johnston, R.W., *Follow Me: The story of the Second Marine Division in World War II* (New York: Random House, 1948).

Kater, M.H., 'Forbidden fruit? Jazz in the Third Reich', *American Historical Review*, vol. 94, no. 1, 1989, 11–43.

Kay, Robin (ed.), *Documents on New Zealand External Relations, vol. II: The surrender and occupation of Japan* (Wellington: Department of Internal Affairs, 1982).

Kennedy, Greg, *Anglo-American Strategic Relations and the Far East 1933–1939* (London & Portland: Frank Cass, 2002).

Kennedy, Paul, *The Rise and Fall of the Great Powers* (London: Random House, 1989).

King, Michael, *Frank Sargeson: A life* (Auckland: Auckland University Press, 1995).

——, *Te Puea: A life* (Auckland: Reed, 2003).

Koonz, Claudia. *Mothers in the Fatherland: Women, the family, and Nazi politics* (New York: St Martin's Press, 1987).

Koshiro, Yukiko, 'Eurasian eclipse: Japan's end game in World War II', *American Historical Review*, vol. 109, no. 2, 2004, 417–44.

Kudaisya, Gyanesh, '"In aid of civil power": The colonial army in northern India, c. 1919–42', *Journal of Imperial and Commonwealth History*, vol. 32, no. 1, 2004, 41–68.

Lambert, Max, *Night after Night: New Zealanders in Bomber Command* (Auckland: HarperCollins, 2007).

Lambie, M.I., *My Story: Memoirs of a New Zealand nurse* (Christchurch: N.M. Peryer, 1956).

Larsen, C.R., *Pacific Commandos: New Zealanders and Fijians in Action: A history of Southern Independent Commando and First Commando Fiji Guerillas* (Wellington: Department of Internal Affairs, 1946).

Lary, Diana, *The Chinese People at War: Human suffering and social transformation, 1937–1945*, vol. 6 (Cambridge: Cambridge University Press, 2010).

Lee, John A., *The John A. Lee Diaries 1936–40* (Christchurch: Whitcoulls, 1981).

Lewis, E.M., *Joy in the Caring* (Christchurch: N.M. Peryer, 1963).

Lissington, M.P., *New Zealand and Japan 1900–1941* (Wellington: Department of Internal Affairs, 1972).

——, *New Zealand and the United States 1840–1944* (Wellington: Department of Internal Affairs, 1972).

Locke, Elsie (ed.), *Gordon Watson, New Zealander: 1912–45* (Auckland: Forward Press, 1949).

Löffler, Christina, *Die Rolle und Bedeutung der Frau im Nationalsozialismus: Antifeminismus oder moderne Emanzipationsförderung?* (Saarbrücken: VDM Verlag, 2007).

Lu, D.J., *Agony of Choice: Matsuoka Yōsuke and the rise and fall of the Japanese Empire, 1880–1946* (Washington: Rowman & Littlefield, 2002).

Macdonald, Joyce, *Away from Home* (Christchurch: Bookroom, 1945).

McAloon, Jim, *Judgements of all Kinds: Economic policy-making in New Zealand 1945–1984* (Wellington: Victoria University Press, 2013).

McClain, J.L., *Japan: A modern history* (New York: W.W. Norton & Co., 2002).

McCormick, E.H. (Dennis McEldowney, ed.), *An Absurd Ambition: Autobiographical writings* (Auckland: Auckland University Press, 1996).

McCraw, David, 'Reluctant ally: New Zealand's entry into the Vietnam War', *New Zealand Journal of History*, 1981, vol. 15, no. 1, 49–60.

McDiarmid, A.B., *Totalitarianism and Christianity* (Wellington: G. Deslandes, 1941).

MacDonogh, Giles, *After the Reich: The brutal history of the Allied occupation* (New York: Basic Books, 2007).

McDonald, Donald, *Sidi Reszegh and other verses* (Wellington: Progressive Publishing, 1944).

McDonald, J.D., *The Pitcher and the Well* (Hamilton: Paul's Book Arcade, 1961).

McDonald, Lachie, *Bylines: Memoirs of a war correspondent* (East Roseville: Kangaroo Press, 1998).

McGibbon, Ian, *Blue-water Rationale: The naval defence of New Zealand 1914–1942* (Wellington: Department of Internal Affairs, 1981).

——, *New Zealand and the Second World War: The people, the battles and the legacy* (Auckland: Penguin, 2003).

—— (ed.), *Undiplomatic Dialogue: Letters between Carl Berendsen and Alister McIntosh, 1943–52* (Auckland: Auckland University Press, 1993).

McIntyre, David W., *New Zealand Prepares for War: Defence policy 1919–39* (Christchurch: University of Canterbury Press, 1988).

McKenna, N.C., *Angel in God's Office: My wartime diaries* (Auckland: Tandem, 1996).

McKercher, B.J.C., *Transition of Power: Britain's loss of global pre-eminence to the United States, 1930–1945* (New York: Cambridge University Press, 1999).

McKinnon, Malcolm, *The Broken Decade: Prosperity, depression and recovery in New Zealand, 1928–1939* (Dunedin: Otago University Press, 2016).

——, 'The impact of war: Anglo-New Zealand economic diplomacy 1939–1954', PhD thesis, Victoria University of Wellington, 1981.

——, *Independence and Foreign Policy: New Zealand in the world since 1935* (Auckland: Auckland University Press, 1993).

McLeod, John, *Myth and Reality: The New Zealand soldier in World War II* (Auckland: Reed Methuen, 1986).

McNeish, James, *The Sixth Man: The extraordinary life of Paddy Costello* (Auckland: Penguin, 2007).
Maga, Timothy, '"Away From Tokyo": The Pacific Islands war crimes trials, 1945–1949', *Journal of Pacific History*, vol. 36, no. 1, 2001, 37–50.
Marsh, Ngaio, *Died in the Wool* (London: Collins, 1944).
Marshall, John, *Memoirs, vol. 1: 1912 to 1960* (Auckland: Collins, 1983).
Martin, D.M., *The War Behind the War* (Christchurch: Left Book Club, 1940).
Mason, R.A.K., *Frontier Forsaken: An outline history of the Cook Islands* (Auckland: Auckland Labourers Union, 1947).
Mason, W.W., *Prisoners of War* (Wellington: Department of Internal Affairs, 1954).
Matangi Tokelau: History and Traditions of Tokelau (Apia: Office for Tokelau Affairs, 1991).
Megaw, M.R., 'The scramble for the Pacific: Anglo-United States rivalry in the 1930s', *Historical Studies*, vol. 17, 1977, 458–73.
Melrose, T.H., *Sound the Tocsin: Japanese menace* (Hamilton: Waikato Times, 1942).
Mergendahl, C.H., *This Spring of Love* (New York: Doubleday, 1948).
Michener, James A., *Return to Paradise* (New York: Random House, c. 1951).
Milner, I.F.G., *New Zealand's Interests and Policies in the Far East* (New York: Institute of Pacific Relations, 1940).
Mitchell, L.C., *The Book of the Guard* (Wellington: Coulls Somerville Wilkie, 1943).
Montgomerie, Deborah, 'GI Joe down under: American infantrymen in New Zealand during World War II', *New Zealand Journal of History*, vol. 34, no. 2, 2000, 262–76.
——, *Love in Time of War: Letter writing in the Second World War* (Auckland: Auckland University Press, 2005).
——, *The Women's War: New Zealand women 1939–45* (Auckland: Auckland University Press, 2001).
Moore, Edith, *No Friend of Democracy* (Auckland: Lee's Weekly, c. 1945).
Morley, J.W. (ed.), *Japan's Foreign Policy 1868–1941: A research guide* (New York: Columbia University Press, 1974).
Motherhood of Man Movement, *Children First is the Motto of the Motherhood of Man Movement* (Auckland: Motherhood of Man Movement, c. 1943).
Naanen, Ben, '"You are demanding tax from the dead": The introduction of direct taxation and its aftermath in South-Eastern Nigeria, 1928–39', *African Economic History*, vol. 34, 2006, 69–102.
New Zealand Educational Institute, *Wealth: Reconstruction in primary education* (Wellington: New Zealand Educational Institute, 1944).
Newman, Keith, *Ratana the Prophet* (Auckland: Penguin, 2009).
Newnham, T.O., *He Mingqing: The life of Kathleen Hall* (Beijing: New World Press, 1992).
Ngata, A.T., *The Price of Citizenship: Ngarimu V.C.* (Wellington: Whitcombe & Tombs, 1943).
Nish, Ian, *Japanese Foreign Policy in the Interwar Period* (Westport & London: Praeger, 2002).
Ogilvie, Gordon, *Denis Glover: His life* (Auckland: Godwit, 1999).
Ooka, Shohei (Ivan Morris, trans.), *Fires on the Plain* (London: Corgi, 1980).
Orange, Claudia, 'An exercise in Maori autonomy: The rise and demise of the Maori War Effort Organisation', *New Zealand Journal of History*, vol. 21, no. 1, 1987, 156–72.
O'Sullivan, Vincent, *Long Journey to the Border: A life of John Mulgan* (Auckland: Penguin, 2003).
Parillo, M.P., *The Japanese Merchant Marine in World War II* (Annapolis: Naval Institute Press, 1993).
Parr, Alison, *Home: Civilian New Zealanders remember the Second World War* (Auckland: Penguin, 2010).
——, *Silent Casualties: New Zealand's unspoken legacy of the Second World War* (Auckland: Tandem, 1995).
Peacocke, Isabel M., *April, May, June* (London: Ward, Lock & Co., 1943).
Pearson, Bill, 'Beginnings and endings', *Sport* 5, spring 1990: www.nzetc.org/tm/scholarly/tei-Ba05Spo-_div1-N10638.html
Peren, Roger (ed.), *Japan and New Zealand: 150 Years* (Palmerston North: Massey University, 1999).
Phillips, C.E., *The People's Plan for a New Order* (Auckland: Unity Press, 1942).
Rabel, Roberto, *New Zealand and the Vietnam War: Politics and diplomacy* (Auckland: Auckland University Press, 2005).
Reid, Bryan, *After the Fireworks: A life of David Ballantyne* (Auckland: Auckland University Press, 2004).
Reid, Nicholas, *James Michael Liston: A life* (Wellington: Victoria University Press, 2006).
Reynolds, David, 'From world war to cold war: The wartime alliance and post-war transitions, 1941–1947', *Historical Journal*, vol. 45, no. 1, 2002, 211–27.
Rogers, Anna, *While You're Away: New Zealand nurses at war 1899–1946* (Auckland: Auckland University Press, 2003).

Ross, Angus (ed.), *New Zealand's Record in the Pacific Islands in the Twentieth Century* (London & New York: Longman Paul, 1969).

Ross, J.M.S., *The Assault on Rabaul* (Wellington: Department of Internal Affairs, 1948).

Sale, E.V., *Shovel, Sword and Scalpel: A record of service of medical units of the Second New Zealand Expeditionary Force in the Pacific* (Wellington: Department of Internal Affairs, 1945).

Sargent, Winston, *The Palms Bend Down* (Christchurch: Caxton, 1945).

Sargeson, Frank, *More Than Enough* (Wellington: Reed, 1975).

——, *The Stories of Frank Sargeson* (Auckland: Penguin, 1982).

Saunders, Hilary Aidan St George, *Return at Dawn* (Wellington: Director of Publicity, 1942).

Scanlan, Nelle, *Road to Pencarrow* (Christchurch: Whitcombe & Tombs, 1963).

Schabas, W.A. & Nadia Bernaz (eds), *Routledge Handbook of International Criminal Law* (New York: Routledge, 2010).

Schaller, Michael, 'American air strategy in China, 1939–1941: The origins of clandestine air warfare', *American Quarterly*, vol. 28, no. 1, 1976, 3–19.

Scott, Dick, *Years of the Pooh-Bah: A Cook Islands history* (Rarotonga & Auckland: Hodder & Stoughton, 1991).

Scott, R.G., *Dick Scott: A radical writer's life* (Auckland: Reed, 2004).

Scotter, W.H., *A History of Canterbury, Vol III: 1876–1950* (Christchurch: Canterbury Centennial Historical and Literary Committee, 1965).

Seddon, Rosalie L., *Whims of a WAAF* (Auckland: Oswald Sealy, 1945).

Sedgwick, Charles P., 'The politics of survival: A social history of the Chinese in New Zealand', PhD thesis, University of Canterbury, 1982.

Self, Robert, *Neville Chamberlain: A biography* (Aldershot: Ashgate, 2006).

Sen, Amartya, *Poverty and Famines* (Oxford: Clarendon Press, 1981).

Shone, Gerald, *U-boat in New Zealand Waters* (Auckland: Pahiatua Publications, 2016).

Sinclair, Keith, *Walter Nash* (Auckland: Auckland University Press, 1976).

Sinclair, Keith & W.F. Mandle, *Open Account: A history of the Bank of New South Wales in New Zealand, 1861–1961* (Wellington: Whitcombe & Tombs, 1961).

Slatter, G.C., *A Gun in My Hand* (Christchurch: Pegasus, 1959).

Smith, H.K., *The State of Europe* (Sydney & London: Angus & Robertson, 1950).

Sparrow, Margaret, *Abortion Then and Now: New Zealand abortion stories from 1940 to 1980* (Wellington: Victoria University Press, 2010).

Stackelberg, Roderick & S.A. Winkle, *The Nazi Germany Sourcebook: An anthology of texts* (Oxford: Taylor & Francis, 2003).

Stafford, Jane & Mark Williams (eds), *The Auckland University Press Anthology of New Zealand Literature* (Auckland: Auckland University Press, 2012).

Stead, C.K. (ed.), *Maurice Duggan: Collected stories* (Auckland: Auckland University Press, 1981).

Stephenson, Jill, *Women in Nazi Germany* (Harlow: Longman, 2001).

Stevens, W.G., *Problems of 2NZEF* (Wellington: Department of Internal Affairs, 1958).

Stewart, Andrew, *Empire Lost: Britain, the dominions and the Second World War* (London: Continuum, 2008).

Stoler, Mark A., *Allies and Adversaries: The Joint Chiefs of Staff, the Grand Alliance, and US strategy in World War II* (Chapel Hill: University of North Carolina Press, 2000).

Stout, T.D.M., *War Surgery and Medicine* (Wellington: Department of Internal Affairs, 1954).

Sturm, Terry, *An Unsettled Spirit: The life and frontier fiction of Edith Lyttleton (G.B. Lancaster)* (Auckland: Auckland University Press, 2003).

Sutch, W.B., *Workers and the War Effort* (Wellington: New Zealand Co-operative Publishing Society, 1941).

Sutherland, I.L.G. (ed.), *The Maori People Today* (Wellington: New Zealand Institute of International Affairs & NZCER, 1940).

Takatori, Yuki, '"America's" war crimes trial? Commonwealth leadership at the International Military Tribunal for the Far East, 1946–48', *Journal of Imperial and Commonwealth History*, vol. 35, no. 4, 2007, 549–68.

Tarling, Nicholas, *A Sudden Rampage: The Japanese occupation of Southeast Asia 1941–1945* (Honolulu: University of Hawai`i Press, 2001).

Taylor, Nancy M., *The Home Front: The New Zealand People at War* series (Wellington: Department of Internal Affairs, 1986).

Thomas, Martin, 'Economic conditions and the limits to mobilization in the French Empire, 1936–1939', *Historical Journal*, vol. 48, no. 2, 2005, 471–98.

Thompson, H.L., *New Zealanders with the Royal Air Force, vols 1–3* (Wellington: Department of Internal Affairs, 1953–59).

Thompson, Martyn, *Our War – The Grim Digs: New Zealand soldiers in North Africa, 1940–1943* (Auckland: Penguin, 2005).

Thompson, R.S., *A Time for War: Franklin D. Roosevelt and the path to Pearl Harbor* (New York: Prentice Hall, 1991).
Thompson, R.S., *Empires on the Pacific: World War II and the struggle for the mastery of Asia* (New York: Basic Books, 2001).
Thomson, Helen, *Happy Voyage* (Christchurch: Helen Thomson, c. 1987).
Touwen-Bouwsma, Elly, 'The Indonesian nationalists and the Japanese "liberation" of Indonesia: Visions and reactions', *Journal of Southeast Asian Studies*, vol. 27, no. 1, 1996, 1–18.
Trotter, Ann (ed.), *New Zealand and China: The papers of the Twenty-first Foreign Policy School* (Dunedin: Foreign Policy School, University of Otago, 1986).
——, *New Zealand and Japan 1945–1952: The occupation and the peace treaty* (London: Athlone Press, 1990).
Trussell, Denys, *Fairburn* (Auckland: Auckland University Press/Oxford University Press, 1984).
The University and the Community: Essays in honour of Thomas Alexander Hunter (Wellington: Victoria University College, 1946). Two essays of most interest: J.C. Beaglehole, 'History & the New Zealander' and Leslie Lipson, 'The university, the civil service & democracy'.
van Vliet, P., 'The Dutch East Indies', *Fourth International*, vol. 4, 1943, 149–52.
Vennell, C.W., *Risks and Rewards: A policy of enterprise* (Auckland: South British Insurance, 1972).
Vercoe, Tony, *Yesterday's Drums: Echoes from the wasteland of war* (Wellington: Steele Roberts, 1996).
Ward, G.F., *The League of the Brown Skirts* (Timaru: G.F. Ward & Co., 1944).
Warlimont, Walter (R.H. Barry translator), *Inside Hitler's Headquarters, 1939–1945* (Novato (CA): Presidio Press, 1991).
Watt, Lawrence, *Mates and Mayhem: World War II: Frontline Kiwis remember* (Auckland: HarperCollins, 1996).
Webby, Elizabeth & Lydia Wevers, *Goodbye to Romance: Stories by New Zealand and Australian women writers 1930–1988* (Wellington: Allen & Unwin, 1988).
Weir, J.E. (ed.), *Collected Poems: James K. Baxter* (Wellington: Oxford University Press, 1979).
Weyher, Kurt & H.J. Ehrlich, *The Black Raider* (London: Elek Books, 1955).
White, Osmar, *Green Armor* (Sydney: Angus & Robertson, 1945).
Whitelaw, M.D., *When the Boys Come Home: Marriage, reunion and readjustment after the war* (Blenheim: H. Duckworth, 1943).
Williams, J.C., *Slate Pencil to Word-processor* (Christchurch: Waverley Press, 1995).
Williams, Tony (ed.), *Anzacs: Stories from New Zealanders at war* (Auckland: Hodder Moa Beckett, 2000).
Willmott, Bill, *The Chinese Communities in the Smaller Countries of the South Pacific* (Christchurch: Macmillan Brown Centre for Pacific Studies, 2007).
Wills, Clair, *That Neutral Island: A cultural history of Ireland during the Second World War* (London: Faber & Faber, 2007).
Wilson, G.E.M., *Brave Company* (London: Robert Hale, 1951).
——, *Sweet White Wine* (London: Hale, 1956).
Wilson, Phillip, *Pacific Star* (Wellington: Alister Taylor, 1976).
Witheford, Hubert, *Shadow of the Flame: Poems 1942–47* (Auckland: Pelorus, 1950).
Wood, F.L.W., *Political and External Affairs*: *The New Zealand People at War* series (Wellington: Department of Internal Affairs, 1958).
Wood, I.S., *Britain, Ireland and the Second World War* (Edinburgh: Edinburgh University Press, 2010).
Wright, Matthew, *Pacific War: New Zealand and Japan 1941–45* (Auckland: Reed, 2003).
Zimmerman, J.L., *Where the People Sing: Green land of the Maoris* (New York: Alfred A. Knopf, 1946).

OFFICIAL

Appendix to the Journals of the House of Representatives (*AJHR*): http://atojs.natlib.govt.nz/cgi-bin/atojs
New Zealand Official Yearbook (*NZYB*): www.stats.govt.nz/yearbooks
New Zealand Parliamentary Debates (*NZPD*)

SERIALS

Auckland Star
Bay of Plenty Beacon
Contact
Dominion
Ellesmere Guardian
Evening Post
New Zealand Herald
New Zealand Memories

New Zealand Observer
New Zealand Railways Magazine
New Zealand Tablet
Otago Daily Times
People's Voice
Press
Rodney and Otamatea Times
Southland Daily News
Spike; or Victoria College Review
Standard
Star-Sun
Truth
Waiapu Church Gazette
Weekly Press

WEBSITES

Atlantic Archive: http://archive.atlantic-archive.org
Avalon Project, Yale Law School: http://avalon.law.yale.edu/20th_century
BBC Archive: www.bbc.co.uk/archive
Cleveland, Les, 'Soldiers' songs: The folklore of the powerless': http://faculty.buffalostate.edu/fishlm/folksongs/les01.htm
Dictionary of New Zealand Biography: www.teara.govt.nz/en/biographies
EyeWitness to History: www.eyewitnesstohistory.com
Learning Memory: http://learnmem.cshlp.org
Maddison, Angus, 'Statistics on world population, GDP and per capita GDP, 1–2008AD': www.ggdc.net/MADDISON/oriindex.htm
National Army Museum: www.armymuseum.co.nz
New Zealand History Net: www.nzhistory.net.nz
NZ On Screen: www.nzonscreen.com
Online Cenotaph, Auckland War Museum: www.aucklandmuseum.com/war-memorial/online-cenotaph
Papers Past: www.paperspast.natlib.govt.nz
Penny Arcade: www.penny-arcade.com/comic/2005/05/24
SciencesPo: www.massviolence.org
Stanley, Peter, '"He's (not) coming south": The invasion that wasn't': www.awm.gov.au/events/conference/2002/stanley_paper.pdf
Statistics of Democide: www.hawaii.edu/powerkills/SOD.CHAP6.HTM
Statistics New Zealand, long-term data series: www.stats.govt.nz/methods_and_services/access-data/tables/long-term-data-series/national-income.aspx
Te Ara – the Encyclopedia of New Zealand: www.teara.govt.nz

INDEX

Page numbers in **bold** *refer to illustrations.*

absenteeism 147–48, 248, 299, 300
Achilles 57, 87, **89**, 171
Acland, John 313
Acland, Phillipa 123
Adams, Barbara 323
Adjutant 125–26
Africa 351; British colonies 42, 43, 44, 353; *see also* North Africa; South Africa
agriculture, *see* primary industries
air-raid shelters and drills 145, 198, **198**, 203, 205
air war 121–23, 237, 238; *see also* bombing
Aitken, Judy 86
Albania 349
Alexander, Stella 62
Algeria 351
Algie, Ronald 151
Alien Control Emergency Regulations 1939 102
Aliens Appeal Tribunal 152
aliens 102, **103**, 150–52, 293, 295
Allen, Sir James 47
Alley, Rewi 38
Allied Expeditionary Air Force 238
Allied powers: moral viewpoints 10–11; New Zealand's contribution insignificant 11–12, 72, 78, 243, 364; and Norway 87, 88; war aims 12, 67, 165–67; *see also* United Nations; and names of individual powers
Allum, John 281, 282
Alport, Cuthbert, *Kingdoms in Partnership* 41
Amala, Apo 230
'Amazon Battalion', Edgecumbe 272, 279
ambulance services 108
Amery, Bankes 251
Amery, Leo 251
Anderson, Hugh 344
Anderson, William 344
Andersons engineering company 109
Anderton, William 39
Andrews, Isobel, 'Bondsmen and Free' 248
Anglo-Iranian Oil Company 135
Annual Holidays Act 1944 314
Anti-Comintern Pact 39
Anzac Day 26
appeasement policy, British 50
Applebee, Charles 265
Are, Nio 297
Argentina 139
Arkinstall, Keith 335
armed forces, New Zealand *see* military, New Zealand
Armstrong, Ronald 130
Ashton-Warner, Evadne 199
Astwood, Arthur 173
Athenia 63–64, **64**
Atlantic Charter 166–67, 353, 354
Atlantic Monthly 223–24
Atmore, Dorothy 149
atomic bombing of Hiroshima and Nagasaki 321, 324–27, 328
atrocities, Pacific War 223–24
Attlee, Clement 353
Auckland 85–86, 87, 108, 113, 116, 140, 151, **198**, 244, 287, 302; American servicemen 215, 220, **221**, 224, 226–28; appeal boards 130; Communist Party 23, 100; Home Guard 143; housing 255; mines in surrounding waters 118–19, 124; peace and prosperity 111, 164; peace celebrations, surrender of Japan 323, 324; 'sly grog' vendors 265; submarines in surrounding waters 196, 240; theft and pilfering 266; weaponry 57
Auckland Amalgamated Society of Carpenters and Joiners 163
Auckland Chamber of Commerce 37, 97, 160, 267
Auckland Drivers Union 163

Auckland Farmers Union 166, 244; Meat Committee 139
Auckland Girls Grammar School 111
Auckland Harbour Board Employees Union 312
Auckland Medical Association 34–35
Auckland Provincial Freedom League 24
Auckland Racing Club 164
Auckland War Memorial **26**
Aunt Daisy (Maud Basham) 220–21, **222**
Australia 41, 45, 48, 50, 55, 65, 97, 138, 139, 172, 175–76, 182, 184, 185, 201, 258; Canberra Pact, 1944 261, 262–63; colonies 171, 262; Declaration of the United Nations, 1942 210; fearful of invasion from 'Near North' 261; food production 253; Pacific Defence Conference, 1939 55, 56; Pacific War Council 216; parliamentary system 348; poster, construction of Bristol Beaufort warplanes **261**; subsidisation of British war effort 332; and United States 180, 216, 221, 348; war with Japan 171, 177, 181–82, 191–92, 208, 214, 217, 230, 261, 318
Averill, Alfred 267
Awake, New Zealand 199–200
Axis powers 10–11, 132, 181, 183; *see also* names of individual powers
Ayson, Hugh 154

Baddeley, Walter 230
Baker Island 53–54
Baker, Jack 332
Balkans 132–34
Ballantyne, David, *The Cunninghams* 26, 129
banking 40, 69, 93, 97, 99
Baptist Assembly 130
Bargh, Victor 194
Barker, Constance 255
Barkle, Clifford 341
Barnard, William 85, 98
Barron, Charles 267
Basham, Maud (Aunt Daisy) 220–21, **222**
Basile, Vincent 152
Baskett, Frederick 267
Batterbee, Sir Harold 65, 79, 108, 119, 120, 141, 196, 252
Battle of Britain 121
Baxter, James K. 343
Bay of Plenty 70, 108, 119, 164, 196, 279, 302
Beagle, Thomas 227
Beaglehole, Ernest 283
Beaglehole, John 42, 98, 158
Begg, James 253
Belgium: colonialism 86–87, 351; German invasion 115; surrender to German troops, 1940 115
Bell, Cheviot Dillon 76
Bell, Jean 63
Bell, William 279
Bengal famine 250, **250**, 251
Bennett, Agnes 148–49
Bennett, Frederick 295–96, 326
Berendsen, Carl 47, 174, 263, 348, 350–51
Bergen, Etna 128–29
Berlin, bombing 122–23, 239
Bertram, James 82, 111, 193, 239, 320; *Crisis in China* 38; *North China Front* 38
Best, Arthur 264
Bevan-Brown, Charles 342
Beyer, Kelso 265
Binswanger, Ottilia 288
Birchfield, Connie 306
Bishop, Clarence 226
Black, Helen 255–56
black market 167, 226, 255, 264–66, 267
blackouts: England 62; New Zealand 12, 145, 204, 206, 233, 343
Blair, Mary 61
Blenheim 317–18
Bloodworth, Thomas 303
Blue Cliffs estate, Canterbury 275
Blue, William 264
Blundell, James 324
Blyde, Henry 97
Bolitho, Hector 61, 121, 223
bombing: air raids 121–23, 231–32, **232**, **233**, 237, 239–40; area bombing 122–23; citizens' fears 73, **73**, 320; Japan **239**, 239–40, **319**, 320, 321, **321**, 324–27; moral questioning 360; *Return at Dawn* (Saunders) 357; Solomon Islands 263, **263**, 345–46; strategic bombing 122
Borneo 169, 193, 244
borrowing to finance war effort *see* loans to finance war effort
Boyd, Max 187, 194, 342
Brasch, Charles 46, 58–59, 63, 110, 121–22
Brathwaite, Errol 324, 335
Brazil 66, 74, 210
Britain: and Canberra Pact, 1944 262–63; collective security 72; Conference of Paris 349; and Czechoslovakia 50; Declaration of the United Nations, 1942 210; and Dutch East Indies 187–88; and Ethiopia 47, 49–50; and Indonesia 352–53; oil interests in Iran and Iraq 178; parliamentary system 348; proposal for talks with Japan and United States 175–76; and Sino-Japanese War 36, 37, 38–39; and Soviet Union 39, 88, 337; and Thailand 184, 185, 191–92; trade with Argentina 139; trade with China 37; and United Nations 350; and United States 52–54, 55, 139, 334, 337; *see also* Royal Air Force; Royal Navy

Britain and New Zealand: belief in British protection of New Zealand 70–71; Britain as 'Motherland' or 'Home' 22, 40, 41, 42, **52**, 65, 70, 76, 77, 115, 252, 363; British ancestry of most New Zealanders 19, 76, 178; British news coverage of the war 259–60; cars imported by New Zealand 23, **23**; Labour government opposition to British foreign policy 47–51; New Zealand food production 68, 69, 79, 126, 241–45, 251–52, 253–54, 347, 363; New Zealand loyalty to Britain **76**, 76–77, 98, 99, **120**, 120–21, 127, **137**, 200–01, 334, 338, 362–63; New Zealand subsidisation of British war effort 331–32; New Zealand's support for Britain at expense of own defence 71, 79–80, 120–21, 200–01, 217, 241, 249, 258–63, 362, 363; trade 23, 34, 40–41, 68–70, 79, 97, 123, 139, 146, 241–42, 251, 331–34, **333**, 336, 363

Britain, Second World War: air raids 121–23, 292; Atlantic Charter 166–67; Battle of Britain 121; Churchill's cable re continuation of war or peace talks 119–21; cost of war 333; declaration of war 61, 63, 65; economic mobilisation 141; financing of war effort 138, 331–32; first phoney war 87; German plan to invade 131, 182; naval blockade 123; New Zealand civilian volunteers for military and other groups 109–10; no longer a world power 337; Pacific Defence Conference, 1939 55; Pacific War Council 216; plans for invasion of Ireland 208; Potsdam Declaration, 1945 320; war economic controls 97; war with Japan 169, 171, 176, 179, 181, 186, 187–88, 191–92, 200–01, 230, 318, 319; *see also* Royal Air Force; Royal Navy

British military 88–89; New Zealanders in 109, 272

British Broadcasting Corporation (BBC) 61, 259–60, 357–58

British Commonwealth 12, 36, 38, 39, 40, 41–42, 48, 127, 131, 156, 171, 238; agreement with Soviet Union 156–57, 158–59; British proposal for talks with Japan and United States 175–76; Cairo Conference 261–62; dominions' freedom of choice 78; and Dutch East Indies 187–88; and French Polynesia 171; and Japan 176, 181, 183, 184, 186, 187, 189; new order statements 166; New Zealand belief that the key player in Second World War 157; use of Egypt as a military base 91; war aims 67, 328; war with Japan 191–92, 194–95, 217, 318; *see also* names of individual countries

British Empire 12, 74, 351–52; Atlantic Charter 167; China 35, 37; democracy 42, 46, 348; differing views within New Zealand 28, 29, 38, 40, 41, 42, 43–44, 46–47, 74–75, 76–77, 85, 97, 98, 156; trusteeships 350; white superiority 223; *see also* colonialism – Britain; and names of individual countries

British Pacific Fleet (Royal Navy) 240

British Pathé 259

British Somaliland 42

Broadfoot, Walter 319

Brocklehurst, Joseph 288

Brodie, William 321

Brown, Donald 32

Browne, Dewi 238

Browne, Mervyn 71

Bryant, James 173

Buick-Constable, Lindsay 81

building industry 96, 138–39, 140, 247, 255

Bulfin, Peggy 284, 338

Bulgaria 132, 349

Bulge, Battle of the 238

Bullen, Nancy 199

Burma 184, 187, 188, 191, 194, **207**

Burrow, James 335

Burton, Ormond 101, 283

Bysshe, Ernest 187

Cabinet Committee on Readjustment of Industry 246

Cadogan, Sir Alexander 350

Cairo Conference, 1943 261–62

Calhoun, William 242

Cameron, Alexander 85

Camp, Charles 314

Campaign for Christian Order 289, 290

Canada 41, 48, 50, 62, 65, 175, 185, 251, 348; Declaration of the United Nations, 1942 210; Pacific War Council 216

Canberra Pact, 1944 261, 262–63

Canterbury 83, 119, 131, 242, 302, 303; 'English' Canterbury 52

Canterbury Education Board 162

Canterbury Navy League 25

Canterbury Trades Council 251

Canton Island 54

Cantonese labour, Samoa, Nauru and New Zealand 45–46, 47, 104

capitalism 22, 25, 27, 33, 38, 41, 50, 53, 75, 100, 156, 160–61, 282, 301, 331

car buying, New Zealand 141, **141**

Caro, Arthur 192–93

Carpenters Union 158

Carr, Clyde 162, 178

cars imported from Britain 23, **23**

Carter, Clare 63–64

Carter, Elsie 238

Cartwright, William 26

casualties of Second World War 328; *Athenia* torpedoing 63–64, **64**; *Casualty List* **134**; civilians 123–24, 232, 233, 328, 343–47; diseases, wounds and injuries 338–43, **341**; 'friendly fire' 338; killed by New Zealand troops 233, 345–47, **346**; Māori 355; New Zealand troops 64–65, 132, 134, 164, 165, 232, 338–40
Catholic church, New Zealand 66; centennial celebrations 46; and Labour Party 292; opposition to conscription 85; preference for keeping volunteer army in New Zealand 79; views on atomic bomb 326–27; views on fascist Italy 32; views on Nazi Party 20; *see also* Irish Catholic New Zealanders
Caulfield, John 107–08
Caves, Denis 90, 340
Caves, John 356
censorship 14, 62, 158, 267, 268, 294, 305, 308, 356–57
centennial, New Zealand: 'After a Hundred Years' poster **75**; Centennial Exhibition (Wellington), poster **16**
Challenge Phosphate Company 45–46
Chamberlain, Neville 43, 50, 51, 54, 61, 67, 78, 80, 87, 98, 332–33
chambers of commerce, New Zealand 14, 37, 96, 97, 115, 118, 160, 311, 313
Chandler, Charles 194, 288, 289–90, 350
Chapman, Charles 314
Charters, Thomas 25–26
Chatfield, Edward 80
Chau Yan Sham 104
Chilvers, Cyril 129
Chilvers, Ronald 130
China 17, 32, 35–36, 37, 74; casualties 328; Declaration of the United Nations, 1942 210; indentured workers in Samoa, Nauru and New Zealand 45–46, 47, 104; and Japan 177, 184, 216; and New Zealand 210; Sino-Japanese War 20, 35, 36–39, 80, 104, 175, 176, 177, 182, 190, 191, 212, 235; and United Nations 350; and United States 35, 54, 175, 183, 186, 240, 261; *see also* Guomindang
Chinese Association 104
Chinese New Zealanders 17, 20, 77, 104, 221
Chorlton, Anthony 32–33
Christchurch **52**, 107, 108–09, 117, 130, 143, 148, 244, 255, 264, 269, 317, 318, 323
Christian Pacifist Society 26
Christophers, Gwenda 63, 280
Churchill, Winston 119–20, 166–67, 181, 187, 334, 337, **337**; Bengal famine 251; Cairo Conference 261; and New Zealand Division 258; trusteeships 350; victory 'at any cost' 333; and war with Japan 177, 179, 182, 186, 192, 200–01, 217
civil defence, New Zealand 145, 202, 203, 233
civilian life: summer 1940–41 163–65; a wartime winter day in Wellington **165**
civilian war work 142–48
Clark, George 84, 101–02
Clark-Hall, Rosemary 273
class divisions, New Zealand 13, 20–21, 24–25, 92, 156, 301–14; *see also* left-wing views, New Zealand; right-wing views, New Zealand
clergy, New Zealand 29, 33, 44, 82–83, 130, 166, 209, 223, 230, 241, 287, 288, 300, 317, 326, 329; *see also* Catholic church, New Zealand; religion, New Zealand
Cleveland, Leslie 226, 267
clothing, austerity 205, 258
Coal Mines Council 146
coastwatchers 174, 196
Coates, Gordon 95, **96**, 97, 121, 159, 160, 178, 180–81, **181**
Cocker, Ada 150
Cole, John Reece 300, 334–35, 343
collective security doctrine 27, 48, 72
Colonial Sugar Refinery Company 172
colonialism and imperialism: African countries 351; Australia 171, 262; Britain 35, 42–44, 45, 46, 54, 72, 74, 86–87, 167, 171, 175, 182, 186–87, 188, 262, 348, 351–52, 353–54 (*see also* British Empire); British proposal for talks with Japan and United States re colonies 175; Declaration of the United Nations, 1942 210; France 30, 35, 42, 72, 74, 86–87, 115, 171, 175, 182, 184–86, 188, 351–52, 354; Germany 32–33; Italy 32; Japan 39, 86–87, 208; Japanese threat to European colonial possessions **170**; Netherlands 35, 86–87, 169, **170**, 171, 175, 178, 181, 182, 187–89, 195, **352**, 352–53, 354; New Zealand (*see* Pacific colonies of New Zealand); postwar imperialism 349–54, **354**; Soviet Union 30, 349; trusteeships 262, 349–50, 354; United States 52, 53–54, 55, 167, 171, 175, **179**, 180, 182, 183, 188, 261, 262, 351–52, 354
Colson, John 324
communism: Catholic clergy views 20; China 20; Soviet Union 30; Vietnam War 361
Communist Party, New Zealand 23, 39, 99–100, 111, 143, 156, 157–59, 292; election, 1943 305, 306, **307**, 309
compulsory military training 29–30, 57
Condliffe, John 41, 332
Coningham, Sir Arthur 238
conscientious objectors 127–28, 129, 162, 248–49; political 129–30; religious 129, 130; *see also* pacifism
conscription 29–30, 78, 85, 101, 116, 118, 126–31, 135–36, 158, 202, 245, 358; appeal boards 127–

28, 129, 130; balloting system 127, 128–29, 244; Māori not conscripted 153; medical test 129
Conservative Party, British 37, 38, 43, 50–51, 63, 98
conservatives, New Zealand *see* right-wing views, New Zealand
construction industry 96, 138–39, 140, 247, 255
Cook Islands 17, 20, 40, 44, 47, 104, 105, 188, 207, 262; air-force transport plane **298**; call for independence 354; colonial administration buildings, Avarua **155**; economic impact of the war 110–11, 155–56; Home Guard 219; participation in war effort 153–54; United States military occupation 217, 220
Cook Islands Māori 297
Cooke, Janet 280
Cooper, Duff 166
Coral Sea, Battle of 214
Corner, Frank 74, 349, 361–62
Cornish, Henry 65
Corsair Bay, Canterbury **234**
Costello, Patrick 349
costs of waging war 70; First World War 91; Second World War 92–95, 99, 142, 330–38 (*see also* casualties of Second World War)
Country Lads 74
country quota 24
county council elections 24, 314
Cox, Geoffrey 61, 88, 216
Craigie–Arita Agreement 38–39
Crawford, John 226
Creed, Nelson 264
Crete 133–34
Crispe, Peter 328
Cruickshank, George 297, 299
Curnow, Allen 357–58, 364, 365
currency crisis, 1939 50–51
Curtin, John 262
Curtis, Wiha 299
Cusack, James 83
cynicism about the war 167, 209, 264, 266–68
Czechoslovakia 50, 349

Dairy Board 318
Daitoa Kyoeiken (Greater East Asia Co-Prosperity Sphere) 11, 182, 206–07
Daladier, Édouard 30
Darbyshire, Harold 158
Dare, Jane 143, 274
Davidson, Norma 110
Davies, David 241
Davin, Dan 225, 364
Davis, Cecil 38
Davis, Eliot 62
Davis, Hazel 272
Davis, Joseph 228
Davis, Sir Ernest 143, 223, 297
D-Day 238
de Beer, Dora 110
de Beer, Mary 109–10, 121
de Valera, Eamon 46, 65
death duties 304
Debreceny, Douglas 82
Declaration of the United Nations, 1942 210
Dee, Colleen 283–84
defaulters 130–31, 248–49
Defence League 29–30, 57, 85
democracy: British colonies 42, 46, 348; county council elections 24, 314; former dictatorships 348–49; France 30, 348; great powers 30; Māori 104; New Zealand colonies 44; safeguarding, as a reason for going to war 73–75, 82, 83, 98, 101, 126, 132, 244, 348–55, 359–60, 364; silencing of New Zealand anti-war protest 100, 101; United States 30, 52
Democratic Labour Party 99, 305, 306, 309, 318
Denmark 87, 88, 89
deserters 269–70
detention camps for defaulters 130–31
dictatorships: colonial empires 74; great powers 30; Greece 132; Labour Party opposition 27, 35, 73; Poland 74; postwar parliamentary states 348–49; as a reason for going to war 73–74, 119, 364; *see also* China; Germany; Italy; Japan; Soviet Union
'Dig for Victory' campaign **253**, 253–54
Diggle, Jack 82
Dittmer, Felix 103
Docherty, Neil 340
Dominion Council of Co-ordinated Business Associations 313–14
Dominion Monarch 62
Donald, Haddon 81
Donaldson, Trevar 266
Dönitz, Karl 123
Donnelly, Sir Arthur 142
Doric Star 87
Dreaver, Mary 274, 277, 282
Duff, Oliver 25, 53, 80–81, 288–89
Duggan, Maurice 287
Dumbarton Oaks conference 350
Dunedin 117, 130, 158, 302, 317, 323
Dunedin Federated Furniture and Related Trades Industrial Union of Workers 158
Dunlop, John Bonar 88
Dunningham, Margaret, *Three Brown Bears and the Manpower Man* 254–55
Dunnottar Castle 270
Dunstan, Peggy 133
Dutch East Indies 107, 169, 178, **179**, 181, 182, 184, 187–89, 191, 195, 212, 347, 353
Dyson, Hedda 166

earthquake, June 1942 **213**, 213–14
East Asia 39, 54, 165, 171, 174, 176, 179, 216; *see also* Southeast Asia; and names of individual countries
Economic Stabilisation Committee 142
Economic Stabilisation Conference, 1940 142
economy, New Zealand: currency controls 36, 50–51, 161; economic waste of going to war 334–35; financing of New Zealand war effort 92–95, 99, 121, 126, 136–38, 301–05, 312; military spending 141, 334; money supply 93, 310; pre-war 17–18, 22, 42, 58; safeguarding, as a reason for going to war 67–70, 330–37, **331**, 364; shrinking economy, last year of war 310; stabilisation policy 310; thriving economy, and prosperity 138–39, 141–42, **142**, 309–10, 330–31, 364; wages, price and cost control 141–42; war controls 95–98, 161; withdrawal of people from productive economy 335–36, **336**; *see also* trade, New Zealand
Edmond, Lauris (née Scott) 26, 99, 224, 225, 246, 306, 342, 364
education 337
Edwards, Lawrence 64–65
Egypt: British withdrawal 351; impact of occupation 88–91, **90**; North African campaign 134, **135**, 217, 229; prostitutes 283, **284**
election, 1943, New Zealand 305–09, **307**, **309**
electricity controls 254
Elkind, Dorée 34
Elliott, Keith 86
Ellis, Sir Albert 125, 327, 328
Ellison, Nancy 342
Ellison, Terry 342
Ely, Arnold 97
Emergency Precautions Committee 57
Emergency Precautions Scheme 145, 150, 202–03, **203** 206, 245
Emergency Regulations Act 1939 95–96
Emergency Regulations Amendment Act 1941 117
Emery, Clifford 194
Employers Association 249
Enderbury Island 54
enemy attack as a reason for New Zealand going to war 70–73, 337, 360–63, 364
Eritrea 187
Eslava, Domingo 227
essential industries 146, 202, 205–06, 246, 296, 297
Estonia 349
Ethiopia 47, 49–50, 187
Evatt, Herbert 261–62
exports *see* trade, New Zealand

factory workers 146, 147, 202, **245**, 246, 248; absenteeism 147–48, 248, 299, 300; Māori 296, 299; women 108–09, **109**, 150, 276–77, **277**, 280
Fairburn, A.R.D. (Rex) 20–21, 75, 329, 364; 'Modern Love' 288
Falck, Bernhard 34
Falla, Paul 110
Fanning Island 62
Farmers Union 97, 116, 139, 246, 249, 299, 308, 314; Otago Provincial Council 85
farming *see* primary industries
fascism 32, 46; belief in defeat by fighting 73–74, 82; Defence League linked to 29; Federation of Labour condemnation 23; Italy 32, 33; Labour Party opposition 27; *see also* Nazism
Featherston 256–57
Federation of Labour 22–23, 29–30, 33, 38, 78, 100, 102, 117, 126, 159, 201, 228, 249, 312, 314, 353
fictional accounts of Second World War 14–15; *see also* names of individual authors
Field, Arthur 34
Field, Estelle 196
Fiji 40, 55–56, 262, 353–54; Indian people 172–73, **173**, 218; New Zealand military occupation 172–73, 218, 338; sugar industry 172, **172**; United States military occupation 217, 218; war with Japan 196, 212, 223, 230
Fiji Infantry Regiment 172
Fijian army 212, 223
films: American 52, 53, 224; British 53
films, New Zealand: censorship 356, 357; New Zealanders inside a cinema **54**; news 82, 356; propaganda 74, 357
Finland 87–88, 349
First World War: casualties 164; Catholic/Protestant split 292; conscription 128; Cook Islands men 154; currency inflation 141, 310; deserters 269; 'dictated peace' 67; Egypt 89; financing 91, 92, 93, 94, 302, 305; German colonies 32; Germans in New Zealand 101, 102; New Zealand casualties 17, 63, 80, 84; opening battles 86; peace settlement impact on Germany 33, 39, 48; shortages, hoarding and profiteering 96, 107, 141; views of New Zealanders 25, 26, 27, 29, 79, 80–81, 83, 84–85, 111; women's dress and behaviour 277
Fischer, Qualbert 102
Fisken, Geoffrey 194
flag flying **137**, 161–62
Fleming, June 199
Fletcher, Anne 64
Fletcher family 161
Fletcher, James 247
food production 68, 69, 79, 126, 241–45, 247, 249–50, 253, 274, 296, 347, 363; 'Dig for Victory' campaign **253**, 253–54; 'vegetable census' 253

Forbes, George 97
Forbes, Valerie 199
Four Peaks estate, Canterbury 255, **255**
Frame, Janet 63, 246
France: collective security 72; colonialism and imperialism 30, 35, 42, 72, 74, 86–87, 115, 171, 175, 182, 184–86, 188, 351–52, 354; democracy 30, 348; and Ethiopia 47; links to New Zealand 30; and Soviet Union 88; and United States 52–53
France, Second World War: D-Day 238; declaration of war 61, 65; German soldiers relaxing **114**; impact of fall of France in New Zealand 118, 119, 120, 126, 139, 143, 146, 148, 150, 156, 159–60, 162, 175, 289; invasion by Germany and armistice 115, 116, 118, 131, 138; Italian invasion 118; Vichy Republic 115, 119, **119**, 134, 171, 184
Franks, Wilfrid 129
Fraser, Janet 149, 272, 282
Fraser, Peter 47, 50, 66, 84, 87, 101, 111, 233; Battle of Britain 121; cable to Churchill re continuation of war or peace talks 119, 120; Canberra Pact 262; Communist Party 158; conscription 126–27; election, 1943 305–06, 308, 309; food production 79, 249; French Polynesia 171, 352; Greece 132; holocaust 293; Italy 258; Japan 188, 348; loyalty to Britain 22, 38, 77; manpower requirements of war and industry 244; Māori 335; Pacific colonies 354; plane shelled in Iraq 134–35; Potsdam Declaration, 1945 320; prices, wartime trade with Britain 331–32; prime minister 113, 115, 117; strikes and lockouts 312; surrender of Axis troops in North Africa 241; trusteeships 349, 350; United Nations 216; United States 180, 191, 216, 260–61; War Administration 212–23, 228; war aims and reasons for going to war 67, 70, 74–75; war cabinet 121; war with Japan 80, 169, 177–79, 182, 186, 191, 201, 206, 260–61, 319; Women's War Service Auxiliary 148–49
Fraser, Sir Bruce 240
freedom: Māori 104; Nash's view 309; safeguarding, as a reason for going to war 73–75, 98, 101, 126, **197**, 244, 348–55, 359–60, 364; silencing of New Zealand anti-war protest 100, 101
Freedom League 151
French Polynesia 171, 352
Freyberg, Bernard 103, 132
Friends of the Soviet Union 23
Front Populaire 30
Fukama Toyokichi 107
Fullarton, John, *Troop Target* **236**
fundraising for war effort 92–93, 121, 138, **138**, 154, 296, 301–02; goods stolen 266
furlough men **268**, 268–70
Fury, Charles 130

Galbraith, Alexander 158
Galway, George 63
Gambia 321, 327
gambling 139, 257
Gardiner, Noel 81
Garland, Warren 36–37
Garry, Francis 62
Gaskell, A.P. 82–83, 345
Gatman, Owen 289
Gaulle, Charles de 171
Gee, Lyndahl Chapple 286
Geering, Lloyd 197
General Motors New Zealand **249**
Gerard, George 288
Gerard, Richard 313
German navy (*Kriegsmarine*) 87, 123–26, 145, 232, 235, 240
Germans in New Zealand: German ancestry of New Zealand citizens 19, 20, 32, 34–35; Jewish refugees 34–35, 103, 151, 152, 293–95; wartime treatment 62, 101–03, 150–51, 152
Germany 32–33; Anti-Comintern Pact 39; British Commonwealth views on war, 1937 48; and Czechoslovakia 50; democracy 348; expansionary policies 32, 33, 39, 74; First World War peace settlement 33, 39, 48; postwar civilian starvation 347; and Soviet Union 67; trade with New Zealand 33–34; and United States 52–53; *see also* Nazism
Germany, Second World War: air raids 121–23, 231–32, **232**, **233**, 237, 290, 292; casualties 328, 346; first phoney war 86–87; German–Soviet non-aggression pact 61, 156, 176, 183, 292; Greece and Crete 132–34; invasion of Denmark and Norway 87, 88, 89, 115; invasion of France and armistice 115, 116, 118, 131, 138; invasion of Soviet Union 131, 156–58, 179, 183, 229, 235, **242**; Middle East 134–35; naval war 87, 123–26, 145, 232, 235, 240; New Zealand civilians in Germany 62, 110; New Zealand war participation compared to Vietnam War 360–61; peace talks 67, 87, 119–21, 131, 329–30; plan to invade Britain 131, 182; and Poland **60**, 61, 74, 86–87, 98, 99, 134; prisoners of war 340; risk of attack as a reason for New Zealand going to war 70–73, 337, 360–63; surrender 317–18; treaty of military alliance with Japan and Italy 176; Tripartite Pact 131–32; 'turning of the tide' 237–38; and United States 240; war crimes trials, Nuremburg 358; women's war work 281, **282**; *see also* names of campaigns and theatres of war
Géry, Jean de 171

Gibbard, Edward 317
Giesen, Gordon 95
Gilbert and Ellice Islands 43, 174, 196
Gilbertson, Mavis 274
Gilmour, Robert 356
Gisborne 240
Glenburn estate, Hawke's Bay 274
Glover, Denis 34, 113, 232, 238, 283, 364; 'A Sailor Finds Love' 283
Goosman, William 136, 311
Gordon, Doris and William 110
Göring, Hermann 87, 232
Gornall, Edgar 283
Graf Spee 87, **89**
Granville, Mary 274–75
Gray, Gay 209, 223
great powers 30–35; *see also* Britain; China; France; Germany; Italy; Japan; Soviet Union; United States
Greater East Asia Co-Prosperity Sphere (Daitoa Kyoeiken) 11, 182, 206–07
Greater Japan Women's Society 281
Greece 132–33, **133**, 134, 152, 165, 335
Green, E.K. 221
Greene, Mark 218, 258
Greville, Alice 283
Grigg, Gilbert 318
Grigg, Mary 274
Guomindang 20, 32, 35, 36, 37, 38, 39, 74, 104, 175, 176, 184, 186, 191, 212, 240, 261, 348; Declaration of the United Nations, 1942 210; Pacific War Council 216

Haare, Waitai 228
Hale, William 318
Hall, William 321
Halsey, William 245
Hamilton 130, 199, 269, 303
Hamilton, Adam 24, 34, 41, 50, 65, 76, 84, **96**, 97, 116, 121, 151, 159, 160, 289
Hamilton, Andrew 196, 200
Hamilton, Ian 131
Hampson-Tindale, Vere 254
Hanan, Josiah 57
Hanger, Paula 223
Hara Yoshimichi 190
Harawira, Kahi 300
Hargest, James 57
Harper, Sarah 64
Hartley, Nell 42, 272–73
Harvey, Marian 198–99
Hauraki 237
Hawai`i 52, 169, 192, 195, 212
Hawker, Maurice 173
Hawkins, Kathleen 276
Hawkins, Victor 130
Haworth, Patricia 227–28
Haworth, Thomas 227–28
Hayter, Adrian 41–42, 341
Hearnshaw, Leslie, *Hours of Work in Wartime* 248
Heaslip, Harold 287
Hedges, Frank 39
Heihei, Hawerati 266
Henderson, James 290, 341–42
Henry, Albert 44
Herangi, Te Puea 77, **77**, 104, 295
Herlihy, Francis 192
Herries-Davis, Thomas 155–56, 354
Higgins, Beatrice 324
Hill, Mavis 281, 282, 344
Hindle, William 252
Hindrup, Leonard 226
Hino Ashihei 223
Hislop, Ailsa 203
Hislop, Thomas 76, 84, 287
historiography 15
Hitler, Adolf 32, 50, 70, 71, 74, 83, 131, 160; cartoons **33**, **232**; Catholic clergy views 20
hoarding 62, 107, 197
Hodgens, Joseph 136–37
Hodgson, John 44
Hogan, John 166, 308
Hogg, David 94
Holcroft, Monte 356
Holland, Henry St Barbe 212, 313, 329
Holland, Sidney 83, **96**, 137, 159, **160**, 233, 242; county council elections 314; furlough men 268; manpower requirements of war and industry 244; socialism 313; strikes and lockouts 310–11; views on New Zealand Division in Italy 258–59; War Administration 212–13, 228, 310; and war with Japan 169
Holm, Sydney 69
Holmwood 124
Holyoake, Keith 313, 361, 362
home front 95–106
Home Guard, New Zealand 143–45, **144**, 150, 199, 202, **203**, 204, 206, 209, 233, 245, 272, 279, 296, 343
homosexuality, New Zealand servicemen 283, **285**
Hong Kong 35, 45, 193
Hore-Belisha, Leslie 80
Horrobin, William 314
horse racing 139, 256–57, **257**
Horton, Sir Henry 304
house building 139, 161, 254–55
household wealth 69
Howard, Louis 345
Howard, Mabel 23, 101
Howe, Richard 166
Howland Island 54

Hudson, Charlotte 199
Hughes, Percy 116
Hull, Cordell 180, 263
Hulme, Clive 200
Hungary 74, 110, 132, 295, 349
Hyde, Robin, *Dragon Rampant* 38

Ickes, Harold 221
imperialism *see* colonialism and imperialism
India 41–42, 43, 46, 74, 89, 181, 201, **201**, 212; Bengal famine 250, **250**, 328, 347, 363; and Britain 353
Indian Army 42, 43, **43**, 187
Indochina, French 183, 184, 188, 190, 347
Indonesian nationalists 189, 352–53
Industrial Emergency Council 146
industrial production, New Zealand 36, 50, 95–96, 249, **249**; essential industries 146, 202, 205–06, 246, 296, 297; non-essential industries 246; *see also* building industry; manufacturing; mining industry; primary industries
inflation 141–42
Insull, James 237
insurance 40, 69, 331
International Labour Organization 309
Invercargill 57, 118, 137, 158, 161, 303
Iran 134–35
Iraq 134–35
Iraq Petroleum Company 135
Ireland 41, 46, 48, 65, 66, 208, 292–93
Irish Catholic New Zealanders 19, 20, 46; hostility to Protestants 292–93
Irving, John Carlyle 147
Isitt, Leonard 325, 327
Italians in New Zealand 152
Italy 32, 217, 235; attack on Ethiopia 47, 49–50; declaration of war on Britain and France 115; invasion of France 118; naval blockade 123; New Zealand troops 258, 259, 263, 270, 271, **271**, 283, 289, 338, 339, 340; New Zealand's declaration of war makes Italy an enemy 360; peace treaty 349; treaty of military alliance with Japan and Germany 176; Tripartite Pact 131–32; *see also* names of campaigns and theatres of war

Jack, James 62
Jackson, Gainor 119
Jacobs, Bertram 267
James Kok Tanzorchester 53
Jansen, Elwyn 35
Japan 35–40; and British Commonwealth 176, 181, 183, 186, 187, 189; British proposal for talks with Japan and United States 175–76; and China 177, 184, 216; colonialism and imperialism 86–87, 208; democracy 348; and Dutch East Indies 178, **179**, 181, 182, 189, 191; economy 35, 39; Federation of Labour condemnation 23; hierarchy of world races 223; and Indonesia 352–53; Māori support 47; Nagoya Pan-Pacific Peace Exposition poster **37**; naval power 71, 171, 337; New Zealand unwillingness to negotiate 177–78; pact with Western powers on status quo in Asia 36; possible alliances or understandings **188**; postwar civilian starvation 347; postwar forced labour by soldiers 347; Sino-Japanese War 20, 35, 36–39, 80, 104, 175, 176, 177, 182, 190, 191, 212, 235; and Southeast Asia 182, 183, 184–86, 189, 216; and Soviet Union 39, 80, 132, 176, 186, 191, 239; *Tōa Shin Chitsujo* (new order in East Asia) 165; trade with New Zealand 36–37, 38, 139, 182, 183, 204; treaty of military alliance with Germany and Italy 176; and United States 53–54, 80, 175, 176, 177, 179, 180, 181, 183, 184, 186, 190, 348
Japan, Second World War: Axis power 131–32, 181, 183; naval and military power 171, 191, 195, 206, 208, 210, 212, 214–15, 235, 237, 337; neutrality 79–80, 107; propaganda **182**, **201**, **207**; trade embargo and freezing of assets 183, 184, 189, 190; Tripartite Pact 131–32; women's war work 281
Japan, war in Southeast Asia and the Pacific: Allied bombing **239**, 239–40, **319**, 320, 321, **321**, 324–27, 328; Allied declarations of war 169, 171; atomic bombing of Hiroshima and Nagasaki 321, 324–27, 328; attack on Pearl Harbor 169, 192, 196, 360; Battle of Midway 215, 247; Battle of the Coral Sea 214; Borneo 193; Burma 194, **207**; casualties 328, 345, 346, **346**; defeat 230, 238–39; diplomatic background 186, 189–91, 201; Dutch East Indies 191, 195, 212; exit strategy 215–16; Fiji 196; Hong Kong 193; Japanese civilian war weariness 320; Malaya 192, 193, 194, 196; Pacific Defence Conference, 1939 40, 55–56, 71, 150; peace cabinet 320; planning 191; Potsdam Declaration, 1945 320, 322; racist quality 221, 223–24, **224**; Samoa 196; Singapore **193**, 194–95, **195**, 197; Solomon Islands 196, 230, 237; surrender 322–24, 325, 327–28; threat to New Zealand 55, 71, 72, 79–80, 120, 145, 169, 177, 178–79, 181–82, 216; war crimes trials, Tokyo 358, **359**
Japan, war in Southeast Asia and the Pacific – New Zealand involvement: Catholic views 292; civilian fears, and effects of war 196–200, 202–06, 209, 214, 215, 319–20; civilian optimism, cynicism and fatalism **209**, 209–10; civilians in lands occupied by

Japan 192–95, 196; *Dead Sniper, Mono* (Reed) **231**; declaration of war 169, 171; following surrender of Germany 318–19, 321; military participation 194, 196, 202, 217; New Zealand's declaration of war makes Japan an enemy 360; New Zealand's support for Britain at expense of own defence 71, 79–80, 200–01, 217, 241, 249, 258–63, 362, 363; prisoners of war 340; shelling of steelworks, Kamaishi 321; shipping losses 240; Solomon Islands 230, 321; submarines in New Zealand waters 195–96, 235, 237; total war policy 150, 202–06, 272, 282, 312; United States views 242, 260–61, 263; unlikelihood of Japanese invasion of New Zealand 206–12
Jarvis Island 54
Jennings, Margaret 193–94
Jews in New Zealand 34–35, 103, 151, 152, 293–95
Jiang Jieshi (Chiang Kaishek) 32, 104, 212, 261
Jodl, Alfred 131
Jones, Edgar 223–24
Jones family, Woodfield estate 275–76
Jones, Frederick 27–28, 56, 87, 121
Jordan, William 37, 47, 48, 49, 50, 221, 349
Joseph, M.K., 'The Girl Who Stayed at Home' 286
Jowsey, Clare 306

Kanak people 352
Kane, Amy 276, 278
Katz, Solomon 293
Kawase Isamu 206, 208
Keefe, James 108
Keys, Lillian 326
King, Ernest 221
Kingston, Bryan 116
Kippenberger, Howard 103, 229
Koiso Kuniaki 238–39
Kokusaku Kenkyu Kai 206
Komet 124, 125
Konoe Fumimaro 181, 183–84, 190
Korea 192
Kursk, Battle of 235

Labour government, New Zealand: conflict between left and centrist groups 21–22, 23; currency controls 36, 50–51, 161; and imperial foreign policy 47–51, 361; Iraqi independence 135; and Japan 35, 36–37, 38, 39, 40, 80, 178–80, 181; League of Nations 27, 36, 38, 48, 72; and Netherlands 353; pacifism and anti-imperialism 361; partnerships with capitalists 161; and Sino-Japanese War 37–38, 39, 175; and Soviet Union 88, 156; strengthening of the military 27–29, 30; and Thailand 185; trade with Germany 33–34; United Nations Organisation 350
Labour government, New Zealand, Second World War 18, 20, 21; aliens authority 151–52; atomic bomb project 326; British proposal for talks with Japan and United States 175–76; cable to Churchill re continuation of war or peace talks 119–21; censorship 356; and colonies held by Allies and United States 188; conscription 126–28, 135–36; criticism of support for Britain at expense of defending New Zealand 200–01, 258–60; declaration of war against Germany 63, 65–66; declaration of war against Italy 118; election, 1943 305–09, **309**; financing of military participation 92–95, 99, 121, 126, 136–38, 301–05, 312; and Finland 88; food rationing 252; manpower policy 202, 206, 246; options for participation in war 78–80, 362–63; Pacific Defence Conference, 1939 40, 55–56; recruitment of armed forces 80–85, **81**; strikes and lockouts 312–13; total war policy 202–06, 272, 282, 312; treatment of deserters 269, 270; and United Nations 216; and United States 176, 177, 180–81, 183, 191; war aims 67, 165–67; war controls over the economy 95–98, 161; war council proposal 117–18; war emergency powers 100, 101, 102–03, 107, 108; war planning 55–59, 99; war regulations 62; wartime coalition government 163, 212–13, 228–29; *see also* War Administration, New Zealand; war cabinet, New Zealand
Labour Party, British 43
Labour Party, New Zealand: anti-conscription tradition 25, 27, 29, 57, 126; and Catholic church 20, 292; and Communist Party 23, 100, 156, 158–59; conflict with National 21, **96**, 312; Māori autonomy 19; pacifism 27; and Rarotonga Labour Party 44; reasons given for going to war 74–75; rightwards drift 158; and Social Credit movement 23, 24; socialism still the goal 313; socialist left *versus* less socialist right 312; views on empire 43–44, 74–75, 77; views on German people 33, 74, 102; views on Nazi Party 33, 74; views on United States 53; war council proposal 117; wartime coalition government proposal 163; working-class emphasis 21
Ladies Patriotic Guild of Rarotonga 154
Laird, John 33
Lambie, Mary 344
Lang, Samuel 192
Langstone, Frank 45, 68, 126, 180–81, **181**
Lao Ma 193
Larsen, Colin 345
Latvia 349
Laughton, John 300
Laver, Derek 226

League of Nations 27, 36, 37, 38, 45, 47, 48, 49, 50, 72, 350
League of Nations Union 26
Leander 57, 62, 338, 344
Lee, John A. 21–22, 23, 27, 28, 29, 34, 56, 62, 68, 73, 84, 94, 99, **99**, 130, 158, 306
Lee, Marjorie 280
Left Book Club 46
left-wing views, New Zealand: British Commonwealth 41, 42, 157; British Empire 28, 41, 42, 43–44, 46, 74–75, 77, 156; Communist Party 156, 158–59; conscription 85, 126, 129–30, 135–36, 158; economic controls for total war policy 312; financing of war effort 302, 304–05; food and industrial production *versus* military 244; geographic isolation of New Zealand as defence 73; German people 102–03, 150; imperial foreign policy 47–51; Japan 35, 37–39; Manpower policy 246, 247, 312; Nazi Party 23, 33, 74; neutrality 66; new world order 166, 329; options for New Zealand participation in the war 78–80; pacifism and opposition to war 26–27, 101, 117, 120, 129–30, 248–49, 361; pre-war militarisation 56; rationing 252–53, 255; Soviet Union 88, 156; strikes and lockouts 310; trade 41; United States 52; war cabinet 121; war policy 98–100; war with Japan 200–01; wartime coalition government 118, 163, 228–29; women 282
Lennox-King, Gilbert 192
letters, censorship 356–57
Levien, Hec 283
Lewis, Edith 272
Liberty Loans **294**, 303
Libya 134, 229
Lion, Ernst 151
Liston, James 20, 46, 327
Lithuania 349
Litvinov, Maxim 37
living standards 141, 160, 310
Llewellin, John 241–42
loans to finance war effort, Britain and Australia 138
loans to finance war effort, New Zealand 92–93, 121, 136, 138, **197**, 302–03; compulsory loans 136; Liberty Loan advertisement, 1943 **294**; war bonds **127**, 136, 302–03
London 61, 62
Lorigan, Barbara 282
Los Angeles Times 250
Loudon, Agnes 111
Louisson, Alfred 93
Low, Cora 299
Luxford, John 67
Lyttleton, Edith 62
Macdonald, Joyce 90, 134
Macey, Florence 264
MacGibbon, Thomas 119
Macindoe, Joan 197
Mackenzie, Hugo, Maria and Herbert 110
MacLean, William 324
Magill, Jeremiah 228
Mahir, Ali 91, 229
Majelis Rakyat Indonesia (Indonesian People's Council) 189
Makatea, phosphate workers 297
Malabar 42
Malaya 169, 178, 181, 183, 184, 186–87, 188, 192, 193, 194, 196, 347
Maltby, Walter 210
Manchester, Elizabeth 110
Mannheim, bombing 122
Manpower Office 202, 206, 247–48
manufacturing 22, **22**, 108–09, **109**, 146, 147–48, 224, 331; loss of workers to the military 242–45, 249, 318, 337; manpowering of workers 246; *see also* factory workers; food production; industrial production
Māori: casualties, Second World War 355; changes brought about by the war 295–96, 297, 299–301; children playing in Waikato River, 1938 **19**; discrimination 300–01; furlough men 269; imagery as emblems of New Zealand 105, **105**; interrelations with Pākehā 18–19; mana motuhake (autonomy) 19, 354–55; military participation in the war 103–04, 152–53, **153**, 296, 299, 300; New Zealand and British military power linked with war god Tū **291**; population 17, 18–19; racism of American troops stationed in New Zealand 221; support for Japan 47, 208; tribal committees 355; tribal social organisation 19; views on British Empire 46–47, 77; views on the war 66, 103–04, 153, 295–96; *see also* Cook Islands Māori
Maori Battalion 103–04, 152–53, 296, 297, 299, 300, 355
Maori Land Court 44
Maori Social and Economic Advancement Act 1945 355
Maori War Effort Organisation 296, 299, 355
Mapp, Richard 223
Marquis, Frederick 139
Marsden, Ernest 325–26
Marsh, Ngaio 33
Marshall, George 186, 189
Marshall, John 62, 361
Martin, Douglas 100, 158
Martin, John 76, 331
Martin, W. Lee 96

Mason, R.A.K. 25, 44, 98; *Help Russia or Help Hitler* 157
Mason, Rex 70, 152, 162, 349, 355
Mason, Walter Wynne 289
Masterton 166, 213, 214, 301
Matenga, Isaac 299
Matsuoka Yosuke 177, 182, 183
Matthews, Lyla 34
Mau movement, Samoa 45
Mawhete, Rangi 153
May, Thomas 338, 343
McCarthy, Darry 277
McCaul, Malcolm 136
McCombs, Terence 210
McCormick, Eric 98, 118, 283
McCowen, Elizabeth 194
McCready, Thomas 269
McDiarmid, Allan, *Totalitarianism and Christianity* 292
McDonald, Donald 134
McDonald, John (air-force officer) 290
McDonald, John (army officer) 67, 359
McDonald, Lachie 320
McDougall, James 304
McIntosh, Alister 47, 258, 262, 263, 305, 349, 361
McIntyre, Agnes 265
McIntyre, Peter, *The Breakthrough, Mingar Qa'im* **229**
McKeen, Robert 39
McKinney, Jack 340
McKinnon, Janet 344
McLagan, Angus 314
McLaughlin, John 110
McLean, Doris 266
McMaster, Lendrick 230
McRae, Henry 91
Mea`ole, Tupua Tamasese 354
Meat Producers Board 318
medical care 344
Meek, Ronald 75
Melrose, Thomas, *Sound the Tocsin* 199–200
Menzies, Eric 266
Menzies, Robert 55
Mercantile Gazette 214
Mergendahl, Charles 286
Merrick, Charles 227
Merrick, Elsie 227
Merry, Alice 304
metahistory 11
Mexico 74
Michener, James 225
Micronesia 352
middle class 34, 91, 107, 310, 314, 324; death duties 304; financing of war effort 91, 92, 121, 301, 302, 304; Home Guard 143–44; recruitment and enlistment in military 82, 84; views on Britain and British Empire 40, 42; views on rationing 252, 255–56; views on United States 53, 225, 226; women's war work 148, **149**, 150, 276–77, 278, 279–81
Middle East 42, 80, 88, 134–35, 201, 217, 338; *see also* Egypt; North Africa
Midway, Battle of 215, 247
militarism 358–60
military, New Zealand 25–27, 73; black market in supplies 265–66; diseases, wounds and injuries 338–40; financing 91–95, 141, 301–05; Labour government policy of strengthening 27–29, 30; laws and customs, differences from civilian laws and customs 358–60; loss of agricultural and industrial workers to the military 147, 241–45; manufacturing of clothing and goods 108–09, 141; at outbreak of war 62–63; peak mobilisation 228, 301; reduction in numbers after surrender of Germany 319; stationed on or near battlefields 263; training 335, 338; war planning 56–59; winding down 244–45, 249, 263; women 148–50, 272–73, 279–81, **280**; *see also* New Zealand Army; Royal New Zealand Air Force; Royal New Zealand Navy
military reserve, New Zealand 202
Milner, Ian 101
Minhinnick, Gordon: cartoon, mood on the eve of war **58**; Munich Pact cartoon **51**
mining industry 146, 152, 158, 202, 208, 228
Mitchell, William 187, 194, 237
Mohaia, Rotahi 299
Moke, Sydney 299
Monaghan, Harold 209
Monckton-Arundell, Lucia 92
Monowai 196
Monterey 62
Moody, Allan 151
Moore, Edith, *No Friend of Democracy* 292–93
Moral Rearmament 289
Morgenthau, Henry 221
Morpeth, Charlton 137
Morrison, Neva 344
Morton, Elsie 163–64
Moss, Lewis 186–87
Motherhood of Man Movement 287
Mulgan, Alan 98
Mulgan, John 77, 194, 357
Mulholland, William 116, 139, 160, 162
Munich Pact 50, **51**
munitions manufacturing and exporting, New Zealand 146, 276–77, **277**
Murland, George 226
Murphy, James 338
Murrell, Allan 226
Mussolini, Benito 32, **33**

Myers, Kenneth 20, 303–04
Myers, Sir Michael 95

Nagoya Pan-Pacific Peace Exposition poster **37**
Nakafuji Norito 178, 180
napalm 239–40, 320
Napier 130, 240
Nash, Walter 22, 51, 66, 70, 78, 92, 156, 289; Atlantic Charter 167; economic stabilisation policy 309–10; Egypt 351; financing of war effort 92, 93, 94, 136; food production 245, 249; imperial foreign policy 47; Japanese troops in French Indochina 184; League of Nations 27; loyalty to Britain 22, 77, 122; Netherlands 352; trade agreement with Germany 33–34; trusteeships 349–50; war cabinet 121; war portfolio 28; war with Japan 177–78, 202, 318, 319; welfare state 94, **117**, 309
Nasser, Gamal 89
National Council of Women 282
National Film Unit 347
National government, New Zealand 29; and Vietnam War 360–62
National Military Reserve 57
National Party, New Zealand 24, 25, 65, 66, 74, 92; approval of Munich Pact 50; attack on working hours and wages 159–60; Britain and British Empire, loyalty to 34, 41, 42, 49, 76; compulsory military training support 29–30, 57; conflict with Labour 21, **96**, 312; election, 1943 305–09; and enemy aliens 294; and furlough men 268; Labour's currency controls 50; leadership 97, 159; and manpower policy 246; right-wing group membership 159; and Sino-Japanese war 37, 38; strikes and lockouts 310–11; and trade agreement with Germany 34; views on keeping volunteer army in New Zealand 79; views on New Zealand Division in Italy 258–59; war cabinet 121; and war controls over the economy 95; war hysteria 115; and war with Japan 200, 318, 319; wartime coalition government 116, 117, 118, 162–63, 212–13, 228–29
National Patriotic Fund Board 92, 138, 266, 301
National Peace Council 27
National Recruiting Council 84
National Service Department 146, 246
National Service Movement 116–17
Nativc Affairs Committee 154
Native Department 355
Nauru 32, 45–46, 47, 104, 105, 110, 111, 125, 139, 145, 188, 207; surrender of Japanese troops 327–28
naval blockades 123, 177
naval war 123–25, 139, 140–41, 145, 240, 241; Germany 87, 123–26, 145, 232, 235, 240; Japanese submarines 195–96, 235, 237; New Zealanders on board mined, shelled or torpedoed ships 123–25, **124**
Nazism: Catholic clergy views 20, 292; Federation of Labour condemnation 23, 33; Labour Party views 33, 72; *Neuordnung Europas* (new order in Europe) 165; New Zealand church and working people's views 33, **33**, 118; New Zealand conservatives' support 32–33; socialism 313–14; views of Germans in New Zealand 101, 103; *see also* Germany
Nelson 264
Nelson Farmers Union 118
Netherlands 39, 74, 115, 216; colonies 35, 86–87, 169, **170**, 171, 175, 178, 181, 182, 187–89, 195, **352**, 352–53, 354; German invasion 115; Japanese assets frozen 183, 184; and New Zealand 189; Pacific War Council 216; and war with Japan 169, **170**, 181, 186
neutrality 12, 65, 66, 73, 292–93
New Caledonia 30, 212, 260, 338, 352
New Guinea 212, 230, 262
New Liberal Party, New Zealand 97–98
new order 165–66, 329
New Plymouth 266
New Zealand army 56, 58–59; clothing manufacturing 108, 141; medical corps 148; mutiny of soldiers 270; occupation of Egypt 88–91, 134; overseas shipment of soldiers 85–86; in Pacific colonies 172, 173, 174, **174**; recruitment and enlistment of volunteers 80–85, 118, 126, 128, 358; rivalry between various groups 270–71; soldiers doing a haka in Egypt **135**; soldiers on furlough **268**, 268–70; soldiers' questioning of morality of killing 360; women 148, 272, 279; *see also* conscription; and names of campaigns and theatres of war
New Zealand Bomber Squadron 122
New Zealand Broadcasting Service 61, 357
New Zealand Dental Association 35
New Zealand Educational Institute 329
New Zealand Educational Institute, North Canterbury branch 26
New Zealand Employers Federation 314
New Zealand Forces Club, Cairo 351
New Zealand Investment, Mortgage and Deposit Company 137
New Zealand Law Journal 128
New Zealand Manufacturers Federation 118, 136, 244, 249, 294
New Zealand Shipping Company 123
New Zealand Wars 46, 104, 295, 297
New Zealand Workers Union 96
Newall, Sir Cyril 157, 169
Newfoundland 41, 51

Newlands, Ian 195
Newspaper Proprietors Association 357
newspapers, New Zealand 37, 40, 70, 74, 75, 82, 83, 116, 152, 229; Allied viewpoint 122–23, 232, **237**, 251, 263; atomic bomb news and opinions 326; British news sources 259–60; censorship 158, 268, 356, 357; election, 1943 308; propaganda 121, 123; right-wing views 25, 51, 66, 88, 98, 103, 119, 121, 160, 245, 308; war hysteria 115
Ney, Marie 195
Ngāi Tahu 104
Ngāpuhi 104
Ngata, Sir Apirana 46, 103, 104, 354
Ngata, Henare 355
Ngāti Porou 46, 103–04, 153
Ngāti Toa 104
Niagara 118–19, 124
Nicholls, Charles 263
Nigeria 42
Nimmo, Robert 79
Niue 17, 20, 44, 47, 104, 110, 154, 188, 219, 354
Nordmeyer, Arnold 19, 38, 103, 163
Norgrove, Dorothy 85–86, 111, 290
Norman, Montagu 34, 51
North Africa 134–35, 152, 217, 235, 270, 285, 336, 338, 344; *Breakthrough, Mingar Qa'im, The* (McIntyre) **229**; 'browned off' infantrymen **259**; surrender of Axis troops 241, 258; *Troop Target* (Fullarton) **236**
Northcroft, Erima 358
Norway 62, 87, 88, 115
Norwood, Rosina, Lady Norwood 303
Norwood, Sir Charles 303
Nuqrashi, Mahmud 351
nurses 108, 110, 148, 272

Observer 286–87
oil industry and trade 178, 188, 208; *see also* petrol
Okirae estate, Hawke's Bay 274
Onozuka Kiheiji 192
Ooka Shohei 192
Operation Barbarossa 156–58
Order of St John 138
Organisation for National Security 57–58, 62–63
Orion 124, 125
Osgood, Bernard 227
O'Shea, Thomas 292
Otago 131, 302; 'Scottish' Otago 52
Otago Returned Soldiers Association 103
Otaki War Memorial Hall window **365**
Ozaki Yukio 182

Pacific: British colonies 42–43, 45, 54, 262, 351–52, 353; French Polynesia 171; New Zealand society's Eurocentric views 259–60; trade with New Zealand 41; and United States 53–54, 55, 261, 262, 318; *see also* Japan, war in Southeast Asia and the Pacific
Pacific colonies of New Zealand 17, 20, 44–46, 47, 55, 66, 104–06, 110–11, 188, 207, 354; military strengthening, Second World War 172–74; participation in war effort 153–56; trusteeships 262, 354; United States military occupation 217–220
Pacific Defence Conference, 1939 40, 55–56, 71, 150
pacifism 11, 26–27, 100–01, 111, 117, 120, 127–28, 129–30, 200, 248–49, 361
Paikea, Paraire 19, 103, 153, 296
Pal, Radhabinod 358
Palmer, Kyle 250
Pan American Airways 105, **105**
Panhuys, Willem van 353
paper regulations 254
Papua 230, 262
Parakoti, Agnes 297
paramilitary, New Zealand *see* Home Guard, New Zealand
Paris 61
Paris Conference, 1946 349
Parker, Wesley 324
Parkes, Judy 274
Parkes, William 343
Parr, Sir James 47
Parry, William 92
Parvin, George 233
Patara, John 228
Patea 143
Patrick, Ruth 326
Paul, Marjorie 255
Pavlovich, John 340
peace: celebrations after the surrender of Germany 317–18; celebrations after the surrender of Japan 322–24; planning 216; Savage's definition 17
Peace and Anti-Conscription Council 101
Peace Pledge Union 27
peace treaties 9, 48, 67, 87, 119–20, 131, 156, 165, 177, 191, 215, 262, 318, 320, 322, 330, 349
Peacocke, Isabel 83, 223
Pearl Harbor 169, 192, 196, 360
Pearson, William 26
Pemberton-Pigott, Bunty 199
People's Movement 98, 159, 161, **161**, 308
People's Voice 25, 39, 99, 100, 156, 306
Perry, William 29, 65, 178, 289
Pétain, Philippe 115
petrol: black market 167, 265; impact of war with Japan 197–98; rationing 107–08, **108**, 111, 139, 255, 343
Pewhairangi, Whetukamokamo 226
Philippines 52, 169, 183, 186, 192, 193, 216, 347

phoney war: first, September 1939 to June 1940 61–113, 115, 126; second, January 1943 to September 1945 **234**, 235–315
phosphate: Makatea 297; Nauru 45–46, 111, 125, 297; rationing 125, 139
Pinguin 124
Pirie, Margaret 20
Pius XII, Pope 166
poetry of Second World War 14–15, 364; *see also* names of individual poets
Poland **60**, 61, 65, 74, 86–87, 98, 99, 134, 235, 328, 349; New Zealanders in 110, 272
Pollard, Gwen 213, 225
Polson, William 294, 314
population, New Zealand 17; British ancestry 19, 76, 178; German ancestry 19, 20, 32, 34–35, 293–95; Māori 17, 18–19; nationalities 19–20, 34–35, 77, 101–03, 150–52, 221; *see also* Chinese New Zealanders; Germans in New Zealand; Irish Catholics in New Zealand; Italians in New Zealand; Jews in New Zealand
Port Hobart 123
Port Wellington 124
Porter, Hilton 64
Portugal 74, 86–87, 351
Potsdam Declaration, 1945 320, 322
Pouvanaa a Oopa 352
Press 30, 40, 83, 145, 191, 260, 309
Price, Charles **218**
price control 141, 142, 310
primary industries 17, 22, 24, 68–69, 79, 96, 97, 126, 146–47; loss of agricultural workers to the military 147, 241–45, 249, 318, 337; mechanisation 147, 246; student workers 245–46; *see also* food production
prisoners of war, New Zealand 263, 289, 321, **322**, 335–36, 338, 340
Pritchard, Zita 277
propaganda 12, 13, 74, 123, 158, 166, 167, 175, **182**, **201**, **207**, **211**, 267, 276, 357–58
Protestants, New Zealand, hostility to Catholics 292–93
psychological illness, Second World War 341–43, 344–45
Public Safety Emergency Regulations 1940 101
Puerto Rico 52
Pukekohe Programme 200

Q-Sing Times 104
Quakers (Society of Friends) 11, 44, 129
queen carnivals 138, **138**

racism: Pacific War 221, 223–24, **224**; Pākehā, towards Māori 300–01
radio broadcasts 21, 53, 56, 65, 70, 77, 102, 107, 121, 122, 152, 184, 229, 232, 259, 263, 270, 272, 274–75, 294, 317; censorship 356, 357; coastwatching network 174; propaganda 357–58
Raglan county 24
railways, New Zealand 334, 335, 336–37
Ramsay, Rollo 314
Ramsbottom-Isherwood, Henry 156
Randolph, Francis 266
Rangitane 124–25; survivors **124**
Rangitikei 123–24
Ransom, Sir Alfred 136
Rapana, Arnold 227
Rarotonga Island Council 154
Rarotonga Labour Party 44
Rarotonga Returned Soldiers Association 104–05
Rātana 47, 103, 295–96, 321
Ratana, Haami 20, 113
Ratana, Tahupotiki 47, 321
rationing 254; Britain 256; Germany 254, **254**, 347; Japan 347
rationing, New Zealand 141, 204–05, 206, 251–54, 255, **265**, 266, 282; butter 251–52, **252**, 256; meat 252–53, 256, 264; petrol 107–08, **108**, 111, 139, 255, 343; phosphate 125, 139; rubber goods **204**, 205
Rautahi, Reihana 89–90
Real Democracy Movement 308
reasons for New Zealand going to war 65–67, 78, 98, 328–30, 364–65; hardheaded reasons 67–73, 330–38, 364; softhearted reasons 67, 73–77, 82, 83, 98, 101, 126, 132, **197**, 244, 348–55, 359–60, 364
Red Cross 138, 154
Redman, John 151
Rees, Rosemary 121
refugees, New Zealand, German Jews 34–35, 103, 151, 152, 293–95
regulations, New Zealand 62, 158, 205, 246, 254–55, 267; Alien Control Emergency Regulations 1939 102; economic stabilisation policy 310; Emergency Regulations Act 1939 95–96; Emergency Regulations Amendment Act 1941 117; Public Safety Emergency Regulations 1940 101
Reid, Ian 122–23
Reifer, Isidor 74
Reiffenstuhl, Günther 240
Reithmaier, Gregor 102
religion, New Zealand 288–93; Christian pacifists 26–27; prisoners of war 289; servicemen 289, 290–91, **291**; *see also* Catholic church, New Zealand; clergy, New Zealand
returned servicemen, New Zealand 84–85, **322**, **325**, **327**, **328**, 329, **330**; psychological illness 341, 342–43; wounds and injuries 339

Returned Soldiers/Services Association 46–47, 57, 196, 289, 295
Rich, Eric 166, 301
Richards, Arthur 300–01
Richwhite, Cleave 45–46
right-wing views, New Zealand: atomic bombing of Japan 326; British Commonwealth 41–42, 157; British Empire 41, 42, 43–44, 97; Communist Party 156; conscription 85, 116; county council elections 24, 314; flag flying 161–62; food and industrial production *versus* military 244–45, 249; Germans in New Zealand 103, 151; Home Guard 143–44; imperial foreign policy 49–50, 151; Japan 35, 36–37; Jews in New Zealand 151; Manpower policy 246–47; Nazi Party 32–33; neutrality 66; new world order 166, 329; newspaper representation 25, 51, 66, 88, 98, 103, 119, 121, 160, 245, 308; options for New Zealand participation in the war 79; pre-war militarisation 57; rationing 252, 253, 255–56; sexual behaviour during the war 286–87, 288; socialism and welfare state 97, 98, 160, 161, 305, **311**, 313–14, 331; Soviet Union 156; strikes and lockouts 310–13; taxation and financing of the war effort 92, 95, 136–37, 301–02, 303–04, **304**; trade 40–41; United States 53; war cabinet 121; war controls over the economy 95, 96–97, 98, 161; war hysteria 115; war with Japan 200–01, 318–19; wartime coalition government 115, 116–18, 121, 162–63, 228–29; women 281–82
roads 334–35, 336–37
Roberts, James 166
Roberts, Owen 283
Robertson, John 38–39
Robertson, Sir Carrick 151
Rodger, Mills 218
Romania 110, 132, 349
Roosevelt, Franklin D. 53, 166–67, 174–75, 181, **181**, 190, 221, 258, 334, 337; Cairo Conference 261; and food production in New Zealand 249; Pacific War Council 216; unconditional surrender doctrine 330; and war with Japan 177, 192, 217, 242
Rothschild, Edward 151
Rotorua 123
Royal Air Force 87; New Zealanders in 109, 122, 231–32, 233, 272
Royal Dutch Shell 188
Royal Navy 71, 87, 123, 171, 176, 232, 240; British Pacific Fleet 240; New Zealand Division (*see* Royal New Zealand Navy)
Royal New Zealand Air Force 56, 57, 325; recruitment of volunteers **81**, 84; in Solomon Islands **243**, **315**; training **128**; war with Japan 194; women 148, 272–73, 279–80, 317
Royal New Zealand Navy 56, 57, 87; recruitment and enlistment of volunteers 84, 118; war with Japan 196; women 148, 280
rubber goods: black market 265; rationing and recycling **204**, 205
rural–urban divisions 24
Rutini, Uru 248
Rydal Downs estate, Canterbury **273**

Saipan 238
Sale, E.V. 218
Salmon, Hazel 226
Salote Tupou III **174**, 218
Samoa: and Canberra Pact 262; Cantonese indentured workers 45–46, 47, 104; Chinese traders 154, 155; economic impact of war 110, 111, 155; German colony 32, 48; military strengthening after outbreak of war with Japan 173–74; peace celebrations 317, 323; street scene in Apia, 1945 **106**; territorial army 56, 62; United States military occupation 217, 218–19, **219**; views on the war 104–06, 154–55; war with Japan 196; Western Samoa, New Zealand government 17, 20, 40, 45, **45**, 47, 48, 56, 188, 207, 354
Samoan Nazi Party 103
Sanderson, Phoebe 247–48
Sargent, Winston 90, 91, 285–86
Sargeson, Frank 86, 152, 286, 345
Sato Naotake 39
Saunders, Hilary, *Return at Dawn* 357
Savage, Michael Joseph 20, 24, **28**, 51, 85, 92, 98, 361; conscription 30; Czechoslovakia 50; death and funeral **112**, 113; Ethiopia 49; League of Nations 27, 36, 47, 48, 49; military policy 28, 56, 57–58, 361; peace 17–18, 27, 48; Samoa 45, 48; speech on declaration of war 65–66, 98; and Te Puea Herangi 77, 104; working class origins 21
Scanlan, Nelle 187
Schacht, Hjalmar 33–34
Scheele, Elizabeth 62
Scholefield, Guy 197, 203
School Journal 26
Schramm, Frederick 20, 100, 103
Schramm, Paul 152, 294
Scott, Archibald 338
Scott, David 345
Scott, Evelyn 63
Scott, Lauris (later Edmond) 26, 99, 224, 225, 246, 306, 342, 364
Scott, Lewis 23–24
Scott, Richard 82, 157, 270, 291
Second New Zealand Expeditionary Force Association 329

Second World War: briefness, and expansive reach 9–10; civilian cynicism, New Zealand 167, 209, 264, 266–68; divisions created in New Zealand society 13; financing of New Zealand participation 92–95, 99, 121, 126, 136–38, 301–05, 312; first phoney war, September 1939 to June 1940 61–113, 115, 126; Minhinnick cartoon, mood on the eve of war **58**; New Zealand options for participation 11–12, 78–80, 362–63; New Zealand war planning 56–59, 99; outbreak of war 61–65; Pacific Defence Conference, 1939 40, 55–56, 71, 150; postwar world 363–64; reasons for New Zealand going to war 65–78, 82, 83, 98, 126, 132, **197**, 244, 328–38, 364–65; second phoney war, January 1943 to September 1945 **234**, 235–315; 'turning of the tide' 229–33, 237–38; United Nations world strategy 216; war aims 12, 67, 165–67, 328; war hysteria 115–21, 283; *see also* air war; casualties of Second World War; naval war; and under individual countries and theatres of war

Seddon, Rosalie 280

Selby, Margaret 109

Semple, Robert 100, 143, 148, 312, 313

servants, Cook Islands Māori 297

service industries 17, 22

sexual behaviour by New Zealanders 283; conservative views 286–87; contraception and abortion 287–88; peace celebrations, surrender of Japan 324; sexualised stage shows **284**; troops overseas 283, **284**, **285**; with United States troops 224, 225–28, **227**, 285, 286; women at home 283–84, 285–86

Shannon, Ruth 124

Shaw, Sylvia 265

Sheehan, Patrick 360

Shinya Michiharu 256–57

shipping: New Zealand civilians heading home at outbreak of war 62; New Zealand state orders for shipping 62; risk to New Zealand shipping of war with Germany 72–73; shipping industry earnings, New Zealand 69; *see also* naval war

shortages, New Zealand 139–41, 282; *see also* rationing, New Zealand

Sick, Wounded and Distress Fund 138

Silverstone, Harold 306

Simpson, Gordon 123

Simpson, Wallis 48

Singapore 80, 178, 182, 186, 187, 189, **193**, 194–95, 197

Sino-Japanese War 35, 36–39, 80, 104, 175, 176, 177, 182, 190, 191, 212, 235

Skellerup factories 109

Skelton, Joan 109

Slatter, Gordon 283, 290, 341

'sly grog' vendors 264–65

Smith, Archibald 264

Smith, Elsie 109

Smith, Lorna 284

Social Credit movement 23–24, 34, 99, 166, 305, 308; *The People's Plan for a New Order* 329

social democracy 22, 29, 53, 75, 94, 98, 166, 206, 277, 307, 314, 348

social security, New Zealand *see* welfare state and social security, New Zealand

society, New Zealand: divisions 18–25; divisions caused by war 13

Society of Friends (Quakers) 44

Soeda Hisayuki 328

Soldiers and Workers 158

Solomon Islands 43, 191, 196, 214, 215, 223, 262, 338, 339, 345, **346**; New Zealand air-force ground crew **315**; New Zealand air-force men **243**; New Zealand bombing 263, **263**, 321, 345–46; New Zealand soldiers **243**, **260**, **351**

Somaliland 187

Somare, Michael 230

Somes Island, Wellington Harbour **103**

Song Meiling 104

South Africa 41, 48, 50, 65, 348; Declaration of the United Nations, 1942 210

South British Insurance 331

Southeast Asia 41, 169, **170**, 178, 182, 183, **185**, 186, 189, 190, 216, 223, 353; starvation of civilians 347; *see also* names of individual countries

Southern Development Bank Notes 207–08

Southland 131, 257, 272, 279, 312, 356

sovereignty: Māori 19, 47; Pākehā views 19

Soviet Union 30, 67, 130, 348; agreement with British Commonwealth 156–57, 158–59; attack on Iran 134; and Britain 39, 88, 337; casualties in Second World War 328; Catholic views 292; Declaration of the United Nations, 1942 210; Defence Ministry poster **31**; and Ethiopia 49, 50; and Finland 87–88; and France 39, 88; German invasion 131, 156–58, 179, 183, 229, 235, **242**; German–Soviet non-aggression pact 61, 156, 176, 183, 292; and Japan 39, 80, 132, 176, 186, 191, 239, 320, 322; and New Zealand 37, 88, 210; New Zealand opinion 23, 24, 32; and Poland **60**, 61, 235, 349; Potsdam Declaration, 1945 320; and United Nations 350; and United States 240, 261, 337, 363–64

Spain, colonies 351

Spanish Civil War 48–49, **49**

Spence, Alistair 82

Spencer, Harry 63

Spencer, Norman 160

Spike 163
St John Ambulance Association 108
Stables, Joyce 317–18
stage shows, sexualised **284**
Stalin, Iosif 30, 100, 337
Stalingrad, Battle of 229
Stanley, Thomas, *The Real Criminals* 158
Stark, James 83
Star-Sun 116, 187, 214, 245, 303
Stevenson, Ian 62
Stevenson, Joanna 164
Stewart, Ronald 290
'stockings scare,' rationing and ersatz silks 140, 205, 267, **267**
Stone, Dorothy 265
Stout, Duncan 342
Strang, David 335
Street, Alister 225, 276
Strewe, Odo 152
strikes and lockouts 310–11
Stunzner, Kurt **103**
Sturgeon 240
submarines: British 338; German 64, 123, **127**, 139, 235, 240, 241; Italian 123; Japanese 195–96, 205, 235, 237; United States 240, 347
subversion trials 100, 101
Sudan 42
Suez Canal 89, 351
Sukuna, Ratu Lala 172
Sullivan, Daniel 19, 205, 253, 312, 326
superstition 290
Sutch, W.B. 146
Sutherland, Joan 166
Suzuki Kantaro 320
Swan, Owen 107–08
Swift, James 122
Swinburn, Helen 275
swing music 52–53
Sydney, Simon 283
Syria 134

Tablet 79, 248, 326
Tairoa 87
Takagi Sokichi 239
Taranaki iwi 153, 296
Tasker, Una 265
taxation: as a means of financing war effort 94–95, **95**, 136–37, 302, 303–05, **304**, 312; wartime increases 136–37
Taylor, Nancy 107, 111, 123, 137, 177, 202, 277, 282, 310, 332
Te Aonui, John 299
Te Arawa 103, 104, 153
Te Kanawa 153
Te Kiri, Ellen 299
Te Puea Herangi 77, **77**, 104, 295
Te Rangi Hiroa 19, 104
teaching profession, views on the military 25–26
Teheran Conference, 1943 349
Territorial Association of Canterbury 57
Territorial Force, New Zealand 28, 29, 57, 73, 202, 245
Texidor, Greville 81, 129
Thailand 74, 184–86, 191–92
theft and pilfering 265–66
Thomas, John 264
Thomson, Helen 40
Thomson, John 196
Thomson, Kathleen 194
Thyne, Mavis 339
Tianjin crisis 38
Timaru 119, 323
Tirikatene, Eruera 20, 103
Tojo Hideki 190, 208, 215, 238
Tokelau 17, 20, 44, 47, 104, 110, 219, 354; participation in war effort 154
Tomlinson, Charles 64
Tomorrow 59, 79, 119
Tonga 43, 173, 230, 260, 262, 338; United States military occupation 217, 218
Tongan Defence Force 173, **174**
Tonkin, famine 347
Toop, Ernest 98, 159
Tossman, Betty 225
total war 10; New Zealand policy 202–06, 272, 282, 312
Total War Research Institute 207
Townend, M.G. 326
Toyama Maru 240
trade, New Zealand 67–68, 97; Britain 23, 34, 40–41, 68–70, 79, 97, 123, 139, 146, 241–42, 251, 331–34, **333**, 336, 363; bulk contracts 332; contents of a typical cargo ship, *Empire Trader* **69**; Dutch East Indies 178; Germany 33–34, 68; Japan 36–37, 38, 139, 182, 183, 204; Malaya 178; munitions exporting 146; Pacific islands 41, 44; tariffs 23, 40, 41, 58, 161, 164; United States 139, 241, 245, 332; wartime shortages of imported goods 139–41, **140**, 164
trade unions 22–23, 27, 37–38, 95, 126, 158, 160, 244, 252, 310–12, 353; division between unions of left and right 312; *see also* Federation of Labour; and names of individual unions
Treaty of Versailles 33, 39, 48, 67
Treaty of Waitangi 19, 75, 104, 153, 355
Triaster 125
Tripartite Pact, 1940 131–32
Truman, Harry S. 324–25
trusteeships 262, 349–50
Truth, New Zealand 25, 119, 293–94
Tsukuda Keiji 190, 191

Tūhoe 153
'Tuis' 150
Turakina 124
Turnbull, Alfred 56, 106, 155, 173–74, **218**
Tweedy, William 119

Umizo Yoshijuri 327
Union Française 352
Union Record 89
Union Steam Ship Company 171
United Nations 210, 216, 235, 237, 238, 242, 243; Charter 350; Declaration of the United Nations, 1942 210; Japanese surrender 322, 327; propaganda poster 210, **211**; Trusteeship Committee 349–50; world strategy for Second World War 216
United Nations Organisation 350
United States 52–54, 62; annexation of Pacific islands 53–54, 55; and Australia 180, 216, 221, 348; and Britain 52–54, 55, 139, 334, 337; British proposal for talks with Japan and United States 175–76; and Canberra Pact, 1944 262, 263; and China 35, 54, 175, 183, 186, 261; colonialism and imperialism 52, 53–54, 55, 167, 171, 175, **179**, 180, 182, 183, 188, 261, 262, 351–52, 354; Conference of Paris 349; Declaration of the United Nations, 1942 210; four 'principles' statement to Japan 180; German migrants 221; and Japan 53–54, 80, 175, 176, 177, 179, 180, 181, 183, 184, 186, 190, 348; and Malaya 187; naval power 71, 171; and New Zealand 39, 55, 139, 176, 180–81, 183, 191, 208, 210, 216, 221, 241, 245, 332, 348; in the Pacific 53–54, 55, 261, 262, 318, 337, **339**; soft imperial power 52–53; and Soviet Union 240, 261, 337, 363–64; and Thailand 184, 185; and United Nations 350; Vietnam War 360–62; War Plan Red 54
United States, Second World War: Atlantic Charter 166–67; declaration of war 66, 169; Germany, Soviet Union and China 240; napalm development 239; naval and military power 171, 191, 240; neutrality 66; and New Zealand food production 241, 242, 245, 249–50, 251, 252, 253; New Zealand soldiers sidelined for garrison duty 260–61; New Zealand subsidisation of war effort 332; only great power left in the Pacific **339**; policy for war in Asia and the Pacific 216, 237–38; servicemen in New Zealand 215, 217, 220–21, **221**, 224–28, **227**; strengthening of defences, Southeast Asia 190; unconditional surrender doctrine 330
United States, Second World War, war with Japan 212, 215, 216, 239, 243; air raids 239–40, **319**, 320; atomic bombing of Hiroshima and Nagasaki 324–27; Battle of Midway 215; Battle of the Coral Sea 214; diplomatic background 174–75, 179, 186, 188, 189–91; 'island hopping' strategy 237; Japanese attack on Pearl Harbor 192; New Zealand interests 180–81, 191, 216, 217, 318–19; New Zealand troops sidelined 260–61; occupation of Pacific islands 217–20; Potsdam Declaration, 1945 320; Solomon Islands 230; *see also* Japan, war in Southeast Asia and the Pacific
urban–rural divisions, New Zealand 24

van Staveren, Herman 294–95
Varian, Frank 90
Vautier, Winifred 339
Vercoe, Tony 336, 341
Vietnam War 360–61
Vile, Sonja 163–64, 226, 288
Voelcker, Francis W. 103
Vogt, Anton 163
volunteering, by civilians 108

Wadman, Howard 44
wage control, New Zealand 141–42
Waikato Farmers Co-operative Auctioneering Company 304
Waikato Farmers Union 96
Waikato iwi 104, 153, 296
Waiotira 123
Walker, Laurie 269
Walsh, Fintan 303
Walter, Detlef 345
war: costs of waging war 70; Labour belief that war provoked by class and money 47; *see also* First World War; Second World War
War Administration, New Zealand: demands for wartime coalition government 115, 116–18, 121, 162–63, 212; establishment 212–13; National Party walkout, and collapse 228–29, 305, 310
war aims 67, 165–67, 328
War and the Working Class, The 158
war bonds 136; advertisement **127**
War Book (New Zealand Labour government) 58
war cabinet, New Zealand: decision to keep New Zealand Division in Italy 258–59; demands for wartime coalition government 115, 116–18, 121, 162–63, 212; establishment 121; as executive of War Administration 213; food rationing 253; furlough men 268–69; manpower policy 246; release of conscientious objectors and defaulters 249; strengthening of Home Guard 204; and United States 352; war with Japan 169, 178, 192; *see also* War Administration, New Zealand

war conference, Wellington, 1939 *see* Pacific Defence Conference, 1939
war crimes trials, Nuremburg and Tokyo 358, **359**
War Disablement Pension 341
War Expenses Act 1939 93
war hysteria 115–21, 283
war memorials 26, **365**
War Purposes Fund 121
war regulations, New Zealand *see* regulations, New Zealand
war work, civilian 142–48
Ward, George 109
Ward, Gilbert, *The League of the Brown Skirts* 281
Warkworth Left Book Club 46
Warren, Ernest 82
Watson, Gordon 99–100, 224, 244
Watson, John 81, 343
Wavell, Archibald 251
wealth gap 20–21
Webb, Patrick 95, 146, 150, 313
welfare state and social security 21, 50, 51, 58, 78–79, 94, 95, 117, 141, 160, 161, 305, 306–07, 309, 313–14, 331
Wellington **18**, 26, 46, 57, 92, 199, 228, 270, 287, 303; 1939 **18**; absenteeism 148; American servicemen 215, 220, 221, 225, 226; appeal boards 130; Battle of Manners Street 226; Centennial Exhibition poster, 1939 **16**; Communist Party 23, 158; earthquake, June 1942 **213**, 213–14; housing 255; peace celebrations 318, 323–24; People's Movement 98; Savage's funeral **112**, 113; 'sly grog' vendors 264–65; submarines in surrounding waters 195–96; theft on wharves 266
Wellington Automobile Association 108
Wellington Chamber of Commerce 160, 252
Wellington Employers Association 160
Wellington Hospital Board 294
Wellington Victory Queen Carnival **138**
West Coast 131
West Coast Trades Council 99
Western Samoa *see under* Samoa
Westmacott, Spencer 46–47
Weyher, Kurt 124–25
Whanganui iwi 104
Whangarei 130, 143
Whangarei Primary Production Council 299
white feathers 83
White, Osmar 230, 243
White, Thomas 223
Whitelaw, Mary 286, 344
Whitton, Marjorie 64
Wickliffe, Ceylon **355**
Wigram, Agnes, Lady Wigram 301–02
Wild and Robertson, Greymouth 93
Wild, Richard 193
Wilkinson, Ellen 110
Wilkinson, Theodore 242
Williams, Gordon 283
Williams, Ralph 223
Williams, 'Willie' 194
Wilson, Cynthia 272
Wilson, David 34, 65, 73
Wilson, Guthrie 335; *Brave Company* 83, 271, 338, 356, 357
Wilson, Philip 345–46
Wilson, Phillip 360
Wilson, Robert 358
Winder, Charles 304
Windsor, Edward 48
Winstone, Jane 272
Wipiti, Bert 194
Witariana, Bert 299
Witheford, Hubert 268
Woman's Weekly 166
women 281; Germany 281, **282**; Japan 281
women, New Zealand: in British military and other groups 109–10, 272; changes in dress and behaviour 277, 278, **278**, 282; civilian reactions to war with Japan 198, 199; factory jobs 108–09, **109**, 150, 276–77, **277**, 280; land girls and farm workers 147, **273**, 273–76; Manpowering proposal 246; Manpowering system class differences 278–79; Manpowering work seen as women's work 278–79; and new order 166, 329; in New Zealand military 148–50, 272–73, 279–80; passive acceptance of wartime life 282; psychological illness 344–45; recruited into auxiliary tasks 148–50, **149**, 279; sexual behaviour during the war 283–84, 286–87; voluntary drill and war training 108
Women's Auxiliary Air Force (WAAF) 148, **149**, 197, 277, **279**, 280, **280**
Women's Auxiliary Army Corps 148
Women's Christian Temperance Union 27
Women's Land Army 109
Women's Land Service 274–75
Women's National Service Corps 108
Women's Royal New Zealand Naval Service 148
Women's War Service Auxiliary 148–50, 281; land corps 273–74
Wood, Edward 50, 78, 80
Wood, Frederick 65, 111, 116, 209, 270
wood use regulations 254
Woodfield estate, Canterbury 275–76
Woodhouse, Airini 275
Woodhouse, Carne 275
working class **21**, 200, 246, 247, **248**, 314; and American servicemen in New Zealand 224; conscription and conscientious objectors 25, 29, 128, 129, 130, 135–36; fundraising 302;

Māori 295, 299–300; and neutrality 66; opposition to war 120; prosperity 18; raids for errant workers by Manpower 247–48; war bonds and savings accounts 136; war donations 93; wealth gap 20, 21; women's war work 108–09, **109**, 150, 275, 276–77, 278, 279, 280–81; *see also* factory workers; left-wing views; trade unions; welfare state

working hours and conditions, New Zealand 146–48, **147**, 159–60, 246–47; forty-eight-hour working week 246–47; forty-hour working week 159–60, **162**; *Hours of Work in Wartime* (Hearnshaw) 248

Wright, Stephenson and Company 161, 331

Yamamoto Isoroku 215

York, Noel 266

You Noy Sum 265

Young, Robert 143, 144

Yugoslavia 132, 349

Zimmerman, John 221